Traditions in Contact and Change

Selected Proceedings of the XIVth Congress of the International Association for the History of Religions

edited by Peter Slater and Donald Wiebe
with Maurice Boutin and Harold Coward

Published for the Canadian Corporation for Studies in Religion/
Corporation Canadienne des Sciences Religieuses
by Wilfrid Laurier University Press

Canadian Cataloguing in Publication Data

International Association for the History of
Religions Congress. (14th : 1980 : Winnipeg, Man.).
  Traditions in contact and change

(Editions SR ; 3)
Bibliography; p.
Includes index.
ISBN 0-88920-142-0

1. Religion – History – Congresses. 2. Religion –
Congresses. I. Slater, Peter, 1934-   II. Wiebe,
Donald. III. Title. IV. Series.

BL21.I57 1980   200'.9   C83-098002-4

© 1983 Corporation Canadienne des Sciences Religieuses/
   Canadian Corporation for Studies in Religion

83 84 85 86 4 3 2 1

No part of this book may be stored in a retrieval system, translated or reproduced in any form, by print, photoprint, microfilm, microfiche, or any other means, without written permission from the publisher.

Cover design by Michael Baldwin, MSIAD

Order from:
Wilfrid Laurier University Press
Wilfrid Laurier University
Waterloo, Ontario, Canada N2L 3C5

TABLE OF CONTENTS

Preface ix

Traditions in Contact and Change: Towards a
History of Religion in the Singular
Wilfred Cantwell Smith 1

I. Indian Traditions and Western Interaction

The Flood Story in Vedic Ritual
J. C. Heesterman 25

Hindu Formulas for the Facilitation of Change
Norvin Hein 39

The Role of the Śaivagama in the Emergence of
Śaivasiddhanta: A Philosophical Interpretation
K. Sivaraman 53

Some Western Interpretations of the Bhagavad Gītā,
1785-1885
Eric J. Sharpe 65

From Hindu Strīdharma to Universal Feminism: A Study
of the Women of the Nehru Family
K. Young 87

Social Change and Religious Transformation among
Bombay Parsis in the Early Twentieth Century
John R. Hinnells .105

Christliche Interpretamente in der Khasi-Renaissance:
Zur religiösen Bedeutung einer Reformbewegung bei den
Hochland-Khasi von Meghalaya
P. Gerlitz 127

II. Buddhist, Chinese and Japanese Studies

Buddhism Through Hindu Eyes: Śaivas and Buddhists in
Medieval Tamilnad
Glenn E. Yocum 143

The Problem of the Origin of the Mahayana
Andrew Rawlinson .163

Filial Piety and Buddhism: The Indian Antecedents to
a "Chinese" Problem
J. Strong 171

Once-Born, Twice-Born Zen: William James and the
Rinzai and Sōtō Schools of Japanese Buddhism
Conrad Hyers 187

Lyrical Imagery and Religious Content in Japanese Art: The Pictorial Biography of Ippen the Holy Man
Laura S. Kaufman. 201

Japanese Rural Communities and Shinto Shrines Since the Meiji Restoration (1868): A Case Study in the Central Area of Mie Prefecture
Haruo Sakurai. 231

Symposium Canada-Chine
Jacques Langlais. 241

Three Religious Ontological Claims: "Being-Itself," "Nothingness within Somethingness," and "The Field of Emptiness"
Frederick J. Streng .249

III. Mediterranean Cultures

Die Bedeutung der Apokryphen Salomo-Oden für die Neutestamentliche Wissenschaft
Michael Lattke. 267

L'Importance du "Rouleau de Temple" pour l'identification de la Communauté de Qumran
Witold Tyloch 285

Terminological Boobytraps and Real Problems in Second-Temple Judaeo-Christian Studies
Morton Smith. 295

The Foster Child: A Neglected Theme in Early Christian Life and Thought
John H. Corbett 307

Mani's Opposition to the Elchasaites: A Question of Ritual
Jorunn Jacobsen Buckley 323

The Transformation of Christianity into Roman Religion
John Helgeland. 337

Le Sopravvivenze Pagane Nel Medioevo
Pierre Boglioni 347

Israel and Byzantium: A Case of Socio-Religious Acculturation
John Wortley. 361

The Change in Status of Women in Iceland from Pagan to Christian Times
Ellen Johns 377

Contribution à l'Etude de la sacralisation de l'espace: le cas de la Paroisse Québécoise
Louis Rousseau. 383

Table of Contents

L'Axe de l'interiorité en architecture religieuse
contemporaire 409
Norman Pagé

IV. Islamic, African and Amerindian Developments

Tradition, Contact and Change in Indian Islam
Exemplified in Muhammad Iqbal's Work 427
Annemarie Schimmel

Shades of Shī^{c}ism in the Tracts of the Brethren of
Purity 447
Abbas Hamdani

Islam, Polity and Society in Turkey: A Middle Eastern
Perspective 461
M. Heper

Sacramental Food Transactions among South Asian Muslims
and Hindus 481
John P. Thorp

Otatha: Probings into Isoko Concepts of Predestiny 503
S. G. A. Osovo Onibere

Religions in Conflict and Change in the Works of Modern
African Novelists 515
Azim Nanji

Three Types of Religious Acculturation Among the
Oglala Lakota 527
Paul B. Steinmetz

The Struggle against Dependency: Equality as
Individuals or as People .543
Patrick Kerans

V. Methodological and Theoretical Discussions

Humanistic and Theological History of Religions with
Special Reference to the North American Scene 553
Joseph M. Kitagawa

The Significance of the Japanese Intellectual Tradition
for the History of Religions 565
Michael Pye

Women's Studies in Religion: The State of the Art,
1980 579
Rita M. Gross

Western Perceptions of Asia: The Romantic Vision of
Max Müller 593
Ronald W. Neufeldt

Les Reins et les Coeurs: Peut-on écrire une histoire
religieuse sur traces? 607
Michel Vovelle

Structure in Jung and Lévi-Strauss
Adrian Cunningham .621

An Analytical Philosopher looks at Oriental Mysticism
James R. Horne. 635

Truth and Dialogue in Religion: Some Cognitive-Developmental Speculations
Thomas Dean 649

Endnotes and Bibliography 671

Authors 750

Acknowledgements. .751

PREFACE

Traditions in Contact and Change contains a selection of papers from the XIVth quinquennial congress of the International Association for the History of Religions (IAHR) held in Winnipeg, Canada, August 15-20, 1980.

The theme of the Congress, which serves as the title of this volume, was reflected in the plenary addresses and in many of the papers as this selection bears witness, although scholars were given the freedom to discuss other topics of their own choosing. The programme of the Congress was carried in twenty sections covering the traditional disciplines and customary specialist areas of study. New among the sections were those for women's studies, religion and literature, and Amerindian religion. All these are established subjects of specialization in North America, but departures from the history and philosophy of religions pattern of previous Congresses. The Canadian Society for the Study of Religion/La Société canadienne pour l'Etude de la Religion, (CSSR/SCER), followed North American custom, when it hosted and organized the Congress.

The Congress attracted about 650 participants from more than thirty countries, although, given the geographic location of Winnipeg and the economic constraints on many scholars, North Americans naturally constituted the majority. A particular highlight was the participation of three scholars from the Peoples Republic of China, attending an IAHR Congress for the first time. The higher than average attendance at the Congress was in part due to the fact that the International Association for Buddhist Studies (IABS) held its third international congress conjointly with that of the IAHR. In consequence, nearly 450 academic papers and reports of one sort or another were presented, supplemented by special symposia, films and exhibitions. For financial reasons, an exhaustive set of these proceedings is not feasible. Since a more comprehensive record of Congress proceedings was provided in a book of abstracts (273 pp.) and a programme booklet (113 pp.) presented to participants at the Congress, it was decided that a selection of representative papers from each section, bearing on the theme of the Congress, would best augment and complete the official record of activities.

The essays included here represent less than a tenth of all the presentations made at the Congress. They were initially recommended by the steering committees for each section, then screened by the four editors, often in consultation with further specialists. The selections are grouped according to major traditions or families of interest, regardless of the sections in which they were given. Together they provide a fair sample of the overall thrust of the Congress. The plenary addresses were delivered by Wilfred Cantwell Smith and Annemarie Schimmel (the newly elected President of the IAHR), Joseph Kitagawa and W.S. Karunaratne, then Ambassador of Sri Lanka to the United States. We have included the three for which we received texts. (It should be pointed out that although illustrations and tables appear in the text of the papers printed here, the notes for each essay have been placed at the end of the volume. We have not included an index for the volume. Given the wide diversity of materials included it would, we think, be of little or no real value.)

Congresses do not just occur. Such gatherings involve a great deal of advance preparation involving literally hundreds of persons both academic and non-academic. It is impractical to attempt to acknowledge all those who assisted in this work individually, especially those who assisted so ably with the full programme of social and cultural events, tours and displays, that supplemented the usual academic fare. Nevertheless, there are some whose labours on behalf of the Congress cannot pass without mention. Winnipeg became the site of the XIVth Congress because of the vision of William Klassen, then Head of the

Preface

Department of Religion, and the active support of Fred Stambrook, the Dean of Arts, at the University of Manitoba. H.R.H. Prince Mikasa of Japan was our gracious and active patron.

Past Presidents of the Canadian Society, Cathleen Going and Louis Rousseau, worked closely with Dean Kitagawa, R.J. Zwi Werblowsky and H.J. van Lier, of the IAHR Secretariat, in preparing for the Congress. Y-h. Jan arranged the plenary sessions and Leslie Kawamura ably assisted us in coordinating the joint session with the IABS. The Congress owed much of its success to the programme planning of Harold Coward and the Section committees, and to the infinite patience and attention to detail of the Congress Secretariat. We especially thank Darlene Clare for her administrative and secretarial assistance and the Conference Office of the University of Manitoba.

The editors of this volume also wish to thank Harold Remus of Wilfrid Laurier University Press, in preparing the final text for publication and Valerie Perlmutter, who tirelessly keyed the text into a not entirely co-operative word-processor.

Finally, we record our thanks to the benefactors and government agencies listed on pp.754/55 who made our meeting financially viable. Special thanks is made here for the support offered the Congress by the International Council for Philosophy and Humanistic Studies/Conseil International de la Philosophie et des Sciences Humaines and for its longstanding co-operation with the IAHR, and to the Social Sciences and Humanities Research Council of Canada for its continuing support of the CSSR/SCER including its sponsorship of this Congress. The Congress was indeed a co-operative enterprise of private and government agencies at all levels.

Peter Slater
Donald Wiebe

THE FLOOD STORY IN VEDIC RITUAL

J.C. Heesterman

The flood story, like all myth, is not just an edifying or comforting tale for homiletic purposes. Perhaps we should even say that myth is not the place to look for any comfort or edification. It is concerned with the incompatible, the insoluble, with conflict and disorder. The only comfort myth may offer is that it provides us with the words, the terms, the "code" for grasping, mentally and verbally, the perplexities of the human condition. This is no mean thing, but it is not a definitive answer to the problem of existence. So also the flood story. It may be too simplistic to see it only as the onset of a new beginning, a cosmogony establishing a new and better order of life. This is, of course, an important aspect of the story. But underneath is the awesome intrusion of chaos and destruction. Even when the flood is given as a cleansing or purification necessitated by the sinful disorder of the world,[1] the overriding motif is the havoc and violence of the catastrophe. Dealing as it does with the intractable antithesis of continuity and violent break, of order and irruption of chaos, it is a deeply disturbing story.

In the oldest extant Indian versions of the flood story no reason at all is given for the catastrophe. There is no mention of any disorder or sinfulness in the human world. On the contrary, the world seems to be in good order, ritual correctness is upheld and there is no apparent need for a cataclysmic purification. This is the more remarkable since the oldest versions occur in the context of ritualistic exposition. Given the ritual's emphatic concern with order, correctness and purity, one would expect the cataclysm to be directly connected with these concerns, or even with a fatal breakdown in their observance, but no connection is made. In fact, the flood story stands strangely apart from the ritual. The only ostensible reason for its introduction in the exposition of the ritual is to provide a "founding charter" to a rite that is central to the sacrifice, the invocation of the goddess Iḍā. But the link between flood and Iḍā, as we shall see, appears to be rather tenuous if not factitious.

What then is the reason for the insertion of the flood story at this point? The present paper intends to investigate this question. It will then appear that the insertion is related to a fundamental reorientation of sacrificial ritual. Being itself violent in origin, the flood story is used to handle the critical problem of sacrificial violence in a new way. On this, rather than on its tenuous connection with Iḍā, rests its claim to be a "charter myth."

But first let us look at the flood story as it is told in the 'Satapathabrāhmaṇa.[2] A small fish comes accidentally between the hands of Manu - always a paragon of ritualistic correctness - when he properly starts the day with his morning ablutions. The small fish pleads with Manu to save him from the rapaciousness of the other fishes and offers in return to save Manu's life. Undaunted rather than unbelieving, Manu asks from what mortal danger the fish will save him and is told of the coming flood. Manu's next question is how he should save the fish. He is then instructed to transvase it during the successive stages of its growth from a water pot to a tank, from there to the river Ganges and finally, when full-grown, to the ocean. Before finally setting out into the ocean the now mighty fish tells Manu when the flood will occur and instructs him to build a ship. The fish promises to return and to guide Manu through the flood. So it happens. The fish has Manu tie the ship to the horn on its head and draws it safely across to the northern mountain. There Manu is told to moor the ship to a tree and to descend gradually after the retreating waters. The text then states laconically: "the flood had swept away all creatures, only Manu was left." This leaves the problem how to set life into motion again, for Manu did not take with him aboard the ship (as in the later Indian versions) the seeds of all manner of life.[3] This is not fortuitious. The restoration of life has to be brought about by the ritual. And so Manu, "desirous of offspring," engages in "worship and austerities" and makes an offering of milk products - ghee, sour milk, whey and curds - in the (now retreated) waters. In a year's time there arises from this offering a resplendent woman, in whose footstep ghee gathers. Here the story brings in another theme: the woman encounters the gods Mitra and Varuna who want to claim her as theirs. She tells them, however, that she is Manu's daughter. The two gods nevertheless claim the right to a share (*apitya*) in her. The text then drops this theme again, only telling us that the woman neither acknowledged nor rejected the claims on her and passed them by to go to Manu. When asked by Manu who she is, she explains that, having arisen from his offering in the waters, she is his daughter. By employing her in the middle part of the sacrifice, she tells him, he will become rich in offspring and cattle. And so, "worshipping and exerting himself with her," as the text puts it ambiguously, Manu generated through her the human race and obtained all the blessings he wished for. The text then rounds off the story with its punch-line: "This woman is the same as the Idā [that is: the deified sacrificial food] and whosoever knowing this performs the sacrificial ritual with the Idā thereby propagates, like Manu, the human race and obtains all blessings." So the main point of the flood story in the Satapathabrāhmana is the deft interweaving of sacrifice and procreation in the figure of the woman who is at the same time the Idā invoked in the middle of the sacrifical ritual.[4] By the same token the obvious incest motif - otherwise prominent in cosmogony, as in the case of Prajāpati and his daughter - is de-emphasized or even avoided.

Although the purpose of the food story is ostensibly to provide a basis for the Idā ceremony of the sacrificial ritual, the linkage between food and Idā is not as obvious as the text wants to make it. The story clearly falls into two independent parts, the flood on the one hand, the Idā on the other. At the hinge between the two parts we already noticed some uneasiness, namely where Mitra and Varuṇa intervene but immediately and inconclusively drop out of the story. More important, however, is the fact that the Śatapathabrāhmaṇa is alone in including the flood story at this point, if at all. The other brāhmaṇas give a different account of the Idā, where Mitra and Varuṇa do indeed play an important part but where there is no question of a cosmic flood. Conversely, the other mention of the flood - a short reference in the Kāṭhakasaṃhitā[5] - puts it in a different context and has nothing to say about the Idā. Here too Manu, only survivor of the flood, makes an offering somewhat resembling the one in the Śatapathabrāhmaṇa's story. "With that [offering] he performed the sacrifice," this text tells us, "with that [offering] he spread out [aprathata], with that [offering] he came to this plenitude [imaṃ bhūmānam agacchat]." Although the image of spreading out the plenitude (or the earth's plenitude) could conceivably be linked, or rather conflated, with the Idā theme, it belongs to a different context, namely the cosmogonic scenario of the demiurge spreading out and fastening the earth that has emerged from or floats on the primeval waters.[6] The theme of the primeval waters and the *terra instabilis* blends easily enough with that of the flood, but the ghee-filled footprint, characteristic of the Idā, has little if anything to do with either the floating earth or the flood.

But perhaps the flood story, apart from introducing the Idā, is meant to account in its own right for the ritual. Evidently there is a telling parallelism: as a new world arises from the devastation of the deluge, so new life is created out of the destruction of sacrifice. Moreover, as the primeval waters are the basic element in the diluvial cosmogony, so water is prominent in the ritual. Thus the Soma sacrifice begins and ends with a bath. In connection with the final bath (*avabhṛtha*) it is stated that the ocean is the womb (*yoni*) of the sacrifice. At the *avabhṛtha*, it is said, "one makes the sacrifice go

[back] to its own womb."[7] The sacrifice, then, arises cyclically from the waters and is made to return to its aquatic birthplace. One is tempted to think of Manu's fish coming out of the water and finally, when full-grown, brought back to the ocean, as is the sacrifice after its completion. Similarly there is the recurrent theme of the sacrifice or of the sacrificial fire fleeing from service with gods and men and taking refuge in the waters.[8]

Particularly interesting for our purpose is the way this theme is used in a Vādhūla text[9] because of the part fishes play in it. The gods want to rearrange the universe so that the gods representing the elements of fire, sun, wind and waters, who were at first differently located, can take up their residences in the spaces proper to each of them. To that end the gods seek to perform a sacrifice, but are in doubt as to the ways and means of this sacrifice. Agni, the Fire, then offers to have himself immolated as a sacrifice (*medha*) to himself. However, when immolated, *medha* (sacrifice) and *asu* (life) escape. The sacrifice is then repeated by immolation - again the escaped and recaptured *medha* part.[10] But each time the double residue of *medha* and *asu* escapes taking the form of particular creatures. In this way a double series of creatures is successively brought about by the sacrifice, the *medha* creatures being each time immolated, while the *asu* ones - apparently unfit for sacrifice - are left alone. Finally the last *medha* residue, in the form of rice and barley, escapes, hides in the waters and is swallowed by two fishes, the rice by a *rohita* fish and the barley by a fish called *caṣa*. The two fishes clearly represent sacrifice. Not only are they equated with the sacrificial substance they have swallowed, but they are also said to carry on their heads sacrificial implements, the *rohita* fish mortar and pestle, the *caṣa* a winnowing basket. When the gods finally catch them the fishes - or rather the two sacrificial substances, rice and barley - explain that by immolating them the sacrifice would be as small as they are themselves. First the gods should allow them to multiply. When the gods ask how this should be brought about, they are given the plough and instructed about agriculture. Only after the rice and the barley have grown and multiplied do the gods successfully complete their sacrifice for the re-arrangement of the universe.

    The Vādhūla text summarized here raises an abundance of interesting leads: sacrifice as cosmogony, the interplay of the two basic elements of fire and water, the creative as well as the threatening, destructive aspect of sacrifice, the residual essence of sacrifice that through its flight under different guises establishes the diversity and plenitude of life and finally the founding of agriculture together with vegetal sacrifice. For our purpose the main interest attaches to a comparison of the two fishes with the one in the flood story. Thus the *caṣa* fish of Vādhūla immediately recalls the *jhaṣa* in the flood story.[11] More importantly, in both cases life is represented by the fish. In Vādhūla's text it is the life-giving essence of sacrifice that is carried by the two fishes. In the flood story too we see that life and its dynamics are represented by the fish. For on Manu's ark life is entirely in abeyance. As we saw, not even the seeds of life have been taken on board. All life and action are in the waters with the fish who safely carries Manu across. Similarly, in both cases there is an emphasis on the need to let the fish grow or multiply. In Vādhūla's account this entails the founding of agriculture with a view to the growth and multiplication of rice and barley. In the flood story great attention is given to Manu's efforts to have the fish grow to an enormous size exceeding even the capacity of the Ganges. Here still another point suggests itself. One easily imagines that the release of a sea-monster , like Manu's full-grown *jhaṣa*, would by itself be sufficient to unleash the flood. Or, in other words, the growth of the fish seems tantamount to a swelling of the waters that ends in the catastrophic deluge. Indeed the flood story begins with an insignificant amount of washing water brought to Manu in the morning with the equally harmless fish in it. At the turning point both waters and fish have developed to monstrous proportions. The life-force contained in the fish and in the waters is ambivalent. When fully developed it brings both destruction and salvation. This seems already to be anticipated in the beginning of the story when the little fish refers to the internecine rapaciousness among the fishes. The motif of life's ambivalence does not come out so clearly in Vādhūla. There more attention is given to the violence of sacrifice that causes its essence to flee. But it seems significant that the two fishes swallow and do not want to give up the life-giving essence of sacrifice. Only by exercising their force as well as their wits are the gods able to catch them and force them to give up the secret.

Finally the fishes have in both cases striking excrescences on their heads. With Vādhūla the two fishes carry sacrificial implements on their heads, manifesting thereby their sacrificial identity. In the case of Manu's fish there is no such clear-cut reference to sacrifice. It has, however, been suggested that the horn, to which Manu's boat is tied, may represent the sacrificial pole ($y\bar{u}pa$).[12] If so, the fish in the flood story - though otherwise unrelated to sacrifice - would not only be the life force active in the waters, but would also represent sacrifice. Whether we are justified in equating the horn with the $y\bar{u}pa$ or not is perhaps not so important as the point that the flood story seems to fit in with the course of sacrificial ritual in yet another respect. I refer to the *avabhṛtha*. There, as already mentioned, the sacrifice is brought back to its birthplace, the waters, like Manu's fish. Also Manu's offering in the waters would seem to parallel the offering in the avabhrtha water (*avabhṛtheṣṭi*).[13] Perhaps we may even go further. After the final bath there comes yet another sacrifice, that of a cow, to Mitra and Varuṇa,[14] starting as it were a new sacrificial cycle. Would it be possible to connect this sacrifice with the intervention of Mitra and Varuṇa after the flood in Manu's story?

The flood story, then, when compared with Vādhūla's account of the sacrifice's origins, seems to be rich in ritual symbolism. However, the comparison also shows that the flood story proper - that is, the first part ending with Manu's descent from the northern mountain - is strangely lacking in direct references to sacrificial ritual. While Vādhūla's account from beginning to end turns on sacrifice, the flood story proper does not even allude to it. It is only against the general backdrop of the association of sacrifice with the waters - as, for instance, in the fairly common identification of sacrifice and waters[15] - that the connection with the ritual seems to impose itself. Once one starts looking for connecting points, one does indeed find many leads. But, even so, the story as told in the Śatapathabrāhmaṇa does not follow up any of the possible leads. It steers clear of the ritual and its terminology. Only in the second part of the story, when the Iḍā rises from Manu's offering in the waters, is the connection with the ritual made. But, as we already observed, the hinge between the two parts looks curiously factitious. The waters in which Manu makes his offering are, strictly speaking, no longer those of the flood. The flood has retreated and Manu has completed his descent from the mountain. The fish that instructed Manu on all manner of detail, has nothing to say about offerings. And when the Iḍā finally comes out of the water Manu does not even recognize her at first. The only connection between flood and Iḍā is, in fact, a somewhat spurious *post hoc ergo propter hoc*. The flood story looks like an erratic insertion, interrupting rather than strengthening the course of ritual exposition. The question then is: why was the story of the deluge inserted at all? Perhaps a short investigation of the Iḍā may give us a clue.

The Iḍā is invoked by the *hotṛ* priest in the middle of the sacrificial ritual after the main oblations in the fire.[16] The *adhvaryu* priest meanwhile cuts off some small slices, called *Iḍā*, of the offering substance, which are eaten by the sacrificer and his priests. The Iḍā ceremony stands for the ritual meal at which the participants share the Iḍā, the sacrificial food. The Iḍā, then, is the life-sustaining substance that is released by sacrifice, to be enjoyed by the participants. In this connection it may be mentioned that the Iḍā ceremony also is the time for bringing up and distributing the *dakṣiṇās* or gifts to the priest - another form of the life-sustaining substance.[17] After the destructive part of the sacrifice, signified by offering up the burnt oblation in the fire, the renewed life is set in motion again and distributed in the tangible form of food and gifts. In this way we can easily understand that after the devastation of the flood the Iḍā is essential to set life in motion again. But if this explains the function of the Iḍā *after* the flood, it does not justify that her appearance should be preceded by a flood. Perhaps one should not ask such questions in mythology. But the fact is that, apart from the Śatapathabrāhmaṇa, the texts have no need for the flood to explain the Iḍā's appearance. The Taittirīyasaṃhitā gives the following account:

Manu was looking for (a proper place) of the earth for sacrifice; he then found (a spot with) spilled ghee; he said "Who is able to produce this at the sacrifice also?" Mitra and Varuṇa answered: "It is the cow, we are able to produce (her)"; they then set the cow in motion; wherever she stepped, from there ghee was pressed out; therefore she [i.e. the Iḍā] is called ghee-footed (*ghṛtápadī*); that is her origin.[19]

In the first place Mitra and Varuṇa - in contradistinction to the Śatapatha version - here come into their own as the prime movers of the Iḍā.[20] But the main point is the ghee-dripping foot or footprint of the divine Iḍā cow. This spot, the *iḍas* or *iḍā́yās pada*, is said to be the best spot, the top of the navel of the earth, in other words, the creative centre of the world. There Agni, the offering fire and primordial *hotṛ* priest, has his seat or birthplace.[21] Not surprisingly Iḍā is both the mother and the daughter of Agni.[22] Her footprint is the primeval place of sacrifice and as such associated with Manu, prototype of the sacrificer and progenitor of the human race. This, it would seem, gives the Iḍā a firmer, more cogent ritual charter than the loosely connected flood story. But we still have to look further into the connection of the ghee-filled footprint, characteristic of the Iḍā with the sacrificial meal.

The clearest ritual manifestation of the footprint is not in the Iḍā ceremony but in the rite of the seventh step of the Soma cow, that is, the cow that will function as the barter price at the purchase of the Soma stalks.[23] After a piece of gold - representative of the fire - has been put on the step ghee is poured on it. Then the sand of the footprint is taken up and divided in three parts, two parts being thrown on the hearths of the gārapatya and āhavanīya fires and the third given to the sacrificer's wife. The mantras that accompany this rite call the Soma cow Iḍā and refer to her seventh step as "the head of the earth", "the sacrificial spot of the earth" and "Iḍā's footprint filled with ghee." Interestingly the Soma cow is also called dakṣiṇā.[24] As I have argued elsewhere,[25] the Soma cow and the dakṣiṇā are related to each other as the two poles of the cyclical regeneration process of the goods of life, which starts with the Soma cow and its seventh step and reaches its acme at the distribution of food and gifts. The Iḍā cow, then, covers the whole of the sacrificial process. We may add that the maitrāvaruṇī cow sacrificed at the end of the Soma ritual, after the final bath, seems equally connected with the Iḍā cow. This maitrāvaruṇī cow is a vaśā, that is, a cow that has become barren after having had a calf. This reminds us of the (exhausted) womb that remained after Prajāpati's creation, or rather release, of the different kinds of beings out of himself. "The womb that was left over became the cow; she is 'womb' [yoni] by name."[26] Further on, in the same text, the Iḍā cow is said to have been fashioned by Mitra and Varuna out of an indigesta moles produced by the gods. The different kinds of being exploit her, and, finally, when she is completely exhausted, reject her. Prajāpati, however, takes pity on her and grants her the ghee-dripping foot, in other words, he restores her and makes her inexhaustible.[27] This tale of maltreatment, exhaustion and restoration together with the apparent connection with the maitrāvaruṇī cow seems to suggest that the Iḍā is not only the Soma cow, the dakṣiṇā cow and possibly also the maitrāvaruṇī vaśā, but equally the sacrificial victim in general. Whose meat is shared and eaten at the sacrificial meal. Strangely, however, no explicit connection is made. The nearest we get to this point is when the Idā and *dakṣiṇā* cows are equated, but no direct link is given as regards the *vaśā* cow of Mitra and Varuṇa.

Nevertheless there are several indications that the Idā cow is equally the immolated victim. The mantras addressed to the victim, when it is led up to the sacrificial pole, are equally addressed to the Soma cow.[28] This does not seem to be fortuitous. As we saw, Idā is Manu's daughter as well as his wife, and ritual mythology has it that Manu's obsessive ritual correctness did not even stop at having his own wife immolated.[29] In this respect - as in others - she recalls the goddess Śrī, Prosperity, who comes forth from the exhausted Prajāpati. The gods want to kill and rob her. But Prajāpati objects that one does not kill a woman, instead one takes everything from her while leaving her alive. The gods then do just that, leaving her much like the exploited and rejected Idā.[29] This sorry tale is meant to explain a particular sacrifice, the *mitravindeṣṭi*. It suggests that the gods share Śrī, or Prosperity, among each other at a sacrificial meal, as the participants in any sacrifice share in the Idā. But, as we saw, the critical point of the immolation is eliminated by Prajāpati's intervention.

Now, communal meals are hardly tolerated in the *śrauta* ritual. The perfectly anodyne Idā ceremony is the last vestige of the sacrificial meal and it is of cow's meat, as in the sacrifice for the "Householder" (*gṛhamedhin*) Maruts,[30] or in the case of the cow for whose parts the participants gamble in the rite to establish the sacred fires (*agnyādhāna*).[31] That such cows are the tangible substance of the Idā may by now seem fairly obvious, notwithstanding the reticence of the texts. But there is one instance where they almost seem to give away the game. This is in the rite of the Soma cow's seventh step. When a line is drawn round the ghee-filled footprint with a view to taking it up, the accompanying mantra says: "Here I cut the neck of the evil spirit, here I cut the neck of him who hates us and whom we hate."[32] The ghee-mixed dust of the footprint is equated with cattle and therefore this rite is supposed to make the sacrificer rich in cattle. If we further consider that just before, when the ghee libation was made, the spot of the footprint was called "the head of the goddess Aditi" and "head of the earth," then one can hardly avoid anymore the idea of a killing or immolation of cattle, that is, of cattle belonging to one's rival or enemy. Accordingly the next mantra claims: "With us be wealth." So not only is the Iḍā cow subjected to violence and immolation before she can perform her beneficial life-giving function at the sacrificial meal, she is also the object of agonistic proceedings between rival parties. This seems to be confirmed by a curious passage of the *Maitrāyaṇīsamhitā*.[33] The gods were, as usual, in conflict with their rivals, the asuras. The goddess Aditi was then with the gods, her counterpart, and the otherwise unknown Kustā with the asuras. The gods planned to cut off Kustā's head if they should win. Conversely the asuras had the same in mind for Aditi in case they are victorious. As we expect, the gods won and decapitated the asuras' Kustā. The text continues to tell us that therefore in the house of a victorious conqueror Kustā, apparently in the form of a cow conquered from the other party, is killed. The interesting point is that this passage, together with other no less agonistic ones, occurs in the *gonāmika* part which is an extensive treatment of the Iḍā.

Behind the Iḍā ceremony, then, there lurks the ugly spectre of violent conflict, such as the one between gods and asuras,[34] for the goods of life that moreover must be immolated before they can be enjoyed at an abundant communal meal or distributed as gifts. In this perspective we can see why the Iḍā ceremony is considered to be a violent rending apart, a breaking asunder of the sacrifice.[35] But the puzzling fact is that of all this - conflict, violence, immolation and communal meal, in short of the potlatchlike scenario suggested by several mythological and ritual features - nothing remains in the actual Iḍā ceremony. It is a perfectly peaceful and harmless affair. Even the sacrificial meal, though clearly suggested by the standard phrase in the ritual rules, "they eat the Idā," has been reduced to an almost unrecognizable minimum. The small slices forming the tangible Idā are not even eaten in community. In so far as there is a communal meal of the sacrificial food it is removed from the place of sacrifice and can take place only when the ritual is over. We can now understand why. The meal was intimately connected with intense rivalry and violence. The central thrust in the development of the śrauta ritual as we know it was, however, to exclude all violence and conflict.

The ritualists achieved this by excluding the other party from the sacrifical arena. Though the rival comes in for frequent mention, even to the point of obsession, he nowhere comes in sight anymore. The gods and asuras still had their regular battles on the place of sacrifice. By contrast, the śrauta sacrificer is alone in the sacrificial arena, except for the company of his priestly experts. And alone he strikes out on his own into a transcendent sphere, not hampered by allies and bypassing his enemies. But then the old explanations of the Idā had to go, because next to her life-giving qualities they had to stress the violence and conflict involved. It would seem that here we may find the reason for the insertion of the flood story in the Śatapathabrāhmaṇa, a younger text steeped in the new ritual doctrine. We may then also understand that the violence and devastation of the flood are in the Śatapatha's telling not only deemphasized but also, in so far as they are necessarily implied, totally unconnected with the ritual. For if they were, the destructive violence of the flood would be a recurrent feature of the ever repeated pattern of the ritual, as, for instance, would be the case if the *avabraha* would be explicitly associated with the deluge, or the *maitrāvaruṇī vaśā* with the Idā cow. The flood story is meant to be a once-for-all intrusion of chaos out of which arises the permanent order of the ritual.

The story of the deluge holds the founding charter of the ritual. As is proper for a flood story, it founds the new dispensation of the *śrauta* ritual. And it does so by putting its critical central part, the sacrificial meal, on a new footing. But even so the Iḍā ceremony continues to be viewed as a breach, a tearing apart. Our texts suggest that this refers to the intrusion of an alien element into the ultramundane *śrauta* ritual, namely the eating, the meal, that properly belongs not to the *śrauta* ritual but to the *pākayajña* of the worldly domestic ritual. But at the same time it clearly serves as a reminder of the paradox that the life-giving ritual remains intimately connected with life's opposite, with death and destruction. Manu's unworldly ritual perfection is utterly meritorious but barren. The tale of the fish confronts him with the internecine vitality of life in the depth of the waters. After this vitality has reached its destructive acme in the deluge, life recreated and expanded through the Iḍā had to admit the breaking asunder, the rending apart of the same Iḍā. The new ritual order of the universe established after the flood must give a place, however well-regulated and confined, to evil and destruction in order to perpetuate life.

HINDU FORMULAS FOR THE FACILITATION OF CHANGE

Norvin Hein

My theme has undergone some shrinkage. Many months ago, when all of us were dreaming of how to get our universities to send us to Winnipeg, I conceived a paper that I then called "Hindu Strategies for Change." That is the title you have read, possibly, in the programme of the congress, so you are entitled to expect that I shall survey the whole development of Indian cultural history, and answer all the questions raised by the official theme of our congress as well. But the clear light of the sun of midsummer, when the paper had to be written, has brought me a little sobriety.

Some oriental Aesop tells of a fox who rose at dawn and stepped out to begin his day's work. Seeing his big shadow, he said, "I shall have a *camel* for lunch today!" The morning's hunt proceeded and his shadow grew smaller and smaller. At high noon he looked for his shadow on the ground, and said, " A mouse will do."

The mouse in this case will be a handful of words and numbers, and the theme is "Hindu *Formulas* for innovation." The words and numbers I have in mind appear to have been powerful in the facilitating of change. In a religious tradition presenting very special difficulties to innovators, they were switching-tools by which new directions could be set.

"*What* new directions?" you may ask, "In Hinduism, *what* innovations?" Is Hinduism not the perennial philosophy, the eternal religion, ever the same unchanging truth varied only by insubstantial changes in outward expression? If that is your position, rest in peace: let us talk then about those "changes in outward expression." They are not few. Interpreters of Hinduism of several schools have pictured Hinduism as unchanging, and there is some truth in that generalization; but as a final characterization of Hinduism it will not do. Hinduism has accepted innovations continuously - in doctrine, in religious practice, and in religious experience. My only effort at persuasion shall be a request that you look back upon an academic experience that we all share: your first effort to read through the five volumes of S.N. Dasgupta's *History of Indian Philosophy*, and your early attempts to absorb J.N. Farquhar's dense *Outline of the Religious Literature of India*. Can anyone reflect on the stupifying mass of India's succession of schools and scriptures, and still believe that Hinduism actually stopped up the mouth of innovators? If Hinduism changed less than other traditions, the difference is not great.

What is different in Hinduism is not how *much* it changed, but *how* it changed. That question of "how?" is the question of this paper. The Hindu innovator had to practice tactics that were different indeed. The unbroken hegemony of a single continuing priestly and literary class was an adamantine fact to which all Hindu reformers had to adapt. When we see how they faced this reality, we shall understand why an ever-changing tradition has appeared to be a never-changing tradition.

The age of the Vedas ended with a religious revolution: in the seventh century B.C. the Indian world was being turned upside down. No Hindu ecclesiastical history directly says so, however. Unaided by any internal reporting of great conflicts, scholars read through the chronological strata of Hindu sacred writings, and suddenly they find Upanishads, and suddenly there are *dharmasūtras* and *dharmaśāstras* and suddenly they find themselves in a new world. New types of religious leaders are cultivating new types of relegous experience in the context of new cosmologies and new values. A new social structure has taken shape, governed by a new social ethics. The subversion of the Vedic order was at least as thorough as any transformation wrought by the Protestant Reformation or by the rise of Christianity within Judaism.

Hindu theoreticians picture the transition as a serene course of events: a happy succession of *samhitā*, Brāhmaṇa, Āraṇyaka, Upanishad and so forth, one harmonious line of scriptures revealed to sages of a single spirit. But scholars perceive that the Upanishads were born in tension; reading between the lines they have recovered the usual story of a struggle between old and new. We shall not rehearse here their ingenious account of the processes of this change. Our interest focuses upon the *strategy* of change: How was the acceptance of these strange new scriptures effected? How did this radical innovation succeed? To answer fully would require, by the standards of occidental church history, a multi-volume work. I believe that something of this problem can be understood if we can perceive all the meaning that lies in two Indic terms that served to bridge the gap between old and new in this first of known Indian revolutions.

The first of these relational words is "Vedānta." It occurs twice in the Upanishads. The Muṇḍaka Upanishad 3:2.6-8 speaks of "the Vedānta knowledge," and the chief points of the content of that *vedāntavijñāna* are then mentioned. They are the characteristic teachings of the Upanishads. The Svetāsvatara Upanishad in the finale of its discourse calls its own message "the supreme secret in the Vedānta [*vedānte paramam guhyam*]," 6:22. "Vedānta" is being used as a designation for the "Upanishad tradition." The term stuck.

"Vedānta" is a one-word history of the domestication of an innovation. "Veda-anta" it means, etymologically, the Veda's end - in two senses. The Upanishads were that portion of Vedic canon that was last in the sequence of traditional Veda-recitation, and the portion that was last appended in later written compilations. The Upanishads were the end of the Veda *positionally*. More important, they were the end - i.e. the consummation - of the presentation of Vedic teaching *pedagogically*. By the time the word "Vedānta" came into use, the material at the end of any instructional presentation had been given a special function: it was the phase at which the complete and unqualified doctrine of the teacher was at last clearly presented. Such progressive instruction is found for example in Chāndogya Upanishad 8:7-13 where it is only in the fourth and final stage of indoctrination that Prajāpati tells Indra the full truth about the nature of the Soul.[1] "Vedānta" identifies Upanishad doctrine as the Veda's crowning truth.

In the Upanishads the term "Vedānta" occurs rather late. Its use reflects, then, long consideration of the problem of the relation between the new light and the old. It reveals the tactic by which the producers of the Upanishads succeeded in giving their religion a status not inferior to that of the more ancient sacrificial tradition. In calling their gospel "Vedānta" the reformers are saying that the appearance of the Upanishads involved no disruption: Vedic teaching, whether in premonition or in consummation, is one continuous process. The *rishis* of old had insight into this teaching, says the Svetāsvatara Upanishad in the passage mentioned: the secret had been "proclaimed in olden time," *purākalpe pracoditam*. Now the Upanishads bring fully into the light a primeval truth that had been the secret essence of the Vedas from the start. No new discovery is involved; no change, really, has occurred, but only the faithful stressing of the essence of old truth.

In the Mahābhārata, "Vedānta" has become the commonplace term for the Upanishads, and such it remains until this day. Acceptance of the word continues to involve acceptance of its picture of the relation between *samhitā* and Upanishad. It bridges a chasm still, connecting to the satisfaction of many the mystical religion of the Upanishads with the sacrificial religion against which it revolted 2,500 years ago.

The post-Vedic overturn brought changes in more than religious experience. There was equally radical change in Aryan social structure and social ethics. The mobile Vedic society composed of classes that were few and flexible gave way to a ranked and disciplined society of hereditary occupational groups. The religious ethics that bound this hierarchy of castes and age-groups together was called *varnāśrama dharma*. It was formulated in specialized scriptures of a radically-new type. These scriptures - the *dharmasūtras* and *dharmaśāstras* - were also called *smṛti*. *Smṛti* is the second of our bridge-words, and a concept that facilitated a social innovation of astounding dimension.

A social metamorphosis of the magnitude of the post-Vedic change in India is hard to find elsewhere outside the context of a conversion to a new religion. Muslim Arabs look back across a similar gap and call their former condition "the age of ignorance." Christians look back upon the transition from the Law to the Gospel and consider that they entered then not only a new religion but a new cosmic age. Hindus look back on as drastic an overturn with no sense of change: they live in the "Vedic" society still. And the arch-Vedists among the Hindu learned, the *karmamīmāmsist* scholars who are the guardians of the continuing Vedic religion, heartily agree. The *karma-mīmāmsists* are the very theorists, in fact, who drew up the orthodox formula by which caste-world became Vedic world and *varnāśrama* ethics became "Vedic" ethics. In a thousand years of literary effort they developed in their handbooks the theory of *smṛti*: that the social requirements of the revealed vedas have been re-stated in plain Sanskrit for our convenience in works called *smṛtis*[2] and which in almost all instances lay down our duties with all the authority of Vedic revelation.

Even as early as 200 B.C. we find in the Pūrvamīmām-sasūtras of Jaimini that *smṛtis* have long been known. No-one denies that they are holy books that ought to be obeyed. What the *karma-mīmāmsists* undertake to explain is why the *smṛtis* are valid, even though they are the work of human authors and differ in content from the eternally-revealed Vedas. They explain: the *smṛtis* have authority because they were composed in a better olden time by holy sages who knew the Vedas in their entirety. Though the lawbooks of those sages contain very many rules whose source cannot now be found in any known Veda, we must not assume that they have no Vedic base and no Vedic force. The authors of the *smritis* were trusty persons, and a much more extensive Vedic literature was available to them, including texts that have been lost - or rather that are scattered now in unknown places.³ Those Vedic texts that are no longer available are the invisible source of almost all those *smriti* rules whose authentication cannot be found in the Vedas that we still possess. We may reject commands found in *dharmaśāstras* only when they contradict a plain Vedic text, or when their patent source is the self-interest of a *smriti*-writer. Otherwise they are authentic and advantageous current guides to religious living for those who belong to the Vedic tradition. They are equivalent to Vedas: *vedatulyā hi smriti*.⁴

In its own realm of social thought, the word *smriti*, like the word *vedānta*, minimized the contrast between ages and extended the sanctity of the old to the radically new. *Smriti* made the new society somehow a "Vedic" society, made new moral codes into restatements of eternal regulations, and made the post-Vedic social change into non-change in the Hindu mind.

In time, epics and purānas also were acknowledged to be *smriti*, and even later innovations were clothed in a derivative sanctity by scarcely-conscious extension of this principle of restatement. As a matter of fact, *any* religious writing could gain acceptance in the "Vedic" tradition if it expressed the doctrinal and moral consensus of its time, if it was issued under the nominal authorship of some ancient sage, and if it had the *nihil obstat*, interested or disinterested, of a few approving brahmans. Thus a people who were bound, in theory, to every syllable of a supernatural and infallible scripture, became in fact permissive of change, and uninhibited participants in radical transitions. In the new, when seen through the spectacles of the *smriti* concept, the old truth was present still.

So far we have been studying old formulas that are famous. Let me elaborate now on this same Hindu approach to change as seen in less familiar devices. A cabala of numerology is involved, and an irenic technique for the introduction of the new that I call, in English, the Device of Just-one-more. Indian theorists have not explained it. Neither have its users discussed it. The Just-one-more strategem becomes null when talked about. It has no Indic name. Having become an expert now in the art of authenticizing, I have cooked up for Just-one-more a hoary-sounding Sanskrit name. It shall be known as *ekottaropaya*, "the device of one more (counting finger)."

The preceptor of the art of *ekottaropaya* counsels his radical young disciples thus: "When you must present a teaching that is a recent fabrication, acknowledge only such degree of novelty as is absolutely unconcealable. Attach your new doctrine to the sequence of an unimpeachable old formula. Speak well of that old formula. Do not suggest that its author knew little, but that *you* know a little more. Present your addendum as something that completes rather than contradicts, like the full orb of the waxing moon emerging from shadow. Invite your hearer to move forward with the rhythm of your impeccable counting: ask him to take only one short leap, a leap irresistible in its naturalness and totally faithful to the old direction of his logic."

I shall cite several examples of the use of the Just-one-more technique, from the Śatapatha Brāhmaṇa. The numbers 4, 5, 17 and 34 have been used by its author to introduce important new ideas with minimum shock and with a maximum of conventionality.

In several passages the Śatapatha Brāhmaṇa pronounces in a most solemn manner that Prajāpati, the divine "Lord of Progeny," is the Thirty-fourth.[5] The declaration is weighty, but to the uninitiated its import is not very clear. A study of the context reveals that the puzzling numerical assertion is made in connection with a matter that is not insignificant. The passages constitute one of Hinduism's earliest expositions of a monotheistic theory of the universe. Rigveda 10:129 had suggested only in passing the possibility of a God before the gods. Vishnu and Śiva in the Śatapatha Brāhmaṇa have not yet begun to become foci of monotheistic thought. The great deity of this Brāhmaṇa is Prajāpati and the first serious effort to produce the fabric of a monotheistic cosmology is centering upon him. Prajāpati is said to be sacrifice personified; he possesses therefore all the productive powers of the sacrifice, and thus of the whole Vedic pantheon. He is all-progenitor, the source of all that is and the being of all that is. He was the creator of the gods. It is this newly-postulated One God of the universe who is declared to be the Thirty-fourth! To an adherent of the Biblical tradition this seems a peculiar way of reinforcing one's monotheistic position. What is the logic of this statement?

The significance of Prajāpati's status as the Thirty-fourth lies in the fact that, by general agreement since Indo-Iranian times, the gods of the Aryan pantheon are properly thirty-three. The early Buddhists were familiar with this statistic of the celestial census: the Buddha descends to earth from Trayastriṁśa, the Heaven of the Thirty-three. The Śatapatha Brāhmaṇa itself gives lists in which the roster of the gods is made somehow to add up to that total. Thirty-three is the total of the gods of earth, atmosphere and heaven - all the gods there are. It is in *that* context that it makes sense to say that Prajāpati is Thirty-fourth. The statement has a double significance.

First, there is an aggressiveness here, negative toward teaching of the past. If Prajāpati is Thirty-fourth, he is not one of the familiar old *devas*, the nature-gods. The *devas* are only thirty-three. Prajāpati belongs to a new order and probably to a superior order. He is a *different* kind of divinity.

Another passage in the Śatapatha Brāhmaṇa[6] confirms its stress on the differentness of Prajāpati, in a similar arithmetic claim. It is a cryptic statement, in this case, that Prajāpati is the *Fourth*. His Fourthness is in relation to the three *lokas*. These are the three strata of the natural world - earth, atmosphere, and heaven - in one or another of which each of the 33 *devas* is said to reside. Prajāpati's abode, we are to understand, is none of these regions of nature, but in a loftier fourth transcendant realm. He is not *in* nature, but above nature.

Transcendance of another kind is asserted in an esoteric statement, elsewhere, that the number of Prajāpati is Seventeen. What is transcended in this enumeration is the aggregate of the 16 *tattvas* or metaphysical elements in the composition of the human psyche. As Seventeenth, Prajāpati is beyond the competence of human understanding, he is not mentally penetrable. Neither is he, as Seventeenth, further factorable or measurable. He is explicable only in terms of himself.[7]

Whether proclaiming a God who is 17th, or 4th, or 34th, the proclaimer of Prajāpati announces an unprecedented kind of God who is not included in or comprehended by the natural world, who in some way surpasses the category of the known gods. Something of the historic offensiveness of the world's original monotheistic proclamations is found here in India also.

Yet all of these figures, in a second unfolding of their meaning, soften the shock of the proclamation of the new God's otherness. A God who is really 34th could not be so if 33 gods do not exist, or if the 33 belong to an utterly unrelated genus, a non-comparable order of being. Prajāpati surpasses but he does not contradict the nature of the *devas*, nor does he require their elimination. The Śatapatha proposes a monotheism that should be intelligible and acceptable because it goes only *one step beyond* conceptions of deity that have long been familiar. What the author asks is an extension, not a reversal, of the old understanding of the sacred. Just one more insight is required.

Hindu monotheists in a later and different confrontation used the *ekottara* device in proclaiming their Lord to be the Twenty-sixth! Their audiences in that case were not worshippers of 33 gods but of none. These are the adherents of the atheistic Sāmkhya system. In their metaphysics these thinkers acknowledged 24 material realities, and one spiritual category to which individual souls belonged: 25 in total, and that is all. This Sāmkhya analysis had its supporting Upanishad texts, and it provided a useful analysis of the psyche that enjoyed wide acceptance. The Indian evangelists of monotheism embraced the doctrine as far as it went, and proclaimed that, beyond it, there is a Twenty-Sixth Reality. It is Isvara, the Lord who presides over all these twenty-five, and is the giver of salvation. In their approach to believers in Sāmkhya these monotheists continued the familiar old Indian method of One-upsmanship.[8]

Such accommodation to polytheism has been characteristic of Indian monotheism. Contrast it with Isaiah's "I am the Lord and there is no other; besides me there is no God" (45:5). Remember also the Occident's thousand years of battle between polytheism and monotheism, from Zarathustra to Muhammad. Our undertaking today is not to evaluate Hindu strategy, however, but to depict its tendency: India's nascent monotheism, like all else new in India, gained a place for itself by a policy of minimizing the difference of the new.

The most audacious of all operations of One-upsmanship has been the attempt to add to the number of the Vedas. The first campaign of this kind appears to have been successful. In the earliest period of our knowledge the Vedic wisdom is a *trayī vidyā* and the number of the Vedas is three. They are known as three in early Buddhist literature,[9] and there are brahmans in South India still who recognize no more.[10] But in Mundaka Upanishad 1.1.5 the priests called Atharvans have already "made it" with some high-placed persons: their hymns are mentioned as constituting an Atharva-*veda*. In the Mahābhārata that acceptance has become general: the Vedas when numbered are accounted to be four. The trick had been done.

And if done once, why not again? If there could be a fourth Veda, why not a fifth? New Vedas could not be written *de novo*, of course, for all true Vedas have existed from eternity. But Vedas now unknown could be newly discovered; and among old books of unknown origin, some could be newly discovered to be Vedas. As we have seen, Vedas have been lost, and as eternal books they could not have been destroyed. They are in existence somewhere. And why should someone not find them?[11]

Not surprisingly, some were found. No sooner had the Atharvan collection obtained secure Vedic status than writers began to push the candidacy of others. Many Mahābhārata readings claim Vedic status for the Mahābhārata itself.[12] The theologian Madhva in the thirteenth century calls the epics, *purāṇas* and the Vaishnava *saṃhitās* a fifth Veda for the lower castes.[13]

But the really daring Hindu claim to Vedahood was made on behalf of the tāntra literature that began to appear about the middle of the first millennium A.D. If tāntrism was not a revolution against the Vedic tradition, the tradition has not known one. Just here, where the challenge to Vedic ideals was greatest, the claim to Vedic status is made with special persistence. Some tāntric writers are content to have the tantras viewed, like the *smṛtis*, as no more than the practical equivalent of Vedas - restatements and adaptations of archaic codes, remade to suit the capacity of weak humanity in the evil Kali age. But the Niruttara Tantra and the Meru Tantra include the tantras in the Vedas themselves. The Niruttara says they are a fifth Veda. Other Tantras elaborate on the claim, saying that the Tantras were revealed from the lips of the fifth face of Śiva, just as the familiar ones issued from the other four. Because Śiva himself was the utterer of the tantras, they are of course fully revealed and fully equivalent to the other four, and absolutely independent sources of highest truth.[14]

Was a more audacious legitimation ever proposed?

Well, perhaps. The most dashing attempt to promote a scripture by adding it to the Vedas may have been a Christian one. The notion of a lost Veda was sufficiently alive in South India in the Seventeenth century to attract the attention of the sharp-minded Jesuit missionary, Roberto di Nobili. In a letter from Madurai, sent to the chief of his order on December 24, 1608, he says:

The local brahmans acknowledge three Vedas or codes, and they admit that none of the three offers access to eternal salvation. They say that they possessed, once upon a time, a fourth Veda, a scripture through which salvation *had* been possible; but the greater part of that saving Veda has been lost, and its few remmants lie entangled and confused in the other three.[15]

Nobili explains his tactic for getting a respectful hearing for his Christian teaching. Just as the Apostle Paul spoke to the philosophers of Athens about their unknown god, he too accommodates to the conceptions of the country. He tells the brahmans that he has come from a far country for the express purpose of bringing to them the saving law that they believe to have been lost. If they wish to know that Veda and have salvation, they need only to come to him for instruction, for he brings the forgotten teaching that they long to hear.

It appears that the brahman establishment of Madurai did not hasten to adjoin the New Testament to the canon of the Vedas. But neither were they outraged. The attempt was polite, and graced with a certain learning. In a few years' stay in India, Nobili had learned how to make a good case for acceptance of a new teaching.

I have now expended all my little hoard of change-facilitating Hindu slogans. They are mere flecks of evidence regarding the nature of culture-absorbing struggles for change about which we know very little. They provide a base, however, for a few generalizations about the operating principles of traditional Hindu innovation.

Hindu innovation was not confrontational. It never confessed that radical displacement was its purpose. Its departures from current views were not admitted to be new. They were a rehabilitation of the teaching of the sages of ideal former times; or they were the clear articulation, at last of what is implicit in established truths.

Is there anything peculiar to Hinduism in such irenic tactics? It is for comparativists to utter the last word on that question. But a *first* word, of rash surmise is as usual not repressible.

The reformers of all traditions, I believe, have rested their proposals when possible upon the ancient values of their cultures, and have stressed the continuity of their proposals with the honored past. In many societies, however, the utility of this appraoch has been limited by the existence of an effective historiography. The floating of interested interpretations of the past is often curbed by substantial information about the actualities of the past. The Western reformer, for instance, has often been compelled to label the new as new, because his hearers knew very well that it was new. The reformer had no alternative - he *had* to argue that even the *new* can be *true*. To justify such an evaluation of the new the innovating thinkers of Western culture developed an array of theologies of revolution: Revelation is progressive, and time makes ancient good uncouth. The Kingdom of God is coming in power, and the codes of former ages have lapsed and are of no effect. Evolution bears us ever onward and upward into increasing light. Thesis, antithesis and synthesis are the process of realization. Confrontation and the elimination of the old is the pathway to truth.

Not even Western religion, of course, holds that the new is necessarily true just because it is new, but we approach that position in the secular religion of Western academia, where the goddess Nova is the principal object of worship. The Apostle Paul found the philosophers of Athens spending their time "in nothing except telling or hearing something new." When we decided to come and present something at Winnipeg, we realized that our offering would have to seem new, or it would not do. You smiled knowingly, I hope, if you read the abstract in which I did my best to persuade you that the findings of this paper would be positively revolutionary. You are tolerant, because you know my necessities. Slanting material to make it seem worthy of a hearing has been a vital game in both East and West.

But the direction of the slant has often differed in the two cultures. The Western reformer can slant his message either way, according to the main chance: he can say, "I speak the truth because what I say is very old," or he can if necessary say, "I speak the truth because what I say is utterly unprecedented." The Hindu reformer had no such option: his credit rested entirely on the primeval nature of his proclamation.

The Hindu strategists of change were distinctive, then, not in the tactics used but in the tactics not used. They could not justify the deliberate destruction of tradition. They could not propose that the good and the true lie in the future rather than in the past. They could not use newness itself as the measure of truth.

THE ROLE OF THE ŚAIVĀGAMA IN THE EMERGENCE OF ŚAIVASIDDHĀNTA: A PHILOSOPHICAL INTERPRETATION

K. Sivaraman

To contemplate the phenomenon of religious traditions in contact and change, it is profitable to reflect on the commonplace truth that they are internally diverse as well as multiple. The religions of India are not only many, as any book on world religions will tell, but some of them are, internally, multiple. By multiplicity is meant that they can be tabulated numerically as six, nine, sixteen, twenty-four, or three hundred and sixty-three depending on the purpose or the vantage point of the one who contemplates them.[1] They are also multiple in the radical sense of each implying in terms of doctrine and guidance a rejection of the other, which, paradoxically, is the same as inclusion. This may be illustrated by saying that inclusion and exclusion pertain to the existential demand for a true understanding of the inter-relatedness of God, self, and the world on the part of the seeker of knowledge. We find here all varieties of opinions from a total 'otherness' of God to an ideal of Advaitic monism. Nevertheless, all these points of view, including monism, continue to be treated as '*pūrvapakṣa*' by Śaivasiddhānta. Freedom is not a self-dissolving dispersal for Saivasiddhānta. It is the integrative experience of Bliss. The true knowledge (*Siddhānta*) is self-revelatory as intuitive experience of Self-Realization.

The preliminary point of this paper, therefore, is that a shift in points of view is integral to the interpretation of a tradition and does not call for, or lend itself to, theory regarding chronology or increasing 'Sanskritisation', as maintained by some Indologists.[2]

It is to be seen that each of these traditions, while maintaining an identifiable continuity as structures existing, as it were, in space and time, appears also in a baffling variety of forms. Regarded from the angle of self-understanding of a tradition the texts present facets of the tradition selectively and often in tension with others, each facet that is emphasized claiming adequacy and relevance as true representations of 'original' intention. The community proclaiming adherence to the tradition does not claim to belong or believe in it without also selecting the specific form under which it is presented, laying claim to be closest to the heart and essence of the tradition. This methodology is followed uniformly by all philosophical perspectives and is known as the method of *Samanvaya*, that is, an integrated interpretation of texts.

The issue of the formative role of the Śaivāgama texts[3] in the emergence of the tradition of Tamil Saivism known as Śaivasiddhānta[4] is an illustration in point. In a very trivial and tautological sense Śaivasiddhānta *is* the Śaivāgama. The label also denotes a significant proper name of a historically identifiable structure, originating as interpretation of the program and purport of the Śaivāgama.[5]

In retrospect the extension of Śaivasiddhānta as interpretation of the Text, renders the original role of the Śaivāgama even more explicit and univocal, thus re-creating coherence and harmony where diversity prevailed and proved baffling to comprehension. Incidentally, and obliquely one may say, it also wins for itself a new perspective in self-understanding, i.e., as the cream and quintessence of Vedanta. In this context, it may be stated here that there are no clear indications in Śaivasiddhānta literature of an orientation toward Vedanta philosophy in the Sanskrit writing of Sadyajyoti, Bhoja, Narayana Kantha, Soma Sambhu, Sarvatma Sambhu, Trilocanasiva, Sri Surya, Aghora Siva and others. It is only in the 'Tamil' tradition of Meykantar, and expressly in Umapati that we perceive answers to the questions of Vedanta as well.

The broader context within which falls the specific problem of the present issue pertains to the problematic text of *Śivajñānabodham*, the canon of Śaivasiddhānta. Perhaps the world's most concise religious canon, it is a closely articulated text of twelve short aphorisms or, to be more correct, *anustubh* verses[6] in Sanskrit. It distils a multitude of scriptural writings, concluding with the line *evam Vidyācchivajñāna bodham Śaivārtha nirnayam*.[7] The title *Śivajñānaboddham* derived from this line is a significant proper name, by which the text came to be known to posterity, meaning 'instruction of the gnosis of Śivam.'

What is of interest especially from the perspective of the theme of 'tradition in contact and change' is that the text which was decisive for the literary, theological and institutional sides of the continuous tradition historically identified as Śaivasiddhānta was not the Sanskrit text (from which its concluding line was quoted above) but a Tamil *Civañānapotham* of twelve aphorisms interspersed with cryptic explanations in Tamil prose and verse.[8] Its author is believed to be a historical figure of the twelfth century. His name as the 'Perceiver of the true' (Meykantar) recurs as an interesting refrain in the explanatory verses of the text. It serves to label the literary and preceptorial lineage of the tradition continuing to this day as *Meykanta Santhānam*.

Are these twelve aphorisms translated from the original Sanskrit into Tamil "for the benefit of the vast multitudes of the non-Sanskritic knowing," as the tradition with a surprising unanimity averred until recently, or is this a case of the rare instance of feed-back into Sanskrit from a non-Sanskritic source, as is suspected by one section of contemporary scholars?[9] What gives a small edge to the latter position (which in this instance, from the very nature of the case, seems an unresovable question), is that the Sanskrit *Sivajñānabodham*, said to be an actual insert of *Raurava Agama* (*bodhitam raurava tantra antagatam śivajñānabodhākhvam upadiśati*, etc), does not find a place in the critical edition of Rauravagama, viz., by Publications de l'Institut Français d'Indologie, Pondicherry

Vols. 1 (1956) and 2 (1968).[10] The Sanskritic text also stands isolated without antecedents and with no follow-up except for a massive commentary (sixteenth - seventeenth century) by Sivagrayogin of Susyanarkoil, who is considered to be the Saiva counterpart of Vedanta Desika of the Vaisnava *Sampradāya*. Both scholars wrote in Sanskrit as well as in Tamil, giving importance to either language.[11]

A rather unfortunate idea prevails that a 'translation' is meant for those readers who do not understand the original and, therefore, is merely a verbatim repetition of the text. I will briefly summarise my reflections on this issue because these are not without considerable relevance for comprehending the meaning of contact between the Tamil and the Sanskritic tradition of Śaivasiddhānta.

Translations mark the stages of continued life of a text comparable to a work of art which lives through continual representations. Each artist imparts something of his own genius to the subject under contemplation. Translations ultimately serve the purpose of expressing the central reciprocity between linguistic structures which are trying to converge on the same conceptual mold of ideas. As a matter of fact a great many texts of the Tamil religious literature - mythologies, regional sacred myths, epics, hagiologies as well as theologies - have gained in depth of meaning and a more robust life through translations into contemporary structures of living languages. This is, at any rate, the basic law of the philosophy of language, reflected, e.g., in the Śaivasiddhānta concept of *nāda*, according to which the "original," through its renderings, far from being "translated" can conceivably rise into a higher and purer linguistic air.

So, instead of viewing the "Sanskritic" contents of Tamil literary and religio-philosophical works as instances of "Sanskritization" in a cultural-anthropological sense or, worse still, as cases of "translation" from one language to another, one must rather look upon them in terms of mediation and understanding, a translation of past meaning into present situation. In this context I may refer to Hans Gadamer's celebrated interpretation of understanding as a process of "presencings," through which the past already functions in and shapes the interpreter's present horizon. Understanding is language-bound, and yet, says Gadamer, there is absolutely no captivity within a language, not even within our native language. Any language in which we live is infinite because a speaking, even a stammering is a case of "being opened into the infinite realm of possible expression...." It is completely mistaken to infer that reason is fragmented (and I may add here *apropos* the theme of this paper, that revelation is fragmented) because there are various languages. Just the opposite is the case.[12]

A translation, therefore, is mediation between two worlds through language and even history. Texts, distant in time, space and language, come to speak in the words that are "our" world, "our" medium of seeing what is. This way of looking at the phenomenon as an instance of the "meeting of the horizons" of "our" world of understanding with that of the understanding of the "original" texts has the promise of accounting for the very distinctive tone of the Śaiva and Vaiṣṇava Tamil religious and literary writings.[13]

It can be seen that this way of understanding texts accords with Tamil grammatical conventions. Tolkappyam, the oldest extant Tamil grammatical treatise (*ca.* third century B.C.), defines an Urtext ('*mutal nul*') as one that was "perceived" (i.e. spoken) by Him of the beginning (*munaivan*) of (ever) manifest wisdom free from the (taint) of deed (*vinai*) (*Porul, Marapial* 66). The "original" text is thus idealised as originating from perfected wisdom unsullied by empiricality, the sphere of action and reaction, which thus becomes normative and qualifies at once as authority to judge and validate texts that are subsequent to it.

The question of the relative originality of the Tamil or the Sanskritic versions of the text, therefore, is not very relevant for this paper. The one point of immediate concern is: What are the formative factors definitive to the structure that is discernibly intrinsic to the text of

Śivajñānabodham? This question raises a problem in its own right and again of the kind that seems meaningfully resolvable only when perceived as belonging with the question of understanding. Underlying this question is the issue of the great Sanskritic and philosophical tradition and the little popular regional tradition, comprised pre-eminently of observances, beliefs and practices not documented in the acclaimed Sanskritic originals.[14]

Scholars like Gonda, Singer, Ingalls, Raghavan and others approach this question from the historical and functional points of view and generally by reference to the contemporary scene.[15] I want to contemplate the question within the terms of my approach from the comprehensive angle of philosophical hermeneutics. By philosophical hermeneutics I mean the broad context of moving toward an adequate approach to textual interpretation on a philosophical level. This is consistent with the spirit and sense of Indian philosophical traditions wherein "philosophy" itself is hermeneutical, that is, an interpretation, even if the subject be logic or ontology. This is not to overlook that what is involved here is perhaps the contact and tension between two kinds of people; between two similarly "calibrated" (arranged in terms of linguistically similar backgrounds) though different "philosophical" languages; between two strands or components of Indian culture like the archaic and the classical; between two stages clearly demarcated in the evolution of Hinduism, viz., proto-Hinduism and Hinduism of the post-Mahabharata period; and lastly, between two "theologies" perhaps that apparently repel each other like those of total immanence and total transcendence. What is rather being attempted is to point to philosophic complementariness over-reaching these divisions, representing efforts at mutuality in the sphere of understanding.

What is the principal factor that shapes the format and the substance of Śivajñānabodham so that, if we can isolate it, we may assign to it the major formative role in the emergence of the neo-classical tradition of Saivasiddhānta? The laconic and cryptic text itself, with its twelve short aphorisms, is not easily understood without help from the massive prose Sanskrit commentary of the early seventeenth century, and also the most comprehensive and incisive Tamil commentary that came to be written a century or more later.

The text, in the light of these commentaries, can be understood in accordance with the scheme of theological categories of interpretation of the Vedanta, and also their transformation in terms of the concepts and categories of the Śaivāgama, as well as those of the hymns of *Tirumurai*.[16] The latter dimension, i.e., a connection with Tamil hymns or litanies, which is naturally highlighted in the Tamil commentary, presents no special problem. It is yet another instance of synthesis of a devotional stream of writing and the theistic current of philosophical texts comparable to the assimilation of Sri-Vaisnavism into the body of Vedanta.[17] The problem in the case of Śaivasiddhānta is its actual relation to the Śaivāgama, lending substance to its claim, not simply to the title of Vedanta, but to represent or recreate its very quintessence. The question, therefore, is how does Śaivasiddhānta mediate between the Tamil tradition of the Śaivāgama and the Sanskrit tradition of the (*Sivādvaita*) *Vedanta*?

Vedanta, literally the end and aim of the Veda ('*vedasya antah*'), is *prima facie* not a synonym of the Upanisads but stands for the classical exegesis and the critical systematization of the teachings of the Upanisads, in the manual called the *Vedanta Sutras*. Thematically, however, Vedanta points to the import of the Upanisads, to its method and to its mystery. A distinction of approach and purport has gradually come to outlive its original sense of a name (*yoganāma*) for a given body of sacred texts.[18] The Veda is surely the one and only source by which the supreme or the Ultimate comes to be known. But Vedanta signifies the "knowing" itself, in the rigorous sense of pure gnosis, beyond the empirical and the discursive *aparokṣānubhūti* or *jñapti* (Śankara) or, alternately speaking, in the ecstatic sense of participation *bhaktirupāpannam jñānam* (Ramanuja).[19]

The term Śaivasiddhānta' has a similar history. In its original sense it was a name for the body of scriptural literature emanating from Śiva himself, viz., the Śaivāgama.[20] Śaivasiddhānta as the name for Śaivāgama is naturally the earlier and more popular label by which it was known even outside the tradition.[21] Whatever may be the historical circumstances under which this body of sacred literature might have arisen, the point of interest from the perspective of this paper is that in its own self-understanding it originated in answer to the need for "exegetical" access to the Veda. The unaided free-lance exegeses developed through the refractory media of "human" agencies are not acceptable in this sphere of understanding. The "human" approaches even though illumined by the same invariable sources of illumination can only approximate in different degrees to the Truth, limited by the very structure of human understanding to what lies within its scope. *Sugato yadi sarvajñah kapilo ne'ti kā pramā? Athobhayopi sarvajñau matibhedas-tayoh katham?* This is an oft-quoted verse in the *prakarana* text relating to Śaivāgama.

The need was felt for an authentic representation of the Vedic revelation, accomplished and final in character, like the Vedas themselves. An expansion of the *Śruti* was required, resulting in something like a self-commentary which gives one the discerning eye to perceive the meaning of the original intention of the text. This, technically, is Śaivasiddhānta - the accomplished and final truth relating to the Ultimate grasped as "The Benign" (*Śivam*) - the only legitimate complement to the Veda which is traceable to that very source to which the Vedas themselves are traced. The Agama may be taken to represent an attempt to rediscover the eternal message *within* the Veda and its tradition over against a distorted and "humanly" misused Veda.

One may thus interpret the distinction between the Veda and the Śaivāgama as one of method, rather than their vehicular nature as revelation, although the latter may be called "specific," according to the vogue of the best in Tamil authority, viz., the *Tirumantiram*, a sixth-century text.[22] The Veda is definitionally the revelation of Truth itself eternal and inerrant. It cannot be superseded by another revelation which also proclaims the Truth. The Vedas, however, can be further supplemented, the supplementation answering to the requirement of the seeker who is prepared for more specific and exclusive inculcation of knowledge. The Vedantic texts themselves *inter se* admit of supplementation without the implication of supersession.[23] The logic is simply stretched. In the true sense supplementation marks the quality of interpretative understanding of revelation.

"I see no difference between the Veda and the Śivāgama" (*vayam tu Vedaśivāgamayor bhedam na paśyāmah*) runs the oft-quoted words of Srikantha, the commentator of *Brahma Sutra* in the context of the Sutra *Patyūr assamanjasyāt*.[24] This ruling amounts apparently to a rejection of Śaiva "theology" but in the commentator's opinion it is only a critique of a purely theistic doctrine of the externality of the world to God, which presumably is not or, rather, could not be the standpoint of the Śaivāgama also. The "personalism" of the Śaivāgama and the philosophical ontology of Vedanta are in the commentator's view eminently compatible.

In fact he even goes to the extent of saying that the two are sematically equivalent: *vede'pi śivāgama iti vyavaharo vuktah*, on the ground that both are alike revealed ultimately through the agency of *Śiva: tat kartrukatvāt*. Ostensibly there is, of course, a difference: the study of the Veda is restricted to the first three of the four castes while the Agama is open to all: *dvividhah traivarnaka visayas-sarva visayasceti*.

The distinction apparently made in sociological terms seems to conceal a deeper truth. Srikantha does not say that the Veda is meant for the three castes and the Agama for the fourth. The distinction is not so much by way of endorsing the caste-based orientation of the Vedanta as it is, in connection with the question of competence between the initiate and the non-initiate (the Śuddha and the Aśuddha), from all the four classes or castes.²⁵ For the initiate who is imbued with the divine eros, a progressive approach through privileges of class and learning is insignificant. The eligibility for supreme knowledge cuts across all caste barriers. The Veda points beyond itself to such men whose life is directed towards the higher value disclosed to it in a "descent."

The Veda exists primarily for the average man, for whom the state, the family, the law and other social organisations have been created. In its supreme expression, however, which constitutes the "limit" (*paryavasāna*), as it were, of its meaningfulness, i.e. in Vedanta, it addresses itself to the specially competent who, in principle, is beyond class distinctions, To him, Vedanta discloses its inner wisdom.²⁶

The Śaivāgama is precisely this very adaptation of Veda and Vedanta, for the ulterior goal of freedom or salvation. It represents the effort to recover the deeper import of its orthodoxy and to recapture its hidden universalism over against its express hierarchism, its implied posture of realisation over against the moment of quest and inquiry. This makes it theologically plausible even within the bounds of Hindu orthodoxy to admit the existence of Āgama and Śāstra literature in languages other than the normative medium of Sanskrit and to accord the intrinsic status of language of revelation to them: *Saṁskṛtaiḥ prākṛtair vākyair yaś-ca śiṣyānurūpataḥ deśabhāṣād yupāyaiśca bodhayet sa guruḥ smṛtaḥ*; such is the admission of Āgama itself.²⁷ The Tamil text *Tirumantiram* discourses not only about different Saivagamas but claims the status of Āgama for its own discourse: *Sindai Cheydu agamam seppalutrene*.²⁸

To return briefly again to the question of "translation," if we permit ourselves to describe "that" by which the "original" is connected with its "translation," as the very virtue of *being translatable*, we must concede a specific significance to be intrinsic to the structure of the Āgama which manifests itself in its translatability. The essence of the Āgama is its very transmission, its being received in understanding. It is like life being connected with expressions of its nature, with representations of its significance. In the sphere of linguistic life at least this seems to be the case as may be seen in the instance of Tamil writings, religious and philosophical, *vis-à-vis* existent and non-existent Sanskrit originals.

Let me return to the question of the role of the Śaivāgama in the emergence of Śaivasiddhānta of *Śivajñānabodham* and look at the philosophical differences that the concept introduces. These differences at the same time do not mark a departure from Vedanta but instead serve to recreate the heart and essence of Vedanta, at least in the self-understanding of the text and the tradition that it founded.

Vedanta in general, and one may include Sankhya-yoga also, understands man in terms of his destined transition from "ignorance" to saving knowledge. Man, "beginninglessly" ignorant and subject, consequently, to the wearying rounds of *saṁsāra*, overcomes ignorance through "gnosis." The Śaivāgama, one may say, strives for an ontological clarification of this fundamental insight. We must understand the being of man to be such that "ignorance" and its offshoot is a possible way of being for him. This is in no way less important than the demand to understand the nature of man comprehensively, including the very ground which makes it possible for him to overcome his ignorance. For Śaivasiddhānta, not only a materialistic and mechanistic view of man, but a strictly spiritualistic view too, would be an illusion. The monistic Advaita Vedanta from this perspective is a *reductio* of Vedanta because it seems to equate ignorance and the overcoming of it alike with the "illusory," albeit in the technical sense of what has no beginning but comes to an end in consciousness.

The theology of the Hymns (*Tirumurai*) discloses an understanding of the human condition, although no systematic ontology of man is explicitly stated. For comprehending the possibilities of man's being which render intelligible his life in the world subject to the structures of existence as well as his life beyond it, we need a different theoretical framework which would demonstrate how every kind of *reality*, ethical, eschatological, epistemic and metaphysical, is rooted in the whole breadth of living existence and ultimately in the structure of being itself.

The Śaivāgama understanding of reality, which comprehends man and his destiny through its intricate and complex doctrine of multiple *tattvas*, provides the general basis for such an approach.[29] More specifically, the kind of Śaivāgama which contemplates life and its world, its structure and values in terms of explicitly thematized ontology seems relevant. The in-depth use that is made of the two Śaivāgama texts - the *Pauṣkara* and the *Sarvajñānottara*[30] in the Tamil and Sanskrit commentaries of *Sivajñāna-bodham* - in answer to these requirements, thus seem to be integral to the formation of Śaivasiddhānta. It may be said, in conclusion, therefore, that Śaivasiddhānta holds together the Tamil tradition of the Āgamas and the Hymns, and the Sanskritic tradition of Upaniṣadic thought. This holding together is not an overcoming of tensions but a flowing convergence which adds to our greater understanding.

SOME WESTERN INTERPRETATIONS OF THE BHAGAVAD GĪTĀ, 1785-1885

Eric J. Sharpe

In 1985, the *Bhagavad Gītā* (hereinafter abbreviated to the simpler form "Gita," without diacritical marks) will have been available to English-speaking readers for two hundred years. Appearing in English in 1785, during the middle years of the nineteenth century Latin, German and French translations followed, providing the reading public in much of Europe and America with an incomparable and at the same time compact first-hand insight into Hindu religion and philosophy. Since 1785, translations of the Gita have indeed provided the Western world with its most usual introduction to Hindu thought - often a solitary and self-sufficient introduction, since many readers appear not to have found it necessary to pass beyond the Gita, preferring its consummate synthesis to the study of the independent elements out of which it emerged.

With the forthcoming bicentenary in mind, I have begun to prepare a survey, not of the Gita's many European-language translations, but rather of the reactions of the Western mind on reading them. It is unlikely that this survey will be fully comprehensive, however. Up and down the Western world, the Gita was read assiduously, inspiring not only more and more translations, but also numerous detached observations, systematic commentaries and the occasional partisan squabble. To have read and digested all the publications involved is therefore a vast undertaking, and probably incapable of completion. The broad outlines are, however, clear enough. The study falls conventionally into two parts, in the first of which the Gita was looked upon either as a specimen of the literature of *ancient* India, inviting comparison with Greek and Latin writings; or as a source-book in the transcendental wisdom of the East. In the second period, beginning in the years around 1885, the Gita came to occupy a position of central importance in the ideology of the Indian national movement. From being regarded as a survival out of India's remote past, it won a position (which it has since those days never lost) as the inspiration of India's present and the promise of India's future. It was only natural, therefore, that in this second period, new questions should have been asked and answered by Western readers, while some of the older questions retreated into the background.

This present paper is limited in two ways. First, in that it deals only with the West's *initial* encounter with the Gita down to approximately 1885, the year in which Edwin Arnold published *The Song Celestial*. And secondly, in being, even within the limits of one hundred years, severely selective. On this occasion I can do little save merely to point to a few of the landmarks along the way, and to narrate rather than analyse. Doubtless there will therefore be as many omissions as there are inclusions - a distortion which I trust will be rectified when my fuller study finally sees the light of day.

Before I proceed, I should like to take a moment to justify more fully my choice of subject, and to locate it within the category of "intercultural hermeneutics." That it likewise provides an excellent example of "Traditions in Contact and Change" I believe goes without saying.

Hermeneutics as such is of course a widely-accepted concept in the study of religion, and needs no explanation from my side. Mostly, however, it has operated from a position within a given tradition, and has directed its attentions mainly toward whatever scripture may be considered as authoritative by that tradition. Clearly, though, there is a growing need for a study of comparative, or intercultural hermeneutics - by which I mean the study of the interpretation of scriptural data provided from within someone else's tradition. During the last two centuries in particular, believers the world over have had, at least in principle, wide and in the end almost unrestricted access to one another's holy scriptures. In view of this, it is surprising that scholars should not have devoted more time to considering precisely how believers (and non-believers) react to the perusal of scripture originating in traditions other than their own.

In 1968 Guy Richard Welbon published his book *The Buddhist Nirvāna and its Western Interpreters*, in which he demonstrated some of the principles on which comparative hermeneutics might profitably be pursued. In his preface he wrote, "Problems in intercultural hermeneutics can be approached most satisfactorily *sub specie particularis*."[1] This was sound advice. In isolating a single Buddhist concept, that of *Nirvāna*, and in examining the ways in which a representative selection of Western scholars had dealt with it, he was able to achieve far more than had he chosen, in the grandiose manner of an earlier tradition of scholarship, to discuss the vast and unwieldy question of "Western attitudes to Buddhism."

This present study is intended to be a modest exercise in the comparative, or intercultural hermeneutics of the Gita. Its rationale is similar to that found in Welbon's book: like his, my study "may be taken as a footnote to the comprehensive understanding of European [and in this present case, also American] intellectual history in the nineteenth and twentieth centuries."[2] In this case, though, the encounter is not with an idea, but with an entirely specific scripture of manageable size. Nevertheless in the end it may well prove to be the case that to study Western interpretations of the Gita is in fact tantamount to studying in microcosm Western reactions to something much larger - Indian religion and culture in its entirety.

I

When and how the Gita first came to the attention of European visitors to India I have not been able to ascertain with absolute certainty, and it may be that there is still material to be discovered from Portuguese sources. The West's *effective* encounter with the Gita began, however, at the end of the eighteenth century, when it found its first translator in the person of Charles (later Sir Charles) Wilkins (1749-1836), a senior merchant employed by the East India Company and a man under the direct patronage of the then Governor of Bengal, the ill-fated Warren Hastings.[3] Wilkins had arrived in Bengal in 1770, and took up the study of Sanskrit eight years later, apparently with the ambitious purpose of making a complete translation of the *Mahābhārata*, which was coming to light in a classically educated age as (among other things) an interesting parallel to the works of Homer and as a new and exotic example of the emergent category of "folk poetry." Work proceeded slowly, however, and in the early 1780's Hastings urged Wilkins to print a translation of the Gita separately.[4] By early 1785 it was presented to the Directors of the East India Company, who were sufficiently impressed to order that it be published, provided that the total cost not exceed Ŀ200. Later in 1785, *The Bhagvat-Gēētā*, or *Dialogues of Kreeshna and Arjoon* appeared, announced (in an advertisement dated May 30th, 1785) as "one of the greatest curiosities ever presented to the literary world," and with a prefatory letter, dated October 4th, 1784, from the pen of Warren Hastings himself.[5]

In his letter, Hastings suggested to the Chairman of the East India Company that one might be cool but not unfriendly when reading this strange new document. He called the Gita "a very curious specimen of the Literature, the Mythology, and Morality of the ancient Hindoos"[6] - and we note that he referred it to the "ancient" and not to the "modern" period in Indian history. In judging it, he said the Western reader should exclude from his mind "all rules drawn from the ancient or modern literature of Europe, all references to such sentiments or manners as become the standards of propriety for opinion and action in our own modes of life, and equally all appeals to our revealed tenets of religion, and moral duty."[7] Read it, he seems to be saying, as one would read the *Iliad* or the *Odyssey*, or even as one would read Milton, and no one's susceptibilities need suffer. Not that there was any real danger of offence being created; for in Hastings' opinion, with some few qualifications, the Gita was "a performance of great originality; of a sublimity of conception, reasoning and diction, almost unequalled; and a single exception, among all the known religions of mankind, of a theology accurately corresponding with that of the Christian dispensation, and most powerfully illustrating its fundamental doctrines."[8] It is a little hard to tell what precisely may have been in Hastings' mind in making this particular comment, though it seems to have been prompted by his reading of the Gita as a treatise on the sacredness of moral duty and the necessity for action.[9]

Wilkins for his part had little to say about the personal impression which the Gita had made upon him. In a short Translator's Preface he did however note that the Brahmins had previously been rather reluctant to grant foreigners free access to it;[10] we must remember that in the 1780's it had not yet become the widely-read popular work of the late nineteenth and early twentieth centuries. The Brahmins considered it, he said, to embody "all the grand mysteries of their religion," and "grand mysteries" are not to be disseminated freely to the uninitiated. Otherwise he considered the main purpose of the Gita to have been the setting up of "the doctrine of the unity of the Godhead" over against "idolatrous sacrifices, and the worship of images;" this was certainly an interpretation which appealed to the age of Deism.

It is, however, worth mentioning in passing that a contemporary Hindu theist like Ram Mohum Roy did not in fact appeal to the Gita for confirmation of his religious views, resting his case instead upon the Upanishads and upon inter-religious consensus concerning the nature and attributes of God. This is not to say that he was not well acquainted with the Gita, though. I am assured by a Bengali scholar that he wrote a *bhāshya* on the Gita, though this has been unaccountably lost. That he regarded it as "law" rather than as " gospel" is clear from a polemical pamphlet, *A Second Conference between an advocate for, and an opponent of, the practice of burning widows alive* (1820), in which he calls it "the essence of all Shastrus." But since this hardly falls within the category of "Western" interpretations, it must regretfully be left on one side.[11]

II

During the earlier part of the nineteenth century, Wilkins' translation remained the English-speaking world's major source of information about the Gita; thanks to Wilkins, the Gita was read by *literati* on both sides of the Atlantic, though on the whole not before the sober concerns of the Age of Reason had begun to give place to the enthusiasms of Romanticism.

Some of the interests of the Romantic movement, which began in the years around 1800, have been described (or perhaps caricatured) as "The melancholy sound of the post-horn and the ruined castle by moonlight, the fairy princess, the blue flower and the fountains dreamily playing in the splendour of the summer night..."[12] But these were no more than the stage properties of a movement based on a passionate longing for the unattainable, the remote and the exotic, and on the cultivation of the individual's "feelings." To the Romantics, few of whom actually set foot in India (and those who did, had mixed feelings about it[13]), that mysterious country served temporarily as a focus of beauty and a place of emotional refuge, and as the idealized source of that sense of cosmic oneness which they had failed to find under the analytical and moralistic banner of the Age of Reason. These emotions the Romantics could express in verse or in prose, in music and art - and in antiquarian scholarship. To their enthusiasms the literature of the East, and not least the Gita, made its full contribution.

In Britain, to take only one example, we find the poet Robert Southey writing works like *The Curse of Kehama* (1810), a lurid narrative poem in preparation for which, according to G.D. Bearce, he had read "as widely as possible in the inadequate literature about India. He purported to understand a great deal about the philosophy and society of India from reading translations of Indian law, drama, and the sacred writings of the Hindus, especially the *Bhagavad-gita*."[14]

But it was in the circle of the "New England Transcendentalists" that the Gita made its deepest impression. Although it had come to the notice of Ralph Waldo Emerson in the 1830's, the book itself did not fall into Emerson's hands (on loan from James Elliot Cabot) until 1845; but once arrived, it made a profound impression on the eclectic amateur Orientalists of the group. Its advent was hailed in slightly curious terms by Emerson on June 17, 1845, in a letter to a friend: "The only other event is the arrival in Concord of the Bhagvat-Geeta, the much renowned book of Buddhism [!], extracts from which I have often admired but never before held the book in my hands."[15] Arthur C. Christy has written that "No one Oriental volume that ever came to Concord was more influential than the *Bhagavad-gita*."[16] To Emerson it was "the first of books"; for Thoreau, its philosophy was "stupendous and cosmogonal" - sentiments echoed in various ways by others of the brethren. The general impression is, it can scarcely be denied, one of romantic *Schwärmerei*. And certainly, Emerson and Thoreau were in no way concerned with whatever the Gita might perchance mean, or have meant, to the heart and mind of India. The important thing was that it spoke, and spoke directly, to them, engaged as they were in fighting themselves free from the twin gods of tradition and rhetoric and toward religious and philosophical independence. This being so, it is easy to assume that the Gita was of value to them chiefly because it was a piece of exotic pantheism. This, though, would be to do the Transcendentalists an injustice. Remember what Emerson wrote in his essay on "The Over-Soul": "Let man then learn the revelation of all nature and all thought to his heart; this, namely, that the Highest dwells with him; that the sources of nature are in his own mind, *if the sentiment of duty is there* [my italics]."[17] It was this sense of duty, Wordsworth's "Stern Daughter of the Voice of God," which acted as a brake on the Transcendentalists' speculations. But what is the Gita, if not a treatise on the sacredness of duty (*dharma*)? On this point, Deists, Romantics and Transcendentalists held common ground.

Henry David Thoreau took at least the memory of the Gita with him on the Concord and Merrimac Rivers in the late 1830's, and wrote about it in *A Week on the Concord and Merrimac Rivers*, first published in 1849. Here Thoreau sees the Gita not as pure morality, but pure intellectuality. "The reader is nowhere raised into and sustained in a higher, purer, or *rarer* region of thought than in the Bhagvat-Geeta."[18] To forsake works Thoreau finds to be a somewhat remote ideal; after all, the things that one has to do are so trivial:

The most glorious fact in my experience is not anything I have done or may hope to do, but a transient thought, or vision, or dream, which I have had. I would give all the wealth of the world, and all the deeds of all the heroes, for one true vision. But how can I communicate with the gods who am a pencil-maker on the earth, and not be insane?[19]

In the end, Thoreau reads the Gita almost as a treatise on Eastern "quietism," or at least quietness, from which modern Europe and America desperately need to learn something other than pragmatic activity. The Gita is sane and sublime, and "Its sanity and sublimity have impressed the minds even of soldiers and merchants" - evidently Thoreau is here thinking of Hastings and Wilkins.[20] In comparison with "English sense," "Hindoo sense never perspired."[21] What does it matter if it is not altogether intelligible? "Give me a sentence which no intelligence can understand. There must be a kind of life and palpitation to it, and under its words a kind of blood must circulate for ever."[22]

The Gita is also mentioned in *Walden*, most notably in a celebrated passage prompted in part by the use of Walden ice for refrigeration on the high seas:

In the morning I bathe my intellect in the stupendous and cosmogonal philosophy of the Bhagvat-Geeta, since whose composition years of the gods have elapsed, and in comparison with which our modern world and its literature seem puny and trivial...I lay down the book and go to my well for water, and lo! there I meet the servant of the Bramin, priest of Brahma and Vishnu and Indra....The pure Walden water is mingled with the sacred water of the Ganges.[23]

With this we may compare an entry in Emerson's *Journal*, describing a "magnificent day" spent with the Gita: "It was the first of books; it was as if an empire spoke to us, nothing small or unworthy, but large, serene, consistent, the voice of an old intelligence which in another age and climate had pondered and thus disposed of the same questions which exercise us."[24]

Bronson Alcott is restrained in comparison, though his journal records for January 25, 1849, "I read the Bagvat Geeta" as the only event of the day.[25] He was probably no less enthusiastic about the Gita than were his more famous friends, but he had less ink in his veins.

III

Meanwhile, the Gita had also begun to make its mark on the Continent of Europe, again mainly as a result of the attentions of the Romantics. In 1823 a Latin translation, the work of August Wilhelm von Schlegel, was published in Germany.[26] Concerning this work Wilhelm von Humboldt was later to write: "This translation is so masterly and at the same time so conscientious and faithful, it treats so intelligently the philosophical content of the poem, and is such good Latin besides, that it would be a great pity if it were used only for a better understanding of the text, and not read for its own sake as well."[27] We might well say, in fact, that Schlegel and Humboldt together brought the Gita to the attention of the German-speaking world, Schlegel through his translation and Humboldt mainly through a lecture delivered on June 30, 1825 to the Berlin Academy of Sciences, *Über die unter dem Namen Bhagavad-Gītā bekannte Episode des Mahābhārata* (published in 1826).[28]

A formidable polymath, Humboldt had begun the serious study of the Gita in 1824, partly as a result of his connections with the Sanskritists of Paris, among them Max Müller's teacher Eugène Burnouf. His lecture of 1826 however comprised mainly a summary of the Gita's contents, since he argued, not unreasonably, that knowledge of the text would have to precede the attempt to theorize about it. But it would be wrong to assume that there is no theory in his account. Although Humboldt's biographer Haym calls his lecture "*ein Muster Klarer, vollständiger und treuer Darstellung,*"[29] it was clear enough even at this time that Humboldt was looking at the Gita as a philosophical poem rather than as a religious treatise. He read it as *Naturdichtung*, not essentially different from what he had found in Schiller,[30] and was soothed by it as though listening to music.[31]

It is perhaps not surprising, then, to find that in a fairly recent study, Marianne Cowen says that Humboldt found in the Gita his own "spiritual ancestors."[32] Basically, she says, this is a matter of "the Perennial Philosophy," the essential message of all mysticism, Eastern and Western, past and present.[33] This can be misleading, however - an anachronistic as well as a vague judgment. It was in Humboldt's case not only a matter of reading the Gita with an eye to the spiritual perception of the oneness of all things, or to a discovery of the transcendental essence of all religions. It was equally a deeply moral insight - understandably so, for anyone brought up on the Kantian ideas of duty and the categorical moral imperative was almost bound to respond in some way to the Gita's emphasis on the immutable *dharma*, as well as to the depths of *bhakti* devotion. In this, Humboldt's response was not unlike that of Warren Hastings, or of Emerson, who was never, even in his most visionary moments, free of the profound sense of moral obligation.

Otherwise, what chiefly appealed to Humboldt in the Gita was its originality and its simplicity, at least when compared with the intricacies of the Brahmanical systems. Krishna's doctrine, he wrote, "develops in such a peculiarly individual way, [and] it is, so far as I can judge, so much less burdened with sophistry and mysticism, that it deserves our special attention, standing as it does as an independent work of art...."[34] It is perhaps worth noting that Humboldt was here using the word "mysticism" not to express the heights of spiritual attainment and insight (*Mystik*), but in a pejorative sense (*Mystizismus*), common in the early nineteenth century, meaning an unhealthy reliance on the irrational and the emotional in the realm of religion and thought generally.[35]

Of Humboldt's enthusiasm for the Gita there could be no doubt. He wrote to a friend that it contained "...wohl das Tiefste und Erhabenste, was die Welt aufzuweisen habe,"[36] and his biographer Haym notes that both as a translator (in the broad sense of the word) and expositor, he sought, both spiritually and formally, to make Krishna's teaching his own.[37] This may fairly be described as the Romantic consensus on the Gita, to the extent to which it was actually known: that its contents were universally human, and that its message of oneness, duty and devotion were such as to lift it high above local or partisan concerns.

IV

Before proceeding to a brief review of some of the critical questions raised by Western Indologists faced with the text of the Gita, we may at this stage pause for a moment to glance at another question, that of the "mysticism" of the Gita. We have already noted Humboldt's delight at the *absence* of *Mystizismus* from its pages. A diametrically opposite view was taken, thirty years later, by the English writer Robert Alfred Vaughan (1823-1857).

In 1856 Vaughan published a book entitled *Hours with the Mystics: A Contribution to the History of Religious Opinion* (6th ed. 1893), which for almost half a century was virtually the only book on "mysticism" in the English language. In it, though mentioned only briefly and in passing, the Gita received some unexpected criticism -

unexpected, that is, to those viewing the "mysticism" question in the light of later assumptions. Vaughan was, as it happens, a Free Churchman, whose father had been Principal of a theological college; and he may be taken as an excellent example of a type of intellectual Nonconformity not uncommon in mid-nineteenth century England. He appears to have chosen the subject of "mysticism" rather more as a literary exercise than out of profound conviction - which fact may account, among other things, for the peculiar dialogue form in which the book is cast. Its "Book the Second" is entitled "Early Oriental Mysticism," and it is here that the Gita puts in its appearance.

Vaughan had no knowledge of Sanskrit, nor was he concerned to interpret the Gita independently of other "mystical" writings. His source was of course Wilkins' translation. But for the Gita's brand of "mysticism" he had no manner of use. In Arjuna's being taught "to disregard the consequences of his actions," Vaughan saw something morally reprehensible:

I find here [he wrote] not a "holy indifference," as with the French Quietists, but an indifference which is unholy. The *sainte indifférence* of the west essayed to rise above self, to welcome happiness and misery alike as the will of Supreme Love. The odious indifference of these orientals inculcates the supremacy of selfishness as the wisdom of a god....[38]

What might be the cause of this? In Vaughan's view, the blame was to be placed upon the doctrine of metempsychosis, which resulted-so he believed-in the setting aside of the moral imperative. The "Hindoo adept" was able to set aside good and evil at will, and hence in the Gita, "Mysticism...is born armed completely with its worst extravagances"-a serious and indeed fatal beginning, "for responsibility ends where insanity begins."[39]

It is curious that Vaughan should have been led to this conclusion, since we will recall that it was precisely the Gita's emphasis on duty which seemed to have appealed most strongly to the pragmatic Warren Hastings, and which certainly played a part in the reflections of the New England Transcendentalists where the Gita was concerned.

Carrying out duty for its own (or Krishna's) sake was however evidently not an option which Vaughan could accept; duty to him was the expression of a response to the sovereign will of God, and true mysticism (*Mystik*) consisted in the conforming of self to the "will of Supreme Love." Separate the moral imperative from the notion of the will of God and - so Vaughan thought - what was left was moral indifference. Ally it to the belief in transmigration, and to the conviction that the true Self is merely encapsulated temporarily within a human body, which it casts off on death as a man might cast off his worn-out clothes, and there remains only a non-moral exercise in irrationality and make-believe.

V

Among the Romantics, attention was focussed chiefly on the universal message of the Gita, only incidental notice being taken of the purely literary critical problems posed by its text. But during the whole of the nineteenth century, Western Orientalists showed an understandable interest in questions concerning the date and origin of the Gita. It would be well to remember that at this time, one side of the Western intellectual tradition was almost obsessively historical in its emphases, and also that before branching out into Indology, most Western interpreters had been thoroughly trained in the Latin and Greek classics. In dealing with the Sanskrit texts, therefore, they tended to work along somewhat similar literary critical lines, and produced theories of authorship similar to those which accompanied, for instance, the Homeric corpus of writings. The Hindu Epic material as a whole they looked on as a literary deposit belonging essentially to the remote past, though one which had unaccountably (though excitingly) survived down to modern times. Questions of authorship and date permitted of few firm answers, and the link between the *Mahābhārata* and its traditional author, Vyāsa, appeared to be no greater than that between the Iliad and Homer; probably it was far more tenuous. The events which the

Mahābhārata described might, like the Trojan War, have had some remote foundation in fact, but probably not a large foundation, and there was no Schliemann on hand to attempt to excavate the Kurukshetra battlefield. Arjuna and Krishna might perhaps have been historical figures, but they were probably at best legendary, and might even be completely mythical. The Krishna stories in the *Purāṇas* did nothing to improve matters, since their apparent association with the world of practical erotica created an instinctive barrier which the West was not able to overcome at that time. At all events, Western scholars generally felt that there were two Krishnas in the Indian tradition, bound together by nothing save a name.

However, the connection between the *Purāṇas* and the Gita under the name of Krishna did send some Western scholars off on an independent line of inquiry. Given that some of the birth stories of Krishna were similar to the legends surrounding the birth and childhood of Jesus Christ, and that the *Purāṇas* and the Apocryphal Gospels contained comparable material, might the connection extend to the Gita? Might some of the Gita's devotional teachings be evidence of the early presence of Christianity in India, and might they have come directly from a Christian source? An attempt to demonstrate such a dependence was made by a certain Franz Lorinser, who published in 1869 a metrical translation and commentary on the Gita, *Die Bhagavadgītā, übersetzt und erläutert*, in which he expressed a conviction that the author of the Gita not only knew and in many cases used the writings of the New Testament, but also in general incorporated Christian ideas and views into his system.[40]

Lorinser's theories found surprisingly little support, however. Their credibility depended, among other things, on the Gita being dated to a period subsequent to the arrival of Christianity in India; and even those few scholars who were prepared to date the Gita to, say, AD 200 were in general unwilling to allow that there could have been an established Christian presence in India (the Thomas legends notwithstanding) as early as that. Both were highly controversial questions, on which there was nothing approaching a consensus. Some limited support for Lorinser's theory was however forthcoming from Oxford's Boden Professor of Sanskrit, Sir Monier Monier-Williams, in his book *Hinduism* (1878), though even this staunch Evangelical Christian felt that in the last resort, some of Lorinser's comparisons "...seem mere coincidences of language, which might occur independently."[41]

Otherwise, what Monier-Williams has to say about the Gita may be taken as fairly typical of the conclusions which Western critical scholarship had reached by about the 1870's - that the Gita contains independent Vedāntic, Sāṁkhya, Yoga, and Bhakti lines of thought, which have been brought together to create what Monier-Williams calls "the Eclectic school of Hindu philosophy."[42] But which of these strands might have come first? Monier-Williams' conclusion was that the Gita's root-stock had been Vedāntic (after all, was it not known as an Upanishad?), and that the Sāṁkhya, Yoga and Bhakti elements came later, as the result of the efforts of a poet who, being dissatisfied with the various separate systems which surrounded him, was driven to construct an eclectic school of his own.[43] Oddly, the epic and dramatic element was at that time left out of the reckoning almost entirely. But these were at best speculations.

Toward the end of the first century of Gita interpretation in the West, there can be no doubt as to who was the most influential of scholarly Indologists. Friedrich Max Müller had been working in Oxford since the 1840's, had completed in 1862 his monumental edition of the *Rig Veda*, and had begun his equally monumental series of *Sacred Books of the East*. Oddly, in view of his background in the German Romantic movement, it must be recorded that compared with his beloved and idealized Vedas, his interest in the Gita was slight. Indeed, he was apt to lament that the Gita, along with other specimens of post-Vedic Hindu literature, had aroused more interest in the West than it properly deserved. For instance, lecturing in 1882 to candidates for the Indian Civil Service, he had this to say:

"It was a real misfortune that Sanskrit literature became first known to the learned public in Europe through the second, or, what I have called, the Renaissance Period. The Bhagavadgītā...[and other writings of the period]... are, no doubt, extremely curious...[and when they were discovered, appeared to be of great antiquity]....But all this is now changed."[44]

It was not that the Gita was not old, but that from Max Müller's point of view, it was simply not old enough. Much of this "younger" literature - and here he refers explicitly to *Nāla* and *Śakuntalā* - he went so far as to relegate to the category of entertainment. Burnouf, he wrote, "was not likely to waste his life on pretty Sanskrit ditties"[45]-not that the Gita is a "pretty Sanskrit ditty," but it is not very much more, and the best that he can find to say about it in his lectures is that it is "...a rather popular and exoteric exposition of Vedāntic doctrines...."[46]

In his 1888 Gifford Lectures, incidentally, Max Müller was one of those who took up the subject of Lorinser's theories. Writing on the general subject of *bhakti*, he conceded that there were resemblances between Christian conceptions of faith and love and those qualities as they appear in the Gita. But for all that, he was not prepared to support Lorinser: "It is strange [he wrote] that these scholars should not see that what is natural in one country is natural in another also. If fear, reverence, and worship of the Supreme God could become devotion and love with Semitic people, why not in India also?"[47] Max Müller did not in fact believe the Gita to be of great antiquity, and he was prepared to admit that Christian influence might be a chronological possibility. The theory was not, however, a religious necessity: "Still, even if, chronologically, Christian influences were possible at the time when the poem was finished, there is no necessity for admitting them."[48]

Mention of Max Müller leads naturally to a brief mention that in 1882 there appeared, in the *Sacred Books of the East* series (Volume 8), Kashinath Trimbak Telang's well-known version of the Gita. I do not propose to deal with this work in detail. I would, however, mention that in his introduction, Telang virtually throws up his hands in despair at the complexity of the critical issues involved in the study of the Gita, writing that "...it is almost impossible to lay down even a single proposition respecting any important matter connected with the Bhagavadgītā, about which any...consensus can be said to exist."[49] On the whole, though, Telang opts for a date before the second century BC, at the close of the Upanishadic period, of which the Gita is therefore one of the youngest representatives.

VI

In 1885, the Gita had been in Western hands for a century, and it was in a way appropriate that the unofficial centenary should have been marked by the publication of what is perhaps the most celebrated, and in some ways the most influential, of Gita translations, Edwin Arnold's *The Song Celestial*.

Edwin Arnold (1832-1904) was one of those many Victorian authors and poets who enjoyed enormous fame in their heyday, but who are little read at the present time. In fact almost the only thing for which Arnold is remembered nowadays is the indirect role he played in introducing Gandhi to the Gita. In his autobiography, Gandhi wrote: "I have read almost all the English translations of it [the Gita], and I regard Sir Edwin Arnold's as the best. He has been faithful to the text, and yet it does not read like a translation."[50] It is also significant that Gandhi was persuaded to tackle the Gita by certain Theosophical friends, since as we shall in due course see, the Theosophists were particularly well disposed toward the Gita, and not unnaturally regarded Arnold as an ally.

Arnold's sympathies were, however, theosophical only indirectly and by implication. He might perhaps be characterized as the broadest of a notable generation of broad-church Anglicans. He was influenced by such men as F.D. Maurice and F.W. Farrar, and while at Oxford had been tutored by A.P. Stanley, later Dean of Westminster and a close friend of Friedrich Max Müller. In 1852, at the age

of twenty, Arnold won the Newdigate Poetry Prize for a poem
entitled "The Feast of Belshazzar," which began:

> Not by one portal, or one path alone
> God's holy messages to men are known.[51]

The years 1857 to 1860 he spent in India as the Principal
of the Government School (Deccan College) in Poona, returning to England and a career in journalism and freelance
writing. His interests were world-wide, and his personal
philosophy tended more and more in the direction of a form
of Transcendentalism. In 1868 he married the great-niece
of William Ellery Channing, and he was a friend of Emerson
and of Walt Whitman. It is perhaps also worth noting that
his youngest son became a convert to Theosophy.

Arnold's most celebrated excursion into the world of
Oriental thought, his poem on the Buddha, *The Light of Asia*
(1879) was written, so his most recent biographer tells us,
"as a witness for religious liberalism."[52] Not unnaturally, this gained him a considerable following among the
Theosophists, for whom the most extreme liberalism was part
of the very air they breathed; and he was very well received by the Theosophists (many of whom were at this time
crypto-Buddhists) on a visit which he paid to India and
Ceylon in 1885-1886. But by this time he had further added
to his reputation as a literary Orientalist through his
version of the Gita.

In preparing to write his version, Arnold is said to
have worked with the Latin translation of Schlegel (1823)
and the English translation of John Davies (1882), and
appears not to have used Wilkins. *The Song Celestial* is of
course a free interpretation rather than a literal translation (though it does embrace a few minor ventures in
textual criticism). It has been said that "...there is no
literary translation that has superseded this one. Today
it is the only one of Arnold's poems that is still regularly read and the one on which his future reputation must
rest."

It is sometimes suggested that when in 1891 Arnold
published *The Light of the World* about the life of Jesus,
he did so mainly as a "reversion" to Christianity after too

many dangerous adventures among the religions of the East. This I for one do not believe. Certainly he was aware that he had been criticized for his involvements with Islam, Hinduism, Buddhism and Japan. But to assume that he came to believe that there had been an imbalance in his religious life which was in need of correction, is to misunderstand the nature and ethos of late nineteenth-century liberal Christianity, which in fact saw the great non-Christian traditions less as competitors to the Christian Gospel than as legitimate preparations for its message. The Gita therefore had its own integrity and value, just as had the life of the Buddha; but it was not, in Arnold's view, sufficient of itself, since it needed to find its fulfilment in Christ. Significantly, in *The Light of the World*, Arnold makes the Magi who brought their gifts to the infant Jesus, not Zoroastrians (or whatever) but Buddhists! They might equally have been warriors from the Kurukshetra battlefield.

Perhaps Arnold's personal religion was "magnificently unorthodox," at least by the officially accepted standards of his day, but he was not alone among Christians in seeing the Gita as "celestial," and therefore as worthy of the deepest respect. That he finally, in *The Light of the World*, appeared to be moving back to what his contemporaries clearly regarded for the most part as uniquely revealed Truth, is to misread the evidence. He was not moving back, but (as he saw it) onward and upward, in the manner of all nineteenth-century religious evolutionists.

VII

With the publication of *The Song Celestial* we have come to the end of the first century of Gita interpretation in the West. It is worth noting that practically everything on which we have reported actually took place, geographically speaking, *in* the West, and as a consequence of the publication of a series of more or less adequate translations. Two things have emerged from our survey thus far. On the one hand - and leaving the early Deists aside - we have seen a resolute attempt on the part of some readers to build the central message (or what appeared to be the central message) of the Gita into a system of instinctive, "transcendental" philosophy, and to find in it support for a world-view already held for other reasons; to this enterprise, questions of authorship and dating were strictly irrelevant. On the other, we have seen the beginning of an attempt to subsume the Gita under the categories of literary criticism. Approached from this angle, the general view appears to have been that although nothing could be said with certainty about the absolute age or the origin of the poem, it had apparently begun life as an Upanishad. Its philosophical and religious foundation had therefore seemingly been Vedāntic, though it had afterward had elements of Sāṁkhya, Yoga and Bhakti incorporated into it. In neither case was the Gita considered as a *living* Hindu scripture, part of the ongoing religious tradition of Hindu India.

Beginning at about this time, however, a great change begins to come over the situation, due almost entirely to the new role which the Gita began to play from the 1880's on, in the life of the Indian national movement. Certainly some of the old questions continued to be asked and answered by Western scholars; but to their number were added a host of new questions about the capacity of the Gita to continue to be a source of religious (and increasingly also political) inspiration. Two new interpretative schools emerged, in support of or in response to the challenge of what some called "the neo-Krishna movement" : the Theosophists on the one hand and the Christian missionaries on the other. In comparison with the first century of Gita interpretation in the West, the second century was characterized by being played out less in the geographical West and more in India itself; equally it was characterized by a new spirit of give-and-take (at its best, dialogue, at its worst, mud-slinging). Before 1885, remarkably few Hindus were prepared to rise up and challenge the West's reading of the Gita. After 1885, not only did the Gita rapidly become the supremely authoritative, and in some respects all-sufficient holy scripture for the whole of "educated India;" it became equally the nationally aware Hindu's declaration of spiritual independence, a symbol of nationhood on which the *mleccha* might comment only with the greatest circumspection. The Western interpreter therefore was apt to find his theories and his constructions challenged and contradicted - perhaps most notably in respect of the Gita's unity and with regard to the question of "the Krishna of history."

In short, while from 1785 to 1885 the Gita appeared to the West as a fascinating document, after 1885 it became a powerful symbol, to which the older canons of interpretation were capable of answering only in part. A consideration of these later developments must however await some future occasion.

FROM HINDU STRĪDHARMA TO UNIVERSAL FEMINISM:
A STUDY OF THE WOMEN OF THE NEHRU FAMILY

K. Young

To an outsider familiar with the classical ideal of Hindu womanhood, Indira Gandhi appears as an anomaly. How could India produce an Indira, much less accept a woman Prime Minister? Indeed, how could India cope with the strength (*sakti*) of a woman who strategically defended national borders, boldly kept Western powers and multinationals at bay, declared an emergency and jailed the opposition, even overcame an overwhelming indictment of her leadership at the elections only to return triumphantly to power? Although the saga is not over yet (1981), enough events have transpired to begin an analysis of this seeming contradiction between these images of the feminine. The question becomes: Is Indira really an anomaly given the traditional norms of Hindu womanhood and, if not, whence the evolution that led to this transformation and its acceptance, at least in the role of leadership, by the majority of Hindus?

The contact of the West with India had created a conflict of values that led to polarizations, in the society variously defined as East and West, or tradition and modernity. Women were at the centre of this conflict. The Hindu concept of tradition with reference to the norms that governed the lifestyle of women was deemed objectionable by the West. In fact, the nineteenth-century critique against Hinduism vociferously focused on feminine misery in Hinduism. The Western critique generated in Hindu psychology the tension between tradition and its modern evaluation. In the female psychology this tension was likely to result in the split between Western feminism and Hindu *strīdharma.*

Strīdharma may be defined as the upbringing, conduct, virtues, and ideal of a Hindu woman. Her orientation is characterized by *patiyoga*, union with the husband. Above all she is to be "good" to the husband through devotion to him, self-sacrifice for his sake, and performance of austerities such as fasting for his welfare. Attention to the husband and by extension to the family characterizes her spiritual and psychological frame of mind. Virtues necessary for this orientation involve patience, fortitude, equanimity, and self-denial. These virtues make her *satī*, a good woman.

Despite the likelihood of such a split between Western feminism and *strīdharma*, it may be argued that the result of the contact between West and East was rather on the positive side, which may be described as a creative synthesis of two polar tendencies. The pivotal period for this change was the Indian Independence Movement, for during this period new images were forged to bridge many polarities, including those faced by women.

Since the women of the Nehru family - Swarup Rani, Vijaya Lakshmi Pandit, Kamala Nehru, and Indira Gandhi - were at the centre of the Independence Movement, an understanding of its influence on their personal lives should provide one perspective on women's response to the polarizations of the day. Moreover, in that three generations of women are involved, their perspectives might reveal different stages of the transition period. Because the Nehru women came under Gandhi's influence, which championed the women's cause on a popular basis, they may be considered representative of the women's movement for "liberation." Finally, because they belong to a family at the vortex of modern Indian history, there are sufficient biographies and autobiographies to open up the interior of family life to analysis.

In brief, to begin to understand Indira Gandhi one must look to the Independence Movement and the changing roles of the women in the Nehru family. Herein lie the hermeneutic clues that lead one to conclude that Indira is not an anomaly but rather belongs to a vanguard of the evolution of the image of the feminine in India.

The concept of *satyāgraha* (truth-force; soul-force) was responsible for this progressive step as it helped to resolve tensions between past and present, East and West. *Satyāgraha* was chiefly applied as a political means for the Independence of India, but alongside it became a general principle to handle tensions felt in other arenas of life. *Satyāgraha* not only revitalized the political forces for Independence, it also contributed to the formation of a national identity. This new self-image was shared by its subjects in order to resolve the internal tensions from whatever source they surfaced. Gandhi's efforts stirred the Indian population to serve for the common cause: Indian Independence. Thus on the political level the equal humanity of male and female was witnessed for once in Indian history and that too on a large scale. According to Indira:

Mahatma Gandhi's gentle voice was strong enough to persuade our women to come out of their homes and to share the hardship, the suffering and the sacrifices of the freedom movement. And this is what today has enabled them to participate equally in the work for development. We therefore did not have to fight for our rights from or with our menfolk. We fought for freedom alongside of our men and this is the spirit in India today. Where women are working, it is not to get anything from the men or in rivalry with them, but in partnership with them to create a better India for us all.[1]

This new equality established during the Independence Movement influenced the domestic arena of those families which had been hitherto subjected to a cultural gulf, that is, the husband had often sought Westernization almost as a theological goal and the wife, precisely because of this challenge to her security, had become defensively conservative and obsessive in her protection of household ritual and custom. Since the honour of a woman was traditionally attributed to the preservation of family custom, any change of lifestyle was threatening to her self-image. Also the men in these upper-class families often spoke in English while the women knew only an Indian vernacular; the men were often educated, the women usually illiterate. This tug-of-war between modernity and tradition was bound to result in the polarization between men and women. Before it surfaced concretely in the form of something analogous to modern women's liberation, the concept of *satyāgraha* provided a means to overcome the stalemate between husband and wife, man and woman.

The concept of *satyāgraha*[2] does not belong to Hindu religious vocabulary. Gandhi invented the term as well as the concept by juxtaposing two different concepts belonging to two different realms of life. The word *satya*, meaning "truth," refers to ethics or philosophy. Truth refers to soul, both the supreme soul (*paramātma*) and the individual soul (*jīvātma*). For Gandhi the supreme soul is God. Because man cannot know absolute truth, i.e. God, he is not competent to punish; therefore ethics excludes the use of violence by man. *Āgraha*, a word in common parlance, means, negatively, "grabbing" in the sense of insisting on having something (i.e. the haughty insistence of an unbending person). Positively *āgraha* means "pleading" or "urging" (e.g. when the hostess urges the guest to eat more and more). The compound *satyāgraha* implies a psychological force, both a haughty and gracious insistence on having what is rightfully one's own - one's identity, one's country, one's truth, one's "soul," so to speak. At the same time there is the recognition that the means must not involve violence because God, not man, is the ultimate judge. Gandhi perceived the potential of the *āgraha* psychology and used this concept as a psychological weapon against the British. The term *satyāgraha* thus constitutes an admixture of two opposites, the benevolent and the abrasive facets of human psychology; one must be strong, courageous and obstinately insistent on a just cause. Simultaneously one must have humility and compassion toward the aggressor.

Such admixture was not a novel concoction, for its reality was based on female psychology, especially in the domestic situations where such a pair of opposites was manifestly applied in day-to-day routine by the women of the household. The religious upbringing created in them the imperative behaviour of benevolence and nobility. The harsh reality of coping with the in-laws in the extended family and assuming responsibility for the household's stability, however, generated in women the spirit of aggression which found its outlet in the art of oblique insinuation. This was the traditional domestic psychology of Hindu women who always appeared dignified with pious strength owing to the combination of *satya* and *āgraha*.

Hindu women were trained from early childhood to offer selfless service and devotion to the husband and his family from the time of marriage. They were taught not to complain, much less show hostility or aggression. As a result an innocence marked their behaviour and a basic benevolence characterized their relationships. When conflict occurred, fasting (*upavāsa*) and vow (*vrata*) were religious acts to overcome the difficulty, not through overt aggression, but rather through barter with the deity, i.e. giving up something in return for receiving a boon to overcome the problem. Thus women's psychology and language were couched in religious euphemism; this prevented, for the most part, their conscious contemplation of the strategic dimension of the act of self-denial. This is not to say that the effect was not strategic. By maintaining their nobility and ethical demeanor in the face of adversity, especially male aggression, women subtly chastised and often reformed their men. In turn, men gave due respect to the moral and religious power (*tapas*) that women developed through their self-denial, suffering, and austerities. A woman, while physically weak, yet had a recognized and tested strength. Called *abalā*, the feminine power of the meek had the delicacy of a rose, which by its sheer beauty and fragility could stop an action of physical might and show up the moral weakness of the aggressor.[3]

Gandhi recognized in this potency (*tapas*, *abalā*), derived from self-denial, discipline, and suffering bravely borne, a "force" that was Indian and could provide an alternative to the debilitating weakness before Imperial might and "right." Although it was based on women's training and psychology, it was an idiom known and experienced by men as well. It was clever of Gandhi to detect and isolate this psychology and to experiment with it in order to wage strategic war with the British rulers.

Because *satyāgraha* was primarily derived from classical *strīdharma*, its characteristics consisted of attributes of Hindu female psychology and traditionality. As a *strategic* means, however, it is known to the world as a clever tactic. Thus the feminine benevolence with its oblique aggression is categorically different from its political derivative, which is more strategic, though with strong moral overtones, than religious. In other words, the strategic dimension of the *āgraha* psychology or self-imposed suffering was exposed and the political rather than religious dimension was pushed to the forefront. Gandhi nevertheless enjoyed the religious ambivalence of this concept. It is this ambivalence that gave nobility as well as workability to Gandhi's ideology. Because in the ultimate analysis the concepts of *strīdharma* and *satyāgraha* were cognate, women were attracted unconsciously or spontaneously to *satyāgraha*; they could identify with it, perhaps "not knowing why." Erikson comments:

> ...mastery over anger is less foreign to those who have learned to express anger in traditional and disciplined ways. Besides, to take active charge of senseless suffering by deliberately choosing to court meaningful suffering can be experienced as an exhiliarating mastery over fate within a new ritualization such as Satyagraha.[4]

This insight discloses the key to the transition in women's psychology from the self-denial, even suffering which often occurred in the domestic context to the purposeful suffering encountered in *satyāgraha*. Women were masters of self-control and could easily redirect it toward a noble cause. When it became a tool for *changing* a situation, rather than *coping* with it, they experienced a new freedom.

In South Africa Hindu women quickly grasped the new idiom. They joined Gandhi's marches, as they or their ancestors had traditionally walked for miles during pilgrimage (*tīrthayātrā*) in India. They made vows that they would not break their march or fast, as they had made *vratas* before. They endured suffering with positive thoughts toward the exploiter, as they had been *tapasvinīs* (women who performed austerities) in the past. When the court invalidated all Hindu marriages, they decried it as an affront to Indian womanhood and motherland and used the tactic of *satyāgraha* for change. They formed novel shock troops, known as the Tolstoy Sisters and Phoenix Sisters. With their babies in their arms, they heroically crossed forbidden state lines. In India, Annie Besant assessed the contribution of women to the Movement:

The strength of the Home Rule movement was rendered tenfold great...by the adhesion to it of a number of women who brought to its helping the uncalculating heroism, the endurance, the self-sacrifice of the feminine nature. Our League's best recruits and recruiters are amongst the Women of India.[5]

Gandhi was sensitive to the disadvantages of polarities visible in any dual situation: Brahmin/non-Brahmin; ruler/ruled; West/East; Hindu/Muslim; male/female. He was also influenced by and enamoured of the Western concepts of equality and humanity. For example, to bring polar differences under one broad category, he brought male and female members of the population into one mass of humanity as the seekers of Indian Independence. The joint participation of men and women in the struggle for Indian Independence generated the larger category of humanity in which the difference of male and female was obscured, especially on the higher and nobler levels. According to Vijaya Lakshmi Pandit:

We have never had nor needed a suffragette movement in India, and there was no antagonism between the sexes. Thanks to the wise leadership of Gandhiji, the Indian Woman stepped out of the home into social and political life without opposition from men and functioned as a comrade with great efficiency.[6]

While the political situation gave the basic impetus to this development, Gandhi knew that for the transformation to be complete, daily life itself had to be substantially transformed. Individuals had to learn how to change and, without denying their individuality, to develop a new universal level of awareness. The experimental coccoon for the transformation of daily life was Gandhi's ashram. Women were at the centre of these ashram experiments, which engendered a new awakening through practical training and what today we term conscious-raising techniques that foster confidence, fearlessness and independence. Kakasaheb Kalelkar notes that at the ashram the problem of women were discussed and lectures on women were given. The theme of these talks was freedom for women:

That woman is in fact not weak; that there is no reason why she should be dependent on man; there is no eternal rule that leadership in society should always remain in the hands of men; that woman can shape and develop herself, and thus only can she help in achieving human progress.[7]

The gist of Gandhi's contribution to the evolution of female psychology appears in the following extracts from his letters to the ashram sisters:

Regard the Ashram as one family, and through it cultivate the sense of the whole world as one family ...women hold the key to Swaraj. Become experts in your work, lead pure lives, and spread yourselves throughout India....

Devotion means faith, faith as much in one's self as in God....

In the end, of course, she who is devoted to Dharma will sacrifice herself for the whole world. But one's country does not run counter to the interests of the world, service in the cause of one's country does take one towards salvation....

Woman is the embodiment of self-sacrifice. But at present her self-sacrifice is restricted to her family. Why should she not make for the nation even greater sacrifices than those she has been making for her family....

The ancient laws were made by men. Though these men were sages and seers they show a lack of real knowledge of women....

I feel if Mirabai cannot get salvation, no man would ever get it....[8]

Hence Gandhi helped women to break out of their domestic "prisons" by redirecting their traditional self-sacrifice and service from husband to nation. He helped women to break into new jobs by divorcing occupation from roles defined by sex and caste and by advocating the dignity of all labour. He helped to lessen women's rigid conservatism by promoting women's solidarity. Gandhi constantly encouraged the ashram sisters to travel to different regions of India and to initiate a new awakening among women. When he himself travelled, he provided inspiration to women by reporting on the activities of the women's movement in other parts of the country. Thus women's solidarity advanced by women crossing caste, religious, and regional lines. Finally he put women on an equal traditional footing with men by acknowledging women's capacity for salvation. Hindu women generally are rebirth-oriented while men have liberation (*moksa*) as their ultimate goal. Gandhi, by definitely stating that women have the *capacity for liberation*, took steps to eliminate any possible misogyny on the religious level. Gandhi, who imbibed his mother's religiosity and had to confront his own personal cowardice, identified with women. According to one source: "It is not the slightest exaggeration to say that for the purpose of improving the condition of women, he became a woman himself."[9]

As demonstrated in the first part of this paper, the concept of *satyāgraha* formed the basis for the development of classical *strīdharma* during the Indian Independence Movement and helped to bridge the hiatus of tradition and modernity. The concluding part of this analysis will show how the women of the Nehru family, in particular Indira Gandhi, came to embody the developmental traits of *strīdharma* as contained in the new image of the *satyāgrahinī* (a woman who engages in *satyāgraha*).

Before Nehrus came under the influence of Gandhi, their home Anand Bhavan was a classic example of the polarizations of the age as exemplified in the situation of the traditional Hindu wife and the "progressive" Westernized husband. The house was literally divided into Western and Indian sections. The patriarch Motilal enjoyed his crystal wine glasses, indoor swimming pool and Great Danes. His wife, Swarup Rani - who was reared an orthodox Brahmin, memorized Sanskrit verses, visited temples performed worship (*Pūjā*) and celebrated festivals (*utsava*) - preferred traditional decor, food, and the atmosphere of pious religiosity. As a good *pativratā*, a wife dedicated to her husband, Swarup Rani had to acquiesce on many occasions to her husband's unorthodox ways. When her daughter scolded her for this, she would reply: "My dear, I do what your father likes, and anyway, he knows best."[10] Motilal, with his liberal openness, allowed her her traditional *strīdharma*. Overt conflict was thereby averted by her *pātivratya* and his generosity, but the deep estrangement was all too real to both. When Jawaharlal followed in his father Motilal's footsteps, the same split occurred in the household. His wife, Kamala, came from an orthodox Brahmin background and found even the women of the Nehru family too Westernized. The confrontation of values marked and marred her early years in Anand Bhavan.

Gandhi's concept of *satyāgraha* had tremendous effect on the Nehru family. A family crisis was precipitated by Jawaharlal's recognition that Gandhi had given back to India her identity. Swarup Rani thought that Gandhi was meddling in the family; she had not accepted him as a friend and could not understand his politics. According to her daughter (now known as Vijaya Lakshmi Pandit):

Mother felt acutely miserable over all that was happening. The person she loved most, her son, was deeply disturbed and unhappy. He was obviously on the verge of some action that she would have appreciated in a mythological figure but not one on whom her hopes of happiness on earth and her place in heaven depended. Then there was the serious situation developing between her husband and her son.

Yet with domino effect the family toppled into Gandhi's waiting arms. Jawaharlal became a *satyāgrahi*; Motilal gave up his English finery and followed his son; Swarup Rani, out of fidelity to her husband (*pātivratya*), followed her husband, and her daughter followed the family, as did Kamala.

For all the women of the Nehru family the cognate structures of *strīdharma* provided a theoretic transition that prompted their emancipation. It was participation in Gandhi's ashram life, however, that provided the concrete experiments for their personal transformations. Because these women were influenced by the polarities of the day in different ways, their experiences and resultant liberations differed accordingly.

Swarup Rani, a woman of great wealth and status who felt most happy when observing the norms of classical *strīdharma*, initially resisted the new image that was imposed on her and had a hard time adjusting to the egalitarianism and austerity of the ashram. Nonetheless, she gradually and naturally identified with the nobility and practical psychology of *satyāgraha*. Even in her old age she joined the *satyāgraha* marches and was mercilessly beaten by the lathi charges of colonial troops. As assessed by her daughter: "My mother who had been ailing most of her life, became almost normal when she was faced with the rigors of the freedom movement."[12] *Satyāgraha* provided for Swarup Rani assimilation to a *modern* albeit Indian identity and through that to a greater communication with her husband, son, and daughter. Sharing the difficulties and the rewards of an important cause, they were brought together by the fight for Independence. Then, too, her husband and children had begun to appreciate *satyāgraha* as an *Indian* phenomenon, and she began to lessen her rigidity through the "consciousness-raising" of the women's movement and the appreciation of universal values.

Satyāgraha had the opposite effect on her daughter. Vijaya Lakshmi had been thoroughly Westernized in her youth by her father and brother and admits that she was Indian only by fact of birth. Used to all the comforts of life, she considered the ashram austere beyond belief and had to come to terms with it, "not accepting it but beginning to appreciate the underlying philosophy...."[13] As assessed by herself, she was "swept along with the tide, a willing victim. It was not possible to think logically. 'Sacrifice' was the key note of the movement...."[14] *Satyāgraha* provided for Vijaya Lakshmi assimilation to an *Indian* albeit modern identity and through that to some of the features of Hindu female psychology. Thus the national movement and Gandhi's feminism shaped her psychology. She took up the cause of organizing women to fight for rights, education, and social services, and as a woman and an *Indian* woman tended to engender *causes célèbers* in her later career as ambassador and representative to the U.N.

It was Kamala Nehru who personally, politically, and dare we say spiritually found rebirth through the concept of *satyāgraha*. Kamala was repressed and severely maladjusted during her early years of marriage. Nehru honestly observed that Kamala was "...unsophisticated in the ways of the world.... The difference in our ages was considerable, but greater still was the difference in our mental outlook, for I was far more grownup than she was... our backgrounds were different and there was want of adjustment."[15] For Kamala, participation in the Cause was like a release from bondage. As assessed by one biographer:

On the one hand, she had to meet the modern imperatives posed by the Nehrus and on the other to cope with their recurrent throw backs to convention. She soon acquired the outward trappings of the former, and became ardently feminist as a reaction to the latter, but without losing her restraint or decorum on both counts.[16]

As assessed by her daughter Indira: "Everywhere my father went he received letters of complaint that 'Kamalaji' had been inciting the women. Otherwise she was very gentle."[17] As assessed by her husband when he recalled her comment the first time she was arrested: ("I am happy beyond measure and proud to follow in my husband's footsteps").

Probably she wouldn't have said just that to the [newspaper man] if she had thought over the matter for she considers herself a champion of women's rights against the tyranny of man. But at that moment the Hindu wife in her came uppermost and even man's tyranny was forgotten.[18]

Of all the women of the Nehru family, Kamala most severely experienced as a young wife the polarization between Hindu *strīdharma* and Westernization through the indifference of her husband and the taunting of her sister-in-law. No wonder the pendulum swing of her psychology moved from extreme repression to virtual aggression while her discovery of courage and selfhood almost overstated the feminist potential of *satyāgraha*. If Nehru had been blind to her noble *strīdharma*, he was not to her noble *satyāgraha*. Husband and wife grew close through their participation in the movement and true romance belatedly bloomed. After Kamala's premature death, Nehru, addressing his daughter Indira, referred to Kamala as a "brave little mummie... with a heart of a lioness."[19] Hence it was with emotional appreciation of women as *satyāgrahinī* that he wrote:

The call of freedom, always had a double meaning for them, and the enthusiasm and energy with which they threw themselves into the struggle had no doubt their springs in the vague and hardly conscious but nevertheless intense desire to rid themselves of domestic slavery also.[20]

We felt proud of our people, and especially of our women folk, all over the country. I had a special feeling of satisfaction because of the activities of my mother, wife and sisters, as well as many girl cousins and friends; and...we grew near to each other bound by a new sense of comradeship in a great cause.[21]

It was easier for Indira to acquire freedom as a woman and as a human being than it was for her mother. The reason is given by Indira herself:

'Well, about women,' she said referring to the whole question of rights, freedom and prejudice, and her own subsequent work for women's uplift, 'I would have taken it for granted and not done anything. I had been born in freedom. But she knew what it could be.'[22]

Indira Gandhi is an outcome of the combination of male-female humanity. *Satayāgraha* as devised and envisioned by Gandhi was inherited and internalized by her in early childhood. Her inheritance, both traditional and politically strategic, came from her grandmother and mother. This inheritance had strong overtones of her father's upbringing and his embodiment of *satyāgraha*.

Indira was too young to remember her first stay at Gandhi's ashram. She does remember, however, her earliest childhood play: re-enactment of *satyāgraha*. At the age of four she quietly burned her doll, who was dressed in a Western frock, in imitation of the grown-up's bonfire-destruction of all foreign cloth. She delivered patriotic speeches to the servants of the household. Later she started the children's section of the Cakra Sangh, the spinning association. At twelve, she founded the Vanar Sena (the Monkey Army), eventually numbering 6000 children, which helped Congress members in the perfunctory tasks of the organization as well as the more daring manoeuvres of delivering messages through police lines. Her fantasy in her own words was: "some day I am going to lead my people to freedom just as Joan of Arc did."[23]

Though Indira was born into the "idiom" of *satyā-graha*, yet she encountered and overcame conflicts in her acquisition of personal independence. It can be said that ultimately she was not given freedom; rather, given the key to freedom, she *grew into* freedom, and for this she paid a price.

Indira's decision to marry Feroze Gandhi exemplifies her growth into freedom. While Nehru had always encouraged his daughter to make her own decisions, he objected strongly to her proposed marriage to Feroze. Indira held firm. It was Gandhi who brought Nehru around and calmed the public outcry over the unorthodox wedding by appealing to a universal level of Hinduism: "know that to be true religion which the wise and the good and those who are ever free from passion and hate follow, and which appeals to the heart."[24] Thus Gandhi, discovering scope for universalism in the ancient texts spoke to Nehru in his own langauge of reason and freedom. Even for those who advocated change, change was not always easy. While one would expect Nehru to be most liberal because of his secularism, one finds him in the context of his daughter's marriage more conservative than Gandhi, who did not advocate rejection of caste identity. Yet both realized that forging a new *Indian* identity would involve situations where parochial restraint would be inappropriate. A genuine love relationship was such an exception.

They recognized that the affirmation of universal values would bear such fruit as interfaith and intercaste marriage. To be true to the definition of religion for this new age, Hindus had to be open to situations such as Indira's marriage if not as the general rule (*sāmānya*) at least as a special rule (*viśeṣa*). Nehru, in his public statement regarding the marriage, noted that Indira had been trained to affirm decisions she felt were right in the face of opposition. This training in independent thinking had led to the daughter's decision and the father's inevitable acceptance.

The marriage ceremony was revised to capture the universalism and political dimension of the moment. With portentous symbolism Indira was given a sword (*khadga*) and repeated:

If there are any people in the four quarters of the earth, who venture to deprive us of our freedom, mark! Here I am, sword in hand, prepared to resist them to the last! I pray for the spreading light of freedom; may it envelop us on all sides.[25]

With intimations of the goddess Durgā, who battles, sword in hand, the forces of *adharma* (unrighteousness and social chaos), Indira is requested to battle for freedom.

Nehru once said "But freedom is a goddess hard to win: she demands, as of old, human sacrifices from her votaries."[26] The goddess in India has many images. When married she is *satī*, the good wife, and the compassionate mediatrix between the devotee, overcome by awe, and the omnipotent god, her husband. When single she is *śakti*, the militant power for social and cosmic order or, on the village level, unpredicatable grace and fury.

As wife, Indira desired to be *satī*; she was solicitous to Feroze; she tenderly nursed him when ill; she typed his correspondence. But Indira and Feroze at the time of their marriage had vowed that their first obligation would be to support Nehru as Prime Minister and by extension to work for the welfare of India. When they relegated their marriage to second place, they did not realize what personal chasms would be created by this noble definition of loyalties. Indira acted increasingly as her father's hostess, confidant, unofficial ambassador, and mediatrix between solicitous politicians and the Prime Minister. Feroze, because of the vow, his own political integrity, and perhaps his male psychology, gradually withdrew from the centre of activity, the Prime Minister's house. Estranged but ever tender to Indira, he was a human sacrifice for Freedom.

Just as in the past, *rājadharma*, the duty of a king, had precedence over *kuladharma*, duty to the family, so for Indira *bharatadharma*, duty to India, had precedence over *strīdharma*. Wheras, *satyāgraha* had bridged the tensions of the male-female relationship for the other women of the Nehru family, it failed for Indira. But then the others had to have loyalty only to the Cause and the marital relationship; Indira faced the conflict of husband and father who differed in their politics.

Indira had established her personal independence first in her decision to marry Feroze and secondly in her decision to continue her support of Nehru despite the cracks occurring in her marriage. She had yet to establish her political independence from her father and her husband. The occasion for this definitive stand was in 1957 when the Communists came to power in Kerala through the vote. As President of Congress, Indira took a public stand against her father and her husband. She successfully called for President's rule and thereby moved toward independent leadership, which helped her to overcome the curse that she was "only Nehru's daughter."

While Indira had never observed *strīdharma* in the *traditional sense*, she had been generally cautious not to antagonize Feroze and even more so her father, except for the pivotal episode regarding President's rule in Kerala. One might say that she had been dutiful to the men in her life and constrained by the male power. The death of Feroze in 1960 and Nehru four years later removed any constraints of *strīdharma*.

Through the training provided by *satyāgraha*, Indira became sufficiently matured and independent to assume the role of Prime Minister. It was because of her participation in *satyāgraha* and her personal witness of its effects on the female members of her family, that Indira developed courage, strength, self-confidence, fortitude, stamina, and equanimity. Indeed, the *āgraha* psychology provided her with political acumen, which is negatively perceived as "haughty insistence" by those who disagree with her strategies. This same *āgraha* psychology is positively appreciated by those who agree with her policies as nobility and strength by which she "urges" the country forward.

Just as Gandhi compounded *satya* and *āgraha*, linguistically and psychologically, so Indira Gandhi compounds pragmatism and ideology according to her understanding of *satya*, which is heavily indebted to the Independence Movement for its ideals of self-identity, independence, and integrity. It comes as no surprise to find her autobiography entitled *My Truth*, even as Gandhi had subtitled his *My Experiments with Truth*. In her final chapter "The India of my Dreams" Indira writes: "In India our ideals have mattered.... They provided the strength and the inner resources on which we have been able to call in all periods of crisis...."[27] Again, it comes as no surprise to find this chapter focused on women:

What is remarkable about India is not the number of women who have risen to prominent positions at one time or another but that women of character have been able to break through all barriers and prejudices and, once they have done so, they have been accepted without question by the public. The Indian concept of women has been governed by two parallel currents - the visible one of the woman in a subordinate role, the *abala* or weak one; and underlying it, that of woman as symbol of energy, the active principle. Thus woman is visualized as the stabilizing factor as well as the quickening one.[28]

If strength (*śakti*) was once the foundation, it has become a visible edifice because of the "consciousness-raising" through *satyāgraha*, feministically understood as woman's liberation. Such strength, though more visible as vocal is understood as a co-partnership with men. Indira warns:

The notion of superiority of one race or of one sex is out of date. Hence the movement for women's liberation should not deteriorate into some kind of confrontation between men and women, nor should it lead to women being treated as a separate species. We do not wish to imitate men, we do not seek high positions for a handful of women. What we want is true equality of opportunity to develop our latent talents and an end to discrimination on the basis of sex in training, education or in social attitudes."[29]

Here is the language of universal feminism. For Hindus it has its roots in something Indian: *satyāgraha* based on Hindu woman's psychology. Indira realistically notes that those polarizations between East and West, tradition and modernity, that influenced her family during the struggle for Independence today are influencing families on a mass basis. Consequently, the true challenge now begins as to whether the Indian woman "is able to achieve a harmonious synthesis between the best of our tradition and the most desirable of the modern."[30] Indira writes: "We still want to keep our own rhythm. The world's rhythm is a changing one. Why can't we women influence it and give it the right beat?"[31]

Is Indira an anomoly? Because of *satyāgraha*, no. She has had national support and international respect. At the same time the *āgraha* psychology in the contemporary context frustrates many, Indians and Western politicians alike. Moreover, Indian husbands now teasingly chide their self-confident wives "Don't be a *satyāgrahinī*!"[32] Thanks to the struggle for Independence we can hear the upbeat reply "It's my soul, *my* truth!"

SOCIAL CHANGE AND RELIGIOUS TRANSFORMATION AMONG
BOMBAY PARSIS IN THE EARLY TWENTIETH CENTURY[*]

John R. Hinnells

The Parsis settled in India in A.D. 936. They came as what we might term "the pilgrim fathers" of their Zoroastrian faith, seeking a new land of religious freedom away from the oppressions inflicted by their Muslim conquerors in their Iranian homeland. Indian tolerance and hospitality has permitted this Zoroastrian community to survive in India for over 1,000 years. The caste system has been an important factor in the preservation of religious tradition and communal identity because it has made inter-marriage and social mixing extremely rare.

Under British rule in the eighteenth and especially the nineteenth centuries a large proportion of the community enjoyed the fruits of commercial success, shared in the benefits of a Western education, and relished the taste of real political influence. To acquire fame and fortune, Parsis moved in increasing numbers from the agricultural life of the villages to the growing commercial capital of India, Bombay. So the Parsis experienced a substantial change in their place in society - from that of an insignificant, exiled rural caste, into an important force in late nineteenth century West Indian urban society. The purpose of this paper is not to document the causes, or the progress, of that change, but is rather to look at how the changes affected the religion of the Parsis in the early twentieth century. I will focus on the years 1900-1918 because after the First World War the position of the British in India was never the same again, and with the social and political changes, there came new orientations and emphasis in Parsi belief. Although no study of Parsi religion in this period has previously been undertaken, I believe it is an important era in Parsi history. Further the issues it raises are in a large part those of this congress, namely Parsi tradition in contact with Western culture and the consequent change.

In order to understand the religious changes among the Parsis in our period it is essential to appreciate just how much their conditions had changed. According to the 1901 census there were 46,231 Parsis in Bombay, this represented practically half (49.08%) the Parsi population of India, but they contributed only about 6% of the Bombay population. Yet they were a powerful group. In the textile industry, at the turn of the century they owned one-third of the mills and provided about half the millmanagers.[1] The Indian steel industry was founded by the Parsi Tata family in 1912 and various Parsi families were the major shareholders and managers of the main Bombay banks.[2] The result was that in a 1903 survey they held a foremost position in the High Income Groups in Bombay out of all proportion to their minority status.[3] Their economic success was visible for all to see through their charitable acts. In the previous fifty years, from 1850 to 1900, Parsis built 64 new fire temples.[4] Only recently, in 1897, they had built a new Atash Bahram, "Cathedral" Fire Temple, in Bombay. This was an enormous undertaking, the consecration ceremony alone taking a year. In the thirteen years 1899-1912, Parsis built thirteen hospitals or dispensaries.[5] In the early years of the twentieth century there were several outstanding Parsi charitable bequests. In 1900-1901 the Petit family gave away six million Rupees in public charities.[6] In 1905 Tata left three million Rupees to found a scientific research institute,[7] and in 1909 the Wadia trust was founded with nearly nine million Rupees to help the poor and needy of all communities in any country.[8] The point is that Parsi wealth was both considerable and visible.

One important change to notice in Parsi society was in education. Before the 1820s the Parsi level of education was as low as that of the rest of the population in Western

India. Literacy was practically non-existent. In the 1840s and 1850s Parsis were educational pioneers in that they built more schools and attended them more regularly in proportion to their numbers, than any other Indian community did. In the second half of the nineteenth century they dominated the centres of Higher Education in Bombay.[9] The result was that the general level of education throughout the community by 1900 was very high. The 1901 census, for example, recorded a literacy rate of 87.38%, which was a considerably higher rate than obtained among the Bombay General Public even in the 1970s. A striking feature of Parsi education was its availability for women. In 1901 63% of Parsi females were literate. This high educational attainment was an important factor behind the business success of the community and behind its political influence, which was considerable at the turn of the century.

I suppose the year in which most Parsis probably felt at their most important was 1905-1906. Various Parsi giants strutted the political stage. Dadabhoy Naoroji, the Grand Old Man of India, and the first Indian ever to be elected a Member of Parliament at Westminster, was perhaps at his peak as a figure of national importance. He was the only person who could hold together the moderate and radical wings of the Indian National Congress at the Calcutta meeting.[10] Sir Pherozeshah Mehta, popularly known as the uncrowned king of Bombay, and recently knighted, was at his most dominating height on the political scene of the city and thereby of Western India.[11] Until 1906 Sir Muncherji Bhownagree served as Member of Parliament at Westminster - the second Indian and the second Parsi to do so. Bhownagree was not particularly popular in India. He was so pro-British he was nicknamed "Bow-and-agree." But that did not change the fact that here was another Parsi concerned with national, indeed international, politics.[12] Throughout the whole of our period of 1900-1918 Sir Dinshah Wacha was the organisational heart of the Bombay Presidency Association and for most of the time was Secretary to the Indian National Congress, and one of the leading moderates.[13] There were of course other major figures, such as J.N. Tata the industrialist,[14] but these few illustrate the enormous influence exercised by this small Bombay community. The year 1907 saw an obvious downturn in Parsi prestige, but the effects of this decline on religious beliefs are a topic I will defer until later in the paper.

The point now is that by 1906 the tiny Parsi community, refugees from oppression, the once isolated and insignificant caste, had become wealthy and powerful not only in regional but also national and international terms. The ordinary Parsis knew of, and took intense pride in, the work of their leaders, as well as sharing in the increased affluence and educational achievements of the community in Bombay. Of course things were different for Parsis still living in the villages of Gujarat, but they are not the subject of this paper. How did this change in conditions affect the religion of the urbanised Parsis in Bombay?

To understand the religious changes of the early twentieth century, it is essential first to comment on some nineteenth-century developements in the field of Parsi religion. The first is the work of the Rev. J. Wilson, the Christian missionary with unquestionably the greatest influence on Parsis.[15] He began his work in Bombay in 1829. He resolved to focus his attention on the Parsis because of their influence in the city. In 1835 he opened a boys school near the main Parsi area of Bombay hoping to attract their youth. He was not disappointed. In 1839 he baptised his first two converts. There was such a fierce outcry among the Parsis he obtained few more. In 1843 he published, in Bombay, a book entitled *The Parsi Religion as contained in the Zand Avesta and propounded and defended by the Zoroastrians of India and Persia, unfolded, refuted and contrasted with Christianity*. This book was influential not because it converted the Parsis, but because of the nature of its attack on Zoroastrianism, the form of which largely conditioned the nature of educated Parsi reaction.

First, Wilson attacked Zoroastrian teaching on good and evil as two Ultimate Principles. This belief, he declared, was "both monstrous and unreasonable, robbing God of essential glory and peculiarity." Second, Parsi religion, he said, was a polytheistic nature worship. Third, he attacked the Zoroastrian scriptures, specifically the priestly law code, the *Vendidad*, which he declared was "in style and in substance destitute of all claims to be considered a revelation from God, but that it is from beginning to end most singularly despicable as a human composition." It was, he said, a monument to the errors of the human mind.[16] It is worth noting at this point that Wilson did not read the portion of the *Avesta* or Zoroastrian scriptures which contains Zoroaster's own words, because that was in Gathic which Wilson did not know. There were other features of Zoroastrianism Wilson attacked. For example he condemned the religion because it did not teach that man wallowed in sin, without which realisation, he said, man would not repent and realise his need for Christ.[17] But this had little influence on the Parsis, because Zoroastrians simply cannot understand or accept the Christian emphasis on sin. The points of his attack which did leave their marks were his dismissal of Zoroastrianism as dualistic and polytheistic and his questioning of the Avesta. Wilson's attack went home because no Parsis had the linguistic ability to refute his account of the texts. Avestan was a dead language used for recitation, but not really understood.

After the initial furor, the Parsis began to respond unobtrusively. Time forbids discussion of all the moves, but some have to be noted. The first was the "Religious Reform Association" founded in 1851, only eight years after Wilson's book was published. Its first secretary was Dadabhoy Naoroji. The aims of the Society were to purge contemporary Zoroastrianism of ceremonies and beliefs which made it appear ridiculous in the eyes of the Western educated. The principal calls for reform of practices were for the use of the vernacular in prayers and the eradication of Hindu social and religious accretions.[18]

The foremost figure of nineteenth century Parsi religious history was K.R. Cama. On his way back from a business visit to Britain in 1859 he stayed in Paris and Erlangen to study history of religions, Avestan and Pahlavi under some of the leading Iranists of the day in order first to educate himself and then his community so that they could repel missionary attacks. On his return to Bombay in 1861 he started classes in his own house. In 1864 he began "the Society for researches into the Zoroastrian religion." Through this society, lectures and publications, Cama was a leading figure in the move to educate Parsis. He was instrumental in the establishment of three colleges for the training of Parsi priests, the emphasis of each being on linguistic work. In 1904 he founded a society to spread the teaching of Zoroastrianism in Parsi schools, so that all children in the community might be educated in their faith.[19]

Another aspect of this programme of Parsi religious education was the work of European scholars. Between 1880 and 1887 the three volumed translation of the Avesta in *The Sacred Books of the East* series appeared (as well as five volumes of Pahlavi texts between 1880 and 1897) and these were available in Bombay. This made the Zoroastrian scriptures accessible to all Parsis with a Western education. Important French and German works were translated into English by some of the learned priests so that these also were available to that educated stratum of Parsi society.[20] The assumption was that the provision of sound translations and scholarly accounts of Zoroastrian history would support the faith of the community. So in 1900 an increasing amount of learned material was available for Parsis in English. Material was available in Gujarati also. A major scholarly work was Kanga's *Avesta Dictionary* (1900) and a number of translations of Middle Persian texts were made. Particular interest appears to have been paid in the early twentieth century to translations of the Ancient Iranian epic, the *Shah Name*. A five-volumed history of ancient Iran was published between 1906 and 1912 by J.P. Kapadia. Further important Parsi scholarly studies will be considered later, but at this point the focus must be primarily on the impetus for change which came through the contact between cultures and for this subject literature in English is of primary importance.[21]

Some writers were interested not only in the provision of texts but also in how they were to be interpreted. The foremost impetus for change in the sphere of doctrine came from a German, - Martin Haug. In 1859 he was appointed Superintendent of Sanskrit Studies in the Government College of Poona. In 1860 he completed the first Western scholarly translation of Zoroaster's hymns, the Gāthās. In 1861 he lectured to the Parsis in Bombay. The essence of his paper was that Zoroaster had taught a pure ethical monotheism. It was only the prophet's later followers who introduced a dualism, he said, and it was they who reintroduced the old pagan polytheism. Zoroaster, Haug declared, had propounded a theological monotheism and a philosophical dualism - that the one God encompassed the opposites of good and evil in himself. Haug, therefore, urged the Parsis to return to the pure teaching of their prophet as represented in the *Gāthās*, and the *Gāthās* alone. They should reject most of their scriptures because they incorporated later corruptions of the faith. What is more, Haug taught, there is no evidence in the *Gāthās* for the many rituals that Wilson and Parsi reformers attacked. Haug's view were expanded in a book published in 1862 entitled *Essays on the Language, Writings and Religion of the Parsis*. This was a very far cry form Wilson's publication some nineteen years earlier, for here Haug was presenting Zoroastrianism as a religion worthy of respect by the West. The westernised Parsis obviously welcomed the change of emphasis. Some were so impressed they wanted to make him a director of one of the Parsi priestly colleges.

But not all Western authors who inspired doctrinal reform among the Parsis were linguists or scholars. Judging by the frequency with which Parsis quote him, one of the most influential Western writers was Samuel Laing. He was a politician, Minister of Finance in India and business man who wrote three books for the semi-scientific reader, discussing the sort of religious questions that arose from late nineteenth-century science. In 1887 he published, in London, a book entitled *A Modern Zoroastrian*. His general theme was that recent scientific work showed that behind all aspects of life lay a dualism. In science it can be seen in the positive and negative of electricity or the poles of a magnet. True religion he said should reflect this dualism inherent in existence. In his discussion of Zoroastrianism he said his aim was:

To show that in its fundamental ideas and essential spirit [Zoroastrianism] approximates wonderfully to those of the most advanced modern thought, and gives the outline of a creed which goes further than any other to meet the practical wants of the present day and to reconcile the conflict between faith and science (p.198).

He described Zoroastrianism as a monotheism because he said Zoroaster taught that God comprehends within himself both principles of good and evil as a necessary law of existence (p.204). He concluded that Zoroastrianism was "the most complete and comprehensive code of morals to be found in any system of religion" (p.206).

Just as it was important to see what Wilson's criticisms of Zoroastrianism were in order to understand the Parsi response, so now it is important to note what qualities Western authors praised in Zoroastrianism. These were: the abstract nature of Zoroaster's ethical monotheism; his lack of interest in rituals and the consistency of Zoroastrianism and modern science. Whether these Western writers were correct in their assessment of Zoroastrianism is in this context irrelevant.

So at the start of the twentieth century the Parsi community in Bombay was, as a whole, reasonably wealthy, powerful, influential and well educated in Western terms. The educated were conscious of Western attitudes to them and their religion, both in the form of missionary attacks and scholarly interpretations.[22] It is important to note that not all the scholarly work on Zoroastrianism was done by Westerners. A number of Parsis made substantial contributions. Dasturs Sanjana and Jamaspasa, and D.M. Madan undertook important editorial work on editions of Middle Persian texts. In the confines of this particular paper these contributions are not so central because these works were not read or understood by the Parsi public at large. D.F. Karaka's two-volumed *History of the Parsis* (1884), though published in London and intended primarily for the Western reader, appears to have been quite widely read by Parsis. M.M. Murzban in his 1917 publication *The Parsis in India* not only provided a translation of Menant's 1898 French work but also expanded her work quite considerably with the needs of his own community in mind.[23] Perhaps the Parsi lecturer and scholar whose work was most widely known in Bombay during our period was J.J. Modi. Although he had produced little in the way of books by the end of the period he was a prolific producer of articles on ancient Iranian and Parsi subjects as well as broader folklore and anthropological topics. He was honoured by Swedish, French, German, Hungarian and British institutions. He also wrote on religion as a priest, mainly in Gujarati, but also in English.[24] Modi apart, most Parsi historians of the early twentieth century were concerned with Parsi history. Foremost amongst them was B.B. Patel and his successor R.B. Paymaster, compilers of the *Parsi Prakash* (vol.II appeared in the middle of our period, 1910). This multi-volumed work collects newspaper entries from earliest times to the Present and provides the basic tool for any Parsi historian. Less prolific, but with high scholarly standards, was S.H. Hodivala, noted for his studies of early Parsi history.[25] The significance of the work of these Parsis for this paper is that Western historical methods of scholarship had been absorbed by various Parsi scholars whose work was known and respected by the public at large, providing them with learned accounts both of their ancient religion and community history. The contact between the traditions of Bombay Parsis and Western scholarship was real, deep and widespread. The question now is what changes did it effect on religious beliefs in the early twentieth century?

It was perhaps inevitable that one problem was a serious identity crisis in the community. As the calls for Indian Independence grew, and especially as the militants such as Tilak gained influence, so the Parsis were forced to consider which side of the growing divide they stood on. The educated leaders such as Naoroji and Mehta, although often considered pro-British, in fact identified themselves first and foremost with India. Naoroji, for example, affirmed in 1893: "Whether I am a Hindu, a Muhammadan, a Parsi, a Christian, or of any other creed, I am above all an Indian. Our country is India; our nationality is Indian."[26] Madame Cama, the daughter in law of K.R. Cama, identified herself so strongly with India and the rising Hindu militancy that after 1902 she lived in exile in France working with leading revolutionaries.[27]

But she was far from typical. Most Parsis who had received a Western education, and that meant most Parsis in Bombay, were pro-British. This is understandable in that any small community, especially one having a vivid memory of persecution, which is then given the scope to flourish as Parsis were, will naturally hold a favourable attitude to the ruling power. These Western leanings were expressed in various ways, through social customs like dress and hobbies,[28] and in diverse publications. A good example of the latter is *The Parsi* which began in 1905 as a glossy magazine, somewhat in the style of *The Illustrated London News*. It constantly exhorted Parsis to disassociate themselves from Indian traditions and identity themselves with the West. Just one quotation must serve to illustrate the tone:

The closer union of Europeans and Parsis is the finest thing that can happen to our race. It will mean the *lifting up* of a people who are lying low, though possessing all the qualities of a European race. It will make our men more of men than they are at present and will make our women better women. The complete Europeanization of the Parsis is now a mere matter of time.[29]

With such a divide running through the community as far as self-identity was concerned we might expect similarly deep divides over religous issues. I can find no clear example of Hindu influence in the beliefs of Parsi writers between 1900 and 1918;[30] the divide is rather in terms of the orthodox and the reformists, or as the orthodox called them, the 'Protestant Party'. This label is not without significance, because most of the Westerners who influenced reforming Parsis were Protestants.

Perhaps the foremost example of a reformist was M.N. Dhalla. He was born into a poor priestly family in 1875 in Bombay but early on moved to Karachi where he grew up as a strict orthodox. In 1901 he moved back to Bombay to study and progressed so well that the community, led by K.R. Cama, raised the funds for Dhalla to go to Columbia University, New York, in 1905. There he studied under the Iranian specialist, Professor A.V.W. Jackson, first for an M.A., then a Ph.D. Dhalla also attended courses in a whole range of subjects, history of religions, anthropology, sociology, as well as pursuing his textual studies. His tutor, Jackson, was a staunch Protestant and he exercised considerable influence on him. Dhalla returned to India in 1908 a transformed person, as he himself said:

My 3 years and 9 months of scientific and critical study at Columbia University...eradicated religious misconceptions that had gathered in my mind due to my blinded mental vision, traditional beliefs and upbringing. As the clouds of superstition dispersed, the mist of mental darkness was rent assunder. I was free of the religion of fear that was the belief of infant humanity and turned towards the pure religion of love, the religion as preached by the prophets and uncorrupted by their fanatical followers. Now that I have been enlightened by scientific study, and now that I have come to know and gain so much, I no longer adhered to my old ideas. My thinking, my outlook, my ideals and my philosophy of life changed. The purpose and meaning of life changed-everything changed. I was now eager to become the thinker of new thoughts, the student of new ideas and the propagator of new concepts. In 1905 I had set foot on American soil as an orthodox. Now in 1909 I was leaving the shores of the New World as a reformist.[31]

On his return to India Dhalla was appointed high priest of the Parsis in Karachi. There and in Bombay he was an influential figure through his speeches, writings and a series of annual Zoroastrian conferences he started in 1910. Essentially what he did was to press as a priestly reformer from within the community the sort of doctrinal reform which had been expounded by the outsider Haug. Dhalla stressed the ideas of ethical monotheism, called for the simplification of rituals and for prayers in the vernacular. He denied the traditional Zoroastrian doctrine of a 'devil', Ahriman, saying that evil was a tendency within man. His concern was to preserve the monotheism of the prophet against charges of dualism.[32] Through the medium of the annual conferences Dhalla campaigned vigorously for a better educated priesthood, and by that he meant educated according to Western standards. This presupposition lay behind the work of various reformists, that a Western education was an important component in a priestly life of holiness. Priests not so trained were regarded as ignorant by many of the intelligentsia.

Dhalla was a kindly person who did not press his reforms with the acrimony characteristic of many. He was also very devout and did not press his learning and logic as far as some of his contempories. D.M. Madan, for example, in publications in 1909 and 1916 argued from the educational principle that knowledge gained for oneself is better than knowledge imposed from above to the religious conclusion that revelation is not conducive to real religious insight. He presented Zoroastrianism not as a religion of devotion, but rather as a logical philosophy. He wrote:

[Zoroaster's] philosophy and religion is purely a human conception, and claims but one merit - the greatest merit that could possibly be claimed for any system of philosophy or religion, its entire and uncompromising consistency with human reason, and the entire absence in it of all dogmatic assertions, or claims to arbitrary authority.[33]

Other Parsis, following Laing, were eager to show how Zoroastrianism was entirely consistent with modern science; probably the most common theme was that the purity laws of the ancient faith were in harmony with scientific teachings on hygiene.[34]

For such writers as these, Western education reinforced the traditional Zoroastrian link between religion and knowledge. The reformists were convinced that true religion must be in complete harmony with modern learning. There was no place for 'faith in the unknown'. The educated reformist Parsi of the early twentieth century had immense faith in human reason in general and the potential of his own religion in particular. Several writers compared their rational religion favourably with that of ancient Greece, or Israel, or the modern West, and found there was little difference. Some also quoted the views of L.H. Mills, and others that Zoroastrian teachings influenced Judaeo-Christian belief and so presented the religion of the Parsis as the fountain source of the great religions.[35]

The westernised reformists represented only one religious trend among the Parsis in the early twentieth century. Theosophy was also a powerful influence. Madame Blawatsky and Col. Olcott moved from New York to Bombay in 1879 and the Blawatsky lodge was founded. Parsis were dominant in the history of the lodge from its inception to the end of our period. Over these 36 years they held the post of President for one-third of the time; the post of secretary for two-thirds and treasurer for three-quarters of the time. All the librarians were Parsis, something like three-quarters of listed publications from Blawatsky lodge were written by Parsis.[36] Theosophists had an appreciable influence upon the Parsi community at large. On February 14th, 1882 Col. Olcott delivered a lecture at Bombay Town Hall addressed to the Parsis entitled "The Spirit of the Zoroastrian Religion," which was published that year. He urged Parsis to preserve their ancient prayers and rites and not to dismiss half their scriptures, as Western linguists such as Haug argued, because, he said, none of these scholars has named the true key to Zoroastrian doctrine. The key he said lay not in the dry bones of words, nor in modern physical science, but rather "occult science is the vindicator of Zoroastrianism, and there is none other."

Theosophy obviously attracted those alienated by the reformist calls for the abandonment of half the scriptures and drastic changes in the age old rites. The orthodox, the established community leaders and the Theosophists came together to oppose change. Because the reformists have been linked with Western education it does not follow that their theosophical opponents were associated with the uneducated. Far from it, Theosophy attracted anyone, not least the educated, who feared the loss of everything in the religion which they held dear. It is interesting to note that although one religious educator I have referred to, namely Dhalla, was a vigorous opponent of Theosophy,[37] another, namely K.R. Cama, in later life became a member of the Theosophical Society. Although Theosophists argued science was blind to spiritual phenomena, and therefore not a guide, nevertheless they also stressed there was nothing in science which conflicted with their teachings. Theosophy could be followed by anyone, they declared. So the Parsi barrister, and the main spokesman for the orthodox, J. Vimadalal, wrote a series of articles in the journal *East and West* in 1904 in which he outlined the doctrinal basis of Theosophy in a manner he believed he could commend to the educated both in India and in the West. What he, and others, were attempting to do was to meet the apparently conflicting moods of the time - the anti-Western backlash provoked by the extreme reformists and yet the overpowering impression which Western science and learning had on India at the turn of the century.[38]

One problem Theosophists had in attracting Parsis was that no matter how Olcott and others reaffirmed their regard for Zoroastrianism, Theosophy remained a movement clearly outside the community and therefore potentially a divisive force. In 1907 a movement started which might loosely be called a 'Zoroastrianised Theosophy'. Its followers call it Ilm-i Kshnoom, the Path of Knowledge. The founder was Behramshah Shroff. He claimed that at the age of 17 he had left home and met a wandering group of Muslims who were really secret Zoroastrians. They led him to the homeland of a secret race of giants in the mountains of Iran, in a land known as Firdo, or heaven. There Zoroastrian treasures and teachings are preserved. Everyone lives in a paradisal state in caves with streams of nectar flowing past. After staying for three years Shroff returned home to Surat where he remained silent for 30 years before beginning his teaching mission in 1907.[39] His doctrine encompassed a number of traditional theosophical ideas - an impersonal God, different planes of being, vegetarianism and reincarnation.

The feature to which I want to draw attention now is the image of Iran it displays. In the first place Shroff is replacing the Theosophists' allegiance to the Masters of remote Tibet, with adherence to Zoroastrian giants and religious treasures in the Parsi homeland.[40] Second, it reflects the subtle change in the Parsi image of Iran. In the nineteenth century it was typically perceived as the land where the Good Religion was oppressed. By the early twentieth century it was being emphasised more as the homeland of the religion. In part this was due to the increasing knowledge flowing from scholarly studies. It was also due to the changing political scenes in Iran and India. The ruling Qajar dynasty, in Iran began to ease conditions for Zoroastrians[41] and at the same time the Parsi fortunes appeared to decline, in India. Earlier I said 1906 was probably the time when most Parsis felt most powerful and secure. But in 1907 a series of events seemed to undermine that position. It was in that year Naoroji retired from public life; then the rise of the Hindu militants at the 1907 Congress in Surat appeared threatening. It was in 1907 that for the first time for many years there was no Parsi M.P. at Westminster, because Bhownagree was not re-elected for a third term. In the same year a caucus tried to remove Mehta from power in Bombay. To many it must have seemed the security of the community was suddenly threatened. In fact, of course, it was not so sudden. The seeds of decline had set in earlier. Despite the appearance of 1905 a few lone voices had already been raising questions whether the Parsis were as secure as they thought. What if militant Hinduism should arouse the innumerable people of India to turn on the Parsis with a violence like that of the Muslim Arabs in seventh century Iran? So the calls began for Parsis to move on from India to seek yet another land of religious freedom. This time, so the appeal went, they should not settle in someone else's country but rather create their own nation to be called Parsistan, with their own army, so that they might remain secure for ever. The most popular destination was in the mountain fringes of Iran, in what is now Afghanistan. If tiny Japan could withstand the mighty Russians in the 1904 war, then, it was argued, the Parsis could stand alone with their great traditions behind them. The earliest appeal of this nature that I can find was made by a Parsi from Quetta, Khan Bahadur Patel in 1905.

Even previous to the advent of the British, they [the Parsis] were *not considered natives of India*, and if the British were to leave India, should this ever come to pass, they will still be looked upon as aliens. It is therefore wise and politic for the Parsis to prepare for themselves a haven of refuge...by founding a colony. The example of Japan should serve as an incentive to the Parsis...if the community some day loses the influence and position hitherto accorded it their fate will be no better than that of the Pariahs in India and the Gabars in their fatherland [Persia].^{42}

The formation of the Muslim league in 1906 stimulated this call which excited increasing comment for decades to come.

This description of the different Parsi religious movements must not be left without an account of the orthodox. Just as books on Hinduism are in danger of focussing wholly on the literate tip of the iceberg and forgetting the mass submerged out of sight, so a similar error can be made in Parsi studies. Few of the orthodox wrote books. An outstanding exception was the High Priest Rustomji Edulji Sanjana. In a book published in 1906 he affirmed the revealed nature of *all* Zoroastrian scriptures, the spiritual value of the rituals introduced by the prophet and the traditional Zoroastrian teaching on the resurrection of the body. He is, incidentally, the last Parsi I can find to emphasise this belief. But even Sanjana, orthodox though he was, denied a belief in a devil, arguing that evil was man's own corrupt thought.^{43}

But typically orthodox literary activity was in the form of pamphlets or newspaper articles, generally in Gujarati, opposing changes.^{44} The strength of orthodoxy was felt most in the faithful observance of religious practices and the groundswell of public opinion. Nowhere was this more strongly felt than on the biggest single issue in early twentieth century Parsis religious discussion-whether the community should accept converts, a debate that led to a court case and which enshrines many of the issues I have outlined.

In 1903 R.D. Tata, son of the leading Parsi industrialist, married a French woman, Suzanne Briere, in Paris. On January 8th in Bombay she underwent the Zoroastrian initiation ceremony and then had a Parsi wedding. This was the first known case of a complete outsider, as opposed to the child of a mixed marriage, undergoing initiation. The community was in uproar.[45] The fear was that if non-Parsis were converted into the community, and were legally recognised as Parsis, the charitable Trust Funds would soon be exhausted. The Parsis, no doubt, had in mind that the mass of Indian converts to Christianity in the 1870s came not from the wealthy classes but from the poor and the outcastes. Such a phenomenon would obviously swamp a tiny minority like the Parsis.

A committee was appointed to report on whether conversion was acceptable in Zoroastrianism. After much intrigue, as well as debate, the members decided that it was doctrinally proper, but said nothing on its practicability. The report was to have been submitted to a public meeting, but a powerful lobby prevented this. The traditional governing body of the community, the Parsi Panchayet, decreed that only Parsi Zoroastrians, and not converts, could benefit from the Trusts or buildings under their controls - an important point being that the buildings included Fire Temples. This decision was supported by a public meeting on April 16 with a resolution in these words: "In the interests of the community and looking to the religious and social condition of the Parsi community, it will be incorrect to convert people from other religions, as such a move would be damaging to the community and shatter its ancestry and unity."[46] The meeting confirmed the Panchayet's decision regarding the Trusts and recommended that any priest performing the initiation of a non-Zoroastrian should be boycotted. These directives, it resolved, should be implemented in all Parsi communities, not just Bombay. The so-called Protestant party delivered a solicitor's letter questioning the right of the Panchayet to make such a decision about the Trust funds, and indeed questioning the very validity of the appointment of the members of the Panchayet. And so legal battle was joined.

Judgment was given by two judges in Suit no. 689 of 1906. The senior judge was the Hon. Mr Justice Davar. He was a known orthodox Parsi,[47] and was one of those who had blocked the report saying there were no religious objections to conversion from going to a public meeting. The second judge was the Hon. Mr Justice Beaman, a Theosophist and hardly likely, I would have thought, to be neutral in his attitude to the Reformists. The Suit was in two parts. In the first the Judges found that the Panchayet was not properly constituted, but the existing Trustees were re-appointed by the Court until a proper system of election was established.

It was the second part of the Suit, on whether a non-Parsi could by conversion become eligible for the Trust Funds, i.e. enter a Temple, which is significant for the historian of Parsi religion. At the outset Mr Justice Davar stressed that as Mrs. Tata, the offended party, was not in court, judgment could not be binding on her, or on others who come afterwards, a point which was later raised to question the whole of Davar's subsequent judgment.[48] But as far as I can see this was never pressed; perhaps the community had no heart for tearing itself apart again. Mr Justice Davar concluded that the Trusts had to be for Parsis by birth alone, because if there were no restrictions: "The ruin of the community would be accomplished in as many days as it had taken generations to attain that position of prominence which the Parsis of India have now achieved (p.82 of the Judgment)." He went on to condemn one of the witnesses who argued for conversion for giving 'blind and erratic evidence' because he saw no objection to low castes like sweepers and Dubras being allowed entry to the community (p.83). The basis of Davar's judgment therefore appears to have been not an application of the law, but what he considered to be best for the community. He ruled that the term Parsi was limited to the descendants of the original emigrants, through the line of the father, and to later Zoroastrian emigrés from Iran (p.116).

Mr Justice Beaman stated that he had at first been inclined to disagree, but finally he concurred with the decision of, but not the reasons for, Davar's judgment. He argued that as the Trust Funds had been established by founders who viewed their community as a caste, this is how the law must decree they should continue to function. A convert to the religion of Zoroastrianism could not therefore be entitled to the Trusts for the Parsis (pp.112-15).

The judgment in this case has been followed ever since by Parsis everywhere. In 1914 in Rangoon there was an outcry when a priest initiated the offspring of a Parsi woman married to a non-Parsi. Mr Justice Davar took an active part in the orthodox campaign and the priest duly made a public apology regretting his act.[49] In recent years there has been a similar controversy over an initiation performed by a Parsi priest in the States. But these are the exceptions which prove the rule laid down in the 1906 judgment.

The two sides in this conversion controversy reflect the divide in the Bombay Parsi community at the start of the century. The Reformist, or Protestant, party was confident in its religion as one with universal appeal and relevance. They were keen to launch their faith as a proselytising religion like most great religions of the day. The orthodox, joined by Theosophists and Kshnoomists, were concerned to preserve the practices and racial characteristics of the community, believing this to be the only way to ensure the continuation of their religious and cultural heritage. The recommendations of the public meetings suggest that whatever may be the *appearance* of Parsi attitudes displayed by the plethora of published pamphlets, the majority of Parsis were, at heart, conservative. The court ruling determined that, on what was the biggest issue of the day, caste status rather than westernization remained the most powerful characteristic of the community.

It is tempting in conclusion to draw parallels between Parsi religious changes and those in contemporary Hinduism. The obvious analogy whould be the Parsi reformists and the Brahma Samaj. What is interesting is that despite the reputation of the Parsis as both westernized and quick to adapt, the reforming process among them began much later than the foundation of the Brahma Samaj. In part this may be due to the fact that the home of the Samaj, Calcutta, was more exposed to Western education at an earlier date than Bombay was. But I believe another and vital factor was that although Parsis were, at this time, socially very adaptable, in their religion they were more conservative. The reason was, and is, that Zoroastrianism functions as a binding force to preserve the identity of this microscopic community. Although the Parsis were in contact with Western traditions, and experienced considerable social change, a counterbalancing force in their religion was their consciousness of being a tiny minority in a tolerant but nevertheless alien culture. This consciousness was reinforced by the strong community memory of the oppression in Iran. The analogy with the Brahma Samaj would therefore be superficial. A parallel with Judaism might be more appropriate in that both have experienced exodus, exile and persecution. For both races religion functions as a cohesive force. Parsi contacts with Western traditions in general, and scholarship in particular, brought substantial change, indeed transformation, in the realm of doctrine, but it brought little or no change in the realm of religious practices. In discussions over such issues as the nature and origin of evil, reason could prevail, but where issues impinged upon religious or racial identity then cherished custom had authority over scholarship, however much the latter may be respected.

It would, however, be wrong to leave the Parsis in Bombay in the period 1900-1918 with the impression that all of them were actually religious. One of the most common themes of writers of all persuasions, of columnists and cartoonists, was the decline of religion within the community. Wealth and westernization brought the comforts of affluence, the threat of materialism. Gambling, drinking, the theatre and the racecourse were the foremost concerns of the educated middle classes if we are to judge from the pages of some of the popular press.[50] How true this picture is, it is difficult to say at this distance. Certainly, the urbane Parsi of Bombay in the early twentieth century had lost most of his connections with the agricultural roots of his religion. The seven great festivals, the gahāmbars, for example, which were based on the pastoral life and the seasons, were not celebrated in the traditional festive manner, for their significance was lost. Perhaps the greatest change that contact with Western traditions brought was not the Protestant party, but an apathy towards religion. In the early years of this century we may see the symptoms of what many Parsi religious leaders consider to be the plague of the community - religious indifference. Indifference, that is, until the Parsi identity and heritage appears threatened for example by the conversion of an alien. In Parsi eyes, that is the time of greatest danger; when traditions are in such contact as this, then drastic change is threatened. At such times there is no indifference.

CHRISTLICHE INTERPRETAMENTE IN DER KHASI-RENAISSANCE:
ZUR RELIGIÖSEN BEDEUTUNG EINER REFORMBEWEGUNG BEI
DEN HOCHLAND-KHASI VON MEGHALAYA

Peter Gerlitz

1. Die Gründung des Seng Khasi im Jahre 1899 hatte zunächst keineswegs zur Folge, daß man die nationalistischen Ziele dieser Organisation und ihre religiösen Reformvorstellungen im damals britisch verwalteten Assam ernst nahm. Man schien im Gegenteil davon überzeugt, daß diese für das ausgehende 19. Jahrhundert so typische antiwestliche und damit auch antichristliche bewegung von einigen wenigen Intellektuellen der Khasi und Jaintia nur eine kurze Episode bleiben würde; denn die schweigende Mehrheit der Stammesbevölkerung akzeptierte den politischen wie den religiösen[1] Einfluß des Westens. Ein politischer Druck seitens der britischen Besatzungsmacht ist nur in wenigen Fällen nachweisbar.[2]

Dieser nahezu kritiklos erfolgten Bejahung des westlichen Einflusses in den Khasi und Jaintia Hills ist es zuzuschreiben, daß die Literatur aus der Gründerzeit des Seng Khasi nahezu unbekannt blieb. Selbst die Bücher Jeebon Roys (1838-1903), der heute allgemein als der "Apostel der Khasi-Renaissance"[3] und als "Pionier einer reinen Khasi-Literatur"[4] gefeiert wird, fanden kaum Beachtung. Seine zwei Jahre vor der Gründung des Seng Khasi erschienene kleine Schrift mit dem Titel Ka Niam Jong Ki Khasi (Die Religion der Khasi),[5] in der der Verfasser seine Landsleute über die in Vergessenheit geratende Religion der Väter informiert und ihnen die Pflichten des matrilinearen Gesellschaftssystems in Erinnerung ruft, erschien nur in einer unbedeutenden Auflage. Ähnlich erging es seinem Kitab Shaphang Uwei U Blei (ed. 1900), in dem er zum ersten Male die Monotheismusthese vertrat und den Nachweis führte, daß die ursprüngliche Khasi-Religion eine omnipotente Gotteskonzeption besaß. Ja, selbst seine aggressive Monatszeitschrift U Nongphira, "Der Beobachter," in der er zusammen mit seinem Sohn Sibcharan Roy seine Leser katechismusartig über den Kultus der Stammesreligion informierte, wurde erst 15 Jahre nach ihrem ersten Erscheinen (1903) für die Öffentlichkeit interessant, als die britische Regierung ihre antichristlichen Tendenzen bemerkte und darum ihre Einstellung anordnete (1918). P.R. Gurdon, der Nestor der Khasiforschung, erwähnt in seinem 1907 geschriebenen[6] Buch nicht einmal den Seng Khasi, geschweige denn seinen Gründer und dessen literarische Zeugnisse.

So entwickelte sich gleichsam im Verborgenen und neben der offiziellen Literatur der Missionare, insbesondere der Welsh Calvinistic Methodist Mission[7] in Shillong und der römischen Katholiken von Shillong und Cherrapunjee, eine genuine Khasi-Literatur, die ausschließlich in der Khasi-Sprache verbreitet wurde und sich ausnahmslos kritisch, in den meisten Fällen polemisch mit der Praxis der Missionare wie dem christlichen Dogma auseinandersetzte. Andererseits scheint gerade diese "Untergrund-Literatur" bereits erste Anzeichen einer synkretistischen Verarbeitung bestimmter Grundbegriffe aus der christlichen Dogmatik zu tragen. In gewisser Weise typisch dafür sind z.B. U Rabon Singh's Ka Niam Khein Ki Khasi (1905?), ein Buch, in dem die Khasi-Religion in ihrem gegenwärtigen Zustand als polytheistische Verfälschung eines urmonotheistischen Grundmodells dargestellt wird,[8] und Sibcharan Roy's Ka Niam Ki Khasi (1919), eine Schrift, die sich ontologisch mit der Gottesfrage und den monotheistischen Zügen der alten Stammesreligion beschäftigt.

In den Publikationen nach dem 1. Weltkrieg scheinen sich Seng-Khasi-Autoren, wie U Homiwell Lyngdoh, Hormu Roy Diengdoh[9] und der Dichter Soso Tham (1873-1941) verstärkt mit der Khasi-Kultur, dem Bestattungsritual und den damit zusammenhängenden matrilinearen Strukturen in Familie und Clan sowie der eschatologischen Dichtung zu befassen[10] -

jedenfalls läßt die Polemik gegen eine westlich-religiöse Überfremdung deutlich nach. Dennoch kann man auch die Literatur zwischen den beiden Kriegen nur vom östlich-westlichen Gegensatz her verstehen: Sie behandelt fast ausschließlich das kulturelle Erbe der Khasi und sucht dieses der westlichen Importkultur gleichzustellen und ebenbürtig zu machen, und - was mindestens ebenso wichtig ist - sie spricht nur in der Khasi-Sprache.

Erst nach dem 2. Weltkrieg, mit der Unabhängigkeit Indiens und vollends mit der Gründung des neuen Unionsstaates Meghalaya im Jahre 1970 bzw. 1972 wagte sich der Seng Khasi mit seinen Ideen an die Öffentlichkeit. Um eine möglichst breite Leserschaft, auch unter den Assamesen und den aus Bangladesch geflüchteten Bengalen sowie im westlichen Ausland zu erreichen, bediente er sich jetzt auch des Englischen. Hier ist vor allem die Sammlung von Essays über Religion und Kultur der Khasi zu nennen, die U Hipshon Roy, der derzeitige Generalsekretär des Seng Khasi, unter dem Titel "Khasi Heritage"[11] herausgegeben hat. Die darin enthaltenen Beiträge von H.O. Mawrie und R.T. Rymbai zur Stammesreligion der Khasi und Jaintia weisen eine starke Ambivalenz auf: Sie beziehen einerseits grundsätzlich einen antiwestlich-antichristlichen Standpunkt, und sie versuchen andererseits ihre eigenen religiösen Aussagen in Begriffen und Inhalten eben dieser von ihnen abgelehnten "westlichen Ideologie" darzustellen. Ihre Religionskritik bezieht sich also nur auf die ideologische Komponente der Verwestlichung, nicht auf den Inhalt derselben.

Diese These wollen wir jetzt im einzelnen untersuchen.
2.1. Die Verfassung des Seng Khasi von 1913[12] beruft sich in ihrer Präambel ausdrücklich auf die religiöse Stammestradition: "Der Seng Khasi ist eine Organisation aller Khasi, die an der traditionellen Khasi-Religion festhalten.... Die Mitgliedschaft steht allen Khasi offen, die an die traditionelle Religion glauben [sic!]" Mit dieser Einladung an die Stammesangehörigen ist zugleich der Ausschluß aller derjenigen verbunden, die die traditionelle Religion verlassen haben bzw. den Grundsatz Ka Niam

Tipbriew Ka Niam Tipblei[13], "Die Religion, die den Menschen kennt und die Gott kennt", nicht beachten. Davon waren die Christen aller Denominationen betroffen.

Diese Exklusivität bedeutete zunächst einen Widerspruch, denn das oberste Ziel des Seng Khasi besteht nach der Satzung darin, "Liebe, Wahrheit, Recht und andere fundamentale Grundsätze der Khasi-Religion überall in den Khasi- und Jaintia Hills zu verbreiten."[14] Doch schon der Zusatz "...der Khasi-Religion" zeigt, daß es sich dabei ausschließlich um das "soziokulturelle und religiöse Erbe"[15] der Khasi handelt. Bereits die folgenden Grundsätze machen deutlich, daß wir es beim Seng Khasi keineswegs nur um eine sozio-kulturelle Einrichtung zu tun haben, sondern in höchstem Maße um eine orthodoxe Reformbewegung mit religiösem Absolutheitsanspruch: Die Mitglieder des Seng Khasi verpflichten sich, "für die Bewahrung des kulturellen Erbes der Khasi zu arbeiten und sich für Solidarität und Bruderschaft unter den Khasi zu begeistern [!]" (2); "die Sache der Aufklärung unter den Khasi durch die Gründung von Schulen zu fördern ";(4) "um die Feuerbestattung [eigentl. the cremation ground] zu bewahren und weiterzuentwickeln und die Interessen derjenigen Khasi zu schützen, die mit ihren Toten gemäß der Tradition verfahren "(6); "um die Sache des traditionellen Khasi-Sports, nämlich des Bogenschießens, zu bewahren und zu schützen, desgleichen die kulturellen Tänze und andere Feste, an welchen die Khasi überall in den Khasi- und Jaintia Hills seit jeher teilgenommen haben" (7).[16] R.T. Rymbai faßt die Ziele - noch enger - in den drei Hauptgeboten zusammen: Kamai ia ka Hok - Gerechtigkeit erwerben - Tipbriew-Tipblei - den Menschen kennen und Gott kennen-und Tip-kur-Tip-kha - die matrilinearen und die patrilinearen Verwandschaftsverhältnisse kennen.[17]

2.2. Die Verbindung von "Matrilinearer Gesellschaftsstruktur und Religion"[18] ist offensichtlich, kann aber hier nur gestreift werden. Khasi wie Jaintia/ Pnar sind matrilinear strukturiert und leiten ihren Stammbaum von der Urahnin Ka Jawbei her. Alle auf diese Weise matrilinear miteinander verwandten Familien- oder Clanmitglieder bilden eine sogen. Kur, die gewöhnlich in eine Reihe von Untergruppen, die ebenfalls kur heißen und den gleichen matrilinear vererbten Familiennamen tragen, aufgespalten ist.[19] Jede kur bildet eine streng exogame Gruppe, so daß Ehen innerhalb dieses Sippenverbandes - und sei er noch so groß - verboten sind.[20] Nach außen hin vertreten wird die kur durch den matrilinearen Onkel, u kni, der den Ehrentitel U kni ha ka iap ka im, "ein Onkel im Leben und im Tode," trägt. Die kleinste aber wichtigste Einheit ist die iing, der "Haushalt", die Familie im engeren Sinne, die von Mutter (i mei) und Kindern bzw. - wenn die Mutter nicht mehr am Leben ist - von der jüngsten Tochter der Familie (ka khun khadduh) und deren Geschwistern gebildet wird. Hier, im eigenen Hause, nimmt der Vater (i pa) eine untergeordnete Stellung ein,[21] während er als u kni die iing bzw. die kur seiner jüngsten Schwester nach außen vertritt.[22]

Die iing ist die zweifellos wichtigste Institution in der Khasi-Gesellschaft und ist für alle Khasi verbindlich, ob sie Christen sind oder nicht. Sie bildet zugleich die grundlegende religiöse Einheit. Denn hier wird das Eigentum der Vorfahren bewahrt, und hier werden die Bestattungszeremonien gehalten. Mit Recht bezeichnet Chie Nakane die iing als "the key to the whole Khasi social organization"[23] Über ihr, wie über allen iing, die durch matrilineare Deszendenz mit der kur verbunden sind, "wacht" die Urahnin Ka Jawbei. Ka Jawbei ist die Urmutter des Clan, ihr zur Seite steht U Thawlang, der Urvater, beide werden von dem Uronkel U Suidnia beraten. Der Grundsatz Ka Niam Tipbriew ka Niam Tipblei - "Die Religion, die den Menschen kennt und die Gott kennt" - ist nur von dieser Clanstruktur her verständlich.

2.3. Bereits Gurdon hat darauf aufmerksam gemacht, daß Ka Jawbei für die Khasi das bedeutet, was die Göttin Brigit für die Kelten war, nämlich Mutter und Begründerin des Stammes.[24] Sie ruft man während des Eierwerfens oder beim Hahnenopfer an.[25] Hier wird sie Ka Blei Ka Jawbei, die Göttin Jawbei, genannt.[26] Die gleiche Deifizierung geschieht mit U Thawlang, dem man im Falle von häuslichen

Schwierigkeiten einen Hahn opfert,[27] und mit U Suidnia, dem der größte und zentrale senkrecht stehende Monolith der mawbynna geweiht ist.[28] In den Gebeten, die F. Stegmiller gesammelt hat,[29] fällt auf, daß in der Anrede das Geschlecht der Gottheit wechseln kann, d.h., daß die Gottheit mal als U Blei Trai Kynrad, Gott und Herr, mal als Ka Blei Ka Jawbei, Göttin Jawbei, angesprochen wird. Das Genus wechselt oder wird gar zur unauflöslichen polymorphen Einheit. Das Numen wird also sowohl als Gott wie als Göttin angesprochen.[30] U Blei und Ka Blei werden synonym oder gar androgyn gebraucht. Von Ehrenfels hat darum die These vom "Doppelgeschlecht und Götterpaar in der Religion der Khasi" aufgestellt.[31] Diese doppelgeschlechtliche Konzeption der Gottheit ist allen Khasistämmen von Meghalaya gemeinsam, wobei die Lyngnam-Khasi den weiblichen Aspekt der Gottheit offenbar stärker betonen als den männlichen,[32] und alle Khasi in Ka Blei den dem Beter zugänglichen Aspekt des männlichen Deus Absconditus erblicken.[33]

2.4. Neben den drei Hauptgottheiten weist das Khasi-Pantheon eine Fülle von Natur-, Haus- und Schutzgottheiten, sowie Dämonen und hauptsächlich Dämoninnen auf, die Stegmiller in seinem Anthropos-Artikel aus den Jahren 1921/22 nach Nomen, Genus und Funktion aufgelistet hat.[34] Der animistisch-polytheistische Charakter des Pantheons ist dabei unverkennbar.

3. Die Vertreter des Seng Khasi haben die These, bei der Khasi-Religion handele es sich um einen durch Naturgottheiten angereicherten Animismus, von Anfang an als eine böswillige Unterstellung der westlichen Religionswissenschaft bezeichnet, deren Urheber P.R.T. Gurdon gewesen sei.[35] Sie gestehen zwar die Verehrung der Ahnen[36] und bestimmter hervorragender Orte, Haine, Bäume, Flüsse und Berge,[37] wie z.B., des Shillong Peak ein und postulieren auch einen gewissen naturphilosophischen Pantheismus,[38] aber sie wehren sich dagegen, daß die Stammesreligion im Westen als animistisch-polytheistische Naturreligion eingestuft wird. Dieser, der animistischpolytheistische Charakter des vorfindlichen Stammesglaubens, sei vielmehr

die neuzeitliche Entartung einer monotheistischen Urreligion des Stammes der Khasi. "Khasi religion (Ka Niam Khasi)," schreibt Hamlet Bareh,[39] "was entirely monotheistic at first but became polluted afterwards with the polytheistic trends - beliefs in other deities, appeasement rituals of both good and evil spirits, propitiation of the ancestors and others." Und was die vielen Götter betreffe, die Götter der Natur und die Ahnengeister, deren Existenz keineswegs geleugnet wird, so handele es sich dabei lediglich um Aspekte des einen und einzigen Gottes U Blei Nongthaw. "As Creator we call him 'U Nongbuh U Nongthaw', sagt der Religionspädagoge H.Onderson Mawrie, ein ehemaliger Christ und führendes Mitglied des Seng Khasi.[40]

As Maker of Man He is "U Nongthaw-bynriew Nongbuhbynriew"; as the Protector and Guardian of our "Iing" He is our "Leilongiing Leilongsem" or "Ka Blei ha Iing".... As the mainstay of our economic welfare He is our "Leilongspah Leilongphew"; as defender of our village He is our "Lei khyrdop Leikharai", and of our territory and state He is our "Leimuluk Leijaka" and "Leihima Leisima"... In sum, in all spheres of our life and in all aspects of His creation He is there with a name."

Doch schon bei der Definition des Gottesbegriffs bedient sich Mawrie bereits christlicher Glaubensaussagen:[41]

U Blei is the Creator and the Sustainer of this Universe. He is almighty and all-powerful, omniscient and omnipresent. Being all in all. He is above GENDER so we may call Him "U Blei" or "Ka Blei"; He is also above NUMBER and we may call Him "U Blei" and "Ka Blei" or "Ki Blei."

Onderson Mawrie will damit offenbar einen mystischen Gottesbegriff auf die doppelgeschlechtliche Gottheit U Blei-Ka Blei übertragen, ein Verfahren, das die ursprüngliche Bedeutung des Gottesnamens durchaus angemessen und legitim interpretiert. Er findet dafür bei dem langjährigen Vizepräsidenten des Seng Khasi, Kynpham Singh, Unterstützung. Dieser schreibt in seinem Essay "Khasi and Jaintia Religion"[42] : "God is ethereal and formless. He is in us and around us. He is infinite (U Blei najrong na tbian).... God is indivisible and, therefore, He is One. Being indivisible there can be no other gods." Jedoch an anderer Stelle⁴³ wird U Blei-Ka Blei ausdrücklich durch eine trinitarische Formel erklärt: Bei den Haruspiyien, besonders bei der Hepatoskopie, wird die Triade Ka Jawbei, U Thawlang und U Suidnia angerufen und diese als die in die Transzendenz projizierte Familien-Trias, bestehend aus dem Urelternpaar und dem matrilinearen Onkel, verehrt. "Jeder Clan hat seine Trias", sagt Kynpham Singh,⁴⁴ "Ka Jawbei, die Ahnenmutter, die Vorfahrin; U Thawlang, den Ahnherrn,...den Begründer des Clan...und U Suidnia, den Ahnenonkel mütterlicherseits.... Die Khasi glauben, daß es eine enge und direkte Gemeinschaft [communion] gibt zwischen Gott und Mensch und, daß es einen Bund zwischen ihnen gibt von Anbeginn der Zeiten...." Ahnlich wie in der christlichen Dogmengeschichte⁴⁵ wird in Analogia Entis vom Geschöpf auf den Schöpfer projiziert: Die in der Khasi-Gesellschaft angelegte Trias findet ihre Entsprechung in einem trinitarischen Gottesbegriff, und dieser wiederum - jetzt als Glaubenssatz verstanden - reflektiert sich in der Trias von Ureltern und Uronkel "The Tripersonal concept is reflected in the family unit, the father representing U Thawlang, the mother Ka Jawbei, and the mother's brothers, Ki Saidnia."⁴⁶

Zuweilen wird die Trias der Ahnengottheiten abstrahiert, und es bleiben nur ihre Eigenschaften übrig: Die Omnipotenz⁴⁷ des Gottes U Thawlang, die Omnipräsenz der Göttin Ka Jawbei und die Omniszienz des Gottes U Suidnia. Um jedem Mißverständnis vorzubeugen, bei der Trias dieser Ahnengottheiten handele es sich lediglich um einen Kryptopolytheismus und nicht um eine hypostatische Einheit, um ein "homoousios," stellt die Seng-Khasi-Dogmatik von vornherein klar: "The Khasi-Pnars⁴⁸ believe that God is omnipotent, omnipresent and omniscient."⁴⁹

4. Auch das Hahnenopfer (jingknia syiar) hat im Seng Khasi einen Bedeutungswandel erfahren. Offenbar erscheint der Hahn schon in der vorchristlichen Periode der Khasi-Religion als eine Art Mediator zwischen Gott und Mensch, jedoch wird man nicht mit Sicherheit sagen können, ob der Sühne-Charakter des Hahnenopfers bereits aus der vorchristlichen Periode stammt und Gurdon's These, "that the

covenant of the cock is the foundation of the Khasi religion,"[50] zu Recht besteht. Denn ein solcher Bund zwischen Gott und den Menschen, der mit dem Sühnopfer des Hahnes besiegelt wird, ist theologisch nur dann verifizierbar, wenn auch ein dem entsprechendes Sündenverständnis vorliegt. Zwar erzählt die Schöpfungsmythe der Khasi von einem Urzustand, in dem Himmel und Erde einander nahe waren und Gott mit den Menschen unmittelbaren Kontakt hatte, von einem Zustand ohne Sünde also,[51] und sie erzählt auch von einem "Sündenfall", dessen sich die Menschen schuldig gemacht haben;[52] - aber schon das Auftreten des Hahnes und sein Angebot, Mittler, ksiang, zwischen Gott und den Menschen zu werden und die Konsequenzen der menschlichen Schuld tragen zu wollen, läßt einen christlichen Einfluß nicht unwahrscheinlich erscheinen. Und Bezeichnungen wie "U khun ka Blei uba kit ryndang ba shah ryndang na ka bynta jong nga u briew," "Der Sohn Gottes, der seinen Hals für mich, den Menschen, niederbeugt," oder das Gebet "ap jutang me U Blei ieng rangbah me u briew," "O Gott, vergiß nicht den Bund, stehe auf, o Mensch!"[53] beweisen wohl eher, daß bereits ein christlicher Einfluß[54] auf gewisse Rituale der Khasi-Religion stattgefunden hat, bevor man sich der wissenschaftlichen Erforschung eben dieser Rituale widmete. Kein Zweifel kann allerdings darüber bestehen, daß das Hahnenopfer und die danach erfolgende Eingeweideschau für die Feststellung von Krankheit und Unglück in der Stammesreligion seit jeher einen wichtigen Platz einnimmt. F. Stegmiller hat uns ein gutes Beispiel eines solchen Opfergebets überliefert, von dem anzunehmen ist, daß es die ursprüngliche und unverfälschte Form bewahrt hat.[55]

Der Seng Khasi möchte offenbar beide Traditionen des jingknia syiar aufnehmen, die klassisch-genuine und die krypto-christliche. Hamlet Bareh z.B. preist die vielerlei symbolischen Kräfte, die in einem Hahn stecken und die von der Ankündigung des Tageslichts beim ersten Hahnenschrei bis zum Symbol für geistige Befreiung reichen;[56] aber er nennt den Hahn gleichzeitig auch U bah ryndang, "den Märtyrer," Ka bikur, "das Signal des Bundes," ka snam, "das Blut," und U krad lynti ka jingiap, "den, der den Pfad der

Toten gen Himmel aufkratzt/=scharrt." Er gebraucht also biblische Begriffe, um seinen Lesern alte rituelle Vorgänge aus der Khasi-Religion nahezubringen und um diese dadurch vor der Vergessenheit zu bewahren.

Als am 23. Nov. 1899 der Seng Khasi gegründet wurde, wählte er eine rote Flagge mit einem weißen Kreis in der Mitte, der einen krähenden Hahn zeigt, das Symbol eines neuen heraufziehenden Zeitalters, in dem es für die Khasistämme ein nationales und ein religiöses Wiedererwachen geben werde. Hipshon Roy, der Generalsekretär des Seng Khasi, interpretiert das Symbol mit großem Pathos:

Der rote Hintergrund bedeutet Mut. Der weiße Kreis stellt die Welt dar. Weiß bedeutet das fundamentale Vertrauen des Khasi-Volkes und seinen Glauben, daß es in die Welt gekommen ist, um die Wahrheit zu verkündigen und zu erlangen. Der krähende Hahn symbolisiert die alte Kultur und Tradition der Khasi, so daß, wenn die Sünde den Weg des Menschen verdunkelt, - er vorankräht [!], um die Sonne hervorzubringen, die Licht gibt - so daß der Mensch den Pfad der Reinheit, der Menschlichkeit und der Göttlichkeit voranschreiten kann.[57]

5. Sehr viel weniger Schwierigkeiten machte es offenbar dem Seng Khasi, sich der Ethik der westlichen Eroberer anzupassen. Hier hieß der alte Grundsatz der Stammesreligion Tip-kur - Tip-kha, "die verwandtschaftlichen Beziehungen mütterlicherseits wie väterlicherseits (=nichtmatrilinear) kennen," keinen Zweifel darüber offen, daß die strengen Reglementierungen innerhalb der Familie und des Clan sich auch auf die ethischen Prinzipien auswirken würden. Tip-kur - Tip-kha bezieht sich nicht nur auf die oben kurz skizzierten Verhältnisse in kur und iing, sondern viel mehr noch auf die außerordentlich komplizierten Heiratsvorschriften. Nicht nur, daß für die Mitglieder der kur strikte Exogamie besteht und ein Überschreiten dieses Gebots "sang" ist und schlimme Folgen nachsichzieht,[58] - auch die Erziehung der Kinder und das gesamte Erbrecht der Khasi ist - wie schon Sir Keith Cantlie gezeigt hat -[59] in die matrilinearen Strukturen der KhasiGesellschaft eingebettet und nur von diesen her zu verstehen. Wenn Tip-kur die Kenntnis der verwandschaftlichen und erbrechtlichen Verhältnisse voraussetzt, so ist - gleichsam mit

negativem Verzeichen versehen - das Wissen um die Tabus, die dem Kur-Mitglied von väterlicher Seite drohen, ebenso wichtig.

Der Seng Khasi übernimmt diese Vorschriften und Restriktionen aus der Tradition scheinbar kritiklos. Das alte Sprichwort "long jaid na ka kynthai," "aus einer Frau ging der Clan hervor," gilt nach wie vor,[60] so daß - wie man sich denken kann - das Thema "Gleichberechtigung der Frau" für die Vertreter des Seng Khasi ein willkommener Anlaß ist, um den Fortschritt in diesem Lande zu preisen oder westlichen Besuchern die "seit Jahrhunderten in Meghalaya praktizierte Frauen-Emanzipation" vorzustellen,[61] oder auf die Tatsache hinzuweisen, daß es bei den Khasi nicht den Status des "unehelich geborenen Kindes" gibt, weil jedes Kind den Namen der Mutter trägt, der Mutter gehört und Erbe der Mutter ist, gleich wer auch immer der Vater des Kindes sein mag.[62]

Diese Hochachtung vor der matrilinearen Deszendenz hat sich auch in den Vier Prinzipien des Seng Khasi niedergeschlagen, wo das "Festhalten an den Grundsätzen der Verwandtschaft, wie sie durch die Ahnen der Khasi dargelegt worden sind," an erster Stelle genannt wird. Hier ist schließlich auch der Impuls für alle ethischen Weisungen zu suchen. R.T. Rymbai nennt als oberste Weisung das "Kamai ia ka Hok," eigentlich: das "Verdienen von Gerechtigkeit," den Erwerb des Rechts, das die Sieben Urfamilien (Ki Hynniew Trep) ihren Nachkommen hinterlassen haben.[63] Gerechtigkeit (ka hok) bedeutet das praktische Verhalten gegenüber dem Nächsten in Wort und Tat.

Sibcharan Roy, dessen literarische Tätigkeit in die Zeit vor und während des 1. Weltkriegs fällt, hat in seinem Ka Niam Ki Khasi von 1919 bereits den Versuch gemacht, das Prinzip der Gerechtigkeit den Maximen der christlichen Verkündigung gleichzusetzen, indem er eine Reihe von Geboten formulierte: Allen voran stellt er als 1. Gebot ein Wort, das Lukas 17,21 ähnelt: "... Denke immer wieder darüber nach, daß Gott in dir und du in ihm wohnst, daß dein inneres Leben erleuchtet werden kann und alle deine Zweifel vertrieben werden können!" Sein 2. Gebot heißt -

entsprechend dem des AT - :"Mache dir kein geschnitztes Symbol...! Halte dich zurück von jeder Idolatrie!" Auf Amos 5 könnte die Weisung zurückgehen: "Sprich mit aufrechtem Herzen, ordne alles mit einem göttlichen Wort! Rechtschaffene Taten sind weit besser als Zeremonien." Ein anderes - vielleicht mit dem alttestamentlichen Gebot der Elternliebe zusammenhängendes - Gebot lautet: "Mache die Verhältnisse unter dem Dach deines Hauses zu herzlichen Beziehungen!" Was die tägliche Arbeit betrifft, so heißt es: "Verdiene dir deinen Lebensunterhalt mit deinem Schweiß! Halte dich von der Begierde fern!" Und schließlich nimmt Charan Roy gar Bezug auf die zwei Pforten und zwei Wege, von denen Jesus in der Bergpredigt (Mt.7, 13 + 14) spricht: "Es gibt zwei Wege, die uns zu unserer letzten Bestimmung führen, der eine führt uns ins Haus Gottes, und der andere in das Höllenhaus."

Noch deutlicher wird in Kynpham Singh's Essay über die Khasi und Jaintia Religion[64] die Verschmelzung von Tradition, Mission und Aufklärung. In vierzehn Geboten und Verboten, von denen er eingangs sagt, daß sie bereits während der schriftlosen Zeit den Khasi mündlich überliefert worden seien, faßt er das gesamte ethische Verhalten des modernen Khasi zusammen. Es mag für die von ihm beabsichtigte Wirkung bezeichnend sein, daß er sich dabei des Englischen bedient:

1. Those who are guilty of intra-clan sexual relationship, those who commit suicide, those who commit murder in their own clan, those who commit abortion, and male-female twins are never cremated by their relatives or clans, no funeral rites are performed and no bones are gathered.
2. Do not commit murder.
3. Do not steal.
4. Love and respect your mother and father. We cannot see God but they represent Him on earth.
5. Respect your uncles, who are your mother's brothers and cousins, the clan relatives of your father, and all elderly people.
6. Live a clean and moral life.
7. Money gained other than by one's own just effort is unclean. Stolen money, bribe and gambling money bring misfortune, misery and poverty to the house.
8. All men are born equal before God. Richness or poverty are outcomes of ones ability, diligence and conduct. Do not envy others because of their wealth, their homes, their riches else God will strike you blind.

9. If misfortune and misery comes to you, do not blame God, blame yourself. If blessings are showered upon you, give thanks to God.
10. Do not do any act which would bring shame and sorrow to another man's home. The same misfortune will follow you back.
11. No matter how rich, no matter how superior, no matter how powerful, do not be proud and arrogant. But rather be rich in humility.
12. Do not acquire what is not rightly yours, be it a cowrie or gold. The sin is the same.
13. Do not laugh at ugly people or deformed people. They are created by God.
14. The end in Life is to do Good. To work honestly to gain riches for bringing comfort is not a sin...

In enger Folge stehen Gebote aus der Periode der alten Khasi-Religion (1,5,10) und der Periode der christlichen Mission (2,3,4,11) neben den Grundsätzen der modernen Aufklärung (6,8,10,13,14). Auf den ersten Blick gesehen haben wir hier einen moralischen Synkretismus vor uns; aber dieser moralische Synkretismus und relativiert harmoni=siert nicht und gleicht die Gegensätze nicht aus, sondern stellt das Erbe der einzelnen Perioden nebeneinander, wobei z.B. auch so einander widersprechende oder gar ausschließende Gebote wie das erste und das achte (bzw. dreizehnte) Gebot ohne weiteres ihren Platz behalten. Die vom Seng Khasi verkündigten ethischen Grundsätze spiegeln also alle kulturellen und geschichtlichen Epochen wider, die sich von der mythischen Urzeit bis in die säkulare Neuzeit in den Khasi Hills abgespielt haben.

6. Die religiösen Aktivitäten des Seng Khasi erschöpfen sich aber nicht in der Neuinterpretation bzw. Revitalisierung von religiösen Begriffen und ethischen Grundsätzen, sondern haben es in der Praxis weit häufiger mit der Selbstdarstellung dieser nationalistisch-religiösen Reformbewegung zu tun. Dazu bieten sich am besten die alten Feste und Tänze der Hochland-Khasi an.

Dem Shad Suk Mynsiem, dem "Thanksgiving Dance," wie der Präsident des Seng Khasi, A.S. Khongphai, übersetzt,[65] der Mitte April in Weiking, nordwestlich von Shillong (darum auch "Weiking-Tanz" genannt) gefeiert wird, kommt dabei eine besondere Bedeutung zu. Es handelt sich um einen alten Stammestanz von ursprünglich nur geringer religiöser Bedeutung,[66] bei dem die Tanzenden - nach Geschlechtern geordnet - einen inneren und einen äußeren Kreis bilden und aufeinander zuschreiten. Die Attraktion des Tanzes besteht hauptsächlich in der bunten Festkleidung der unverheirateten Mädchen, die Kronen aus Silber oder gar Gold tragen, während die jungen Männer silberne Pfeile, die in silbernen Köchern stecken, bei sich haben.

Die Festlichkeiten dauern drei Tage[67] und werden jeweils vom Präsidenten des Seng Khasi mit einem Gebet zum Gotte U Blei Nongthaw, dem Schöpfer, eingeleitet. Bezeichnenderweise findet der Weikingtanz auf einem Gelände statt, das der Seng Khasi im Jahre 1911 eigens für diesen Zweck erworben hat. Das beweist die nationalistische Tendez des Unternehmens. A.S. Khongphai verschweigt auch nicht, daß der Hauptzweck des Shad Suk Mynsiem-Tanzes darin bestehe, "to bring together the Khasis folks from the four corners of the Khasi and Jaintia Hills into one gathering once a year, to enjoy together that collective feeling [sic!] of 'peace of mind' (suk mynsiem)."[68] J. B. Bhattacharjee sagt in seinem Messenger of Khasi Heritage,[69] daß der Shad Suk Mynsiem den Khasi geholfen habe, "to revive and preserve their traditional dances which was fast dying out due to the lack of patronage and depreciation by the missionaries." Und ärgerlich bemerkt er: "Die Missionare schauten auf den Seng Khasi nicht gerade mit Wohlwollen und vermuteten in dem Tanz ein Symptom des Wiedererwachens [der Stammerreligion, der Vf.] Die Welsh Mission startete praktisch eine Kampagne gegen ihn, indem sie jeden von der Kirche exkommunizierte, der dem Tanz beigewohnt haben könnte...." Das war der Grund, weshalb sich die Mitglieder des Seng Khasi entschlossen, "to combat the detribalising and denationalising impact of Christianity and Christian education by promoting nationalist education and love for the country and traditional culture."[70]

Das sind harte Worte gegen die christliche Missionspraxis, doch sie scheinen nicht übertrieben zu sein. Auch die christliche Soziologin Nalini Natarajan bestätigt sowohl das Verbot einer Teilnahme von Christen an den Weiking-Feierlichkeiten wie die heftige Reaktion der orthodoxen Khasi, die ihre alte Kultur durch die christliche Überfremdung bedroht sahen.[71] Allerdings weiß sowohl sie als auch P.R.G. Mathur[72] zu berichten, daß liberale christliche Kreise ihre Teilnahme am Shad Suk Mynsiem und an anderen religiösen Festen, die der Seng Khasi fördert, erwägen oder gar schon daran aktiv teilgenommen haben. Am 15. April 1969 hätten sogar einige römisch-katholische Nonnen zugeschaut. Diese Entwicklung scheint anzudeuten, daß der Seng Khasi mehr und mehr an Bedeutung gewinnt, zumal er sich durch die aktive Förderung der traditionellen Feste und ihre zeitgemäße Interpretation im Volk Anerkennung verschafft. Wenn sich nun auch die Christen nach den langen Jahren ihrer Gegnerschaft dazu entschließen, die religiösen Feste und Tänze der Khasi als Ausdruck ihrer traditionellen Kultur zu verstehen, dann bedeutet das zwar keine Akkulturation, aber ist doch als Zeichen einer ernsthaften Auseinandersetzung mit den Zielen des Seng Khasi zu sehen.

7. Der Seng Khasi hatte sich seit seiner Gründung im Jahre 1899 gegen eine christliche Überfremdung und damit gegen eine Verwestlichung der Khasi-Stämme gewehrt. Mit dieser Zielsetzung war er ins Leben gerufen worden. Aber es erweist sich jetzt, daß seine ideologischen Vorstellungen von einer religiösen Renaissance in nationalem Gewande nicht ohne Hilfe westlicher und vor allem christlicher Ideen[73] zu verwirklichen sind. Nationalismus[74] und religiöse Traditionen allein genügen offenbar nicht, um eine Reformbewegung wie den Seng Khasi entstehen zu lassen. Man kann nicht an der christlichen Missionsgeschichte in den Khasi Hills vorübergehen, ohne ihren Einfluß auf Gesellschaft und Kultur zu erkennen. Dafür ist diese christliche Missionsgeschichte zu intensiv gewesen. Sie hat weitgehend die Erziehung im Lande bestimmt und humanitäre Einrichtungen inauguriert, sie hat westlichen Denkstrukturen Eingang verschafft und Begriffe geprägt, die die Intellektuellen heute nicht mehr entbehren können. Diese Denkstrukturen und Begriffe hat sich auch der Seng Khasi zu eigen gemacht,[75] um alte stammesgeschichtliche Überlieferungen neu zu interpretieren und für das Khasi-Volk verbindlich zu

machen. Nur so konnte es ihm gelingen, den Stämmen wieder zu ihrer Identität zu verhelfen, die sie unter britischer Besatzung und christlicher Mission verloren hatten. Daß dabei auch Christen unter den Stammesangehörigen eine wichtige Aufgabe zufällt, ist ohne Frage. Wir kennen einige Fälle von praktischem Synkretismus aus der jüngsten Zeit, in denen sich führende christliche Persönlichkeiten, wie der sziem von Mylliem und der Lynskor (Premierminister) von Khyrim zusammen mit orthodoxen Khasi an Opferfesten beteiligt und die gemeinsamen Ahnen angerufen haben.[76] Die vom Seng Khasi ins Leben gerufene Reformbewegung hat also nicht nur ein Nehmen, sondern auch ein Geben zur Folge gehabt, weil sich die Religionskritik des Seng Khasi gegen die ideologische Gefahr der Verwestlichung, nicht gegen die Inhalte des Christentums als solche richtete. Dem entspricht, was Nalini Natarajan beobachtet hat:[77]

There is also increasing rapport between Christians and orthodox Khasis. Both sections have moved away from their original rigid positions and towards each other. While Christian preachings nowadays refer to the common concept with Khasi Niam, the orthodox realise the logic in many Christian teachings. This is contrary to the attitude in the early days, when Christianity was considered an exclusive religion and often, propagating it meant preaching against other religions."

BUDDHISM THROUGH HINDU EYES:
ŚAIVAS AND BUDDHISTS IN MEDIEVAL TAMILNAD*

Glenn E. Yocum

It is commonly recognized that Buddhism in the Tamil-speaking areas of South India suffered a severe and ultimately fatal setback at the hands of a renascent form of popular theistic Hinduism. The Tamil bhakti movements of the seventh through ninth centuries were not merely characterized by an emotionally-charged devotionalism directed toward Śiva and Viṣṇu, here typically conceived as deities concretely manifested at various temples and sacred places; a number of the leading saint-poets are also pictured as having been in fairly frequent struggle with Buddhists and especially Jains. The conflict with these "heretical" traditions continued to receive prominent attention in the hagiographical literature stemming from the centuries after the initial wave of devotional enthusiasm. This was a time when the insights of the early poets were being elaborated in philosophical treatises, in puranic narratives - particularly those recording the saints' lives, and in an increasingly complex and magnificent temple cult patronized above all by the Cōḻa kings.

This paper will focus on one aspect of this time of religious ferment, namely, the conflict between Buddhists and devotees of Śiva, although in the process it is hoped that some insight will be gained into the wider dimensions of the issues at stake. In a sense Śaivas and Buddhists represent the two extremes of the religious turmoil in medieval South India. The Vaiṣṇava Āḻvārs - and certainly their later followers in the Śrī Vaiṣṇava sect - were never so distinctively Tamil in thought and expression as their Śaiva counterparts. And unlike Buddhism, the Jains, apparently willing to assimilate certain important aspects of the Hindu tradition, at least managed to survive in South India. For one, Jainism is far better represented in the Tamil literary tradition than Buddhism, and several Jain works or Jain-inspired works are among the very finest to be found in the entire corpus of pre-modern Tamil literature. Thus, in attending to the extremes of this broader religious antagonism certain contrasts emerge in perhaps somewhat higher relief than they might otherwise.

Our discussion will be limited almost entirely to Śaiva literature; for there are no extant Buddhist works which describe the conflict with Tamil Hindus. First, we shall examine a chapter which records a religious debate between Śaivas and Buddhists in the legendary biography of Māṇikkavācakar, the premier poet of Tamil Śaivism. Moving back through time, a similar incident in the life history of Tiruñāṇacampantar, another major Śaiva poet, will come under consideration. In this instance the hagiographical material can be supplemented by the evidence of Campantar's own poems, which contain rather frequent disparaging references to Buddhism. And finally, widening our scope still further, some general suggestions will be made about the incompatibility of Tamil Śaivism - indeed of what might be called traditional Tamil religiosity - with the kind of Buddhism apparently present in South India. Since this last item will involve some discussion of what I would call non-Sanskritic Tamil ideas, it will lead us still further back into the past in an attempt to get at the roots - at least in so far as they are discoverable in texts - of important indigenous Tamil religious ideas, ideas which then later re-emerge in a Śaiva tradition that sees itself in opposition to Buddhism.

1. **Māṇikkācakai's Debate with the Buddhists from Sri Lanka**

The *Tiruvātavūrar Purāṇam* by Kaṭavuḷmāmuṉivar is a hagiography devoted entirely to the life of the ninth-century Tamil Śaiva poet Māṇikkavācakar.[1] It probably stems from the fifteenth century in its present form, although some of the incidents, particularly those pertaining to the Madurai region, have been recorded in Śaiva hagiographical literature as early as the twelfth century.[2] The *Tiruvātavūrar Purāṇam* has seven chapters (*carukkam*, Skt. *sarga*) containing a total of 544 four-line verses. The sixth *carukkam* is entitled "The Chapter about the Conquest of the Buddhists in Debate" and deals exclusively with an incident foretold in earlier sections of the text. It recounts Māṇikkavācakar's miraculous victory over a delegation of Buddhists from Sri Lanka in a debate held at Chidambaram. Although this work is of small literary merit, the content is interesting and a complete translation of the sixth chapter of the purāṇa is available from the author.[3]

Certainly the conflict between Śaivas and Buddhists which is depicted in this text is quite sharp. It is not my intention here to dwell on the details of the debate itself. The reasoning employed is hardly a model of logic, although it is worth nothing that the Buddhist doctrines and practices which are held up for criticism do seem to imply that some form of Theravāda is probably under discussion. In fact, it is not the argumentation, marred as it is by inconsistency and opacity, which impresses one but the vehemence of the debaters, particularly Māṇikkavācakar and his Saiva colleagues. What we have turns out to be more a contest of power than a debate, culminating in the Buddhist debaters' being struck dumb, the Sinhalese king's previously dumb daughter articulately defending Śaivism, and all the Buddhists becoming Śaivas and regaining their speech. The intensity and tone of the whole encounter is heralded by the "debate's" opening salvo of the my-god-is-greater-than-your-god variety. Indeed, we are confronted here with the essentially monotheistic character and style of Tamil bhakti in both its Śaiva and Vaiṣṇava forms, monotheisms which, if we are to believe their own reports, condoned and even encouraged persecutions which are, to the best of my knowledge, unprecedented in pre-Muslim India.

Debate has had an impressive history in Indian education and religious controversy.[4] And while the particular instance under discussion may not exemplify the well-defined elements of formal reasoning expounded in the classical treatises on logic, it is an example of a longstanding South Asian practice of attempting to resolve religious controversy in public disputations, often under royal patronage in the king's presence as is the case here. One thinks of Hsuan Tsang at Kanauj in a debate sponsored by king Harṣa.[5] It is debates like these that occasioned the writing of Buddhist *vāda*-manuals such as those by Maitreyanātha and Vasubandhu.[6] Down to the early eighteenth century there are reports of debates sponsored by the Kandyan kings of Ceylon between Buddhists, Calvinists, Catholics, and Muslims.[7] The sponsorship of such debates doubtless also served political ends. In the case of Hsuan Tsang previously mentioned, it is fairly clear that Harṣa used the debate to force one of his feudatories to appear at court. And at one point (v.441) the *Tiruvātavūrar Purāṇam* implies - although its own participants do not completely live up to this ideal - that such debates were a good method of guiding religious controversy into channels that would not result in unrest and violence.

Serious questions, however, can be raised regarding the historicity of Māṇikkavācakar's debate with the Sinhalese Buddhists. There are only two references to Buddhists or the Buddha in the entire *Tiruvācakam*, a collection of Māṇikkavācakar's devotional poetry arranged in 51 hymns totalling 3414 lines. In one instance Māṇikkavācakar simply dismisses Buddhists along with the ignorant practitioners of other sects (*camayam*) as adhering to religious tenents which leave their own followers in bewilderment (*Tiruvācakam* 15:6). This is the only belittling reference to Buddhism from Māṇikkavākar's own hand.

Tiruvātavūrar Purāṇam 449, however, claims that hymn 12 of the *Tiruvācakam*, "Tiruccalal," stems from Māṇikkavācakar's debate with the Buddhists in Chidambaram. While this hymn is in question-and-answer form similar to the style of a debate, there is nothing in the content of "Tiruccalal" itself to suggest that the questioner argues from a Buddhist point of view, as is required by the hagiographical account. The hymn deals exclusively with various aspects of Śiva's persona, the first two lines of each of its twenty verses stating a question or problem about one of Śiva's features (e.g., his bearing Gaṅgā in his hair, v. 7), to which the remaining two lines give an explanation. Certainly the tone of the questions and answers is less heated than the rhetoric recorded in the purāṇa. As the purāṇa notes (v.499), the setting of the hymn is that of a girls' game involving question and response. In fact, "Tiruccaḻal" is one of a whole series of hymns in the *Tiruvācakam* (hymns 7-19) intended to be sung by women while performing certain domestic activities or in accompaniment to female village games which were at one time popular in the Tamil country. All presuppose that those singing these hymns have psychologically/spiritually cast themselves in the role of females devoted to Śiva, their beloved or husband. Rather than a hymn written to summarize a debate, a more likely explanation of "Tiruccaḻal's origins is suggested by its general context in this series of "female" hymns. In the absence of other evidence from Māṇikkavācakar's own poetry which would confirm a debate with Buddhists, I would speculate that the later hagiographical tradition attempted to read the story of the debate into the *Tiruvācakam* itself, where no such a debate is explicitly mentioned.

We know that by Māṇikkavācakar's time, i.e., the ninth century, Buddhism was in decline in the Tamil country; for Hsuan Tsang had already noted the plight of Buddhist institutions in the far South two centuries earlier.[8] In certain respects it is perhaps surprising that Māṇikkavācakar refers to Buddhists at all, particularly so in view of his failure to mention Jains, who in all probability were more numerous in ninth-century Tamilnad than were adherents of Buddhism. If, however, there is a historical kernel to the story of the poet's debate with Buddhists from Sri Lanka, his pejorative reference to Buddhism is more understandable. Certainly, the South Indian and Sinhalese kings' plundering of each other's territories makes an encounter with foreign Buddhists possible.[9] Indeed, the Sinhalese king Sena II supposedly avenged the humiliation suffered by his predecessor at the hands of Śri Māra Śrivallabha when his army overran the Pāntiyan capital of Madurai in the 850's.[10] This event could have occurred close to the time Māṇikkavācakar is reputed to have been active at the Pāntiyan court in Madurai (probably during the reign of Varaguṇavaman II, whose regnal years were 862-885). Thus, it may be more noteworthy that there are so few disparaging references to Buddhism in Māṇikkavācakar's poems. For someone supposed to have been a high-ranking civil servant of the Pāntiyan king, Māṇikkavācakar reveals singularly little - in fact, nothing at all - about the political situation of his day.

Turning to the other mention of Buddhism in the *Tiruvācakam*, one begins to gain some notion of why the general orientation of Tamil Śaiva bhakti was uncongenial to Buddhism. In this verse, the Buddha appears as a devotee of Śiva.

> The Buddha, Indra, Brahmā, Viṣṇu -
> all offer praises to
>   the Madman,
>   the Lord who dwells in Perunturai,
>   the Father who cuts off rebirth,
>   the One who inhabits beautiful Tillai's hall.
>
> Let us sing about this -
> and also about how His gracious feet entered our minds,
>   while we clap and play *tellēnam*. (*Tiruvācakam* 11:16)[11]

Here in one brief verse are several of the salient features of Tamil Śaiva bhakti. It is popular, as evidenced by this particular poem's being set to the women's game of *tellēnam*, a game which involved singing and clapping. Śiva is praised as a madman who intervenes in his devotees' lives by destroying rebirth. For the Buddha to extol a mad god who annuls the workings of karma and rebirth seems most peculiar indeed. And this mad god is concretely manifested, according to this verse in Perunturai and Tillai, two locations of great personal significance in Māṇikkavācakar's life. He is not just Śiva, not just the Madman. He is the mad Śiva at a particular place, who furthermore enters his devotees' minds. In short, he possesses them, making them ecstatic, intoxicated, mad. All of this, of course, is a far cry from the control of mind and body aimed at by Buddhist codes of conduct and meditation.

2. Campantar and the Buddhists

Of all the leading Śaivas of the Tamil bhakti movements Tiruñānacampantar was certainly the most vociferous in his opposition to non-Brahmanical traditions. The story of this seventh-century poet's debate-contest with a group of Jains at Madurai claims that his victory resulted not only in the conversion of the Pāntiyan king to Śaivism but also in the impalement of 8000 of Campantar's Jain opponents.[12] According to the *Periyapurāṇam*, upon defeating the Jains at Madurai, Campantar travelled north into the Cōḻa country. After a miraculous crossing of the Kāvēri and visits to several Śaiva temples north of the river, Campantar and colleagues arrived at a place called "Pōtimaṅkai inhabited by ignorant Buddhists *(cākkiyar)*" (*Periyapurāṇam* Tiruñāanacampantamūrttināyaṉār Purāṇam 904). Pōtimaṅkai is probably to be identified with Pōtimaṅkalam where Buddha images have been found in recent times.[13] Apparently the place was a Buddhist settlement in the seventh century; for upon arrival Campantar and his Śaiva cohorts announced their presence with a great din of trumpets and conches, challenging the local Buddhists to debate. Here we have the reverse of the situation described in Māṇikkavācakar's hagiography. The Śaivas are the ones making a foray into Buddhist territory.

The Buddhists were led by one Buddha Nandi, the leading Thera (Tamil *tērar*) at Pōtimaṅkai (905-906). Buddha Nandi was angered by what he took to be the blowing of victory trumpets before the debate had even begun. But then occurred what surely must be one of the more bizarre incidents in the records of Indian debates. One of the Śaiva devotees, who happened to be Campantar's amanuensis (he "wrote down the sacred *patikams* when they were uttered"), said, "By Alutaiya Pillaiyār's [i.e., Campantar's] holy word let a thunderbolt fall and cause that Buddhist's head to fall off and tumble to the ground" (908).[14] These words, of course, were no sooner spoken than Buddha Nandi's head was blown to bits. Buddha Nandi's followers were naturally thrown into confusion but nonetheless were able to regroup under the leadership of one Sāriputta and engage the Śaivas in debate.

The substance of the debate is little more interesting than that of the one noted in the first section of this paper. It is noteworthy, however, that Campantar, though present, does not speak himself, but rather allows his above-mentioned secretary to argue the Śaiva position. Discussion turns on how the Buddha can receive the homage of his devotees and reward their worship, if in his case the five *khandhas* have been destroyed and he is no longer present. Also challenged is the notion of the Buddha's omniscience. On both points Sāriputta is vanquished. Thereupon all the Buddhists bow before Campantar's feet and become Śaivas.

From this account it is fairly clear that the Buddhists of Pōtimaṅkai were Theravādins. Not only are they referred to as Theras, but their doctrinal position also seems to be consonant with Theravāda ideas.[15]

In contrast to Māṇikkavācakar, there is ample evidence of Campantar's dislike of Buddhism in his own devotional poems. Campantar's poetry is rather different from Māṇikkavācakar's in that the great bulk of it falls into a very well-defined form, that of the *patikam*, a hymn of ten (to twelve) stanzas usually praising a manifestation of Śiva at a particular temple. In Campantar's *patikams* the last stanza contains the poet's signature and states the benefits that will accrue to those who sing his hymns. For example,

> Those who are able to sing
>   this garland of ten verses
>   arranged according to the seven-toned scale,
>   which the learned Nāṇacampantar from Kāḻinakar
>   [i.e.,Cīkāḻi]
>   sang when he extolled the Lord of Maraikkaṭu,
> will receive the good wishes of those who live on
>   earth and attain eternal bliss.[16]

Other *patikams* promise release from rebirth, wisdom, the company of the celestials, the removal of all doubt, and other such rewards to those who sing them. Thus, Campantar's hymns claim to be efficacious in and of themselves. They are a type of mantra. It is then little wonder that their power could be so effectively invoked against the opponents of Śaivism.

Moving back to the penultimate stanzas of Campantar's *patikams*, i.e., the tenth verse in most cases, one typically finds here a derogatory reference to Buddhists and/or Jains. Since there are 385 extant hymns by Campantar, there is no dearth of anti-Buddhist polemics in his poetic corpus. The Buddhists are commonly denounced in brief epithets, many of which reveal nothing more than Campantar's hostility towards them. Hence, Buddhists are said to be ignorant, foolish, evil, "dark" (a term of abuse), and, of course, are criticized for not following certain Śaiva practices such as wearing the sacred ashes. The level of discourse in this regard is rather similar to that of the *Tiruvātavūrar Purāṇam:* Buddhists are bad; Śaivas are good, although one senses that the underlying reasons for this antagonism are never clearly stated.

Some of Campantar's hymns contain more extensive condemnations of Buddhists and Jains, and in these instances we are treated to a longer list of what the poet finds disgusting about these non-Hindu traditions. The 366th *patikam* of the Campantar *Tēvāram*, addressed to Śiva as the lord of Tiruvālavāy (i.e., Madurai), is one such hymn. It is reputed to have been sung at Campantar's great confrontation with the Jains at Madurai and is consequently more vehement in its denunciation of Jains than of Buddhists.

    1. O highest One,
       half of whom is a woman
         it is Your holy purpose
            to conquer and exterminate in debate
               the Buddhists [*tērar*] and Jains [*amaṇ*, Skt.
                                   śramana]
            who have no real underpinnings,
            wandering about,
            scoffing at Vedic sacrifice.

       May Your fame on earth be great,
       O our Source who dwells in Ālavāy!

2.   O You whose throat gleams darkly like a precious gem, it is Your holy purpose
      to go debate
         the cunning, black Buddhists and Jains
           who do not live according to Vedic rules.

       May Your fame on earth be great,
       O our Source who dwells in Ālavāy!

3.   O You who carry the battle axe and deer in Your hands, it is Your holy purpose
      to debate and break
         those who clad themselves in mats [i.e., Jains],
         those who pluck all the hair from their heads, [i.e., Jains],
         those evil ones who do not live by the Vedas.

       May Your fame on earth be great.
       O our Source who dwells in Ālavāy!

4.   O First One,
       who wears the lustrous moon as a wreath on Your head,
     it is Your holy purpose
      to debate and subdue
        the evil Jains
          who try to darken the goodness
         of the six-fold way which brings release.

       May Your fame on earth be great,
       O our Source who dwells in Ālavāy!

5.   O One different from the world,
      who wears the excellent sacred ashes,
     it is Your holy purpose
      to debate and scatter
         those who do not direct their minds to the precious Vedas
        on which Brahmins meditate.

       May Your fame on earth be great,
       O our Source who dwells in Ālavāy!

6.   O our Thief,
      who skinned the wild elephant,
     it is Your holy purpose
      to debate and put to flight
         those Jains of low character (*kuṇṭar*)
          who intend to destroy the sacrifice.

       May Your fame on earth be great,
       O our Source who dwells in Ālavāy!

7. O Śiva,
   whose sacred form is like the gleaming fire,
   it is Your holy purpose
      to debate and cause those Jains [*arukar*] to
                                                flee
   who say that the path of those who know the
                                  Vedas is worthless
      so that they burn with rage.

   May Your fame on earth be great,
   O our Source who dwells in Ālavāy!

8. O You,
   who graciously bestowed a sword on the demon
                                    [i.e., Rāvana],
   it is Your holy purpose
      to debate and convince
         those Jains who avoid the wind
            which blows upon the body of one
                              wearing sacred ashes.

   May Your fame on earth be great,
   O our Source who dwells in Ālavāy!

9. O Mountain,
   whose beautiful form neither Viṣṇu
      nor the four-faced one [i.e., Brahmā] is
      able to see,
   it is Your holy purpose
      to debate about Your nature
         with those dark-bodied Jains.

   May Your fame on earth be great,
   O our Source who dwells in Ālavāy!

10. O Lord,
    whom those exhausted Buddhists [*cākkiyar*] do
                                           not see,
    it is Your holy purpose
       to debate and split to pieces
          those Jains who do not cherish Your
          coral-like feet which subdued the three
          fortresses that day.

    May Your fame on earth be great,
    O our Source who dwells in Ālavāy!

11. Blessed are those who can sing this song
       of Campantar from Cīkāḻi,
          which he sang
             upon receiving permission from the King
                                          of Ālavāy,
             when he defeated those withered-bodied
                                              Jains.[17]

Again, it is the tone of denunciation rather than the

content of the criticism that is most noteworthy. Condemnation of Jains and Buddhists for being non-Vedic is not surprising, although it is interesting how little concerned with Vedic thought and ritual Tamil Śaiva bhakti tends to be. The Vedas are hardly important sources of inspiration for Tamil Śaiva poets and philosophers. One frequently gets the impression that reference is made to the Vedas simply to establish the legitimacy of bhakti or the philosophical position being assumed, while the texts themselves are hardly known, or if known are not related in any significant sense to the expression of Tamil Śaivism.[18] Perhaps the prominent presence of several Brahmins in the Tamil Śaiva tradition accounts for such references to the authority of the Vedas (e.g., both Campantar and Māṇikkavācakar were Brahmins). In any case, I do not think that it is rejection of Vedic authority that lies at the heart of Tamil Śaivism's antagonism toward Buddhism. More significant perhaps are those references to ascetic and monastic practice. The Jains receive particularly harsh treatment in this regard, but some Buddhist practices (e.g., the wearing of monastic robes) are also sometimes held up for ridicule. Despite frequent mention of Śiva's asceticism, of sacred ashes, and less often of *tapas*, Tamil Śaivism is not an ascetic, renunciatory tradition. Its texts make quite clear that devotion to Śiva is possible for all people. One need not become a samnyāsin to be a bhakta. Bhakti is definitely not limited to a monastic elite. Nor does it depend on a strict discipline which makes a strong distinction between monks and laymen. Ideologically at least, Tamil devotionalism has been a great leveller of hierarchy and distinction.

Apparently the Śaiva outrage at "heretical" behaviour was sometimes reciprocated; for we note above in verse 8 how Jains sought to avoid contact with the wind coming from the direction of a Śaiva who had smeared ashes on his body. There are several other interesting features about Campantar's hymns which can be mentioned only in passing. The ninth verse typically establishes Śiva's superiority vis-à-vis Viṣṇu and Brahmā, and the eighth stanza usually mentions Rāvaṇa. Also, it is not uncommon for Campantar to extol the excellence of the Tamil language in the signature stanzas, which is relevant to a point made in the last section of this paper.

A final example from Tamil Śaiva devotional literature which mentions Buddhism is the story of Cākkiyanāyanār in the *Periyapurāṇam*.[19] As this Nāyaṉār's name indicates, he was a Buddhist (*śākya*, Tamil *cākkiyar*). The story is instructive not for what it says about Buddhism but for the light it sheds on the eccentric forms which devotion to Śiva tended to take in Tamilnad. Cākkiyanāyanār was a member of the Veḷḷāḷa caste (a cultivator caste). He was troubled about rebirth and sought a way to be released from samsāra. At Kāñci he studied the Buddhist scriptures and decided to become a Buddhist. But the more he learned about Buddhism, the more he became convinced that Buddhism was not the answer. Eventually he found what he was seeking in Śaivism and became utterly devoted to the veneration of Śiva's feet. Since he was convinced that one's social position and appearance were irrelevant to devotion, he never gave up his Buddhist robes. Cākkiyanāyaṉār always worshipped a śivaliṅga before he ate his meals. One day he happened upon a śivaliṅga in an open field and immediately became enraptured. In his ecstasy he picked up a stone and threw it at the liṅga. The text says that Śiva took pleasure in Cākkiyanāyanār's action, just as parents sometimes enjoy the silly actions of their young children. In any case, Cākkiyanāyanār decided to do his stone-throwing *pūjā* to Śiva on a regular basis, since he felt it to have been an act of Śiva's grace that he first performed this odd form of worship. The story ends by saying that once Cākkiyanāyaṉār started to eat before he had thrown a stone at the liṅga. Suddenly he realized his oversight and immediately got up from his dinner to pelt the god in the usual manner. At this point Śiva appeared with his spouse and bestowed on Cākkiyanāyaṉār a place in Śivaloka.

What is striking here is the discontinuity with Buddhist practice, the incongruity of the situation.

Ecstatic stonethrowing is hardly the kind of behaviour one would expect of a Buddhist monk. But, as will be seen, it is not particularly unusual behaviour given Tamil Śaiva notions of the sacred.

3. Tamil Śaivism and Buddhism

In the final section of this paper, I should like to outline some of those features of Tamil Śaiva religiosity which make Śaiva bhakti incompatible with Buddhism. Furthermore, I shall claim that many of these characteristics are traceable to, and hence gain their force from, a pre-bhakti stratum of Tamil culture. But before I sketch these general features, an observation about South Indian political history is in order. For a period of about three hundred years before the rise of Pallava power at the end of the sixth century, there is a lacuna in our knowledge about the political situation in Tamilnad. Apparently the traditional Tamil dynasties, the Cōḻas, Pāṇṭiyas, and Cēras, went into eclipse during this time. The end of this "dark period" of South Indian political history is marked by the appearance of "a mysterious and ubiquitous enemy of civilization, the evil rulers called Kalabhras (Kaḷappāḷar)."[20] Despite the political instability, this was a time when several significant works of Tamil literature were written, e.g. *Tirukkuṛaḷ*, *Cilappatikāram*, and *Maṇimēkalai*, which were Jain or Buddhist inspired. The inclination of these texts toward Jainism or Buddhism is more understandable if K.A. Nilakanta Sastri's suggestion is correct that the Kalabhras were probably Buddhists and that their rise to power may have been motivated by religion.[21] It was during the reign of the Kalabhra king Accutavikanta that the Theravāda monk Buddhadatta wrote his *Abhidhammāvatāra* and *Vinayaviniccaya* while residing in traditional Cōḻa heartland of the Kāvēri delta.[22] There is a late Tamil legend which claims that Accutavikanta imprisoned the Cōḻa, Pāṇṭiya and Cēra kings.[23]

Perhaps some of the bhakti poets' opposition to Jains and Buddhists stems from persecutions suffered at the hands of the Kalabhras. In the bhakti movements of the seventh through ninth centuries, there are indications of a revival, a reassertion of distinctively Tamil elements, which may have been suppressed during a period of Jain and Buddhist cultural and political hegemony. Of course, if Tamil bhakti is a revival of sorts, it does not simply reproduce a *status quo ante*. Far from it. The longing for a soteriological goal is a feature shared with Jainism and Buddhism which does not appear in the earliest written evidence of Tamil religious thought and practice, the Caṅkam poetry of the first to third centuries A.D. The deities to whom devotion is directed are mainly Brahmanical gods who came to the Tamil country from the North. But the expression of Tamil bhakti, I would argue, is in certain important respects quite peculiarly Tamil. Kamil Zvelebil has noted well the revivalistic aspect of Tamil bhakti, particularly as it parallels Tamil political reassertion:

> The anti-Buddhist and anti-Jain *bhakti* movement coincides in Tamilnad in time and content with the establishment and spread of a strong Tamil national feeling and with the political expression of this fact - the origin and spread of the powerful Tamil kingdom of the Pallavas under Mahendravarman I (580-630 A.D.) and his son Narasimhavarman I (630-668 A.D.). In the second half of the first millennium, Buddhism and Jainism are regarded as something alien, something which is inimical to this national self-identification of the Tamils.[24]

The Buddhist and Jain traditions are alien not simply because they appear to have enjoyed the support of an unpopular regime. The roots of Buddhism's conflict with Tamil Śaivism lie deeper than that. To try to get at this incompatibility, some general features of Saiva bhakti need be described.

Śaiva bhakti in its early stages in Tamilnad is above all affective, ecstatic bhakti. It is distinctly non-intellectualized. Devotion to Śiva is accompanied by behaviour which, if we are to believe the tradition itself, often bordered on the hysterical. Dancing, weeping, laughing, babbling, and horripilation are some of the visible signs of the infusion of Śiva's grace in his devotees, whom non-devotees understandably sometimes accuse of being crazy. As already noted, Śiva himself is called a madman. Indeed, the opening phrase of Cuntarar's *Tēvāram* addresses Śiva as *pittaṉ*, a madman. Tamil bhakti is "hot"; it is passionate, emotional, frenzied, indeed slightly mad. Śiva is the dancer *par excellence*, his devotees dance in ecstasy.

In reading Tamil Śaiva bhakti poems I am often struck by the similarity between ecstatic devotion and possession by a god. The sense of being overpowered, enslaved, and even entered by Śiva is much like that of possession. Possession and ecstatic dancing were well-known features of early Tamil cultic practice, so far as we are able to glimpse the shape of religious ritual in early Tamilnad from occasional references in Caṅkam poetry, the earliest extant Tamil literature, which largely reflects a culture not yet "Aryanized." Such examples of dancing and possession are especially associated with the god Murukaṉ, a peculiarly Tamil deity. These forms are notably brought together in the god-possessed dance of the Vēlaṉ, the priest of Murukaṉ. Vēlaṉ means "spearman," because like Murukaṉ himself this religious functionary carries a spear. Murukaṉ too can be called Vēlaṉ, thus confirming the temporary identity of deity and god-possessed priest. The Vēlaṉ's dance is sometimes called the *veṟiyāṭṭu* or *veṟi ayartal*.[25] The word *veṟi* indicates the ecstatic nature of the dance; for it connotes drunkenness, giddiness, intoxication.

There are other forms of religious dancing associated with Murukaṉ, but not directly involving possession as does the dancing of the Vēlaṉ priest. *Maturaikkāñci* 612-617 and *Tirumurukāṟṟuppaṭai* 215-216 mention the *kuravai* dance done by women. Mention of ecstatic dancing occurs elsewhere in the Caṅkam corpus.[26] And possession and frenzied dancing also appear in the post-Caṅkam but pre-bhakti *Cilappatikāram*.[27] Possession continues to be an important aspect of South Indian folk religion, as the ethnographic literature makes plain.[28]

It is apparent, I think, how the Tamil propensity to see the gods as powers periodically taking possession of individual humans, who at these times act very differently from "normal" people, might well have prepared the ground for the ecstatic bhakti of Tamil Śaivism. In this regard the indebtedness of Tamil bhakti to its South Indian cultural milieu has not gone unrecognized by other scholars. George Hart has written that:

> the custom of ecstasy in worship survived in Tamilnad to produce the Nāyaṉmārs and Āḻvārs, who went about Tamilnad singing ecstatic devotional songs about Śiva and Vishnu, and were largely responsible in later times for the position of pre-eminence those gods attained as well as for the Bhakti movement, which produced the *Bhāgavata Purāṇa* and spread all over India.[29]

And Louis Dumont has noted the similarity of bhakti to possession in folk religion.[30]

There is a sense of concrete experience of the sacred in Tamil Śaivism that is quite notable. Śiva is understood as having manifested himself at particular sacred places, on which sites temples are built where his sacred presence is perpetuated.[31] The god is usually sung as specifically revealed at particular temples. This is a crucial aspect of the bhakti movements. God is not abstract. He is very concrete, embodied in temple icons. Whoever would be devoted must be devoted to particular manifestations of the deity enshrined at sacred places. There is, of course, some parallel here to stupa worship and pilgrimage centers in Buddhism, though the emphasis on concreteness in Tamil Śaivism is extreme. Zvelebil touches upon a number of points made so far in the following rather exuberant and exaggerated passage:

> ...the cult of sacred places, a feature so typical for both Śaiva and Vaiṣṇava *bhakti* in the South, which was probably the most "popular" element of the movement, added much to its spread and attraction. The theology of *bhakti* was realistic to the extent that it did not accept the conception of the phenomenal world as an illusion; it was theistic: God was individualized and made completely real, so to say "solidified" in a very concrete form of the idol worshipped in the temple; at a given moment in time, God was dwelling in a concrete and near place, in a familiar local shrine. And what kind of God! Śiva took on a colourful, vital personality, absorbing much of the local *couleur*, and the attention of the people; and perhaps even more absorbing became the personality of Viṣṇu - in the role of child, lover, and intimate companion of the

devotees. So, in comparison with the decayed, deteriorated Southern Buddhism and Jainism we see in the Tamil Hindu revival the triumph of emotion over intellect, of the concrete over the abstract, of the acceptance of life over its ascetic denial, of something near and homely against something alien and distant, and, above all, the acceptance of positive love against cold morality or intellectually coloured compassion.³²

Śiva is sometimes identified with a region, e.g., the Pāntiyan kingdom in Māṇikkavācakar's poetry. He "patronizes refreshing Tamil" (*Tiruvācakam* 8:10). He is thus affiliated with the land and the language, both of which are important components of the Tamil cultural tradition. Perhaps one of the reasons why Buddhism failed to take root in the Tamil imagination is because of this tremendous affection for landscape and language which the Tamil literate tradition had already developed before the large-scale incursion of Buddhism into the far South. Certainly the love for the language exhibited in Tamil literature prevented Buddhists in the South, who were apparently content to write in Pali and Sanskrit (with the notable exception of the Tamil "epic" *Manimēkalai*), from fully penetrating Tamil consciousness.

George Hart has claimed that ancient Tamil literature exhibits an understanding of the sacred fundamentally different from that of North India. The deities of ancient Tamilnad, he claims, "were not transcendent beings, but rather immanent powers, present in objects encountered every day and involved in every aspect of ordinary life."³³ Even though the Tamil bhakti movements represent a great infusion of northern traditions into the South Indian cultural milieu, the old fascination with nature, with the idea of an immanent sacred, still finds a voice in a number of forms in bhakti poetry.³⁴ Hart has argued that this early Tamil sense of an immanent sacred power was particularly focussed on women and kings (i.e., chieftains).³⁵ With regard to kings, Hart does succeed in showing that the person of the king was surrounded by an aura of sanctity for the ancient Tamils, but he does not convince me that this was peculiarly Tamil. I find his case somewhat more persuasive as it pertains to women. And there is a special kind of fascination with the feminine sacred later in some of the Śaiva bhakti literature[36] and in the myths associated with particular temples.[37] It is perhaps not insignificant that the major Buddhist work in Tamil, *Manimēkalai*, has a heroine whose name is identical with the title of the work. A goddess of the same name also figures prominently in this epic. It is a very "female" work, and perhaps in this sense not a very typically Southern Buddhist one.

The early Tamil focus on women and consequently also on the household and family life, the love of nature, the notion of concreteness and ecstasy in religion, the affection for a vernacular language, all were factors conducing to make Tamil culture a popular one; or at least they were factors which gave this culture easy access to the minds of the non-literati. The bhakti movements were certainly popular. To be sure, they later developed sophisticated philosophical expression, but in their origins and to some large degree in their continued expression they represent not an elitist tradition but one which could easily be appropriated by a wide range of people. Bhakti hymns are still sung by many Tamil villagers, and stories about the Nāyan̲ārs continue to fascinate many Tamils.

From the meager evidence available it appears that Buddhism in the far South developed neither a flourishing lay life nor a close identification with royal sovereignty, perhaps in the latter case simply because Aśoka's empire did not extend to the southernmost regions of the peninsula. Be that as it may, both ordinary people ("the masses") and their rulers could take their religious cues elsewhere. Indeed, it is my argument that they took such cues from a largely indigenous Tamil tradition and from its later Brahmanized forms in the bhakti movements. This tradition already in some sense affirmed the sanctity of kings, the near sacrality of the land, the importance of marriage and family life, and the experience of religious ecstasy attendant on possession by a god. From the beginning, it seems to have incorporated popular elements. In short, neither it nor its Brahmanized expression in the bhakti movements could be called virtuoso, elitist, ascetic, or monastic.

The Tamil tradition of which I speak was already firmly established when Buddhism became a force to be reckoned with in the South. It had already achieved a literary expression of considerable depth and sophistication. It was not easily dislodged. While Tamil culture and religion did undergo change in the bhakti movements, what emerged was a new synthesis which in turn acted upon the wider Hindu tradition, particularly in its devotional forms. Buddhism never became fully assimilated to the primary elements of local Tamil culture.

THE PROBLEM OF THE ORIGIN OF THE MAHAYANA

Andrew Rawlinson

Everyone knows that the origin of the Mahayana is a mystery. Suddenly, there appeared a number of sutras, all claiming to be *Buddha-vacana*, which criticize, in varying degrees of hostility, the Hinayana, and frequently refer to themselves as the Mahayana. Where did they come from, and why?

The usual answer, pioneered by Bareau[1] and augmented by Lamotte[2] and Conze,[3] has been a *historical* one.

According to this view, the Mahayana has its sources primarily among the Mahāsaṃghikas.[4] The school of that name held that the Buddha was infinite[5] and *lokottara*,[6] and two of its offshoots, the Prajñaptivādins and the Bahuśrutīyas, taught some form of the doctrines of *prajñapti* and *śūnyatā*.[7]

In addition, we have to recognize the influence of other schools: the Sarvāstivādin Abhidharma at the back of the Prajñāpāramitā literature, according to Conze;[8] and the *dhāraṇī-piṭaka* of the Dharmaguptakas.[9] Then there is the probable Zoroastrian influence on the Sukhāvatī-vyūha.[10] And generally speaking, the impetus behind this new movement was the pressure of the laity, which the Mahāsaṃghikas were open to anyway.

Unfortunately, the argument goes, we have lost almost the entire canon of the Mahāsaṃghikas and their subschools, and we therefore have a very incomplete picture of the emergence of the Mahayana. But we can assume that it developed gradually out of this branch of traditional Buddhism, though not unaffected by a few extraneous influences.

This account, which is carefully argued and based on scrupulous scholarship, is very tempting. But when we examine it closely it appears even more full of holes than its proponents admit.

To begin with, it is exceedingly vague - so vague, in fact that it may be unfalsifiable. How, for example, are we to explain that the Mahāsamghikas agree with the Theravādins and the Sarvāstivādins in omitting *tathatā* (or *dharma-sthitatā*) from the list of *asamskrta-dharmas*?[11]

If the *śūnyatā* wing of the Mahayana is influenced by the Prajñaptivādins, why does the term *prajñapti* occur only twice in the whole of the Astasāhasrikā Prajñāpāramitā?[12]

The Mahāsamghikas, though accepting the *mūlavijñāna*,[13] reject the teaching of *vāsanā* and *bīja*;[14] yet the early Mahayana includes them,[15] presumably taking them from the Sautrāntikas.[16] So now we have to add this school to the Mahāsamghikas, Prajñaptivādins, Bahuśrutīyas, Sarvāstivādins and Dharmaguptakas as sources for seminal Mahayana ideas. This calls for an explanation that is stronger than the "missing evidence" thesis.

Similarly, at least four Mahāsamghika doctrines seem to be in direct conflict with the *śūnyatāvāda*.[17] Not only that, but the Prajñaptivādins and the Bahuśrutīyas clearly split from the original Mahāsamghikas because of their teachings on *śūnyatā*. How is it, then, that the Mahayana manages to bring back together the Buddhology of the Mahāsamghikas and the *śūnyatāvāda* of their offshoots?

Again, the Gokulikas, who gave rise to the Prajñaptivādins and the Bahuśrutīyas, rejected the sutras and the Vinaya, and regarded the Abhidharma alone as the *Buddha-śāsana*.[18] This does not square with the total reliance of the Mahayana on its own sutras, nor with the complete absence of a Mahayana equivalent of the Vinaya or Abhidharma (until very late).

Another question: how are we to explain the emergence of the Bodhisattva as the Mahayana ideal? The references to the Bodhisattva by the Mahāsamghikas are few, and the term is understood in the usual Hinayana sense of Śākyamuni before his enlightenment.[19] Moreover, these references are restricted to the Bodhisattva's birth - hardly Mahayana material. Scholars have frequently pointed out the importance of the Jātakas and Avadānas (this is part of the argument for the lay influence on the emergence of the Mahayana), as well as the occurrence of scenes illustrating the *pāramitās* on the *stūpas* at Sāñcī, Bhārahat and Amarāvatī. But we must assume that these were common Buddhist property. What we know of the Mahāsaṃghikas does not lead us to believe that it was this school that developed them.[20]

Yet another question: if the Mahayana was influenced by the laity, or was even a concession to it, why does the Aṣṭasāhasrikā Prajñāpāramitā say that it is practically impossible to understand the *śūnyatāvāda*?[21] Why does the Saddharmapuṇḍarīka say that the Dharma is deep and difficult to know?[22] These texts advocate considerable extensions and subtle transformations of the Dharma, not a dilution of it.

All of these points can be summed up very simply: many new ideas were available to Buddhists, some of which were particularly favoured or developed by specific schools. But it is not obvious that the Mahayana, which synthesised these ideas into a whole, is *based* on any one of these schools.

This is indicated by the fact, as Bareau notes,[23] that not one work of any Hinayana school mentions the Mahayana by name - the very word is entirely missing. And not only that, but the Mahayana sutras also do not refer to any specific school - they simply use their own blanket term "hinayana". Now if the Mahayana had evolved out of the Mahāsaṃghikas, is it not likely that there would be *some* reference to them, *some*where, at *some* time? But there isn't. Are the Mahāsaṃghikas and their offshoots included in the Hinayana or not? We just don't know - the Mahayana sutras are silent.

I suggest that a purely historical approach will never answer the questions I have raised. And this is not because we do not have the evidence to hand, but rather because we *first* need to answer the question: *how* and *why* are the main strands of the Mahayana related (namely: Buddhology, the *Bodhisattva-caryā*, *śūnyatā* and *prabhāsvara-citta*)? This is a religious question, not a historical one. And as we indicated above, even if we accept that the Mahayana did grow out of the Mahāsaṃghikas and their offshoots (though personally I do not think it did), the question still remains of how the very different ideas of this tradition were united in the Mahayana.

Before going on to try and answer this basic question of the how and why of the Mahayana, we must be aware of two important facts established by recent scholarship.

First, the earliest Mahayana sutras were much shorter than the versions we have now. I have summarized the evidence for this elsewhere.[24] Here we need only mention the following vital points: the earliest Mahayana teachings were transmitted *orally*,[25] *secretly*[26] and probably *in small groups*.[27]

Secondly, and following from the first point, the ideas and doctrines of the earliest strata of the earliest sutras cannot easily be placed in a linear order of development. The concepts of Bodhisattva, *śūnyatā*, *tathatā*, *Buddha-jñāna*, *pariṇāma*, *upāya*, *pāramitā*, *prabhāsvara--citta*, *Buddha-kāya* etc., are found with various senses, and in various relationships with each other, in different sutras.[28] As we discover how the texts themselves have evolved over the centuries, we find that we cannot use the later, established senses of these terms to understand their usage in the earliest strata. Lancaster, for example, has shown that the concept of *upāya* in the first Chinese translation of the Astasāhasrikā Prajñāpāramitā is mainly restricted to the Bodhisattva's use of *upāya* to gain enlightenment for himself. This is very different from the way the concept is used in the later recensions of the same text.[29] I have shown that the earliest layer of the Saddharmapuṇḍarīka is not unduly critical of the Śrāvakas (i.e. the Hīnayāna), and that it says that even *avaivartika* Bodhisattvas cannot know the range (*viṣaya*) of the *Buddha-jñāna* - not at all what one would believe from reading the expanded Nepalese version that we now have.[30]

The fact is that *all* the seminal Mahayana concepts of the Mahayana are found early on, but with an extremely uneven development in the various texts. The simplest way of explaining this is to postulate a *multi-origin* of the Mahayana. But this is not primarily a historical claim, but a religious one. I propose a *three-fold transformation* of Buddhism, the interactions of which gave rise to the many-faceted phenomenon we call the Mahayana. These transformations are:

1. A *fragmentation* of *transmission*. By a division of labour, some monks specialized in the sutras, some in the Vinaya, some in the Abhidharma, some in the Jātakas and Avadānas.[31] Each of these divisions created its own peculiar biases and developments.

2. The *dimensions* of the Buddhist tradition were also *separated out* and, more than that, *extended*. These dimensions are:

(a) śīla: **Key terms**: *viśuddha, puṇya, guṇa, kuśala-mūlā, pūjā, śraddhā*; **Main theme**: glorification of the Buddha; **Base** the *stūpa*

(b) samādhi: **Key terms**: (i) the *nature* of *citta: prabhāsvara-citta, bodhicitta, mūlā-vijñāna, āśraya, bīja*; (ii) the *manifestations* of *citta: ṛddhi, vikurvana, nirmāṇa, anubhāva, adhiṣṭhāna*: **Main theme**: magical and spiritual transformation; **Base**: the *araṇyāyatana*.[32]

(c) prajñā: **Key terms**: *Buddha-jñāna, śunyatā, samatā, tathatā, dharmadhātu*; **Main theme**: *paramārtha*; **Base**: the *vihāra*.[33]

3. The underlying *motif* of the Dharma was *altered*. It was now immeasurableness (*aprameya*) or infinity (*ananta*): the Buddha is infinite (*śīla* dimension);[34] *citta* and its manifestations are infinite (*samādhi* dimension);[35] the *prajñāpāramitā* is infinite (*prajñā* dimension).[36]

I now present a hypothesis concerning the origin of the Mahayana, a hypothesis that is tacitly based on these transformations. I am in effect placing the emergence of the new yana in a religious context, i.e., I am attempting to explain the how and the why of the Mahayana.

I suggest that there were separate groups of Buddhists, both monk and lay, which claimed direct contact with the Buddha, or some Mahāśrāvaka (e.g. the opening of the Ratnaguṇasaṃcayagāthā, or some Bodhisativa (e.g. Mañjuśrī in the Saddharmapuṇḍarīka). This was an inspirational, in some cases even visionary, contact that was extremely powerful, totally convincing to those who experienced it, and passed on from person to person (not unlike the Subud latihan). It was independent of any school or group of schools; in other words, it occurred spontaneously or by direct transmission among groups of Buddhists that belonged to many different affiliations.

The claim of the Mahayana sutras (which were, remember, originally concise oral teachings) to be *Buddha-vacana* is not, therefore, a propaganda device or a pious fiction. The authors of these works genuinely thought of themselves as channels for a *śāsana* that needed to make no appeal to existing teachings. That is why the sutras make no mention of schools by name.

The result of this new inspiration was the realization that the Dharma had been straitjacketed by conservatism; doctrinally, socially and most importantly, in its relitious aspiration. The guiding force of the new awareness was *aprameya*.

But this realization was itself filtered through one of the three dimensions of *śīla*, *samādhi* or *prajñā* (with varying combinations, of course; see the end of my Conze Festschrift article). The *stūpa*-based *śīla* groups were lay oriented; the more retired *samādhi* groups were probably mainly monks but there may well have been lay members also; the *vihāra*-based *prajñā* groups were entirely composed of monks. All of these groups (which were separated geographically as well as being centred on different buildings or institutions, with all the social differences that these imply) contributed to the Mahayana. The Bodhisattva is in fact an amalgam of these three, which explains why, for example, the Prajñāpāramitā literature is obviously non-lay while Vimalakīrti is a wealthy merchant. And, of course, these inspired groups could have any number of prior allegiances: Mahāsamghika, Prajñaptivādin, Bahuśrutīya, Dharmaguptaka, Sarvāstivādin, Sautrāntika and so on. These traditional distinctions were irrelevant and were swept away under the inspiration of the new *śāsana*.

So the Mahayana has a multi-origin that is varied in time (some elements of it are very old, some very new), in provenance (some groups in the northwest, some in the southwest, some maybe even in Central Asia) and in religious dimension (i.e., *śīla*, *samādhi* or *prajñā*). This is why the term *mahāyāna* itself is used so casually in the earliest sutras. Other terms such as *Buddha-yāna*, *eka-yāna*, *agra-yāna*, *udāra-yāna* etc., in fact occur more often. There are several instances in the Saddharma-pundarīka, the text that is most concerned with this subject, where some recensions have one of these terms and other recensions have another.[37] The Astasahsrikā Prajñāpāramitā has only one occurrence of *buddhayāna*,[38] but in its earliest stratum specifically says that the *mahāyāna* is *aprameya* and *ananta*.[39] The Sukhāvatī-vyūha sutras do not use the term *mahāyāna* once.

In fact, the Mahayana was not a school at all and did not evolve out of a school or schools. It was a transforming movement which accepted anyone regardless of his/her background, and in its earliest phases, at least, relied exclusively on its own independent inspiration. In this it is not unlike Pentecostalism, which includes both Catholics and Protestants, but which in the last analysis claims the Holy Spirit as its justification. And we know that, historically, Pentecostalism did not grow out of either Catholicism or Protestantism, but was rather a pan-Christian movement that spread by virtue of the shared experience of its practitioners. This is not to say, of course, that Pentecostalism does not have demonstrable roots in traditional Christianity. The point is that it does not need to go back to traditional Christianity as a source for its teaching. (Another analogy with the Mahayana might be Gnosticism, which was larger than Christianity but was also found within it but in fact is independent of it.)

We will not be surprised to find, therefore, that the Mahayana, like Pentecostalism and Gnosticism, used varied sources in order to flesh out its teaching. These included:

1. *reinterpretations* of the Nikāyas, including specific passages,[40] by those who were conversant with them;

2. *speculations* of every description from the more progressive schools (e.g. the Mahāsaṃghikas and their offshoots);

3. *reassessment* of traditional techniques (e.g. the Prajñāpāramitā literature's radical re-orientation of Abhidharma practice);

4. *inclusion* of non-exclusive practices (e.g. the pāramitās; stūpa worship);

5. *acceptance* of foreign influences (e.g. Amitāyus; the Buddha image in northwest India).

We are asking the wrong question if we try and find *an* origin of the Mahayana (allowing for a few extraneous additions.) We will not find it among the laity or the Mahāsaṃghikas or among rebel monks or breakaway Abhidharmists or among the invading tribes of northwest India. All of these made a contribution, but the contribution of each was controlled by the multi-dimensional model of the Mahayana that existed from the beginning.

The multi-origin that I propose has, as one of its attractions, that it takes the Mahayana sutras themselves seriously. There was a reason why they claim to be *Buddhavacana*. In an important religious sense, they are: they were received by the few and transmitted to the many. It is likely that the Mahayana's early spread was very rapid, and, like any inspirational movement, its adherents were tenacious and influential out of all proportion to their numbers. The bulky and somewhat laborious nature of the sutras as we now have them has obscured this possibility, as has the ponderous response of the traditional schools, which were probably barely aware of the new phenomenon. But hidden beneath all these textual elaborations and sectarian accretions is a simple and perennial truth: that the spring of spirituality is inexhaustible and wells up in the most unexpected places.

FILIAL PIETY AND BUDDHISM:
THE INDIAN ANTECEDENTS TO A "CHINESE" PROBLEM

John Strong

One of the classic topics in the study of religious change and interaction in Asia is that of Buddhism's transformation after its introduction into China. The story is a familiar one: as Buddhism - an essentially Indian faith - sought to establish itself in its new Chinese context, it came face to face with Confucian and Taoist ethics and culture and so was forced to adapt in a variety of significant ways.

The question, of course, is much more complex than this. Religious traditions, in a given area, are almost constantly in a process of interaction with each other. They are hardly static entities that are modified only when they come into contact with a radically different ideology. Thus the way in which a religious tradition does change, as it moves into and adapts to a brand new situation, is itself not always new. In fact, "change," in such cases often moves along lines or patterns of change that have already been opened up by earlier contacts with other traditions.

If this is true, the transformations of Buddhism as it moves into China should be examined not only in terms of its contact with the "new" traditions of Confucianism and Taoism, but also in light of the "avenues of change" already opened up for Buddhism by its contacts with religious traditions in India and Central Asia.

In an effort to do this, I propose to focus in this paper on one particular aspect of Buddhism's encounter with its "new" Chinese context: its reaction to and espousal of the Confucian virtue of filial piety.

Fifty years ago, Jean Przyluski pointed out that there was no solid basis for thinking that the "concessions" Buddhism made to the practices of filial piety and ancestor worship were exclusively an East-Asian development. Indeed, he insisted, without, however, presenting much evidence in support of his view, that the need to reconcile the tradition of Buddhist monasticism with a more general family-oriented ethic "was felt in India as well as in China."[1]

Clearly, Buddhism nowhere existed in a religious or ethical vacuum. In its homeland as much as in China it developed in contact with and in the context of other faiths. One of these faiths in India was, of course, the Hindu Brahmanical tradition in which, according to some, service to and reverence for one's parents (living and dead) were as crucial a duty as they were in China.[2]

This does not mean that filial piety and ancestor worship in the two countries were identical. Nonetheless, it is a fact that for the Indian householder, "the parents were the highest idol," and the father was "one hundred times more venerable than the teacher."[3] Duties of the Hindu son included devotional offerings to the ancestors as well as having a son in turn to perpetuate these practices. Indeed the Indian family was defined as the group which made offerings together to common departed *manes*.[4]

In this context, Indian Buddhists, with their nominal rejection of the householder's life and advocacy of celibacy, understandably were open to criticism from certain Brahmanical circles on this very issue of unfiliality and neglect of the family and ancestors. The situation, of course, was by no means identical to that which developed in China, and one should not expect to find in Indian sources counterparts to the apologetics of Mou-tzu, or the pointed accusations made against the Buddhists by Fu-I, Han Yü and Chu-hsi, or the articulate defences of the faith by Tsung-mi, Ming-chi Ch'i-sung.[5] Nevertheless, as we shall see, Indian Buddhists did have to face - if not overt charges of unfiliality and neglect of the ancestors - at least suspicions of such on the part of some of their

Brahmanical contemporaries. The Chinese Buddhist need to deal with this issue therefore was nothing new; the Indian Buddhists had already had to address it, and, most interestingly, they did so in ways that often foreshadowed those of their later Chinese brethren. As we shall see, at least some of the Chinese Buddhist reactions to Confucian accusations of unfiliality had their models in Indian Buddhist responses to Brahmanical charges of the same thing.

I propose to discuss this issue by examining a number of popular Buddhist stories taken from canonical and non-canonical Pali and Sanskrit sources and then tracing their fortunes in the Chinese setting. Because of considerations of space, I will limit myself here to stories focussing on three distinct themes: (1) the Buddha's praise of monks who materially support and honour their parents in this life; (2) the claim that the greatest filial act is to convert one's parents to Buddhism; and (3) the continuation of support for one's parents after their death.

1. Supporting One's Parents in This Life

From the beginning, Buddhism clearly maintained the principle of filial piety insofar as the laity was concerned. In the well-known *Sigālovāda-sutta*, which is often called "the Vinaya of the layman," the Buddha himself preaches that a good son should serve and respect his parents in five ways: he should support them, perform duties incumbent on them, keep up the lineage by having children, maintain the family traditions, and in every way make himself worthy of his heritage.[6]

This sutra, which was clearly written as a response or alternative proposal to specific Brahmanical practices,[7] was translated no less than four times into Chinese between the second and the fifth century, and commonly used by Buddhists in China to show their religion's support for Confucian filiality.[8] In a sense, however, it begs the issue: the Sigālovāda ethic is presented as one for *lay* householders while the Indian and Chinese detractors of Buddhism were concerned more with the lack of filial conduct on the part of the *monks* who abandoned their families, shaved their heads and wandered forth in the homeless life. What lifestyle vis-à-vis one's parents did the Buddha advocate for monks?

The answer to this question inevitably involves us in a consideration of the *Sāma* (Skt. Syāma, Ch. Shan-tzu) *jātaka*, an important "non-canonical" text which was used to promote the Buddhist doctrine of filiality in both India and China. Like most jātakas it consists of two main parts: (1) an introductory tale which sets the occasion for the telling of part (2) the jātaka per se, i.e., the tale of the Buddha's past life. Both parts of the *Sāma jātaka* are of particular interest to our theme, and we shall consider them in turn. The introductory tale may be summarized as follows:

The son of a wealthy couple from the town of Sāvatthi happens to go to the Jetavana monastery where he hears the Buddha preaching a sermon and decides he wants to become ordained a monk. The Buddha, quite properly, tells him that in order to do so he must first obtain his parents permission.[9] Since he is their only child, they are reluctant to grant him leave, but he is determined, and when he fasts for seven days to show his commitment, they finally agree to let him go. He is duly ordained, and promptly decides to become a forest monk devoted to meditation; he goes off to a small hermitage, leads an ascetic life and strives for arhatship.

In the meantime, his parents get older and are robbed of all their wealth by their unfaithful serfs who realize that they can safely rebel as there is now no son in the family to demand payments from them. Destitute, the parents become beggars.

The son learns of their plight, and resolves to quit his ascetic striving in the forest and to return to the lay householder's life in order to support them. On the way home, however, he comes to a fork in the road; one path leads to his parents in Sāvatthi, the other to the Buddha at the Jetavana. "Shall I see my parents first or the Buddha"? he wonders, and decides that since this may well be his last opportunity to see the Buddha as a monk, he will go to him first, take his leave, and then return home to take care of his parents.[10]

Up to this point, then, the story appears to assume that the two lifestyles - that of eremetical striving as a monk and that of supporting one's parents as a filial son - are mutually exclusive and fundamentally opposed to one another. The fork in the road symbolizes the young man's dilemma: he cannot go both ways at once.

The Buddha, however, shows him that he can. In his omniscience, he is aware of the young man's quandary, and as soon as the latter arrives at the Jetavana, he preaches to him the "Mother-maintainer sutta" (Mātuposaka sutta).

This convinces the young man that he does not have to choose between his life as a monk and his life as a good son. "I will now support my parents," he resolves, "while still remaining an ascetic without becoming a householder."[11] He accomplishes this simply by sharing with them the food he receives on his alms rounds, going out begging, as a monk, first for them and then separately for himself. Likewise he shares with his parents other gifts (such as robes) which he receives from lay people.[12]

Soon, however, certain members of the Sangha find out what he is doing and accuse him of violating the monastic rules. "Sir," they admonish him, "the Master does not allow us to waste the offerings of the faithful; you do an unlawful act in giving to laymen the offerings of the faithful."[13] They report his actions to the Buddha. He, however, praises the monk instead of reprimanding him, and encouraging him to continue in this apparently legitimate practice, he proceeds to tell him of the time when, long ago, he himself supported his parents, "while going the round for alms."[14]

There follows, then, the second part of the jātaka, the story of the Buddha's previous life as the ascetic Sāma. It may briefly be summarized as follows: Sāma (the bodhisattva) lives in a forest hermitage with his blind parents and is very devoted to caring for them. Every morning he sweeps their room, fetches water, prepares food for them, gives them the best dishes, and eats only after they have finished. So they live until, one day, a king, passing through the forest on a hunting expedition mistakes Sāma for a deer and mortally wounds him with a poisoned arrow. Filial to the end, Sāma, as he lies dying, is chiefly concerned not for himself but for the welfare of his parents. He asks the king (who is aggrieved at having shot an ascetic) to go to the hermitage and take care of them. The king agrees to do so, finds the parents, gently tells them of their son's death and assures them he will care for them.[15]

The ending, however, is to be even happier than this. The parents are led to their son's body, where the mother performs an Act of Truth, declaring, among other things, that "if it be true that in old days he [Sāma] nursed his parents night and day, then may this poison in his veins be overpowered and ebb away." The magical power of truth proves effective and Sāma revives. His parents, moreover, recover their sight, and the jātaka ends with Sāma preaching a sermon to the king on the advantages of filiality.[16]

The *Sāma jātaka* is the prototype for several other jātakas in which the filiality of the bodhisattva is praised.[17] In all of these, although the story of the Buddha's former life may vary, the introductory tale which sets the occasion for the story is the same: a monk wants to take care of his parents while remaining a monk. His desire to do so is criticized by other monks but praised by the Buddha who then recounts a jātaka to further legitimate the practice.

Clearly the issue is one which was controversial within the ancient Sangha. It is interesting, however, that the story, although it appears in the *Jātaka*, bears all the earmarks of the formulation of a *Vinaya* rule. It would seem, then, that despite the fact that a monk had nominally cut all ties with his family and despite the quite strict Buddhist rules about mendicancy and what could be done with the alms received, the community did allow for monks to share their alms food with their parents, and praised the filial sentiments which led them to do this.

My suggestion is that this exception, which our story presents as being granted by the Buddha himself, represents a Buddhist compromise with the Brahmanical ethic of filiality operating at the popular level towards which the jātakas were geared.[18]

Of crucial import in making this argument is the short sutta called the "Mother-maintainer sutta"[19] which, as we have seen, is referred to in the introductory text of the Jātaka. In this sutta, a brahmin mendicant, *who is in the habit of supporting his parents with the alms which he gathers*, becomes interested in the Buddha and his teachings. He is worried, however, that he may have to give up this feature of his lifestyle if he converts to Buddhism, and so asks the Buddha: "Of a Truth, Master Gotama, I seek my alms after the normal manner [i.e., according to Dharma] and so seeking them I maintain my parents. Am I not, sir, in so doing, doing what ought to be done?"[20]

The Buddha's answer, in light of what we have seen in the jātaka, comes as no surprise. He praises the brahmin's action, fully agrees that he is doing the right thing, and further adds that in supporting his parents he is thereby engendering much merit. The brahmin is impressed; he had come to the Buddha expecting a dispute over this issue, instead he finds only agreement. The way is now open for him and he does not hesitate: he converts to Buddhism.[21]

The "Mother-maintainer sutta," and, to an even greater extent, the *Sāma jātaka* were popular texts in ancient Indian Buddhism. The story of Sāma, for example, was among those depicted on the great stupa at Sanchi;[22] images of him were fashioned for certain great festivals in ancient Sri Lanka;[23] and a stupa in Gandhara which marked the reputed spot of his death became a Buddhist site of pilgrimage.[24] Moreover, later Sanskrit texts, discussing the karmic effectiveness of filial deeds, refer repeatedly to the story of Sāma for their paradigmatic example of such action.[25]

It comes as no surprise, then, that in China, the *Sāma jātaka* should also have been used as one of the prime texts for convincing persons that the Buddha himself supported filial action.[26] The introductory tale seems to have been less used to this effect than the jātaka itself, (perhaps because of the Chinese Sangha's deemphasis on the practice of begging) but the whole tale of Sāma was very well-known and, in fact, was given "canonical" status in China as the "*Sutra* of the bodhisattva Shan-tzu [Sāma]" *(P'u-sa Shan-tzu ching).*[27]

What is fascinating is that this tale, which we have seen responding in India to a Brahmanical setting, was so readily interpreted, in China, in the context of Confucian standards. In fact, as Kenneth Ch'en has pointed out, the tale of Sāma's filiality so well illustrated the classical Confucian virtue of *hsiao* that "by the Sung dynasty it was accepted in the popular literature as one of the twenty-four standard models of piety."[28] Ironically, however, Sāma (Shan-tzu) himself ceased to be a Buddhist in the process; he was metamorphosized into the Confucian Yen-tzu, assigned to the Chou Dynasty, and only as such was he invoked as one of the twenty-four paradigms of *hsiao*.[29] Bluntly, put, then, the story of Sāma, told to convince the Chinese of Buddhism's support for filiality, instead ended up convincing them that Sāma was no Buddhist but a Confucian.

2. Converting one's Parents to Buddhism

In this irony which, to be sure, I have much oversimplified, we have an illustration of one of the complex difficulties which Buddhist missionaries in China faced. Proof-texting to show their religion's "canonical" support for the principles of filial piety was clearly not sufficient. A distinctly Buddhist doctrine of filiality needed to be propounded. As Professor Ch'en put it:

The Buddhists were quick to realize that mere refutation of the Confucian charges was negative in spirit and not sufficient to gain a favourable hearing for Buddhism among the Chinese. In a society where filial piety was emphasized, the Buddhists recognized clearly that their religion must develop and stress its own ideas concerning piety if it were to flourish in China.[30]

One of the strongest positive arguments developed by Chinese Buddhists, according to Ch'en, was the claim that by joining the monastic order, an individual would then better be able to convert his parents to Buddhism, and they would thereby be saved from "repeated misery in the endless cycle of transmigration."[31]

For example, the Hua-yen patriarch Tsung-mi (780-841) argued that the Buddha himself had left his family and sought enlightenment so as to be able to repay the kindness of his parents by preaching to them the true doctrine.[32] It was a view which obviously could be reinforced by the well known legends of the Buddha returning home to Kapilavastu to convert his father[33] and of his ascending to the Trayāstriṃśat Heaven to preach to his mother. The same point may be found even more explicitly stated (by the Buddha himself) in the much earlier *Fo-shuo hsiao-tzu-ching* (the Sutra on a filial son). In this text, the Buddha praises the virtues of both father and mother, the care they take for the safety of their child, and the worry they have over nurturing and raising him. The monks listening to the Buddha then opine that, in order to repay this kindness of his parents, a good son should "satiate their tastes with delicious foods, please their ears with heavenly music, adorn them with the choicest raiments, and carry them on his shoulders over the four seas to the end of his life."[34] The Buddha, however, states that none of these actions, although perhaps commendable, is nearly as filial as the act of converting one's parents to the faith and causing them to take refuge in the Buddha.[35]

Some have claimed that the contents of the *Fo-shuo-hsiao-tzu-ching* are such that "one is inclined to think it was composed by a Chinese and not a translation of a foreign text."[36] It is true that the name of the translator of the text has been lost and that no extant Sanskrit or Central Asian original has been found. Nonetheless its message and some of the specific imagery it uses have clear roots in Indian sources. Let us consider for example a story in the Sanskrit text of the *Pūrṇāvadāna* which is particularly relevant in this regard because it concerns one of the subsequently great heroes of Chinese Buddhist filiality, Mahā-Maudgalyāyana (Mu-lien). The relevant portion of the tale can be translated as follows:

The Venerable Mahā Maudgalyāyana reflected: "The Blessed One once said, 'Monks, truly, a mother and a father do what is difficult for their son: giving him milk and showing him the many things of this world, they feed, nourish and rear him. If a man were to carry his mother on one shoulder and his father on the other for a full hundred years, or if he were to establish them in supremacy and lordship over this[37] great earth, and give them all of its various riches, he would not be doing as much for them... as the son who introduces, instructs, establishes and confirms his doubting parents in the fullness of faith, his sinning parents in the fullness of morality, his greedy parents in the fullness of renunciation or his weak-minded parents in the fullness of wisdom.' Now I [thought Maudgalyāyana] have failed to attend to my mother; I must consider where she has been reborn."
   Fixing his attention, he saw that she had been reborn in the Marīcika World System (lokadhātu). He then pondered the matter of who it was who was going to convert her and he saw that it was to be the Blessed One.... [Maudgalyāyana, therefore, goes to the Buddha] and says: "Bhadnata, the Blessed One once said, 'Truly, a mother and a father do what is difficult for their son....' Now my mother has been reborn in the Marīcika World System and is to be converted by the Blessed One. The Blessed One is able to convert her: let him therefore have compassion on her."
   Then the Blessed One said: "Maudgalyāyana, by whose magical power shall we go there?" "By mine, Blessed One." Then the Blessed One and the Venerable Mahā Maudgalyāyana placed their feet on the summit of Mount Meru and set forth, and in seven days they reached the Marīcika World System.
   From afar, [Maudgalyāyana's mother] Bhadrakanyā saw her son, and, as soon as she saw him, she rushed up to him exclaiming, "Ah! At long last I see my little boy!" Thereupon the crowd of people who had assembled said: "He is an aged wandering monk, and she is a young girl - how can she be his mother"? But the Venerable Mahā Maudgalyāyana replied, "Sirs, these skandhas of mine were fostered by her; therefore she is my mother."
   Then the Blessed One, knowing the disposition, propensity, nature and circumstances of Bhadrakanyā, preached a sermon fully penetrating the meaning of the Four Noble Truths. And when Bhadrakanyā had heard it, she was brought to the realization of the fruit of entering the stream.[38]

I would like to put off until later the question of the relationship between this seemingly rather primitive version of the Maudgalyāyana story and the full development of his legend in China in the *Yü-lan-p'en-ching* (Avalambana sūtra) and the various *pien-wen* dealing with Mu-lien and his mother.

For the present, it is important to focus on the theme that the best way for a monk to repay the kindness of his parents is to preach (or have someone else preach) the Dharma to them. In our avadāna text, there is in fact no question of Maudgalyāyana helping his mother in any other way. She is not presented as physically in need of support and Maudgalyāyana is not about to try to feed her or help her in any material way. The Buddha, he recalls, thought this not nearly so filial as introducing her to and confirming her in the faith.[39]

What is remarkable here, of course, is that this filial obligation extends over the boundaries of rebirth. The story is quite explicit about this: the inhabitants of Marīcika are surprised that Maudgalyāyana, an old man, should call Bhadrakanyā, a young girl, his mother. Maudgalyāyana, as we have seen, sets them straight, insisting that the relationship in one life continues on in the next.

From this it was just one step to the conclusion that all sentient beings in all the realms of rebirth may, at one point in the cycle of samsāra, have been one's mother or father and so should be treated accordingly.

This was a view which was picked up by the Chinese Buddhists as well and developed into the notion of *ta-hsiao* (great filial piety), superior to the Confucian virtue precisely in that it embraces all living beings rather than just one's present parents.[40]

Mahāyānists, as is well known, were motivated to seek enlightenment precisely out of compassion for all sentient beings, and the recollection of their suffering formed an important first step of the bodhisattva's meditative path.[41] In some cases, the identification (and in tantric meditations the visualization) of all sentient beings as one's mother and father seems to have been used to stress the intensity of the compassion one should feel for them. At times this compassion could be expressed by physically aiding suffering sentient beings, but the major thrust of the bodhisattva ideal, at least in its early forms, was upon leading all sentient beings to *enlightenment*, just as the thrust of the stories we have been considering is on leading one's parents to the same goal.

3. Filial Support for the Departed

So far we have seen two elements in the Buddhist apologetic whether in the Indian or Chinese context. On the one hand, there is a focus on material support and service to one's parents (or at least alleviation of their physical suffering) in this life - a practice commended by the Buddha for monks and laymen alike and practiced by him in his countless previous lives. On the other hand, there is an emphasis on converting one's parents to Buddhism by preaching the Dharma to them, either in this life or, if they have passed on, wherever they have been reborn.

It was inevitable, perhaps, that when these two strains came together attention should be given to the problem of how to provide material support or alleviate the suffering of one's parents, not in this life but after their death and rebirth elsewhere.

This is one of the major questions addressed by the fully developed Mu-lien story in which Mu-lien's mother is reborn as a hungry ghost. Mu-lien's primary aim, in this case, is not to convert her to Buddhism but to relieve her intense hunger and thirst. As is well known, in the *Yü-lan-p'en-ching*, he is presented as trying first to do this on his own, but finding he cannot as the food he brings her turns to charcoal as soon as she tries to eat it. In despair he turns to the Buddha who then instructs him to prepare a great feast for the community of monks whose collective merit alone is enough to relieve the suffering of his mother.[42] This, then, is the origin of the Yü-lan-p'en or Avalambana feast commonly prepared by devout Chinese Buddhists for the Sangha to ensure the well-being of their ancestors.[43]

The Avalambana festival (and the whole practice of making food offerings to or for the sake of one's deceased parents) has been seen in the context of ancestor worship in China, but it must also be seen in that context in India.

Since at least Vedic times, it was customary for Indians to make regular offerings (śrāddha) of lumps of rice (piṇḍa[44]) to the spirits of their deceased ancestors (pitṛs). These offerings, ideally to be made by the eldest son, start upon the death of the parent and then are made with declining frequency as grief (and the danger of a malevolent ghost) fade. In post-Vedic Hindu practice, a differentiation is made between the pitṛs and the pretas. The latter are thought of as the ghosts of newly deceased parents who need to be given special attention and food offerings until the performance of the Sapiṇḍi Karaṇa, a ceremony which takes place about one year after death and ensures the transition of the suffering preta to the happier state of pitṛ.[45]

As several scholars have pointed out, the word *preta*, although it could theoretically refer to any departed ghost, actually meant, in the context of religious practice, the spirits of one's own departed ancestors.[46] This was true in the Buddhist context as well.[47] There are, in the Pali Canon and commentaries, several examples of offerings made to hungry ghosts in this sense of the word,[48] and both G. P. Malalasekera and Richard Gombrich have pointed out that the whole Buddhist practice of feeding the pretas is an adaptation of the age-old Hindu filial ritual of making śrāddha offering to one's dead ancestors so that they may rest peacefully.[49]

That the Buddhist practice of making offerings to the pretas was also perhaps a *concession* to this Hindu custom of ancestor worship is indicated in a noteworthy sutta preserved in the *Aṅguttara Nikāya*: A brahmin named Jāṇussoṇi comes to see the Buddha and confronts him on this very issue of ancestor worship:

Master Gotama, let me tell you we brahmins so-called give charitable gifts: we make the *(shrāddha)* offerings to the dead, saying: "May this gift to our kinsmen and blood-relations who are dead and gone be of profit. May our kinsmen and blood-relations who are dead and gone enjoy this offering." Pray, Master Gotama, does that gift profit our kinsmen and blood-relations dead and gone? Do they really enjoy that gift?[50]

The Buddha's answer is significant. He says that the gifts will indeed be enjoyed by the departed ancestors, but only if they have been reborn among the *pretas*. If they have been reborn in hell, or as animals, or humans, or deities, the offerings will not profit them at all. The Brahmin presses him on this point: "But Master Gotama, suppose that the blood relation who is dead and gone has not reached that place, who then enjoys that offering"? "In that case, brahmin, other blood-relations dead and gone, who have reached that place, enjoy it." "But suppose, Master Gotama, that both that blood-relation and the others who are dead and gone, have not reached that place, who then enjoys that offering"? "That, brahmin, is impossible, it cannot come to pass that that place should be empty for so long a time of blood-relations dead and gone."[51]

This formulation should not necessarily be taken as the definitive one. What we can see in it, however, is a struggle by Buddhists to find some sort of compromise between their rather rigid doctrine of karma and rebirth, on the one hand, and the ancient and popular practice of making offerings to the dead, on the other. The Buddha admits to the efficacy of these offerings to the ancestors but only if they have become *pretas* and so, in this way, are both traditional recipients of śrāddha and have a place in the scheme of rebirth.

It comes as no surprise then, that Mu-lien's mother should be a hungry ghost;[52] the preta realm was, already in India, the place in the Buddhist cosmological scheme where some room had been made for the spirits of one's dead parents and for the traditional practices of ancestor worship.[53]

4. Conclusion

By focussing on the question of filial piety, I have tried, in this paper, to examine the transformation of Buddhism in the context of both its Indian and Chinese settings. In so doing, I have looked at several relevant popular stories and found similar examples of interaction taking place in both of these countries.

In our first example - the *Sāma jātaka* and the related "Mother-Maintainer Sutta" - we saw the emphasis placed on the *physical* support which a son owes his parents. This was advocated not only for laymen but for monks as well. It is true that, in the case of monks, the parents seem to have been in exceptional need of such support for it to become an issue. However, the overall thrust of the stories in both the Indian and Chinese contexts was that monastic and filial lives are not necessarily incompatible.[54]

In our second example, we saw the emphasis put on the *spiritual* or dharmalogical support which a son owes to his parents. Filiality comes to center on the conversion of one's parents to Buddhism, and leading them to the True Dharma. There is correspondingly a certain maligning of the final values of mere physical support. This is evident in the *Fo-shuo-hsiao-tzu-ching*, in China, and in India in the *Purṇāvadāna's* story of Mahā Maudgalyāyana which, as we saw, anticipated many of its themes.

In our third example, the emphasis was put on the *ritual* support which a son owes his deceased parents. This is most clearly found in the paradigmatic story of Mu-lien and his preta-mother, in which physical and spiritual interests are combined in the solution of making food offerings to the Sangha for the sake of the dead parent (preta). The roots of this solution, however, were also traced to Indian Buddhism and the context of Hindu ancestor worship.

The Buddhist doctrine of filial piety thus was formulated, in both India and China, on three different but related levels - the physical, spiritual and ritual planes.[55] This fact, however, should not make us blind to some real differences between the two situations.

In India, for example, Buddhism was far from unique in being a religion which advocated abandoning the householder's life for a celibate and monastic existence. In so doing, in fact, it was merely following a legitimate, if "heterodox," pattern shared by many other sramana movements of its time, and which was to some extent incorporated into the mainline Hindu tradition as well. The question of filiality and ancestor worship was thus applicable not only to Buddhism but to a large number of religious movements, and in this company Buddhists perhaps felt less pressure to be explicit about their stance on these issues than they did in China.

Indeed, in China, the Buddhist response to the question of filiality seems to have been more systematically and self-consciously developed. Only there did Buddhist scholars sit down to spell out in detail their position on this matter. Only there, also, did certain patterns of change become fully realized. For instance, the whole Avalambana ritual really took wings in China, becoming by T'ang times "a most flourishing festival."[56] The same can hardly be said to have been the case in India where we have no good evidence for the existence of a fully developed and popular Avalambana festival, although, as we have seen, we can clearly find its antecedents in legend and in Brahmanical ritual.

Nevertheless, it seems to me that the similarities in the patterns of change in Buddhism in the two countries are great enough to warrant seeing genuine parallels between them.

Buddhism has often been called a missionary religion. What we usually forget, however, when this statement is made, is that it was so in India as well as in China. This fact is especially evident when one looks at the popular literature of Buddhism - the stories, avadānas and jātakas - which provided much of the material for the sermons of Buddhist preachers and proselytizers in both countries.

In my view, then, the question of the establishment of Buddhism in China (which for so long centered on the much debated issue of whether Buddhism influenced China more than China influenced Buddhism) must be considered as an extension to the question of the establishment of Buddhism in India.

ONCE-BORN, TWICE-BORN ZEN:
WILLIAM JAMES AND THE RINZAI AND SŌTŌ SCHOOLS
OF JAPANESE BUDDHISM

Conrad Hyers

In his Gifford Lectures of 1901-2 William James developed a typology of once-born and twice-born forms of religious experience and expression.[1] It was a distinction which he had adopted from Francis Newman's work of a half-century earlier on *The Soul, its Sorrows and Aspirations*. In his *Varieties of Religious Experience*, James considerably elaborated upon this distinction through categories such as "healthy-minded" and "sick-minded," the "harmonious self" and the "divided self." But while James expanded the purview of the discussion considerably, and cited a wide variety of cases in doing so, he limited himself to the Western, largely Christian tradition. James' typology may, however, be useful in an Oriental, Buddhist context, especially in elucidating the contrasts between Rinzai and Sōtō Zen.

Western books on Zen have tended to present Zen as a relatively homogeneous experience and teaching, a kind of seamless garment of truth. But this is not the case, either in its Chinese or later Japanese forms. Part of the monolithic image of Zen in the West is the result of the fact that, prior to 1970, most of the literature in English on Zen was derived from the Rinzai school - and most of that written either by the Rinzai scholar, D.T. Suzuki, who dominated the field for half a century with many books and articles, or those who based their work on his. Only in the last decade has a literature developed in English out of Sōtō Zen, with the work of emigrated Sōtō masters such as Shunryu Suzuki and Taizan Maezumi,[2] and various efforts at translating Dōgen's *Shōbōgenzō* and *Zuimonki*.[3]

In his preface to Shunryu Suzuki's book, *Zen Mind, Beginner's Mind*, Huston Smith notes the marked contrast between the two Suzuki's: "Whereas Daisetz Suzuki's Zen was dramatic, Shunryu Suzuki's is ordinary. *Satori* was focal for Daisetz, and it was in large part the fascination of this extraordinary state that made his writings so compelling. In Shunryu Suzuki's book the words *satori* and *Kensho*, its near-equivalent, never appear."[4] The observation is quite telling. Rinzai Zen aims at precipitating an ecstatic experience of enlightenment through such devices as unrelenting concentration on one's *kōan* and daily *sanzen* sessions with the master in which the *kōan* is "thrown" again and again at the monk. Sōtō Zen stresses the act of "just-sitting" (*shikantaza*) in meditation, allowing one's original, Buddha-mind to manifest itself. Rinzai sees *zazen* primarily in terms of meditating on the *kōan* with a view to breaking down the hold of ego, desire and discrimination. In Sōtō one does not meditate *on* anything, but rather sits in the primordial purity of the mind, clear of any point of focus; *zazen* does not progress toward, but proceeds from, enlightenment.

In sorting out these differences, William James' once-born/twice-born typology offers some helpful insights. When one examines, in particular, the reported religious experiences of the pivotal figures of the two Japanese Zen sects, Dōgen and Hakuin, they seem remarkably "true to type." And their subsequent teachings, pedagogical methods, and understandings of meditation and enlightenment seem quite consistent with the differences between a once-born and twice-born religious psychology.

1. Hakuin and Twice-Born Zen

The first experience mentioned in Hakuin's *Orategama* already offers an autobiographical report familiar to the psychic odysseys of the twice-born. When Hakuin was seven or eight he was profoundly disquieted by a sermon delivered on the eight hot and eight cold hells described in a Tendai Buddhist text: "Returning home, I took stock of the deeds of my short life and felt there was but little hope for me. I did not know which way to turn and was gooseflesh all over."[5] Secretly he began to chant passages from the *Lotus Sutra* "day and night," but to little avail. Even a hot bath and the crackling of the wood fire beneath so reminded him of the cauldrons of the eight hot hells that he gave a shriek of terror heard throughout the neighborhood. In Hakuin's impressionable mind his condition was so desperate that he became convinced that his only hope lay in monkhood. His parents refused to consider the proposition. But young Hakuin continued to spend inordinate amounts of time at home and in the temple studying and reciting sutras, and finally at the age of fifteen he entered monastic training.

Already Hakuin had begun to manifest the characteristic turmoil to which James applied the term "soul-sickness." James describes the symptoms as those of melancholy, fear, dread, depression, anxiety, guilt, anguish, and despair. Hakuin also manifested the traits of what James termed the "divided self." The individual experiences a profound inner conflict, feeling on the one hand wretchedly sinful and deserving of suffering, yet on the other hand possessed by an equally holy desire to be righteous. Religious efforts of the most diligent sort are confounded and sabotaged by desperate feelings of lostness, darkness, bondage and doubt. There is often a heavy burden of guilt, yet over matters that to others may seem normal, minor or even trifling. (Hakuin recalled being conscience-stricken over having committed the heinous sins of killing small birds and insects). Nothing but a radical transformation in the depths of one's being would seem to offer any promise of salvation from such a depraved condition.

Such a state of affairs persisted until Hakuin was twenty-four, when matters reached a breaking point which he later designates as the "Great Doubt" (*daigi*) and makes one of the preconditions of enlightenment. "Night and day I did not sleep; I forgot both to eat and rest. Suddenly a great doubt manifested itself before me. It was as though

I were frozen solid in the midst of an ice sheet extending tens of thousands of miles....To all intents and purposes I was out of my mind and the *Mu* [*kōan*] remained."[6] After several days in this condition, which he also later designated the "Great Death" (*daishi*) and interpreted as the dying of ego and desire, he recounts how he "chanced to hear the sound of the temple bell and...was suddenly transformed. It was as if a sheet of ice had been smashed or a jade tower had fallen with a crash. Suddenly I returned to my senses....All my former doubts vanished as though ice had melted away. In a loud voice I called: 'Wonderful! Wonderful!'[7]

To such an enlightenment experience Hakuin gave the designation the "Great Joy" (*daikangi*). It is later described as the "joyous delight of that single victorious cry of 'Ka!' [in one who has] cut off the root-force of life - that cast of the mind of ignorance which has come down through countless past ages."[8] In order to reach the manic heights of this "Great Joy" it was necessary to fall to the depressive depths of the "Great Doubt" and disappear into the "Great Death." In fact, Hakuin argued, the intensity of joy and the degree of understanding were directly proportional to the intensity of doubt that preceded it. "If your doubt measures ten degrees so will your enlightenment."[9] Note the remarkably similar comment made by William James: "The rapturous sorts of happiness of which the twice-born make report has as an historic matter of fact been through a more radical pessimism than anything we have yet considered."[10]

Ecstatic experiences continued to characterize Hakuin's Zen life for many years, leading to his belief that there was not just one enlightenment, but a succession of possible enlightenments - as in mining a rock quarry one does not break up all the stubborn strata with but one blast. In one case he was reading from the Zen anecdotal records; in another he gained an enlightenment from the sound of snow falling; in another he was "overcome by a great surge of joy" while practicing walking meditation; and in yet another he was wading in water during a rainstorm when he suddenly received an even deeper understanding of the verse on the Roundness of the Lotus Leaf. "I roared with laughter and everyone there thought I was mad."[11]

One of the characteristics of autobiographies of the twice-born is that they make good stories - which is also the reason they tend to predominate in religious literatures. Unlike the more commonplace autobiographies of the once-born - if they are reported at all - they make for good press. There are dramatic conflicts, titanic struggles, exuberant passions, emotional extremes, vivid contrasts, heroic actions. There are powerful temptations to be overcome, tortuous ordeals to be passed, awesome heights to climb and terrible abysses to fall into. Extraordinary sensations, supranormal visions, ecstatic transports, dreams and fantasies are the stuff that twice-born tales are made of. One sees these elements not only in Hakuin's own story, but in those stories which inspired him in his quest, or which he uses as exemplary models for his monks to emulate: Sekisō who meditated for long hours, keeping a sharp awl beside him to stab his flesh should he start to doze; Gudō who meditated in a grove of bamboo without a stitch of clothing covering his body, while great swarms of mosquitoes covered his skin with bites; or the second Ch'an Patriarch who reputedly cut off his forearm in demonstration of his utter determination to find peace of mind.

The imagery which Hakuin uses in his teaching is likewise heroic in character. Life is a battleground of contending forces, requiring spiritual warriors and warfare. "At all times in your study of Zen," he counsels, "*fight against* delusions and worldly thoughts, *battle* the *black demon* of sleep, *attack* concepts of active and passive, order and disorder, right and wrong, hate and love, and *join battle* with all things of the mundane world. Then in *pushing forward* with true meditation and *struggling fiercely*, there unexpectedly will come true enlightenment"[12] It is no surprise, then, to find that the pedagogical techniques used by Hakuin are similarly conflict and crisis oriented. On the basis of his own twice-born experiences, and those commonly reported in the Zen anecdotal tradition, Hakuin's mission is to precipitate similar twice-born experiences in his monks and lay followers. By verbal abuse, physical abuse, rejection and frustration the psyche of the monk is brought to a breaking point, beyond which, hopefully, will come light and liberation. Zen anecdotes, particularly those stressed in Rinzai, frequently refer to "roughhouse" treatment: shouting, slapping, striking, kicking. The most important technique, however, is the *kōan*. This is the principle weapon used in the battlefield of the spirit. In fact, meditation is largely understood as meditation on a *kōan*, whose purpose is to frustrate totally and thwart illusory ways of thinking and being. In this manner a crisis of consciousness is to be brought about. At "wit's end" one may then, for Hakuin, be able to experience that Great Doubt and Great Death which lead to Great Joy and Light.

Hakuin recounts how, when he was a young monk, he had experienced great difficulty in meditation (*zazen*). He had tried the more quietistic approach of emptying the mind in accord with Buddhist teachings concerning emptiness (*sūnyatā*) and no-thought (*mushin*). He had believed that "absolute tranquillity of the source of the mind was the Buddha Way," but the more he tried to achieve emptiness, the less tranquil his mind became.

Trivial and mundane matters pressed against my chest and a fire mounted in my heart. I was unable to enter wholeheartedly into the active practice of Zen. My manner became irascible and fears assailed me. Both my mind and my body felt continually weak, sweat poured endlessly from my armpits, and my eyes constantly filled with tears. My mind was in a continual state of depression and I made not the slightest advance towards gaining the benefits that result from the study of Buddhism.[13]

Because of Hakuin's failure in the *zazen*-only way and his subsequent successes with the *kōan* method, he became an unrelenting advocate of *kōan*-meditation. And he became an arch-critic of what he called "dead sitting" (*shiza*) and the "silent-illumination heretics" that practiced it. Thus, for Hakuin, the teaching of "sudden enlightenment" advocated by the Southern Ch'an school - over against the "gradual enlightenment" approach of the Northern ~Ch'an school - was fully confirmed in his own experience.

2. Dōgen and Once-Born Zen

In Japanese Zen the great advocate of "*zazen* only" was Dōgen, the founder of the Sōtō school in the thirteenth-century. Dōgen had, in fact, begun his Zen practice under the first Japanese teacher of Rinzai, Eisai, but came to reject the *kōan* method, particularly a meditation on *kōans* in the expectation that one might arrive thereby at enlightenment and Buddhahood. Dōgen taught instead that one should "just sit," for what one is attempting to realize one already *is* at the center of one's being. One already *is* a Buddha, *is* enlightened, *is* fundamentally at peace. One should therefore "just sit" within one's Buddha-nature and allow it to flow out into all of one's being and life. So, whereas Hakuin talks about "dead sitting" (*shiza*), Dōgen talks about "just sitting" (*shikantaza*), "nothing other than sitting." Such sitting for Dōgen is by no means futile or dead, for it is sitting within the fullness of the life of Buddha. Nor is it "gradual enlightenment" for enlightenment is the logical and ontological basis of all practice of the Way.

Early in Dōgen's monastic studies one question had troubled him, and it is the key to his Zen understanding. If, as Mahayana Buddhism teaches, we are all endowed with the Dharma from birth, and are therefore already in the truth, why is it necessary for all - even those exalted beings called Buddhas - to seek enlightenment and pursue arduous spiritual disciplines? In Mahayana Buddhism there had developed the distinction between original enlightenment (*hongaku*) and acquired enlightenment (*shikaku*). The Tendai sect in which Dōgen had begun his monastic practice had given special emphasis to original enlightenment. And by Dōgen's time Tendai teaching had carried the doctrine to the radical conclusion that enlightenment was an eternal reality, not a temporal occurrence. If such teachings were correct, what was the place or purpose of religious practice? Why any special exertion at all, let alone the long road of exertion in the hope of being enlightened and achieving *nirvana*? In searching for an answer to his conundrum Dōgen was referred to Eisai, known for his introduction of Rinzai Zen teachings from China. When Eisai died the following year, Dōgen continued his study and practice for nine years under Eisai's leading disciple, Myōzen. At the age of twenty-three Dōgen accompanied Myōzen on a journey to China to study in some of the leading Ch'an monasteries. There a resolution to his problem came during a period of meditation when the monk next to him had fallen asleep. The master, Ju-ching, shouted at the sleeping monk: "In *zazen* you must cast off body and mind. How can you give in to sleep? The remark - or the shouting - jolted Dōgen into an understanding of the dilemmas he had been pondering, and he experienced a great sense of joy at his new-found discovery.

At first glance this scenario looks roughly parallel to that of Hakuin's early life and first enlightenment at twenty-four: troubled soul, searching for an answer, finding a solution, experiencing liberation and joy. On closer examination, however, there are important differences. Dōgen was not troubled in the same traumatic way as Hakuin, nor with the same kind of problem. Dōgen's problem was not some deep *internal* conflict issuing in emotional crises of doubt, depression and guilt. It was more of an *external* problem in the traditional teachings of Mahayana Buddhism, a philosophical puzzle posed by an apparent contradiction in Mahayana doctrine and practice. Dōgen *himself* was not the problem. There is no suggestion of alienation from the Buddhist Way, or anguished torture of soul. In searching for an answer to his questions he does not evidence a feeling of lostness, hopelessness or condemnation. The issues do not seem to have tormented him, or driven him to the depths of melancholy and despair. He dealt with the matter in what William James would have called a "healthy-minded" way: probing, testing, sifting, challenging, working through to a solution.

In a sense Dōgen's *kōan* was the very teaching and

practice of Mahayana Buddhism itself. And the resolution at which Dōgen arrived is not that of twice-born experience. The resolution is that the religious practices of Buddhism are not means to some higher end: enlightenment, Buddhahood, *nirvana*. The religious practices are *themselves* the goal of Buddhism. They are not means at all, but ends in themselves. *Zazen* - which for Dōgen is the heart of Buddhist practice - is not a technique for searching after and gaining something. Sitting in meditation is to be practiced for its own sake. This is, so to speak, the way Buddhas sit.

In all this one sees a religious understanding which is in the order of what William James characterizes as the healthy-minded, once-born perspective. One is not fundamentally sick, but healthy; not sinful but pure; not broken but whole; not in bondage but free; not in error but in the truth. There are some persons, wrote James, who are "born with an inner constitution which is harmonious and well-balanced from the outset. Their impulses are consistent with one another, their will follows without trouble the guidance of their intellect, their passions are not excessive, and their lives are little haunted by regrets."[14] For them goodness is conceived as the central and all-embracing aspect of being. Instead of dwelling on the evils and woes of the world they emphasize "the dignity rather than the depravity of man."[15] There is no felt necessity for a radical reconstitution of the psyche or world, for "we are already one with the Divine without any miracle of grace, or abrupt creation of a new inner man."[16] The watchwords, therefore, are not conversion and rebirth, but growth and maturation; not eradicating one's deluded and sinful inclinations, but nurturing one's natural propensities to goodness and harmony. To use Dōgen's own watchwords: the task is to allow one's Buddha-nature to manifest or realize itself (*genjō*) and thus to be confirmed (*shō*) in the Dharma.

One should not presume from this that Dōgen's life was altogether tranquil and bright. His father died when Dōgen was two; his mother when he was seven leaving a dying request that he would become a monk and search out the truths of Buddhism. The death of his mother did not, however, lead to some deep spiritual crisis, nor did the heightened sense of the ephemerality of life lead to melancholy. Human existence, however brief, was read as a great opportunity. Dōgen's monastic career began at the age of thirteen and was characterized by considerable energy and diligence in the learning and pursuit of the Buddhist Way. One has the impression of singleness of purpose, constancy of zeal and direction, and naturalness of religious practice. Instead of being influenced by the fatalism and melancholy that marked the spirit of the age in both its secular and religious literatures, he moved forward in gratitude for the privilege of human birth and the present moment that was available to him. Life was perceived as a gift, not a prisonhouse or a battleground.

One is reminded here in particular of William James' description of the religious outlook of the once-born, even in the face of the harsher realities and readings of life. They persist in "flinging themselves upon their sense of the goodness of life, in spite of the hardships of their own condition, and in spite of the sinister theologies into which they may be born. From the outset their religion is one of union with the divine."[17] Relative to any excuses that might be offered in terms of the misfortunes of life, the doubtfulness of significant achievement in such a brief life-span, the seemingly arduous path to enlightenment, or the degeneracy of the age, Dōgen responds: "Those who have faith in the Way should know for certain that they are unfailingly in the Way from the beginning - thus free from confusions, delusions, being upside down, increase and decrease, and errors."[18]

If, then, the Zen of Rinzai and Hakuin stresses the twice-born experience of "sudden enlightenment," perhaps the Sōtō Zen of Dōgen stresses "gradual enlightenment." Yet this is not Dōgen's position. Dōgen, in fact, proposes the most radical once-born position imaginable. He insists that gradualism is heretical, for it suggests a long, slow climb from a place one wishes to abandon to a place one desires to be. He even rejects the analogy of a seed of potentiality growing gradually into a mature plant or tree.[19] Dōgen, in fact, argues that his position is the authentic "sudden enlightenment" teaching; for what could be more sudden than to realize that one is already where one has decided to journey, and what one has aspired to be. On the other hand, Rinzai Zen, for all its emphasis upon, and attempts to foster, an experience of sudden enlightenment, is seen as having the look of gradualism about it; for one is given a *kōan* with which to wrestle in the hope of eventually achieving an awakening - like ripening fruit to the moment that it suddenly falls from the tree.

3. Reassessing James' Typology

These contrasts between the biographies and teachings of Hakuin and Dōgen leave a major issue in interpreting Zen. Do the once-born and twice-born kinds of religious experience lead to radically different forms of Zen? When one examines the actual consequences of these two different readings of Zen experience, they do seem considerable in the areas of Zen training and pedagogical techniques, and in the understandings of Zen that accompany these. Yet they seem minimal in the areas of religious perspective and teaching.

Rinzai as well as Sōtō claims to be non-dualist, the *satori* experience itself being one in which dualistic modes of thinking and perceiving are seen as collapsed and transcended. And even though Dōgen relentlessly attacks dualisms of many sorts, including those which the Rinzai sect seems to foster, he must still acknowledge some distinctions along the way, such as between those who are aware of their Buddha-nature and those who are not. "Although the Dharma is amply present in every person, unless one practices, it is not manifested; unless there is realization, it is not attained."[20]

Rinzai as well as Sōtō agrees that one's original nature is pure and enlightened, needing to be awakened from the depths of one's being. Hakuin, for example, frequently speaks of *satori* as an experience in which one gains an "awareness of True Self" and in which "our own Original Self-Nature presents itself in direct immediacy."[21] But for Hakuin this awareness comes suddenly after a period of time in which one seems quite removed from such a realization, if not moving in an opposite direction.

The issue between Rinzai and Sōtō, then, seems to boil down to a difference in method rather than a difference in result, a difference in psychology more than in philosophy. The Rinzai method and psychology is that of bursting the bonds of ego, desire, attachment and ignorance. In Christmas Humphreys' helpful analogy, the Rinzai approach, "like the explosives used in logging, is designed to break the jam in the river, and let the waters and all which float thereon ride free."[22] The Sōtō approach on the other hand, in Alan Watts' imagery, is that "muddy water is best cleared by leaving it alone." To dynamite the pond would only make the pond muddier.

The implication of this would seem to be that, originally, these two approaches have arisen out of and addressed themselves to two different human conditions. Subsequently they have tended to become a matter of orthopraxy, rather than means for accommodating individual differences - though there are masters in both the Rinzai and Sōtō schools who have used the techniques of both traditions.

Whatever the approach, both Zen schools recognize that at a certain point (either from the beginning in "just sitting" or through some dramatic change in the psyche) the goal must become a non-goal, seeking must turn into no-seeking, action into non-action. As Hui-nēng preached, "When there is no abiding of thought anywhere on anything - this is being unbound. This not abiding anywhere is the root of our life." On this point both Hakuin and Dōgen agree. Not only does Dōgen advise, "Do not think about how to become a Buddha," but Lin-chi (Rinzai) before him had also characterized the true Zen individual as one who has "not a thought of running after Buddhahood." If, for Lin-chi, "Your searching minds really come to an end, there will be no more anxiety for anything."[24]

The problem, still, is how searching minds are really to come to end. Judging from Hakuin's own testimony, Dōgen's "just sitting" would not have worked for him. He was too inwardly divided and too beset by melancholy, guilt and doubt. "Just sitting" for Hakuin became "dead sitting," and if anything aroused the opposite of its intention: he became increasingly agitated, anxious, distracted and depressed. Hakuin needed something that would bring his internal conflicts out into the open and to a climax. And for this the *kōan* served admirably as a device for "snapping the bonds of ignorance." On the other hand one might ask whether all who enter a Rinzai monastery are to be seen as similarly troubled souls in need of such dramatic techniques, or whether instead the techniques are sometimes being used to create in relatively stable spirits a sense of doubt, anxiety and despair, from which they can in turn have a sense of release.

Of the two types, the healthy-minded and the sick-souled, both psychology and religion have displayed considerable interest, energy and ingenuity in dealing with the latter but very little in dealing with the former. The religious insights and experiences of the once-born - even for William James - have often been seen as less profound, mature and complete. What is most needed both in psychology and religion - and the psychology of religion - is a comparable development of an understanding of the once-born, and an interpretation of the religious profundity and maturity of such a perspective on life. In the Zen context, Dōgen and the Sōtō tradition provide a very helpful starting point for this, both psychologically and religiously.

LYRICAL IMAGERY AND RELIGIOUS CONTENT IN JAPANESE ART:
THE PICTORIAL BIOGRAPHY OF IPPEN THE HOLY MAN

Laura S. Kaufman

Within the Buddhist art tradition of Japan, two seemingly contradictory tendencies coexist: one is a respectful preservation of forms and meanings transmitted from the Asian mainland; the other is a propensity to abandon formal Buddhist imagery, or to mingle it with elements drawn from the profane sphere. If the former attitude reflects appreciation of a precious heritage, the latter reveals the confidence of people who have identified fully with a religion received from afar. The world view that leads the Japanese to cross the boundaries between the secular and religious realms is no doubt traceable to the native religion of Shinto, which celebrates the numinousness of the natural world. It is not, however, inimical to the values of Buddhism, particularly the great Mahāyāna tradition of East Asia, with its teaching that the absolute and the relative worlds interpenetrate. The uniquely Japanese aesthetic response to the Buddhist teachings takes forms as varied as the *Fan-Shaped Lotus Sūtra* of Shitennōji, written in the late Heian period (795-1185) over paintings of everyday scenes, and the *kara senzui*, the "dry" or waterless stone gardens first constructed in Zen temples of the Muromachi period (1392-1573). Yet another example is the *kōsōden*, the "biographies of illustrious priests" that were made in great numbers in handscroll (*emaki*) form in the Kamakura period (1185-1333).

Because the secular art tradition upon which they draw is well preserved, the *kōsōden* offer fertile ground for study of the interaction between secular and religious imagery. And among all the priests' biographies, secular imagery is employed most conspicuously in the *Ippen Hijiri-e*, the Pictorial Biography of Ippen the Holy Man, a cycle of twelve handscrolls executed in 1299. Its forty-eight illustrations comprise an array of landscapes and detailed views of holy places that is unparalleled in *emaki* of any subject (figs.1 & 2 pp.220,221). The lyrical atmosphere created by these encompassing settings might well lead one to surmise that secularizing tendencies have overwhelmed the biography's religious content. Indeed, writings on the *emaki* tradition often describe the *Ippen Hijiri-e* much in these terms. However, a close examination of the illustrations, taking into account the accompanying text, suggests the quite different conclusion that the religious themes of the story of Ippen the holy man have not been abandoned.

Ippen Shōnin (1239-1289) is remembered today as the founder of the Ji-shū, the Ji Sect, and as the third and last of the important Pure Land teachers of Kamakura Japan. Like his two great predecessors, Hōnen Shōnin (1133-1212) and Shinran Shōnin (1173-1262), Ippen taught that the only Buddhist path appropriate to the degenerate times was devotion to Amida Buddha through recitation of the *nembutsu* (the invocation of Amida's name). However, Ippen's career differed significantly from those of Hōnen and Shinran, who saw in their teachings the same orthodoxy as the older sects transmitted from China. Ippen had strong ties with the folk religion of his day, which contained a pronounced strain of Amidism. He patterned his life upon the model of the *hijiri*, the wandering holy men who flourished outside the framework of organized religion. Renouncing any fixed abode, he traveled constantly and preached to people of every station in life. He was accompanied by a group of monks and nuns that he called the Ji-shū, meaning the Ji Band, which became the Ji Sect only after his lifetime. Ippen's methods of religious propagation, such as distribution of *nembutsu* cards and dancing *nembutsu* services, were those of the folk religion. Moreover, he revered the Shinto gods and the many holy places that were pilgrimage centres of the folk; indeed, he based his religious mission upon the revelation he received in 1274 from Ketsumiko no kami, a god of the Kumano Hongū who was considered a manifestation of Amida Buddha.

The *Ippen Hijiri-e* was dedicated in 1299 on the occasion of the tenth anniversary of Ippen's death.[1] The biography was deposited in Kankikōji, the temple in Kyoto that still owns it. According to the scrolls' dedicatory inscription, the text was written by Shōkai, the founder of Kankikōji, who was related to Ippen, having been either his nephew or younger brother. Thus Shōkai knew Ippen personally, as may have been the case with other participants in the biographical project. The inscription cites Hōgen En'i as the painter, but no Kamakura-period artist of that name is recorded elsewhere.[2] The patron remained anonymous; it is apparent, however, that he was wealthy and highly placed. Atypically, the work is executed on silk, which was inordinately more costly than the customary material of paper. The support of a patron is also suggested by the paintings' length and complexity. Moreover, the silk of the text portions is stained various colours and delicately underpainted with designs, recalling the aristocratic *shikishi* style of decorating calligraphy paper.

The events portrayed in the *Ippen Hijiri-e* are set into the familiar world of Japan in the not-too-distant past. This is true as well of the biographies of other Pure Land founders, such as the *Hōnen Shōnin Eden* (an illustrated biography of Hōnen) and the *Zenshin Shōnin-e* (an illustrated biography of Shinran).[3] However, the *Ippen Hijiri-e* uses far more sparingly the idealizing techniques that make the religious intent of most other *kōsōden* much more obvious. There is almost no trace of the traditional iconography of the Buddhas and Bodhisattvas that is elsewhere interjected into miraculous episodes and death scenes. Furthermore, the usual emphasis upon the protagonist's superiority is absent here. It is true that the portrayal of Ippen is somewhat idealized, for his buckteeth and oddly shaped head, known from contemporary accounts and posthumous portraits, are merely hinted at (figs. 3 & 9 pp. 222, 227). On the whole, however, he is shown as a gaunt, gentle person, not as a perfect being who towers above others physically or spiritually (see especially figs.6 & 10 pp.224,228).

Also noteworthy is the panoramic scale of the paintings, which makes emphatic characterization of Ippen almost impossible. We may cite as an example the illustration of Ippen preaching in 1284 at the Shakadō, a temple at Shijō-Kyōgoku in Kyoto (Scroll VII, section 2; fig.2 pp.221). According to the text, "Rich and poor, high and low flocked to see him. The people had no space to turn around and look; their carriages were unable to turn about."[4] The painting encompasses the Shakadō, the surrounding streets, and the approach across the Shijō Bridge. This ample setting accommodates dozens of figures, who run across the bridge, struggle to squeeze through the crowd, or watch the proceedings from adjacent rooftops. The mass propagation of Buddhism in Kamakura Japan is portrayed in the liveliest terms, yet the figures are so tiny that Ippen is necessarily inconspicuous. He is in the temple courtyard, where he distributes *nembutsu* cards from the shoulders of a husky young monk (fig.3 pp.222). Beside him is the temporary plankroofed chapel in which his monks and nuns are performing the dancing *nembutsu* service. Thus the narrative elements correspond with the text, but are rendered in small scale.

The *Ippen Hijiri-e* was certainly the first artistic and literary work devoted to the life of Ippen. Yet it was soon followed by others. The *Ippen Shōnin Ekotoba Den* (known today only by numerous copies) emerged in about 1304 to 1307 from the circle of Taamidabutsu (or Shinkyō), who was Ippen's official successor as Ji-shū leader.[5] It was Taa who began the process of molding the informal Ji Band into an organization that could be perpetuated into future generations. Although animosity seems to have developed between Taa and Shōkai, the *Ippen Shōnin Ekotoba Den* - actually a joint biography of Ippen and Taa - draws upon the compositions of the *Ippen Hijiri-e*. Yet the differences between the two works, which may have become even more exaggerated with successive copying of the *Ippen Shōnin Ekotoba Den*, are striking. Reflecting no doubt

Taa's own point of view, the *Ippen Shōnin Ekotoba Den* characterizes Ippen as the first patriarch - and Taa as the second - of a distinctive religious movement. This notion is enhanced by recourse to the conventional devices of didactic storytelling: idealization and emphasis. A section from the Kōmyōji copy of the *Ippen Shōnin Ekotoba Den*, executed in the sixteenth century following closely a version of the mid-fourteenth century, offers a clear contrast with the narrative methods of the *Ippen Hijiri-e* (fig.4 pp.222). Illustrating the same events of 1284 that are represented in the Shakadō scene of the *Ippen Hijiri-e* (fig.1 pp.220), it shows Ippen and his disciples crossing the Shijō Bridge. Insofar as he is extremely homely, Ippen is depicted here more as he actually looked than in the *Ippen Hijiri-e*. But he is larger than the other figures and darker in colour; the people he encounters stare and point at him. The attempt to make Ippen conspicuous and important-looking deprives him of his humanity.

In contrast with the mythic characterization of the *Ippen Shōnin Ekotoba Den*, Shōkai and his associates may have had uppermost in their minds their living memory of Ippen as a great and beloved human being. They may have viewed Ippen's career, too, much as Ippen himself had, as that of a holy man rather than that of a patriarch. In fact, the text of the *Ippen Hijiri-e* itself suggests that Shōkai did not intend to write the biography of a more-than-human patriarch.

The text recounts the usual events in the life of a Buddhist teacher, describing Ippen's travels, his devotions and realizations, his preaching and triumphant encounters with both the pious and the doubting. It quotes documents containing Ippen's teachings, such as sermons, letters, and Chinese hymns. At the same time, however, the text goes beyond the conventional formulae of a priest's biography. It employs freely the enriching literary devices of secular prose literature. As in works such as the great thirteenth-century war tale, the *Heike Monogatari*, and Kamo no Chōmei's contemplative essay of 1212, *Hōjōki*, lyrical intensity is achieved in prose passages by using parallel construction of sentences and phrases. Often this device occurs in descriptions of Ippen's travels, as in the following account of his journey to Kumano (Scroll III, section 1):

Crossing mountains and seas over the thousand-fold cloud ways, he dipped the sleeves of his robe in the current of the Iwada River. He worshipped at the many shrines to godlings along the route, and opened the fastness of his heart by the water's edge near the Gate of First Aspiration. At the densely overgrown shrines of Fujishiro and Iwashiro the dew of the Manifest Traces sparkled like jewels; at the altars of Hongū and Shingū the subdued brilliance of the moon hung like a mirror....[6]

Also in common with the secular prose style are frequent allusions to Buddhist legend and to Chinese history, and lengthy accounts of pious or historical lore concerning the temples and shrines that Ippen visits.

The frequent quotation of Ippen's *waka* (Japanese poems of thirty-one syllables) is yet another point of resemblance to contemporary secular literature. Because writing poetry was an everyday occurrence in medieval Japan, most Buddhist teachers composed *waka*. The *Ippen Hijiri-e*, however, places unusual emphasis upon poetry, including forty-seven of Ippen's *waka* and over a dozen more poems written by others. Ippen's poems are strongly Buddhist in content, suggesting that they were written mainly as teaching devices. But as is typical of religious *waka* generally, they draw upon the lyricism and the nature imagery that were the basis of the native poetic tradition.

In sum, the text of the *Ippen Hijiri-e* does not present Ippen as a saint of superhuman perfection. Its intensely lyrical mood introduces a tone of warmth and affection, characterizing Ippen as someone whose greatness as a religious teacher cannot be separated from his human sensibility.

Although the unconventional elements in the written biography must be taken into account in any study of the illustrations, the paintings cannot be explained simply as responses to the text, for the written and pictorial biographies were conceived of as a single project. To the extent that the paintings were more costly to sponsor and more time-consuming to execute, they may well have had primacy in the planning. Shōkai must have known before writing the text what sort of accompanying illustrations the patron desired.

In the paintings, it is the landscape elements that are the enriching elements equivalent to the poems and lyrical passages in the text. In some sections, the landscape motifs have no special role beyond creating a convincing setting for the action. Elsewhere, however, they exploit the correspondence between the natural world and the realm of human feeling that had for centuries been a premise of the Japanese poetic tradition and the arts based upon it.

One way in which landscape contributes to the storytelling is by means of natural motifs that mirror and intensify the emotional tone of the events portrayed. For example, in the spring of 1274, Ippen determined finally to renounce his home and embark upon a life of wandering and pilgrimage (Scroll II, section 2). As he left his ancestral home in Iyo on Shikoku, he was seen off by Shōkai, who accompanied him part way. In the illustration of the final parting (fig.5 pp.223), Shōkai looks back at Ippen and his company as they walk past a conspicuous ancient cherry tree covered with bright round blossoms. The tree has just passed the peak of bloom; a few petals are fluttering to the ground, joining the clusters of fallen petals that are already beginning to gather. It is the briefness of the cherry flower's bloom and the scattering of its petals that give the flower its conventional significance as the embodiment of the fragility of youth and beauty. Thus the motif of the cherry evokes the poignancy of Ippen's separation from his family. Further, because it helps to make the parting from Shōkai an emotionally charged, vivid event, it enhances the notion that Ippen and Shōkai were very close - an idea that Shōkai may well have wished to see incorporated subtly into the pictorial biography.

Yet another motif that lends itself to association with human emotion is the flock of migrating birds. It is employed, for example, in the scene of Ippen's departure in the winter of 1279 from the house of Ōi no Tarō and his sister, who had invited the holy man to hold a *nembutsu* service at their house (Scroll V, section 1; fig.6 pp.224). As Ippen and his band depart across barren winter fields, the wild geese flying overhead mirror the freedom and vulnerability of their wandering life. The motif is employed with a realism characteristic of the scrolls: Ippen is setting out toward the north and the birds are flying south, in the opposite direction. In poetry, migrating geese often stand for a deceased loved one - someone who has departed but cannot return. This symbolism suggests another level of meaning for the motif in the painting: the geese fly toward the people gathered at the samurai's house as though to express their helpless desire that Ippen return to their midst. Thus a poetic image becomes a vehicle for suggesting the intense devotion that Ippen inspired in those he met.

In the two paintings just cited, a specific, conventionally meaningful natural motif is introduced into the setting to enhance the story's emotional content. This is a simple device that was often used by Kamakura-period illustrators of both secular and religious narratives in emotionally charged scenes. Elsewhere in the Ippen scrolls, however, the settings are employed more ambitiously: they contribute to the characterization of the hero Ippen. In these scenes, specific motifs may again be significant, but the mood or ambience created by the entire landscape is also crucial. These are illustrations in which poetry and travel, themes that were also established by lyrical techniques in the text, are dominant.

One poetic episode occurred in about 1279 at Onodera (Scroll V, section 2). The text reads:

At a place called Onodera in Shimotsuke Province, when suddenly a violent rain fell, Ippen saw the nuns drying off their *kesa* and robes, and wrote:

  Fureba nure   When it rains they get soaked
  Nurureba kawaku When they get soaked they dry off
  Sode no ue wo   How evanescent are the people
  Ame tote itou   Who shirk from the rain upon their
  Hito zo hakanaki   sleeves.7

The text offers no indication of season, but the artist interpreted the storm as a rain of early spring (fig.1 pp.220). This required taking some liberty with the poetic tradition that assigns gentle showers (*harusame*) to the spring season and heavy downpours of the type Ippen encountered to summer. The strong association of the vernal season with poetry and lyricism must have influenced this decision. The painting shows Ippen and the Ji-shū taking shelter from the storm. Ippen, already seated within a hut, watches his disciples tend to their damp clothes in a flurry of activity. The artist depicts the rain that was the subject of the poem with an unusual pictorial device - fine ink lines lying diagonally across the landscape. Yet this motif alone would not have created the lyric intensity that evokes a mood of poetic inspiration. This is achieved by the soft, almost melting beauty of the scene, which is replete with traditional poetic spring motifs: budding trees in mountain forests, blossoming cherry trees, birds returning from winter migrations, soft hazes, and pale green new vegetation.

The significant features of the illustration - particularly the prominence of seasonal motifs, the panoramic scale of the landscapes, and the small size of the figures - appear to be typical of the secular tradition of poetic illustration. They occur in the paintings and decorative objects that document this tradition from the mid-Heian through the Kamakura periods.[8] Moreover, the Onodera scene, and the Ippen scrolls as a whole, correspond to the characteristic style of other poetic paintings of the late thirteenth century, when the scattered, delicate landscapes of the Heian period gave way to more detailed, spatially coherent scenes.

A work that is particularly close in style and spirit to the Ippen scrolls is the *Saigyō Monogatari Emaki*, the Illustrated Scroll of the Life of Saigyō. This undated and only partially preserved set of handscrolls was probably executed in the latter part of the thirteenth century. Saigyō Hōshi (1118-1190) was one of the great poets of the late Heian period; he renounced his life as a courtier, becoming a monk, and traveled throughout Japan in search of poetic inspiration. In the process of narrating his biography, the handscroll paintings illustrate some of the circumstances under which Saigyō wrote his verse. In the section from the Ōhara Collection's scroll illustrated here (fig.7 pp.225), he is on a journey to Kumano when he stops at one of the small shrines en route, the Yagami Ōji. Composing a poem about the blossoming cherry trees, he writes it upon the fence of the shrine. His poem reads:

>   Machitsukuru   The cherries of Yagami
>   Yagami no sakura   That I was waiting for
>   Sakinikeru   Have blossomed.
>   Araku orosu na   Do not blow down roughly
>   Mine no matsukaze   Wind, in the pines on the peak.[9]

The important elements of both the poem and the story of its composition are present in the painting: the cherry trees, the Yagami Shrine, and Saigyō's act of dedication. As in the Onodera illustration, the figure of the protagonist is small and relatively inconspicuous, but the intensity of his response to nature is suggested by his immersion in an encompassing setting. The fact that the *Saigyō Monogatari Emaki* was conceived as a biography and not just as a cycle of poetic illustrations seems typical of the Kamakura mentality, which took interest in great people and their distinctive personalities. Its attempt simultaneously to document the protagonist's life and to illustrate his poem also characterizes the Onodera scene.

Another section of the *Ippen Hijiri-e* demonstrates still more clearly the painter's immersion in the poetic tradition. It is the first part of a double illustration representing Ippen at the Shirakawa Barrier and his subsequent visit to the grave of his grandfather Kōno Michinobu, who died in exile in the far north (Scroll V, section 3). The first portion of the text reads:

In Kōan 3 (1280), when Ippen went from Zenkōji to Ōshū [the Northern Provinces], in many days of travel there was not one famous place. There were spots where the moon emerged from the dew on the wild grasses and brushed the distant tree tops. There were places where the sun came through the fog in the seaside pines and inclined toward the waves on the horizon. He followed the routes of fishermen and merchants. Although they did not know who he was, he exchanged pledges with them. Without waiting for the pitiful contributions of the old folks of the hamlets and the elders of the villages, he tied karmic bonds with them. In this way, Ippen arrived at the Shirakawa Barrier, and fastened this to the pillar of the deity of the barrier:

> Yukuhito wo So that travelers
> Mida no chikai ni Will not be excluded
> Morasaji to From Amida's vow
> Na wo koso tomure I affix his name
> Shirakawa no seki At Shirakawa Barrier.[10]

It is not surprising that Ippen wrote a poem at Shirakawa. As the gateway in medieval times between civilized Japan and the wild regions of the north, the Shirakawa Barrier evoked in travelers deep emotion and was a popular subject of poetry. In the background of the painting, Ippen is depicted, much as Saigyō was at the Yagami Ōji, seated in front of the tiny tutelary shrine (figs.8 & 9 pp.226, 227). The rustic guard house of the barrier occupies the foreground. Surrounding all is a landscape of dancing mountain forms; it is disorderly spatially, but conveys a heightened intensity of feeling suggestive of Ippen's exhilaration at reaching this remote outpost. Adding to the almost joyous mood is the bright autumn foliage - red maples and ivy vines in the foreground and yellow, orange, and russet trees on the distant mountains.

Here again, as in the Onodera section, the season is supplied by the painter, not by the text. The selection of autumn was not arbitrary, however, for the poetic tradition associated Shirakawa Barrier with the fall season. Most notably, about a century before Ippen, Saigyō Hōshi, the archetype of the poet-wanderer, visited Shirakawa, leaving the following poem on a pillar of the barrier house:

> Shirakawa no Shirakawa barrier house
> Sekiya wo tsuki no Guarded by the moon -
> Moru kage wa Its light leaking in
> Hito no kokoro wo Holds back my human heart.[11]
> Tomuru narikeri

Ippen was apparently familiar with this verse by Saigyō, for, using the classical poetic technique of *honkadōri* (allusive variation), he enriched his poem by borrowing from Saigyō some elements of the basic situation and some words (*moru*, to escape, and *tomaru*, to hold back). As is typical of the technique, Ippen's poem conveys an entirely new meaning, for it has a strongly Buddhist significance. Most likely Saigyō's act of writing the poem upon the barrier house pillar also served as a model for Ippen; characteristically, however, Ippen left his verse at the local shrine, thus reinforcing its religious meaning.

That the illustrator understood the source of Ippen's poem is suggested, first, by the emphatic autumnal imagery: the moon - the principal image of Saigyō's poem - is conventionally associated with autumn. Moreover, though the episode is depicted as occurring in broad daylight, the artist painted a tiny full moon (inconspicuous in black-and-white illustration) in the sky beyond the far mountains in the upper left portion of the scene. The painting thus illustrates both Ippen's act of dedicating a *waka* and the poem by Saigyō from which it derives. This seems to be the only extant painting of the Kamakura period that establishes a visual correlate for the poetic technique of allusive variation. It may be the only surviving work to embody a degree of refinement that was characteristic of the most sophisticated poem illustrations.

Both the Onodera and the Shirakawa episodes seem intended to suggest Ippen's way of responding to the people and places he encounters in his daily life. At Onodera, he criticizes his disciples' frivolousness with a poem that draws upon the immediate situation of being caught in the rain: presumably this is a more gentle and efficacious method than delivering a straightforward admonition. At Shirakawa the obligatory traveler's verse becomes the occasion for a *nembutsu* poem. In these episodes Ippen employs poetry both as a teaching device and to express his transformation of ordinary experience into spiritual inspiration

Throughout the Mahāyāna Buddhist world, there have been saints and holy men who expressed their understanding in poetry.[12] It is only natural to turn to verse when attempting to suggest with words an experience that transcends conceptualization. Moreover, the principles of expedient means (hōben in Japanese; upāya in Sanskrit) and of the identity of the phenomenal realm and the absolute - taught in all Mahāyāna schools - justified the practice. Thus, although their native poetic tradition encouraged in them an unusual reliance upon lyricism and nature imagery, the Japanese who wrote religious poems were not unique. Yet the Japanese view of the relationship between poetry and religious realization was extreme. The Japanese of the Heian and Kamakura periods valued poetic sensibility to an extraordinary degree, associating it with human worth in general. That they went so far as to identify poetic sensibility and spiritual greatness is demonstrated by this passage from the writings of Myōe Shōnin (1173-1232), a priest of the Kegon Sect who was an influential figure in early Kamakura Buddhism:

Through all ages eminent Buddhists emerge from men of taste. Although the poems both in Chinese and Japanese and the poetical dialogues in Japanese are not Buddhism in themselves, those who have taste for these things are certain to extend their taste to Buddhism and become wise and very kind men.... Buddhism should be taught to those who, from childhood, have delicate taste and truthful heart.[13]

Only in light of this attitude can we appreciate the frequent inclusion of Ippen's poems in the text of the *Ippen Hijiri-e*. The poems demonstrate that Ippen was not a common or vulgar itinerant preacher, but someone who could and did realize the highest spiritual state. They reflect Ippen's greatness both as a human being and as a Buddhist teacher. In turn, the illustrations of Ippen at Onodera and Shirakawa embrace the poetic aspects of their stories. While they reflect an extraordinary enthusiasm for poetry and lyrical depiction on the part of those who made or planned the paintings, they do not signify indifference to the stories' religious content. The tradition of poetic illustration had developed means to convey the ineffable in a painting, and these means are employed to suggest Ippen's inspiration, both poetic and religious. The illustrator eschewed the visual prose of conventional religious narrative, which tended to depict someone as saintly by separating him from the human condition. Instead he attempted to evoke the warm atmosphere that surrounds a masterful and truly generous teacher. No doubt the ambition to portray Ippen's greatness in lyrical terms was nourished by the memory of his actual personality.

Another theme expressed in the paintings, largely in lyrical terms, is Ippen's unceasing travel. There was a practical side to Ippen's life of wandering. It permitted him to preach in the towns, markets, and pilgrimage sites where many people gathered at once; he also ventured to remote areas where the folk had few opportunities to hear the Buddhist teachings. However, Ippen's understanding of Buddhism must also have been a factor in his adoption of a journeying life. Unlike the earlier Pure Land teachers, who had stressed the cultivation of faith in Amida Buddha, Ippen emphasized renunciation of all dualistic notions through complete abandonment to Amida.[14] He embodied this teaching in his own life most conspicuously by giving up the security of a fixed dwelling and becoming truly homeless. His popular epithets, *yūgyō shōnin* (traveling saint) and *sute hijiri* (renunciant holy man), suggest that this gesture made a profound impression upon his contemporaries.

Because the teaching of impermanence is so fundamental in Buddhism, the journey had often before been seen as a metaphor for the spiritual path that the individual pursues in an everchanging world. Thus Ippen's contemporaries were well prepared to recognize the religious significance of his life of wandering. At the same time, however, the notion of travel also had strong literary and even romantic overtones for them. The Japanese of medieval times - as today - were enthusiastic travelers and sightseers. They viewed travel as an occasion to come into contact with the natural world and with life's beauty and profundity, and so regarded it as the very stuff of poetic inspiration. In this poetic view of travel there is an element of aesthetic appreciation of impermanence - a notion that in itself is a response to the Buddhist teachings. Saigyō Hōshi's *uta angya*, or poetic pilgrimages, typify the association made between travel and poetry, as well as the compatibility of both with a life of religious renunciation.

Travel was the hallmark of Ippen's career, and it is emphasized accordingly in the paintings of the *Ippen Hijiri-e*. Further, the complex of meanings attached to the notion of travel made it only natural to render this religious theme vivid and memorable by employing lyrical vocabulary derived from the poetic tradition.

The theme of travel is indeed a leitmotif that runs throughout virtually all the paintings of the cycle. The opening section shows Ippen setting out on his first journey to study Buddhism; subsequently he is never shown in the same place in successive paintings until the last four sections, which depict his final illness. Twelve illustrations - one quarter of the set - show Ippen arriving somewhere, setting out, or in the course of his journeys (see, for example, figs.1,5,6 & 10 pp.220,223,224, 228). Frequently this subject matter offers fertile opportunity to create arresting landscape settings, and these are important in making the theme of Ippen as a traveler come to life. As we observe Ippen immersed time and time again in lovely and varied surroundings, we instinctively empathize with him, assuming that he was deeply inspired by the beauty all around him. Yet these adventures which are so appealingly portrayed stand as well for Ippen's spiritual journey.

One painting in which the travel motif is linked specifically with the notion of religious inspiration depicts a turning point in Ippen's life: in about 1270, after a lengthy return to secular life, he suddenly decided to resume his spiritual practice (Scroll I, section 2). The text describes the event as follows:

Playing with children, he amused them with the game of spinning a top. One time, the top fell to the ground, ceasing to turn. Contemplating this, he realized that if you turn it, it spins; but if you do not turn it, it does not spin. Because we create the three kinds of action, our transmigration through the six realms never ceases. But if our own efforts stop, how can we wander on? Ippen told me that here for the first time he realized in his heart the nature of birth and death and grasped the meaning of the Buddhist teachings.... So, in order to renounce human affection and enter the unconditioned path, he resolved to see his teacher once again....

At the time of the top-spinning incident, he saw this poem in a dream:

Yo wo watari	The clouds in the sky on the
Somete takane no	high peaks
Sora no kumo	That were stained
Tayuru wa moto no	As they began to pass through
Kokoro narikeri	the world
	Have vanished to their true nature.¹⁵

The latter portion of the illustration depicts the journey to Kyushu to revisit Shōdatsu, Ippen's former teacher (fig. 10 pp.228). Ippen and his traveling companions are walking along a seashore with wind-twisted pines. The subdued tonality and empty spaces of the landscape create a still, austere mood. But on the distant shore a single cherry tree is blossoming at the foot of the mountain, hinting at the promise of the spring season; overhead, a flock of geese returning from winter migrations wings through the mist. Thus the notion of reawakening religious inspiration is transposed into lyrical terms; it is evoked both through the reawakening of the natural world and through Ippen's apparent absorption in the sights around him. We may note that Shōkai resorted to a similar device in the text: using a convention from the secular prose tradition, he ended the episode by quoting the poem Ippen wrote in response to the events described. Ippen's insight into the nature of cause and effect is thus crystallized in a *waka* recording a dream of clouds.

In the course of Ippen's travels, he visited many of the most flourishing pilgrimage centres of medieval Japan, especially those associated with the careers of the early *nembutsu* preachers or with the folk cult of Amida. His reverence for the Buddhist and Shinto deities was profound. Several episodes of the written biography indicate how deeply his pilgimages moved him. At Enkyōji, for example, Ippen emerges from the inner sanctuary in tears after viewing the temple's sacred image of Nyoirin Kannon (Scroll IX, section 4). Of Enkyōji and its founder, Shōku Shōnin, he observes: "It is difficult to express in words the marvelous virtues of the Shōnin's practice of the *buddha-dharma*. My only goal in traveling through the various provinces has been a pilgrimage to this temple."[16]

The notion of pilgrimage is strongly emphasized in the text of the *Ippen Hijiri-e*. Over and over, Shōkai digresses from his account of Ippen's life and teachings to present the histories, legends, and good qualities of the places Ippen visits. Some of these passages are surprisingly lengthy; some are documented with quotations from temple records and other sources.

Ippen's enthusiasm for pilgrimage is reflected as well in the illustrations, which depict him at no less than eleven Shinto shrines and sixteen named Buddhist temples and pilgrimage sites. Sometimes Ippen is characterized as a pilgrim who prays, watches sacred dances, or visits with local priests; at other sites, he performs the duties of a teacher by delivering sermons, distributing *nembutsu* cards, or celebrating the dancing *nembutsu* service (fig.3 pp.222). Yet in all these paintings Ippen's specific actions are less important to the notion of pilgrimage than the vivid portrayal of the holy sites themselves. Thus the pilgrimage theme, like the themes of poetry and travel, is considerably enhanced by the elaborate settings. In this case, however, the crucial factor is not the lyricism of landscape passages but strikingly realistic and accurate architectural depictions.

Almost inevitably, great care is taken in representing the shrines and temples that Ippen visits. The distinctive architectural features of layout and construction style are shown, as is the topographical relationship of the buildings to their site. Probably few, if any, of these views of holy places were invented by the painter. Since physical, written, or pictorial evidence provides some kind of information about the appearance of most of these sites in Kamakura times, it is possible to verify that many of the representations in the *Ippen Hijiri-e* are at least partially accurate architecturally and topographically.[17] Considering that these holy places are widely scattered throughout Japan, much effort at gathering information must have accompanied the execution of the scrolls.

Various types of information seem to have been available to the painter. He knew some sites from personal experience. In other cases, he may have consulted travelers' descriptions, maps, or drawings. One useful source was sacred *mandara* paintings consisting of highly detailed representations of shrine compounds. For example, the representation of the Shakadō, located at one of the major crossroads of Kyoto, was no doubt based upon on-the-spot observation (fig.2 p.221). The temple itself is not elaborate or distinctive architecturally, but subsidiary elements - the fields of the *kawaramono* on the flats of the Kamo river and the *torii* of the Gion Shrine - make the representation specific and vivid. The portrayal of the Hongū (the upper or main shrine) of the Iwashimizu Hachimangū, on the other hand, was based upon a painted model; it follows the composition found also in a fourteenth-century *Iwashimizu Hachimangū Mandara* in the Ōkura Shūkokan, Tokyo, which depicts both the upper and lower shrines (figs.11 & 12 pp.229,230). The handscroll and the *mandara* are alike in their immense complexity. In both, the principal shrine buildings and the outbuildings situated below on the mountainside are disposed with tight precision on a steep angle of recession.

The type and degree of realism differ in the representations of the Shakadō and the Iwashimizu Hachiman Shrine, but each in its own way achieves a high degree of completeness and accuracy. In this respect, they are both comparable to Shinto *mandara* paintings. The architectural *mandara* are unusual and uniquely Japanese religious paintings. Although Buddhist versions were also made, the religious values they express are essentially Shinto: their literal realism seems intended to evoke the numinousness of the holy places they represent. A similar significance attaches to the scrupulously rendered views of temples and shrines in the *Ippen Hijiri-e*. They create a mood of sanctity and respectfulness, suggesting the intensity of Ippen's experiences as a pilgrim.

The literal representation of architectural settings

serves, therefore, the theme of pilgrimage in much the same way that the gentle lyricism of the landscapes contributes to the themes of poetic inspiration and travel. The method is similar in both instances: the emphasis and clarity of narrative that would result from adopting a large scale for the figures is sacrificed in order to create subtly meaningful settings. In the case of the architectural depictions, however, it is not the world of poetry and lyrical illustration that is drawn upon as the source of imagery, but a type of religious art with little intrinsic connection to the teachings of Pure Land Buddhism.

Ippen Shōnin did not aspire to elegance. His earnest desire to preach the *nembutsu* as universally as possible led him to employ both the dramatic methods of mass proselytizing and the subtleties of *waka* poetry. The *Ippen Hijiri-e*, on the other hand, is the product of an aristocratic sensibility. But the lyricism that dominates its paintings is not arbitrary or ornamental. Rather, it inspires the viewer's admiration for the vitality of Ippen's personality and the authenticity of his spiritual realization. Furthermore, the artist has not bound himself to the dreamy world of seasonal imagery but has drawn as well upon the austere and literal style of Shinto *mandara* painting.

In later generations the complex, subtle characterization of Ippen in the *Ippen Hijiri-e* did not prove as useful to the Ji-shū as the didactic clarity, achieved by more conventional methods, of the *Ippen Shōnin Ekotoba Den*. Yet we have seen that the *Ippen Hijiri-e* also reflects a serious effort to portray religious themes. And we must acknowledge the validity of its characterization of Ippen. It mirrors the blend of orthodox Buddhist, folk, and Shinto elements that constituted his unique version of Amidism. Moreover, it touches upon the aspects of Ippen's career that have left the most enduring impression upon the Japanese popular imagination. In the twentieth century, when Buddhism no longer dominates Japanese culture, "Ippen-san" is still fondly remembered for his wandering life and for the uniquely Japanese quality of his presentation of Buddhism.

Figure 1: Ippen Hijiri-e, V,2: Onodera. Kankikōji, Kyoto

Figure 2: *Ippen Hijiri-e*, VII,2: The Shakadō. Tokyo National Museum, Tokyo

Figure 3: <u>Ippen Hijiri-e</u>, VII,2, detail: Ippen at the Shakadō. Tokyo National Museum, Tokyo

Figure 4: <u>Ippen Shōnin Ekotoba Den</u>, III,3, detail: Ippen at the Shijō Bridge. Kōmyōji, Yamagata.

Figure 5: *Ippen Hijiri-e*, II,2, detail: Ippen parts from Shōkai. Kankikōji, Kyoto.

Figure 6: Ippen Hijiri-e, V,1: Ōi no Tarō's house. Kankikōji, Kyoto.

Figure 7: Saigyo Monogatari Emaki, section 4: Yagami Ōji. Ōhara Collection, Okayama.

Figure 8: Ippen Hijiri-e, V,3: Shirakawa Barrier. Kankikōji, Kyoto

Figure 9: Ippen Hijiri-e, V,3, detail: Ippen at Shirakawa. Kankikōji, Kyoto.

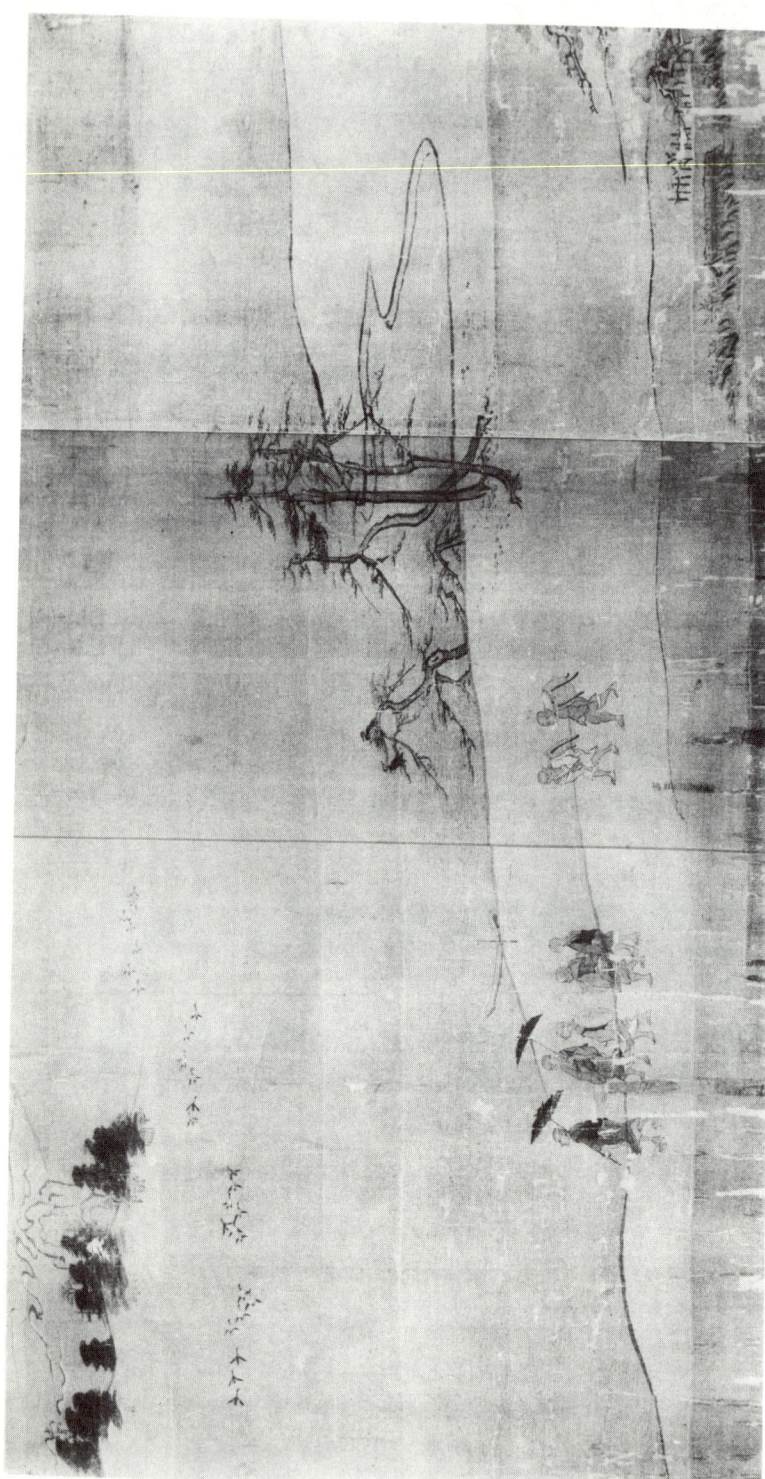

Figure 10: Ippen Hijiri-e, I,2: Journey to Kyushu. Kankikōji, Kyoto.

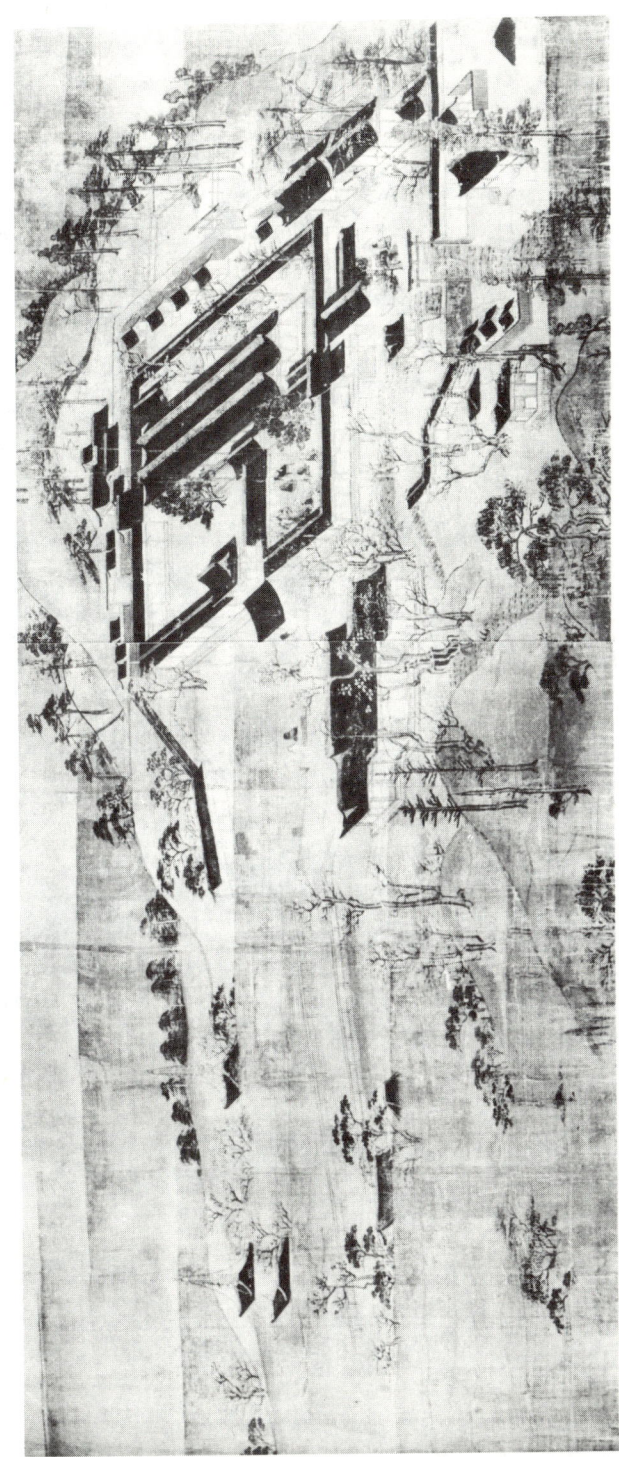

Figure 11: *Ippen Hijiri-e*, IX,1: Iwashimizu Hachiman Shrine. Kankikōji, Kyoto.

Figure 12: Iwashimizu Hachimangu Mandara. Ōkura Shūkokan, Tokyo.

JAPANESE RURAL COMMUNITIES AND SHINTO SHRINES SINCE THE MEIJI RESTORATION (1868) - A CASE STUDY IN THE CENTRAL AREA OF MIE PREFECTURE

Haruo Sakurai

Modern life for the Japanese people started with the Meiji Restoration in 1868. From this time on we can see the radical changes caused by the contact with foreign cultures. The new Meiji government developed a comprehensive policy for the religious life of the Japanese people. The most important religious policy was to make Shinto the sole spiritual center of the state by separating Shinto from other religions. In general the movements known as Sect Shinto (Kyoha Shinto) were also treated as religious organizations, such as Buddhism and Christianity. Therefore the new government had carried out many elaborate policies for Shinto Shrines, which were the local foundation of Shinto.

Shinto Shrines were traditionally divided into two groups. One group was the Shinto Shrines which had special connection with the state and the other group was the Shinto Shrines which had close connection with the rural communities surrounding them. The new Meiji government made an effort to have a close combination with Shinto Shrines. As the first stage of this effort the government ordered that local administrative officials should carry out research on the name of Kami (deities) which were enshrined, the history of the Shrines, the dimensions of Shrine buildings and Shrine area, and so forth, and should register all Shinto Shrines in the country. The government used these materials to strengthen its administration of Shinto Shrines. As part of this administration the government determined the Shrine rank (Shakaku) for each Shrine, which signified its relative position among Shinto Shrines. Shrine ranks for individual Shrines were specified in the period from 1868 to 1872.

The complete system of ranks was separated into eleven ranks, but they were divided into two big groups: the higher ranking group was Central Government Shrines called "Kansha;" the lower ranking group was Shrines below Prefectural rank called "Minsha." And the Minsha rank was broken down into the following four ranks by regional criteria: Prefectural Shrines (Fuken-sha), District Shrines (Go-sha), Village Shrines (Son-sha), and Ungraded Shrines (Mukaku-sha). Out of all these shrines, the ones with Village Shrine rank are very closely related to rural communities. From the early Meiji period the government presented ceremonial offerings to Kansha shrines and from 1882 also to Prefectural Shrines. But there were no such offerings to District Shrines, Village Shrines, and Ungraded Shrines.

Therefore many people who favored the enhancement of Shinto and Shinto priests requested that the government also present ceremonial offerings to District and Village Shrines at the annual festivals of those Shrines. The rationale of this proposal was that by this offering the government would concretely express its intention to make Shinto the sole spiritual center of the state. In accepting this proposal, in 1907 the government agreed that local governors should present ceremonial offerings to District and Village Shrines. Before this agreement the government officers began to decrease the number of these Shrines, mainly Village Shrines.

This movement of decreasing the number of Shrines was called the policy of Shrine Mergers (Jinja-gappei). One of the most important reasons for Shrine Mergers was that the government officers (the Bureau of Shinto in the Department of Home Affairs) thought that each rural Shinto Shrine had to be merged in order to unite the spirit of people in local communities.

After the Russo-Japanese War (1904-1906), the financial condition of local communities became worse. The local bureau of the Department of Home Affairs felt the need of economic reconstruction in each local community. At that time there was a campaign of local reform in line with the purpose of the 1908 "Boshin" Rescript. The intention of the campaign was to emphasize the necessity of the unity of the spirit of people for the development of industry in the local area. The Bureau of Shinto joined in this campaign.

This movement of Shrine Mergers was implemented throughout Japan. For this purpose the central movement used as its model case Mie Prefecture, the site of the Grand Shrine of Ise, the highest ranking of all Shinto Shrines.

This Shrine Merger movement was developed mainly from 1906 to 1910. The chart, (Table 1, pp.239), shows the number of Shinto Shrines in Mie Prefecture.

Although there were no direct governmental commands for Shrine Mergers, nevertheless many people felt that to merge Shinto Shrines actually was the will of the state or the Rescript of the Emperor. A general method of Shrine Mergers was to enshrine the "kami" from "A" Shrine to "B" Shrine and then to destroy the buildings and the grounds of the "A" Shrine. And the parishioners ("Ujiko") of "A" Shrine were regarded as the new parishioners of "B" Shrine. "B" Shrine was generally called the Central Shrine of the Shrine Merger. Usually this movement of Shrine Mergers was directed at several Shrines, sometimes as many as a dozen.

This program of Shrine Mergers was a great shock to the people. And many people, especially the parishioners of merged Shrines, were displeased with such control over their religous life, but they had to obey this Merger. Then in 1930 and 1936, after the peak period (1906-1910) of Shrine Mergers, there were two interesting announcements by the Mie Prefectural Office. These two announcements are almost the same in content, to the effect that the people who lost their Shrine through the Shrine Merger program should never reestablish new Shrines or provide the area for such new Shrines. By these announcements we can understand that many people were displeased with the Shrine

Merger and made an effort to reestablish former Shinto Shrines which had been merged into other Shrines.

The movement for the reestablishment of Shrines is called Jinja-Fukushi (Shrine Reestablishment). After World War II (1945), when the close connection between Shinto and the state was abolished by G.H.Q., this movement of Shrine Reestablishment was actively carried out and many new Shrines were created. The administration of Shinto Shrines by the state was changed and many Shinto Shrines were under the jurisdiction of the law of Religious Juridical Persons (Shukyo-hojin-ho), the same as were Buddhist Temples and Christian Churches.

I was very interested in this phenomenon of Shrine Reestablishment, so in 1970 I distributed a questionnaire about this movement throughout Mie Prefecture. I sent the questionnaire to 374 chief priests of Shinto Shrines located in Mie Prefecture. My questionnaire included the following four points:

1. How many Village Shrines were merged into your Shrine?
2. Have the Shrines which were merged into your Shrine separated from your Shrine or not?
3. If the Shrines were separated, when was it done?
4. What kind of relationship is there now between your Shrine and the separated Shrines?

I received answers from 189 chief priests for a return rate of 54.5%. The results are as follows:

1. The number of Merged Village Shrines was 766 and the number of separated Shrines was 217.
2. The period of separation:
    a. before 1945   27 Shrines
    b. 1946-1954   124 Shrines
    c. 1955-1964   39 Shrines
    d. 1965-1970   9 Shrines
    e. unknown   18 Shrines

3. The relationship between the Central Shrine and the reestablished Shrines:
   a. continue   88 Shrines
   b. no relationship 104 Shrines
   c. no answer   25 Shrines

From these results two important facts emerge. One is that after World War II, from 1946 to 1954, many Shrines were reestablished, although there were many radical changes in the policy and society of Japan. This means that the strong desire of people to separate their "Kami" from the Central Shrine of Shrine Mergers appeared in the period of Shrine Reestablishment at the time of social changes and religious freedom which occurred at the end of World War II. We must pay attention to this behavior, i.e. the method of reestablishing former Shinto Shrines.

The other important thing is that the number of Shrines which have no relationship with the Central Shrine is more than the number of Shrines which have some relationship with it. This result shows us that one of the most important purposes of Shrine Mergers, i.e. to unite the spirit of the people by Shrine Mergers, had not been completely achieved. Even in the case of affirmative answers for continuing relationship (3.a), there are some problems. For example, Shinto priests answered that the relationship between the Central Shrine and Reestablished Shrines continues now; but in interviews I found out that the parishioners of Reestablished Shrines did not really revere the Central Shrine. I think there is a significant difference between the attitude of Shinto priests and that of the parishioners of Reestablished Shrines.

Now let me describe a typical case of Shrine Reestablishment. The area of this research is seven villages which are located in the central part of Mie Prefecture, and the periods are 1979 and 1980. The names of these seven villages are Hoda, Yokochi, Iseba, Inagi, Meta, Hayamaze, and Takagi. These villages belonged to two feudal clans in the Edo period (1600-1867): toba feudal clan (Hoda, Yokochi, Iseba, and Inagi) and Tsu feudal clan (Meta, Hayamaze, and Takagi). In 1871 after the Meiji

Restoration, the administration of feudal clans was reformed and seven villages were affiliated to Watarai Prefecture, which was one of the former names of Mie Prefecture. In 1889 these were organized into one large village called Koishiro Village. (There are two meanings for the word "village." So I use "Mura [natural village]" when I indicate the seven small communities and only for Koishiro do I use "village.")

The Shrine Merger in Koishiro Village was carried out through the following process. In 1907 the prefectural governor of Mie Prefecture decided to present the prefectural ceremonial offering to Hoda-Shrine in Hoda-mura, and Hoda-Shrine was regarded as the Central Shrine of this Shrine Merger. And every Shrine in Koishiro Village was merged into Hoda-Shrine in 1908. The name of Hoda-Shrine was changed to Koishiro-Shrine and all Shrines in Koishiro Village were destroyed. The chart, (Table 2, pp.239), shows the names of the seven "Mura" and Village Shrines, and the number of their parish families.

The reasons why Hoda-Shrine was regarded as the Central Shrine are as follows:
1. The buildings and the ground of Hoda-Shrine were the most complete, compared with other Shrines.
2. Hoda-mura was the most powerful, economically and politically, in Koishiro Village.
3. Hoda-mura had the advantage in water for irrigation of rice. Because the main industry of Koishiro Village was agriculture, much water was needed to grow rice. These seven villages got water from two rivers, and Hoda-mura was located at the upper part of these rivers and occupied the closest position to the water gate.

For all these reasons the leaders of the Shrine Merger thought that this merger would be successful, and they hoped that all villagers would be eager to attend the festivals of Koishiro-Shrine. Instead, except for the inhabitants of Hoda-mura, many villagers declined to visit Koishiro-Shrine. In interviews I conducted some old people said that they felt loneliness (samishisa) or emptiness (munashisa) because they had lost their own Shrine. Although people formally agreed to merge their Village Shrine, in their hearts they had been resisting such control of their religious lives.

After the Shrine Merger in Koishiro Village, the inhabitants of these villages, except Hoda-mura, made an effort to maintain the grounds of each of their Village Shrines. Such a place is called "Yohai-jo" - the place to worship a Shrine from afar. Though the government never permitted them to maintain such places they continued their own village festivals there. So at the time of festivals of the Koishiro-Shrine, the inhabitants of six small "Mura", except Hoda-mura, never visited there and only a few people attended the festivals.

After World War II each of the six "Mura" reestablished their respective Shrines: Yokochi-Shrine in Yokochimura, Iseba-Shrine in Iseba-mura, Inagi-Shrine in Inagimura, Ukehi-Kumano-Shrine in Meta-mura, Hayamaze-Shrine in Hayamaze-mura, and Kogaki-Shrine in Takagi-mura. These new Shrines were established at the place of "Yohai-jo," except Inagi-mura and Hayamaze-mura. These two "Mura" obtained other sites, because they lost the former grounds of their Village Shrines a few years after the Shrine Merger. And the "Kami" for the Village Shrines were separated from Koishiro-Shrine and re-enshrined at each new Shrine in 1953. At the time of Shrine Reestablishment, the name of Koishiro-Shrine was changed to the former name of Hoda-Shrine by the inhabitants of Hoda-mura. So now there is no relationship between Hoda-Shrine and the other six Shrines. There is no Shinto priest in the six Shrines: only Hoda-Shrine has one Shinto priest, who performs the rituals of the six Shrines whenever he is asked. Usually the parishioner in charge of the Shrine prepares for and performs the ritual for the respective Shrine in the six "Mura."

In interviews most people said that they wished to have their own Shrine and to take care of their Shine by themselves. This is the most obvious reason why they separated their Shrine from the Central Shrine. And the success of Shrine Reestablishment is demonstrated by the fact that the inhabitants of the six "Mura" have maintained the areas for their new Shrines.

From this research I can appreciate the close connection between the local inhabitants and their Shrines. That is, the local shrine actually defines the local community and in turn the Shrine is the symbol of the rural community. For these people, official government policies (such as Shrine Mergers) were not so important as their perception of the sacredness of their local Shrine site. The nature of local Shrines, of course, is related to the structure of the traditional Japanese community, but this is a subject that goes beyond the present paper.

(Table 1) The number of Shinto Shrines and Village Shrines in Mie Prefecture

Period	The Total number of Shinto Shrines	The number of Village Shrines
1903	10524	1699
1904	10473	1694
1905	10413	1692
1906	9851	1676
1907	5908	1435
1908	2048	803
1909	1630	708
1910	1415	659
1911	1272	629
1912	1198	617
1913	1165	613

(Table 2) The names of seven "mura" and Village Shrines, and the number of their parish families

The names of seven mura	Village Shrine name	Parish families
Hoda	Hoda-Shrine	118
Yokochi	Yokochi-Shrine	61
Iseba	Iseba-Shrine	54
Inagi	Kaze-Shrine, Ishii-Shrine, Inagi-Shrine	125
Meta	Ukehi-Shrine	27
Hayamaze	Ukehi-Shrine	57
Takagi	Kogaki-Shrine	74

SYMPOSIUM CANADA-CHINE,
dans le cadre du 14e Congrès de l'I.A.H.R.

Condensé par Jacques Langlais

Pour la première fois depuis l'avènement de la République Populaire de Chine, trois membres de l'Institut de Recherche sur les Religions Mondiales, à l'Université de Pékin, ont partagé les résultats de leurs travaux avec des collègues occidentaux. Leur participation au 14e Congrès de l'I.A.H.R. a été rendue possible en grande partie grâce à l'initiative du Dr. Jan Yun-hua, de l'Université McMaster (Hamilton, Ontario). Voici un résumé de leurs communications.

"Contribution de Chen Yuan à l'étude de
l'histoire des religions"

Gao Wangzhi

Chen Yuan ou Chen Yuan-an (1880-1971) compte parmi les grands historiens de la Chine moderne. Il a consacré près de 60 ans de sa vie à la recherche historique. Professeur, dès les années 30, à l'Université de Pékin et dans d'autres universités, il a dirigé la Bibliothèque Métropolitaine (aujourd'hui Bibliothèque de Pékin) ainsi que la Bibliothèque du Musée du Palais. Membre de l'Académie Centrale, il a été président de l'Université Catholique de Pékin (1926-1952) et de l'Université Normale de Pékin (1952-1971).

Une grande partie de ses travaux porte sur l'histoire des religions de la Chine et notamment sur le christianisme. Son ouvrage, *Survol historique de la diffusion du christianisme en Chine* (1924), est une contribution unique à l'histoire du christianisme chinois. Il s'est intéressé particulièrement à la période nestorienne, à partir de 635, et à celle des Jésuites (Ricci, Schall et leurs compagnons). Il compléta son oeuvre par d'importantes monographies comme *Les catholiques de la famille impériale sous les règnes de Yongzheng et de Quianlung* (1932).

En ce qui concerne le bouddhisme chinois, son apport le plus marquant est une série d'ouvrages de références, en particulier son *Introduction à la bibliographie de l'histoire du bouddhisme chinois* (1942) et ses *Chroniques sur les bouddhistes* (1934). Le premier classe 35 ouvrages bouddhiques parus depuis le 3e siècle en diverses catégories (bibliographies, biographies, apologétique, lexicographie, etc.). Le second tente de préciser les dates de naissance et de décès de plus de 2,800 moines qui vécurent depuis le 3e siècle jusqu'au début des Qing. Il faudrait mentionner aussi de nombreuses monographies comme sa *Postface à la biographie de Ci En (ou Xuan Zhuang) publiée par le Collège Bouddhique* (1924) ou des traités comme *Pourquoi le bouddhisme a pu se répandre en Chine?* (1932).

Chen Yuan s'est également intéressé au taoïsme. De 1923 à 1924, il a colligé plus de 1000 épigraphes taoïstes de la période s'étendant des Han jusqu'aux Ming. Il les a réunies dans une collection de 100 volumes intitulé *Recueil d'épitaphes taoïstes*, maintenant en voie de publication à Pékin. Cette oeuvre est destinée à rendre de grands services aux chercheurs chinois et étrangers. Ici encore, Chen Yuan a publié des monographies comme *Le néo-taoïsme au nord du Fleuve Jaune sous les Song du Sud* (1941) et des traités comme *Les sympathies divergentes de Yelü Chucai et de son fils* (1929). Dans ce dernier ouvrage, il montre comment le père, un favori de Genghis Khan, préférait le bouddhisme au taoïsme, alors que le fils, un temps premier ministre à la cour mongole, inclinait vers le taoïsme, fait significatif du point-de-vue des rapports entre les deux religions.

Avec sa *Brève histoire de la diffusion de l'islam en Chine* (1928), Chen Yuan a fait oeuvre de pionnier dans l'histoire de l'islam chinois. Il y a retracé entre autres les premiers rapports officiels sino-arabes dès 651, ainsi que le récit de voyage de Du Huan, qui séjourna chez les Arabes au milieu de 8e siècle. Il faut mentionner également une oeuvre maîtresse publiée dans les années 20: *L'assimilation chinoise des autochtones du Xiyu sous la Dynastie Yuan*.

De côté du judaïsme, Chen Yuan s'est révélé, là encore, un pionnier avec la publication à Kaifeng, en 1920, d'un important traité intitulé *Yi Ci Le Yi*. *Yi Ci Le Yi* est la translittération chinoise d'Israël. L'épigraphe de la synagogue de Kaifeng (1486) est le plus ancien monument littéraire du judaïsme chinois. Ce document fait remonter la fondation de la synagogue à 1163.

Enfin on doit à Chen Yuan deux traités sur l'histoire des zoroastriens et des manichéens en Chine. Les premiers arrivèrent en Chine entre 516 et 519 et ils se multiplièrent avec l'occupation par les Arabes de l'Asie Centrale. Mais leurs présence en Chine aura été relativement brève si l'on songe que depuis les Song de Sud, il ne subsiste aucune trace d'eux dans la littérature historique chinoise. Il en est autrement des seconds. Arrivés en 694, les manichéens se répandront le long du Fleuve Jaune parmi les Uighurs, jusqu'à la défaite de ceux-ci par les Kirghis en 841. Ils entreront alors dans leur déclin et survivront, après les Song, comme religion secrète. Fait à signaler, Chen Yuan n'a pas eu connaissance des travaux sur le manichéisme que Pelliot et Chavannes publièrent conjointement dans le *Journal Asiatique*, en 1911 et 1913. De part et d'autre, ils arrivèrent cependant aux mêmes conclusions. Et quand Pelliot écrivit en 1923 son petit article sur les reliques manichéennes du Fujian, il emprunta à Chen Yuan une citation du *Livre sur le Fujian* de He Qiao-yuan qu'il avait cherché en vain à se procurer.

Après tout, la poursuite de la vérité scientifique impose aux chercheurs chinois et étrangers l'échange et la coopération et, de ce point de vue, le progrès des relations amicales entre la Chine et le Canada autorise, chez les historiens de la religion, les plus grands espoirs.

II

"La recherche des 30 dernières années
sur l'histoire des religions chinoise"

Lin Ying

En matière de recherche socio-historique, la grande tendance des 30 dernières années, chez les universitaires chinois, a été l'approche marxiste. La religion, en tant que phénomène social, est la produit des conditions sociales. Dans la Chine féodale, le bouddhisme, le taoïsme et le confucianisme se sont opposés et influencés mutuellement et ils ont constitué l'idéologie dominante de la société chinoise.

En ce qui concerne l'idéologie bouddhique, la première décennie de la République Populaire de Chine a connu le début des recherches de type marxiste dans ce domaine. Deux titres dominent cette période: l'*Histoire générale de l'idéologie chinoise* en 5 volumes de Hou Wai-lu (édition revue et corrigée de 1957) et une *Collection des ouvrages sur l'idéologie bouddhique depuis les Han jusqu'aux Tang* (1963).

D'autres travaux importants sont parus dans cette période, entre autres l'*Histoire générale de la Chine* de Fan Wen-lan, qui traite de la propagation du bouddhisme parmi les diverses nationalités de la Chine, ainsi que de son influence sur l'art et la culture depuis le 1er siècle jusqu'au 8e. Il faut signaler également *Les contacts antiques avec les régions occidentales et le pèlerinage de Fa Xian en Inde*, de He Chang-qun, de même que la contribution, en 1955, de l'Association Bouddhique Chinoise à l'Encyclopédie bouddhique dont le premier tome est paru en langue anglaise, cette année, au Sri Lanka.

Malgré le malheureux hiatus de la recherche universitaire, de 1966 à 1976, des progrès ont été réalisés ces dernières années, grâce en particulier aux travaux de Ren Jiyu qui paraîtront d'ici cinq ans en 8 volumes. Ils constituent la première histoire générale du bouddhisme chinois à paraître depuis l'avènement de la République Populaire.

Comme pour le bouddhisme, les historiens du taoïsme religieux - qu'ils tiennent à dissocier du taoïsme philosophique - se sont intéressés surtout à ses aspects idéologiques. Mais le taoïsme a joué de ce point de vue un rôle moins significatif que le bouddhisme, étant moins systématique et plus hétérogène que lui.

L'*Histoire générale de l'idéologie chinoise* d'Hou Wai-lu, citée plus haut, est le premier ouvrage à donner une vue d'ensemble de l'évolution du taoïsme d'avant le 13e siècle. Il faut également citer la monographie de Yang Xiang-kui, *Etudes sur la société et l'idéologie de la Chine antique*, qui retrace les origines du taoïsme et en identifie la source au mélange des superstitions populaires avec le confucianisme de tendance religieuse de l'école Jin Wen.

Un thème qui a vivement préoccupé les historiens chinois d'avant 1966 a été celui de la relation entre la religion taoïste et les guerres de paysans, à la fin des Han Postérieurs. On doit à Wang Ming l'édition critique du *Tai Ping Jin He Jiao* (1960) dont 57 des 170 volumes originaux nous sont parvenus. En plus de faciliter la recherches sur les guerres de paysans, la publication de cette collection a contribué à l'étude de l'histoire du taoïsme ancien. En outre, des collègues de la section "confucianisme et taoïsme", à l'institut de recherche sur les religions du monde à Pékin, préparent depuis deux ans une *Bibliographie du Dao Zang avec index* dans le but de faciliter aux chercheurs l'accès à cette énorme collection de textes taoïstes. L'un d'eux doit rencontrer à Paris, en septembre prochain, l'équipe du Professeur K. Shipper qui travaille également sur le Dao Zang.

Un problème qui a également préoccupé les historiens chinois est celui de savoir si le confucianisme est une religion. Traditionnellement, le confucianisme, en Chine, a été étudié avec le bouddhisme et le taoïsme. D'après Ren Jiyu, dont le traité s'intitule *Formation du confucianisme en tant que religion*, le confucianisme s'est transformé en une véritable religion à partir des Song. D'autres chercheurs ne voient dans le confucianisme qu'une école philosophique.

Il faudrait mentionner en terminant l'absence de données concernant les travaux de nos collègues de Taiwan. Elle est due à l'isolement d'une époque révolue. Nous espérons que dans le proche avenir, la situation sera corrigée.

III

"Le Coran en Chine"
Jin Yi Jiu

Dans son *Survol historique de la diffusion de l'islam en Chine*, Chen Yuan date les débuts de la propagation de l'islam en Chine depuis le contact établi, par le troisième calife Uthmân avec la cour des Tang (651). C'était à l'époque où les marchands perses et arabes se rendaient en Chine par mer ou par terre, à Chang-an (aujourd'hui Xian) ou dans les villes côtières comme Guangzhou (Canton).

Jusqu'à l'époque des Song, les lettrés chinois connaissaient mal l'islam et l'interprétataient d'un point de vue bouddhique. Ainsi Zheng suo-nan dans le *Xin Shi (Le répertoire du coeur)* affirme que "les Hui-hui vénèrent le Bouddha et ont construit une haute tour d'où ils appellent continuellement la Bouddha à haute voix".

A partir du 13e siècle, une forte vague d'immigrants musulmans, persans, arabes et de l'Asie Centrale, se mêlèrent aux populations nan, uighur et mongoles pour former une nouvelle nationalité, les Hui. Mais pendant de longs siècles, le Coran ne sera pas identifié comme tel et continuera d'être recensé parmi les écritures bouddhiques. Ce n'est que sous les Ching que le nom de Coran sera translittéré de diverses façons, dont celle qui a prévalu chez les lettrés musulmans: "Gu-ran".

Ces faits révèlent l'ignorance de l'islam chez l'intelligentsia chinoise de temps, ignorance attribuable surtout au fait que l'islam s'est répandu parmi les marchands étrangers et le peuple Hui, et qu'il ne disposait d'aucune organisation missionnaire. La transmission de la tradition musulmane s'est faite d'abord oralement. Il faut attendre au 16e siècle, avec Hu Pu-zhao (1522-1597), pour voir l'établissement d'une système d'éducation monastique pour les Akhunds. Les étudiants devaient copier le Coran de leur main, de sorte qu'il se développa divers styles calligraphiques. La première édition imprimée du Coran en Chine date de 1862.

Quant aux traductions, elles viendront tardivement et d'abord sous la forme de passages intégrés aux écrits des lettrés, tels Wang Dai-yu (1570?-1660) et Ma Zhu (1640-1711). Avec la dernière moitié du 18e siècle s'ouvre la période des extraits que l'on transpose en caractères chinois pour permettre aux musulmans de réciter le Coran sans l'assistance d'un maître. C'est le cas, par exemple, du *Han Zi He Ting (Sélections du Coran translitérées en caractère chinois)* paru en 1882

Ce n'est qu'au 20e siècle, à partir des années 20, qu'apparaissent les traductions complètes du Coran, telle le *Ke Lan Jing*, Le Coran (1927) de Li Tie Zheng, d'après la traduction japonaise de Kamoto Ken'ichi et la traduction anglaise de Rodwell. Une autre traduction, cette fois l'oeuvre d'un musulman, Akhund Wang Wen-qing ou Wang Jingzhai, parut à Pékin en 1932 sous le titre de *Gu Lan Jing Yi Jie, Traduction du Coran avec commentaire*. Comme pour les autres traductions musulmanes de cette période, la langue en est assez difficile et souvent obscure.

Enfin, on doit à l'islamologue bien connu Ma Jian, de l'Université de Pékin, la traduction du Coran à partir du texte arabe. Déjà huit volumes sont parus en 1952 et la Maison d'édition des Sciences sociales chinoises la publiera prochainement au complet.

Avec ces traductions a débuté en Chine la recherche sur le Coran, ainsi que l'enseignement, dans certains collèges, de la pensée coranique.

THREE RELIGIOUS ONTOLOGICAL CLAIMS: "BEING-ITSELF," "NOTHINGNESS WITHIN SOMETHINGNESS," AND "THE FIELD OF EMPTINESS"

Frederick J. Streng

A common religious claim is that human beings must know and actualize "the nature of things" if they are to live authentically. For people to live out their fullest potential they need to awaken to the deepest reality in existence. This call to perceive the most comprehensive reality of life has two interrelated aspects: that the notion of reality is intended to account for *all* existence, and that the grasp of the nature of reality is used as a criterion for determining the difference between a lesser and greater *quality* of "being in the world." Thus, while an understanding of the nature of things applies to all existence, it also expresses the claim that some moments and forms of existence are better or more authentic, than - not just different from - others.

By focussing on these aspects of religious ontologies, we are calling attention to the existential character of such ontological formulations. Ontological claims, then, are not just obscure abstractions, but forces in the selection of "better" or "worse"; such perceptual forces are constituents in the formation of self-awareness. By accenting the dynamic character of ontological claims in a religious context we are led to raise questions about the relation of the ontological terms to the creation of a mental world in which there is not only a selection of what *is* seen, but what *can be* seen.

We will examine key positive and negative ontological terms in the writings of three contemporary religious philosophers: Paul Tillich, a Christian; Chün-i T'ang, a

Confucian; and Keiji Nishitani, a Buddhist. They are twentieth-century thinkers who are well-read in scientific thought, aware of the modern malaise of human self-alienation, and recognize that they live in a religiously plural world. They are sensitive to the limitations in the formulations given in their respective religious traditions, but wish to expose the vitality and insight of "true spirituality" as they have reformulated "the best" from their religious and cultural backgrounds. What is most crucial for this analysis, however, is that they attempt to provide an understanding of the inner nature of existence in light of the general human situation; then, they give their prescription for authentic living in the context of cross-cultural human experience.

Nevertheless, each philosopher expresses the "true nature of things" differently, and gives a different prescription for living authentically. Tillich asserts that all existence depends on unconditional "being-itself," and that the anxiety produced by the dialectical nature of non-being and being in existence is overcome by *individual acts of creating meaning*. Chün-i T'ang holds that the very nature of existence is a harmonious rhythm of "nothingness within somethingness," and that conflict can be creatively reformed when people fulfil their true humanity by establishing *their appropriate position within the cosmic process*. Keiji Nishitani states that the deepest reality that human beings can know is "the field of emptiness," and the solution to self-destroying delusions is to *transform the quality of one's consciousness*.

In comparing the use of different positive and negative terms in the three ontologies, we suggest that these are not only interestingly different formulations of ultimate reality, but that each of these formulations correlates with a particular "manner" or "way" of achieving authentic living. The three approaches represent different ways in which these philosophers have integrated the actual positive and negative impact of common human experience. That is, most people affirm that there is both continuity and change in the world. The world is directly perceived as "being there" while *at the same time* nothing particular seems to last - whether it is a concrete thing, emotion, or idea. This is complicated by the fact that the experience of the human presence in the world is determined by *giving* more value to one thing rather than to another. Thus, reflective human beings have often recognized that *what* is seen as *real* is connected to the *act of giving value*. We hope to show that these three spokespersons in describing different ontologies give weight to different aspects of the human experience: Tillich gives greatest weight to creative meaning, T'ang to social harmony, and Nishitani to the quality of consciousness.

1. Being-Itself

Paul Tillich, in his *Systematic Theology*, states that "being-itself" is the ground of all existence, and that finitude is the expression of the interaction between nonbeing and being. He asserts:

> The power of infinite self-transcendence is an expression of man belonging to that which is beyond nonbeing, namely, to being-itself....
> The dialectical problem of nonbeing is inescapable. It is the problem of finitude. Finitude unites being with dialectical nonbeing. Man's finitude, or creatureliness, is unintelligible without the concept of dialectical nonbeing.[1]

Here we see that the dialectical relationship between nonbeing and being is inescapable for anyone or anything in existence. Tillich points out that within Christian understanding there are two ways that nonbeing is related to being. First, nonbeing is expressed through the notion of the Greek phrase *ouk on*. This is the recognition that humanity is created out of nothing and must return to nothing. He points out: "The *nihil* out of which God creates is *ouk on*, the undialectical negation of being."[2] This leads human beings to a sense of radical negation, a sense of "being not."

The other understanding of nonbeing that was integrated into Christian theology, according to Tillich, is one that is called "the dialectical form of nonbeing" in

relation to being. This is expressed in the Greek phrase
mē on.[3] The dialectical form of nonbeing is experienced
existentially in the anxiety about the transience of life.
For Tillich, *this anxiety is rooted in the very structure
of being-in-the-world;* it is not a distortion of this
structure.[4] The direct experience of nonbeing is the
anxiety that every person has in having to die; it is an
automatic direct experience that every person has of the
dialectical relationship between nonbeing and being.

The experience of nonbeing, according to this
position, is entirely dependent on being for any
ontological value. Unlike the subsequent examples that we
are going to consider, Tillich insists that "nonbeing is
literally nothing except in relation to being."[5] Even in
the direct experience of human finitude people must look at
themselves and experience nonbeing from the viewpoint of "a
potential infinity."[6] The power of being as being-itself
cannot have a beginning or an end; it is simply the basic
presupposition for anything to be. This power of being as
experienced in the individual is the power of infinite
self-transcendence. We should note, however, that infinity
is not being-itself; because being-itself lies beyond "the
polarity of finitude and self-transcendence."[7] The power
of infinite self-transcendence as it is related to being-
itself is a very important notion in that one's reality is
manifested by an *activity of self-transcendence*. The
infinite self-transcendence is a negation of the finitude
experienced in life. Thus, while being-itself precedes
both finitude and the infinite self-transcendence, infinite
self-transcendence is the expression of being-itself within
finitude.

While Tillich holds that in finitude "being is
essentially related to nonbeing,"[8] being-itself is not
essentially related to nonbeing. (In contrast, as we will
note below, T'ang's position is that "nothingness" is
inherent in "somethingness" as a principle of change, and
Nishitani says that "being" becomes possible only within "a
field of emptiness.") In a view asserting that
being-itself is ultimate reality, a relation between being

and nonbeing leads to disruption and chaos. Being-itself is the primal *a priori*. Continuity in life is therefore credited to the presence of "being," and any change is understood to be real where it is identified substantially as a causal force that arises from the being of something or "what is" from one moment to another. That which remains the same from one moment to the next is what "is." The "courage to be" is a human act of finite self-transcendence through dependence on being-itself manifested in the infinite drive to seek self-transcendence.

For Tillich human existence is that sort of reality whose fulfillment is in or through *meaning*; to be human means that a person tries to unify all the elements of one's consciousness, both the ideal or theoretical aspects and the material or practical aspects of one's experience. Reality is not exterior to the act of the human spirit that seeks to either receive or bestow a unifying awareness to all facets of life. He makes clear that meaning is the core of conscious existence when he says:

Meaning is the common characteristic of the ultimate unity of the theoretical and the practical sphere of spirit, of scientific and aesthetic, of legal and social structures. The spiritual reality in which the spirit-bearing form (*Gestalt*) lives and creates, is a meaning-reality [*Sinnwirklichkeit*].⁹

There are three elements in every expression of meaning: (1) an awareness of the interconnection of the separate aspects of meaning, (2) the awareness that every particular meaning is related to an unconditioned and ultimate meaningfulness, and (3) that while there is no complete unity of meaning in any existing (and, thus, conditioned) meaning there is "the demand to fulfill the unconditioned meaning."[10] Here is the justification for Tillich's claim that every cultural form has as its basis an ontological character; any cultural form can be a medium for the spirit-bearing forces. However, not all cultural expression has an intention to express the unconditioned meaning; in fact, there are demonic expressions when the unconditional meaning is denied. Nevertheless, it is the *demand* for the attempt to present the unity of all meaning that makes the unconditional meaning actual in form.¹¹

The consciousness of meaning, then, is the place where *spirit takes form*. It is an act of ego-consciousness whereby human beings manifest infinite self-transcendence; it expresses the ontological negation of nonbeing. This makes the highest value in human life an act which depends on being itself, and which at the same time is a positive action within finite existence. The role of the personality in exposing both the partially unified cultural meaning and the unconditional ground for all meaning is made clear when Tillich states:

> The real meaning-fulfillment is one in which bestowal of meaning takes place in the sphere of individual reality bound to nature; an ideal fulfillment is one in which the giving of meaning involves no transformation in the material sphere, but rather a fulfillment of the existent thing in its immediate formation.... Personality is the place of meaning-fulfillment, both real and ideal.¹²

Thus, for Tillich, authentic existence is the concrete creation of meaning by an individual who thereby partially transcends the anxiety of nonbeing, and manifests the infinite demand to create a unifying awareness of life.

2. <u>Nothingness within Somethingness</u>

In contrast to Tillich's affirmation of the unconditional being-itself, the Neo-Confucian philosopher Chün-i T'ang stresses that Chinese cosmologies affirm an immanent order of change that involves "nothingness within somethingness." Change, in the Chinese world view, is not a finite order of reality that depends on being-itself. Rather the essence of things, in T'ang's words, "is exhibited in the capacity for adaptation and creation through interaction with the changing environment."¹³ He argues that instead of conceiving the essence of an object as a permanent energy, the dominant Chinese view is that "the nature of an object lies in its capacity [the Chinese original implies the meaning of tolerance - translator] for interaction with other objects."¹⁴ The process of change cannot be avoided, as in some assumed eternal world or abstract infinity; the only options are a harmonious or disharmonious change. The latter is inappropriate change, such as growth taking place where dissolution should prevail, e.g., a cancerous growth. The immanent natural order has an observable regularity. This regularity is not a predetermined force from the outside. Rather, it is a spontaneous and natural development, an inner tendency that brings about abundance and renewal.[15]

According to T'ang the principle of regularity is also a principle of freedom. This is because the life principle (i.e., the Tao) which makes any event possible does not determine the form of a specific event. Since the appearance of concrete objects or events arises through interaction with other objects, its nature is one of (regulated) freedom to interrelate with other things. The life force is not an external divine fate or unchanging essence, but the capacity to adapt or modify a particular object within a set of relationships. This capacity to change is inherent in both material and moral development. Thus human moral development is intrinsically a part of the nature of things. T'ang emphasizes the creative responsibility of humanity by saying:

[H]eaven endows every man with an ability to free himself from the control of his own mechanical habits and external forces, and thus he is able to create along with the change of his environment. An object or event needs interaction with other objects in order that its freedom in the process of creative evolution can be fully manifested.[12]

The basic ontological concept that places change in the center of the life principle is that there is "nothingness within somethingness." Both "nothingness" and "somethingness" are important aspects of change whereby existence can be seen to have regular change without predetermined control and maintain individual freedom in every occasion of existence without chaos. Every event or entity in existence has in its nature the capacity to "prehend other objects. Its ability to prehend lies in its nothingness [$hsü$]."[17] He elaborates the importance of "nothingness" by commenting:

The prehensive nature of an object is its Yin aspect. The essence of matter is its Yin nature. This Yin or prehensive nature lies in its nothingness, which not only takes external forces as somethingness but also renders them recessed.... The externalization of the power of an object is what we call *shih* [somethingness or substantiveness]. This externalized power depends on the power's being prehended by other objects and thus being dissipated and transformed into nothingness.[18]

The "nothingness" of T'ang's "nothingness within somethingness" is neither the dramatic claim of *ouk on* that is overcome by God's omnipotence, nor that of *mē on* which is an agonizing recognition that what "is" ends in death (what is not) - as described by Tillich. Rather by making something depend on nothing (i.e., dying or dissipation) in the very nature of things - just as much as nothing depends on something - there is a recognition that change is authentic and necessary. In this view anxiety over an individual entity becoming nothing is seen as unnatural, or a misapprehension of the inherent structure of life.

At the same time, the openness for relatedness, or prehension, is not sufficient to account for the manifestation of things. The ability to relate results in the actual formation of a particular thing or event. Thus, it is the interaction of nothingness *and* somethingness in all existing things that exposes the life principle. Because of the prehensive capacity, or nothingness, self-realization and self-fulfillment of something are possible. In describing the importance of the hexagrams in the *I Ching* for symbolizing the interaction of nothingness [*hsü*] and somethingness [*shih*] T'ang states:

The sixty-four hexagrams symbolically characterize that all existences interact with one another through their virtues or power, so that they give rise to new events or objects. The fundamental principle of giving birth to new events or new objects lies in the occasion that the firm matches the receptive and the moving matches the rest, so that there is interprehension between "somethingness" and "nothingness." This is why the concept *chung ho* [comprehensive and dynamic harmony] is an ultimate value.[19]

The immanent interaction of "nothingness" and "somethingness" is at the base also of T'ang's understanding that there is a natural harmony in life; even conflicts lead to harmony. The process of natural development is an extension of any identifiable entity while at the same time the entity is open to interaction. What appears to be a conflict in the short-term view is a development and reintegration in a long term view. He describes the resolution by pointing out that it

> lies in the two interacting objects' conscious expansion of their interactive perspectives through their own exploration of a broader path, so that they can form two broader evolutionary processes and these two processes interact with each other again.... Only because of this, all existence can continue to be born and to grow, and the universe thus can perpetuate its existence.[20]

This understanding of the inner bipolar interaction of prehending "nothingness" and actualization of "somethingness" is quite different from that found in Tillich's understanding of the nature of things as unconditional "being-itself" which is only partially experienced in conditioned existence, where nonbeing is in conflict with being-itself. From T'ang's perspective, the dissolution of entities or events is in the nature of things; to become anxious about it is to be ignorant of the "nothingness" which is one necessary pole of the creative life principle. Inherent in any positive, or firm, aspect of life there is a force that simultaneously pushes toward the negative, or yielding. Similarly the yielding process, or "nothingness," becomes eventually an expression of the firm, or "somethingness."

For Chün-i T'ang the deepest religious realization is not a symbolic grasp of the unconditional object of knowledge, God, as suggested by Tillich, nor the empty mode of consciousness that is totally unattached to any form - as we will see in Nishitani's insight into the nature of things. For T'ang the demand of spiritual knowledge is a self-awareness that arises from humanity's transcendent nature. In true self-awareness a person grasps the highest values rooted in human nature itself. He points to a reality of human life that transcends any formal claims by the major religious traditions, and comments as follows: "The moment in which [man] is engaged in the 'authentic' self-awareness is the moment in which he transcends his own religious spirit, confirming and intuitively apprehending man's spirit of self-confidence which comprehends and is on and above the religious spirit."[21]

The actualization of transcendent knowledge, however, does not mean that one can leave the interaction of concrete form and universal ideals; this knowledge does not eliminate the ordered rhythm of change or transport one to a divine or unconditioned realm. Rather, it leads to a self-confidence in the capacity of human nature which is always extending beyond the fulfillment of any given moment. Confucianism, he insists, shares with all major religions the central demand of religious life: "Man lives to find a sure place to establish himself and his 'fate'."[22] Human beings "establish" themselves within the order of the universe by realizing that their well-being is inseparable from that of all other beings.

By doing an appropriate moral-spiritual action a person expresses the inherent value in the "human-heart." The highest expression of value in the universe is self-confidence arising from the intuitive participation in the rhythm of change. T'ang says:

[T]he final stage of the development of man's religious spirit ends in approaching the spirit of self-confidence.... Since Confucius and Mencius, the Confucianist has emphasized the spirit of self-reflection, self-awareness, and self-confidence. This spirit will become the convergence of all religions in the long run.[23]

This manifestation of the highest human value is not separate from values inherent within all nature. Ultimately, all existence is an expression of value, and every human act which appropriately, ethically and naturally, places a person in the cosmic rhythm is an authentic expression of life.

3. <u>The Field of Emptiness</u>
The last expression of "the nature of things" which we will examine is the affirmation made by Keiji Nishitani, a philosopher speaking out of the background of Zen Buddhism.

He claims that the most comprehensive understanding of "being" in relation to the experience of change and disappearance is found in the standpoint of "emptiness." He summarizes his position by saying, "It is only in a field where the 'being of all things is a being at one with emptiness that it is possible for all things to gather into one, even while each is a reality as an absolutely unique being."[24] This notion of emptiness is not the negative principle (mē on) that calls into question the reality of life, as we saw in Tillich's ontology, nor is it a negative (hsü) pole in the bipolar rhythm of change, as in T'ang's understanding. Rather it is the root, or basic, field in which the affirmative and negative are possible at all. In emphasizing the relativity and temporality of the basic character of "being" he writes:

A system of "being" becomes really possible, not on a field where the system of "being" is seen only as a system of "being," but on the field of emptiness where being is seen in a place where the reality of being is seen as being-nothingness as well as nothingness-being; namely, in a place where the reality of beings, at the same time, takes on a temporary and so far basically "illusory" character; in a place where the mode of being becomes possible whereby things precisely in their true reality are temporary appearance, and precisely as things-in-themselves are phenomena.[25]

At this point we should already note that the "field of emptiness" is not a substantive reality, but much more a state of consciousness which gives a certain quality or character to the arising and dissipation of existence. The emptiness which Nishitani talks about is not a *nihilum (ouk on)*. Rather it is a continual emptying of the self-centered grasp of personality and attachments to things.[26] The interplay between the affirmative and negative aspects in emptiness, however, is perceived only when one realizes that it requires a complete negation of any abstraction of emptiness or being-in-itself. Thus, this is a radical kind of negativity which seeks to plumb the very depths of a notion of emptiness by negating even "emptiness" as a notion. Only by negating the particular forms of one's experience can one get beyond the negation itself to a sense that there is an intrinsic relatedness between all things. One must pass through the nihilism of nihilistic existentialism, which, in simply negating essences, judges life to be absurd. Nishitani claims that once a person passes through the claim of absolute negativity as the opposite to a universal essence (i.e., "being-itself"), then one does not perceive life as absurd when confronted with nonbeing; nor need a person develop his or her ego strength as a superman or wonder woman. Rather, a new "mode of being" (nonattaching to being-itself) takes form as one moves through the depth of nihilism.

The deep realization of the emptiness of everything makes it possible to penetrate the ontological reality of all particular things while at the same time affirming the relative reality of particular things in existence. Emptiness, as understood here, is not the reality of being-itself, nor as a part of the intrinsic rhythm of all change; there is no reality outside the language system that correlates with the notion of emptiness. This is affirmed not because there is nothing whatsoever outside the language system, but because words are seen to be powerful, but inaccurate, constructors of experienced reality. Ontological terms should not be seen primarily as indicators of something outside of the language system in a one-to-one correlation with any concept. Thus, to perceive the nature of emptiness - in distinction to the notion of "emptiness" - is to avoid identifying this term with some presumed substance or principle. As soon as emptiness is taken as a reality either in the subject, or as a reality outside of self, it is no longer the root source for both the subjective and objective experience.

The effort to avoid both an absolute nihilism and the negative pole of a bipolar dialectic process is matched only by the intensity with which Nishitani affirms that one must perceive the relationships between particular things while at the same time maintaining their particularity. He says that from the standpoint of emptiness,

each thing is itself while not being itself, is not itself while being itself; its "being" is unreal in its truth and true in its unreality. This may sound queer at first but, in fact, through such a view, we are enabled for the first time to conceive a "force" by virtue of which all things are gathered and brought into relationship to one another - a "force" which, since ancient times, has been called nature *(physis, natura).*[27]

If one were *not* to assume this intrinsic relatedness through the "ground of emptiness," Nishitani is ready to admit, something would exist "in-itself," namely, when it is separate from everything outside of itself. In everyday conventional subject-object awareness, the identification of something-in-itself is significant because it excludes what is not-itself. This results in a total lack of being able to perceive the nature of anything outside of oneself, and finally ends up in a chaotic awareness. "Only on the field of emptiness," Nishitani continues, "where being is being-nothingness as well as nothingness-being, is it possible that each being is itself in the face of all the other, and thus, at the same time, is not itself to all the others."[28]

The result of perceiving the world from this standpoint is that the *uniqueness* of a thing requires that it is situated as the root *center of all other things.* The relationship that particular unique things have with each other while being essentially interrelated is called "circuminsessional" by Nishitani. When a particular thing recognizes its basic character as "no-self nature" it recognizes that its being is one with emptiness; by letting go of its own "self" it becomes a participant in the center of all other unique particulars. From the standpoint of emptiness, then, a thing "is" in terms of its own "selfhood" when it both is subordinate to all other things and *at the same time* becomes the center for all other things.

Since the field of emptiness is also identified as the field of the "circuminsessional relationship," all things manifest their own reality when they have let go of grasping after some unique essence of themselves and found their own absolute selfhood in complete interrelatedness. The mode of being which is the genuine "suchness" of a thing is that it is inaccessible to identifying it simply with either the subject or the object; rather, something really "is" when it is identical with itself and at the same time with other things. All things in the world, then, are seen to be interrelated. To be interrelated means being both the center and the supportive aspect of, subordinate to, another thing at the same time. The absolute interdependency that one thing has with another for its own unique selfhood is expressed by the term "circuminsessional" in which "all things in their 'being' thus enter into another home-ground, are not themselves and, nevertheless precisely as such (i.e., on the field of emptiness) are themselves to the very end."[29] This web of circuminsessional interpenetration is called by Nishitani a "mode of being"; it is "the thing's in-itself mode of being, its non-objective mode of being as 'middle,' its selfness."[30]

For Nishitani religion is defined as "an existential exposure of the problematical which is contained in the usual mode of self-being."[31] While all of life is transient, and human beings encounter the reality of non-being at each step, it is only in religion that human beings reach a deepening of the perception of their transience so that they see nothingness manifest in their own being. In Zen this awareness is called "coming to oneself." Nishitani explains such a moment of awareness when he writes:

The opening up of the horizon of nothingness out of the ground of our life is the occasion of the radical about-face in our life itself. This turn-about is no other than the transformation from the self-centered (or man-centered) attitude which asks concerning all things, what is their use to us (or to man) to that of asking for what purpose do we ourselves exist.[32]

This awareness must be more than an intellectual comprehension of reality; it has to be a total realization in spirit, soul and body, and is sometimes termed "the Great Doubt." As Tillich spoke of "meaning-reality" - i.e., of the reality of our being known through meaning - and T'ang called for the actualization of one's "human-heart" to make oneself "a 'real' man," so Nishitani says that placing our self in the "horizon of nothingness" is the moment when "reality itself comes to its own realization."[33]

While both T'ang and Nishitani recognize that existence is basically a process of interrelations, rather than materializations of essences, T'ang insists that "somethingness" (substance, materiality) as it appears in naive perception is an essential part of the rhythm of change, while Nishitani holds that in the most profound level of awareness there is only co-dependent arising of changing forms. Nishitani thus rejects the notion that there is anything essentially real external to us; there is only that reality that emerges in relation to certain processes of awareness, some of which include more attachment to external things than others. There is no entity nor principle, such as the "rhythm of change," that maintains itself in an unchanging way. The standpoint of emptiness requires that a person penetrate directly to the precise point of what makes something what it is: the field of emptiness; otherwise it cannot really be known.

The mode of being called "emptiness" is also regarded by Nishitani as a standpoint or perspective. To perceive emptiness requires converting one's consciousness to the place of emptiness, and thereby stopping the ego-identification with the particular forms of things as if they had independent essential being. It is to accept that while one is thinking, perceiving, and feeling, one recognizes the lack of selfhood in oneself and in all other things. To let go of either absolute subjectivity or absolute objectivity is to transcend the conventional standpoint. Therefore, in emptiness nonbeing is not a threat-producing anxiety of an ego-centered consciousness. Nor is it a threat to a person trying to transcend the limitations of a finite self.

In converting to the standpoint of emptiness there is a release from the assumption that the self-transcendence is a particular act or a series of acts to become something - in contrast to the significance of personal action as suggested by Tillich. It is the recognition that one already *is* a particular entity while at the same time transcending that particularity. The shift to a process of knowing designated as the "standpoint of emptiness" is a shift from a mode of constructive consciousness that is fundamentally an "act of designation" - designating, or separating one thing from another - to the negation of substantiation and specification of one thing over against another. This is to know that the true selfness of fire, for example, is non-fire, or that the selfness of a tree is "no tree." What we perceive, then, is that the selfhood of any particular thing is known by its context, and that there is no self-identifying essence that separates it from all other things. The shift to the standpoint of emptiness, then, for Nishitani, is shift in the quality of consciousness whereby both the world that is seen by a person and the perceiving subject arise in mutual dependence without attachment to the form (the actuality) of any given moment.

4. Summary

These different approaches describe authenticity in relation to different modes of experiencing life: through the creation of meaning under the demand of being-itself, by establishment of one's place in the cosmic rhythm of change through moral choice, and through full awareness of the transience and interrelated arising of existence. While in each case these religious philosophers wrestle with the relation of changing (dying) existence to regularity or order that is permanent to some degree, they describe the nature of existence differently and thereby give value to different dimensions of human experience.

The differences of the three approaches can be summarized as follows. Tillich advocates the actualization of authentic living through an individual's creation of meaning. The source for the reality of meaning is the unconditional "being-itself"; it is basic to, but distant from, existence which is defined by the threat of nonbeing. To know the nature of things requires an act of ego-consciousness whereby a person transcends the tension of being and nonbeing through symbols. Symbols give the reality of meaning to life. This sense of reality assumes ideal essences which provide life with value. Therefore, life has a reason and meaning through a categorization of what "is," and through symbolic meaning that partially reflects the unconditional source of all events.

T'ang advocates the actualization of authentic living through establishing one's "self" within the transcendent order of change. This order of change (or life-principle) is expressed as "nothingness within somethingness." It is the basis for any existing form; however, any form has the freedom to manifest its basic character in an individual way. The knowledge of oneself in the other order (rhythm) of change is possible because "human-nature" is essentially transcendent and infinite. Through actualizing human-nature in everyday affairs a person becomes a "true" person, thereby fulfilling one's cosmic moral obligations. The fulfillment of moral obligations are the manifestation of one's nature in relation to the order of change.

Nishitani advocates the actualization of authentic living through developing full awareness of the habitual self-constricting force of conventional ego-consciousness. For him, authentic "being" is becoming fully aware that the "field of emptiness" is the basic nature of all being. The emptiness of all things is directly perceived by dropping attachment to a subject-object dualism. This perception is possible through the Great Doubt. Authentic living, according to Nishitani, does not come about through the activity of ego-consciousness to create meaning, or through an intuitive grasp of the transcendent order of change; rather, it comes from a quality of consciousness known as "no-self" or "empty mind."

Each philosopher's use of positive and negative ontological terms is both a process and mode of valuing which molds the character of an experience of ultimate reality. To reduce any process to that of another distorts the intentionality found in the alternate process. To the extent that we can accurately describe three different processes for defining reality (as expressed in key positive and negative ontological terms), we call into question the assumption that "religion" is only one basic structure of experience. It is an umbrella term covering a complex of different structures of ultimate valorization in human experience.

DIE BEDEUTUNG DER APOKRYPHEN SALOMO-ODEN FÜR DIE
NEUTESTAMENTLICHE WISSENSCHAFT

Michael Lattke

1. <u>Die Oden Salomos als pseudepigraphischer Teil der
sogenannten neutestamentlichen Apokryphen</u>

In dem auch ins Englische übersetzten bedeutenden Sammelwerk "Neutestamentliche Apokryphen in deutscher Übersetzung" von Hennecke/Schneemelcher, das im ersten Band neben der allgemeinen Einleitung vor allem evangelienartige Texte und im zweiten Band neben apostolischen Pseudepigraphen, Apostelakten und den Pseudo-Klementinen apokalyptische Texte bietet, findet sich auch ein "Dichtungen"-Anhang, der ausser dem christianisierten kurzen heidnischen "Naassenerpsalm"[1] die "Oden Salomos" enthält,[2] und zwar in Übersetzung und Bearbeitung durch den berühmten Neutestamentler und Philologen Walter Bauer. (In der von R. Wilson edierten englischen Ausgabe fehlt dieser Anhang seltsamerweise!)

Der Terminus "apokryph" ist ein wissenschaftlich äusserst unscharfer Begriff. Er bedeutet - soviel kann hier gesagt werden - literaturhistorisch und kanongeschichtlich viel mehr als bloss die wörtliche Übersetzung des griechischen Wortes ἀπόκρυφος. In den wenigsten Fällen der alt - und neutestamentlichen Apokryphen handelte es sich um Geheimschriften, die vor der Allgemeinheit und Öffentlichkeit "verborgen" gehalten werden sollten, jedenfalls zur Zeit ihrer Entstehung und auch ihrer Intention nach.

Zunächst ist davon auszugehen, dass in den ersten zwei Jahrhunderten das Christentum - darin ähnlich dem Frühjudentum - in seinen Richtungen, Schattierungen und Entwicklungslinien vielgestaltiger war, als es die spätere Dogmatik und Dekretierung der Kirche wahrhaben wollte, oft im Gegensatz zur Volks- bzw. Gemeindefrömmigkeit (bis ins hohe Mittelalter).[3] Das betrifft auch die literarische und dichterische Produktion der Frühzeit. Glücklicherweise sind ja Kanonsverzeichnisse[4] erhalten und Kirchenvätertestimonien,[5] die nicht nur die verschieden zahlreichen Schriftentitel bezeugen, sondern auch Aufschluss geben über die begrifflichen Etiketten und sogar über die Differenzen der Zuordnung (sc. zu "kanonisch" etc.)

Was hier ferner wichtig ist, ist die häufige Synonymität von κανονιζόμενος und ἐκκλησιαζόμενος d.h. von kanonisch und kirchlich, was natürlich eine gegenseitige Verengung darstellt.

Schliesslich ist festzustellen, dass der dem Kanon entgegengesetzte Begriff der Apokryphen relativ jung ist, dass vielmehr die damit gemeinten Schriften als "ausserkanonisch" oder "umstritten" bezeichnet wurden, als "Schriften, die nicht in der Kirche, wohl aber vor den Katechumenen verlesen werden."[6]

Auf dem Hintergrund solcher vermeintlich "orthodoxen" Abwertung wird hier versucht, die Apokryphen in einem historisch und literaturgeschichtlich "neutralen" Sinn zu sehen und zu verstehen.

Was die Oden Salomos angeht, so sind zwei Vorbemerkungen angebracht. Die erste besteht in der meiner Erfahrung nach nicht überflüssigen Warnung, die 42 *Oden* Salomos nicht zu verwechseln mit den 18 älteren pharisäischen *Psalmen* unter demselben Pseudonym. Die zweite Bemerkung betrifft die Rechtfertigung der Tatsache, dass die Oden seit Entdeckung des fast vollständigen syrischen Kodex Harris, also seit 1909 zu den Apokryphen des *Neuen* Testaments gestellt wurden. Wenn man sich nämlich an die Angaben der Stichometrie des Nikephorus und an die der in ihrer Echtheit bezweifelten Synopsis des Athanasius halten würde, dann gehörten die Oden (mit den Psalmen) Salomos zu den ἀντιλεγόμενα des *Alten* Testaments. Aus den fünf Odenzitaten in der koptischen Pistis Sophia könnte man sogar schliessen, das sie für den gnostischen Verfasser neben den davidischen Psalmen ein Teil des Kanons waren. Womit dies zusammenhängt, kann nur vermutet werden: ihre frühe, später ja auch handschriftlich belegte, gemeinsame

Überlieferung mit den Psalmen Salomos bzw. überhaupt ihr Verfasserpseudonym. Ob dieses Pseudonym von Anfang an schon vom Verfasser oder von den Verfassern oder von dem Sammler bzw. Redaktor als Überschrift gewählt wurde, bleibt wohl für immer im Dunkel der frühchristlichen Geschichte. Vielleicht war ihre Verfasserschaft auch nur anonym. *dass* die Oden aber schon sehr bald unter dem Namen des alten Königs Salomon kursierten und damit hohe Autorität beanspruchten, zeigen die koptischen Zitate, vor allem aber die handschriftliche Überschrift von Ode 11 im Papyrus Bodmer XI: ᾠδὴ Σολομῶντος

Die Tatsache als solche, dass diese Oden oder Hymnen oder Lieder anonym oder sogar pseudepigraphisch sind, ist kein Grund zur Beunruhigung, Geringschätzung oder Abwertung. Sind doch zahlreiche der kanonischen und apokryphischen Schriften von unbekannter Hand verfasst und redigiert und "fälschlich" - doch in durchaus verschiedenartiger Intention - einer bestimmten und berühmten, wenn auch nicht immer wirklich bekannten "Persönlichkeit" zugeschrieben! Hat man doch auch bereits die ganze apostolische und nachapostolische Zeit als Ära der Pseudepigraphie wissenschaftlich qualifiziert![7]

Aus der Forschungsgeschichte, deren kritische Darstellung meine augenblickliche Hauptarbeit darstellt, seien hier nur Ausgangs- und vorläufiger Endpunkt genannt. Der eigentliche Beginn der Odenforschung ist fest mit dem Namen des englischen Forschers J. Rendel Harris verbunden, während heute - nach Qumran und Nag Hammadi freilich in ziemlich veränderter Situation-die Arbeiten von J.H. Charlesworth und meine eigene Edition (Band I und Ia) und Konkordanz (Band II) zu neuer Beschäftigung herausfordern. Worin in erster Linie - und im Grunde genommen immer noch - die Bedeutung der Oden Salomos liegt, habe ich versucht, im Titel meiner auf vier Bände veranschlagten Arbeit anzuzeigen: "Die Oden Salomos in ihrer Bedeutung für Neues Testament und Gnosis."[8]

2. <u>Die Bedeutung der Oden Salomos für den Gnostizismus</u>

Da dieser Aspekt heute nicht meine Aufgabe ist, kann ich mich ganz kurz fassen. Faktum ist einmal

a. Die gnostische Interpretation der Oden Salomos in der koptisch-gnostischen Schrift "Pistis Sophia."

Ich habe 1978 auf der International Conference on Gnosticism at Yale zu diesem Thema ein paper vorgetragen, dessen überarbeitete deutsche Fassung in einem hermeneutischen Anhang meiner Oden-Edition publiziert ist.[9] Dass den Oden Salomos neben anderen Schriften von einer gnostischen Gruppe zitier- und auslegungswürdige Bedeutung beigemessen worden ist, steht also fest. Viel schwieriger und offener ist

b. Das kontroverse Problem des gnostischen Charakters der Oden Salomos.

In neuester Zeit ist sogar die seit H. Gunkel weithin geltende und sehr weit gefasste "Auffassung, dass wir es mit einem gnostischen Hymnenbuch aus dem 2. Jh. zu tun haben,"[10] bei vielen Gnosisforschern unter den Religionswissenschaftlern und Patrologen ins Wanken geraten. Das hängt vor allem mit der intensiven und kritischen Bemühung um dieses interessante Phänomen des spätantiken Synkretismus zusammen. Ich persönlich bin noch nicht zu einem ganz endgültigen Urteil gelangt. Wahrscheinlich wird man-und dies in Analogie zu mancher Schrift der Kodizes aus der Bibliothek von Nag Hammadi- *nie* sagen können, die Oden Salomos seien gnostisch im Sinne eines vollständigen Kosmogonie- und Erlösungsmythos. Wenn man aber berücksichtigt, dass auch im ausgereiften Gnostizismus nicht alles so heterodox und abstrus war, wie es die verzerrenden Darstellungen der amtlichen und grosskirchlichen Häresiologen behaupten, dann wird man unbefangenerweise in den Oden Salomos mythologisch-soteriologische Aussagen, Motive, Vorstellungen, Begriffe und Bilder entdecken, die sich auch bei den späteren Gnostikern grosser Beliebtheit erfreuen. Wichtiger ist schon jetzt in unserem speziellen Zusammenhang die Erinnerung an die unausgebildete Frühphase der Gnosis, deren Existenz nicht zuletzt auch gerade durch neutestamentliche Schriften der zweiten Hälfte des ersten Jahrhunderts und der ersten Hälfte des zweiten Jahrhunderts erhärtet zu werden scheint, und zwar in doppelter Tendenz: negativ bekämpft einerseits und positiv aufgenommen andererseits. Ist darauf gleich zurückzukommen, so geht es nun als Hauptaspekt um:

3. Die gegenseitige Bedeutsamkeit von Salomo-Oden und neutestamentlicher Literatur

Wie ein roter Faden zieht sich durch die nicht allzu lange Geschichte der Beschäftigung mit den Oden Salomos die Betonung der Wichtigkeit dieser Jahrhundertentdeckung für die formgeschichtliche und religionsgeschichtliche Erforschung und Interpretation des Neuen Testaments. Drei Aussagen verschiedener Zeiten mögen das beleuchten:

1. Ein Jahr nach der editio princeps von Harris, also im Jahre 1910, sagte Adolf Harnack: "Das ist geschichtlich die wichtigste Frucht, welche uns diese Oden bringen, dass sie in doppelter Weise das vierte Evangelium, d.h. seine Religion und seine Theologie, beleuchten. Was sie hier lehren, ist ebenso neu wie aufklärend zugleich und wird die Kirchenhistoriker noch lange beschäftigen. Man hat hier den Steinbruch vor sich, aus dem die johanneischen Quadern gehauen sind!"[11] (Mit Kirchenhistorikern meinte Harnack natürlich auch die historisch arbeitenden Neutestamentler.)

2. C. H. Kraeling urteilte 1927: "Among these finds of greater importance the most recent and significant, by reason of its bearing on the New Testament itself, is the discovery of the collection of early Christian hymns which in the later tradition passed under the name of the Odes of Solomon."[12]

3. Zusammen mit R. A. Culpepper beginnt J. H. Charlesworth einen seiner Artikel 1973: "The Odes of Solomon are a neglected key for unlocking the historical and theological enigmas of John."[13]

Abgesehen davon, dass bis heute sich kein allgemeiner Konsens über Tatsache, Art und Umfang der gegenseitigen Beeinflussung abzeichnet, ist es auffällig, dass ein fortlaufender vollständiger Kommentar zu den Oden Salomos immer noch fehlt. Ich habe einen solchen als Band IV meiner Arbeit geplant und angekündigt. Dort wo man in neutestamentlichen Kommentaren und Monographien vor allem zum Johannesevangelium die Oden heranzieht, geschieht es meist in der gleichen eklektizistischen und ausschlachtenden Weise wie mit anderen Texten. Die intensivere Heranziehung aber geschieht mit Recht in zweifacher Richtung, einmal unter formgeschichtlichen Gesichtspunkten, zum anderen zur Lösung des johanneischen Rätsels.

a. Formgeschichtliche Gesichtspunkte

"Die bekannten parallelen Stellen im Epheserbrief (5,19) und Colosserbrief (3,16) reden von 'Psalmen, Hymnen und geistlichen Oden,' ohne dass wir daraus die Berechtigung entnehmen dürfen, von drei scharf gesonderten Formen urchristlicher Lieder zu reden."[14] Das Muratorische Fragment nennt im 2. Jh. ein "novum psalmorum librum Marcioni" - "ein neues Psalmenbuch für Marcion."[15] Über die Christen am Anfang des 2. Jh. berichtet Plinius (Briefe X, 96f), sie sängen oder rezitierten bei ihren Treffen "carmenque Christo quasi Deo," womit nach R. P. Martin am wahrscheinlichsten ein Hymnus gemeint ist: "The conclusion that carmen means a hymn addressed to Christ seems more likely."[16]

Bis zur Entdeckung der Oden Salomos war man zur Verifizierung solcher Angaben auf frühchristliche Fragmente angewiesen und beschränkt, die in den - vor allem späteren - neutestamentlichen Schriften selbst bewahrt und überliefert sind, und die form- und redaktionsgeschichtliche Betrachtungsweise in den letzten Jahrzehnten kritisch herausgearbeitet und untersucht hat. Damit sind nicht so sehr diejenigen Lieder bzw. Stücke gemeint, die mehr oder weniger ganz in Inhalt und Form aus alttestamentlichen Zitaten zusammengesetzt sind (wie bes. in Lk, Hebr und Apk), auch nicht in erster Linie hymnische Briefschlüsse (wie Röm 16, 25-27 oder Judas 24-25), die ebenso ad hoc gebildet wurden wie das sogenannte Hohelied der Liebe (I Kor 13) oder wie der kleine, vom Johannesevangelium (3,16 u.a.) abhängige Hymnus auf Gott, die Liebe und die Liebenden (I Joh 4,7-10). Auch innerchristlich entstandene und tradierte Bekenntnisformeln (wie I Kor 15,3ff oder Eph 4,5f) seien hier ausgeklammert, obwohl sie manchmal formal und inhaltlich mit eben den vorgeformten, teils vorchristlichen, teils verchristlichten, teils schon christlichen Hymnen eng zusammenhängen, auf die es dann ankommt, wenn ein solcher lückenschliessender Schatz frühchristlicher Poesie wie die Oden Salomos recht gewürdigt werden soll. Die wichtigsten neutestamentlichen Hymnen, auf die auch in Punkt 4 zurückzukommen sein wird, sind: Joh 1,1ff, Phil 2,6-11, Kol 1,15-18, Eph 5,14, I Tim 3,16 und 6,15f, II Tim 1,9f und 2,11-13, Tit 3,4-7, Hebr 1,3f, I Petr 1,18-21 und 3,18f.

Nachdem J. Kroll schon 1921/22 die Oden Salomos für "Die christliche Hymnodik bis zu Klemens von Alexandreia" als "ein wichtiges Glied in der Rekonstruktion der christlichen Dichtung"[17] ausführlich berücksichtigt hatte (bes. S. 70ff), so hat erst G. Schille 1965 in seiner Arbeit "Frühchristliche Hymnen" in Bezug auf die genannten neutestamentlichen Hymnen "die Gattungsfrage gestellt und versucht, auf eine methodische Hymnodik zuzusteuern,"[18] wobei er u.a. besonders die Oden Salomos in einem bisher nicht gekannten Ausmass in seine Untersuchung einbezog. Jede formgeschichtliche Hymnenforschung dieses Zeitraums hat dort anzuknüpfen. Allerdings kann auch die alttestamentliche Psalmenforschung von und seit H. Gunkel immer noch wichtige Aspekte beisteuern; man denke vor allem an den auch die Oden Salomos gestaltenden parallelismus membrorum.

Übrigens begegnen in den Oden auffällig oft über die reinen (Schluss-) Doxologien hinaus - und nicht nur imperativisch - Aussagen, die man hymnologische Selbstreflexionen nennen kann. Typisches Beispiel neben Ode 16,1ff ist dafür Ode 26. Dieses Lied kann man geradezu als einen Hymnus über die (eigenen?) Hymnen bezeichnen. Auch Ode 40 gehört mit seiner hymnologischen Terminologie in diesen formgebenden Zusammenhang, aus dem heraus sich letztlich die häufige Verwendung der teils bildlich, teils real gemeinten Begriffe Herz, Mund und Lippen erklärt.

b. Die Oden Salomos und das Johannesevangelium - zwei frühchristliche Texte voller Rätsel

Es ist - wie gesagt - vor allem das Johannesevangelium zusammen mit dem davon abhängigen ersten Johannesbrief, das durch die Oden Salomos in neues Licht gerät. Wo die spezifische Eigenart und Sonderstellung des vierten

Evangeliums innerhalb der frühchristlichen Literatur empfunden und gesehen wird, ist man wissenschaftlich froh darüber, dass diese Isolation aufgehoben ist, um es ganz vorsichtig und allgemein zu sagen. Wenn man von den drei Möglichkeiten der Beziehung zwischen den Oden und dem unter dem Pseudonym "Johannes" überlieferten Schrifttum weder die literarische Abhängigkeit der Oden von Johannes noch die quellenmässige Abhängigkeit des Johannes von den Oden in ernsthaften Betracht ziehen möchte, sondern mit Charlesworth/Culpepper und anderen der dritten Hypothese zustimmt "that the Odes and John come from the same religious environment,"[19] verbreitet sich die textliche Basis beträchtlich für eines der wichtigsten und schwierigsten religionsgeschichtlichen Probleme der neutestamentlichen Wissenschaft.

Ohne auf die letztlich unlösbare literarkritische Quellenfrage des Johannesevangeliums eingehen zu müssen, lässt sich das "eigentliche geschichtliche Problem" auf die "völlig andere Sprache" und die "Herkunft der Begriffswelt" insbesondere der johanneischen Reden fixieren.[20] Klammert man einmal aus verschiedenen Gründen Qumran, Philo, das Corpus Hermeticum, die Ignatianen und die Mandaica aus, so bleiben in erster Linie die literarisch einheitlichen Oden Salomos als erhellende Parallelen einerseits, doch als analoges Problem andererseits. In gewisser Weise verdoppelt sich so das johanneische Rätsel, für das W. G. Kümmel eine Lösung anbietet, nämlich die Annahme einer sich an den Rändern des Frühjudentums bildenden vor- und dann auch innerchristlichen *Gnosis*.[21]

Wenn J. R. Harris in seiner editio princeps ein wenig lapidar feststellte, die Oden seien "as gnostic as the New Testament,"[22] dann liegt darin eine gewisse Ironie der Geschichte dergestalt, dass heute - wie schon angedeutet - das Verhältnis der Gnosis zum Neuen Testament durchaus diskussionswürdig ist. Geht es - wie bei Paulus - um Polemik gegen Gnostiker, z.ß. in Korinth, zeigt sich Bereitschaft zur Anerkennung historischer Sachverhalte auf breiter Front. Geht es aber - wie beim Johannesevangelium - um die auch nur partielle Möglichkeit akuter Gnostisierung

christlicher Kreise, deren Schriftprodukte später kirchlich
kanonisiert wurden, setzt sehr häufig eine Abwehrsperre
ein. Die Frage sei erlaubt, ob damit nicht die Reserve
zusammenhängt, die Oden Salomos als gnostische oder
wenigstens gnostisierende Dokumente zu betrachten und zu
interpretieren.

Damit sei die hypothetische Frage verbunden, ob das
johanneisch-salomonische Doppelrätsel sich nicht vielleicht
doch am leichtesten und so umfassend wie möglich lösen
lässt, wenn man als ihr gemeinsames Entstehungsmilieu eine
aus heterodoxem Judentum sich speisende, aber wohl immer
schon synkretistisch gefärbte Frühgnosis annimmt, in die
spezifisch christliche Gedanken verschieden stark und
literarisch mehr oder weniger wirksam eindrangen (vgl. die
bis heute nicht befriedigend geklärten Probleme des
sogenannten Judenchristentums). Wenn man auch selbstver-
ständlich nicht den gesamten späteren Gnostizismus in die
Frühzeit transponieren darf, so hat sich doch in neuester
Zeit durch die zahlreichen Entdeckungen originaler Gnostica
ein Vorverständnis von Gnosis herausgebildet, dessen
Authentizität und lebensnähere Differenziertheit manche
Rückschlüsse zulässt und so auch eine Verstehenshilfe für
den status nascendi darstellen kann.

Solch grosse Linien und mehr allgemeine Erwägungen
bleiben für eine Entwicklungsgeschichte antiker religiöser
Literatur natürlich von eminenter Bedeutung. Von gleicher
Wichtigkeit aber ist die jeweilige kontextuelle Einzel-
analyse und - besonders im zeitlich begrenzten Rahmen
dieses Kongresspapers - im Einzelvergleich die Beschränkung
auf wenige

4. Inhaltliche Zusammenhänge zwischen einzelnen Stellen
   der Oden Salomos und Aussagen des kanonischen Neuen
   Testaments

Zu dieser wissenschaftlichen Aufgabe gibt es schon recht
umfassende Voruntersuchungen: etwa die Johanneskommentare
von W. Bauer (^{4}1933), R. Bultmann (1941) und R. Schnacken-
burg (1965); die Monographien von H. Becker (1956) und E.
Schweizer (1939) zu den johanneischen Offenbarungs- bzw.
Bildreden, von W. Langbrandtner (1977) und M. Lattke (1975)

zum johanneischen Begriff der Liebe, von F. G. Untergassmeir (1974) zum johanneischen Namensbegriff, von J. Ernst (1970) zu Pleroma in den paulinischen Antilegomena, usw. *Ein* mythologisches Thema ist besonders oft schon untersucht worden, nämlich die sowohl in den Oden (17, 22, 42, u.ö.) als auch in I Petr 3,18ff begegnende Höllenfahrt Christi.[23] Auch die Taube in Ode 24 ist im Vergleich mit den neutestamentlichen Taufgeschichten immer wieder, zuletzt sehr gründlich von Stephen Gero (Nov. Test. XVIII, 1976, 17-35) thematisiert worden.

Schliesslich ist ganz besonders hinzuweisen auf die allerdings nur teilweise kommentierten Zusammenstellungen von Parallelen, z.B. auf die von R. Abramowski, R. Bultmann, J. H. Charlesworth/R. A. Culpepper, P. Kleinert, É. Massaux, F. Spitta und R. H. Strachan.[24]

Diese und ähnliche Sammlungen, die meist nach der jeweiligen Textfolge angeordnet sind, können nicht und müssen auch nicht in all ihren Einzelheiten wiedergegeben werden. Da auch Vollständigkeit hier nicht angestrebt zu werden braucht, konzentriere ich mich a) auf einige interessante, selbst zusammengesuchte Merkmale der - um es noch einmal zu betonen: *nicht* literarischen - Verwandtschaft zwischen den Oden Salomos und dem Corpus Johanneum, und b) auf weitere markante neutestamentliche Parallelen zu ausgewählten Odentexten. Ich werde versuchen, neben bestimmten aussagekräftigen Einzelstellen vor allem Themen und Begriffe herauszustellen, die qualitativ wie quantitativ als repräsentative erscheinen, und die auch sprachlich, d.h. vor allem griechisch und syrisch, als kongruent angenommen werden können. Was diesen letztgenannten Punkt betrifft, kommt der einzigen syrisch-griechisch erhaltenen elften Ode eine gewisse Schlüsselstellung zu.[25]

Dabei werden zwangsläufig jeweilige spezifische Eigenartigkeiten, von denen bei aller Verwandtschaft und Ähnlichkeit nicht nur das Neue Testament, sondern auch die Oden Salomos voll sind, unterdrückt. Auf eines dieser Kennzeichen, das schon öfter kritisch beobachtet worden ist, möchte ich jedoch wenigstens hinweisen: in den Oden spielt die Ethik so gut wie keine Rolle! Die meisten der gar nicht so seltenen Imperative sind entweder Aufforderungen zum Lobpreis, also doxologischer Natur, oder von der Art und Weise, die ich einmal "Heilsimperative" nennen will, z.B. Ode 34,6: "Glaubet, lebet und seid erlöst!" Indem ich aber meiner ganz persönlichen Überzeugung Ausdruck gebe, dass auch das Johannesevangelium die ethische Komponente - besonders im Vergleich mit Jesus und Paulus - vernachlässigt oder sogar bewusst, vielleicht "gnostisch" missachtet hat, komme ich zu sprechen auf:

a. Merkmale der Verwandtschaft zwischen den Oden Salomos und johanneischen Theologumena

Am Begriff "Bewahren" (griech. τηρέω, syr. ܢܛܪ) lässt sich gleich Mehreres zeigen. Einmal fällt formal die Reziprozität auf, die auch zur typischen johanneischen Sprachstruktur gehört (bei ἀγαπᾶν γινώσκειν, εἶναι ἐν und μένειν ἐν). Während das johanneische "Bewahren" einer der "Aspekte der soteriologischen Beziehung zum Wort des Lebens"[26] ist, redet der Heilsimperativ Ode 8,10f von der gegenseitigen Relation zwischen den Erlösten und dem Mysterium bzw. dem Glauben, also wahrscheinlich - in synthetischem parallelismus membrorum - dem Glaubensgeheimnis: "Bewahrt mein Mysterium, die ihr durch es bewahrt seid! Bewahrt meinen Glauben, die ihr durch ihn bewahrt seid!" Andere Stellen, nämlich Ode 18,7 und 35,2, an denen vom "Bewahrtwerden" durch den Herrn die Rede ist, leiten durch ihren Kontext unmittelbar zu einem der wichtigsten Begriffskomplexe der Salomo-Oden über, nämlich zu dem der "Erlösung" griech. σωτηρία, syr. ܦܘܪܩܢܐ), dem sogleich als ebenso wichtig der des unsterblichen Lebens (griech. ζωή syr. ܚܝܐ) gleichbedeutend an die Seite gestellt werden muss.

Nicht nur die Tatsache, dass das Leben in den Oden quasi personifiziert erscheint (3,8f; 28,6 u.ö.), lässt an die Selbstprädikation des johanneischen Jesus denken, z.B. 14,6: "ἐγώ εἰμι ἡ ὁδὸς καὶ ἡ ἀλήθεια καὶ ἡ ζωή " - "Ich bin der Weg und die Wahrheit und das Leben." Auch die Weitergabe des Heilsgutes des ewigen Lebens, die abbildhafte (vgl. Joh!) Ausstattung der Erlösten damit zur

Unvergänglichkeit und die Veranstaltung der Sammlung von "Lebendigen" sind Topoi, die als johanneisch gelten können.

Was die reinen Begriffe "erlösen, Erlöser und Erlösung" angeht, so muss man feststellen, dass die Wortgruppe um σῴζω im Johannesevangelium zwar selten ist, dass aber die Soteriologie so stark dominiert, dass man mit Recht das vierte Evangelium durch das paradoxe Schlagwort von der "realized eschatology" (C.H. Dodd u.a.) charakterisiert hat, was sich ohne weiteres auch auf die Oden Salomos übertragen lässt.

Übrigens dienen die meisten der nicht sehr zahlreichen Mythologumena in den Oden der Beschreibung des Erlösungsgeschehens. Das Johannesevangelium ist gemessen an den späteren Mythos-Systemen noch zurückhaltender in der Verwendung mythologischer Elemente, was mit der Aufnahme von und Verbindung mit "Jesus" zusammenhängt, dessen Name ja in den Oden überhaupt nicht erscheint. Doch gilt für beide Schriften, dass nicht die Kosmogonie, sondern die prädestinatianische Soteriologie-mehr oder weniger mythologisch, mehr oder weniger kosmologisch-die Hauptrolle spielt, und dass diese auch in beiden primär bezogen ist auf die erlösten Einzelnen.

Bei den wichtigen, teils bildlichen, teils abstrakten, Begriffen: Erkenntnis, Licht/Finsternis, Liebe, Wahrheit/ Irrtum (Lüge), Wasser des Lebens, Weg und Wort sind die johanneisch-salomonischen Übereinstimmungen so deutlich und zahlreich, dass ich mir Einzelnachweise und eingehendere Erörterungen hier ersparen kann. Ich komme damit zu:

   b. Weitere neutestamentliche Parallelen ausgewählter Odentexte

Auf Parallelen wie den Mythos vom Abstieg des Erlösers ins Totenreich (Scheol), wie das Motiv von der Taube oder wie den kosmischen Erlösungsbegriff der "Fülle", "Vollendung" (griech. πλήρωμα, syr. ܡܠܝܘܬܐ von ܡܠܐ) wurde schon hingewiesen. Letzterer Begriff, im Gnostizismus ein beliebter terminus technicus, führt in die deuteropaulinischen, also auch pseudepigraphischen Briefe an die Kolosser und Epheser, die neben ihrer deutlichen Abhängigkeit von paulinischer Theologie manche Analogie zum

Johannesvangelium aufweisen. Diese beiden Briefe werden darum jetzt etwas ausgeblendet. Ebenfalls weitgehend ausser Betracht bleiben Parallelen, die auf gemeinsame alttestamentlich-jüdische Tradition zurückgehen, wie z.B. die Vorstellung vom Joch (Ode 42, 7, Mt 11, 29f) oder das Bild von der Beschneidung des Herzens (Ode 11, 1-3, Röm 2, 29). Zahlreiche der hier einschlägigen Parallelen wie etwa noch das Schema "Erniedrigung/Erhöhung bzw. Rechtfertigung als Sieg" in Phil 2 und I Tim 3, 16 finden sich in den neutestamentlichen Hymnen-Fragmenten, deren formgeschichtliche Behandlung unter Punkt 3a somit auch inhaltlich gerechtfertigt erscheint.

Ich beginne mit dem apokalyptischen Motiv der "Ankunft" des Herrn (griech. παρουσία, syr. ܡܐܬܝܬܐ von ܐܬܐ) in Ode 7,17-19, wozu das für den späteren Paulus gar nicht so typische Stück I Thess 4, 15-17 zu vergleichen ist. An beiden Stellen schimmert die Vorstellung einer feierlichen, prozessionsartigen Einholung des Kyrios durch (εἰς ἀπάντησιν - "entgegen").

Der metaphorische Gebrauch des Wortes "anziehen" (manchmal auch im dualistisch begründeten Gegensatz zu "ausziehen") verbindet die Oden mit Paulus. Ausgangspunkt ist Gal 3, 27: ὅσοι γὰρ εἰς χριστὸν ἐβαπτίσθητε, χριστὸν ἐνδύσασθε - "die ihr auf Christus getauft wurdet, habt Chr. angezogen". Imperativisch dann in paränetischem Zusammenhang Röm 13, 14: ἐνδύσασθε τὸν κύριον Ἰησοῦν χριστόν - "zieht vielmehr den Herrn Jesus Christus an!"

In den Oden Salomos kann nicht nur der sich gleichgestaltende Herr (7, 4), sondern auch die Gnade (4, 6, 20, 7), das Siegel (4, 8), die Heiligkeit (13, 3), der Name des Höchsten (39, 8), die Freude (23, 1) und die Liebe (23, 3) angezogen werden. An den letzten Stellen zeigt der parallele Vers 2 (Gnade, s.o.), dass mit "anziehen" ein "Nehmen" oder "Empfangen" gemeint ist. Die an die Sophia (Weisheit) erinnerude[27] Jungfrau (Ode 33, 5ff) predigt denen, die sie angezogen haben, eschatologische Unzerstörbarkeit (V. 12), wozu das Anziehen des neuen Menschen in Kol 3, 10 und Eph 4, 24 herangezogen werden mag. Wichtiger und unabweisbarer ist die Parallelität von I Kor 15, 53-55 mit Ode 15, 8, wo der Verfasser singt: "Ich habe die Unvergänglichkeit durch seinen Namen angezogen, und ich habe die Vergänglichkeit durch seine Gnade ausgezogen." Der Unterschied zu Paulus, der hier wohl sprachlich eingewirkt hat, besteht allerdings darin, dass in Ode 15 das Ende schon realisiert, der Tod schon zerstört ist, während in I Kor 15 gut paulinisch die eschatologische Spannung gehalten wird.

Ich beschliesse diesen Punkt einmal mit dem Hinweis auf ein bereits mehrfach untersuchtes, durchaus nicht unproblematisches Oden-Motiv und dann mit einer Frage.

In den salomonischen Oden ist von der Erhebung der Arme zum Herrn die Rede (21, 1), womit sicher die auch in I Tim 2, 8 beschriebene jüdische und christliche "Gebärde des Beters"[28] gemeint ist. Der Parallelismus "Ausstreckung der Hände"/ "Erhebung der Stimme" (Ode 37, 1f) bestätigt dies. In der nicht ganz wörtlichen Dublette Ode 27 / 42, 1f ist darüberhinaus eine Deutung der ausgebreiteten Hände auf "sein Zeichen" hin gegeben. Wenn dies gleichzeitig als das "richtige Holz" bezeichnet wird, so kann darin durchaus Polemik gegen das Kreuz des historischen Jesus liegen.

Nun die Frage: Hat in Ode 22, 12 der "Fels" (syr. ܟܐܦܐ der Kopte hat hier "Licht"), der nach Auflösung der Welt Fundament für alles ist, und auf den Gott seine Königsherrschaft syr. ܡܠܟܘܬܗ der Kopte hat hier "Reichtum") gebaut hat als einen Wohnort der Heiligen, hat dieser Fels im Sinne literarischer und sachlicher Übereinstimmung etwas zu tun mit der berühmt-berüchtigten Stelle Mt 16, 18f ("Du bist Petrus, und auf diesen Felsen etc.") *oder* liegt auch hier Polemik vor *oder* handelt es sich gar um eine andere Felsen-Tradition?

Nach allem generell wie speziell Gesagten möchte ich nicht abbrechen ohne einige sehr vorläufige und thesenhafte

5. <u>Hermeneutische Erwägungen zur religionsgeschichtlich vernachlässigten Interdependenz von Kanon und Apokryphen des Neuen Testaments</u> [29]

1. Der Kanon als kirchliche "Heilige Schrift" ist nicht nur ein fragmentarisches Geschichtszeugnis, sondern in seiner Abgrenzung und Ausschliesslichkeit ein künstliches

Gebilde des 3. und 4. Jahrhunderts. Die neutestamentliche Wissenschaft ist eine ebenso künstliche, aus der Glorifizierung des Kanons wie aus praktisch- kirchlichen Bedürfnissen projizierte Einzeldisziplin. In ihrer doppelten Isolation von der alttestamentlichen Wissenschaft und von der Patrologie[30] steht sie in der ständigen Gefahr, sich zu intensiv, zu häufig und oft auch methodisch zu verfeinert mit jedem "heiligen" Wort zu beschäftigen, um immer wieder und noch einmal einen tieferen Sinn oder eine neue Nuance zu entdecken.

2. Es wird nicht bestritten, dass die analysierende und kommentierende Exegese des Neuen Testaments als ihren literatur- und religionsgeschichtlichen Rahmen die hebräischjüdische und griechisch-hellenistische Umwelt beleuchtend und kontrastierend berücksichtigt. Auch lässt sich nicht übersehen, dass Christentum und Kirche von Anfang an soziologisch und literarisch eigene Entwicklungslinien[31] hervorgebracht haben, die einerseits einen partiellen Bruch mit der jüdischen Wurzel und andererseits eine wachsende Emanzipation von der griechisch-römischen Antike darstellten. Darin liegt eine gewisse Berechtigung, die frühe Geschichte der christlichen Religion und Literatur gesondert zu betrachten und zu interpretieren.

3. Für eine solche innerchristliche Geschichte der beiden ersten Jahrhunderte,[32] also desjenigen Zeitraumes, der gemeinhin die apostolische und nachapostolische Ära sowie die Jahrzehnte der apostolischen Väter und frühen Apologeten umfasst, häufen sich die Probleme. Zunächst wird man bedauern, dass sich eine auch nur annähernde Lückenlosigkeit bei derzeitiger Quellenlage nicht erreichen lässt. Je weiter man auf den Ursprung der christlichen Bewegung zurückgeht, desto weniger lässt sich historisch getreu rekonstruieren. Will man sich ein lebendiges und der Frühzeit entsprechendes Bild machen von dem, was die christlichen Gruppen von Syrien bis Rom, von Mazedonien bis Ägypten religiös und erbaulich, theologisch und ethisch bestimmte, dann darf man dies nicht allein bewerkstelligen mit den Augen der späteren idealisierenden Kirchenge-

schichtsschreibung und ketzerbekämpfenden Amtskirchenmentalität. Nicht nur auf die Umwelt nämlich, sondern auch auf das Christentum selbst muss man den Massstab des Synkretismus anlegen.

4. Der Kanon des Neuen Testaments als *eine* Quelle für die Zeit von 50 bis 110 besteht bis auf die echten Paulus-Briefe aus anonymen Schriften bzw. aus Pseudepigraphen.[33] Nicht bloss über die Verfasser bleibt man im Ungewissen, auch die Entstehungsorte, Abfassungszeiten und Adressaten sind in den meisten Fällen unsicher oder gar unbekannt. Manche der später kanonisierten, z.T. noch lange umstrittenen Schriften sind gleich alt wie bzw. sogar jünger als der Hirte des Hermas, der erste Clemensbrief, die Briefe des Ignatius, der Polykarpbrief, der Barnabasbrief oder die Didache. Diese Tatsache ist nicht nur äusserlich chronologisch zu berücksichtigen, wie es etwa Ph. Vielhauer in seiner "Geschichte der urchristlichen Literatur"[34] dankenswerterweise durchgeführt hat.

5. Vielmehr-und damit komme ich zu meinem eigentlichen Anliegen - muss man als Neutestamentler diese Texte und vor allem auch einen Grossteil der neutestamentlichen Apokryphen inclusive der erhaltenen "häretischen" sprich gnostischen Literatur in sein Arbeitsgebiet einbeziehen. Dies heisst, sie genauso intensiv zu studieren und - wenigstens arbeitsteilig - auszulegen wie den Kanon selbst, sie nicht nur nebenbei und abfällig als Wort- und Begriffssteinbrüche zu benutzen. Zwar haben die frühen und wichtigsten neutestamentlichen Schriften hier schon fast überall literarisch eingewirkt, woraus sich auch einiges für das frühe, fast zeitgenössische Verstehen lernen lässt. Da es aber vor, neben und nach den spärlichen Resten von Literatur immer auch lebendige mündliche Traditionen gegeben hat, enthalten die späteren und nicht-kanonischen Evangelien, Apostelgeschichten, Briefe, Apokalypsen und eben auch Hymnenbücher wie die Oden Salomos umgekehrt vieles für das bessere Verständnis der Geschichte der kanonischen Schriften, ihrer Inhalte und Aussageformen, ihrer Verfasser und Entstehungskreise, ihrer Urheber und Anlässe, ihrer Leser und Hörer. Die neutestamentliche

Wissenschaft ist noch weit davon entfernt, mit dieser Interdependenz in ihrer Forschungskonzeption und Lehrtätigkeit wirklich Ernst zu machen.

L'IMPORTANCE DU "ROULEAU DE TEMPLE" POUR L'IDENTIFICATION DE LA COMMUNAUTE DE QUMRAN

Witold Tyloch

Les manuscrits découverts près de la Mer Morte ont signalé l'existence, au sein du judaïsme, d'une communauté bien organisée et active pendant plus de deux siècles. La durée de l'existence de cette communauté fut déterminée grâce aux résultats de travaux archéologiques menés dans les grottes où les manuscrits ont été trouvés, ainsi que dans les ruines de Qumrân et d'Ain Feshka. Ces travaux archéologiques ont permis de constater que la communauté de Qumrân fut fondée au milieu du deuxième siècle avant notre ère,[1] et qu'elle continua d'exister, avec une interruption d'environ trente ans, jusqu'à l'an 68 de notre ère. Cette constatation fut confirmée ensuite par les recherches paléographiques[2] et linguistiques.[3]

I

Dès le début de la discussion scientifique qui suivit de près la découverte des manuscrits, on a proposé d'identifier cette commnunauté avec l'un ou l'autre des groupes existant dans le judaïsme au cours de la dernière période du Second Temple. Ces groupes étaient connus surtout grâce aux descriptions de Flavius Josèphe qui ne mentionne toutefois que les plus grands groupes au sein du judaïsme d'alors: les Pharisiens, les Sadducéens et les Esséniens.[4] Flavius Josèphe les appelle "écoles philosophiques" afin de les rendre ainsi plus facilement reconnaissables à ses lecturs païens, et il mentionne aussi les Zélotes.[5] Mais on sait, grâce à d'autres témoignages anciens, que les groupes au sein du judaïsme d'alors étaient beaucoup plus nombreux.[6]

Un examen plus approfondi des manuscrits de la Mer Morte a fourni des arguments supplémentaires pour l'identification de la communauté qui a écrit ou transcrit ces documents, avec les Esséniens. Les premiers à proposer cette identification furent E.L. Sukenik[7] et A. Dupont-Sommer[8] qui justifia amplement, d'une manière élaborée et convaincante, l'hypothèse de l'origine essénienne de ces documents. Au fur et à mesure de la publication des textes trouvés dans les grottes de la Mer Morte, cette hypothèse gagna des partisans, d'autant plus que les informations de Philon d'Alexandrie,[9] de Flavius Josèphe,[10] de Pline l'Ancien[11] et d'Hippolyte[12] appuyaient cette hypothèse. La confrontation des indications transmises par ces auteurs sur l'organisation, l'idéologie, les institutions et les pratiques des Esséniens plaidait pour l'identification de la communauté des manuscrits avec ce groupe au sein du judaïsme.

Malgré ces constatations, cette hypothèse n'a toutefois pas été accueillie sans réserves et l'on a tenté d'autres essais d'identification de la communauté des manuscrits de Qumrân avec les Sadducéens,[13] les Pharisiens,[14] les Zélotes,[15] ou avec un groupe juif inconnu auquel on donnait le nom de Sadoquites.[16] On l'a identifiée également avec les Karaïtes,[17] et l'on est même allé jusqu'à nier l'existence des Esséniens.[18] Etant donné cette situation, j'ai tenté, dans mon livre sur "Les aspects sociaux de la communauté de Qumrân" publié il y a douze ans,[19] de reconsidérer à nouveau le problème de l'identification du groupe au sein duquel les manuscrits de la Mer Morte ont pris naissance.

Les auteurs qui avaient alors écrit sur les manuscrits de la Mer Morte s'étaient presque tous penchés sur le rapport entre la communauté de Qumrân et les Esséniens, la plupart ne faisant que répéter les arguments qui mettaient en évidence les affinités révélées par les manuscrits entre les Esséniens et la communauté. C'est pourquoi, dans mon livre, je n'ai pas répété leurs arguments et me suis plutôt attaché à souligner les traits les plus marquants du point de vue des aspects sociaux, et qui témoignaient du caractère essénien de la communauté de Qumrân. Trois de ces aspects me semblaient particulièrement importants: la communauté des biens, du travail et de la vie.

Confrontés aux données fournies par les documents de Qumrân sur la communauté des biens et le mode de vie des responsables de la création des manuscrits et de leur transcription, les textes de Philon d'Alexandrie, de Flavius Josèphe, de Pline l'Ancien et d'Hippolyte sur les Esséniens semblaient constituer un argument décisif en faveur de l'identification de la communauté de Qumrân avec les Esséniens. Ceci fut également confirmé par la comparaison de l'organisation de la communauté de Qumrân avec celle des Esséniens, puisque ces deux communautés comprenaient deux branches différentes et qu'au sein de chacune de ces communautés, la plus petite unité structurale était composée de dix personnes.[20] De plus, la procédure d'admission des nouveaux membres était semblable,[21] et chacune des deux communautés divisait ces derniers selon leur degré de zèle dans l'application des principes en vigueur dans la communauté.[22] L'ordre hiérarchique observé par les Esséniens ainsi que l'ordre selon lequel ils prenaient la parole dans leurs assemblées étaient les même que ceux imposés par la Règle de la communauté de Qumrân.[23] Parmi les autres similitudes, on peut énumérer encore l'importance attachée aux repas pris en commun, les décisions sur l'admission des nouveaux membres, des principes hygiéniques semblables,[24] l'attention particulière attachée à l'étude et à l'explication de la Bible[25] dont la lecture constituait un élément important au cours des repas pris en commun. Le système pénal menaçait les membres des deux groupes de peines similaires pour des transgressions analogues, comme par exemple - il s'agit bien sûr d'un simple détail - la punition encourue pour avoir craché pendant les réunions, ou encore les peines sévères, allant même jusqu'à l'exclusion totale, infligées en cas d'infractions à la communauté des biens.[26] L'attitude morale des Esséniens décrite par Philon est aussi entièrement confirmée par la Règle de la communauté de Qumrân, et d'autres traits communs sont également visibles dans la doctrine en ce qui touche les pratiques rituelles et leur observance.

Toutes ces similitudes constituent déjà une preuve assez convaincante du caractère essénien de la communauté de Qumrân et une indication que les manuscrits découverts dans les grottes sont une source directe pour la connaissance du mouvement essénien. Toutes ces observations ont trouvé néanmoins un appui nouveau permet- tant de trancher définitivement la question: la découverte du "Rouleau du Temple" et sa publication.

II

Devenu accessible aux chercheurs seulement en 1967, ce rouleau intriguait fortement les spécialistes intéressés aux manuscrits de Qumrân. Il se trouva entre les mains du professeur Y. Yadin qui publia les premières informations sur la découvertes du rouleau et, après une analyse préliminaire de son contenu, lui donna le nom de "Rouleau du Temple".[27] Ce rouleau, qui mesure 8,6 m. de longueur, s'avéra le plus long de tous les manuscrits de la Mer Morte et aussi le plus important. Pour cette raison, tout le monde savant attendait avec impatience la publication définitive de ce précieux document édité en trois volumes par le professeur Y. Yadin, en 1977.[28]

Le texte de ce rouleau s'étend sur 66 colonnes dont la partie supérieure est complètement disparue. En dépit du mauvais état de préservation du manuscrit, la majeure partie du texte est lisible grâce aux nouveaux procédés techniques utilisés pour son déchiffrement. Dans cette tâche, Y. Yadin ne s'est pas borné seulement à ce rouleau; il a utilisé aussi les fragments de deux ou trois copies de ce document provenant de la grotte IV et conservées au Musée Rockefeller de Jérusalem. Il a réussi à combler ainsi les différentes lacunes du texte et à en reconstituer des parties considérables.

La forme de l'écriture du "Rouleau du Temple" montre qu'il fut écrit par deux scribes qui étaient d'habiles calligraphes. Le premier a écrit les cinq premières colonnes, l'autre tout le reste du rouleau.²⁹ En s'appuyant sur l'analyse paléographique, on peut facilement constater que leur écriture est de type hérodien.³⁰ On peut donc penser que ce rouleau ainsi qu'une des copies furent écrits dans la seconde moitié du premier siècle avant notre ère, ou dans la première moitié du premier siècle de notre ère. La troisième copie de ce document présente aussi un type hérodien d'écriture. C'est le fragment Rock. 4375. Mais l'écriture de la seconde copie conservée au Musée Rockefeller est de type hasmonéen. C'est le fragment Rock. 43366. Ce fait suggère que le document fut composé à la fin du deuxième siècle avant notre ère.³¹

III

En substance, le "Rouleau du Temple" se compose de commandements et de prescriptions concernant différents domaines de la vie religieuse: renouvellement de l'alliance (col. I), pureté et impureté rituelles (col. XLV-LII), construction et aménagement du Temple, avec description de son équipement et de ses ustensiles (col. III-XII; XXIX-XLIV; LIII-LV). Le rouleau contient aussi des règles pour le roi et son armée (col. LVI-LIX), et des prescriptions pour les prêtres et les lévites dans le style du Deutéronome (col. LX-LXVI).

Une partie assez importante du rouleau contient des ordonnances sur les fêtes, les sacrifices et les offrandes prescrites à ces occasions (col XIII-XXXIX). Il s'agit d'une collection des différentes prescriptions du Pentateuque tirées de l'Exode, du Lévitique, des Nombres et surtout du Deutéronome. Mais chose intéressante, en citant le texte biblique, l'auteur du "Rouleau du Temple" le change souvent, mettant à la première personne le sujet de ses citations, au lieu de la troisième personne comme dans1 la Bible.³² Ce procédé semble indiquer que l'auteur du "Rouleau du Temple" croyait ou voulait faire croire à ses lecteurs que son oeuvre constitue la Loi véritable révélée à Moïse par Dieu. En même temps, on peut supposer qu'il voulait donner à son oeuvre une plus grande autorité. Cette supposition peut être appuyée par le fait que dans ce rouleau, le no de Dieu: YHWH, est toujours écrit normalement dans la même écriture que le reste du texte, contrairement à l'usage connu dans d'autres manuscrits de Qumrân où, pour écrire le nom de Dieu, on employait des lettres paléohébraïques ou simplement quatre points. C'est aussi l'usage bien connu des manuscrits des livres de la Bible et des commentaires bibliques.

Les prescriptions concernant les fêtes et les sacrifices et offrandes qu'on devait faire à l'occasion de ces fêtes sont particulièrement intéressantes. Outre les jours fériés connus du judaïsme officiel, le "Rouleau du Temple" contient des informations sur des fêtes demeurées inconnues jusqu'ici. C'est ainsi qu'en plus de la Fête des Semaines, le "Rouleau du Temple" mentionne deux autres fêtes qu'on devait célébrer cinquante et cent jours après: la Fête du Nouveau Vin, et la Fête de la Nouvelle Huile. Toutes ces fêtes étaient célébrées selon le calendrier en vigueur dans la communauté essénienne de Qumrân et d'après le comput reçu dans ce milieu,[33] c'est-à-dire le calendrier connu par le Livre des Jubilés. Ce fait semble donc indiquer que l'auteur du "Rouleau du Temple", ainsi que celui du Livre des Jubilés, étaient des Esséniens.

IV

Cette indication trouve appui également dans le contenu du "Rouleau du Temple", surtout dans le fragment concernant la Fête de la Nouvelle Huile. Voici la traduction de ce fragment, d'après le texte reconstitué par Y. Yadin:[34]

 (col. XXI, 12) Depuis ce jour vous compterez sept
   sabbats, sept fois
  (13) quarante-neuf jours. Sept sabbats
   pleins il y aura jusqu'au lendemain du
   septième sabbat. (35)
  (14) Vous compterez cinquante jours (36) et
   vous offrirez l'huile nouvelle de la
   part des demeures

(15) des tribus des fils d'Israël, la moitié d'un hin (37) par tribu, l'huile nouvelle des olives concassées. (38)

(16) De cette huile vous offrirez les prémices de l'huile d'olive sur l'autel. C'est le sacrifice des prémices (39) devant Yahvé.

(col. XXII,01) (........)

(02) (.....) d'expier par cela pour toute la communauté devant (Yahvé) et son offrande

(03) en fleur de farine, trois dixième (40) bien mêlé (?) (41) avec un demi hîn de cette huile.

(04) On encensera sa graisse, son offrande et sa libation (?) conformément à la loi du sacrifice. C'est l'holocauste en parfum

(05) (d'apaisement pour Yahvé (42) .....). Cette huile,

(1) ils la verseront dans les lampes (43) avec les(quelles illumineront (?) ...)

(2) (.....) les étendards des chefs des milliers avec les chefs (.....)

(3) (.....) quatorze (agneaux et) moutons. Les lévites abattront (.....)

(5) les prêtres fils d'Aaron (asper)geront leur sang (sur l'autel tout autour...)

(6) (.....et) leur graisse ils encenseront sur l'autel de l'ho(locauste.....)

(7) (leur offrande) et leur libation ils encenseront sur les graiss(es....holocaustes en parfum)

(8) d'apaisement (pour) Yahvé. (Des moutons et des agneaux ils prélèveront) comme don

(9) la cuisse droite et la poitrine (dans) le geste de présentation, le commencement (de l'épaule) et

(10) les mâchoires et l'estomac aux prêtres comme leur portion selon leur loi, et aux lévites

(11) le dos. Après, ils distribueront aux fils d'Israël. Et les fils d'Israël donneront aux prêtres

(12) un mouton et un agneau, aux lévites un mouton et un agneau, et à chaque tribu

(13) un mouton et un agneau. Ils les mangeront le même jour dans la cour extérieure

(14) devant Yahvé.[44] C'est la loi éternelle pour leurs générations. Chaque année après cela

(15) ils mangeront [45] et ils s'oindront de la nouvelle huile des olives, car en ce jour-là, ils expieront

(16) pour toute l'huile d'olive de la terre devant Yahvé, une fois dans l'année. Ils se réjouiront,

(col. XXIII,01) tous les fils d'Israël, dans toutes (leurs résidences devant Yahvé. C'est la loi éternelle)

(02) (pour leurs générations).

Ce fragment du "Rouleau du Temple" me paraît très important pour la solution définitive du problème de l'identification de la communauté de Qumrân avec les Esséniens. En effet, les indications de ce fragment, et particulièrement les prescriptions, tranchent la question d'une manière décisive, en plus d'expliquer l'information étrange fournie par Flavius Josèphe sur l'attitude des Esséniens envers l'huile et l'onction.

Flavius Josèphe, qui prétendait avoir passé quelque temps chez les Esséniens et avoir donc une connaissance directe de leurs coutumes et de leur pratiques, écrit entre autres ceci: les Esséniens "regardent l'huile comme une souillure, et si quelqu'un a été oint malgré lui, il s'essuie le corps; ils se font un devoir, en effet, d'avoir la peau sèche et d'être toujours vêtus de blanc".[46] Cette information semble indiquer que les Esséniens n'avaient pas l'habitude de se servir de l'huile pour l'onction de corps. Le "Rouleau du Temple", de son côté, précise que les membres de la communauté de Qumrân ne rejetaient pas complètement l'habitude de l'onction du corps avec l'huile, mais qu'ils pratiquaient cet usage seulement une fois l'an (col. XXII, 16). D'après le "Rouleau du Temple", il s'agit là d'une pratique rituelle signifiant expiation et purification: à la Fête de la Nouvelle Huile, les membres de la communauté de Qumrân purifiaient l'huile de toute la terre [47] par le rite de consécration, et pour obtenir le pardon de Dieu et gagner sa grâce, ils s'oignaient le corps ce jour-là.

Les indications fournies par le "Rouleau du Temple" montrent bien que les Esséniens n'excluaient pas entièrement l'onction du corps. Leur attitude envers cet usage semble causée, comme l'a suggéré Y. Yadin,[48] par le fait que durant leur habitation à Qumrân, les Esséniens n'avaient pas d'huile convenable, d'huile épurée qu'on ne pouvait obtenir, comme le "Rouleau du Temple" le montre, que par les rites d'offrande et de sacrifice de l'huile au temple de Jérusalem. Flavius Josèphe ne pouvait pas connaître les vraies raisons de cette habitude des Esséniens lorsqu'il écrit qu'ils se font un devoir d'avoir la peau sèche. Le passage du "Rouleau du Temple" sur la Fête de la Nouvelle Huile constitue en fait une preuve nouvelle et décisive pour l'identification de la communauté de Qumrân avec les Esséniens. Cette opinion est corroborée par d'autres données de ce document qui, même s'ils attendent encore une analyse détaillée, montrent dans leur ensemble qu'on ne peut plus mettre en doute cette identification, voire même la contester.

TERMINOLOGICAL BOOBYTRAPS AND REAL PROBLEMS IN SECOND-TEMPLE JUDAEO-CHRISTIAN STUDIES

Morton Smith

Let me begin with some reasons for not presenting this paper: In the first place, there is a prejudice in favor of any established terminology; from infancy we have been trained to believe that what we have been taught is right. Moreover, this belief is convenient. Secondly, to discuss the established terminology one has to use it, so the discussion involves a sort of begging the question, what the rabbis called *sbat be sbat*. Finally, those who may to some extent agree with me will want to go on to the question, what can be done about the faults of the terminology? But there is little likelihood that the established usages can soon or greatly be changed. Consequently I shall probably get some blame for wasting time.

Nevertheless, the present system seems to me so unfortunate that I want to try to describe some of the damage it does, and to indicate an alternative conceptual structure by which I think our studies could be better oriented.

First, let us look at our terminology for the sources. We commonly describe the Jewish and Christian books of this period (which, for convenience, I shall extend to about the end of the first century A.D.) as either "biblical" or "extra-biblical." "Biblical" books are classified as "Old Testament" and "New Testament," while the "extra-biblical" are apt to be called "post-biblical," "intertestamental," "pseudepigrapha," etc. "The Apocrypha" are a little, second-class canonical group of not quite definite content, a sort of theological *demi-monde*, while "apocryphal," when not referring to members of this group, is a term of abuse implying that the user disbelieves, or at least dislikes and wants to discredit, the document referred to.

This common usage conceals the fact that there is no such thing as "*the* Bible." There are many different "Bibles," accepted by many different religious organizations, but it hardly needs arguing that the question of what was or is accepted by the Samaritans or the Ethiopians or the Mormons or the Council of Trent or the sanhedrin of Yabneh has no importance for questions about the original significance of books written before their times. On such matters the Holy Ghost was not a reliable source of information.

Hence to classify the finds at Qumran, for instance, into "biblical" and "extra-biblical" books is to commit a gross anachronism which, having been committed, has concealed from many scholars the question of the actual relations between the texts found there. Probably no one would deny that the Qumran sect (or the several sects from which works somehow got into the Qumran manuscripts) did distinguish between books of what they thought greater or less legal authority, supernatural inspiration, sanctity, etc. But we should not assume that their judgements about these matters coincided with those of the rabbis of Yabneh. Given the Qumran remarks about "those who plaster the wall" and "those who seek after smooth things," there seems a strong likelihood that their opinions would have differed. Consequently we should not assume that the Qumran authorities thought Genesis more sacred than Jubilees - indeed, the reverse is probable. And for practical legal questions the Damascus Document may have taken precedence of both, as Mishnah and Talmud take precedence of Old Testament texts in Jewish law. Undoubtedly, too, the Qumran sectarians revered the biblical prophets, but they also thought they themselves could do better. The secrets hidden in the prophetic texts had been revealed to the teacher of righteousness (pHab. 7.4f.); his followers were the instruments of further revelations given in their study groups, and were pledged to obey everything "that might be revealed" "from time to time" (Manual 9.13). The author of the Hodayot repeatedly claims prophetic inspiration. What evidence, then, have we for supposing that whenever Qumran texts speak of "the prophets" they refer only to those canonical in the present Hebrew Bible? Given such uncertainties, grouping of the texts by literary types - legendary, legal, prophetic, etc. - would have given a better impression of the Qumran literature *as the sectarians saw it* than would the division into our anachronistic categories of "biblical" and "extra-biblical."

These categories cannot be defended by the argument that the "biblical" texts belong to an older literary period, the others are "post-biblical" or "intertestamental." "Post-biblical" is defensible only from a Jewish point of view; the New Testament texts, undoubtedly "biblical" by ordinary standards, are of course later. Even if they are left out of consideration, "post-biblical" is hard to defend: Daniel and Esther may be later than Jubilees and the Temple Scroll. "Intertestamental" is not equally bad; it is worse. It suggests that this literature can be arranged on a single line leading from one Testament to the other, whereas in fact there were many different lines of development, some running counter to others. Moreover, we need a term to describe all of this sort of literature, not only that preserved in Qumran, but also the works of the same sort that continued to be produced long after the completion of the texts eventually canonized in the New Testament. The closest relatives of the Hodayot, for instance, are the Odes of Solomon; the early apocalypses, visions of Enoch, and testaments of the patriarchs are the first examples of lines that run far down into the Middle Ages. "Intertestamental," therefore, will not do. Neither will "pseudepigrapha." Many of these texts (indeed, most of those at Qumran) are not pseudepigraphic, while many biblical texts are so (see my article in *Pseudepigrapha I, Fondation Hardt Entretiens* 18.189ff.)

In sum, the current terminology is unsatisfactory because it tries to describe the material by reference to a criterion, canonicity, which is both ambiguous and, for questions of origin and original significance, irrelevant.

Given such confusion in the description of the sources, we should not be surprised to find even more confusion in the historical terms based on the sources. Here the worst causes of trouble are the "sectarian" terms and their subdivisions. "Late Judaism" (*Spätjudentum*) I mention only to dismiss; the application of such a term to the Judaism of two thousand years ago should have immediately been laughed out of usage. The best to be said in its defense is that, by its survival, it warns us against those foolish enough to use it.

"Hellenistic" and "Palestinian" Judaism are more pretentious contenders because they seem to be supported by impressive bodies of evidence. On the one side are commonly marshalled the LXX, the Letter of Aristeas, Philo, the remains of the other so-called "hellenistic Jewish authors," and those Greek works of Israelite forms - in common parlance, "apocrypha and pseudepigrapha" - usually assigned to the diaspora. The impression these give is supported by the great predominance of Greek in Jewish inscriptions outside Palestine and by many miscellaneous diasporic archaeological remains. On the other side are set Ben Sira, the lost Semitic originals of many other works from the latter days of the Second Temple, the great predominance of Hebrew and Aramaic at Qumran, their less marked (roughly 65/35) predominance in Judean inscriptions before 70, Josephus' report that he first wrote his *War* in Aramaic and needed secretarial help to put it into decent Greek, and the development of rabbinic Judaism in the years after 70. Neither of these lists is anything like exhaustive; both are intended merely to indicate the sorts and extent of the evidence that has led to the common distinction of "hellenistic" or "diasporic" from "Palestinian" Judaism.

This distinction has been particularly mischievous because it has led to much circular argumentation. On the basis of supposedly Semitic or Greek traits, works of unknown origin have been attributed to Palestine or

Alexandria (Alexandria being the central dump for works of allegedly "hellenistic" Judaism) and these attributions have then been used as further evidence for the supposedly different characters of the Judaism of these different localities. Thus the field is now encumbered by a mass of so-called "knowledge" that is really clotted conjecture, and this pseudo-knowledge has contributed to seriously one-sided pictures of Palestinian Judaism. The most influential were probably those of George Foot Moore and of Bousset from whose *Kyrios Christos* came Bultmann's attempt to dismiss as secondary everything in the Gospels that he could represent as "hellenistic." "Hellenistic" is a particularly unfortunate term because of its ambiguity; it had better be used to refer to the historical period, B.C. 323-30.

As soon as one looks more closely at the above mentioned bodies of evidence they disintegrate, and so does the case for a general distinction between Palestinian and diasporic Judaism. First of all, what is "diasporic"? Does "Palestine" include Ptolemais, Sepphoris, Sebaste, Tiberias, Scythopolis, Caesarea, Apollonia, Antipatris, Azotus, Ascalon, Anthedon, Gaza - to mention only the bigger places? Was the Judaism in these "Palestinian" or "diasporic"? Next the authors: The Septuagintal translation (of the Pentateuch only) was reportedly made in Alexandria and the report by "Aristeas" is presumably Alexandrian. Most will dismiss without thinking what he also reported, that the translators came from Palestine. As for the translation of the other books, the field is free and the presence of Greek translations even at Qumran should warn against the assumption that they could not have been made in Palestine. Ben Sira indeed wrote in Hebrew and his work was translated by his grandson when the latter went to Egypt, but the grandson's Greek had presumably been learned in Palestine. Of the so-called "hellenistic Jewish authors" half a dozen - Eupolemus and "pseudo-Eupolemus", Cleodemus-Malchus, Theodotus, Philo the elder, and one of the authors used in Sibyllines III - have plausibly been assigned to Palestine. On the other hand, a diasporic work gives us the most dramatic glorification of martyrdom to preserve purity (IV Macc., from Antioch). Again, the most picturesque miracle stories to demonstrate the sanctity and divine protection of the Jerusalem temple, those of II Macc., are commonly assigned to the diaspora, because the author was Jason of Cyrene. But the fact that Jason came from Cyrene does not prove that he worked only there (cp. Menippus of Gadara and Paul of Tarsus), and the letters prefixed to II Macc. do prove that our text came to Egypt from Palestine. As for the inscriptions, what they prove is that there were plenty of Jews in Judea who preferred Greek to any Semitic language, and a few in the diaspora who preferred Hebrew or Aramaic to Greek. Archaelogically, the rarity of iconic decoration in Judea (but not in the rest of Palestine) before 70 is indeed remarkable, but even in Judea and Jerusalem itself there are some exceptions - the tomb of Jason, for instance ('*Atiqot* 4).

All in all the evidence seems to indicate that while Hebrew and Aramaic elements were more frequent in Palestine, and especially in Judea, and while Greek elements were more frequent elsewhere in Roman territory, nevertheless, the range of possible variations was everywhere roughly the same. Even rather extreme variants turn up where we should least expect them, e.g. substantial evidence for Essene influence has been found in the Epistle to the Ephesians (Kuhn, *NTS* 7.334ff.). It would not be implausible to suppose that a few aristocrats in Jerusalem had the sort of Greek education and philosophical attitude that we find in Philo. Although Josephus' Greek was none too good, his rival, Justus of Tiberias, was much better at home in the language (Josephus, *Vita* 40 and 340) and was remembered in philosophical literature for one of his anecdotes about Plato (Diogenes Laertius 2.41).

Consequently the common *in toto* distinction of "Palestinian" from "diasporic" (not to mention "hellenistic") Judaism is simply unjustified. One can speak only of a difference *a potiori*, and of a few particular groups which, so far as we can judge from the preserved evidence, seem to have been peculiar to one or another district, for instance, the circle around the Onias temple in Egypt, or the therapeutaes, *perhaps* the baptist groups in the Jordan valley, and so on. Sometimes such groups can be connected with unique figures - John "the baptizer," Simon "the magician" *(magos)*, Judas of Galilee, Jesus of Nazareth.

Nobody thinks of excluding Judas of Galilee and his followers from accounts of first century Judaism, though their practise of killing without trial not only gentiles, but even Jews of whom they strongly disapproved, would seem to have put them rather far outside ordinary interpretations of Jewish law. Promiscuous murder might be thought to indicate a more serious break with Jewish tradition than did healing on the Sabbath or eating with publicans and sinners. But Judas' followers were saved from schism by suicide, while the success of Jesus' followers has made "Christianity" a category distinct from "Judaism." Consequently, in spite of the recent fashion of declaring that "Jesus was a Jew," it is rare to find an account of first-century Judaism which recognizes that Christianity was one of its most important forms. Conversely, how many accounts of early Christianity treat it as an exceptional form of first-century Judaism? What goes for the movements goes also for the men. The only Pharisee about whom we are really well informed is St. Paul, but how many accounts of Pharisaism have taken account of him? John the baptist and Simon *Magus*, too, are commonly treated as peripheral figures of "Christianity," not as evidence of the various forms of Judaism - this although "Christianity" as such did not come into existence until John was dead and Simon's connection (if any) with the followers of Jesus had probably been terminated.

But Simon was a Samaritan. And what were the Samaritans? The destruction of the Gerizim temple in Hyrcanus' time is most plausibly understood as an attempt at religious *Anschluss*: Thereby the Samaritans would be forced to bring their sacrifices to Jerusalem and subject themselves to the Hasmonean High-Priesthood, which evidently considered them as potential *Ioudaioi* - adherents of the Judean cult. How many of them consented to enter the fold? How many refused and resorted to surreptitious sacrifices without a temple, or contented themselves with synagogue worship? We have no way of telling. Josephus distinguished "Samaritans" as an ethnic group, and was contemptuous of them as he was of Idumeans and Galileans, who by this time were undoubtedly "Jews" - i.e. adherents of the Jerusalem cult - but whom Josephus often distinguished from *Ioudaioi* when he used the latter term to mean (territorial) "Judeans."

It is time to tear away this cobweb of nomenclature and try to see the facts it conceals. We have to do with the gradual extension through the Greco-Roman world (and through Arabia, Mesopotamia, Armenia, and Iran, which are usually ignored) of a peculiar cult and its associated literary, legal, and social traditions.

Part of the literary tradition was the legend that the cult had once been peculiar to a single family - allied tribes are often linked by such familial legends. This legend has persisted to the present: Christians, like Jews, are still theoretically one family, "the Israel of God." However, already in antiquity the members of this theoretical family seem to have showed no significant physical uniformity. I do not recall any ancient reference to a man's being recognized, from his physical appearance, as a Jew, except when the recognition was an inference from circumcision. (And even circumcision was not specific; it occurred among Arabs and Egyptians.) We can be reasonably sure that in the Greco-Roman period the followers of this cult had been so diversified by intermarriage, adoption, conversion, and adherence, that its spread cannot be considered as that of a single genetic stock.

The one thing common to all forms of the cult was the god called Yahweh, Yah, Iao, etc., who was often associated with various titles and epithets - Elohim, Adonai, Sabaoth, He who hears prayer, He whose name is blessed, etc. Most of these epithets, in one place or another, seem to have been hypostatized as independent but associated deities.

Yahweh might also be associated with other gods, of whom a long list could be compiled from Old Testament times on. His most famous associate, of course, was to be Jesus. In a few systems of the sort usually called "gnostic" Yahweh appears as an inferior god, and he so appears, too, in a good many unsystematic magical texts. He was also included in various syncretistic expressions of late Roman paganism, for instance the famous Clarian oracle; "I declare Iao to be the highest god of all, the Hades for winter, Zeus of beginning spring, Helios of summer, and splendid Iao of autumn." (Macrobius, *Sat*. I.18).

To what extent such theological effusions implied worship is uncertain, but there is no question that the worship of Yahweh by pagans was ancient and extensive. Ezra proudly records the offerings made to Yahweh by the Persian emperors; the refusal of the Jerusalem temple staff to accept sacrifices offered by the Romans was the official beginning of the revolt of A.D.66 (Josephus, *War* 2.409). Therefore to discuss the spread of this cult in terms of "the extension of Judaism" - whatever one means by "Judaism"- is to discuss only one part of a complex process. The neglected part of this process, which badly needs study, was an important factor in the extension of declared "Judaism," since Dio Cassius reports that the name *Ioudaioi* was commonly applied to whatever men followed Jewish customs (37.17.1).

This report illustrates our need for another study - that of the ancient definitions of "Jew" and "Judaism," with careful attention to the different users of the terms and the circumstances of the usage. We have already seen some of the ambiguities of the terms in antiquity - the fluctuation between religious and territorial usage (the Idumeans were *Ioudaioi* because adherents of the Jerusalem temple, but not *Ioudaioi* because not natives of Judea), the fluctuation between references to temple adherence and reference to general religious pattern (the adherents of the Onias temple were *Ioudaioi* by general pattern, in spite of their rejection of Jerusalem), the uncertainty as to which variations of the pattern, and how many of its elements, are referred to. (Were the Samaritans *Ioudaioi*, or the Christians, or the *sebomenoi*? And so on.) An even more serious difficulty results from the modern specialization of "Jew" to refer to the adherents of rabbinic Judaism and their descendants, plus a few minor groups - the Karaites, the Falashas, and the like. Because of this modern usage, students of first century "Judaism" commonly take for granted that, even though rabbinic Judaism had not yet developed, something very like it was the common form of the religion, at least in Palestine, and all other groups are to be seen as divergent from this primitive stock. An extreme of absurdity is reached from this notion when the Judaism of the high-priestly families of the Jerusalem temple itself, who are supposed to have been mostly Sadducean, is represented as a divergence from pretendently "normative" Pharisaic Judaism.

This simply begs the question: What actually were the beliefs and observances of "the average Palestine Jew" - if there was any such animal - before 70? We have reports in rabbinic literature and in Josephus' later works that most people followed the rulings of the Pharisees (N.B. *not* that they "were Pharisees"), but these reports are suspect as self-interested. Josephus knew nothing of this when he was writing his earlier works; by the time he came to his later he had himself become a follower of the Pharisees. Moreover, his claims about their influence are contradicted by his reports about the course of events, in which they repeatedly appear as advocates of persons and policies that failed to gain general support. The later rabbis, for their part, had an obvious, practical interest in representing their spiritual ancestors, the Pharisees, as already enjoying the sort of authority they themselves hoped to achieve. Accordingly, neither rabbis nor Josephus can be trusted on this matter. We had better think of pre-70 Judaism simply as the sum of its known parts, plus other elements of which we know little more than that they existed, plus yet more elements of which even the existence is now unknown. To make students aware of this special meaning of "Judaism" is one of the most difficult aspects of presenting the subject.

What we do know of the various forms of Judaism before A.D.70 is derived mainly from their literary remains. Therefore, another question that needs looking into is the relation between the cult of Yahweh and the Israelite literary tradition. Unfortunately, the study of this literary tradition is dominated by and neglected for the study of the various canonical anthologies made from it - i.e. the different Old and New Testaments. What we need is a history of the literature as a whole, a history based not only on what has been preserved, but on the evidence of what has been lost, and tracing not only the development of characteristic Israelite forms and themes, but also the various combinations and developments that resulted when this literary tradition came into contact with that of Greece. The beginnings of this work - to the end of the Persian period - have often been attempted, but I do not know of any adequate history of the Israelite literary tradition in the Greco-Roman world.[1] Such a history would have to place the development of important new forms - e.g. the gospel - in proper context, explore the ways in which Israelite content was adapted to Greek forms and so changed them (as, for instance, in the Pauline "epistles"), and follow out the resultant combinations and compromises to their issuance in the new literary forms characteristic of the Middle Ages (for instance, the new histories, beginning with that of Eusebius, produced by the fusion of Israelite and Greek historical conventions and concerns).

There is so much to be done here that I hesitate even to mention the other fields for research, for instance, the study of Israelite legal traditions and their adjustments to and influences on their Greek and Roman counterparts, or the similar study of liturgical traditions. I hope that what has been said will at least suggest my desiderata for investigation of the cult of Yahweh in the Greco-Roman period. The investigation should take account of all the evidence, and should not impose on any part of it categories and distinctions which were developed only in later times. What was indefinite must carefully be kept indefinite. Indeed, the gradual development of the later categories is one of the most important topics of the study and is only now beginning to receive the attention it deserves. Here the McMaster project is an example of what needs to be done. As such projects are gradually completed and their results assimilated, it is possible that the maleficent effects of our inherited terminology may to some extent be corrected.

Postscript: In the light of the discussion elicited by this paper and of problems raised by several other papers at the Congress I should like to add a further desideratum for research in this field. As far as possible the topics studied should be specific and clearly defined or definable; abstract terms and enormous subjects should be avoided. For example, accounts of ascents into the heavens and of means to ascend can be discussed with useful precision; so can conversations with angels, predictions of impending disasters, etc. But no good is likely to come of attempts to decide just which combinations of these and other elements constituted, *at that time*, an "apocalypse" - especially since, before A.D. 70, no writer of any work now called an apocalypse ever used this title for his composition. Similarly, discussions of the "gnosticism" of those who never called themselves "gnostics," the "mystical religion" of those who never spoke of any, and suchlike great, unsubstantial generalizations, are verbose inanities. At present we need precise accounts of the preserved data.

THE FOSTER CHILD: A NEGLECTED THEME IN EARLY CHRISTIAN LIFE AND THOUGHT

John H. Corbett

Foster children were to be found almost everywhere in the Greco-Roman world in ancient times; but nowhere is the foster child to be identified with an adopted one; for the practices of fostering and adoption were distinctly different. Whereas adoption was a formal process usually legally recognized, the practice of rearing foster children was essentially a pragmatic one; surplus children were fed and reared as fosterlings by someone other than their natural parents; and it is from this relationship that their name derived (*threptos/alumnus*). Their legal status was always vexed and their social position uncertain, as we shall see. It is true, nonetheless, that the decision to adopt a child often arose from the same source as the impulse to rear a fosterling; in antiquity marriage was often viewed with a mistrust rooted in misogyny; and adoption or fostering were often viewed as preferable to procreation, in part at least, no doubt, because of the widespread fear of excessive fertility, a fear well founded in the demographic experience of antiquity.[1]

The evidence clearly indicates that the most common sources of foster children were the streets and other public places where unwanted infants were abandoned to die by exposure, and sometimes rescued to be reared as foundlings by would-be foster parents. Fostering thus presupposes infanticide; and, indeed, infanticide was universal in the Greco-Roman world except among the Jews and, later, the Christians.[2] Among the other Semitic peoples, the prevalent form of infanticide at one time was infant sacrifice;[3] more common, and more important for this study was the practice of exposing children, especially girls, "potting" them as the Greeks sometimes called it from the widespread use of pots for this purpose.[4] Infanticide has obvious social and demographic implications which should not be overlooked; it is an efficient and selective technique for the control of fertility, especially when more female infants are killed; and infanticide was common in the Western world until pre-modern times.[5] That it was widely practiced is no indication that infanticide caused no concern; it is perhaps easier to suppose than to demonstrate a close connexion with the widespread ancient anxiety concerning sexuality. It stands to reason that children chosen for sacrifice or simple exposure had a special quality or were the focus of a special concern; foundlings who were reared as foster children retained this special quality, as this paper shall suggest. They had been marked out for death by exposure, indeed to all intents they had been put to death; and subsequently they were reborn when taken up as fosterlings; they had passed through death to life, and acquired thereby the special quality of "liminal beings," as I shall argue. It is for this reason that their legal and social status remained ambiguous. Reared by someone other than their natural parents, by whom however they could be reclaimed, they could be treated as slave or child, concubine or spouse, as our sources clearly indicate. In other words the social status of the foster child is best understood in relationship to his paradoxical social experience; and this is no less true for Christian than for pre-christian times. It is thus appropriate to begin with a glance at the practice of fostering among the Greeks and Romans before the time of Christ.[6]

If we look first at the legal and anecdotal evidence, already in the early *Law Code of Gortyna* (ca. 480-460 B.C.) we find exposure of children casually mentioned as a practice taken for granted; although no explicit terminology is used, the Code allows masters to take up, and presumably rear, the children of serfs under various conditions (*Code* IV); this is clearly contrasted with the practice of formal adoption among the free-born, dealt with at length in another place (*Code* X, XI).[7] A speech attributed to Demosthenes (ca. 350 B.C.) informs us of a woman purchased as a slave girl and raised for prostitution; the point at issue is her civil status, for her owner had raised her (*threpsai* cognate with *threptos*) as a daughter and passed her off as free-born to increase the profits of her trade, so we are told. Again the ambiguous status of the fosterling.[8] Similarly, at Rome, the jurist Scaevola (consul 95 B.C.) had experience of a case involving a divorced woman who had exposed her son; the son was taken up and reared by another but was adjudged by the jurist to be his father's heir although unknown to him, for he had never been disinherited (*Digest* XL 4, 29).

The legal experience of *alumni* was apparently fraught with ambiguity; Scaevola was consulted as to the provisions made for the support of an *alumnus* in a will - are they binding on the heirs (*Digest* XXXIV 1, 15)? Suetonius tells us of two distinguished grammarians of the first-century B.C., both of them free born, exposed, reared and trained by their foster father (*nutritor, educator: On Grammarians* VII, XXI); one of them actually preferred to remain a slave despite his mother's attempt to assert his freedom (ibid. XXI). Both attained considerable eminence despite their ambiguous social status; we should note that their private histories were well-known. The oratorical literature of the early Empire contains a number of vivid hypothetical but not altogether fictitious cases pertaining to exposed children; sometimes the natural father is portrayed as trying to claim them back (Seneca *Controv.* IX 3); some might be deliberately crippled by their foster-fathers to make them more effective beggars (ibid. X 4). A father seeks to reclaim his exposed son by repaying the cost of maintenance; but the son prefers to be associated with the family of his *educator*, however poor; he wishes to marry the man's daughter (Quintilian *Inst. Orat.* VII i, 14).[9] It is completely consistent with the picture that our other evidence presents that an *alumnus* could aspire to marry his foster sister. Jurists in the time of Justinian were well aware that doubt had been felt *apud antiquos* regarding the legitimacy of marriage between a man and his *alumna* (*Cod. Just.* V 4, 26 of 530 A.D.); the Christian Emperor is prepared to allow it - so long as she was not his godchild; the Emperor feels that such an *alumna* must have been reared and freed not as a daughter but with marriage in mind. Such ambiguities were common and often vexing; Pliny asks Trajan for guidance in dealing with *threptoi* who were apparently common in his province of Pontus and Bithynia; how was their status to be clarified? Who was liable for their maintenance? Trajan replied that these *liberi nati deinde sublate a quibusdam et in servitute educati* were to be declared free, even without the repayment of their maintenance by the natural parents who were now presumably asserting their freedom. Roman law from the early Principate protected the freedom of exposed freeborn children; but in not requiring repayment of maintenance Trajan is clearly following the Greek rather than the Roman custom (Pliny *Letters* X 65/6).[10] The whole contentious case illustrates the ambiguous status of *threptoi*, a social not legal description of these fosterlings, and the extreme diversity of practice in their regard throughout the Empire in the time of Trajan as before - and since.

Space does not permit me to discuss in detail the fascinating case of Petronia Iusta, known to us at first hand from a body of documents recently discovered.[11] But the evidence seems to indicate that Petronia was an *alumna*, taken up and reared by her natural mother's patron, who well may himself have been her natural father, though not prepared to admit it. In any case her social status was much contested and the evidence confirms everything that we know about the ambiguous nature of fosterlings. They are the children of their foster-parents and then again not children but freedmen or slaves. Their origins are mysterious, their paternity especially so, whether they come from the gutter or from nearer home. They have a special relationship with their foster-parents but it is not such as necessarily to exclude a more intimate liaison with foster siblings or parents, an observation which gives substance to some of the charges made by the Church Fathers (though Christian *practice* was not much different, as we shall see.) All in all, foster-children are rather unusual people, they defy exact social classification, a condition which anthropologists have noted to endow such people with a special significance for good or evil.

The epigraphic evidence confirms this general picture. In the Greek East we find that most of the inscriptions concerning *threptoi* were either votive or sepulchral; others relate to the manumission of slave *threptoi*. As Nani correctly observes, on the basis of the epigraphic evidence, the term *threptos* is clearly a word drawn from daily speech without a technical legal meaning, indicating a child or adult who is being or has been reared by people other than its natural parents.[12] As such we find the term applied to people of many different social conditions; it is used of slaves, whether they were exposed children or sold at birth or born and raised in the master's household. It is also used to describe freed slaves. But in the Greek East we find the term used of free foster-children, whether adopted or simply wards of their foster-parents, and of students or apprentices in relationship to their teachers or masters. The evidence from the Latin world gives almost the same picture. Notable among names born by fosterlings are ones which mark them as lucky or as gifts from the gods, an interesting point given what we have observed about the special status of foster-children.

If the evidence which we have been examining helps establish the scope and importance of the social practice of fostering, the literary evidence contributes much to our understanding of its social meaning. Stories from Homer or Hellenistic comedy help us to flesh out the details of the practice which we have already outlined. The tale of the swineherd Eumaeus in the *Odyssey* (XV 364 ff), Euripides' play, *Ion*, about an exposed child of mysterious origins and unusual sagacity, and the comedies of Menander and Plautus (Menander *The Arbitration*, Plautus *Cistellaria*; cf. *Casina*) all contribute to our understanding of the special status and significance of the foster child. But the most famous literary foundling of antiquity is Oedipus. Crippled and exposed on a hillside to die, he was rescued by a shepherd and brought up as a king's son. The prophecy which led his parents to expose him already marked him out for death, as it appeared, but for a special fate in fact; he was a child who was not a child, a child who became husband of his own mother, after killing his "real" father and bringing a curse on Thebes, a man of great power and virtue driven to uncover the mystery of his own birth only to destroy himself. This story bears much reflexion, the tragic working out of an old mythic theme rich with resonances on the themes of kinship and identity but for us also a classic statement of the "special" status of the exposed child, the foundling, a status defying conventional classification and clearly associated, for good and bad, with social marginality. The foundling is related to the community in some way, but not well integrated with it; he has been left for dead and, in a manner, reborn; but the associations of his previous life can return to haunt him. The story of Oedipus illustrates the dangers posed to the community by foundlings and the potentially tragic consequences arising from clarification of their status; in such cases discovery leads to a tragic reversal of fortune and integration with the community is achieved only at great cost. The Oedipus story has great symbolic meaning for our study.

The common recurrence of the themes of exposure, fostering and discovery of identity in Hellenistic New Comedy and at Rome attests merely to the domestication of the myth in the Greco-Roman world. The fosterling is still a socially marginal character, now usually a heroine in disguise, who still requires to be integrated into the community through a clarification of status, a clarification achieved through comic reversal and leading to a positive comic resolution. We might say that the tragic theme had lost some of its potential in becoming domesticated; we are clearly dealing here with a form of secularization parallel to the experience of the modern world so familiar to the social sciences.[13] The gods have withdrawn somewhat, social definitions are less clear cut in the cosmopolitan Hellenistic world, or at least cause less anxiety; characters and experiences which call into question these social definitions are now seen as less threatening; they can, perhaps, be handled in new ways. Mary Douglas has shown how fears of pollution are related to social anxiety about group self-definition, and also that there is a close correlation between social images of the body and the structure of a society.[14] As Greco-Roman society became increasingly cosmopolitan in the Hellenistic period (moved, that is, from a society with strong "group" to one with strong "grid," in the useful terminology of Mary Douglas)[15], it came increasingly to feel less threatened by the social anomaly represented by foster-children. And the newly articulated structures of law, education and administration made such anomalies more easy to deal with. However, as we shall see, foster-children again became an area of concern and potential difficulty in the early Christian period.

It might also be useful to introduce into our consideration of the special status of the foster-child, the concept of "liminality" as developed by Victor Turner;[16] it harmonizes well with the theoretical perspective adopted from Mary Douglas but allows for a more dynamic interpretation. Briefly stated, Turner's theory draws attention to the special qualities associated, for good and bad, with people passing through any important change of status; societies develop *rites de passage* to regulate such important changes and to reduce the danger which they pose to social stability by calling into question conventional social classifications.[17] People passing through such changes are said by Turner to acquire a quality of liminality, such as shamans do by their rites of initiation, or the mystic initiates in the ancient mystery cults.[18] Exposed children do pass through such a stage of liminality and when taken up as fosterlings they retain some of the qualities associated with the liminal process of death and rebirth. By following Turner's lead we can win a powerful ally in our quest for understanding, in the form of a successful methodology for analysis and a convincing body of analogous cases. I consider these advantages to be decisive; the case is strong for considering the ancient foster-child as a liminal being and it will be further strengthened when we turn to the Christian evidence.

Almost from its earliest days the Christian church was much concerned with the two practices of infant exposure and fostering; the early Christians, like the Jews, saw their own rejection of infanticide as a fundamental, one might almost say *the* fundamental difference separating them from the pagans. In this way the *Epistle of Barnabas* from the first century lays it down as an absolute injunction (chapter 19); "Thou shalt not slay the child by procuring abortion; nor again shalt thou destroy it after it is born"; again, those in the "Way of Darkness" are characterized as "murderers of children, destroyers of the workmanship of the Lord" (chapter 20). Justin, in the second century, argues that, so far from being guilty of infanticide, Christians "have been taught that to expose newly born children is the part of wicked men" (*Apology* I 27); rather than engage in exposure and infanticide, Christians chose continence (*ibid.* I 29). This opposition of infanticide and continence is of the very greatest importance, and I shall return to it again; suffice it to note here that the condemnation of infanticide is a dominant theme among the Church Fathers.[19] Nothing very much is said in this early apologetic literature about fosterlings. It is presumably taken for granted that Christian families will not produce any surplus children for fostering in the normal course of things. What, we may ask, of infants exposed by pagans? The *Apostolic Constitutions*, one of the earliest guides to church practice, make explicit provisions for the adoption of *Christian orphans* and entrust the general responsibility for their welfare to the bishop (*Apostolic Constitutions* IV 1-2; cf. *The Didascalia Apostolorum in Syriac* XVII). The way this service is organized under the bishop is analogous to the procedure later adopted for the protection of

Christian *alumni* and we are probably entitled to assume that Christians rescued exposed children of whatever background from the earliest period and reared them as foundlings. There are some precious pieces of information suggesting that this was happening commonly by the fourth century at the latest.

In a letter to Boniface Augustine discusses the baptism of infants and their sponsorship at baptism by adults who may or may not be their parents (Augustine *Letters* 98; see *PL* #33; 362); some infants are sponsored by strangers; sometimes masters sponsor their own slave children; sometimes the parents are dead and others act as sponsors as a form of charity. "From time to time (infants) whom their parents have cruelly exposed to be reared by anybody (who took them up) are gathered up by holy virgins and sponsored for baptism by them." This letter was probably written around A.D. 400: it certainly suggests that holy virgins had been accustomed for a considerable time to take up foster-children and have them baptized certainly Augustine does not consider it a novel idea. But we should note carefully the association of holy virgins and foster-children; Augustine considers their action as a cardinal work of mercy, explicitly comparing it to the deed of the Good Samaritan. That famous deed is, of course, not only an example of charity but a type of the redemption; it is certainly in place here, for the "redemption" of abandoned children is at the very heart of Christian belief and practice.

As we might imagine there is abundant epigraphic evidence for the practice of fostering among Christians.[20] The theme is especially common in the Christian inscriptions of Rome. The early evidence from the catacomb of Priscilla, which is generally dated to the first and second centuries, is apparently not yet available in a complete and accurate modern edition. However, it appears that there are some half-dozen or more inscriptions from this early cemetery mentioning *alumni* and attesting to their close relationship with their foster-parents, and there may be some others of equal antiquity.[21] I should add that there is often little in form or content to distinguish the Christian inscriptions relating to *alumni* apart from the form of names, an occasional clearly Christian expression or the location in which the inscription was found. In form and in its more restricted social significance the Christian practice of fostering clearly has little to distinguish it from the non-Christian practice which it resembles; as we shall see, the value attached to the practice of fostering by Christians is somewhat different.

From the time of Constantine on, there is abundant legal evidence of the concern which the Roman Christian Emperors felt for exposed children and fosterlings. Even Diocletian, as early as A.D. 294, had taken steps to forbid the sale of newborn children (*Cod. Just.* IV 43,1); and, in order to prevent poor parents from exposing their children, Constantine was obliged to provide food and clothing at state expense first in Italy (A.D. 315) and subsequently in Africa (A.D. 322; *Cod. Theod.* XI 27,1 & 2); the details of these laws suggest the dimensions of the problem and Constantine's concern to find adequate remedies.[22] The problem obviously was a thorny one; accepting sale and fostering of children might seem to encourage the practice; but giving natural parents or former masters unrestricted rights of recovery would effectively discourage fostering of slave or free children by making the rights of the foster-parents rather uncertain. This latter situation could be avoided by eliminating the right of recovery altogether; in any case by 412 the rights of the foster-parents were established as absolute provided only that a bishop had witnessed the act of fostering with his signature (*Cod. Theod.* V #9, 2). We must assume that exposure, though illegal, continued, for the church was soon concerned to establish a regular procedure for fostering. About the sale of infants we must be content to remain in the dark. It is a possibility, of course, that the readiness of Christians to be foster-parents effectively ended the need for infanticide by exposure; the presence of a regular procedure for fostering, perhaps even of church-organized foundling homes, would probably have made it unnecessary for parents of surplus children to resort to exposure and infanticide.[23]

At the church council held at Vaison in France during 442, the status of foster-children seems to have been a subject of some concern; in any case, two canons of the council were devoted to this question; they make interesting reading. We are told that complaints had been voiced on all sides because children were being exposed and left for the dogs while those charitable persons who were inclined to take them up were restrained from doing so by their fear of malicious gossip. What such gossip was we are not informed; the context might suggest that Christians were being accused of using unscrupulous means to recruit new members of their "cult" from among the abandoned children whom they rescued.[24] This must remain open to question; but again we are certainly justified in concluding that by 442, in France at least, the fostering of exposed children was a widespread and recognized practice among Christians. The canon is concerned to encourage the practice in accordance with imperial statute and it enjoins that the person who takes up an exposed child should call on the church as witness to his act and obtain a document attesting to church approval. Likewise the priest is required to make an announcement from the altar on the Lord's day "so that the church may know that the exposed child has been taken up"; ten days only are allowed for recovery of the child by the natural parents, counting from the day of exposure. And even in the event of some claim on the child a debt of gratitude is owed to the person who has taken up the foundling. Canon X of the same council adds that anyone who seeks to reclaim such children after this procedure or who engages in malicious gossip will be subject to the (ecclesiastical) punishment reserved for homicides! This is strong language, but the implications are clear; and the same provisions are tersely restated ten years later in Canon LI of the Council of Arles.[25] Obviously people, probably even Christians (to whom in the first place the announcement from the altar was directed), were still in the middle of the fifth century, in France at least, in the habit of exposing children on a regular basis. Such children were being taken up by Christian foster-parents, perhaps even by holy virgins of the sort mentioned by Augustine in the same context in Africa about a generation earlier (Augustine *Letters* 98; see above); the involvement of holy virgins would suggest an organized institutional effort on the part of the church, something which seems very probable. In any case the natural parents of the exposed children were apparently in the habit of reclaiming their offspring at a later point, perhaps to save them from Christian indoctrination (but this remains mere speculation); or if they did not reclaim them, they contented themselves with malicious gossip directed against the foster-parents. The equation of the crime to homicide shows how seriously the church responded to this threat and suggests that we are dealing here with a central Christian institution, a conclusion also suggested by the involvement of the holy virgins and the interest of the Christian legislator.[26] As it happens we have sufficient evidence to suggest that in fifth- and sixth-century France the foster-child played as central a role in Christian belief as it must have in Christian practice.

Anyone who looks through the article "*alumnus (alumna)*" in the *Thesaurus Linguae Latinae* will note that there is a considerable body of evidence for the use of these words in a transferred sense to describe a dependent or disciple;[27] there is an ancient precedent for such an important metaphorical usage, but much of the evidence is drawn from Christian Latin literature, where from the time of Tertullian on, Christians are referred to as *alumnus dei, alumnus Christi* or as the foster-child of some martyr (e.g. Prudentius *Peristeph*. 2, 570, of the followers of St. Lawrence). I should emphasize that this is not simply a picturesque figure of speech; such "alumni by devotion" are well known to the students of Christian epigraphy.[28] We should reflect at length on what it means in a Latin and Christian society to be addressed as Salvian addresses a correspondent in fifth century France when he distinguishes her with the title *alumna Christi* (Salvian *Letters* V, to Cattura). Or again when Gregory of Tours, to whom we owe so much of our knowledge and understanding of Latin Christian society in sixth century France, refers to one of his close friends and associates, the priest Arridius, as *peculiarem beati confessoris* [*i.e.* Martin] *alumnum* (*Miracles of St. Martin* III 24; cf. III 8, 42), to what extent are we to take these expressions as mere figures of speech, to what extent do they reflect a central preoccupation of Christian society with the special relationship that exists between a foundling and his fosterparents? I have argued at length in another place that saints such as St. Martin, in the world of Gregory of Tours, are quite clearly seen as the spiritual equivalent of powerful secular patrons who help the poor and sickly and weak, sometimes indeed in what we would call "miraculous" fashion but always with the effect of bringing believers under their powerful protection.[29] In Latin society with its hierarchical, patriarchal and authoritarian tendencies, the patron-client relationship served as a most influential model of human organization and spiritual values in the Roman Christian world. A special place in this complex of social and spiritual dependency which binds together believers, the saints and God himself, was occupied by the relationship between foster-children and parents. And so it was natural for Gregory of Tours and others to refer to believers as foster-children of St. Martin or St. Lawrence or of Christ himself. But it was the more natural to do so inasmuch as foster-children were a common feature of Christian life and had probably always been so. Clustered around the bishop's seat, living in or near the shrine of some great patron saint, fosterchildren probably had a place on the ecclesiastical dole, together with the beggars and cripples whom we find supported so commonly by *ecclesia mater* in Gregory's world. In fact the word used for that dole, *matricula*, probably was originally used for the charitable institutions which fostered children as a living mother from the time of the early church; an attentive study of Gregory of Tours would turn up evidence that infanticide was still practiced in sixth-century France, and, together with infanticide, the fostering of exposed or abandoned children.[30] Further research in the primary sources, I firmly believe, would do much to clarify this picture and to confirm my suggestion that foster children occupied an important place in early Christian life and thought.[31]

Infant sacrifice was common practice in the ancient Semitic world; it must have been seen to confer some social and spiritual benefits on those who practiced it - to have had some "redemptive" effect, as we might say. In the Hellenistic and Roman world the religious aspects of infanticide seem to have been consciously deemphasized; but it was certainly a regular aspect of everyday life in Greece and Rome. The early Christians resolutely opposed themselves to infanticide and replaced it with a new, almost frantic insistence on sexual continence and a re-emphasis of the importance of fostering as it was currently practiced. This is the more comprehensible inasmuch as fertility or over-fertility, sexuality or excesses of sexuality had become a dominant obsession in the ancient world - and with reason whether considered from the demographic and biological, the social or the ideological point of view. We see this obsession reflected in the Gospels;[32] Christ himself in his preaching and healing around the Sea of Galilee appears always as the resolver of the dominant paradoxes of life and death, not least the paradox of sexuality and chastity. Christ can do this because in his person he embodies the ultimate (child) sacrifice which transcends and brings to an end all the fruitless re-enactments of child sacrifice since Abraham was freed from sacrificing Isaac and before; Christ ends the old order and establishes a new one in which slaves and prisoners are delivered from bondage - and infants, we might add, from death - to become the social basis of the new Christian order as it spread from Syria to Rome, long threatened but finally triumphant. Christ, the "Beloved Son"[33] of God, in his body had passed from death to life and his resurrected body became the church - not simply a religious image or an article of faith, but a social and human reality. Mary Douglas has convincingly demonstrated that the body is the ultimate natural symbol in all human society; how is it surprising, then, that the body of Christ has such redemptive power? In it were the seeds of the new social order, the reconstituted patriarchal family which gathered around the bishop as representative of God on earth and later as delegate for the saintly patron who acts as *pater* and *dominus* to the new family of servants, widows, virgins and fosterlings, and other dependents among the sickly or possessed who assembled around his shrine in every community of the Latin West.[34] Despite the early tendencies of some Christians to reject sexuality, marriage and family life out of hand (such "encratite" tendencies were notably marked in the founding Syrian church), the new model of family life proved too effective in social and ideological terms to be so easily eclipsed - it had too great a "redemptive" power - it simply worked too well as the basis of the new Christian synthesis. The foster-child is only one element in this new synthesis, but it is a most important element, very close to the social and symbolic heart of the new enterprise, inasmuch as the *alumnus* shares the "liminal" quality of the risen Saviour and represents Christ himself in a very real way, "the first born from the dead" (Revelations 1:5). Unfortunately, as with redeemed slaves and prisoners, foster children were not only the first born and foundation of the new social order, they all too often proved its victims as well; but that is a chapter in the story of the growth of the institutional church, and, as such, beyond the scope of my present enquiry.

MANI'S OPPOSITION TO THE ELCHASAITES:
A QUESTION OF RITUAL

Jorunn Jacobsen Buckley

1. Introduction

Between 1970 and 1978, a new Manichaean source became available to the scholarly public. The Greek text, "On the Becoming of His Life," contained in a minute book 4.5 X 3,5cm., had been totally unknown before 1970, when it was brought to light as the "Manichaean Cologne Codex" (*Codex Manichaicus Coloniensis*). In 1970 A. Henrichs and L. Koenen published, in *Zeitschrift für Papyrologie und Epigraphik*, the first article on this text, with excerpts translated from the Greek.[1] A partial transcription and translation followed in two installments, published by the same authors in 1975 and 1978.[2]

A translation from Syriac or East-Aramaic[3] into Greek, the text discloses a particular development within a religious tradition of Late Antiquity. Presented partly as Mani's own words, the Codex states that Mani grew up in the Mesopotamean Jewish-Christian sect of the Elchasaites. There are hitherto unknown discussions between Mani and his fellow-sectarians regarding the group's rituals. Of special interest to the present investigation, the book also relates why Mani broke away from the group, preparing to start a new religion.

The Arabian historian Ibn al-Nadim referred to the Elchasaites in his *Fihrist al-'Ulum* (ca. 988 A.D.) in a passage deserving new consideration, in light of the Codex:

They observe ablution as a rite and wash everything which they eat. Their head is known as al-Hasih and it is he who instituted their sect.... They agreed with the Manichaeans about the two elemental (principles), but later their sect became separate.[4]

The disagreement between the two sects concerns the proper way of dealing with these opposed elements, light (upper world) and darkness (lower world).

The new Codex gives us a glimpse into the events leading up to this schism. Specifically, the disagreements regarding the value of baptism and purification concern me in the present study. Here, a brief presentation of Mani's refutations of Elchasaite rituals of ablution and baptism is followed by consideration of several questions: First, what are the cruces of the arguments between the Elchasaites and Mani, the budding apostate, concerning problems of purity and pollution? Secondly, questions regarding mixtures of dirty and clean elements must be addressed. Specifically, is it held possible for believers to extricate themselves from such divine/demonic blends? This problem is, of course, one of salvation and leads one to question whether salvation can come about directly, through individual baptism, or if sinners have lost their chances of such direct redemption? The conclusions will seek to pull these issues together, formulating the conflicts between Mani and the Elchasaites in terms of basic principles of thought and action in the two religious traditions.[5]

2. <u>Mani's Challenge to the Elchasaite Ritual Tradition.</u>
The Elchasaites trace their teachings and practices back to the prophet Elchasai ("hidden power," "hidden god"[6]) who flourished around A.D. 100.[7] According to tradition, he was the last in a line of prophets anticipating the "Seal," the ultimate prophet who was to herald the end of the world. In Mani's time, then, the sect was waiting for this "Seal," preparing itself for his appearance by practicing daily baptism.

Mani's father, Patik, was a Parthian who had joined the Elchasaites while Mani was still an infant (around A.D. 215-16).[8] Indeed, in the Codex the Elchasaites say of Mani, "From youth you have been with us, doing well in the ordinances and customs of our Law."[9] However, Mani experienced two revelations, one in his twelfth and the other in his twenty-fourth year, in which an angel appeared to him, predicting Mani's break with the Elchasaites.[10] The ensuing debates between Mani and the baptists occurred, as one might expect, just before the rebel went his own way.

Referring to the Elchasaite custom of immersing their food in water before eating, Mani makes the following statement,

[This] washing by which you wash your food is of [no avail]. For this body is defiled and molded from a mold of defilement. You can see how, whenever someone cleanses his food and partakes of that (food) which has just been washed, it seems to us that from it still come blood and bile and flatulence and excrements of shame and (the) defilement of the body.[11]

Mani goes on to assert that baptizing food makes no difference whatsoever. Food sustains the human body, whether one prefers to dwell on the beauty or on the ugliness of that body.

Next Mani states,

Now the fact that you wash in water each day is of no avail. For having been washed and purified once and for all, why do you wash again each day? So that also by this it is manifest that you are disgusted with yourselves each day and that you must wash yourselves on account of loathsomeness before you can become purified. And by this too it is clear most evidently that all the foulness is from the body. And, indeed, [you] also have put it (i.e., the body) on.
Therefore, [make an inspection of] yourselves as to [what] your purity [really is. For it is] impossible to purify your bodies entirely - for each day the body is disturbed and comes to rest through the excretions of feces from it - so that the action comes about without a commandment from the Savior.[12]

Mani asserts here that if baptism is necessary at all, the initiatory rite ought to suffice. But since the group insists on daily baptism, Mani claims that the stains of sin cannot be removed by any external purification. Again, he draws the connection to eating. As long as the human body needs food, it remains impure: no ritual of baptism can ameliorate the situation.

More dramatically, Mani strikes yet another blow to the Elchasaites' hallowed tradition of baptism:

If, then, you accuse me (Mani) about the washing, look, again I prove to you from your Law and from those things revealed to your leaders that it is not necessary to wash. For Elchasai, the founder of your Law, points this out: when he was going to bathe in the waters, an image of a man appeared to him from the source of the waters, saying to him: "Is it not enough that your animals injure me, but do you [yourself] also mistreat [me without reason] and profane [my waters]?" Elchasai [marveled and] said to it: "Fornication, defilement, and impurity of the world are thrown into you and you do not refuse (them), but are you grieved with me"? It said to him: "Granting that all these have not recognized me (as to) who I am, you, who say that you are a servant and righteous, why have you not guarded my honor"? And then Elchasai was upset and did not bathe in the waters.[13]

It is worth noting that here, Mani does not refute Elchasai but, from an Elchasaite point of view, interprets the incident in an heretical manner.[14] Elchasai behaves surprisingly, not at all like a founder of a baptist sect. The human body impairs the water by immersion; the element seems to be divine to such an extent that humans may not deal with it. Water is not, therefore, a vehicle for salvation, so the rite must be repealed and water be left alone and revered. No place is left for an optimistic view of the body. That which is already condemned cannot be purified by water.

According to Mani, Elchasai made a second attempt to bathe in water, but the image in the water spoke to him again: "'We and those waters are one. You have come, therefore, even here to wrong and injure us.' Trembling greatly and upset, Elchasai allowed the mud upon his head to dry and thus he pointed it out."[15]

In these tendentious accounts of baptism the central ritual of the Elchasaites is rendered in a clearly derogatory manner. The question arises, what could replace the baptism-ritual or, more correctly, what is the "right" way of practice originally intended by the founder? Mani answers:

The purity, then, which was spoken about, is that which comes through knowledge, a separation of light from darkness, of death from life, of living waters from turbid, so that [you] may know [that] each is [...] one another and [...] the commandments of the Savior, [so that...] might redeem the soul from [annihilation] and destruction. This is in truth the genuine purity, which you were commended to do; but you departed from it and began to bathe, and have held on to the purification of the body, (a thing) most defiled and fashioned through foulness; through it (i.e., foulness) it (the body) was coagulated and having been founded came into existence.[16]

Appealing to "Scripture," Mani radically re-interprets the means to achieve purity. This seems to be an argument in favour of intellectual Gnosis in contradistinction to external rituals of purification. Baptism, an apostasy according to Mani, only serves to keep up the illusion that it is possible to purify the loathsome material body. The "living water" mentioned above is not tangible water, but denotes a spiritual reality outside of this world.[17] Mani advocates a thorough dualism in which salvation is available solely through a knowledge that separates the opposing elements.

The Elchasaites ask themselves whether Mani's new preaching is a valid re-evaluation of the group. Since they have been waiting for a prophet, the "Seal," the "eternal rest of the garment,"[18] some of them are willing to accept Mani as this prophet. As a previously good Elchasaite, Mani knows very well what the expectations of his fellow-sectarians are, and he conforms in some crucial ways to the manner in which the last prophet is supposed to act.[19] The majority of the members, however, are against Mani, and he breaks his ties with the group, taking with him two disciples and Patik, his father. The angel's prediction comes true and the innovator starts proclaiming an essentially new religion (around A.D. 240).[20]

3. The Opposing Presuppositions

A picture of seriously conflicting views of the world and of the human being emerges in these debates. Mani has ceased to baptize himself, to behave like a pious Elchasaite. Why? In Mani's first statement, his refutation of the food-ablution,[21] the human being, not the food, seems to be polluted. Essentially, Mani says that even if one cleanses the food, it gets transformed into dirt by passing through the unclean human body. An image of impure creation, the human body cannot turn even cleansed food into anything pure. Already doomed beyond redemption, the body's problem is not anything external; it is, indeed, its own problem.

Elaborations on this first conclusion follow in Mani's diatribe against daily baptism, the Elchasaite remedy for pollution and sin. Precisely because the Elchasaites insist on repeated baptism, they must have committed sins heavier than they can atone for, Mani argues. Again, since the body constantly needs aliment, it cannot attain to total purity. Bodily movement, realistically portrayed as the process of digestion, prevents lasting quietude of the body. The body's own needs account for this unhappy state of affairs; the ideal seems to be a virtually unattainable stillness of the body.

Mani's evaluation of water offers some further food for thought, so to speak. Seemingly adapting a "holier-than-thou" attitude towards his audience, Mani holds water in even greater esteem than do the errant baptizers. In the slyly tilted story of the Water's accusation against Elchasai, Mani shows that even the founder of the baptist-group is unfit for the pure water.

Finally, the apostate sums up his refutations by saying that purity comes through knowledge that separates the contrasting elements. This kind of purity seems different from that obtainable through rites in which the believers employ external ablutions. Baptism is futile; sheer negativity seems to characterize Mani's attitude towards the human form and content.

The "soul" mentioned in the *CMC* quotation[22] cannot be saved by baptism. Mani sees water as holy and *out* of human reach, while the Elchasaites hold water in utmost respect and understand it to be *within* human reach. Both body and water are amalgams. Consisting of lowly material as well as of an imprisoned soul, the human being is only able to free itself (i.e., its soul) by knowledge without specified, accompanying ritual action. Similarly, the water is composed of light and dark parts, i.e., divine and demonic particles. These are intermingled to such an extent, however, that there is no method by which to separate them. So water is not ritually efficacious for the human being, who is characterized by the same deplorable mixture of heavenly and demonic elements.

It becomes important to differentiate between the traditional Elchasaite view and that of the challenger by asking questions about the nature of the mixture of good and evil. If the mixture is "evil" in itself, what does one do with the divine part of it? If not irredeemably evil, may the blend be approached ritually, so that believers can separate the warring elements?

According to Mani, the condition of the redemption of the soul is knowledge, i.e., separation of oppositions: light/darkness, death/life, living water/turbid water.[23] Purity, denoting eligibility for salvation, is available if one can distinguish these dichotomons principles and elements.

One may discern a peculiar logic in Mani's evaluation of water. Tangible water is made up of counteracting elements, divine and demonic. The mixture is unfortunate, but the "living water" part seems to predominate so that water acquires a positive value. In fact, water is *too* divine to do humans any good. Revered for its inherent light-particles, the water still belongs in a negatively judged mixture.[24] According to Mani's equations, the devalued human body can in no tangible or practical way overcome the dichotomy residing in the water. Thus resigned, Mani seems to assert that theoretical knowledge, not ritual understanding, marks the correct way of religion.

How, then, could the Elchasaites ever perceive water as being efficacious in ritual? The positivity of water in Elchasaism is of a different kind than that preached by Mani. When the apostate declares that daily baptism has no value, he means that it does not work. The question is how *did* it work in Elchasaism before Mani's re-evaluation?

In the Elchasaite schema, conditioned statements predominate. If the right food is immersed, the purificatory aims are achieved. Similarly, when an Elchasaite baptizes himself according to the religious rules, he cleanses himself of sin and anticipates full, future salvation. Elchasaites can turn both food and themselves into pure entities by correct ritual practice. They do not operate with any stark dualism (à la Mani), but possess instead a practically applicable view of themselves and the world. Fully confident in their religious action, the Elchasaites can be said to mediate earth and heaven. Also, the ritual of baptism seems to enable one further step: actually making the earthly into the divine. Baptism of food as well as of humans is a transformatory endeavour through which interaction between the two worlds is made possible. Bringing his self - and world - understanding into play in ritual, the Elchasaite overcomes the distance between the below and the above.

Mani, on the other hand, rejects water as a means towards bridging the two realms. He advocates what looks like an ideal of conceptual knowledge severed from practical, ritual understanding. For the Elchasaites baptism "works" because they, when properly purified, are compatible with the nature of the water. But Mani asserts that the ritual is futile. Is thought the only remedy for this breach?

4. Mani's Religious Appropriation

In *CMC* Mani does not offer a new ritual solution to the problem of purification. Salvation of the soul requires knowledge which, in its turn, depends on acts of separation of opposed elements. Might such separations entail new means of transformation, offering paths from the earthly to the heavenly realm?

Turning to evidences for the hierarchical structures of Manichaeism, one finds solutions to questions regarding practical implementation of Mani's doctrine of separation. Mani divided his community into classes patterned, it seems, on Christian organization. Listing the five classes - apostles (teachers), bishops, priests, Elect and Hearers - Asmussen observes, "Christian writers from the fourth century onwards ... openly state that when Mani chose the number twelve [for the first class] he followed the example of the Church."[25]

The four first classes are all "upper-level" Manichaeans, while the Hearers comprise the laypeople.[26] The relationship between the Elect (monks) and the Hearers is of special significance to the present investigation because it illuminates Mani's new interpretation of avenues towards purity and salvation. A division of labour between the Elect and the Hearers suggests that (1) the "chosen ones," the Elect, take the place of the purifying element of water in Elchasaism, and that (2) the separation of tasks for Elect and Hearers implies an indirect path to salvation for the latter.[27] This two-fold interpretation is to be supported in the following. One must, above all, avoid interpretations of the prescribed "separation" in purely theoretical terms. Mani's message does not speak of any intellectual endeavour aimed at an ideal of philosophical sifting and sorting out of opposites.

Returning to *CMC*, we find teachers, bishops, Elect and Hearers (but not priests) listed.[28] Importantly, this organization is divinely decreed, being part of the revelation by Mani's heavenly Twin.[29] The division of labour between the Elect and the Hearers expresses, in its own unique way, the "separation between light and darkness." In view of the Manichaean negative evaluation of matter and body, the salvation work of the Elect and the Hearers paradoxically turns out to be a very physical one.[30] A farmer, baker and servant for the Electus, the Hearer grows, prepares, and gives the food to the pure Electus. The latter's dealings with the material world are extremely restricted; otherwise, his purity would be endangered. Any work, particularly agricultural activity, is indeed murder of the light particles inherent in all living elements. The Hearers alone devote themselves to these worldy tasks, incurring sins which the Elect have the power to forgive. Like a Theravadin *arhat*, the Electus depends on the Hearer, the layman, to materially support him. In return, the Electus furnishes the servant with spiritual merit.[31] Helping the Electus to attain and keep the purest possible condition, the Hearer indirectly works for his own salvation too. Eating foods containing large concentrations of divine light, the Electus aids these elements by letting them return to their home in the light-world. The digestion specialist becomes a machine[32] to purify and liberate the captured light. This process *is*, in fact, "the separation of light from darkness."[33]

When the Auditor brings the daily meal, consisting mostly of bread and fruit, to the Electus, the latter poses the prescribed question, "Whose flesh and blood is this?"[34] In addition, he pronounces the negative confession of sins; "'I did not mow thee, did not grind thee, nor knead, nor lay thee in the oven. But another did do this and bring thee to me. I eat thee without sin.' Thereafter he said to the catechumen who had brought him the bread, 'I have prayed for thee,' whereupon the other went."[35] Another food-meditation is attested in a Soghdian Manichaean text, to which Vööbus observes,

Preparation for eating forms an indispensable part of this almost mystical action. At first the monk thinks with grateful heart of God and Buddha. It becomes evident from the text that he has certain mythological scenes of the primeval struggle before his eyes. Then he thinks of what it is that he eats...it is clear enough that two thoughts were connected with this: the guilt caused by the preparation of the food, and the part which the monk had to perform in the process of liberating the particles of light which were hidden in the food."[36]

Both the differentiation between servant and monk, and the seemingly hypocritical attitude of the latter infuriate early critics of Manichaeism.[37] Even from within the Manichaean fold the Elect and the Hearers might seem to belong to different worlds. Countering such suspicions the *Šahpuhrakan* states that the Hearers are indeed "Children of the living Family and the Lightworld."[38]

The Hearers may even be able to save themselves in *this* life, without having to be reborn, if they become "perfect" Hearers. "The sign of that perfect catechumen is this: you find his wife in the house with him, but she is with him as the strangers [are]. His house, too, is like an inn to him, and he says, 'I live in a house, renting it by days and months.'"[39] This kind of Hearer has made the transition to the stage of the Electus, and he will therefore avoid rebirth.[40]

The Elect separate light and darkness; the auditors, too, are said to have made the same separation.[41] At first glance this seems inconsistent. But the Hearers have made a *mental* separation, even though they do not practice their insights. Alfaric, citing Augustine, explains about the Hearers,

They behave like the crowd that used to go to listen to the Saviour without having the courage to attach themselves to the small group of disciples. This is precisely where the name one gives them comes from. One calls them "Auditors" because they listen to the words of life without putting them into practice."[42]

Awareness of the necessity to sever light from darkness is itself a form of knowledge, a first stage in the Hearers' commitment and a prerequisite for the practical application of the Elects' religious insight. Salvation, whether at the end of the present life (for Elect and perfected Hearers) or later on (for the majority of the Hearers), depends on both classes to carry out their duties.

Even as Mani reinterprets his native religion, then, he keeps its orientation towards practice. His revisions do not demand a rejection of cultic means as such; the Electus is not to be an isolated philosopher devoted to a purely intellectual ideal of knowledge. In *CMC*, when Mani twists the traditions about Elchasai, sarcastically letting the water rebuke the baptist, he presents him as an Electus.[43] Not only does the water accuse Elchasai of polluting it, the earth, too, protests against his agricultural activities. He realizes that the earth is "the flesh and blood of my Lord."[44]

Mani has other bones to pick with the baptists: he ridicules them for their wheatbread prohibition.[45] Adducing proofs from the Gospel traditions that Jesus did not distinguish between kinds of bread, Mani reminds the Elchasaites that the Master ate with women and common people.[46] The Master's disciples, it is added, did not carry around mills and baking ovens.[47] Mani clearly makes fun of those who worry where their food will come from.

But this raises another issue, viz. that one must rely on a class of servants, i.e., the Hearers; Jesus' disciples, as Elect before their time, had no need to worry as long as the lower-level faithful provided them with food. Bread-baking is an activity unworthy of the core of devotees.[48]

The Elchasaites shun certain, unspecified vegetables and fruits.[49] Again, Mani rejects such dogmas on Gospel grounds.[50] Conspicuously, though, Mani has his own, strong feelings about vegetables, feelings which upset his fellow baptists. In one incident Mani tells of an Elchasaite on his way to sell vegetables to people outside the sect. The produce complains, saying, "Are you not righteous? Are [you] not pure? Why do you carry us away to the fornicators?" The baptist, alarmed, returns the vegetables.[51] To sell or give away food to outsiders would be blasphemous since such people cannot digest and free the divine particles in it.[52]

In a previous episode the Elchasaites have observed that Mani declines to harvest vegetables from the garden" ... but instead asked them (for the vegetables) as a pious gift."[53] Shunning sinful harvesting, Mani already behaves like an Electus. Mani's lack of differentiation between vegetables and fruits does not last long, however. The Electus' discriminatory eating habits become the major vehicle for salvation in Manichaeism.

What might have threatened to turn into an entirely intellectual doctrine, alien to cultic institutions, addresses, instead, the immediate need for religious practices. Purity comes about, not by lofty *gnosis* alone, but by rites of separation and purification. The division of labour between Hearers and Elect furnishes Manichaeism with a solution to the problem of correct action.

5. Conclusion

Water, in Elchasaism the workable implement for personal and direct dealings with the upper forces, is replaced, in Manichaeism, with an interceding elite of pure human beings, the Elect. Also, the separation between Hearers and Elect signals another telling shift away from

Elchasaism. An Elchasaite performs his own baptism. This rite of self-immersion requires no higher-ranking, officiating figure.[54] The development of the Manichaean form of religious hierarchy, on the other hand, illuminates a two-step path to salvation, a transition from direct (water in Elchasaism) to indirect (the Hearers' soul-service to the Elect) dealings with the divine element. The Elect become the prerequisites for salvation. No longer effected by an external rite of purification, the redemption process now requires the inner workings of the religious specialist.

As in Elchasaism, the food, the salvific element, and the human being must be compatible with each other. But purity of aliments and believers no longer depends on water-ablutions. Isolated in the body of the Electus, the light food-particles are carried to their redemption. In Manichaeism the purifying element and the pure person have merged. In Mani's exegesis of Elchasaism, the identification could not have been accomplished in the old religion since the body could never have achieved real purity. Salvation in Elchasaism required immersion in an external element, water; in Manichaeism the light-elements' immersion into the internal body of the Electus guarantees their salvation.

The thesis of salvation by digestion points to a concern with internalization, though this internal process is of a different kind than one might have expected. There has long been a tendency to discredit cultic components in the area of Gnostic studies. Often, Gnosticism itself has been understood to illustrate a development from external, cultic practices to a concern with inner, metaphysical knowledge. The theory of a shift in interest, from ritual to thought, or "from Myth to Logos," distorts the Manichaean picture, though, since the tradition insists on keeping both aspects. The "internalization" encountered in Manichaeism destroys immediate expectations of an equation between inner reality and purely theoretical *gnosis*. A metaphysical understanding of the separation between light and darkness does not suffice, the *real* differentiation goes on in the body. Again, internalization does not mean theoretization!

The mixture, then, of light and darkness can be broken up through correct practice. Another form of separation is expressed in the division of duties between Hearers and Elect. In this manner, the Manichaeans aim at the salvation of the light-particles in the food and in their bodies. The Elchasaites, on the other hand, while agreeing with the new view as regards the importance of correct aliments, seek to save themselves only, by entirely external means. The "knowledge" advocated by Mani implies a cosmic salvation-program which transcends the limits of his native group. He seeks to accomplish this goal, not by stressing sheer, pious adherence to certain doctrines, but, curiously, by emphasizing the importance of organizational and physical control.

It is, I think, doubtful whether any Gnosis, however discursive and loftily theoretical, can persist without any cultic life. In the example presented here, one discerns the persistence of ritual and the stress on material prerequisites for salvation, *across* the decisive break between the Elchasaite position and the view attributed to Mani.

THE TRANSFORMATION OF CHRISTIANITY INTO ROMAN RELIGION

John Helgeland

Introduction
Recently, the religions of antiquity have been recipients of attention from the social sciences. Of these disciplines, those of psychology and sociology have been the most often employed.[1] In this paper we shall draw upon cultural anthropology, not for the sake solely of its "being there" but to show how it is able to illuminate one aspect of this question: How did Christianity change from the religious style reflected in the New Testament to that of the popular religion of the early Middle Ages? We will argue that one of the primary factors involved was the church's perception of time and space. Moreover, it is to be contended that the cultural forces which produced the changes operated independently of the conscious reflection of the participants of this tradition. The models and structures which the Christians encountered in moving into the Roman culture overwhelmed them and became the receptacles which both shaped the tradition and determined what would be carried along and what would be left behind.

Time and Space
One of the central topics of the movement we are studying is that of time and space. Certainly the thought of Jesus and of Paul presupposed that time was the medium through which salvation was made available to people.[2] Much of their thought revolved around the subject of what God's future would be like and that one is to wait expectantly for that future to take place. In the process of waiting for that future they counseled men to change their minds

and to conform to what that reality would resemble. Jesus' parables of the Kingdom of God teach what he thought that reality would be. So, too, Paul's emphasis on faith had a similar intent, namely, to convince the Christian to be transformed inwardly to how God will behave toward man. In a word, people must be *converted*.[3] They were to reorient their attitudes to become worthy recipients of what was to come. Behavior was secondary in the sense that it was shaped and molded to inner convictions. Even though the intensity of the expectation of the return of Jesus evaporated in the later writings of the New Testament, the notion that a Christian had to believe certain things continued. The early Christian religion was an internal one.

What is clear is that the early Christian community did not expect to meet the holy in space, in any object, or in any particular person.[4] For example, even the Eucharist originally was treated as a memorial feast which anticipated the rapid return of Jesus. It was not until the time of Ignatius, however, that the Eucharist received attention in itself by being called the drug of immortality (φάρμακον ἀθανασίας); by so doing, Ignatius makes a thing or a spatial object out of the Eucharist.[5] As emphasis on time fell away, though, the procession was not from time to no-time, but from time to space. Just as primitive Christianity implicitly held that time was the central category, Roman religion was dominated by the motif of space and place. Moving more and more into the Roman world, Christianity became increasingly populated with people who had grown up with spatial models of religion. These people slowly, but relentlessly, helped to displace time centered religion with models which reflected the Roman, not the Hebrew world. Central to our understanding of why this change took place is the Roman concept of *numen*.

As the work of the cultural anthropologist Mary Douglas persuasively argues, the fundamental act in forming a culture is the process of drawing boundaries.[6] To avoid falling into chaos, people must draw lines of distinction. The first discrimination is between persons, between the me and the not-me. Body fluids, spittle, semen, urine, blood, and tears are dangerous because if these fluids touch someone else, they have the possibility of blurring the distinctions between bodies. In most cultures, this possible situation is prohibited by taboos of various sorts. A taboo prevents the possibility of pollution which is a situation where the space of one body is spatially confused with the fluids from that of another. The danger inherent in these tabooed substances, then, makes them powerful; they are regarded altogether differently from non-tabooed material. Boundaries which are the basic elements of any culture are for the most part arbitrary; it is a religious value judgment to say that they should be drawn in the places where they are. The boundaries extend outward from the body to create the substratum of a culture.[7]

One effect of drawing boundaries is that this action produces a highly differentiated world. So, to one tribe, the land on the other side of the river is not simply more land, it is dangerous territory where one might lose one's self or soul as well as one's physical life. From this differentiated world springs the notion that some places, some objects, or some actions possess constructive or destructive, good or bad attributes. In the Roman world *numen* was the word used to designate this powerful attribute; it was a sort of spiritual electricity the presence of which produced good, the absence chaos. We use the model of electricity advisedly. It is used simply to offer a mental picture of how *numen* was communicated and not to support an evolutionist theory of Roman religious development as earlier historians of religion have portrayed it.

Georges Dumezil is highly critical of what has just been said.[8] He objects to the work of Rose and Wagenvoort in that they uncritically applied the concept of *mana* from studies in Polynesian religion to the Roman situation. Dumezil goes to great lengths to show why *mana* does not accurately duplicate Roman *numen*. For the purpose of this paper the relevant issue is whether there is *numen* in objects alone as in the concept of *mana* or whether *numen*

only exists as the will of a particular deity. He argues
the latter, that where there is *numen* there is always a
deity which stands behind it. In our previous work on the
religion of the Roman Army it seemed as though *numen* was
both the expression of the will of a deity and the property
of objects in isolation.[9] In army religion one can find
numen associated with objects such as weapons, places, the
walls of the camp. It would seem fruitless to look beyond
these objects to find a particular deity who was symbolized
in these particulars. Nevertheless, we agree with Dumezil
that *numen* is the major component in a religious *system*
which, we must add, was almost exclusively spatial in
nature.

We have said that *numen* was very much like a spiritual
electricity; it could not be created, but it could be
channeled. It did not come to one without a physical,
spatial medium and, when so transmitted, it had great power
to produce benefits of various kinds. This spatial model
became the property of Christians in the middle second
century in the form of the cult of relics.

Relics and the Church

Eusebius tells of the struggle over the remains of the
Christians executed in the persecution in Lyons-Vienne in
the year 177.[10] Clearly different from the religion of the
New Testament, which had no interest whatsoever in the
topic of burial, the church of Lyons-Vienne went to
extraordinary lengths to retrieve the remains of the
martyrs. And just as energetically, the Romans fought to
keep the Christians from succeeding and did so by burning
the bodies and throwing the ashes into the Rhone river,
"...so that not a single relic of their bodies might be
left on earth."[11] This event was not an isolated incident
for in 259 near Utica Romans destroyed the bodies of
Christian martyrs, this time by means of quicklime.[12] What
was on the minds of the Romans most likely was to prevent
the formation of Christian cemeteries which would become
permanent focal points of Christian communities. On the

other hand, Christians wanted relics as a medium of religious power.

By the third century we find explicit reference to collecting the remains and the personal effects of the martyrs. In the account of the death of St. Cyprian we are told precisely where he is buried.[13] When Maxmillian was martyred in 295, the account of his martydom explicitly tells us that he was buried next to St. Cyprian.[14] The body was brought there by a certain Pompeiana who was herself buried there two weeks later; presumably she wanted her grave to be permeated with the *numen* of Cyprian and Maximillian.

Beginning with the death of Cyprian one begins to find references to clothes and other objects which served as receptacles of holy energy. As he was led to execution, Cyprian removed his outer cloak and knelt upon it and gave his dalmatic to his deacons. Then his fellow-Christians began spreading clothes and napkins in front of him, most likely to catch his blood. This might seem to go further than the evidence would allow, but similar events happen in other accounts. The *Acts of Fructuosus* in 259 make much of his giving up his sandals just before being burned alive, and the onlookers afterward gathered up his ashes.[15] St. Irenaeus, bishop of Sirmium, also took off his clothes before he was martyred and his body thrown into the river.[16] Both recensions of the martyrdom of Agathonice have her taking off her clothes before dying at the stake, and recension A has the Christians secretly collecting her remains which were protected for the glory of Christ.[17]

The fact that the cult of relics dealt as well with objects which were not parts of bodies has precedents in the Roman world.[18] Just one example is the cult of the standards in the Roman army. This cult dealt with standards which were not deities. Even though we do not know how much earlier, by the time of Pope Gregory I the church turned to the use of derivative relics.[19] By then, the custom was to empower an altar by the inclusion of a relic. With the building of new churches, the demand for relics increased although the cessation of the persecutions had made martyr bodies, as economists say, an inelastic commodity. Therefore, the practice of *brandeum* arose; it placed a cloth next to the body of a saint which then took on his powers. Declaring that the derived relic had the same miraculous potency as did the body itself, Gregory made the point vivid by cutting such a cloth which began to bleed.

A further outgrowth of the expanding emphasis on spatial models is the practice of incubation, sleeping in the sanctuary next to the tomb of a saint. Gregory also tells the story, for example, of a mad woman who spent the night in a cave formerly inhabited by St. Benedict and who emerged the next morning sane.[20]

The cult of relics, then, is one example of how the spatial structures of Roman culture altered the time-consciousness of the Christian community. And, as the Christian moved into this world, they encountered a system of models and structures which operated upon them in a subtle yet relentless way; the Christian community at all of its levels of sophistication seemed nearly powerless to resist this transformation. But there are other examples of the Roman space consciousness. We can include only one more - the Roman mental map of how the world radiated outward from Rome itself.

The Shape of the Roman Religious World

From our previous studies in Roman military religion, it is possible to show in some detail how the territory of the empire was related to Rome.[21] We can illustrate this by the excavations of Dura Europos where the Yale expedition unearthed a document now called the *Feriale Duranum*. This was a liturgical calendar which was one of many distributed to every legion and cohort of the army. It specified the festivals and sacrifices the Cohort XX Palmyrenorum was responsible to celebrate during the year A.D.226. Most of the Dura festivals were those celebrated in Rome on that specified day, and the additional festivals were for the military alone such as *armilustrium*, the ritual empowering, with *numen*, the weapons of the soldiers. The army as "the

Roman people at war" celebrated the same festivals as did Rome on those specified days. This had the effect of harmonizing the military with Rome in a liturgical manner. No matter where the unit was stationed within the empire they all were bound to Rome by means of the military religious calendar.

Not only were the camps tied to Rome by means of synchronizing their time with Rome, but each camp was an architectural replication of Rome. The walls around the camp symbolized the walls around Rome. The *praetorium* was the capitol; and the camp itself was the city of Rome on the frontier. Continuing this symbolic configuration, the *limes*, the border around the empire, was symbolically the wall around Rome; both Rome's wall and the *limes* were sacred in Roman eyes. What we have here is the classic navel of the universe with power radiating outward from the sacred centre, Rome itself.[22] Military camps were "real" only when they were set up in standard patterns which in turn reflected and amplified the power of Rome. Every square inch of the imperial Roman soil fell within this sacred configuration.

As the church moved into the Empire, these models became the Christian way as well. It is likely that the struggle over the date of Easter in the middle second century was understood in these terms: like the Army sending out ritual calendars from Rome, so the Roman congregation sent out orders as to the correct Easter date. Much later in the time of Bede we have evidence that the Easter date was quite consciously synchronized with Rome.[23] The priest Wilfrid told the recalcitrant Colman that the Easter date they kept was the same as that where the apostles Peter and Paul were buried and that it was kept uniform in every province and on every continent.[24] When the Picts adopted the Roman tonsure and the Roman Easter date they ceased to be led by error and entered the "real" world which was characterized by uniformity with Rome. For Bede, Rome was the primary sacred place because it was there that Peter and Paul were buried and the Eucharist was celebrated over their graves.[25] Episcopal succession was, for Bede and for many others, a spatial concept in that Peter was regarded as having consecrated Clement in Rome. It was, therefore, the place where other bishops ought also to be consecrated whenever possible.

Architecturally, the churches in the outlying territories imitated the practice of the army in that they both tried to reproduce Rome symbolically. The English obtained builders from Rome to build a church in the Roman fashion and named it after Peter.[26] In France, too, they took the Roman world as a blueprint. Altars became abbreviations of types of parish churches in Rome; they needed numbers of priests to attend the altars. They did not construct multiple altars because there were so many priests, as we had thought previously.[27]

Conclusion

As early as the time of Irenaeus in the second century, who said that every church must be in agreement with Rome, we can see the church moving into the mental map of the Roman world.[28] We have seen that this development had powerful consequences for the nature of Christian self-understanding and self-expression. In a few centuries the structure of Christianity had been changed from one religion into another, from a religion oblivious of space and objects to one where these were actually the bearers of the holy. Accordingly, the whole understanding of what constituted the holy underwent transformation. Grace, for example, in the New Testament specified an attitude of God toward man, but in several centuries it came to designate a quantifiable power very much like *numen*.

A concluding note concerning the place of theology within this process may be pertinent. As we have argued, much of what is described here went on at an unreflective, perhaps preconscious, level. In the face of what took place, most theologians seemed powerless to change the course of things. Some bishops had misgivings regarding the cult of relics and there is evidence they spoke against it. Interestingly, one finds no mention of relics in the martyr accounts from Montanist circles;[29] probably their continuing emphasis on time prevented them from moving in that direction. There were attempts, moreover, to use the cult of relics in tandem with classical Christian motifs. The relic, it was said, communicated confidence to the people because, since the body of the martyr was certain to be raised, they would be resurrected along with it.[30] Of course, such a notion cannot serve as any kind of explanation of the martyr cult because many inanimate objects were used in connection with the cult, as the practice of *brandeum* illustrated. So theology, as one of many categories of religious behavior, came in after the fact attempting to provide an aesthetic bond between the folk religion and the high culture of the theologian. But whether the folk religion of space or the theological religion predominates is a function of the sociological and anthropological accidents which condition societies.[31]

LE SOPRAVVIVENZE PAGANE NEL MEDIOEVO

Pierre Boglioni

In un congresso che si propone di studiare le tradizioni religiose "in contatto e in trasformazione", il tema delle sopravvivenze pagane nell' Europa medievale appare di particolare pertinenza. Agli storici del cristianesimo ed ai teologi, come agli antropologi ed ai folkloristi, esso pone problemi capitali sulle capacità di espansione del cristianesimo e sulle modificazioni che esso ha potuto subire nella lotta contro il paganesimo. Lo scopo del presente rapporto è di evocare in breve le principali configurazioni della problematica di questo tema nei diversi momenti storici e nelle diverse discipline.

Non mi nascondo il carattere necessariamente schematico del mio esposto, che sorvola in poche pagine una materia vastissima. La nozione di sopravvivenza (*survival*, *survivance*, *Fortleben*) è vaga, come lo sono le nozioni complementari o parallele (resti, reliquie, tracce, etc.). Anche la nozione di paganesimo è generica e può denotare secondo le circostanze strati assai diversi di cultura religiosa: paganesimo greco - romano classico, elementi indoeuropei, elementi italici, iberici, celti, germanici e - più addietro nel tempo - quegli elementi delle religioni preistoriche, specie del neolitico, che sono malagevoli da definire ma essenziali nella composizione dei sincretismi locali. E' inoltre difficile distinguere in questo "paganesimo" la dimensione religiosa da quella magica e da quella puramente profana. L'interesse eventuale di questa comunicazione consiste nella varietà stessa dei punti di vista evocati e nell'incontro auspicato di discipline diverse.

1. Le sopravvivenze come persistenze

La problematica più semplice intorno alle sopravvivenze pagane riguarda la fase iniziale della diffusione del cristianesimo, quando per un certo periodo le antiche religioni coesistono con la nuova, conservando una coscienza netta della reciproca diversità. In tale momento storico la sopravvivenza del paganesimo è di fatto una persistenza, che può divenire resistenza là dove la coscienza della diversità religiosa sia abbastanza forte da provocare una reazione attiva al processo di acculturazione.

Nel medioevo tali persistenze riguardano solo in modo sporadico il paganesimo strutturato della religione classica, del quale già nel 391 Teodosio aveva interdetto la pratica e chiuso i templi. Esse riguardano piuttosto la religione dei popoli di conversione recente e ancor più la religione delle popolazioni rurali, presso le quali il cristianesimo non si era ancora radicato con strutture capillari adeguate. Il crollo della struttura unificante dell'impero aveva infatti ridato nuova vitalità alle culture indigene e favorito il risveglio di forme religiose arcaicizzanti.

Le sopravvivenze del paganesimo inteso in questo senso sono state studiate principalmente dagli storici della missione cristiana, della quale costituiscono il limite e, per così dire, il rovescio. Dal punto di vista dell'espansione cristiana gli studi sono molto numerosi. Si sono identificate le diverse strategie della missione di fronte al paganesimo: distruzione violenta, contraffazione o sostituzione, trasformazione di senso o di contenuto. Si è riconosciuta l'importanza primordiale della taumaturgia. Si è cercato di stabilire il ritmo di diffusione del cristianesimo e si sono studiate le modalità sociali della sua propagazione: dall'alto in basso, dal gruppo alla coscienza individuale, dal centro alla periferia (cf. nella bibl. *La conversione al cristianesimo*, *La christianisation*, J. Le Goff).

Gli studi sono invece meno dettagliati per quanto riguarda le persistenze stesse. Certo, gli storici delle religioni hanno minuziosamente rastrellato i testi ufficiali dell'alto medioevo, specie per la religione dei Germani. Esistono monografie ed opere di sintesi (W. Boudriot, S. McKenna, D. Harmening, etc.). Ma il quadro storico delle persistenze non ha la medesima nettezza di quello dell'espansione cristiana. Si è data un'importanza maggiore ai testi ufficiali (concili, penitenziali, prediche), ma non si è costituito un inventario sistematico degli elementi fattuali che si possono ricavare da tutti i documenti (agiografie, miracoli, lettere, carte): geografia precisa dei luoghi e delle forme di culto evocate; casi di "revivals" di antiche tradizioni; cronologia delle menzioni di riti o feste. Salvo per la Gallia merovingia (E. Salin), non si è sfruttato l'apporto essenziale dell'archeologia funeraria. Un tale inventario di dettaglio permetterebbe una storia più sfumata del trionfo del cristianesimo e fornirebbe riferimenti circostanziati per la storia del folklore.

2. Sopravvivenze e "superstitiones"

Anche dopo la conversione ufficiale di tutta l'Europa al cristianesimo, la chiesa medievale non si è mai illusa sul grado di cristianizzazione delle masse. Dal VI al XVI secolo, una serie di testi pastorali, giuridici o teologici, mostra la preoccupazione costante di sradicare un mondo religioso alternativo, designato principalmente col termine di *superstitiones*. Non è facile tradurre questo termine nelle lingue moderne, conservando le sfumature che gli attribuiscono gli autori medievali, ma è certo che una componente fondamentale della nozione di *superstitio* è costitutita dal suo legame con un passato precristiano. La problematica delle *superstitiones*, si potrebbe dire, è la problematica delle sopravvivenze pagane quale percepita dagli intellettuali del medioevo. Essa costituisce dunque un luogo essenziale per studiare sia l'esito oggettivo dell'antico paganesimo, sia l'idea che se ne facevano gli autori medievali (D. Harmening).

Un'analisi globale dei testi medievali che riguardano la *superstitio* mostra che il senso del termine si trova in equilibrio instabile fra tre dimensioni divergenti, benchè complementari. Una prima dimensione è di ordine storico: mediante le categorie di resto, tradizione, origine, la *superstitio* è ricollegata alla cultura religiosa pre-cristiana e designata con termini quali "vetustus error", "ex vetusta consuetudine paganorum", "quod adhuc de paganis residet". La seconda dimensione è di ordine culturale o sociologico: la *superstitio* è interpretata come sciempiaggine d'ignoranti, ovvero collegata alla nozione di inferiorità sociale o di marginalità. I termini che l'esprimono sono allora "fatuitas", "dementia", "phantasma", "vanitas", i qualificativi sono quelli di "stultus", "ignorans", "insipiens", e le classi sociali sono quelle dei "rustici", "pauperes", "populares", "vetulae". Tale senso è gia vicino a quello profano e secolarizzato che le lingue moderne attribuiscono al termine di superstizione. La terza dimensione interpreta la *superstitio* mediante categorie strettamente teologiche: invenzione di Satana e suo strumento di dominio sull'uomo. In tale prospettiva essa è qualificata come "turpis", "perversa", "nefaria", "nequitia". E' ovvio che tali dimensioni non si escludono reciprocamente e che anzi non sono mai interamente assenti l'una dall'altra. Ma la loro importanza rispettiva non è la stessa nel corso del medioevo. Agli inizi (VI-XI s.) la coscienza delle radici storiche della *superstitio* è ancora viva e tale dimensione predomina sulle altre: i fenomeni descritti come "superstitiones" sono anche designati come "paganitates", "paganiae", "paganae observationes", secondo una terminologia che vede in essi vere persistenze. Dal XII al XIV secolo si incontra di più la spiegazione mediante l'ignoranza o la marginalità. La coscienza di una certa "secolarizzazione" o folklorizzazione della *superstitio* sembra compiuta verso gli anni 1220/1250. Il nemico principale della Chiesa non è più allora nel passato, ma in quelle eresie popolari attuali che contestanto radicalmente la sua struttura sacerdotale ed i suoi poteri. La cultura ancestrale retrocede di fronte all'urbanizzazione. Cosciente del rinnovato controllo sulla religione della città mendiante gli ordini mendicanti, la Chiesa ufficiale ha creduto che il peso religioso delle *superstitiones* si era indebolito e che si poteva ora considerarle come semplici "superstizioni", curiosità innocue di interesse minore (R. Manselli, F. Cardini). Il mondo della *superstitio* è ancora assai vivo in Guglielmo d'Alvernia, professore di teologia e vescovo di Parigi (+1249). Non sarà più che realtà libresca in Tommaso d'Aquino, appena due generazioni dopo. A partire dagli inizi del XV s., la spiegazione teologica della *superstitio* come opera di Satana cancella le antiche interpretazioni e trova un'intensità drammatica con l'identificazione alla stregoneria. Questa appare a teologi e giuristi non come un resto del passato, ma come un'anti-religione attuale. Improvvisamente, dei resti folklorici sparsi ed incoerenti sono promossi alla dignità di nuova religione e ricollegati non a delle radici storiche o locali, ma ad un'anti-chiesa universale: nella spiegazione della *superstitio* la teologia si sostituisce interamente alla storia e alla sociologia.

A questi tre grandi cicli nella tematica medievale della *superstitio* corrispondono situazioni documentarie e problemi metodologici diversi. Al primo momento corrisponde une documentazione abbondante e diretta. Ricorderò a titolo di esempio i *Sermones* di Cesario d'Arles (+524), il *De correctione rusticorum* di Martino di Braga (+580), gli opuscoli di Agobardo di Lione, i *Dicta Pirmini*, i numerosi *capitula* della legislazione ecclesiastica o civile, e la nutrita serie di penitenziali, con le loro descrizioni talvolta assai precise, come nel caso del più famoso di essi, il *Corrector* du Burcardo di Worms (1025). Tali testi sono conosciuti da sempre. Il problema fondamentale appare quello della loro interpretazione. Al seguito di W. Boudriot, D. Harmening lo ha ripreso in modo sistematico. Il limite documentario di questi testi consiste nel fatto che rappresentano esclusivamente il punto di vista della Chiesa e che mostrano una netta tendenza alla ripetizione: così, possono riferire come fatti ancora vivi dei fenomeni già tramontati, o trasporre ad una regione la descrizione di fenomeni analoghi di un'altra. Malgrado la loro grande quantità e l'apparente abbondanza di dettagli, la religione concreta del popolo minuto ci sfugge, per l'alto medioevo, più che per ogni altra epoca.

Dal XII al XIV secolo, la documentazione diventa più frammentaria e più difficile da reperire. Quando i teologi si occupano di *superstitiones*, come Tommaso d'Aquino (I-II, qq. 92-96), si avverte la discussione teorica più che l'esperienza diretta. Per trovare testimonianze vissute, bisogna scremare grandi quantità di documenti, alla ricerca di incisi occasionali o secondari: il *Verbum abbreviatum* di Petrus Cantor (+1197), la *Historia scholastica* di Petrus Comestor (+1179), il *De Universo* o il *De fide et legibus* di Guglielmo d'Alvernia (+1249). Bisogna seguire pazientemente la pista dell'enorme letteratura omiletica e quella dei commenti al Primo Comandamento. Peraltro, la cultura laica comincia a lasciar trapelare contenuti propri sia con una produzione diretta in lingua volgare come le *Edda*, sia nei diversi filoni che giungono ad innestarsi nella cultura clericale: negli *exempla* dei predicatori (J.-C. Schmitt), nell'arte (R. Sheridan - A. Ross), nelle leggende che affiorano in opere come il *De nugis curialium* di Gualtiero Map e gli *Otia imperialia* di Gervasio di Tilbury.

Col XV secolo, le fonti delle *superstitiones* rividentano esplicite e dettagliate. Ricorderò quel documento eccezionale che è *l'Evangile des quenouilles*, testo piccardo del 1470 c., che sciorina in una grande risata di veglia quelle credenze mitiche, paure cosmologiche e ricette di magia amorosa che avevano proibito con orrore gli antichi penitenziali. Teologi e giuristi ricominciano a scrivere trattati su questi argomenti: dobbiamo così un *De superstitionibus* a Nicola di Jawor (c. 1405), un altro *De superstitionibus* a Giovanni di Francoforte (v. 1412), un *Tractatus de superstitiosis quibusdam casibus* a Enrico di Gorichem (verso 1425), etc. I manuali degli inquisitori se ne occupano esplicitamente e i documenti inquisitoriali, facendo parlare il popolo, ci danno un tipo di documentazione profondamente nuova. Ma ormai la problematica della *superstitio* è diventata quasi esclusivamente quella della stregoneria.

Nella coscienza degli inquisitori, il rapporto fra la

stregoneria ed il mondo pagano del passato è del tutto scomparso. Ma esso si impone inevitabilmente alla critica moderna. Già M.A. Murray avevo proposto una spiegazione essenzialmente storica della stregoneria, postulandone il carattere cultuale e il legame diretto con religioni preistoriche: "Ritual Witchcraft (...) can be traced back to pre-Christian times, and appears to be the ancient religion of Western Europe" (*The Witch-Cult*, p.11-12). In questa forma estrema, la teoria non è più difesa da nessuno. Ma la critica attuale riconosce sempre più chiaramente che nella stregoneria medievale bisogna distinguere il livello dell'interpretazione ideologica, in gran parte costruito dagli intellettuali, e la realtà oggettiva delle credenze e pratiche popolari, proprie di una cultura che trova nel passato pre-cristiano le sue radici. Così, R. Kieckhefer ha potuto, con una ingegnosa critica delle fonti, isolare nella massa dei processi di stregoneria gli elementi di ideologia colta sovrapposti ("the imposition of learned notions") alla cultura popolare. Nel suo saggio sui benandanti, C. Ginzburg aveva già descritto in modo convincente come dei resti di una religione agraria, di cui si trovano tracce da un capo all'altro dell'Europa, finirono per essere assimilati alla stregoneria corrente, sotto la pressione dell'interpretazione ideologica degli inquisitori.

3 Sopravvivenze pagane e cristianesimo

La Riforma imprime alla problematica delle *superstitiones* una svolta decisiva con la violenta polemica sul pagano-papismo: la sopravvivenza dell'antico paganesimo non sarà più ricercata in una marginale cultura popolare, ma nella struttura stessa del cristianesimo medievale, con la sua liturgia, le sue forme di culto e di pietà, i suoi sacramenti e sacramentali, le sue leggende. La tematica delle infiltrazioni pagane e del "paganesimo cristianizzato", tanto forte da dare impulso alle prime ricerche di storia comparata delle religioni, sarà così paradossalmente uno dei luoghi storici e culturali della discussione sulle sopravvivenze del paganesimo.

Tale tematica è già sviluppata nel *De vitandis superstitionibus* e nel *Traité des reliques* di Calvino, ma trova la sua espressione storica e critica più completa nelle vastissime *Centuriae Magdeburgenses*, gigantesco sforzo della storiografia protestante per mostrare nella storia del cristianesimo medievale il progressivo distacco dall'ideale evangelico. Sistematicamente, esse rilevano un vasto materiale sul culto dei santi e della Vergine, le devozioni, i miracoli, le leggende, con lo scopo preciso di identificare nella filosofia e nelle religioni antiche gli elementi che si sono infiltrati nel cristianesimo. Un gran numero di polemisti maggiori e minori riprenderà questi temi. Henri Estienne darà loro lustro letterario nella sua *Introduction au traité de la conformité des merveilles anciennes avec les modernes*, caricatura del cristianesimo medievale che i controversisti saccheggeranno senza scrupolo.

E' da notare che anche la controriforma cattolica fu spinta da questa polemica a valutare in modo più critico che nel medioevo le *consuetudines non laudabiles*. Nasce così nella stessa pastorale cattolica una serie di opere, essenziali per la storia del folklore, che non temono di indagare nel mondo cattolico la possibilità di sopravvivenze di atteggiamenti pagani. Le più importanti sono, verso la fine del XVII secolo, i grandi trattati dell'abbé Jean-Baptiste Thiers, *Traité des superstitions selon l'écriture sainte*, *Traité des superstitions qui regardent tous les sacrements*, e quello di poco posteriore dell'oratoriano Pierre Le Brun, *Histoire critique des pratiques superstitieuses qui ont séduit les peuples et embarassé les savants*.

Il filone della critica protestante è rimasto poi sempre presente sotto diverse forme. Affiora nella polemica razionalista contro il cristianesimo, come nell'opera famosa di C. Middleton, *A letter from Rome, showing the exact conformity between Popery and Paganism* (Londra, 1729), destinata a largo successo. Degrada poi a luogo comune, combinando la polemica confessionale antipapista con vaghe categorie di storia comparata delle religioni, in un insieme di pubblicazioni minori, che sanno insieme del pamphlet e della divulgazione di massa. Ricorderò a titolo di esempio le affermazioni del poligrafo Arthur Weigall: "Una gran parte del cristianesimo confessionale è in realtà così chiaramente une forma di paganesimo rifatto, che se ne può parlare come dell'ultimo baluardo degli dei pagani" (*The Paganism*, p.16). Per Mourant Brock, "la transizione dal paganesimo al papato ha portato poco cambiamento nei principi e nella pratica di Roma, ed ha lasciato la religione molto simile a quello che era prima, salvo che alle deità ed ai riti pagani si davano ora nomi e termini cristiani" (*Rome*, p.269). Anche la propaganda nazista riprederà questo centone di luoghi communi e di temi banali: "il cristianesimo è stato ed è per noi tedeschi la breccia più pericolosa per l'invasione dello spirito, delle credenze e dell'ideologia non solo giudaiche, ma straniere in genere...Dal di dentro come dal di fuori, la religione cristiana dipende dal paganesimo precristiano" (R. Neuwinger, p.242-243).

Sarebbe però altamente inguisto ridurre a questi epigoni risibili l'influsso della critica protestante. Da un lato, essa ha senza dubbio sensibilizzato gli spiriti, nei paesi di cultura tedesca e inglese assai più che in quelli di cultura latina, allo studio comparativo del cristianesimo. Con la critica liberale, ha spinto a studi più rigorosi sulle origini cristiane. Ha finalmente influenzato anche il modernismo cattolico, infondendo in esso un atteggiamento più critico nello studio delle tradizioni religiose. Si pensi all'opera famosa e confusa di Th. Trede sul paganesimo della chiesa romana nell'Italia del Sud, e all'opera vasta di Pierre Saintyves, pseudonimo letterario di qull'Émile Nourry la cui casa editrice pubblicò tanta parte della letterature modernista francese.

Nutrito agli inizi da motivazioni e argomenti teologici, il filone della critica protestante al culto cattolico diventa così fonte di studi storici e folklorici nei quali la problematica delle sopravvivenze pagane trova un altro dei suoi centri maggiori di ispirazione e che interessano tutti in modo più o meno diretto il medioevo.

4. Sopravvivenze pagane e folklore

Non si puo ignorare, infine, come luogo essenziale di discussione e documentazione sulle sopravvivenze pagane nel medioevo, le discussioni degli etnologi ed antropologi sulla problematica più generale delle sopravvivenze culturali.

Già i primi autori che si erano occupati di descrivere i fatti folklorici avevano rilevato il carattere arcaicizzante della cultura popolare, ma l'idea trova una sua precisione concettuale ed un ruolo ermeneutico maggiore nella scuola antropologica inglese del XIX secolo, mediante la nozione tecnica di *survival*. Il primo ad avanzarla e definirla fu E.B.Tylor: "Fra i documenti che ci aiutano a tracciare il corso che la civiltà mondiale ha effettivamente seguito, v'è un'estesa classe di fatti per designare i quali mi sembra conveniente di introcurre il termine di *survivals*. Si tratta di procedimenti, abitudini, opinioni, ecc., trascinati dalla forza dell'abitudine in uno stadio nuovo della società, diverso da quello in cui ebbero la loro origine, e che rimangono così come prove ed esempi di una condizione più antica della cultura" (*Primitive Culture*, I,p.16). Pensando il progresso dell'umanità come un processo cronologicamente diverso ma strutturalmente uniforme in tutti i paesi ed in tutte le civiltà, perchè iscritto in una natura umana che è identica dappertutto, Tylor faceva del *survival* una nozione centrale per fondare il legame organico fra antropologia, folklore e storia, la cultura folklorica essendo una sopravvivenza di quegli strati primitivi della cultura umana, che si possono ancora documentare presso i popoli selvaggi.

Non è nostro compito tracciare la storia successiva della nozione di *survival* che Taylor aveva proposto, nè indicare le applicazioni che essa ha avuto nelle varie branche di studi del folklore contemporaneo, come quello delle favole o dei giochi infantili. G.L. Gomme, teorico della scuola antropologica inglese, definirà il folklore proprio mediante la nozione di *survival*: "il folklore è la scienza che si occupa delle sopravvivenze, delle credenze e dei costumi arcaici nei tempi moderni" ed è "forse il solo mezzo per scoprire gli stati primitivi della storia psicologica, religiosa, sociale e politica dell'uomo moderno" (*Folklore*, p.IX). Fra le critiche interessanti segnalerò quella di Stanley A. Cook e quella luminosa di R.R. Marett, ripresa sostanzialmente da G. Cocchiara (v. Bibl.). L'apporto di queste critiche è di togliere alla nozione tyloriana della sopravvivenza il suo carattere statico di puro detrito della storia, per sottolineare i processi attivi mediante i quali la cultura popolare seleziona le sopravvivenze, ne trasforma il significato inserendole in altri contesti, e le vive non come resto passivo, ma come mezzo attivo di reazione a situazioni vitali. Richiamando costantemente l'attenzione sul pericolo dei falsi parallelismi e delle spiegazioni semplicistiche, questi autori danno finalmente alla nozione di *survival* una complessità ed un valore più grandi.

Resta il fatto che l'idea tyloriana, variamente intesa ed applicata, ha dato origine a ricerche documentarie impressionanti. Si ricorderà l'enorme costruzione di Wilhelm Mannhardt, iniziata con *Der Baumkultus der Germanen* (1875), continuata con *Wald- und Feldkulte*, terminata con le *Mythologische Forschungen*, pubblicate postume nel 1884, nella quale egli si sforza di ricondurre all'unità di una credenza originaria e fondamentale l'enorme varietà di miti, credenze e culti legati alla natura vegetale e alle pratiche agrarie. Con *Mutter Erde* (1905), Albrecht Dieterich intraprendeva una ricerca metodologicamente analoga sull'idea primitiva secondo la quale la terra è percepita come la grande Madre di tutti i viventi. Anche nel *Ramo d'oro*, le cui ambizioni sono più universali, le pagine sulle sopravvivenze degli antichi miti nel folklore attuale sono numerose.

Questo robusto impulso culturale si è poi frammentato, secondo influenze non sempre facili da documentare, in un insieme di ricerche parziali che, per una data regione o un dato popolo, si sforzano di gettare un ponte fra un passato spesso preistorico e il presente folklorico. Ricorderò a titolo d'esempio la ricerca insieme erudita e confusa di C.G. Leland sui resti della religione etrusca e romana nella Romagna del XIX secolo, che lo portava all'affermazione globale: "il contadiname della Romagna Toscana, che ha vissuto sin dai tempi preistorici con pochi cambiamenti, ha conservato attraverso la dominazione etrusca, latina e cristiana un sciamanismo primitivo o un rude animismo" (p.4). In un'opera classica e più sicura, J.C. Lawson sfrutterà sistematicamente lo studio del folklore greco contemporaneo per l'analisi della religione della Grecia antica. In una linea analoga sono anche i lavori, meno impegnativi, di W.W. Hyde e G.J. Laing. L.J.-B. Bérenger-Féraud costituiva, sotto l'influsso della scuola antropologica inglese, un vasto corpus di "superstitions et survivances". Le ricerche sul persistere del culto degli alberi e delle fonti possono essere poste sulla medesima linea (ad es. M. Crampon, P. Audin). Significativa fra tutte, per il suo titolo stesso, l'opera di Paul Sébillot sul paganesimo contemporaneo nei paesi celto-latini: "sorta di sotto-religione, molto più antica, che si rivolgeva a delle divinità locali o alle forze della natura...il paganesimo contemporaneo non differisce spesso nella grandi linee da quello che era praticato migliaia di anni fa, e questa sotto-religione attuale, che siamo lungi dal conoscere a fondo, non è stata intaccata sensibilmente, nelle sue parti essenziali, dalle religioni più colte e più raffinate che si sono succedute, con carattere ufficiale, nelle diverse regioni dell'Europa celto-latina" (p.XVII e XXVI)

Con questo tipo di ricerche e di problematica, sembriamo esserci ormai definitivamente allontanati dal medioevo. Antropologi e folkloristi, infatti, nello stabilire il legame fra antichità e folklore contemporaneo, sono portati abitualmente a "saltare" il medioevo. Ma ciò è dovuto soprattutto alle difficoltà oggettive di documentazione per i non specialisti. Resta il fatto che, per la loro stessa natura, tali ricerche postulano un *continuum* fra antichità e tempi moderni, e possono essere considerate come documentazione almeno ipotetica di una vita sotterranea che ha dovuto continuare anche nel medioevo.

Le testimonianze medievali, spesso sporadiche, scarne, e di difficile interpretazione, su sopravvivenze di antiche religioni, trovano in queste richerche un quadro geografico e tassonomico prezioso, che il medievista non puo ignorare.

ISRAEL AND BYZANTIUM:
A CASE OF SOCIO-RELIGIOUS ACCULTURATION

John Wortley

Of all the major Christian traditions, Eastern Orthodoxy probably remains (as it has long been) the least known and the most misunderstood. This is partly because students of Christianity especially, but not alone, have failed to realise how very different Orthodoxy is from the other, and mutually inter-related, Christianities of the West, Catholic, Anglican, Evangelical, Reformed, etc. Over and over again Western attempts to appreciate Orthodoxy have failed because they made the basic error of trying to view the East through Western eyes, and to describe it in Western terms in the light of the Western experience. Liturgists will readily appreciate (for instance) that to call the Orthodox Liturgy *mass* is to place an almost insuperable block in the path to understanding the Orthodox way of worship. Historians know that it is only in these last decades that we have finally begun to set aside the crashingly anachronistic and occidocentric term *Caesaropapism* which for so long Westerners have used in their vain attempts to grapple with the complex question of church-state relations in the Orthodox sphere. Orthodoxy cannot be known this way, because Orthodoxy is fundamentally different from anything in the Western experience, and as generations of ecumenically-minded Anglicans have painfully learned, Orthodoxy must be studied on and in its own terms.

One important respect in which Orthodoxy is different from anything Western is that, in contradistinction to the churches of the West, all the Orthodox churches derive their origin and much of their substance from a single and highly sophisticated cultural and political experience, that of the East Roman or Byzantine Empire, which (said Gibbon, with customary preponderance of asperity over truth) "subsisted one thousand and fifty-eight years"[1] (i.e. counting from the accession of Arcadius and Honorius) "in a state of premature and perpetual decay." All Orthodoxy is therefore Constantinopolitan to some (usually considerable) extent, in a way that by no means the whole of even Catholic Western Christendom is Roman. An understanding of *Byzance* is therefore an indispensible *eisagogue* to the understanding of orthodoxy.[2]

Now there is much which can already be said about the Byzantine Empire, though it is true that much more yet remains to be discovered or to be ascertained; the extent to which the swaddling cloth which Gibbon gave still clings about it is clear demonstration of the recent infancy of Byzantinology. One thing, however, is clear and becomes clearer with each step: that the Byzantines were an extremely proud people indeed, who (in Gibbon's words) "styled themselves, with some appearance of truth, the most enlightened and civilised portion of the human species."[3] They seem rarely to have doubted but that theirs was the most excellent heritage in the best of possible worlds, the Christian *oikoumenē*; beyond its borders were only barbarian inferiors. Some were more inferior than others it is true; indeed there came to be a recognised scale of degrees of inferiority, but at the head of that scale, very high and exalted, stood the Greek-speaking Christians who obeyed the Emperor of the New Rome on the Bosphorus. It may seem a little strange that a Christian Empire, the first Christian Empire, did not a little more heed Saint Paul's teaching that in Christ there is neither Jew nor Greek, bond nor free, etc., but it was not so. The Christian Greeks fixed a great gulf between themselves and the *barbaroi* beyond their borders, as indeed they did between bond and free within.

On what grounds, then, did the Byzantines base their claim to superiority to the rest of the inhabited world, other than on the simple fact of their physical, military and economic superiority? What were the ideological springs of their *superbia*? There are several possible answers to this questions, each of which was true to a greater or lesser extent at one time or another, for the emphasis shifted with changing conditions. In the earlier centuries, in and after the age of Constantine the Great, they took their greatest pride in being Romans, which is of course precisely what they were, and what they continued to call themselves right down to the final catastrophe in 1453 (they rarely used the terms "Byzantine" to denote other than a resident of Constantinople). Towards the end of the Byzantine epoch, they tended to take pride in a title which they would once have bitterly resented, that of *Hellenes*; in being heirs to the cultural explosion of ancient Hellas. But between the period in which their Neo-Romanism and that in which their Neo-Hellenism was to the fore, a political and a cultural heritage respectively, there was a period of about half a millenium when it was neither the politician nor the scholar who nourished Byzantine pride, but the churchman. This however, must not be allowed to suggest Western patterns of church-state relationship, for these would not be true of Byzantium. There, church and state were rather mutually inter-penetrating entities whose precise limits cannot be detected because they did not exist the way they came to exist in the West. Churchmen, or their disciples, obviously suggested what we are about to discuss, for it is derived from church lore, but what was suggested could only have succeeded with the willing acceptance of it by influential lay members of society, from the emperor down; and it shall be seen that the laity stopped short of accepting all that might have been suggested in this respect by churchmen who lacked the authority to enjoin what they might have preferred.

What was suggested to, and won the willing approval of, the laity, was this: that the New Roman Empire had a sacred vocation also to be the New Israel, the new chosen people of God; an eschatological kingdom established on earth to consummate the divine plan for the world.[4] In a word, the Byzantines saw themselves as fulfilling precisely that role in the new dispensation which the prophets had claimed for the Jews in the old.

It is, of course, a familiar enough feature of New Testament, and especially of Pauline, teaching that Christians are the "new circumcision"; that in rejecting Jesus, Judaism had forfeited its birthright of being the chosen people, and that this, with all the promises and privileges thereunto pertaining, had now been transferred to the new Israel, which was the church of the Christians. Once the church had grasped this message (and it seems not to have done so until the middle of the second century[5]), it was almost inevitable that, with the establishment of Christianity in the Empire, that is, with the near-coincidence of the two spheres of *imperium* and of *Christianitas*, the spiritual idea of the New Israel would be clothed with political flesh, *a fortiori* in view of the undoubtedly political background to the New Israel idea as it appears in the pages of the Old Testament. Indeed, with the exclusive Christianisation of the Empire, it would have been rather strange if there had not been a move to apply New Israel teaching to the entire body politic at Byzantium; and yet it is not so easy to prove beyond reasonable doubt that there was such a move. By the tenth or eleventh century it had probably come to be generally accepted that New Rome was the New Israel,[6] but like most things that were generally accepted, few bold and unambiguous statements to that effect are to be found in the sources. It is the constant complaint of the Byzantinist that he knows far too much about things that were disputed, and far too little about the much larger area in which there was general agreement, a complaint no doubt which future generations of historians will level at the British Constitution and the Canadian sense of national identity.

What the scholar does encounter is random scattered indications; asides in writings, established practices and habits, the curious use of certain terms and so forth, all of which, often by implication rather than directly, seem to indicate *in their totality* that the Byzantines had absorbed much more from their Jewish Progenitors-in-the-faith than merely their scriptures; indeed, that they seem to have identified themselves with the Ancient Jews more closely than has done any other major Christian group before or since. It must be stressed that it is in their *totality* that the indications in question seem to point in this direction. Many of those indications have been noticed elsewhere already;[7] there is scarcely a reputable book on Byzantium which will omit all reference to it as the New Jerusalem, or say nothing of the sacral nature of Byzantine kingship, for instance. What has not yet been done is to take all the indications together and to weigh their effect *in toto*; hence neither has the extent to which the East Romans embraced their Israelite heritage yet been fully appreciated. It would be beyond the scope of a small paper to examine all the implications, but we may pass some of the major ones under review.

The importance of the liturgical evidence has not been fully appreciated. When the Constantinopolitan liturgical calendar first emerges from the long tunnel of obscurity, towards the end of the ninth century that is, this curious detail is to be noted. It begins, as all Byzantine liturgical calendars do, on 1st September, the beginning of the Indiction and therefore a New-Year's day of some importance (not of course the only one). It is called the feast of the "Crown of the year," but 1st September is also - and this is what is very revealing - the feast ($h\bar{e}$ $Mn\bar{e}m\bar{e}$) of Joshua, the son of Nun, who was the successor of Moses and led the Children of Israel into the Promised Land, flowing with milk and honey.[8] Such a choice of patron for the New Year may seem a little strange, and certainly has some very interesting implications, but it is only the tip of a much larger piece of evidence. The old Byzantine calendar shows a very pronounced interest indeed in the personages of the Old Testament. Joshua the son of Nun is no *hapax*; nearly every patriarch, prophet and celebrity of the Jewish scriptures finds his or her feast-day somewhere in the Byzantine calendar, and some of them are feasts of considerable importance, no mere secondary commemorations.[9] Not only that, but oratories and even quite large churches were dedicated in the names of Old Testament heroes, especially in honour of the Prophet Elijah, who was especially beloved of that great persecutor of the Jews, Basil I the Macedonian.[10] And even beyond (or more likely before) that, relics of the old Jewish heroes were sedulously collected from the Holy Land (the axe of Noah amongst them) to become the objects of a devotion no different from and no less intense than that which was offered to the mortal remains of the Christian martyrs and apostles. Now devotion to the Old Testament heroes is by no means unknown in the mediaeval West, as anybody who has studied the glass for instance at Chartres knows well, but it was never anywhere near so intense or so thorough as in the East, where, as the calendar and the dedications testify, it became thoroughly institutionalised. In 787, at the Seventh Ecumenical Council, the Old Testament heroes were specifically accorded the same honours as those of the new dispensation: "All the saints from Creation onward, before the law and after the law, were in a state of grace with God and worthy of veneration. Prayers can be addressed to them: they can intercede."[11] Fully to appreciate the implications of this decision, one would have to consult some of the entries in the *synaxaria* against the commemorations of Old Testament persons. The writers leave one in no doubt whatsoever that they regard these persons very much as *their* heroes, with whom they are linked by a bond which is stronger (because it is a spiritual bond) than any Byzantine ever felt for Scipio or Pompey or Augustus or Hadrian.

Now let us set this side-by-side with the evidence of the chronicles, those "world chronicles" on which we have to depend for much of our knowledge of middle Byzantine history.[12] These measure time not, as one might expect, *ab urbe condita* or by some other calculation of the pagans, but *from the creation of the world* as recorded in the Book of Genesis, and which was computed to have taken place on 25th March, 5508 (or 5492) B.C. Within this chronological framework, the main line of events is traced, not through the fortunes of Greece and Rome (which are not neglected, but are treated as accidental to the main theme), but through the fortunes of ancient Israel as they are recorded by the Old Testament writers,[13] of whom the chronographers treat themselves as the continuators. They tell their story with the same convictions with which the Deuteronomist historians told theirs: that good kings die prosperously in their beds, full of years and success, whilst bad kings suffer catastrophic reverses and bite the dust most horribly and prematurely. Goodness is defined in terms of religious orthodoxy; badness as heterodoxy, "doing that which is evil in the sight of the Lord."[14]

When the chronographers speak of the enemies of the Empire, which, for the most part, means the Muslim, there is a marked tendency to replace the traditional name of Saracens with either Ishmaelites or Hagarenes, and sometimes even with Gentiles, $ethn\bar{e}$.[15] This is balanced by a corresponding tendency to speak of imperial misfortunes in the kind of language which the Old Testament writers use to describe the reverses of Israel, especially in terms of the despoiled vineyard of the Lord.[16] If these tendencies were no more than occasional occurrences, it would be possible to dismiss them as mere literary conceits, but they occur so regularly and persistently that it is impossible to avoid the conclusion that they reveal some deep-seated passionately held convictions that *Romania* really was the New Israel of God.

The chronographers also emphasised the resemblances between Judaic and Byzantine kingship, and in doing so, they pave the way to an understanding of what are otherwise some very puzzling anomalies in the Byzantine system of government. For instance, the apparently erratic system of succession on the throne bears strong resemblance to the way the kings of Israel and Judah succeeded each other.[17] The emperors' obsession with religious orthodoxy and moral purity is remarkably similar to that of the "good" kings of the Old Testament. Whilst the chronographers undoubtedly emphasise this similarity, it is unlikely that they invented it. As early as Constantius' time,[18] the church was offering its own (Old Testament) view of kingship to emperors, though it is interesting to note that, unlike the Western churchmen of the eighth century, those of the East never persuaded, or, for all we know, even attempted to persuade their emperors to accept sacerdotal anointing, nor did coronation, after its inception in the fifth century, ever become an exclusively episcopal prerogative in the East.[19]

For a clear demonstration that the churchmen's lessons had not gone unheeded, we have only to turn to the sixth century, when Byzantium made its last and least successful attempt to re-assert its *Romanitas*, the age of Justinian the Great. When that Emperor first entered the completed Great Church of the Holy Wisdom which he had built to grace (as it still graces) the City of Constantine, he is reputed to have boasted, not without justification, "Glory be to God who hath thought me worthy to accomplish so great a work: I have vanquished thee, O Solomon!"[20] This remark is of double importance, for it implies not only that he had in some way done for Constantine's city what Solomon had done for David's, a point to which we shall return, but also that Justinian in some way identified himself with that old king of the Jews. Not with Augustus, still less with Alexander the Great, for each of whom, as a Roman, he might have felt some affinity, but with an ancient Jewish king whose connection with things Roman was non-existent beyond the realm of legend.

It would be easy to write this identification off as mere fancy, but there is good reason to believe that by the sixth century Byzantine emperors were beginning to take themselves seriously as quasi-Israelite kings, Messianic kings in fact, charged with the shepherding of the New Israel in the paths of righteousness, which is precisely what Justinian's great legislative reforms sought to do. "Righteousness exalteth a nation,"[21] says one Old Testament writer, speaking a common conviction of his time, therefore the law must not only make men obey, but also make them good. That Justinian was guided by this principle is illustrated nowhere more clearly than in the new attitude to homosexuality in his legislation. At a stroke of the pen, the tolerant stance of the Greco-Roman tradition was replaced by laws against and draconian punishments for unnatural sex-acts, which subsequently entered into the Western tradition with the recovery of Justinian's law books in the eleventh century, and have remained with us to this day.[22] The explanation of this curious *volte-face* is surely to be found in the terrible retribution which fell upon the people of Sodom and Gomorrha for their sins.[23] The Shepherd of New Israel had both a responsibility and an obligation to ensure that no such catastrophe befell his empire, therefore he outlaws sin, in order that righteousness might exalt his nation.

So far, we have said little or nothing about emperors which might not be explained as meaning rather less than I am suggesting that it means, but with the accession of the Emperor Heraclius at the beginning of the seventh century, the case is somewhat altered. When Heraclius returned in triumph from the east in 628, the only emperor other than Maurice to have led his troops in battle for more than two hundred years (i.e. since Theodosius the Great), he was welcomed home says Theophanes (who, it should be noted, was writing two hundred years after the event but is hardly likely to have made this up), by the entire clergy and people (*ho laos*) of Constantinople, processing forth with lights and palm branches.[24] It is a passage which has puzzled many and shocked others, for even in the extraordinary circumstances which then obtained (the emperor in question having lately recovered the relic of the True Cross from the Persians), there seems to be something rather blasphemous in greeting him with the actions with which Christ was welcomed to Jerusalem. It would have been much less shocking to the Byzantines, who did indeed regard their emperor as a Christ-figure (witness the famous Dumbarton Oaks ivory of Constantine Porphyrogenitus), and it was in the *centre* of the cenotaphs of the twelve apostles that the *isapostolos*, Constantine the Great, had himself buried; not beyond or below them.[25]

Yet in spite of all this, the welcome of Heraclius ought not perhaps to be interpreted in that way. The reference is back to a pre-Christian, Old Testament meaning of the word "Christ" which would have been familiar to the readers of the Septuagint in a way it no longer is in the vulgar versions which now nourish our piety. There are two important pieces of evidence. One is a sermon preached by Theodore the Syncellus on 7th August 627 to celebrate the failure of the siege of Constantinople by the Avars a year earlier, *porrōthen horōn*.[26] Nowhere else (so far as I am aware) in Byzantine literature is the idea of "*Byzance*," or, to be precise, in this case, Byzantium, as the New Israel so consistently and persistently pursued. The foes of the Empire, Persians and Avars, are called "Gog," which the preacher takes to mean "the gathering together of the Gentiles" (*ta Ethnē*), as Moabites, Hagarenes; as Gebal, Ammon and Amalek. "And I have thought of this City as Israel," he says, "in which God and the Virgin are devoutly worshipped and the mysteries of the faith are performed in their entirety." There is much more in the same vein.

The second piece of evidence is the famous David Plates which, though the precise date may be in dispute, undoubtedly were produced in the reign of Heraclius, and seem to be a deliberate attempt to portray that emperor as a New David, as a new deliverer.[27] This suggests that it was not as *the* Christ that Heraclius was welcomed to his capital in 627, but as a *christos*, a messianic warrior king, the character who is of such great importance in Byzantine apocalyptic literature, which is itself the heir of Jewish apocalyptic.

Heraclius had barely celebrated his triumph before there arose a new and more terrible foe in the East: Islam, whose irruption was to deprive the Empire of several of its most opulent provinces. Even before the full impact of that irruption had taken effect (and some would say because of it), the Romans became deeply involved in another kind of struggle, this time not with the "Ishmaelites" without, but with the "Israelites" within; perhaps one might say (though the Byzantines did not, so far as one can tell) "with the Samaritans." Religious dissent was no new enemy to Byzantium, but this time there was a difference; the point at issue was not primarily one of doctrine and belief, but of practice and of devotion. The dissenters persisted in, the government condemned, the veneration of the holy icons. In this case therefore the dissenters represented established practice (and in the event, were ultimately pronounced orthodox, in 843) whilst the government was the innovator.

By "the government" in this unusual instance we mean the two "iconoclast" emperors, father and son, Leo III the Isaurian and Constantine V Copronymus.[28] These were truly remarkable men by any account, with very strong views on the nature of the office which was successively entrusted to them, an office which they viewed as a kind of Melchizedekian presbyteral kingship. In the *Preface* to the *Ecloga* (726) Leo III combined with this the idea of a pastoral responsibility, derived from Jesus' command to Peter, "Feed my sheep," and also a specific claim to Davidic kingship.[29] There can be little doubt that Leo regarded himself very much as God's appointed servant whose duty it was to interpret and to accomplish the Divine Will. Thus when he set out to eliminate the icons and the devotion which was attached to them, because it seemed to contravene the second commandment, he thought of himself (according to Stephen Gero, an eminent scholar of the *iconomachia*) as a second Hezechiah, or as a Josiah *redivivus*, casting out the idols from the temple of the Lord.[30] But it is the last of the iconoclast emperors, Theophilus, who has left us the most striking statement of the high doctrines of kingship, and once again it takes us right into the heart of the Old Testament. One of the first acts of his reign (in 829) was to punish by death those who had slain the Emperor Leo V in the Palace chapel, "not that their hands were stained with human blood," he says, "but that they also *annihilated the annointed of the Lord within the sanctuary*...."[31]

Yet whilst one might produce more and more examples of how Byzantine emperors seem to have thought of themselves as New Israelite kings, what is to be said of those people who were less than emperors? What indication is there that they shared this supposed imperial identification with the sacral kingship of ancient Israel? There is this: that many of those Byzantines whose writings have survived thought and wrote of their great "God-guarded city of Constantine" not only as New Rome, but also as the "New Jerusalem" or as "New Sion."[32] It used to be supposed that this was precisely what Constantine the Great intended his new capital on the Bosphorus to be: a new and wholly Christian capital, a second Jersalem; but this idea has now been shown to be fallacious. Constantine did take pains, considerable pains it seems, to provide his empire with a Christian capital and a New Jerusalem, but it was the old Jerusalem in Palestine, resurrected and adorned by the agency of the Empress Mother Helena. Evidence is still lacking that Constantine ever made any significant attempt (such as church building) to give Constantinople a Christian character.[33]

After the death of Constantine however, with the accession of exclusively Christian emperors and the growing importance of the new capital, things began to change. Thus the third canon of the Second Ecumenical Council: "The Bishop of Constantinople shall have precedence of honour after the Bishop of Rome, because that city is New Rome." The importance of this, which becomes very clear when the sixth and seventh canons of the First Ecumenical Council at Nicaea in 325 are compared with canons two and three of this at Constantinople in 381, is that it is giving to Constantinople the position of honour formerly occupied by Jerusalem. The New Rome was being ranked as a new Jerusalem.

Of course, there were some ways in which the "New Jerusalem" would always be inferior to the old but, as time went on, it became apparent that the one was increasing in popular esteem at the expense of the other. In the *Life of Saint Daniel the Stylite*, for instance, there is a passage (written early in the sixth century) in which that saint (as a youth) is dissuaded from going up to Jerusalem by an hairy elder, because of a Samaritan uprising. "Go rather to Byzantium," he says; "there you shall see second Jerusalem, Constantinople where you can delight in the *martyria* and great oratories...."[34] There is the clue; prior to the Synod of 381, Constantius had already adorned the capital with two fine great churches, and one of them (Holy Apostles') he had supplied with relics of the Apostle Andrew, Timothy and Luke. By the middle of the next century, largely by the munificence of Pulcheria Augusta, the City had acquired a staggering collection of holy relics, both of old- and new-covenant heroes, and had housed them magnificently in a score of elegant oratories. "And many bodies of the saint who had fallen asleep were raised...and went into the holy city" (Mtt. 27.51-52) is a text which probably occurred to many in this context, and the *mirabilia* of old Jerusalem must have begun to look rather poverty-stricken in comparison.

Yet it was not until after the age of Heraclius that Constantinople came openly and often to be referred to as the New Jerusalem, and then for three very good reasons. Firstly, the Persian conquest in 614 and the Arab of 634 succeeded in removing the Palestinian Jerusalem beyond the borders of the Empire and so in striking a mortal blow to its credibility. Yet again it had failed to save itself or to be saved. Secondly, Jerusalem's greatest treasure, the Wood of the True Cross, the most important of all relics, was removed to Constantinople by Heraclius either in 629 or in 634, a treasure which preachers did not hesitate to hail as the Ark of the New Covenant. Thirdly, the miraculous deliverance of their city in the first and terrible siege of 626 clearly demonstrated to the Byzantines that she was indeed "guarded by God," if not totally unconquerable. It was in the light of these events that Constantine's city came to be named the New Jerusalem, and continued to be so named even by people so sophisticated as Photius, until their hopes were disappointed by the Latin conquest in 1204.

Just as the Old Jerusalem was sanctified and distinguished by its Temple, so was the New by her Great Church of the Holy Wisdom which, together with the sacred palace, dominated the city. It also dominated that city of nearly half-a-thousand churches in a number of other ways, reflected in the tones of highest hyperbole in which the Byzantines were accustomed to speak of it;[35] not only in size and dignity (as the seat of the ecumenical patriarchate and the centre of the imperial liturgy), but also in quality. This is something which it is not easy to apprehend, but the Great Church was certainly something more than a church to those who reverenced that sanctuary. This is clear from its very inception, from Justinian's boast "Solomon, I have outdone thee!" and also from the amazing fact that no relics appear to have been used at its consecration. The Great Church was credited with a sanctity greater than that of other, even older and more venerable shrines, and I suspect that for many people, this was no less than the divine presence Itself, the *shekinah*, as at the old temple of Jerusalem, something which Christians were forbidden from claiming by their scripture which insisted that the Christian God "dwelleth not in temples made with hands." But if simple people thought this privately, others came as near to saying it publicly as they dared; here is Procopius, the contemporary of the building of the Great Church, speaking of it in a celebrated passage which was often quoted and intensified by later writers:

And whenever anyone enter the church to pray, he understands at once that it is not by any human power or skill, but by the influence of God that this work has been so finely turned. And so his mind is lifted up toward God and exalted, feeling that He cannot be far away, but must especially love to dwell in this place which He has chosen.[36]

Many legends gathered around the Great Church to reinforce its superior quality, including one belief that at the last, when the city would perish by flood, the Great Church alone would be saved by being raised up to heaven by the golden thread which invisibly retained its great dome.[37]

It has already been mentioned that no relics seem to have been associated with the Great Church at its inception, contrary to prevailing practice, but in later centuries, it did begin to acquire its own collection. By the end of the twelfth century it was rivalling the *Nea* and the Lighthouse Church in this respect, but with one striking difference: the Great Church relics included a surprisingly high proportion of Old Testament *memorabilia*, and, more especially, of those with Jerusalem connections. Portions of the Holy Sepulchre were reverenced there, for instance, and perhaps even the Throne of David.[38] But most curious, and perhaps most revealing of all, is the testimony of Anthony of Novgorod. Reporting on his experiences at Constantinople in the 1490's he claims that in the sanctuary of the Great Church were conserved the veil of the Temple and the Ark of the Covenant, replete with Manna, the Rod of Aaron, and the two Tables of the Law; and that these last were held by the clergy at the singing of the *Allelujah* in the Liturgy.[39] These appear to be clear indications that the idea of the Great Church as the Holy Temple of the New Jerusalem was both extant and encouraged at Byzantium.

Such, then, are some of the reasons for suspecting that the Byzantines took their heritage more seriously than other Christians have done; it is perhaps not so surprising that this should been so. It has to be borne in mind that from the very inception of Christianity (and indeed before it) the Greek-speaking world had immediate and direct access to the Hebrew literary tradition through the Septuagint, and that the East Roman world remained a highly literate society throughout its existence, whereas literacy was already sadly eroded in the West by the time it received its Vulgate. It must also be remembered that in the earlier centuries, the Eastern Empire included a large population of Syriac-speaking subjects whose Christianity was more Jacobite than Pauline; more Semitic than Hellenistic. It is becoming increasingly clear that these people felt a greater affinity for Jerusalem than for Constantinople, and that, especially before the Muslim conquest and religious dissent cut many of them off from the Empire, they had a pronounced influence on the religious life of the East.

To these considerations must be added the fact that until the seventh century, Palestine was a province and

Jerusalem a city of the Empire. This could not have failed to affect in some way the fortunes of an Empire which was centralised and centripetal to an extent to which no state was ever so organised until the emergence of modern France. All roads led to New Rome, especially the sea-roads, and everything travelled along those roads to the great vacuum (as it was at first) at the centre; goods, services, people and ideas, there to be consumed, assimilated, condemned or imposed on the whole empire by imperial *fiat*. In such circumstances, it is to be expected that something of the Old Israel would be absorbed and appropriated by Constantinople. It was also almost inevitable that the original proprietors of the idea of Israel would be persecuted by those who now made that idea their own. Perhaps the strongest indication of all, and saddest, of Byzantine Neo-Zionism is Byzantium's relentless and almost unceasing persecution of the ancient people of Israel. Did this not happen precisely because *their* continued existence was a denial of the promise which Byzantium would make its own?

THE CHANGE IN STATUS OF WOMEN IN ICELAND
FROM PAGAN TO CHRISTIAN TIMES

Ellen Johns

In the year 1000 Christianity was introduced into Iceland. It went on "peacefully," without the brutal fights that Norway had experienced around fifty years earlier. The Icelanders "chose" Christianity first of all for political reasons. The Norwegian king was holding three sons of the most esteemed families in Iceland as hostage, and the old men on the *Ting* feared his anger if they did not embrace the new faith. Thus, Christianity became the official religion, but those who wanted to remain pagans were still allowed to present offerings to the old gods, only not in public. Many other religious customs from old times were also tolerated. About a hundred years later, when Iceland received bishops and church law, the "climate" became tougher. But for another two hundred years the church had to fight the pagan way of life.

The Icelandic sagas, the history books and the laws were written by men. And there is no doubt that the stress lies on the brave, powerful *man*. When we try to find out something about the status of women, we meet with several problems. The most important is that nothing was written down in pagan times. Furthermore, all writers of history and saga were Christians, mainly priests and thus negative or critical towards the old religion. It has also been discussed whether the sagas are historical or not; that problem will not be dealt with here, but I will follow the scholars who see them as fiction *based on* facts. The saga writer very often has an ambivalence towards the strong and proud woman. He is impressed but also critical, and sometimes he creates a madonna-like type as a contrast to the typical saga woman (Aud in *Gisla*).[1] More trustworthy are the law and history books, but they give a very superficial picture of woman's role in society. In spite of such difficulties, it is not completely impossible to obtain an image of (1) the role and the worship of female divinities, (2) the function of women in religious rites, and (3) the status of women in social and family life.

The Germanic religion can be divided into two main currents, a "power" cult which includes worship of the warrior gods, *Odin* and *Thor*, and the fertility cult of the sister and brother (and lovers) *Frey* and *Freya*. The other gods and godlike figures can also be divided into these two different camps.

Freya is the most worshipped of the female deities. She is famous for her lovers and her love affairs, but she is highly respected. A man was banished from Iceland for calling her "a bitch." As is often the case with the fertility goddess, Freya is also the death goddess. She picks up half of the dead in battle; the other half go to Odin. She is the greatest of the *Valkyries*, the female divinities who follow men in war and can point out those who are going to die. She is also the most important of the *dises*, divinities of the home, birth and fertility. A yearly *disa-blot* (dise offering) was very widespread.

In the fertility cult, the *vättes* (certain "lower" deities) were also important. They lived in waterfalls, stones and trees, and were worshipped and invoked in magical rites. Often each home would have its personal *vätte* and the women in the house had to be on good terms with it.

Fate is an important concept in Germanic religion. No man or woman could escape it; even the gods were under the laws of fate. Fate could be personified as the *nornes*, feared and powerful goddesses.

The women had an important place in the fertility cult, much more than in Odin and Thor worship, which was a religion for men with organized "men's societies." Women could be priestesses in fertility ceremonies, and they were often feared and respected magicians. They could foretell one's destiny, and often in the sagas a tragedy results from neglect of the words of a prophetess. Freya is called the great sorceress. In the ceremonies the masculine sex symbols were (literally) handled by women, a horse phallus being the most powerful symbol.

In family life, the Icelandic woman had much power, but first of all within the house, *"innan Stokks"* - inside the threshold, which was the border between the feminine and the masculine world. She could be forced to marry against her will, since marriage was a legal contract between two clans, and a man was (almost) always the leader of a clan. But the sagas tell us very often of the terrible anger and revenge of the woman who has not been consulted about the marriage; she finds her honour insulted and often has the unwanted man killed so that next time she can choose her marriage partner herself. Erotically, she is rather free. One saga (*Gisla*) gives as the reason for one family's emigration to Iceland the sexual behaviour of a daughter. The daughter had two lovers who were both killed by her brother, not because they had slept with her, but because they belonged to the wrong clan. In Iceland she is still an ideal type for marriage, and she is not criticized for her behaviour. (What she thought of the murders is not told in the tale.)

In another saga (*Njal*) a woman gets a lawful divorce from her husband because he cannot satisfy her sexually.

Economically, women were fairly well protected since they kept their *mundr*, dowry, after marriage and also after divorce. But their husbands had to agree on the management of their money. Married people could not be each other's heirs: the money went to the children or to other members of either the man's or the woman's family.

The saga woman is first of all known as the "instigator" (*Hitserin*), or the woman behind the hero. She acts indirectly, urging men on to fight. In fact, she is very often the cause of the fight. She is extremely proud; a slap in the face can mean divorce or even her husband's death. This "capricious woman" type has a narrative function in the saga: without conflict, no saga. The "indirect acting" also goes back to the mythological ideas of the *Valkyries*, the destiny goddesses who follow Odin and decide who is going to live or die in battle. Maybe the *egging* (urging) was the only way of getting some power *outside* the house, since the battleground was a man's place.

Rather than being the "other sex," the Icelandic woman was the "different sex." The masculine and the feminine had to be separated rigidly. The worst thing one could say to a man was that he was *ergi*, a pervert. And this was mainly said of a man who was suspected of having played the feminine role in a homosexual relationship. Naturally, there is contempt for womanhood in this, but also a fear of the danger of mixing the two sexual spheres. The contempt for woman directed towards an effeminate man could also be very strong: for example, a woman asked for divorce because her husband wore silk trousers, probably indicating that he was a transvestite or *ergi*.

What did Christianity give these women? Glorifying the Viking culture, we could say that the proud *Valkyrie* was destroyed by condemning and intolerant priests. Glorifying Christianity, we could say that at last the capricious whore could learn to be a good and decent woman. Both have been done. Let us look at some of the facts, and also discuss precisely the nature of the change that occurred.

Christianity brought a change in the sex of God. God and Jesus replaced Odin, the *allfadir*, and his son Thor, and the rest of the gods were easily disposed of. The new religion must have been regarded as supermasculine and patriarchal, since the Virgin Mary first became important in Iceland late in the twelfth century. We know little about how the women reacted to the dethroning of their sisters in heaven. If they had any protests they could not write them down. By the time they had learned to write, they were already good Christians.

What is sure is that the fertility rites, the magic and the offerings to the nature spirits, continued for centuries.[2] Often the pagan traditions continued under

Christian disguise.[3] Without holding official "*disa-blots*" and without saying Frey(a)'s name, the female cult continued inside the house, especially at great events such as the birth of a child.[4] One could say that female religious culture went "underground."[5]

The church's view of womanhood was different from the one in pagan times, and had profound consequences for Icelandic society. But the new ideal was slow in gaining authority. Pagan tradition said that the feminine was mystical, powerful, and frightening. Christianity maintained that woman was evil, the first agent of sin. German religion did not know sin, and therefore neither mercy nor salvation. They needed no one to "blame" for the condition of the world, for every man and woman was responsible for his/her and the family's honour, and nothing else. One could say that pagan femininity in its frightening mystique was more *taboo*, while femininity in Christianity was a more or less conscious projection of what man regarded as evil.

The hardest aspect for the church to fight was the sexual freedom in Iceland. The men would not give up their mistresses, and regarded their "illegitimate" children as worthy of inheriting their possessions, not as the fruit of sin and so worthy of condemnation. Women refused to remain alone as widows or as divorcees, but the Church did not want them to remarry. In pagan times, a woman, married or unmarried, could have a lover without being punished. The man would be punished if her family did not approve; they were free to kill him within one year for having taken advantage of an unmarried woman; within three years for having taken advantage of a married woman. This shows that the responsibility for the sexual act rested on men. The church taught that adultery was a deadly sin, which must have been difficult to understand, since old Icelandic language does not even have a word for adultery. The new puritanism was worst for the women, since men had the power to carry on as they had done, and since sexual morality was, in the first instance, connected with the ideal woman. This idea of the pure, non-sexual woman slowly, but surely, undermined female sexuality, in fact until the present day.

Economically, church law provided some rights for women, because women in difficult situations, or without means of any sort, would be protected by the church.[6] By marriage women lost some of their independence, because now the husband could choose if he wanted a separate or a joint estate. But the wife was the primary heir of her husband's estate, preceding even the children. By the middle of the thirteenth century, Norwegian and Icelandic law prevented women from being married against their wills. This law is said to be an enormous step in the direction of the emancipation of women. This law, however, was more *de jure* than *de facto* in its consequences. The possibility for a girl to have her own opinion was smaller under the feudalistic patriarchy in the late (Christian) Middle Ages than in pagan times. "Father's words" were law, even more so in the small family unit than in the clans.

The connection between change in religion and change in society was very intimate in Iceland, since bishops more or less ruled the country throughout the Middle Ages, after a long fight for power with the most important families in the community. The "easy" conversion in the year 1000 turned out to be very hard to carry through in daily Icelandic life; many of the old customs and much of the religious life of pagan times went on for a long time thereafter. The women, as bearers of the family traditions, were important in this underground work. But, at last, they yielded and became the "decent housewives," bearers of the Christian virtues of purity, piety and humility.

There is, however, no need to glorify Icelandic pagan time as being a good time to live in for women. The French anthropologist Claude Lévi-Strauss has said that society is the exchange, or even trade, of women between men. So also in pagan Iceland, women were "given away," though often protesting, to other men. But the new religion in Iceland and the social changes that went with it must be said to have been one step forward and two steps backward for women's status in society.

CONTRIBUTION À L'ETUDE DE LA SACRALISATION DE L'ESPACE:
LE CAS DE LA PAROISSE QUEBECOISE*

Louis Rousseau

Lorsqu'elle s'attaque à l'analyse de l'espace, la religiologie actuelle hérite d'une problématique dont les éléments essentiels ont été graduellement mis en place et synthétisés par van der Leeuw d'abord, puis surtout par Mircea Eliade au tournant des années 1950. L'article "Architecture sacrée et symbolisme" dont la rédaction finale remonte sans doute à 1957 et qui était demeuré inédit jusqu'à sa récente parution dans Les Cahiers de l'Herne (1978) représente sans doute l'expression la plus achevée de cette problématique.

On conviendra aisément que nous nous trouvons là en présence d'un modèle assez complet qui nous fournit une structure et des fonctions spécifiquement religieuses quand à l'organisation de l'espace, et cela à partir d'une méthode comparatiste appliquée aux dossiers des peuples chasseurs et agriculteurs qu'Eliade désigne souvent par l'expression vague de cultures traditionnelles.

Or pour ceux qui trouvent utile de se situer au sein de ce paradygme et tentent de résoudre des questions de description et d'interprétation de l'organisation sacrale de l'espace dans l'occident moderne et contemporain, un certain nombre d'obstacles théoriques et méthodologiques doivent être levés:

1. **L'opposition chaos-cosmos, profane-sacré**
Le premier obstacle et le plus massif tient à l'applicabilité du modèle dans le contexte de cultures pour lesquelles discours et les rituels religieux ne constituent plus l'essentiel des pratiques significantes comme c'est le

cas par exemple en Occident depuis la naissance de discours scientifiques au moment de la Renaissance. L'opposition simple chaos-cosmos, espace désarticulé, sans orientation ni signification versus l'espace ordonné, orienté (centré) et seul significatif, ne fonctionne évidemment plus puisque de nouveaux langages et de nouvelles pratiques (géographiques, économiques, sociaux, politiques) apparaissent et fabriquent des ordonnances qui rompent avec l'hégémonie ou l'englobement des symboliques religieuses. La construction des espaces humains se fait plurielle et si cette autonomisation des différents régistres qui marquent l'espace représente effectivement une brisure avec l'ancienne unité sacrale on ne peut en aucune façon la décrire comme un retour au chaos. Une religiologie de l'espace moderne et contemporain doit donc préciser les nouveaux rapports entre la structuration religieuse de l'espace et sa structuration économique, sociale, politique, etc. Si l'on persiste à utiliser la binarité profane-sacré pour interpréter ces phénomènes, on doit modifier la logique de la relation. L'opposition stricte ordre-absence d'ordre ne s'applique plus. Faut-il parler de complémentarité entre différentes formes d'ordre comme le fait B. RAY (1977, 365) pour analyser les sanctuaires royaux du Bugenda? En réalité le terme de complémentarité ne nous éclaire guère puisque tout reste à faire pour décrire le réseau complexe des relations entre structures signifiantes qui organisent l'espace moderne et contemporain. On discerne, ici le problème central auquel doit s'attaquer une théorie religiologique de l'espace qui aspire à une applicabilité générale.

2. Tous les espaces sont signifiants

Les conséquences méthodologiques de cette question sont également de grande portée. Puisqu'il n'est plus possible de restreindre notre examen aux espaces marqués par la symbolique religieuse et que leurs relations avec d'autres organisations signifiantes font partie de leur mode spécifiques de signifier, il faut procéder à une analyse de l'ensemble des espaces et pour ce faire, se doter d'une procédure adéquate.

Celle-ci est en voie d'élaboration depuis une dizaine d'années dans des travaux que l'on tend à regrouper sous l'appelation de "sémiotique" ou "sémiologie de l'espace"(1). Elle se donne pour tâche "la description, la production, l'interprétation des langages spatiaux" (GREIMAS, 1979, 13). Elle tend à se réaliser selon deux types principaux d'approches. Une première qui cherche à appliquer les lois du discursif au domaine de l'espace qui en tirerait en quelques sorte sa forme; une seconde cherche à dégager les lois spécifiques du spatial à partir du mode d'agencement des éléments spatiaux en eux-mêmes. Dans un cas comme dans l'autre la décision fondatrice consiste à considérer tous les éléments de tous les espaces humanisés comme des signes non verbaux dont l'entreprise sémiologique (ou sémiotique) doit chercher à produire les règles grammaticales et syntaxiques.

Il devient possible dès lors de concevoir et de réaliser une religiologie de l'espace en utilisant des procédures sémiologiques grâce auxquelles les ensembles spatiaux accèdent au statut de langage et ainsi médiatisent concrètement l'image qu'une société donnée construit et reproduit d'elle-même pour elle-même. C'est en cherchant à discerner un ordre dans cette images générale que la religiologie s'appliquera ensuite à son object spécifique, c'est-à-dire à ces ensembles de signes qui n'acquièrent leur lisibilité dernière que dans l'axe de l'opposition sacré/profane.

La recherche dont il sera question dans la présente communication tente d'explorer des voies d'une meilleure articulation entre le niveau des lois qui régissent le processus de signification dans le domaine de l'espace traité comme une instance de langage, et le niveau proprement herméneutique et phénoménologique qui permet de faire apparaître la constitution spécifiquement religieuse de cette organisation de l'espace. Cet objectif méthodologique de portée générale dans le domaine de l'étude de la religion ne sera pas atteint à l'aide de réflexions théoriques, mais plutôt par le biais d'une analyse empirique cherchant à en vérifier la faisabilité.

Nous avons retenu le cas particulièrement intéressant à cet égard, de l'organisation spatiale de la paroisse québécoise. Il s'agit d'un produit de culture chrétienne européenne de l'époque moderne qui s'effectue à partir d'un leg spatial amérindien pouvant être provisoirement considéré, du point de vue de la société blanche qui s'y implante, comme étant à l'état "naturel". Nous nous intéresserons plus particulièrement à l'une d'entre elle (La Nativité de La Prairie, près de Montréal, cf. Y., LaCroix, 1981).

Considérant que les éléments de l'espace paroissial produit sont des *signes* et que l'ensemble de des signes constitue une structure sémiologique qui renvoit d'une manière qui reste à déterminer au texte mythologique fondateur du groupe humain qui a lentement produit cet espace dans le temps, cette étude fait l'hypothèse que l'engendrement historique de l'espace d'une paroisse catholique du Québec provient de l'influence de facteurs de deux types:

- un premier, héritier d'une dominance dans la tradition occidentale de la détermination sacrale de processus de production de l'espace. Cette dominance s'exprime dans le fait que l'architecture générale de cet espace est régie par le code religieux qui prévaut dans cette société de sorte que l'ensemble des points, lignes et surfaces constitue un système signifiant qui renvoie à ce code comme programmeur collectif;

- un second, héritier de la réduction graduelle de ce premier facteur depuis la Renaissance et qui laisse la structuration de l'espace, comme langage, aux mains des sous-codes géographiques, économiques et sociaux (nature du lieu et de ses contraintes, activités économiques, redistribution spatiale des groupes sociaux, etc.).

Ces deux facteurs opèrent simultanément, dans le cas de la paroisse québécoise, et l'étude cherche à découvrir, plus précisément, quel est le message religieux qui s'y manifeste. Nous y découvrirons un système complexe et intégré qui condense l'expérience du sacré et la rend accessible sur tout le territoire familier de la vie quotidienne.

1. <u>Construction d'un modèle</u>

Les problèmes spécifiques de la "lisibilité" de l'espace, lorsqu'on les compare par exemple à la situation plus usuelle de la lecture d'un texte, rendent nécessaire la création d'un modèle théorique de l'objet, préalable à la description et à l'interprétation de tout ensemble spatial particulier. On peut escompter que l'explication de ce modèle permettra à la fois de clarifier l'opération analytique et de vérifier subséquemment la qualité de toute la démarche en permettant à d'autres chercheurs de la critiquer. Est-il téméraire de penser que cette méthode pourrait aider à rendre plus transparent le processus d'interprétation qui, trop souvent dans le cas de la phénoménologie de la religion, se masque en tant que processus conduisant à des résultats?

Nous nous inspirons très largement dans cette étude du travail de A.-Ph. Lagopoulos (1977) qui a tenté de faire le point des principales études contemporaines en sémiologie de l'espace et de dégager les règles de l'organisation sensée tant des espaces de cultures analogiques (correspondant à ce qu'Eliade nomme cultures traditionnelles) que de cultures dialectiques (marquées par la réduction de l'importance des significations mythologiques ou religieuses). Il ne saurait être question ici ni d'énumérer ni de résumer les règles qu'il énonce à propos de l'agglomération urbaine. Il suffira de retenir quelques énoncés fondamentaux qui permettent de lancer la démarche, quitte à indiquer en cours de description de l'espace paroissial québécois les applications plus particulières.

Rappelons la perspective initiale. Nous cherchons à comprendre comment l'organisation humaine de l'espace transforme ses composantes physiques en signes (signifiant - signifié, Sa - Se) et, plus spécifiquement, comment s'opère la mise en relation entre le réseau des significations religieuses et l'organisation de l'espace, ce que l'on désigne comme le processus de sacralisation de l'espace.

Pour tout sujet humain (et tout groupe ou sous-groupe) "la réalité 'physique' se transforme en pré-signifiant (substance de l'expression) renvoyant à une image mentale. Les signes dénotatifs de cette image sont des fonctions-signes" appartenant donc à un système non-isologue. (Lagopoulos, 1977, 74).

Les signifiants dénotatifs (Sa_d) de l'image mentale d'un espace donné "sont classifiés en trois classes de nature paradigmatiques: les *points* (noeud ou points de repère, pour le plan des Signifiés dénotatifs, Se_d), les *lignes* (axes de circulation ou limites, pour le plan des Se_d) et les *surfaces* (régions pour le plan cité)" (ibid)".

Si on applique aux ensembles de signes spatiaux les propositions concernant les modes généraux d'articulation des signes entre eux, on dira finalement qu'ils constituent pour les sujets humains des combinaisons de signes (syntagmes) "régies par des lois syntactiques, dont le substrat de nature générale semble être le couple d'opposition -/0 ou -/- et la triade -/0/-. La forme triadique peut être analysée en deux couples dualistes "marqué-non marqué" dont les termes marqués sont opposés (-/-). Tous deux ont la forme "marqué-degré zéro", avec cette différence que l'un a la forme -/0 et l'autre 0/-. La forme 0/rien correspond aussi au couple "marqué-non marqué" et apparaît aux cas d'omission d'un Sa_d de l'image mentale". (ibid)

2. <u>La sacralisation de l'espace à La Prairie de la Magdeleine</u> (Québec)

Les limites de la présente étude nous interdisent de résumer la genèse historique de l'espace rural québécois. Qu'il nous suffise de dire que dès le début de la colonisation blanche s'instaura une pratique d'occupation du sol en rangs allongés en bordure d'une voie de communication et que cette pratique, contraire aux habitudes françaises et à la volonté politique d'instaurer des établissements nucléaires (R.C. Harris, 1968, 169-181) ne fut influencée en aucune façon par des motifs d'ordre religieux. Le découpage des territoires paroissiaux, les première chapelles rudimentaires et les croix de chemins furent fonction d'un espace déjà organisés par les habitants à partir d'un ensemble de fonctions cohérentes et juxtaposées: politiques, sociales, économiques, et non l'inverse. Notre analyse de l'espace de La Prairie illustera ce processus typique.

2.1 La genèse de l'espace paroissial

Nous avons la chance de posséder une représentation figurée de La Prairie dressée par Champlain en 1611 et avant toute occupation européenne. On aperçoit sur cette esquisse effectuée du point de vue d'un navigateur sensible aux points de repères et aux obstacles une partie de l'Île de Montréal, des îles, un Sault qu'il nomme Saint-Louis et qui borne les eaux navigables aisément à l'ouest, et, sur la rive opposée, derrière un littéral marécageux et une prairie à demi immergée, de grandes prairies naturelles traversées de rivières. Voilà l'ensemble des déterminations géographiques qui donneront les orientations majeurs de l'occupation humaine de cet espace.

Ainsi lorsqu'en 1647 les Jésuites se font concéder par François Lauson de la Citière un arrière-fief avec privilège de franc-alleu (indépendance à l'égard de la Compagnie des Cent-Associés), il tire son nom de la caractéristique principale du sol: La Prairie, et il est borné par deux "rapides" (saults), ce qui donnera voie libre et privilégiée à ses contacts militaires et commerciaux avec l'implantation montréalaise.

Ce n'est toutefois qu'en 1668, suite à la première paix iroquoise, que les Jésuites octroient les 40 premières concessions. Durant les 25 ans qui suivent la guerre avec les Iroquois et les commerçants des Pays-Bas et d'Angleterre demeure endémique. La Prairie joue la rôle de poste français avancé sur ce front; aussi y établit-on des fortifications qui, avec quelques modifications, dureront tout le régime français et joueront, en temps de guerre, un rôle de refuge pour les habitants de la paroisse et abriteront l'église, le presbytère, le Couvent des religieuses enseignants, la résidence des seigneurs jésuites et ses dépendances, les casernes militaires et leurs gardiens.

Le fait que les habitants de La Prairie, jusqu'à tout récemment, parlent du village comme du "vieux fort", nous indique assez l'impact de la fonction originelle de l'enclos villageois dans la signification vécue de l'espace paroissial.

Pourtant même la situation dangereuse de frontière ne modifia pas la forme de lotissement allongé le long des voies d'eau adoptée ailleurs. Entreprise villageoise s'il en fut une en Nouvelle-France, avec un noyau bien identifié et une très vaste commune naturelle ouverte à tous, La Prairie dût se conformer à la volonté populaire de telle sorte qu'en 1692 la rive du fleuve était presqu'entièrement concédée et qu'en 1733 on y comptait 227 rotures assez peu défrichées (agriculture de subsistance), sans divisions internes, signe indubitable d'un développement du territoire de l'intérieur.

Sur la carte dressée sous les ordres du général Murray en 1760 (APC) on découvre ce qui structurera tout l'espace intérieur de cette paroisse: le noyau villageois, les cinq rivières (St-Régis, St-Pierre, La Tortue, St-Lambert (aujourd'hui St-Jacques) et la Ste-Claude) et la rive du St-Laurent, le chemin St-Jean construit en 1748 pour communiquer vers le réseau de fortification le long de la rivière Richelieu et du lac Champlain. En 1831 la carte de Bouchette (fig.1, pp.405) donne une excellente représentation du développement de l'occupation du sol. Les voies d'eau sont maintenant bordées de chemins le long desquels sont implantées les habitations. Les rangs sinueux découpent le territoire avec même des hameaux qui apparaissent à l'intérieur (St-Philippe, St-Pierre qui deviendra St- Constant, St-Matthieu) et qui réduiront le territoire paroissial. La production de cet espace a donc obéit à la logique générale de tout l'espace québécois, compte tenu de ses contraintes physiques particulières.

D'abri qu'il était au début, entouré de son enceinte, le village est devenu la tête de pont des échanges commerciaux avec le sud (principalement les USA) au 19e siècle. En 1832 on y compte environ 1200 habitants, des manufactures (en moulin à scie, une tannerie, une poterie, une brasserie, une manufacture de chapeaux), des entreprises liées à la production agricole environnante (deux moulins à maïs, un moulin banal et un silo à grains) des services socio-éducatifs (un couvent pour filles, un hôpital, des écoles de rangs et l'église avec son presbytère), deux bateaux à vapeur qui assurent le transit en bien et en personnes vers Montréal et neuf tavernes qui témoignent de la vitalité du loisir masculin. Un bon groupe de professionnels et 35 artisans fournissent les services spécialisés requis. Au plan économique le village se définit donc à la fois par rapport à sa propre population et à l'espace rural environnant, et par rapport à l'axe Montréal-USA. Au plan social il concentre les éléments de la petite-bourgeoisie professionnelle et commerciale qui vivent des besoins en services de la population ouvrière du village et agricole de la campagne environnante, tout en détenant les principaux leviers de commande, à l'exclusion bien sûr, du contrôle idéologique et moral.

2.2 L'espace rural

Il nous est possible, après ces notes rapides au sujet de l'espace québécois en général et celui de la paroisse de La Prairie, d'en venir à ce que nous proposons d'analyser depuis le début, les signes déployés et lisibles sur cette surface, afin d'y déceler la place spécifique du régistre sacral. Nous devrons, pour des raisons évidentes de brièveté, procéder à une lecture largement synchronique et normalisée, i.e. ne tenant pas compte des multiples accidents particuliers qui occupent sans doute une place importante dans l'image mentale des habitants.

Pour ses producteurs et reproducteurs le territoire de La Prairie procède d'une opposition fondamentale entre le village et la campagne dont le trait le plus frappant, à écouter nos informateurs, semble l'opposition entre le différencié (là où l'on vit, le village, par example) et l'indifférencié (la campagne, du même point de vue villageois). Ceci nous autorise à diviser la description de la même manière. Nous examinerons donc d'abord l'espace rural, puis l'espace villageois.

Considérant tous les éléments de l'espace comme des signifiants et voulant regrouper ceux-ci en trois classes (points, lignes et surfaces), nous procéderons de la plus englobante à celle qui l'est le moins. Examinons donc les surfaces.

SURFACES

La cartographie contemporaine (fig.2, pp.406) distingue entre le terme *côte* et le terme de *rang*. Le premier désigne une surface, i.e. l'ensemble des lots dont un des côtés est formé par une même voie de communication (fleuve, rivière, ruisseau, chemin). Le second désigne une ligne, un axe de communication le long duquel s'étale la rangée des habitations et bâtiments de ferme (on emploie aussi le terme du chemin dans le même sens). La pratique populaire semble moins précise, mais nous préférons, pour l'analyse, utiliser cette disctinction. Ce qui importe pour nous, c'est la signification sociale. Depuis le régime français, dans la conscience de ses habitants, l'attribution d'un nom particulier à une côte, renvoie à la perception de l'existence d'une communauté humaine distincte à l'interieur de l'ensemble paroissial (2).

Sur l'ancien territoire paroissial (avant ses divisions du 19e et 20e siècle) on compte 32 côtes, y compris les divisions en 1ère et 2ième concessions. Il faut y ajouter l'immense territoire de la Commune situé au sud-est du village. Entre les côte et la commune opère l'opposition habité, d'usage privé et inhabité, d'usage commun. La côte renvoie donc primordialement au découpage de la proprieté privée de l'espace (la roture, sous le régime seigneurial) par un ensemble d'habitants dont les lots sont juxtaposés. Cette propriété ("ma terre") permet l'exploitation agricole y compris celle des parcelles boisées. Le signifié dominant de la côte est donc de nature économique et caractérise l'ensemble des unités familiales par l'exploitation agraire de grandes propriétés, par opposition aux habitants du village qui occupent des lots minuscules et une place différente dans le processus de production.

LIGNES

Toutes ces surfaces "appartiennent" par un de leurs côtés à une ligne qui joue le rôle d'axe de circulation et détermine l'implantation des habitats et de leurs dépendances. Comme nous l'avons indiqué plus haut, le réseau hydrographique de La Prairie a contitué le déterminant majeur de la production de son espace. Le St-Laurent a servi de frontière du côté nord-ouest de la paroisse. Il a fixé les bornes des premiers lotissements, tout en constituant la voie de communication majeure vers le centre montréalais. Les rivières et multiples ruisseaux ont ensuite engendré la plus grande partie de découpage intérieur. Les nécessités de la circulation des personnes et des biens ont fait apparaître les routes de rang qui ont ainsi doublé les axes riverains, et les chemins de traverses (souvent nommées *montées*) permettant de passer d'un rang à un autre. Finalement à ce deuxième système de ligne bien proche encore du réseau hydrographique, s'est ajouté à partir du milieu du 19ième siècle, un système exogène marquant la dépendance croissante de l'espace paroissial par rapport à de plus grands ensembles socio-économiques: la première ligne de chemin de fer au Canada (1836) reliant La Prairie à St-Jean (axe Montréal-USA); puis le système de routes et d'autoroutes de la deuxième partie du 20ième siècle qui indique l'appartenance contemporaine de cette paroisse à l'espace métropolitain.

Depuis la fin du 18ième siècle les axes routiers se sont substitués au réseau hydrographique comme voies de communication intra-paroissiales. Ce dernier conserve cependant sa fonction de frontière indisputable des domaines à propriété privée, par opposition aux "lignes" qui sont produites par l'arpentage sur les trois autres côtés d'un lot et demeurent potentiellement disputables et même transgressables par les propriétaires voisins, ce qui justifie les innombrables procès "de clôture".

D'emblée le "rang" occupe la place la plus signifiante dans la classe ligne pour la période classique. Chemin de terre jusqu'à tout récemment il permet un certain alignement et groupement à distance des maisons. Il détermine donc le devant des maisons, leur côté exposé à la vue des passants et souvent édifié (gallerie avec ses chaises berçantes en belle saison) pour "regarder passer le monde", par opposition à l'arrière tourné vers les champs et la forêt, direction du travail. Comme nous l'avons indiqué au début de cette section le système de lots allongés particulier au Québec permet à la fois un certain éparpillement de la population (par opposition au noyau villageois), mais favorise aussi un intense voisinage. La représentation mentale dominante du rang est de nature sociale: ligne qui réunit des unités familiales qui partagent un identique sentiment d'appartenance ("les gens de tel rang") et qui peut égaler, sinon dépasser en intensité le sentiment d'appartenance au grand ensemble paroissial. Identité et donc différence d'avec les autres rangs. Ici s'ajoute le facteur de parenté. Quelques études (3) ont souligné la tendance endogamique au sein d'un même rang et d'une même paroisse. Compte tenu de la fécondité tout à fait exceptionnelle des canadiens français au 19ième siècle il ne faut donc pas se surprendre que dans l'espace de quelques générations un rang en vienne à pouvoir être surnommé du nom d'une seule famille (par ex., à La Prairie, le Chemin des Prairies fut surnommé le rang Brosseau). Notons, pour clore, la présence d'une signification politique négative du "rang" puisqu'il ne dispose d'aucun pouvoir spécifique et qu'il s'oppose ainsi au village ou résident les notables de la classe politique. Toutefois la solidarité du rang donne souvent lieu à des alignements très forts du vote.

POINTS
Venons-en à la plus petite unité signifiante qui regroupe les points de repères de l'espace rural. C'est ici, comme la théorie phénoménologique le laisse prévoir, que nous découvrirons les marques d'une organisation sacrale de l'espace.

Les rangs de La Prairie disposent de trois types de points de repères: les maisons et l'ensemble voisin des bâtiments de ferme, l'école du rang et la croix de chemin.

Il s'agit là de l'ensemble normal d'un rang parvenu à son occupation humaine à peu près complète.

La maison (dont l'intérieur constitue à son tour un ensemble signifiant que nous n'avons pas le loisir d'analyser ici) renvoie d'abord à ses occupants, la maisonnée, i.e. une famille composé d'un couple de parents et de leurs enfants (plus de six en moyenne au 19ième siècle) et à l'occasion des grands-parents. Mais c'est une maisonnée insérée dans un complexe réseau de parenté et cette signification fait partie intégrante de l'image de ce point (tel noeud de relations parentales) et singularise la maison des nouveaux arrivants (rares) sans lien de parenté, d'avec les autres. A ce signifié social s'ajoute une connotation économique produite par l'état architectural des bâtiments: expression du savoir-faire et de la richesse acquise et transmise de la famille.

Normalement chaque rang (jusqu'à la fin des années 1950) est doté d'une maison d'école qui accueille tous les enfants du rang dans une seule classe pour les études primaires, sous la direction de la "maîtresse d'école". Il s'agit d'une école publique ouverte à tous, mais dans les faits le contenu de l'enseignement est contrôlé par un organisme confessionnel et le curé du village ainsi que les inspecteurs veillent de près sur le confessionnalisme du système et de ses enseignants. En plus des apprentissages de base, l'insistance majeure porte sur la moralisation et la catéchisation des élèves. L'école assume donc une des fonctions essentielles du curé qui réussit moins qu'elle dans l'éducation religieuse des enfants et des jeunes adultes jamais assidus au catéchisme du dimanche donné à l'église du village. Grâce à l'école du rang, l'éducation fait marcher tous les enfants vers un point unique, indépendant des réseaux de parenté. L'école fait échapper les enfants à la famille et toutes les querelles à propos de l'instruction obligatoire soulignent ce trait fondamental qui constitue peut-être la signification majeure de ce foyer éducatif implanté au milieu du rang. Et des deux sociétés qui se disputent le contrôle de l'école, la civile et la religieuse, la seconde domine à peu près totalement jusqu'au début des années 1960. Opposition entre le savoir contrôlé d'en-haut et la transmission de la vérité par la famille et le milieu ambiant, telle apparaît bien être la marque majeure de ce point de repère de l'espace rural présent partout à partir du milieu du 19ième siècle.

Si le foyer éducatif porte déjà la trace de sa fonction de transmission de la vérité religieuse et appartient ainsi pour une part à l'univers des signes religieux, la croix de chemins, quand à elle, condense l'essentiel de la présence de sacré à l'extérieur du village. Nous allons tenter de reconstituer les principaux éléments de la signification de ce foyer rural du sacré à partir des conduites populaires telles que nous les ont décrites nos informateurs de La Prairie et telles que d'autres études nous permettent de les saisir (4).

Les enquêtes conduites sur le terrain entre 1972 et 1980 (5) ont découvert la présence de dix-sept croix de chemins sur le territoire de l'ancienne paroisse de La Prairie. Reportées sur la carte (fig.2, pp.406), ces survivances de la vieilles coutumes apparaissent situées le long des routes de rang, jamais à moins de trois quart d'heure de marche de l'église principale, pas toujours au centre géographique du rang, mais rarement à une extrémité. Nous connaissons le processus menant à l'érection d'une croix. L'initiative est généralement individuelle au départ et le clergé n'y a pas part sauf dans le cas des croix commémoratives d'un événement (trois cas à L., 1, 4, 9). Un cultivateur voudra ériger une croix pour mieux assurer la fécondité de la terre, ou encore parce qu'il en aura fait le voeu (remerciement pour biens matériels obtenus, guérison, faveurs spirituelles obtenues, croix anti-conscription 1914-18). Cependant dès qu'il en parle aux voisins pour discuter du meilleur site, le geste est pris en charge par une unité sociale plus large qui se l'approprie pour en faire non pas la croix d'un tel, mais celle du rang.

Presque toutes les croix au sujet desquelles nous avons des informations à La Prairie sont du type orné de motifs décoratifs ou symboliques (trois ont des corpus).

La forme qui revient la plus souvent est le cercle évoquant le soleil ou la couronne d'épine, et elle constitue le centre des deux axes. On observe quelquefois certains instruments de la passion: un coq formant girouette à l'extrémité de la hampe, une niche-maisonnette au tronc de la hampe pour abriter une statue (mariale). Le plus fréquemment les extrémités se terminent par un motif stylisé (fleur-de-lys, pommette). La présence d'un coeur dans l'axe revoie à la populaire dévotion moderne au Sacré-coeur. On a fréquemment délimité un certain périmètre autour de la croix (petite clôture, par exemple) qui l'isole de l'espace environnant. Le message visuel de ce signe renvoie donc essentiellement au thème de la vie triomphant de la mort à la fois par le rappel de la passion (la victime qui sauve de la mort) et de la symbolique solaire. On pourrait pousser beaucoup plus loin l'interprétation de ce signe complexe, remarquer par exemple qu'il constitue une représentation du centre du monde et de la relation terre-ciel, mais nous préférons accéder au signifié populaire par l'observation des conduites conscientes.

La croix de chemins engendre des comportements spécifiques. Ce n'est pas simplement un point de repère dans l'espace du rang. Bien sûr, tous la remarquent et l'utilisent comme un différenciateur spatial, à l'instar de bien d'autres points de repère (maison, grange, gros arbre, courbe de rivière ou de chemin, etc.). Mais elles fait fonction de centre spécifique pour les habitants du rang et ceux qui y circulent.

On s'y réunit pour prier à la belle saison. Lors des inondations printannières les habitants d'un rang vont à la croix plutôt qu'à l'église, le dimanche. Dans la mémoire des informateurs contemporains cependant, la prière de groupe à la croix s'identifie le plus avec les exercises quotidiens du mois de Marie (mai). Cette dévotion italienne s'introduit en France et au Québec vers la fin des années 1830. Destinées aux "âmes d'élite" (religieuses et religieux) on se rend compte qu'elle a été reprise par le peuple qui l'a implanté solidement dans son propre espace rural, au grand désagrément du curé qui voudrait la centraliser dans l'église du village. Aprés le souper, durant le grand mois des semailles (mai) les femmes et les enfants, souvent encadrés par la maîtresse d'école, se rendaient à la croix pour les exercices pendant que les hommes restaient à la maison. Il est assez probable que cette dévotion à la "mère du ciel", confiée aux femmes, doit être inscrite dans l'univers des rites de fécondité pour la terre tout autour que les hommes ont labourée, hersée et ensemencée dans la journée. D'ailleurs les informateurs mentionnent d'autres occasions de prières communes (ou même individuelles) au pied de la croix qui ont un motif explicitement agraire: demande de pluie pour les légumes en juillet et août, supplications pour éviter ou être délivré des sauterelles au moment des récoltes.

Foyer des réunions de prière en marge de l'église, la croix focalise aussi les gestes individuels dans son aire de vue. Lorsque l'angelus tinte à la cloche du village, on se tourne vers la croix pour réciter la brève suite d'invocations. Tous ceux qui passent devant la croix font un geste de respects; les hommes soulèvent leur coiffure, les femmes saluent de la tête. On récite un ave. Même les passagers d'une automobile ou d'un autobus font de même.

La description des pratiques qui font de la croix un signe sacré nous oriente vers les éléments constituant son langage spatial propre. Elle agit bien comme un centre organisateur du rang. Celui-ci juxtapose des habitants en une suite de lots borné par une ligne de circulation. La croix rassemble la ligne en un point unique, les voisins en cercle de prière. Elle opère ainsi en donnant à lire un message fondamental produit et reproduit dans la société du rang. La croix tire en effet sa signification la plus évidente de l'opposition entre le niveau céleste (Origine absolue de la Vie) et le niveau terrestre (manifestations de la fécondité agraire). La croix permet à l'Origine de la Vie de rejoindre le champ de ses effets. Pour les habitants du rang son langage pourrait donc être ainsi résumé:

```
     origine    /  non-origine   /  effets
                   non-effet

                       ou

     vie        /     rien       /   vie
```

Ceci nous permet de mieux saisir comment, pour les périodes historiques où les habitants de la paroisse partageaient le même mode de vie et le même univers symbolique particulièrement bien condensé dans la croix de chemin, celle-ci parvenait sans doute à assumer en elle les autre grandes fonctions de l'espace rural (l'économie des surfaces terriennes, la société du rang, la famille de la maisonnée et le groupe des jeunes soumis à l'acculturation de l'Eglise). La croix représente la structure signifiante la plus englobante des unités rurales de la paroisse. Elle n'a pas présidé à la production de l'espace qui provient d'autres facteurs, mais une fois celui-ci donné, elle s'en est constitué, pour un temps, le centre symbolique réel, ce qui est peut-être la forme moderne du processus de sacralisation de l'espace.

2.3 L'espace villageois

Dans le grand ensemble de la paroisse de La Prairie, le village peut-être défini comme un noyau ou point central vers où convergent la circulation des campagnes et celle qui relie la paroisse à l'extérieur (par le chemin St-Jean, le quai, le chemin de fer et le vieux chemin le long du fleuve). Nous ne répéterons pas ici la genèse du village résumé en 2.1, nous contentant de rappeler sa plurifonctionnalité. L'analyse de l'espace portera sur le village tel qu'il apparaissait et était vécu par nos informateurs, de la deuxième partie de 18ième siècle jusque vers les années 1930 (6) (cf. fig.3, pp.407).

POINTS
La grande église qui date du milieu du 19ième siècle constitue le point de repère dominant de tout le village. Ce signe sacral condense en lui-même tout l'univers des représentations du Grand Récit chrétien, dans la forme

prise par le catholicisme romain québécois de cette période (ultramontanisme, i.e., renvoyant toutes les médiations au centre romain auquel il manifeste son appartenance; italianisation de la sensibilité religieuse). Il est aussi le lieu ou advient le salut efficacement par son culte multiforme, le centre du temps (éternité). L'église s'ajoint un bâtiment de chaque côté, le presbytère au sud et le couvent des religieuses enseignant aux filles, au nord. A l'arrière, un espace dégagé occupé par le cimetière qui émigrera hors des limites du village à la fin du siècle.

Deux autres édifices à taille imposante se dégagent du côté du port, l'hospice des soeurs de la Providence avec sa chapelle et l'académie des garçons dirigées par des frères enseignants. Cet ensemble de points détermine un secteur visuel très facilement identifiable, physiquement, par la taille des édifices.

Quelques autres points de repères qui se distinguent par la nature collective des activité qui s'y déroulent, sont à signaler: les trois magasins généraux situés en face de l'église, le marché où les ruraux viennent vendre aux villageois, les nombreux hotels et le quai des vapeurs.

On peut donc classer les points saillants du vieux village entre les signifiants qui renvoient à la Vérité et au Salut (le sacré) et ceux qui renvoient à l'ordre des transactions économiques et libidinales.

LIGNES

La plupart des points de repères mentionnés se placent selon deux axes, l'un perpendiculaire à la façade de l'église (laquelle respecte l'orientation symbolico-cosmologique lié au soleil levant), l'actuel chemin de St-Jean qui bipartitionne à peu près complètement l'espace sacré (est) de l'espace profane (ouest), l'autre parallèle à l'axe de l'église, la rue Ste-Marie au bout de laquelle est situé le marché, avec deux hotels importants en bordure. L'ancien chemin St-Jean borne le vieux village à l'est et sert de voie majeure des communications avec l'extérieur du village. Les deux premiers axes se croisent devant l'église et renforcissent ainsi la fonction nodale de ce point où viennent se superposer les principales significations de l'espace villageois.

SURFACES

Dans l'image mentale de la population du village (et sans doute aussi des gens de la campagne) les zones importantes du village naissent de ces axes qui sont les seuls retenus et valorisés par la mémoire. On pourrait ainsi parler de la surface mentale engendrée par le marché (avec police et pompiers) et les hotels de la rue Ste-Marie versus la surface mentale engendrée par l'église et les bâtiments cléricaux situés sur l'autre axe. Les rapports annuels du curé nous donnent accès à un des éléments de la tension latente entre les deux surfaces. Durant les années 1850 et 1860 il fait un décompte annuel des activités dangereuses pour les moeurs de ses fidèles et leur fidélité à la pratique dominicale. Il s'agit du brouhaha inévitable entourant le marché aux viandes qui se tient le dimanche et de la pratique d'utiliser l'espace de stationnement et les étables des hotels, ce qui favorise l'intempérance et les conversations peu chrétiennes. Et tout cela se passe dans la zone Ste-Marie qui s'oppose ainsi à la diffusion de l'aire sacrale qui voudrait régir l'ensemble des conduites du village.

Mais la zone sacrale exerce une très forte attraction sur la vie sociale de la communauté en lui fournissant les services éducatifs, sociaux et liturgiques. Et le curé notera la graduelle intégration des activités commerciales et de loisirs à "l'esprit du dimanche" au fur et à mesure que l'on approche de la fin du 19ième siècle.

On ne se surprend donc pas d'entendre nos informateurs décrire l'unité de la paroisse d'antan en la reliant à la domination du foyer religieux. Ce centre sacral crée l'unité du fait d'un partage indiscuté de l'univers symbolique qu'il reproduit et de la position de contrôle du clergé sur les opinions et les conduites. La fonction sacrale en est venue, pour un temps, à recouvrir toutes les autres, sans les faire disparaître, mais en les articulant ensemble dans les croyances et les conduites quasi unanimes.

D'un tissu spatial beaucoup plus dense et complexe, le foyer sacral structure à la fois la différence interne essentielle (les deux zones mentionnées) et l'organisation mentale unitaire. Le message de cette écriture spatiale du village peut sans doute être réduit aux même éléments fondamentaux que ceux de l'écriture spatiale rurale, à la différence qu'il y a ici saturation maximale de la représentation, ce qui n'est qu'une autre façon de décrire la position nodale du village dans l'ensemble paroissial. A la différence probable, également, d'une plus grande présence de la règle et du contrôle qui jouent le rôle de médiateur de sacré, dans la prédication, et surtout l'importance du personnage clérical pour la période 1840-1950.

Reportée dans la diachronie, la production de l'espace villageois de La Prairie manifeste une assez grande continuité formelle. Le plan de l'ingénieur de Léry du début du 18e siècle destiné à rebâtir un nouveau fort nous montre que la surface sacrale occupe tout le côté est du triangle (cimetière, église, couvent, résidence jésuite et dépendances) alors que la surface restante est livrée au campement militaire et à l'habitation civile. Il y avait là l'embryon de la structure en T décrite plus haut et une sorte de bipartition du monde gravée dans l'espace. On peut probablement conclure que dans ce fort-village, la tradition d'une assignation particulère de l'est comme région sacrale a marqué sinon la planification même de l'espace (puisque la documentation nous laisse dans l'ignorance), du moins sa lecture par les villageois et les paroissiens en général, détenteurs de ce code d'interprétation symbolique jusqu'à une période récente.

CONCLUSION:

Il faut conclure ce qui demeure malgré tout une esquisse bien préliminaire.

- Il y a une organization sacrale de tout l'espace paroissial. Elle opère à partir des points signifiants essentiels que sont l'église et les croix de chemins. Dans le premier cas, la production historique de l'espace villageois garde les traces d'un ancien programme cosmologique qui "obligeait" à respecter l'axe symbolique est-ouest, sans que l'on puisse toutefois réduire toute l'architecture du village à l'effet de domination de la signification sacrale. L'origine religieuse (jésuite) de cet espace a sans doute renforcit la présence de ces traces à La Prairie, relativement à la majorité des villages québécois. Les croix de chemins, de leur côté, n'ont en rien affecté la naissance de l'espace rural dont répondent les facteurs géographiques (réseaux hydrographiques, économiques (propriété terrienne) et sociaux (voisinage, parenté). Mais l'analyse de ces différents réseaux de signifiants conduit infailliblement au point de repère sacral où se manifeste et se reproduit l'unité sociale supérieure du rang dans ses pratiques rituelles et son univers symbolique accrochées de près au mode de production agricole.

- Les différences de l'organisation spatiale du village et des côtes renvoient aux fonctions différentes qui s'y déploient: production commerciale, manufacturière et de service, au village, exploitation terrienne dans les côtes. Nous n'avons pu pousser assez loin l'analyse, mais il est d'ores et déjà plus que probable que ceci introduit une différenciation du vécu de cet espace au plan religieux, l'espace rural générant une signification encore largement liée aux rythmes de la nature par opposition à l'espace villageois marqué par la fonction éthique de contrôle des intentions et des gestes des acteurs villageois. Tout ceci, bien sûr, sans ruptures nettes et avec un très large consensus au niveau des représentations symboliques.

- L'évolution de tout ceci depuis quelques décennies est fort intéressante. Pour la résumer nous dirons que d'un espace transémique, c'est-à-dire constitué de plusieurs fonctions distinctes et perçues comme telles, mais néanmoins articulées par un régistre sacral qui diffuse partout et en chacun, nous sommes passé à un espace à tendance monosémique, marqué par la grande opposition public (travail) / privé (dortoir domestique) ou la campagne évolue vers la banlieu pendant que le village est devenu une petite ville industrielle. L'organisation sacrale de l'espace s'est à peu près totalement défaite.

Pour les habitants de La Prairie ses signes n'ont plus qu'une valeur connotative (7). Renvoyés dans l'aire de la conscience individuelle ils signifient ce que chacun veut bien y mettre et il faudrait maintenant procéder à une enquête non plus auprès de quelques informateurs mais bien de toute la population (ou d'un bon échantillonnage) pour saisir ce qu'ils disent encore. De noyaux signifiants du sacré ils sont devenus des objets du patrimoine, les points de repères d'une mémoire culturelle commune, une classe spécifique d'objets dont doit maintenant s'occuper l'Etat dans sa tentative de créer une mythologie civile.

Fig.1 Laprairie, espace rural (1831)

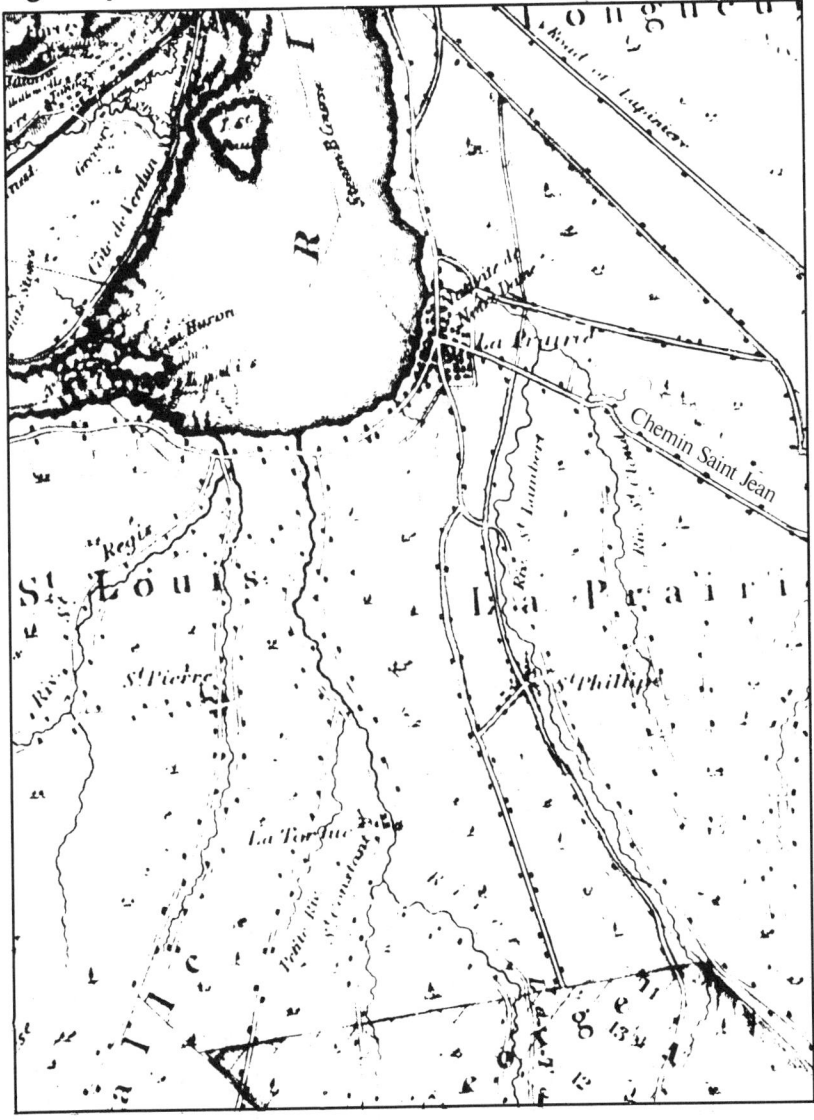

Fig. 2 Les croix de chemin, milieu 20ième s.

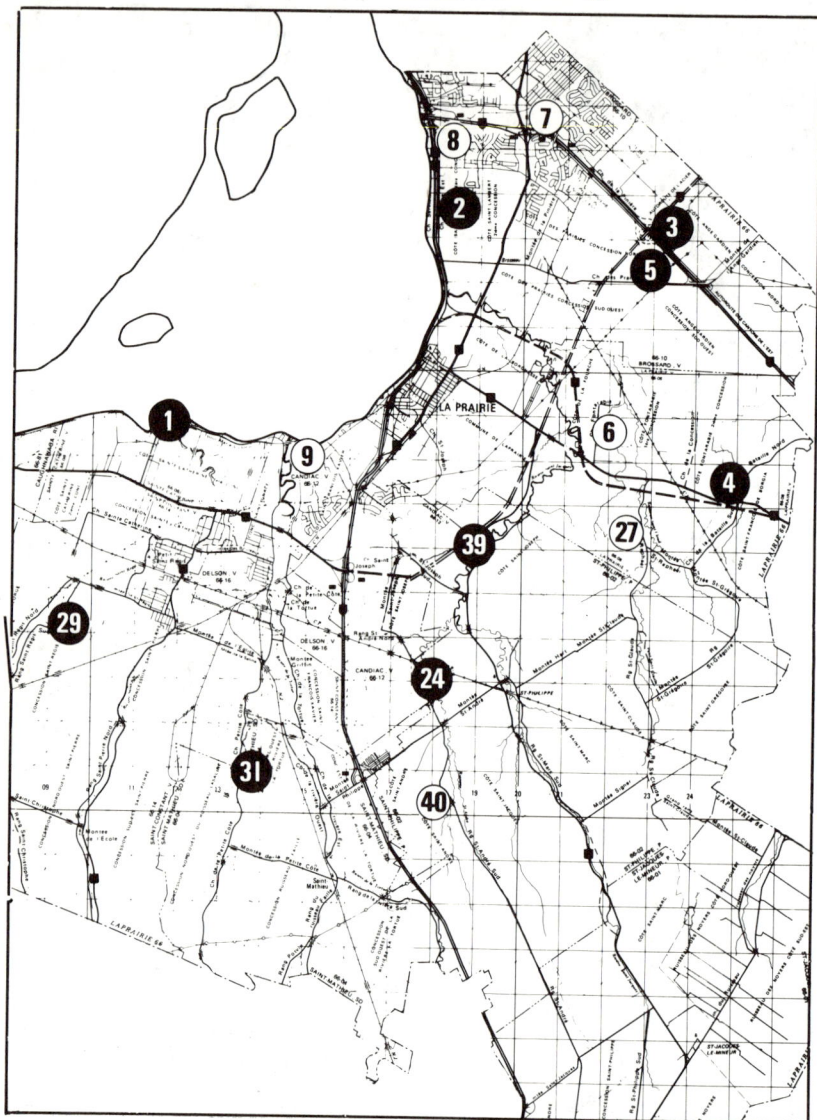

Fig. 3 Village de Laprairie (1894)

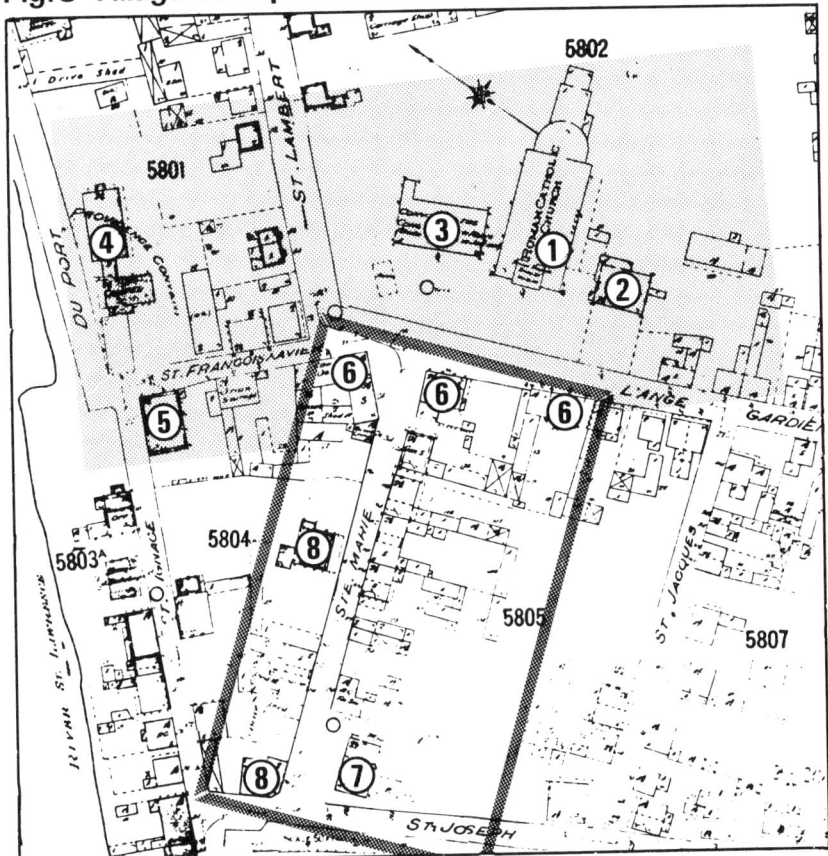

Légende

1. Eglise
2. Presbytere
3. Couvent des enseignantes
4. Hospice
5. Académie
6. Magasins
7. Marché
8. Hôtel

L'AXE DE L'INTERIORITE EN ARCHITECTURE RELIGIEUSE CONTEMPORAINE

Norman Pagé

Durant toute la première moitié de ce XXe siècle - et même jusque vers 1960 - 1965 - l'architecture religieuse, selon une tradition séculaire, rivalise avec l'architecture civile. Parmi les monuments les plus prestigieux et les plus révolutionnaires dont l'histoire de l'art contemporain peut s'enorgueillir, figurent, en nombre étonnant, des cathédrales, églises et sanctuaires.

Depuis près de vingt ans, par ailleurs, ces fiers édifices religieux, à quelques exceptions près, ne surgissent plus de terre. Les silhouettes des nouveaux développements urbains ne comptent plus le point de repère traditionnel. Et même au coeur des villes, comme à la suite d'un puissant raz-de-marée, la morphologie du centre urbain s'est si radicalement transformée que dômes et clochers ont été relégués à l'ombre des gratte-ciel.

Le lieu privilégié de l'audace technique ou de l'inspiration la plus originale n'est plus l'édifice sacré mais le stade olympique, le centre des arts ou le palais des congrès. L'architecture religieuse n'est plus en lice. Plus surprenant encore, ses formes symboliques ont été récupérées par l'architecture civile. L'ampleur ou la majesté d'un édifice, la gratuité surtout de ses structures, sa verticalité, ses arcades, ses vitraux ou mosaiques ne sont plus du monopole de l'architecture religieuse.

Au strict plan du langage des formes architectoniques, en Europe comme en Amérique, on se surprend aujourd'hui à confondre le Civic Center Synagogue de New York, la cathédrale San Sebastian de Rio de Janeiro ou l'église St.

Mary's de Red Deer en Alberta avec le Palais des Congrès de Berlin, l'aéroport Kennedy de New York ou le Poème électronique de Le Corbusier à Bruxelles. Les formes ne parlent plus par elles-mêmes. Leur langage se confond. Au point où dans nombre de banlieues, il faut ajouter à l'édifice un signe, ou une enseigne, qui puisse permettre d'en identifier la fonction.

La transformation de notre société occidentale a-t-elle, en deux décennies, mis un terme à l'histoire de l'architecture dite sacrée? Faut-il sonner le glas, tout au moins, de l'architecture religieuse monumentale? Surgit-il présentement de nouvelles formes architecturales liées au sacré? Quels caractères symboliques nous faut-il retenir de cette longue et riche tradition? Plus concrètement encore, que ressort-il des diverses expériences en cours qui semble caractéristique et déterminant en cette fin de siècle?

Dans ce labyrinthe de questions que l'on est en droit de se poser, je voudrais, aujourd'hui, ne m'arrêter qu'à celles qui permettent de mieux cerner les transformations de l'architecture religieuse traditionnelle et la persistance, au plan symbolique, d'une constante majeure: l'axe de l'intériorité.

LES EGLISES, MONUMENTS D'ARCHITECTURE
Il est difficile d'oublier que notre XXe siècle a été marqué jusqu'à récemment, dans la tradition chrétienne à laquelle je me limite ici plus particulièrement, par la construction d'églises dont l'originalité et la qualité architecturale sont telles que tous les répertoires d'architecture contemporaine nous les présentent voisinant avantageusement avec les plus remarquables des édifices civils.

Nombre de ces édifices religieux constituent même des prototypes d'architecture moderne et les lieux privilégiés où se sont exprimés avec le plus d'imagination créatrice les architectes qui ont fait école au XXe siècle. Rappelons, à titre d'exemples, que parmi les premiers édifices cités pour l'audace de leurs techniques, au tout début du siècle, figure l'église Notre-Dame du Raincy (1922) en France, d'Auguste Perret: première forme monumentale à substituer aux murs de maçonnerie des structures de béton précontraint permettant de transformer l'enceinte en paroi de verre; que c'était également dans une église, la United Church de Oak Park (1907), à Chicago, que Frank Lloyd Wright avait mis à l'épreuve sa technique, déterminante pour le XXe siècle, du béton brut monolithique. C'est également dans une chapelle, celle de Santa Coloma de Cervello (1915), en Espagne, que Antonio Gaudi a pu laisser libre champ à son génie surréaliste. L'église surnommée The Steel Church, de Cologne, est le lieu ou l'architecte Otto Bartning exploite librement ses nouvelles structures d'acier. C'est en construisant l'église de Saint-François d'Assise (1943-46), à Belo Horizonte, au Brésil, que Niemeyer sème la controverse en utilisant pour la première fois à pareille échelle, ses célèbres arcs paraboliques. De même, l'oeuvre reconnue comme la plus parfaite de Saarinen, sa dernière, est l'église Christ Church (1949) de Minneapolis; elle constitue, avec les églises de Moser et Schwarz en Suisse, le prototype de l'église protestante moderne.

On comprend aussi facilement que ce soit dans des édifices religieux, comme la chapelle Palos Verdes de Californie, que l'architecture de verre due à Frank Wright et à son fils John Lloyd Wright ait d'abord pris forme. On ne se surprend pas non plus que ce soit dans une église, celle de la Vierge Miraculeuse de Mexico, que Felix Candela ait pu élever aussi témérairement ses prodigieuses voûtes de béton incurvées. Doit-on s'étonner enfin que l'oeuvre la plus décriée, et la plus citée aujourd'hui, du grand Le Corbusier, ait été une église: Notre-Dame du Haut de Ronchamp (1950-55), en France, oeuvre construite "dans une sorte d'élan sacré", comme le disait son auteur lui-même.

Parmi toutes ces oeuvres célèbres de l'architecture religieuse du XXe siècle, c'est à Ronchamp que je voudrais que, dans un premier temps, l'on s'arrête, puisque de l'avis d'un des théoriciens et critiques de l'architecture des plus rigoureux, Christian Norberg-Schulz, "l'importance de Ronchamp dans l'histoire des formes architecturales est inestimable ...(Ronchamp) marque la renaissance de l'architecture religieuse"...[1] afin de nous permettre de déterminer en quoi ce chef-d'oeuvre d'architecture peut, même aujourd'hui, et dans le contexte de cet exposé, s'avérer inestimable même s'il n'a pas, de fait, marqué la renaissance de l'architecture religieuse.

RONCHAMP: HAUT LIEU DU SACRE
L'oeuvre de Ronchamp a d'abord été décriée, par les architectes les premiers, comme une structure excédant toute norme, comme une forme irrationnelle, un théâtre néobaroque, une sculpture de béton armé. Elle est citée aujourd'hui comme une des oeuvres les plus inspirées, les plus poétiques de l'art contemporain. Elle nous apparaît comme sûrement le chef d'oeuvre de l'architecture religieuse du siècle. Souvent imitée depuis, elle n'a jamais été surpassée.

Techniquement, Ronchamp est une audacieuse structure. Le toit, en forme de coque de crabe renversée, est constitué de deux membranes de béton de 6 centimètres d'épaisseur, distantes entre elle de 2,26 mètres; il ne touche pas aux murs épais qui forment l'enceinte de la chapelle mais repose sur les huit piliers porteurs que ces murs renferment, de sorte qu'un long rais de lumière horizontal de 10 centimètres d'épaisseur court sous lui. Ces murs, irréguliers ou à pans verticaux triangulaires, sont de ciment armé de 16 centimètres d'épaisseur, variant à la base de 3,70 mètres à 1,40 mètre pour un sommet de 50 centimètres. Les autres parois ne sont qu'une pellicule de 4 centimètres de béton projeté sur grillage. À l'intérieur, la chapelle donne l'impression "d'une ronde bosse (en creux)... les quatre parois, le plafond, le sol, tout est mobilisé dans une simplicité désarmante."[2] Les surfaces se raccordent comme des ondes croissantes. Trois tours captent la lumière, "celle de gauche prend la lumière de l'aube et s'éteint vers midi, la seconde prend la relève jusqu'au dernier rayon du soleil couchant. La grande tour ouverte vers le nord, maintient la lumière blanche."[3] Tout le volume intérieur est mouvement et harmonie: le sol descend, la voûte monte, les murs s'écartent mais tout converge vers l'autel, pôle d'aspiration. Même les ouvertures, fenêtres ou baies, ne se comprennent que de l'intérieur, embrasures ou ébrasures.

Ronchamp, c'est l'église-monument, l'espace sacré aux formes renouvelées, le lieu de paix, de prière, de recueillement, le lieu de la rencontre entre l'homme et Dieu, plus centré sur Dieu que sur la communauté, d'édifice-témoin qui parle aux hommes de Dieu, "l'espace indicible" selon l'expression de Le Corbusier. Après 15 ans, le caractère insolite de ses particularités techniques s'est émoussé mais la poésie de ses formes, la puissance de ses volumes, le mystère de ses ombres émeuvent encore le visiteur attardé. Ronchamp, c'est une sorte de lieu sacré à l'état pur.

ARCOSANTI: CIVITAS DEI
Un second prototype d'architecture gratuite, mais d'une toute autre échelle, sur lequel je voudrais maintenant attirer votre attention, démontre bien la persistance de la symbolique religieuse architecturale dans les mentalités, et même dans celle des architectes du XXe siècle les plus futuristes.

Il s'agit de cette oeuvre gigantesque de l'architecte Soleri, qui nous a été présentée lors du dernier Congrès international sur la religion et l'architecture, tenu à San Antonio, Texas, en mai 1978, sous le thème "Renaissance de la vision créatrice". Cette oeuvre est en voie de construction, depuis 10 ans déjà, dans le paysage biblique de l'Arizona, à quelques 70 milles au nord de Phoenix. Son auteur, Paolo Soleri, est considéré aujourd'hui comme un des créateurs les plus visionnaires de notre époque. Il est aussi réputé comme philosophe et théoricien de l'architecture, auteur d'un traité révolutionnaire connu sous le titre d'AR-COLOGIE (AR-chitecture, é-Cologie). Les principaux essais théoriques de Soleri ont été regroupés dans un livre intitulé "Matter becoming Spirit".[4]

Le projet-rêve qu'il est à réaliser présentement sur un territoire de 860 acres dans le désert de l'Arizona est une ville futuriste du nom d'Arcosanti, caractérisée essentiellement par une réorganisation radicale et révolutionnaire des structures traditionnelles d'une cité.

Au plan morphologique, d'après Soleri, la cité future, pour répondre aux besoins de l'avenir, ne peut plus être construite en étendue, elle doit être tri-dimensionnelle. Les nouvelles structures urbaines, en raison des millions d'êtres qu'elles sont appelées à contenir doivent être miniaturisées et, d'autre part, pour être viables, ces nouvelles structures ne peuvent être établies qu'en fonction de nouveaux types de communication, et dans un nouvel esprit, entre l'homme et la société, et entre la société et son environnement. L'homme de demain, pour survivre, sera celui de l'écologie; sa cité sera solaire ou ne sera pas.

Mais les impératifs de Soleri ne sont pas que d'ordre écologique. Sa cité tri-dimensionnelle l'exprime. La verticalité de ses formes structurales évoque, comme les cités-monastères du Moyen Age, une autre dimension de l'homme qu'il appelle trans-rationnelle ou théologique. Arcosanti n'a pas que la forme pyramidale, elle en a aussi le sens. Pour ce créateur qui se dit anti-matérialiste et pour qui la matière est en processus constant de transformation en des formes toujours plus "éthérées ou spirituelles", la cité de l'homme de demain n'est pas qu'une préfiguration de la Jérusalem céleste, elle est déjà Civitas Dei, la cité de Dieu.

Arcosanti se présente donc comme un projet-synthèse futuriste en réponse au rêve d'une portion de l'espèce humaine à la poursuite d'une forme de survie. De l'extérieur, d'après les plans minutieux publiés par Soleri, les structures de cette mégapolis évoquent la plus majesteuse et la plus complexe des cathédrales que l'homme ait pu dresser dans le ciel. Il n'y a pas d'églises à l'intérieur d'Arcosanti (encore qu'il y ait un centre d'études théologiques), mais toute la cité est église, ecclesia, communauté d'esprit et de coeur, cité-symbole, cité parcellaire dont les structures éclateront un jour aux dimensions du monde... Cité étagée qui n'est pas non plus sans évoquer la Tour de Babel.

AMBIGUITE DES ARCHETYPES

Ronchamp et Arcosanti passeront à l'histoire: Ronchamp pour la qualité de ses espaces poétiques et Arcosanti pour sa démesure téméraire, mais les deux soulèvent diverses questions de fond car ni l'un ni l'autre de ces "monuments sacrés" ne peuvent être considérés comme à la source de la renaissance de l'architecture religieuse.

Ronchamp nous apparaît à nous, en cette fin du XXe siècle, plus au terme qu'au sommet de cette longue lignée d'églises monumentales qui jalonnent l'histoire de la chrétienté, depuis les premières basiliques de Rome ou de Byzance jusqu'aux plus impressionnantes cathédrales. Ronchamp a le mérite unique en lui-même de renouveler radicalement par ses formes le bâtiment-église monumental, mais le plan et les structures seulement sont modifiés, si substantiellement que ce soit; l'esprit du lieu sacré traditionnel est le même, exactement. Ronchamp est à la fois "réceptacle et don, forteresse et vision poétique de ce qui est autre".[5] Quel que soit donc son caractère révolutionnaire, cette église est essentiellement dans la lignée des églises monumentales traditionnelles; elle en est même le dernier grand témoin.

Le mystère - et la fascination - de ces hauts lieux du sacré est grand, mais les temps ont changé. Ronchamp, 15 ans seulement après sa construction, n'a plus la teneur de l'archétype qu'on avait cru y discerner. Son caractère reste unique. Un architecte de génie a créé, dans un espace privilégié, comme il le voulait, "un vaisseau d'intime concentration et de méditation" hors de toute contrainte historique, ou socio-économique. Mais l'édifice, il faut bien l'avouer, est plus enraciné dans la tradition que dans son époque et son milieu culturel. La chrétienté n'est plus ce qu'elle était. Et les architectes d'aujourd'hui tout en enviant Le Corbusier, le réalisent, tête basse. Impossible désormais d'envisager, comme en leurs rêves d'antan, la construction d'un de ces hauts lieux du sacré traditionnel, qui soit pour chacun ce jeu de formes poussé à l'extrême limite de l'exploitation de la matière et de la technique. Les exigences sont autres, les contraintes et les limites aussi.

Soleri, pour sa part, a misé sur l'infiniment grand. Son rêve, pour utopique qu'il apparaisse aux yeux d'un grand nombre, repose pourtant aussi sur une tradition bien établie, et bien assortie, dans l'histoire de la chrétienté. Les structures d'Arcosanti, au premier regard, tiennent de la science-fiction mais elles ne sont pas sans évoquer non plus les ensembles monastiques de l'architecture paléochrétienne, ces "îles ordonnées et paisibles à l'intérieur d'une société qui se débattait dans une profonde confusion".[6] A la fois enclos topologique sacré et megapolis, Arcosanti reproduit une interprétation très articulée, dans le contexte d'aujourd'hui, d'une structure urbaine qui se veut "signifiante", intégrant et combinant les données symboliques de l'horizontal et du vertical. La cathédrale de Soleri est également un espace spiritualisé, elle est cette basilique qui illustre, à sa manière, comme à Rome ou à Bysance, le chemin menant au salut et préfigurant la Jérusalem céleste.

Mais pour le chrétien qui a assimilé le Concile, Arcosanti véhicule des valeurs triomphalistes. C'est la cité des privilégiés, des élus. Elle n'est signe de communion que pour ceux qui l'habitent. Ses structures d'oasis et de ghetto, sont élevées "en opposition". Arcosanti exprime avant tout la persistance de la symbolique architecturale monumentale et l'utopie renouvelée.

L'ECROULEMENT DU MONUMENTALISME

Plus à ras de terre, l'implantation d'églises nouvelles soulève aujourd'hui de multiples questions. Pour ne pas dire, au risque de simplification excessive, que tout est remis en question par ce biais. L'on s'interroge plus spécifiquement sur le type même de présence que doit assurer une église en diaspora, sur les nouvelles formes de regroupements possibles face à l'urbanisation, à la mobilité des populations, à la désaffectation voir à la dissolution des paroisses traditionnelles de même qu'aux nouvelles perspectives qu'offrent les regroupements par noyaux multiples ou par zones concentriques. Et plus en profondeur encore, de la portée du retour aux sources véhiculé par Vatican II et de l'accent à mettre sur des valeurs comme l'authenticité, la pauvreté évangélique, l'accueil, le partage et le témoignage.

Si toutes les théories élaborées par ces remises en question n'ont gardé pour la plupart qu'un poids très relatif et n'ont pas donné lieu, loin de là, à des solutions uniformes, il n'en reste pas moins qu'en architecture religieuse, la situation a changé. La construction de nouveaux lieux de culte l'atteste. Les communautés chrétiennes - de même que les diocèses - dans l'ensemble, ne peuvent tout simplement plus assumer les frais de construction de l'église monumentale, même là ou elles le voudraient. Et là où il s'en élève encore, ces églises, cathédrales ou sanctuaires, sont de plus contestées par nombre de chrétiens comme autant de contre-témoignages. La chrétienté est entrée dans cette nouvelle phase de son histoire où le triomphalisme traduit par le monumentalisme en architecture n'est plus possible, phase dans laquelle déjà, par ailleurs, d'autres formes architecturales sont nées, reflétant plus adéquatement un autre mode de vie et de nouvelles valeurs.

Théoriquement, selon un certain consensus, le bâtiment-église est maintenu, comme à la fois "signe et support de la communauté chrétienne"[7] et non, d'abord, comme expression visible d'une forme historique de l'institution ecclésiale. La nouvelle église ne doit pas d'abord apparaître comme le temple majestueux élevé à la gloire de Dieu, mais, plus humblement, comme le lieu de rassemblement d'une communauté.

De fait, comme l'édifice religieux n'est plus, selon la tradition séculaire, désigné comme le centre de la cité, le point de repère axial de la topographie de la nouvelle ville, du faubourg ou de la banlieue, ses formes ont en conséquence été modifiées. De nouvelles formes architectu-

rales ont pris naissance, accordées à de nouveaux modes de
vie des communautés, à de nouveaux besoins, à de nouvelles
contraintes et à de nouvelles tendances. Ce sont la maison
d'église, le centre communautaire et la chapelle du silence.

LA MAISON D'EGLISE

La maison d'église est ainsi appelée communément parce que
sa structure d'ensemble se rapproche plus de l'esprit et
des formes de l'architecture domestique que de l'architecture monumentale. Littéralement, elle traduit pour Dom
Fréderic Debuyst[8] qui en est devenu le théoricien attitré,
l'expression latine *Domus Ecclesiae* et ce, avec toutes les
connotations théologiques qu'a pu en détacher Joseph
Comblin dans sa célèbre Théologie de la ville.[9]

Au plan architectural, de l'extérieur, la maison
d'église ne se distingue guère des autres maisons l'environnant. Implantée par définition parmi d'autres, elle se
situe même de préférence à l'écart plutôt qu'au centre des
nouveaux développements urbains; un signe ou une enseigne
l'identifie comme le lieu de rencontre ouvert aux chrétiens
que les activités quotidiennes ont dispersés et qui
désirent s'y retrouver pour partager, communier, célébrer.
Son ambition n'est ni d'encadrer, ni de dominer, mais
d'être simple présence.

Son plan se caractérise par deux éléments principaux:
un porche ou narthex qui sert de lieu d'accueil et un
espace plus vaste, aéré, lumineux et unifié en faveur d'une
participation active aux célébrations. D'une extrême
simplicité, cette maison tire sa qualité expressive de l'aménagement sensible de son espace et de la vérité de ses
matériaux, en somme d'un dépouillement qui s'apparente à
celui du Centre Zen.

Les plus réussies de ces maisons d'église sont sans
doute, à l'origine et encore aujourd'hui, celles construites par les architectes finlandais Kaija et Heiki
Siren, notamment la chapelle d'Otaniemi, avec ses "parois
englobant le parvis et la nef, une toiture en pente, la
lumière venant de l'arrière, avec vue panoramique au-delà

de l'autel; une simple enveloppe en maçonnerie et en bois. On a rarement obtenu plus avec si peu de moyens".[10]

LE CENTRE COMMUNAUTAIRE

Le centre communautaire se distingue de la maison d'église par ses proportions et la diversité des services qu'il offre plus que par son esprit, car il est, lui aussi, de par ses formes architecturales, édifice parmi d'autre édifices.

Son plan reprend les deux éléments de base de la maison d'église, soit le narthex et le lieu de célébration. S'y rajoutent, selon les besoins du milieu, d'autres lieux de service, salles de réunions, bureaux des animateurs de pastorale, chapelle du Saint-Sacrement ou chapelle de semaine, baptistère, salon funéraire, etc. Défini comme édifice pluri-fonctionnel, le centre communautaire relève d'un programme architectural établi à la fois par les animateurs responsables, l'architecte et les représentants de la communauté. C'est une oeuvre d'équipe. Il est édifié avant tout comme lieu de rassemblement et lieu de célébration. Ses fonctions premières sont les célébrations liturgiques, mais il se prête également aux autres célébrations communautaires ou activités propres à la communauté: réunions de catéchèse, conférences, banquets, fêtes populaires, concerts, etc.

Les centres communautaires les plus réussis que nous connaissions doivent leur cohérence constructive à quelques éléments symboliques fondamentaux: un parvis d'entrée, qui est lieu d'accueil d'abord, et qui chemine ensuite, librement, pour conduire aux autres salles mais aussi à l'espace central qui est le lieu de la célébration avec comme point focal, l'autel. Ni salle de concert, ni théâtre, cet espace central se doit par l'organisation de son volume intérieur de traduire son caractère propre, sans affectation.

Généralement, les centres communautaires contiennent de 200 à 800 personnes lorsque toutes les salles connexes sont ouvertes sur l'espace principal, de sorte que ce lieu central de culte peut substantiellement conserver son caractère d'intimité. Mais le risque chaque fois est grand pour l'architecte de rater l'affirmation claire, cohérente et subtile d'un tel espace.

LA CHAPELLE DU SILENCE

Cette chapelle s'avère de plus en plus nécessaire au coeur des grandes villes. C'est l'espace de recueillement au milieu des trépidations du quotidien. Le lieu de retraite, l'oasis. Elle se caractérise par le dépouillement, ce vide qui est plénitude; aussi par l'accueil inconditionnel, sans échange explicite. Aux heures du repas eucharistique, tout se déroule sans juridisme, ni moralisme, sans emphases mais avec la rigueur et la poésie de la plus pure liturgie. Les détails architectoniques d'une telle chapelle tiennent à rien et à tout. Ses mesures sont celles de l'incommensurable. Au comble, c'est l'espace poétique. Le modèle le plus proche nous vient d'Orient, c'est la "chambre de thé" du Japon: 9 mètres carrés.

Ces chapelles sont lieu de prière et lieu de communion. Elles sont les plus difficiles à construire et à habiter, mais elles sont nécessaires car elles révèlent l'essentiel.

L'Arama, un lieu de retraite méditative du genre situé à Santa Monica, en Californie, a gagné en 1977, sur un total de 619 concurrents, le concours annuel de la revue américaine *Progressive Architecture*. Un membre du jury disait à ce sujet: "Un peu austère,...extrêmement subtil, très esthétique et très soucieux du détail...Plus j'y pense, plus ses qualités se précisent..." Telles sont également les caractéristiques des ermitages du Père de Foucauld, au coeur du désert comme en bordure des faubourgs.

L'AXE DE L'INTERIORITE

Le bâtiment-église aux formes monumentales, révolutionnaires et triomphantes (pour ne pas dire triomphalistes) n'est indéniablement plus, du moins pour la phase que nous traversons, le type d'architecture religieuse que la chrétienté d'aujourd'hui peut se permettre de construire. Conséquemment, il faut bien également l'admettre, une très longue tradition, dans l'histoire de l'Eglise comme en histoire de l'art, est en voie d'extinction.

L'architecture religieuse, pour autant, est-elle en voie de disparaître? Si l'on ne s'arrête qu'aux constructions majeures, aux formes symboliques monumentales, aux église du genre "spectaculaire", comme chacun est enclin à le faire spontanément en raison des schèmes de référence historique les plus familiers (ce qui est le cas du critique d'art ou du théoricien en architecture), il nous faut considérer à juste titre que très peu des édifices religieux construits depuis 20 ans risquent de passer à l'histoire.

Si par ailleurs on analyse l'histoire de l'architecture dans son rapport forme-fonction, si l'on s'arrête à voir d'abord dans la forme architecturale "la forme spatiale qui signifie lieu, parcours et domaine, c'est-à-dire la structure concrète de l'environnement humain",[11] on se surprend à découvrir que la caractéristique distinctive de l'architecture religieuse en Occident, depuis ses origines jusqu'à nos jours, n'est pas la monumentalité mais l'intériorité, ou du moins que l'axe qui traverse toute l'histoire de l'architecture depuis l'époque paléochrétienne jusqu'à la nôtre inclusivement et cela à travers, ou par dessous les formes monumentales traditionnelles, est à proprement parler, l'axe de l'intériorité.

Les premiers lieux de culte relèvent de l'architecture domestique. Les premières églises ont d'abord été conçues comme des mondes intérieurs, et qui plus est, des univers clos. Et c'est "à l'intérieur" des édifices religieux primitifs que le caractère sacré de l'espace a pris forme. Parmi les éléments symboliques architecturaux qui ont fait l'objet d'une réinterprétation, aux origines mêmes de l'architecture chrétienne, se trouvent le concept du "centre" et celui du "parcours".[12]

Ces deux concepts caractérisent les plans et les espaces de toute l'architecture paléochrétienne. L'espace longitudinal (le parcours) exprime la dimension temps et est à l'image de la vie et de l'orientation de l'action humaine. C'est cette longue basilique à colonnes, terminée par une abside où siégeaient l'évêque et son clergé, transposition du palatium sacrum romain. L'espace centralisé, pour sa part, est image du cosmos: la partie inférieure est la zone terrestre, la coupole qui la recouvre figure le ciel d'où provient la lumière qui l'éclaire et la dématérialise; c'est le projet de salut rendu visible. L'Orient a adopté ce dernier plan pour ses principales églises dès l'origine, pour le combiner, par la suite, dans des structures encore plus vastes, avec l'espace longitudinal: d'où les variantes historiques connues: plan polygnal ou cruciforme avec coupole centrale, plan en quinconce, etc.

Ces espaces symboliques, simples ou combinés, se retrouveront par la suite, tout au long de l'histoire, sous des formes variées pour aboutir, à certaines époques, à des images spatiales des mieux articulées ou à de grandioses synthèses symboliques, et tant dans l'agencement des volumes intérieurs que dans l'exploitation des formes extérieures. Fondamentalement, cependant, l'église garde la même signification première: elle est centre et parcours, traduisant à la fois la dimension linéaire de la vie et l'événement total, cosmique qu'est la rédemption. La nouvelle phase dans laquelle l'architecture religieuse est entrée depuis Vatican II ne transmet pas, essentiellement, autre chose; elle l'exprime même plus radicalement, en raison du dépouillement auquel l'accule notre époque.

Dans la maison d'église, comme dans le centre communautaire, les éléments symboliques du parcours et du centre sont repris dans ces variantes que présentent le narthex et l'espace central unifié. Le narthex, porche d'entrée ou préau ouvert, symbolise l'accueil et ouvre dans l'axe, ou par un cheminement plus libre, à l'espace central dont le point focal est l'autel. La dématérialisation de cet espace central s'obtient par une certaine rigueur, une certaine vérité des structures, mais davantage encore par la qualité même de l'organisation spatiale. La lumière, diffuse, tangentielle ou en plongée y joue souvent le rôle le plus délicat: celui de faire parler ou chanter les formes. La verticalité tombe au profit du plan enveloppant de l'espace central. La distinction habituelle entre nef et sanctuaire est modifiée, du moins celle de cette nef avec collatéraux et jubés et vue en perspective de ce sanctuaire "sacro-saint" où se déroulait l'action liturgique. La liturgie n'étant plus "spectacle" mais "participation", le sanctuaire désormais étreint la nef, l'assemblée entoure l'autel. C'est "l'Eglise, peuple de Dieu".

De l'extérieur, la maison d'église, comme le centre communautaire, voisine les autres maisons ou édifices et ne s'en distingue guère, ni par ses formes, ni par ses matériauxé. Elle est, le plus souvent, localisée en périphérie des nouveaux développements urbains, à l'écart des grandes routes et même à distance des trottoirs. Elle exige une démarche seconde. Selon le mot de Rostand, c'est à l'intérieur qu'elle a ses élégances.

Le dernier mot revient à Le Corbusier, lui qui écrivait à propos de Ronchamp: "Des choses sont sacrées, d'autres ne le sont pas, qu'elles soient religieuses ou non"[13]..."L'architecture n'est pas affaire de colonnes mais affaire d'événements plastiques. Les événements plastiques ne se règlent pas sur des formulaires scolaires ou académiques; ils sont libres et innombrables"[14]..."C'est une intimité qui doit s'intégrer en chaque chose, capable de provoquer le rayonnement de l'espace indicible"...[15]

424   Traditions in Contact and Change

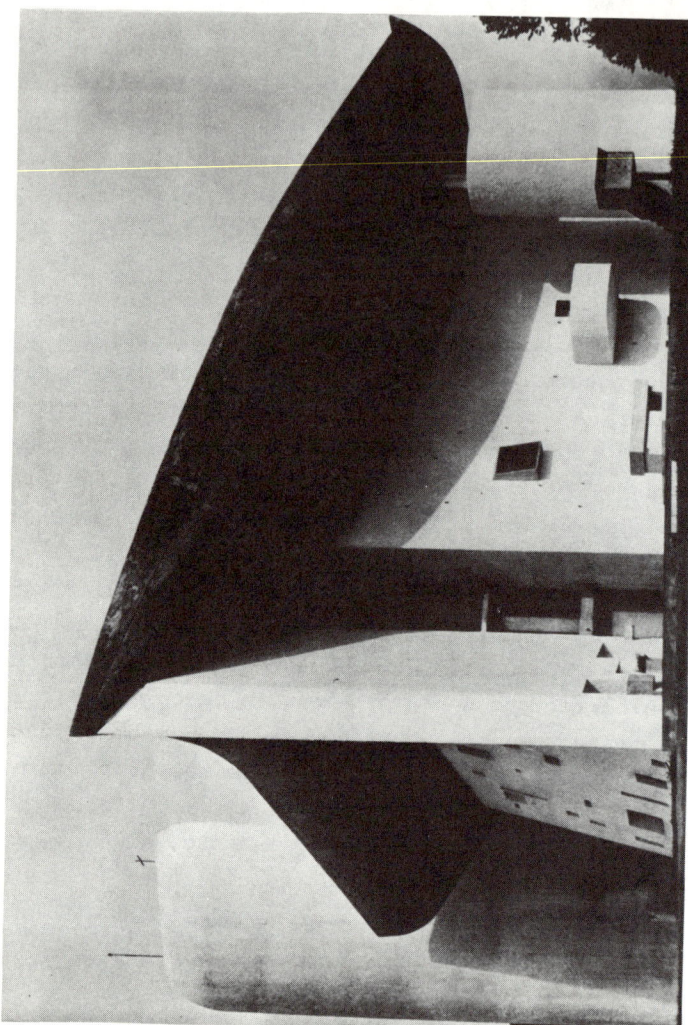

Photo 1: Chapelle Notre-Dame-du-Haut (Face est), Ronchamp. Le Corbusier, architecte. Ex: Ronchamp-Vence, Les chapelles du Rosaire à Vence par Matisse et de Notre-Dame-du-Haut à Ronchamp par Le Corbusier (Paris: Editions du Cerf, 1955), 65.

Photo 2: Hexahedron-Arcosanti. Paolo Soleri, architecte. Ex: *The City in the Image of Man* par Paolo Soleri (Cambridge, MA: MIT Press, 1969), 113.

Photo 3: Salle de méditation, Centre d'études des religions, Université Harvard, Cambridge, Mass. S. Jackson et associés, architectes. Ex: Revue L'Architecture d'aujourd'hui, no. 125 (Avril-Mai, 1966, Boulogne, France), 99.

TRADITION, CONTACT AND CHANGE IN INDIAN ISLAM,
EXEMPLIFIED IN MUHAMMAD IQBAL'S WORK

Annemarie Schimmel

The world of Islam has entered in these days the fifteenth century of its existence. One often divides the past 1400 years into two almost equal halves - the first 700 years comprise the victorious expansion of Islam from its centers in Arabia to Spain, India, and Central Asia as well as the high time of Islamic scholarship, poetry and science. After the Mongol onslaught, however, which culminated in the fall of Baghdad in 1258, the phase of decline set in: the institution of the caliphate was extinguished, and new social and political developments weakened the Muslim countries. In the opinion of many scholars this political and cultural decline and the stagnation of the once so successful scientific activities among the Muslims is due not only to the destructions wrought by the Mongols but also to the expansion of the mystical theories of all-embracing Unity of Being, *waḥdat al-wujūd*, as systematized by the brilliant Spanish-born mystic Ibn ᶜArabī (d.1240). The defenders of orthodox Islam from the days of Ibn Taimiyya (d.1328) as well as Western orientalists see in the victory of this "sweeping pantheism" the greatest danger for the active and dynamic spirit of Islam. The tension between the Living God to whom man turns in trust and obedience because he is aware of his own state as poor servant, is replaced by a system maintaining a situation in which Creator and creature seem to function merely like water and ice, even though the essence of God remains absolutely transcendent and inaccessible. The shortened Persian formula of the believers in *waḥdat al-wujūd*, i.e., *hama ūst*, Everything is He, was repeated in innumerable poems all over the Muslim world, especially in the Persianate world, and thus percolated down into the lowest classes of the population, all the more since it usually constituted the central element in the teachings of the dervish orders which now rapidly spread from Morocco to India. It left no room for the loving person-to-person encounter between God and man, which makes the expressions of early Islamic piety so touching.

But it would be wrong to see the whole history of Islamdom after 1258 under the sign of decline; on the contrary, the most successful Islamic empires emerged around 1500 to prosper for another two centuries: they are the Safavid state in Iran where the Twelver Shia was introduced by the founder, Ismail I, in 1501; the Ottoman Empire which soon extended its borders to Austria as it comprised, from 1517 onward, also the Holy Cities of Mecca and Medina; and the Moghul Empire in India, surpassing the two others in cultural activities and splendor. A new period of decline sets in around 1700. That is particularly true for India, where after Aurangzeb's death in 1707 the vast empire fell to pieces. The weakness of the Moghul rulers in Delhi and their viceregents elsewhere, especially in Bengal, allowed the British East India Company an easy access to the treasures of the Subcontinent.

It has to be remembered that the situation of the Indian Muslims has been peculiar ever since the first invasion of Muhammad ibn al-Qāsim in 711 to Sind, when the lower Indus valley - the southern part of present Pakistan - fell under Muslim control. Sind remained a relais for the introduction of Indian science to Baghdad, but became also the seat of the heterodox Carmathian movement whose presence made itself felt in India throughout the centuries. When Mahmūd of Ghazna conquered large parts of Northwest India in the two decades after the year 1000, Muslim presence, and with it Persian culture, became an integral part of life in the area between the Khyber Pass and Lahore; it soon extended to Delhi and into Bengal and Rajasthan, and in the mid-fourteenth century Muslim kingdoms in the Deccan developed an interesting culture of their own. Not to forget the Arab settlements in South India, particularly in the coastal areas of Malabar, where the traveler Ibn Battuta found flourishing Islamic schools in the 1330's.

The Indian Muslims were always confronted with the problem where they actually belonged. Were they part of Indian culture, and was India part of the Muslim empire? Many would answer this last question in the affirmative, but the majority, at least among the upper classes, felt rather as parts of the Arabo-Persian Islamic homeland: the role of the *ashrāf*, the nobles of non-Indian origin, who constituted the real aristocracy, in Indian Islam, points to this truth. Baranī in his highly revealing chronicle clearly points out that the neo-Muslims of Indian origin are inferior to the Turks, the ruling military aristocracy who came mainly from Central Asia and had indeed played the dominant role in the first three centuries after Mahmūd Ghaznawi's campaigns to Baranī's own time in the mid-fourteenth century. Not in vain has the word 'Turk' become an equivalent of 'Muslim' in many Indian idioms. Likewise the veneration shown to the *sayyids*, the descendants of the Prophet through his daughter Fatima, was in India greater than in any other country. The feeling of being part and parcel of the Arab-Muslim nation permeated the life of many Indian Muslims, and it is no accident that in the numerous eulogies written for the Prophet of Islam first in Persian, then in Urdu, Sindhi, Panjabi, and Pashto, the epithets $^c arabī$, *makkī*, *madanī* are used much more frequently for the Prophet than is the case in other languages. Qudsī Mashhadī's $na^c t$ from the seventeenth century is a good example of this style, as is the remark of the great reformer, Shāh Walīullāh, one century later, when he sighs that the Muslims are "fallen in exile" in India, and demands that Arabic culture and customs should be introduced wherever Muslims live. At the same time, however, another great scholar of central India, Azād Bilgrāmī, tried to show, in his *Subhat al-marjān*, that India is the true home of prophecy, and underlines the close relation between Arabic and Indian culture and poetry.

One may even see the conflict between the two sons of Shāhjahān under this aspect: Dārā Shikōh, the heir apparent, followed his great-grandfather Akbar's inclination to appreciate Indian culture and try to make "the two oceans meet" because he, like many other mystics, sensed the affinity of *waḥdat al-wujūd* and Indian *advaita*. A Persian translation of the Upanishads was meant to serve this purpose, for Dārā Shikōh regarded the Upanishads as the "book that is hidden" as mentioned in the Koran (Sura 68:52). Against this mystic attitude, which was also reflected by the fact that quite a few Indian Sufis had used Hindi for their ecstatic love songs, the law-abiding members of the Muslim society always dwelt upon their loyalty to the Arabic heritage as manifested in the Arabian Prophet so that a constant dichotomy of mystical-Indian and orthodox-Arabo-centered religion is visible in medieval India.

This situation became even more complicated with the British presence in the Subcontinent which began to take shape after the battle of Plassey in 1757. Delhi, still the seat of the Moghul emperor, had been plundered by the Persians under Nādir Shah and by many other invaders, Muslims be they or non-Muslims. Even the troops of Ahmad Shāh Abdālī, called into India by the Delhi nobility and Shāh Walīullāh in the hope of defeating the Marathas, did not refrain from plundering the country and brought certainly no relief to the poverty-stricken population. The British used the confusion to expand their power over the various successor states of the Moghul Empire and over Delhi, where the last Moghul emperors were not more than puppets in their hands.

This change can be sensed in the poetical language as well: formerly the glorious Turk was confronted with the lowly, yet attractive Hindu; from around 1600 the poets prefer to speak of the *qaid-i firang*, the Frankish, i.e., European, prison. This expression goes back to the experience of the Portuguese harrassment of Indian ports, but carries with it also the remembrance of colorful pictures as brought by the European envoys to India. Thus, the expression *qaid-i firang* was not absolutely negative - it was a colorful, charming prison in which the poor Muslim had fallen, and it thus reflects the feeling of being confronted with something which is both an opponent and a model of elegance and sophistication. This attitude prevails almost to our day, for the European world was so glittering and attractive and yet so dangerous for the inherited culture that the choice between complete negation of any Western values and the wholesale acceptance of the new, superior technical models was sometimes not easy.

The situation changed to the worse after the abortive attempt of Indian soldiers to rebel against the British and enthrone the old Moghul emperor Bahadur Shah Zafar as real, not puppet ruler (1857). It resulted, however, in the complete takeover by the British Crown. The social changes which had set in about half a century earlier due to the introduction of British law courts and, in 1835, the scheme for a replacement of Persian as official language by English, had affected the Muslims much more than the Hindus. The new taxation system destroyed many of the large endowments out of which educational institutions had been paid, and the British school system, largely run by missionaries, was not acceptable to traditionalist Muslims. The revolution of 1857 broke the established order almost completely, and only a comparatively small number of Muslims decided to cooperate with the new rulers in order to survive and to secure the survival of their coreligionists. In fact, the situation all over the Muslim world was similar: the political and cultural influence of England and France increased from Northwest Africa to the Arab countries, and therefore everwhere movements sprang up which tried to defend the Islamic ideals. They usually looked up to the Prophet Muhammad as the model of a political leader, and were inspired by his victories over the numerically stronger Meccans.

The first *tarīqa Muhammadiyya*, the "Muhammadan Path," in India was founded in 1734 in Delhi and became very active in the first half of the nineteenth century, fighting first the Sikhs, then the British. Similar mystico-political orders were the Tījāniyya and Sanūsiyya in North Africa, who fought against French and Italian colonial powers. The danger that the Western powers might take over the Muslim world not only politically but culturally and spiritually was felt by many pious; it was articulated in particular by Jamāluddīn Afghānī, who dreamt of a political revival, a pan-Islamic orientation of the Muslim world. He influenced Arab modernists as well as the Ottoman Sultan ᶜAbdul Hamīd II, who cherished dreams of becoming the caliph of an all-embracing Islamic nation. Afgjhānī coined the comfortable phrase of the "spiritual East" and the "material West", which became commonplace with the reformers in the following decades, and is still in use. This contrast was, however, not invented by him but goes back at least to the medieval mystical thinker Suhrawardī Maqtūl, the founder of the *ishrāqī*, illuminist, school; (executed in 1191). He saw the human soul imprisoned in the "Western exile" and taught her to travel East, to the spiritual Yemen.

Contrary to those who advocated a strictly anti-Western attitude, a few reformers, especially in India, understood that the Muslims would be doomed to complete cultural extinction if they did not participate in modern education. It was Sir Sayyid Ahmad Khān who finally succeeded, against the fierce opposition of the orthodox, in founding the Anglo-Muslim College at Aligarh "to preach the gospel of free enquiry, of large-hearted tolerance, and pure morality." He was sure that the work of God as visible in nature could not contradict the word of God as revealed in the Koran (remarkably, the words "work of God" and "word of God" are given in English in the Urdu text!). He took up, therefore, the old Islamic maxim attributed to the Prophet: "Seek knowledge even in China." Why then not in Europe? After all, the Muslims had brought their scholarly achievements to Europe during the Middle Ages, and it was thanks to them that Western philosophers, physicians, and scientists came to know the wisdom which the Muslims had translated from Greek and Syriac but enriched with their own practical knowledge - thus, to take back Western science meant only to take the interest on the scholarly capital which Islam once had given to Europe. To be sure, many of the traditional ulema could not share this view, for $^c ilm$, knowledge, was the knowledge that served to prepare man for the Otherworld, and should not be applied to this life or used for "practical" purposes. (That was one of the reasons why a modern high school, founded in the Arcot area around 1850, soon had to be closed: the leading theologians did not see why one should study to gain one's livelihood.) Such thoughts may have also been on the minds of some of Sir Sayyid's opponents. Besides they declared him, the layman who arrogated to himself the power of interpreting Prophetic traditions, "an instrument of the devil" and even more. However, Sir Sayyid and his collaborators insisted that Islam is not against progress but is compatible with every modern way of life. (That he still advocated purdah for women is one of the inconsistencies which reformers sometimes overlook.) Sir Sayyid's contemporary, Syed Ameer Ali, went even farther than he in his book *The Life of Muhammad or the Spirit of Islam*, which found a wide echo in English speaking circles in India and Europe. He proved that Islam itself *is* progress.

The orthodox schools, though fighting among themselves, attacked the reformers heavily; the *Ahl-i hadīth* spoke about the *fitan*, the disturbances which usher in the Last Judgment, when looking at Sir Sayyid's work. Even more antagonistic were the members of the theological school of Deoband, an institution founded by members of the Shāh Walīullāh school and the Chishtī Sābirī order. They reverted to strict fundamentalism and neglected the "mystical" tradition largely. Sir Sayyid, too, coming from a background where Naqshbandi tendencies were dominant, tried to divest Islam of the all too many mystico-magical and legendary accretions. This in turn led his adversaries to claim that he was a *nēcharī*, "naturalist".

Among the *fitan* mentioned by the *ahl-i hadīth* were also the followers of Mirzā Ghulām Ahmad, whose claims to have some mysterious "prophetic" qualities or to be the *mahdi* caused from the very beginning in the 1890's a wide literary controversy in Urdu and Panjabi. The Ahmadiyya, growing out of a pious, almost ascetic movement, became the main protagonists of Islam in the West and are noted for their untiring missionary activities; the tension between them and the orthodox brought about the first major religious crisis in Pakistan in 1953, and they were finally declared an un-Islamic minority in 1975, despite the services they had rendered to the propagation of Islam in Europe and Africa.

In the colorful picture of Muslim movements towards the end of the nineteenth century some small communities played a particularly important role. Badruddin Tyabjee from the numerically insignificant Sulaimani Bohora group rose to prominence as the first Muslim president of the All India National Congress (founded in 1885), and his family in Bombay was in the forefront of modernization. Likewise, the leader of the other Ismaili group, the Nizārī Khojas, the Aga Khan, succeeded in changing his community into a modern society. The Aga Khan reached India from Iran in 1838, and Aga Khan IV, born in 1877, became one of the outstanding political leaders of the Indian Muslims, but also the ingenious reformer of the Ismailis in Africa.

The problems of Muslim society during that age of spiritual restlessness are reflected in literature as well: the novels of Deputy Nazīr Ahmad show life in middle class homes of Indian Muslims, instead of imitating the traditional fairy tales which continued almost without end and were colored by the constant interference of jinns, fairies, or dervishes. Nazīr Ahmad tried to educate the Muslim woman whom he wanted to be industrious and literate; he criticized polygamy and its evil effects, but also too much leniency toward the British. In Mirzā Qalīch Beg's Sindhi novel *Zīnat* (1892) the heroine even discards the veil and struggles her way through life, at least for some time - an attitude which in notoriously backward areas like Sind was unusually progressive.

Even more than in these novels the new attitude to life is palpable in a poem which a friend of Sir Sayyid published in 1879: it is Hālī's *Ebb and Flood of Islam*, briefly called after its verse form the *Musaddas*, "six-lined stanzas." The *musaddas* form was generally used for the long epical descriptions of the battle of Kerbela by Shia Muslims, mainly in Lucknow, and had thus become a form connected with spiritual, elevating contents. Hālī describes in his poem the greatness of Islam in the days of yore, contrasting it with the present miserable state of the Islamic peoples. From this time onward the romantic glorification of the past remained a standard topic used by all reformers - the love of the Arabs of Andalus, which shows itself in the numerous novels in Urdu, written under the stylistic spell of Sir Walter Scott, and which culminates in Iqbal's programmatic poem *Masjid-i Qurtuba*, is typical of this attitude. Hālī's conclusion is: if Islam is followed *in toto*, people achieve happiness, if not, they decline. Here he stands in the same line with the Egyptian reformers Muhammad ᶜAbduh and Muhammad Rashīd Ridā; and the same argumentation was continued in both form and content by Iqbal in his *Shikwāh* and *Jawāb-i shikwāh* and is today as widespread as it was a century ago.

Iqbal, whose work we just mentioned, is perhaps the most fascinating thinker-poet of the Indo-Muslim, probably even of the whole Muslim world, in the period of critical change. He was born on November 9, 1877, a few days after the Aga Khan; he is thus a contemporary of Teilhard de Chardin, Martin Buber and Sri Aurobindo, with whose philosophical thought his own way of thinking has much in common. After studies in his native place, Sialkot in the northern Panjab, Iqbal studied in Lahore; the great British orientatist Sir Thomas Arnold encouraged him to go to Europe. Study of law and Hegelian philosophy in Cambridge and a short stay in Germany, where he obtained his Dr. Phil. in Munich, followed. In 1908 the scholar, already known as a fine poet in Urdu, returned to Lahore. While mainly practicing law, during the rest of his life Iqbal's true ideal was to disseminate the new ideas which he had developed after his encounter with Western civilisation. In 1915 he published, in Persian verse, his *Asrār-i Khūdī*, "Secrets of the Self", in which the traditional mystical ideas of man dissolving in the ocean of God like a tiny drop were condemned, and man instead was called to develop his self to the utmost possibilities. The influence of Hegel and Ibn ᶜArabī is discarded. Now, Nietzsche, Bergson, and Goethe are Iqbal's mentors, and his spiritual guide is Maulānā Rūmī.

The duties of the ideal man in the ideal Islamic society are discussed, two years later, in the Persian *mathnawī Rumūz-i bēkhūdī*, "Mysteries of Selflessness." Then follows *Payām-i Mashriq*, Iqbal's Persian answer to Goethe's *West-Östlicher Divan*. The collection of his Urdu poetry which was published next has the revealing title *Bāng-i darā*, "The Call of the Caravan-bell," for Iqbal saw himself, as he says at the end of the famous "Indian Song," as the bell of the caravan that leads the Muslims back to the central sanctuary in Mecca. Arabic Islam, unmixed and strong, is contrasted, as in the medieval Indian tradition, with Persian, mystical, hence unhealthy trends in Islam. Despite such verdicts, Iqbal's next work is the *Zabūr-i ᶜAjam*, "Persian Psalms," which contains some of his finest and most daring prayer poems. To it is appended a modern version of the *Gulshan-i rāz*, the "Rose Garden of Mystery," in which Iqbal answers the questions discussed by the medieval Sufi Shabistarī in his own style.

A year after this work was published, Iqbal gave his "Six Lectures on the Reconstruction of Religious Thought in Islam" in various universities of the Subcontinent. The book, to which a seventh chapter was later added, discusses his main ideas of human development and religious experience in a terminology heavily indebted to European, particularly German, philosophy. In 1930, presiding over the annual meeting of the All India Muslim League (a body founded in 1906 to secure the political rights of the Muslims) Iqbal expressed the hope that a Muslim state in the majority provinces of northwestern India should be formed to maintain and guarantee the integrity of Muslim life. This was the nucleus of Pakistan. Iqbal and his followers, including Quaid-i Aᶜzam M.A. Jinnah, who began to work for the Pakistan idea after his return from England in 1936, could not envisage how partition would be achieved, nor did they think of a strained relationship with India. On the contrary, Iqbal's statements stress the role of such a Muslim state for the protection of India's political interests.

Two years later, Iqbal's *magnum opus* appeared. This is the *Jāvīd-nāma*, a journey through the spheres, in which the poet, following Dante's example, discusses burning political and theological issues with the inhabitants of the various spheres, guided by Maulānā Rūmī. After participating twice in the Round Table Conference in London, Iqbal visited France (Bergson and Massignon), Spain, and Italy (where he met Mussolini) as well as Jerusalem. He was also invited to Afghanistan to consult about the foundation of Kabul University. Then, he began to ail, but in 1936 his most mature Urdu poems appeared as *Bāl-i Jibrīl*, "Gabriel's Wing," and one year later another Urdu anthology with poems pertaining to political and social problems was published as *Zarb-i Kalīm*, "The Stroke of Moses." After Iqbal's death on April 21, 1938, his collection of shorter poems in Persian and Urdu was published as *Armaghān-i Hijāz*, "Gift of the Hijaz," a title which expressed his unfulfilled hope to visit the holy places in Arabia which he had extolled as the true centers of Islamic spiritual life.

Iqbal's work is a perfect mirror of the various shades of Indian Islam, and at the same time shows how an intelligent modern Muslim is able to combine (even sometimes in quite unexpected ways) the Islamic and the modern Western philosophical tradition. As he turned away from his inherited mystical attitude, tinged by the centuries-old impact of Ibn^{c}Arabī's *waḥdat al-wujūd* on the poetry of the Subcontinent, he gave up his neo-Hegelian way of thinking, which he had acquired at Cambridge. From Ibn^{c}Arabī he turned to Maulānā Jalāluddīn Rumi, in whose work he discovered once more the dynamic principle of love. He interpreted Rumi, correctly, without the use of the numerous traditional commentaries which had shrouded his message in a web of Ibn ^{c}Arabi's thoughts and terminology. At the same time Iqbal discovered the vitalists, in whose philosophy he saw a similar, positive approach to life. The discussion about Nietzsche's "evil" influence on Iqbal has never ceased, but very often has missed the point. For Iqbal's ideal of the *mard-i mōmin*, the true believer, as it is developed from the *Asrār* onward, is only superficially influenced by Nietzsche's Superman and related concepts of the late nineteenth century. For while Nietzsche's Superman will appear only after "God is dead", Iqbal's ideal man is the one who is closest to God and has reached perfect unity of his will with God's will; he is the true *khalīfa*, God's vicegerent (Sura 2:29), as well as $^c abduhu$ (Sura 17:1), God's most perfect servant. Besides, Iqbal's criticism of Nietzsche's position should not be overlooked. Iqbal saw that man in traditional Islam had become a victim of all too many ritual prescriptions which left no moment of life free. Man was part of a closed system which was, or at least seemed to be, ruled by inscrutable predestination. On the other hand Iqbal discovered the danger inherent in the "pantheistic" system, which did not allow a true personal relation between man and God and was all-inclusive, hence did not leave room for an active ethical system. Iqbal rediscovered in the Koran the Adam's role who is called to be God's *khalīfa* and to ameliorate the earth until he is called to account for his actions on Doomsday to his Creator, Sustainer, and Judge. In Iqbal's *mard-i mōmin* one can also discover traces of the Islamic notion of the *insān-i Kāmil*, the Perfect Man, as developed by Ibn^{c}Arabī and Jīlī, in whose works the Prophet is the Perfect Man who reflects the fullness of the Divine Names.

But even more the Faustian ideal seems to have shaped Iqbal's concept of man. Goethe was his model in the Western world, as was Rūmī in Islam, and he made these two poet-thinkers meet in a famous poem in the *Payām-i Mashriq* where both, each endowed "with a book without being a Prophet," stress the predominance of Love over intellect. It was from Goethe that Iqbal learned the idea of constant striving as the true way to salvation:

> Wer immer strebend sich bemüht,
> den können wir erlösen –

that could be said of Iqbal's ideal man as well. Like Faust, the *mard-i mōmin* will never rest and never ask the fleeting moment to linger on: once he stops on his upward way, be it even to enjoy the perfect beauty of a view, he has lost himself to Satan, because, as Iqbal knows from the mystics of Islam (Ghazzālī, ᶜAttār, Rūmī), the road is endless, and once "the journey to God is finished the journey in God begins" (ᶜAttār), while to stop means to descend. This constant movement never ends, not even after death; here too infinite depths of Divine life open before man, provided he has been strong enough to meet death not as an enemy but as a friend, and has strengthened his personality to overcome the momentous shock of death. Parallels to Iqbal's hope for a dynamic afterlife are found in Goethe, as well as in Heinrich Scholz's and particularly Tor Andrae's ideas.

Goethean is also the role Iqbal allots to Satan. As becomes evident from the *Jāvīdnāma* he was well aware of Hallāj's role in the development of Islamic satanology. According to him, Iblīs's refusal to prostrate himself before Adam is a sign of his overstressed monotheism, which does not allow him to bow before anything but God himself. This Iblisian *tauḥīd*, which however neglects the Divine spark in Adam, has been extolled by various mystics from Ahmad Ghazzālī to Sarmad and Shāh ᶜAbdul Latīf in India. For Iqbal, whose satanology is highly complex, Iblis is not evil in himself, rather, he is the necessary partner of man whom he lures away from the peaceful meadows of Paradise, to teach him the joy of constant struggle. It is through Ahriman's blood that the world becomes colorful (*Jāvīdnāma*). Iblis has no absolute power over man. On the contrary, he longs to be subdued by the true *mard-i mōmin* and will then perform the prostration which he had refused before the immature Adam. Iqbal's Iblis often reminds us of Goethe's description in the "Prologue in Heaven" in *Faust*:

> Des Menschen Tätigkeit kann allzuleicht erschlaffen,
> Er liebt sich bald die unbedingte Ruh;
> Drum geb ich gern ihm den Gesellen zu,
> Der reizt und wirkt und muss als Teufel schaffen.

When Iqbal tried to revive Islam he, like every Muslim, looked in the first place to the Koran. Interpretation of the Koran has always shown the spiritual climate of a certain age. It is understandable that, in a time of political and social changes, the Muslim commentators turned mainly to the ethical contents of the Koran. Others tried to interpret away everything connected with mythological or "non-scientific" statements and thus explained the jinn as microbes, or, more logically, as wild tribes outside the civilized area. Or they were able to detect allusions to electricity and even the A-bomb in the words of the Holy Book. Rarely, as in the case of the Egyptian Khalafullāh, the literary art of the Koran was underlined, an attempt which was sharply rebuked by the authorities of al-Azhar. Very few modernists turned to abstract theological notions, such as the definition of God, and speculations about the eschatological parts of the Koran were generally avoided, or demythologized.

Iqbal once more stresses the personal character of the Koranic God: he is not conceived in philosophical and mystical terms as First Essence or $wājib\ al-wujūd$, the Necessarily Existent. Here again, Iqbal stands in the line of the eighteenth-century reformers in Delhi, who disliked the fact that God was circumscribed by expressions not found in the Koran, where the fullness of His ninety-nine names had been revealed. For Iqbal, God is a super-ego which comprises all the smaller egos of which the cosmos consists. They are part of Him and yet distinct from Him. Friedrich von Hügel's statement comes to mind:

> Indeed we can safely hold with Lotze not only that Personality is compatible with Infinitude, but that the personality of all finite beings can be shown to be imperfect precisely because of the finitude, and hence the "Perfect Personality" is compatible only with the conception of an Infinite Being; finite beings can only achieve an approximation of it.

More relevant for the modern world is the question whether the Koran, being the uncreated Divine word, rules the times or should be interpreted according to the exigencies of time. Iqbal, who devotes a fine chapter in *Jāvīdnāma* to the "World of the Koran" which unfolds afresh every day, would probably have agreed with the interpretation given some time after his death, by the Moroccan thinker Muhammad ᶜAzīz Lahbabī, that not the text in itself is the revelation but what the believer discovers every time afresh when reading the Koran. This idea is basically a Sufi one. It stresses the dynamic quality of the Koran: To read it means to listen to God himself who guides man on the right path. Therefore hundreds of interpretations of a single verse are possible according to the understanding of the reader.

While Iqbal maintains, of course, the position of the Koran as the infallible source of Islamic life, he also discusses problems of prophetology. In the course of time, Muhammad had been surrounded by a wonderful veil of legends, mythical concepts, and loving epithets, and he, who wanted to be nothing but "a slave to whom was revealed," became not only the infallible intercessor at Doomsday, and God's most beloved creature, but assumed the role of the Perfect Man, the meeting point of God and His creation, the primordial essence of light. The poets sang of his miraculous birth and never tired of describing his ascension to heaven; but his historical personality was more or less forgotten. To be sure, the Delhi reformers, as orthodox theologians in general, underlined his political role as founder of a successful community, which proves that he is the God-sent messenger who brings the final revelation to humanity. In the nineteenth-century the accents were shifted - as in Christianity the faith in the mythical Christ was replaced, in some currents, by a growing interest in *Leben-Jesu-Forschung*. Thus the Muslims, defending their Prophet against the unjust attacks of orientalists and missionaries, once more turned to a historical study of his life. The biographies, which appeared in great number from the late nineteenth-century onward, showed not only his political success and his role as a social reformer but highlighted personal virtues such as his kindness and mildness. In the course of time he became the model of all modern achievements, so that Nasser went so far as to call him "the imam of socialism."

Iqbal too discussed the role of the Prophet and very ingeniously contrasted the prophet who returns to the world after having spoken to God without veil, with the mystic who refuses to return from the Divine Presence. He takes up an old Sufi idea, for Sufism had always distinguished between "prophetic sobriety" and "mystical intoxication." The prophet will implement in this world the experiences of his meeting with God, creating an ideal society, while the mystic prefers to live in his dreamy intoxication. Iqbal stands here fully in the Naqshbandi tradition, but at the same time applies to Islam the differentiation of "prophetic" and "mystical" piety, as analyzed in the West by Söderblom and Heiler (of whose work he was not aware). A particularly interesting aspect of Iqbal's prophetology is the discussion of Muhammad's role as the *khātam alanbiyā*, the Seal of Prophets, after whom no other prophet will come to earth because he has completed the Divine revelation. Iqbal speaks here of the birth of inductive intellect, which now does not need any more prophetic instructions - formulations which could lead to dangerous consequences, as becomes clear from the works of modern Indian Marxists. In his poetry, however, Iqbal achieves once more a wonderful blending of all aspects of the Prophet Muhammad, whom he extols in ever new classical and modern formulations.

Iqbal, of course, also turned to the Five Pillars of Islam. Here prayer occupies the largest part of his work. Few poets have written more beautiful but also more daring prayer poems than he. Like the classical mystics, particularly Rūmī, he was aware that the soul can live only in the constant alternation of prayer and activity, called by him *khalwa* and *jilwa*. Again, the "prophetic" character of his piety becomes evident. Besides stressing the role of prayer as an act in which the lonely human soul all of a sudden discovers its place in the Divine Life, Iqbal also dwelt upon the social character of ritual prayer and spoke of the enormous social change which would take place if the proud South Indian brahmin were to stand shoulder to shoulder with the untouchable during the service. Prayer is much more than a personal experience. It is an expression of the unity of mankind who all turn to the same center of worship, Mecca, and recite the same sacred words.

Strangely enough, Iqbal has never theoretically discussed the pilgrimage, so important for the formation of the Muslim community. Mecca was and is not only the center of religious life but also a place where much spiritual exchange between Muslims from all over the world took place, so that many revivalist movements started from Mecca and Medina. One could interpret parts of Iqbal's work as a symbolization of the constant spiritual pilgrimage of the believers to Mecca, where he, "the bell of the caravan," guides the straying modern Muslims, leading them away from the glittering beauty of the "Frankish prison" and the sweet scents of Persian gardens. But a theoretical formulation of these ideals is lacking.

Fasting and *zakāt*, alms-tax, are also mentioned but briefly in his work. He certainly does not go as far as some modernists who interpret hard industrial work as "*jihād* against hunger" which allows man to be exempt from fasting (thus in Tunisia). The alms-tax is seen by him as by many modernists as a perfect state budget and a weapon against both communism and capitalism.

Iqbal's political ideas are expressed mainly in the *Rumūz-i bēkhūdī* but he touches upon them in the Lectures and expresses them more clearly, though often in bitter words, in *Zarb-i Kalīm*. They permeate his whole work even though he is not consistent in his views. Wilfred Cantwell Smith has therefore devoted to him two chapters of *Islam in Modern India*: "Iqbal the Progressive" and "Iqbal the Reactionary." This is correct. Iqbal did not want secularization but doubtlesssly modernization; he wrote a beautiful poem on "Lenin in the Presence of God" and defended the working class against the capitalists. But he was strongly anti-Marxist. He spoke against the return to pre-Islamic ideals which became fashionable in the 1920's in the Middle East, Thus he attacked Iran and Turkey. But his attitude toward the Turkish experiment with secularization was at times very positive, as when he accepted the Grand National Assembly as a legitimate law-giving body replacing the caliph. One wonders whether this was his belated answer to the *khilāfat* movement in India, in which he had not participated. Iqbal saw the danger of the "Pharaonic" and "Tammuzi" movements in Egypt and Iraq respectively, and the triumphant song of the old deities in *Jāvīdnāma*, who extol the orientalists who have dug them out of their tombs, seems, in a nutshell, to foreshadow Edward Said's criticism of "orientalism" as a destructive Western invention.

With all his interest in politics, Iqbal was not a practical politician. He never gave a solution to the problems of the ideal form of an Islamic state. Nationalism was condemned as something satanic. The Muslim owes loyalty to God, not to thrones. He knew well that liberalism could be positive, and was needed, but was aware that liberalism has a tendency to act as a force of disintegration because it does not develop systems in which the believers feel secure. Kenneth Cragg's remark that "serious Islam" is found in the disciples of Maudūdī and Hasan al-Bannā points to the same truth, for the motto of the Muslim Brethren is "Islam is faith and dogma, fatherland and nation, religion and state, spirituality and activity, Koran and sword" - words which could be a quotation from an Iqbalian poem. As much as he was in favor of a dynamic movement in Islam, he believed that it would be dangerous to give up the inherited forms in the present difficult time of transition.

To solve all these problems, as Ilse Lichtenstadter says, Iqbal, like Ghazzālī took "refuge in a quasi-Sufi religion of the heart." The very title of his Lectures, "Reconstruction of Religious Thought in Islam," recalls the title of Ghazzālī's main work, the *Ihyā' ᶜulūm ad-dīn*, "The Revitalization of the Sciences of Religion." As much as Iqbal attacked what he called "Pirism", i.e., the sway which the mystical leaders held over the large masses of their generally illiterate, poor followers, yet he knew of the values of spiritual education and was in contact with the Nizami Dargah in Delhi. And as much as he condemned traditional Sufi poetry, as more dangerous for the spirital health of the Muslims than the hordes of Jingiz Khan and Attila, he was very close to pre-Ibn^{c}Arabī Sufism. Hallāj appears in the *Jāvīdnāma* as a kind of forerunner of the poet himself, as someone who has called spiritually dead people to resurrection and was therefore killed by the establishment. Rūmī's influence is even more tangible than that of other mystics in all of Iqbal's works after 1912. The predominance of love over law was one of the centers of early Sufi life, as was the teaching "Qualify yourselves with the qualities of God." It is one of Iqbal's great contributions to Muslim thought that he rediscovered the dynamic aspects of Rūmī's work, which provided him with ever new answers to his religious questions and guided him in his quest for the Man of God.

Iqbal is as contradictory as modern Islam itself. For even though the forms of behaviour have been modelled according to the example of the Prophet and thus are similar in every nook and corner of the Islamic world, Islam is anything but monolithic. It goes without saying that the confrontation of a world religion, which claims to bring the final revelation to mankind, with the plethora of modern influences, which are both dangerous and fascinating, expresses itself in various shades of reaction. Most of the reformers in the Muslim world were not certain how to answer this challenge. They could use neither the classical Arabic of theology nor modern Western languages, to convey their interpretation of Islam in meaningful words which were acceptable to both elite and masses. Iqbal was lucky in this respect. Being a poet, he could express his message in the poetical imagery of Persian and Urdu, which was well known all over the subcontinent. One of his major contributions to modernization is the way he filled traditional symbols with new content. The most important bird in his cosmos is no longer the complaining nightingale but the lonely, strong falcon (a soul bird which Rūmī had loved very much). The rose of the nicely trimmed garden is not his favorite flower but rather the red tulip, in traditional verse often connected with the bloodstained shroud of the martyrs or with the flame on Mt. Sinai. For Iqbal, the lonely desert tulip is the symbol of man who lives on his own resources in the wilderness and radiates the message of strength and loving activity in the world. Iqbal changes the role of Farhād, the cheated lover of Princess Shīrīn, into that of the worker who is cheated by the capitalists, and in translating freely into Persian verse Goethe's poem "Mahomets Gesang" he revives the classical mystical image of the powerful stream, as representation of the Prophet and his activity. For this reason the poet himself assumed the nom-de-plume *Zindarūd*, "Living Stream," thus pointing to his relation with the living stream of Prophetic tradition.

There are dozens of ways to interpret Iqbal, as became very clear during the symposia held in Delhi, Lahore, and other cities remembering his hundredth birthday in 1977. From the "superb artist" to "ardent communist," from "strictly orthodox Muslim" to "advocate of social justice" - Iqbal was everything. And every interpreter had at least a few verses to defend his or her viewpoint.

In my view, Iqbal's most interesting and probably most lasting aspect is his rediscovery of dynamism in Islam. He tried to show once more that Islam as taught by the Koran and implemented by the Prophet is a powerful, dynamic religion, capable of new developments. The hope of some orientalists that Islam might find a new course by "going back to the Greeks" is exactly the contrary of Iqbal's ideals, for according to him it was the Hellenistic heritage which had destroyed the strength of Islam even as it had tinged Christianity. It is out of this attitude that he, like most modernists, has always repeated one Koranic word which is valid for the whole Islamic world even today: "Verily God will not change the state of a people until they change their own state" (Sura 13:12).

SHADES OF SHIʿISM IN THE TRACTS OF THE BRETHREN OF PURITY*

Abbas Hamdani

The celebrated medievel Ilamic encyclopaedia, the *Rasāʾil Ikhwān al-Safāʾ* has lent itself to several contradictory theories regarding its religious persuasion and its authorship because of the eclectic nature of its views and the anonymity of its authors. It is now generally accepted to be an Ismāʿīlī work[1] although its attribution to Sunnī, Muʿtazilī, Sūfī or Shīʿī schools or to various combinations of these schools continue to be made and defended. There is fragmentary internal evidence for each of these points of view. What is needed, however, is the positioning of one set of such evidence against the other and evaluating the general direction of the *Rasāʾil's* ideas. I would like to concentrate here on what the authors of the *Rasāʾil* say themselves, rather than on what others have said about them.[2]

First of all, I would like to state references that would indicate Sunnī authorship. At one place there is a praiseworthy reference to al-Siddīq, al-Fārūq and Dhuʾl-urayn (IV,269) no doubt speaking of Abū Bakr, ʿUmar and Uthmān. There is an attempt by a late Ismāʿīlī writer to explain it away.[3] On the other hand it might denote a Zaydī shīʿite respect for the first three Caliphs, but as we shall see later, the Zaydī connection of the *Rasāʾil* is contradicted by the *Rasāʾil's* insistence on the esoteric interpretation of the Qurʾān. At another place a hadīth is related on the authority of ʿĀyisha (I,358) which no shīʿī would ever do, unless the introduction of ʿĀyisha's name is an editorial interpolation. Such a doubt is raised by the fact that a report of ʿAlī in the printed text (II,59) is attributed to ʿUmar in one of the manuscripts of the

Rasāʾil.[4] At two places (III,489 and IV,408) there are references to *al-Khulafāʾ al-rāshidūn*, unless the term *al-Rāshidūn* is not intended to refer to the first four Caliphs. Further on there is a passage that denounces, among other religious polemicists, the *Rawāfid* (III,161) which clearly indicates the non-Zaydsī Shīʿa in the terminology of the Sunnī or Zaydī writers. In another article under preparation[5] I have, however, considered this passage as a definite interpolation, on the ground that all the groups criticized and excluded (the Nawāsib, Rawāfid, Jabariyya, Qadariyya, Khawārij and al-Ashāʿira) indicate only one persuasion of the authors namely a Hanbalī traditionalist. This certainly cannot be because of a generally liberal and eclectic thrust of the *Rasāʾil* which we shall presently consider. Two sections on *Ahl al-wajd* (I,240) and another on love entitled *fī māhiyyat al-ʿishq* (III,269-286) are replete with Sūfī terminology. When describing an ideal person, he is referred to as *al-sūfī al-sīra* (II,376) although this is only one of the many attributes. Sayyid Husayn Nasr would, however, consider this to be a Shīʿī Sūfī instead of a Sunnī Sūfī tendency,[6] agreeing with A.L. Tībawī who says "The Ikhwān al-Safāʾ may be taken as symbolizing the Shīʿa attempt, while al-Ghazzālī represents the Sunnī attempt at a synthesis."[7] Susanne Diwald on the other hand would consider the *Rasāʾil* just Sūfī, not Shīʿī, thus implying its Sunnī character.[8] In fact Louis Massignon had pointed out a long time before that an early author Ibn Sabʿīn (d. 669/1270) had considered al-Ghazzālī's (d. 505/1111) ideas derived "mostly from the *Rasāʾil Ikhwān as-Safā*, weak in philosophy like its source"[9] thus emphasizing the *Rasāʾil's* Sunnī Sūfī orientation. Tibawi points out a statement in the *Rasāʾil* to the effect that if an ideal Imām dies and does not leave behind a successor like him, then the community can still continue to be ruled by a consensus (Raʾy Wāhid) because the Reason is the Chief (Al-ʿAql Raʾīsun) (IV,125-126 and 137). Tibawī thinks this is a Sunnī philosophic view that rejects the Shīʿī belief in the continuous hereditary succession of the Imāms.[10] One can point out a Zaydī Shīʿī alternative but I will not press this point, because of evidence contrary to Zaydism mentioned below.

A section in *Al-Risālat al-Jāmiʿa* (p.468) compares the community of believers to a shooting star with a tail of brightness. Its leaders appear "one after another in time after time." Such a position would be contrary to Zaydī acceptance of interrupted Imāmate or of two Imāms at the same time at different places.

This is all the evidence that is advanced to indicate a Sunnī, Sūfī or Zaydī content of the *Rasāʾil* and it is not sufficient to conclusively assign the encyclopaedia to Sunnī, Sūfī or Zaydī authorship. Moreover, what is there is not unequivocal and can be and has been interpreted otherwise. The preponderance of non-Zaydī Shīʿite material, as will be described presently, disproves the Sunnī or Zaydī theory. Yet I would accept a part of it. It is quite possible that the Brethren of Purity had one or two Sunnī fellow-travellers among them dedicated to the overthrow of the ʿAbbāsid state and in the process to not minding the establishment of a Fāṭimid Shīʿite State as long as it was liberal and tolerant. The Shīʿī Brethren's eclectic and interconfessional stand helped these Sunnī collaborators to form a united front with the former for the common opposition to the ʿAbbāsid Caliphate which in the third centruy of Islam was passing through a social malaise and had already generated many kinds of opposition movements both Shīʿite and non-Shīʿite. The inclusion in the *Rasāʾil* therefore, of a few references of a Sunnī character would not only illustrate the Brethren's generally liberal position but also be a good tactical move. It would help camouflage its secret, subversive underground movement against the ʿAbbāsid establishment.

As for the Shīʿite colour of the *Rasāʾil*, the following could be cited: the Prophet Muhammad's saying "I am the city of knowledge and ʿAlī is its gate" is given (IV,460). So also is emphasized the loyal love (walāya) of the Prophet's household (Ahl al-Bayt) (IV,375). The Prophet is reported to have said to ʿAli, "I and you are the parents (abawā) of this community (umma)" (I,385). Notice also the "salawāt" for ᶜAli (II,59 and III,211). This benedictory expression is reserved by the Sunnīs only for the Prophet. The progeny of the Prophet is referred to as the "rightly-guiding Imāms" (al-aᵓimmat al-hudāt) (II,377). In the section on Imāmate (III,493-497) the institution is equated with Caliphate and it is said to be of two kinds: (a) of *nubuwwa* (i.e. prophecy) and (b) of *mulk* (i.e. dominion). People's views are said to be of two kinds: (a) those who consider the Imāma/Khilāfa to belong to the Prophet's family on whom *naṣṣ* (designation) has been made and (b) others (IV,494). The implication is that the Imāmate of prophecy is in the family of the Prophet, although the Imāmate of dominion could be exercised by others. This would indicate the superiority of the Shīᶜite Imāms over the ᶜAbbāsid Caliphs.

The *Rasāᵓil* describe the four festivals of the philosophic year (as-sanat al-falsafiyya) (IV,267-272) the third of which is the ᶜId Ghadīr al-Khumm, the day on which the Prophet designated, according to the Shīᶜa, ᶜAlī as his successor, but the "joy (of the occasion) was marred because it was mixed with the breaking (of the covenant) and treachery" (IV,268). The last festival, ᶜId al-Muṣība (the day of calamity) is once described as the day of the Prophet's death and again as the Battle of Karbalāᵓ (the occasion of Ḥusayn's martyrdom) "which ended - with the killing of the martyrs and the disgrace of Islam" (IV,269). The tone of the whole chapter is unmistakably Shīᶜite.

Again a section (III,511-514) describes the gradation of knowledge from (a) the lower stage of *zāhir* (exoteric) for the *awāmm* (common people) to a higher (b) middle stage that prefers *ijtihād* (independent legal reasoning) in religion to *taqlīd* (blind following of a legal school) and then to the highest stage of (c) *bātin* (esoteric) for the *khawāṣṣ* (the initiated élite) where the true nature of religion is understood. Here we have the typical *taᶜlīmī* Shīᶜite position, the theory of esoteric interpretation and the preference for a continuing legal thinking in opposition to the *taqlīd* of the four schools of Sunnī law. The Brethren also state: "Among people there are groups of intellectuals who would not be satisfied with *taqlīd* but would demand proofs and the uncovering of truths (*haqāʾiq*)[11] and the seeking of *ʿilla* (the motivation and the purpose of the religious law)" (III,379). These are only some examples among many that spell out the Shīʿite character of the *Rasāʾil*.

But the question arises: to what sub-sect of the Shīʿa do the Brethren of Purity belong? We have already pointed out the unlikelihood of their being Zaydī. The above statement in favour of the Bāṭinī (esoteric) knowledge would be repugnant to Zaydism.[12] Let us now consider the Ithnā ʿAsharī (or twelver) possibility. Among the misguided people cited by the *Rasāʾil* are those that are described thus: "So also is considered [erroneous a group] that believes that the great and guiding awaited Imām is hidden and does not appear because of the fear of the opponents. Know that the holder of such opinion remains all his life expectant of the Imām's appearance, wishful of his coming, eager for his advent. He, then, wastes his life and dies in despair and sorrow, not having seen his Imām, nor having known his person." (III,523). This passage, to my mind, clearly opposes the Ithnā ʿAsharī theory of the Awaited Imām (al-Imām al-Muntaẓar). The question may arise: Why particularly the awaited Imām of the Twelvers and not of the Fāṭimids or the Qarmatians? The answer lies in the lines that follow immediately the above passage. As proof of the argument is given a verse of a well-known Ithnā ʿAsharī poet of Caliph al-Maʾmūn's time, Daʿbal al-khuzāʿī, who recited in a dirge written for the Imāms of the Twelvers: "Don't you see, for thirty years I have been pacing up and down in sorrowful expectations." (III,524).

Not only this argument of the Brethren, but also their insistence on Bāṭinī knowledge cited above, that places the Brethren in Ismāʿīlī camp. *Al-Jāmiʿa* declares: "Faith comes in two kinds: *Ẓāhir* (exoteric) and *bāṭin* (esoteric)" (IV,67). The Imām-lawgiver (*wāḍiʿ al-sharīʿa*) lays down the work of the *Duʿāt* (members of the religio-political organization called the *Daʿwa*) "who are the highest ranking individuals." They inform frankly the élite (al-Khawāṣṣ) the secret and open aspects of belief, but they make only indirect references in unclear and suggestive language by esoteric interpretation (taʾwīl) to the masses to win them over. They are bound by fraternal ties and joining of hearts (taʾlīf qulūbihim) so that they can unite in work and word. (IV,130-138).

The Daʿwa of the Brethren needed to penetrate various classes of people in order to be effective. They say: "Know, O brother, may God aid you and us with His Spirit, that we have brethren and friends among the noble and gracious people. Spread out in different places; among them is a group of the sons of kings, amīrs, wazīrs, secretaries (kuttāb) and governors (ʿummāl); among them are the sons of notables, the dihqāns, small-holders (tunnāʾ) and merchants (tujjār) and among them is a group of the sons of ʿulama, men of letters (udabāʾ), jurists (fuqahāʾ) and religious men; and among them is a group of the sons of craftsmen (ṣunnāʿ), local headmen (mutaṣarrifīn) and leaders of crafts and professions (umanāʾ al-nās). We have delegated to each group of them a brother from our brethren, whose knowledge and insight we approve, to represent us in their service by counseling them with fellow-feeling (rifq), kindness (raḥma) and affection (shafaqa)" (IV,188).

Such a role of the Daʿwa was typical of the Ismāʿili way of working; also entering into a covenant or a bond (ʿahd or mīthāq). The Brethren say: "Know that the government of the people of good (ahl al-khayr) begins, firstly by the gathering in a place (town, country) of good and noble people and by their agreeing on one opinion, one faith and one religion, and by binding themselves together by an ʿahd and mīthāq to help each other and not avoid each other, to cooperate with each other and not withdraw from such cooperation." (IV,187). These words are addressed to a new member who has sought admission to the fraternity (al-akh al-mustajīb).

The appeal of the Brethren was to the youth. They say: "It behooves our good and eminent Brethren, may God guide them and us with His spirit, to follow the example of the philosopher in wisely choosing (i.e. seeking the company of) the *aḥdāth* and *fityān* (members of youth groups) who are good and noble; well-mannered and cultured; understanding and intelligent, for substaining our knowledge and the secrets of our wisdom, following the tradition of God. This is because He does not send a Prophet who is not young nor does He give wisdom to any devotee who is not *ḥadath* (a young member) from among the *fityān* (the fraternities of youth)." (IV,151).

This idealistic picture of the *fityān* might give us the impression that they were disinclined to violence. Such an impression would not be absolutely correct. The penetration of the Daᶜwa among the youth as described by the Brethren is, however, not for violent purposes but in a liberal and interconfessional manner. They say: "Do not occupy yourself with reforming of old men who have kept since their childhood false ideas, bad habits and evil qualities, for they will weary you and will not be changed. If they do change, it would be very little and of no avail. Your concern is with young men of sound heart who incline towards letters, begin to study the sciences, seek the path of truth and the other world, believe in the day of reckoning, make use of the religious codes of the Prophets, study the secrets of their books, renounce passion and polemic and are not fanatical in matters of doctrine." (IV,161-168)[13]

The liberalism of the Brethren is further evidenced by passages such as these: "Know that the truth is found in every religion (*dīn*) and is current in every tongue. What you should do, however, is to take the best and to transfer yourself to it. Do not ever occupy yourself with imputing defects to the religions of people; rather try to see whether your religion is free from them." (III,501). Also; "Acquire knowledge, any type of knowledge, philosophical, legal, mathematical, scientific or divine. All that is nourishment for the soul and life for it in this world and the hereafter." (III,538).

The *Rasāʾil* contain a long *Risāla* (no.22) on Animals and Birds (II,178-377). It is an allegory in which man's qualities are compared to those of animals, birds and the *jinn*. Representatives of different species and nationalities speak in a Conference of Creation.[14] At the end, an ideal individual addresses the Assembly. He is described as "excellent, intelligent and possessing insight, [as if] he is Persian in origin, Arab in faith, a *ḥanīf* in religion, an ᶜIrāqī in manners, a Hebrew in tradition, a Christian in conduct, a Syrian in devotion, a Greek in knowledge, an Indian in vision, a mystic (*ṣūfī*) in his way of life (*sīra*), an angel in his morals, a leader (*rabbānī*) in opinion, a divine (*ilāhī*) in gnosticism (*maᶜārif*) and of everlasting qualities (*ṣamdānī*)" (II,376).

The Brethren describe themselves as *Rabbāniyūn*, *Abbār* or *Ḥunafāʾ* (IV,126) which are of course cover-names derived from Judaic, Christian and Ṣabian traditions, intended to attract wider support from people who did not belong to their movement. Their ambiguities, allusions, insinuations and even contradictions were calculated to evade ᶜAbbāsid censorship and attack, which in any case ultimately came. It is for the same reason that one secret remained a closely guarded one; the names of the authors of the *Rasāʾil*. The work, however, is a manifesto of the Ismāᶜīlī movement and is for that reason required to be publicized (I,327).

The ideas of the Brethren are revolutionary and subversive to the ᶜAbbāsid Establishment. They theorize about the change of states (*taᶜāqub al-duwal*) (I,180-181) and the passage of dominion from one nation to another, from one country to another and from one dynasty to another (IV,190). They give the good tiding (*bashāra*) of the Imām's success (IV,146) in the overthrow of the rule of the people of evil (*ahl al-sharr*) and the establishment of the rule of the people of good (*ahl al-khayr*) (I,181; IV,187).

From their ideas and their activities, as stated in their *Rasāʾil* the Brethren do suggest to us their Ismāᶜīlī affiliation although they do not reveal their names and try to camouflage their identity by creating certain ambiguities on purpose. Should we accept, then, their Ismāᶜīlī identity, the question would still remain whether the Brethren were Qarmaṭian, who after the disappearance of their seventh Imām, Muḥammad b. Ismāʿīl b. Jaʿfar al-Ṣādiq, expected his return as Mahdī or Qāʾim and did not believe in the continuity of his line, or were they Fāṭimid who believed in the continuity of the line, in the hidden Imāms of the period of concealment (*al-dawr al-satr*) and the advent of the period of Fāṭimid open rule (*al-dawr al-kashf*).

The *Satr* (concealment) period (148-297 H./765-909 A.D.) is characterized by a peculiar tactic of the Fāṭimid movement. It maintained the *wāqifī* (static) view of the Ismāʿīlī line ending with seventh Imām Muḥammad b. Ismāʿīl just for keeping the messianic hope of the movement alive, in terms of his reappearance. Otherwise it was devoted to continuing underground work led by Muḥammad b. Ismāʿīl's descendants and aided by his dāʿīs for the establishment of a new Caliphate. If it was purely a religous movement the first aspect (messianism) would have been sufficient. Since, however, it had political ambitions, the second aspect (i.e. the establishment of a new Caliphate), had ultimately to prevail. This apparent contradiction has created much confusion in interpreting the movement and detracted from a proper understanding of its dynamic motivation. Since the Imāms were in hiding between 148/765 and 297/909, any attempt at active preaching on their behalf would have led to exposure and repression by the ʿAbbāsid Caliphate; hence it was necessary to make the symbolism of Muḥammad b. Ismāʿīl an ongoing one till such time as it would become expedient to abandon it. Such a tactic had its own danger. Should some of the dāʿīs wish to separate and go their own way, the *wāqifī* belief in the return of Muḥammad b. Ismāʿīl could provide ground for defiance of the continuing line of Imāms in hiding, and might even be successful for two reasons: the inability of the central organization to impose disciplinary action because of its underground existence and the possibility of the support of the mass of ordinary faithful who were, in any case, in the dark. Such separations constituted the ever-growing platform of Qarmaṭianism.

It is in the light of such an interpretation, I believe, that the internal references in the *Rasāʾil Ikhwān al-Safāʾ* must be viewed. On the one hand, the *Rasāʾil* shows a devoted adherence to the Seventh Imām; on the other, they indicate the existence of a later living Imām, or his successor, who is about to establish the new Caliphate. The *Rasāʾil* lay great emphasis on the number seven as the perfect number that includes the meaning of all numbers (I,58) and yet they attack the *Musabbiʿa* (the Seveners) because "their outlook is partial and their dialectic, not universal (I,217); again "the Seveners exaggerate the exposition of sets of seven and exhibit in this field strange instances." (III,180). They speak of *al-Ghāʾib Amīr al-Muʾminīn* who is to return (IV,362) and at the same time they criticize the Shīʿa for holding that "the *Imām Muntazar* is hidden out of fear; nay he is present in their midst." (IV,148). It is only a continuing Imāmate in a period of concealment and expectation that can make the *Rasāʾil* speak of *Al-Aʾimmat al-Mahdiyyūn* (the Mahdī Imāms) in the plural (I,274). In *al-Risālat al-Jāmiʿa* (Beirut ed.) we have reference to "the Seventh *Raʾīs*, who comes at the end of time, the Lord of the Brethren of Purity" and yet he is the initiator of the first cycle (*al-munshiʾ al-nashʾat al-ūla*), also the repeater of another cycle (*muʿīd al-nashʾat al-ukhrā*) (p.286). Then follow three parallel and analogous cycles of Prophethood, embryonic development of the child and Imāmate in the last few sections of *al-Risālat al-Jamiʿa*. What is said about one cycle, could by analogy be applied to the other. Talking of the seventh month of pregnancy, it is stated that the child can be born, but in the eighth month the child does not attain its position, does not rise in rank and is aborted (*sāqit*) from reaching its due place *(martabat al-bala-gh)*. The days of the eighth month pass (or return = *yaʿūd*) into the ninth when delivery takes place, the creation is completed and another cycle begins (p.524). In another passage it is stated that the child dies between the seventh and the eighth months, but can be born in the ninth and sometimes even in the tenth (519-20). If we were to extend the analogy of this process to the Imāms of the *Satr* period, the time of the eighth Imām ᶜAbd Allah was one of difficulty, but that of the ninth, i.e. Aḥmad, was pregnant with possibility. If the mission is not successful at this time, it may be accomplished in the time of the tenth Imām. Again the seventh is mentioned but is identified with Aḥmad *al-mabᶜūth*. He is surrounded by his *ḥudūd* (dāᶜīs). This is described as another cycle and a new *amr* which the reader is going to behold (p.516-17). Although by introducing the epithet *al-mabᶜūth*, we are led to think of the Prophet Muhammad, he is not meant here because it is the Aḥmad of the new *amr* that the Brethren are referring to.

Emphasizing only the *wāqifī* aspect of the *Rasāʾil*, Zāhid ᶜAlī[15] and W. Madelung[16] have described the work as Qarmaṭian. Madelung emphasizes the reference to the son of the Seventh Imām having fallen from his position, but as pointed out above, the complete analogy goes up to the ninth and even the tenth Imām (Aḥmad). The analogy of the months of pregnancy to the continuing Imāmate and the reference to the impending new *amr* should not be missed. Another reason for their acceptance of the Qarmaṭian authorship is their acceptance of Abū Ḥayyān al-Tawḥīdī's (320-414/932-1023) story allegedly giving the names of certain authors of the *Rasāʾil* contemporary to him.[17] Indeed, the names of the Baṣran individuals cited by Abū Ḥayyān indicate Qarmaṭian connections. Moreover, the late date of composition, i.e. 373/983, implied by Abū Ḥayyān may also cover up some internal allusions, such as verses of al-Mutanabbī, al-Fārābī's qualifications of an Ideal Ruler and a reference to Al-Ashāᶜira included in the *Rasāʾil*. I have explained in another article why Abū Ḥayyān's story is not correct; its purpose being to establish the heresy of Zayd b. Rifāᶜa by claiming that he is a companion of the alleged heretical authors of the *Rasāʾil*, rather than to state the correct names of the *Rasāʾil's* authors.[18] Again, I have explained the use of a common source, an early Arabic translation of Plato's *Republic*, by both al-Fārābī and the Ikhwān in their listing of the qualifications of an Ideal Ruler in another article.[19] Citation of al-Mutanabbī's verses, a reference to al-Ashāᶜira and other scattered references of later origin are editorial interpolations, probably inserted by a Sunnī Ṣūfī editor of the post-Ghazzālī period. This I have discussed in yet another article.[20] Fortunately for us, there is preserved a reference to the *Rasāʾil* in an early Fāṭimid source, the *Sīra* of the Sāᶜī Jaᶜfar b. Mansūr al-Yaman (ca.270-360/ 883-970) which mentions the pre-Caliphate Fāṭimid Imām of the *Satr* (concealment) period, Imām Aḥmad b. ᶜAbdAllah b. Muhammad b. Ismāᶜīl b. Jaᶜfar al-Ṣādiq, as the *Munshiʾ* (=issuer, presenter, publicizer) of the *Rasāʾil*. More information on this source can be found in a recent article of mine.[21]

From these studies, I have concluded that, despite later references found in it, the *Rasāʾil* was not a work of the time of al-Tawḥīdī or later, but was a pre-Fāṭimid work; its authors were a group of Fāṭimid dāᶜīs working in collaboration with other colleagues who may have been even Sunnī but who were dedicated to the overthrow of the ᶜAbbāsid Caliphate and the establishment of the Fāṭimid one; the names of the authors would never be known although it is apparent from the language and style that they belonged to the eastern provinces (Iraq and Persia);[22] they composed and revised the *Rasāʾil* at one time and had a coordinator among them;[23] they capitalized on the messianic expectations prevalent among the Shīᶜa, particularly after the disappearance of the Ithnā ᶜAshari Imām Muhammad al-Muntaẓar in 260/873 and used these expectations for the establishment of a Fāṭimid Caliphate in 297/909. The time of Imām Aḥmad was shortly before the latter date, and that must be the time of the composition of the *Rasāʾil*.

The Risāla 48 (IV,145-197) is couched in the words of the Imām himself. He tells the Shīᶜa to give the good tidings (bashāra) of the establishment of his State and government (IV,145). He criticizes some Shīᶜa thus: "A group of evil-doers have taken Shīᶜism as a cover.... They call themselves ᶜAlids, while they are not." (I,147) They are further described as having given up the duties of religion. This sounds like an attack on the Qarmatians.

Again he criticizes another group of the Shīʿa thus: "They have made Shīʿism into an earning for themselves. They are like the mourners and story-tellers and by Shīʿism they understand only *tabarrā* (repudiating the first three Caliphs), indulging in scandal, insult, curse and crying with the mourners..." (IV,147-148). This seems like a criticism of the Twelvers. He describes these Shīʿīs as saying: "The Imām is awaited (muntaẓar). He is hidden because of the fear of the opponents." To them he replies, "Never, on the contrary he (the Imām) is apparent (Ẓāhir) and in their midst (bayn ẓahrānīhum). He knows them but they deny him." (IV,148). It is in this connection that the claim is made that the true "successors to the Prophet (Khulafā) are the Mahdī Imāms (al-Aʾimmat al-Mahdīyūn)." (IV,148). The context suggests that the Imām speaking is making a claim for all the Mahdī Imāms, the Fāṭimid Imām of the *Satr* period. He describes himself as no longer hidden but apparent, and gives the good tidings about the establishment of his State. It is as if the birth of the Fāṭimid Caliphate is quite close. There is an air of imminence about this *Risāla*.

After the establishment of the Fāṭimid Caliphate, *Rasāʾil Ikhwān al-Ṣafāʾ* seems to have been withdrawn.[24] The revolutionary spirit it inculcated had served its purpose. It was not needed any longer, lest it should become dangerous to the Fāṭimid establishment itself. This was done with regard to other works also.[25]

Before the end of the Fāṭimid Caliphate, however, the Nizārī Daʿwa in Persia and Syria beginning in 487/1094[26] and the Ṭayyibī Daʿwa in Yaman beginning in 524/1129 revived the work.[27] They needed the revolutionary spirit of the epistles in order to survive and to strengthen the hope of their followers in the advent of "the rule of the people of Good" (I,181; IV,187).

The threat that the *Rasāʾil* continued to present to the orthodox ʿAbbāsid establishment is illustrated by the fact that the Caliph al-Mustanjid had copies of the work publicly burnt in 545/1150 and shortly after in 566/1170 insisted on Salāḥ al-dīn al-Ayyūbī to discontinue the

Fāṭimid Khuṭba in Egypt.[28] The promise that the *Rasāʾil* gave even to the late Indian Ṭayyibī Daʿwa is illustrated by the fact that the Indian Dāʿī Yūsuf Najmuddīn (d.1798) described the work as the *Qurʾān al-Aʾimma* (Qurʾān of the Immāms) as distinct from the *Qurʾān al-Umma* (the Qurʾān of the muslim community).[29]

ISLAM, POLITY AND SOCIETY IN TURKEY:
A MIDDLE EASTERN PERSPECTIVE*

M. Heper

1. Introduction

A recent typology of state-religion relationships indiscriminately lumps together all those countries with solely or predominantly Muslim population into a single category of religion-dominated polity.[1] Earlier, Lewis had suggested that Islam is a "significant" force in Egypt, Iran and Turkey, and a "major" force in other muslim countries.[2] In the aftermath of the Iranian revolution even the above distinction is not made. "Islamic resurgence" is considered a real possibility in all such countries, including Turkey.[3]

An investigation of whether such a prediction is based upon valid analysis necessitates a clarification of, first, what is "Islamic resurgence," and, second, what brings it about. According to one definition, Islamic resurgence means "the establishment of an Islamic republic by means of a mass movement as in Iran."[4] Less extreme definitions include (1) a more pronounced observance of the Islamic tenets amongst the masses, (2) Islam as a focus of identity, - a "Third World" state of mind, and/or (3) a domestic revival which influences national policies.[5]

What gives alarm, of course, is the possibility of a mass uprising against central political authority. What brings about such an upheaval? Here, there is no clear-cut answer. Rather than attempting to single out the causal factors attention is focused upon what is presumed to be the incipient phase of the movement - the increased visibility of popular Islam. Reduced to its bare essentials, the line of reasoning seems to run as follows:[6] Islam, in the last analysis, is a mysterious force. From time to time "it" decides to act. When exactly "it" would act is also mysterious because such an impulse is unaffected by social, economic, and political factors. One can detect, however, its deciding to act. The unmistakable sign here is a resurgence in popular Islam.

This approach is less than convincing. It is not persuasive to argue that a rise in popular Islam would inevitably lead to a mass movement against the central political authority. Similar structures may have different functions and "consequences." Furthermore, the external causes of religious behaviour are so diverse that an understanding of this behaviour can really be achieved from the viewpoint of the subjective experiences, ideas, and purposes of the individuals concerned - in short, from the viewpoint of the religious behaviour's "meaning."[7]

It is also difficult to act on the assumption that the religious impulse is unaffected by sociological factors. It is clear that religion is not merely an epiphenomenal institution. On the other hand, if Lewis' claim that religion is a significant force in certain countries and a major force in others is valid this difference cannot be explained only in terms of variations in interpretations of theology. Furthermore, religion itself is a multi-functional institution; Islam has been used by particular groups for entirely different purposes.[8]

More generally, theology is not a good predictor of behaviour: "Often religions of mankind...have borne within themselves a series of motives, each of which, if separately and consistently followed through, would have stood in the way of others or run against them head-on."[9] Even if one could explain all cases in terms of theology there are, of course, different theologies in the Muslim context, too, i.e., different branches, and in some cases such as the Sunni branch, different "schools" within the same branch itself.

Thus, an attempt to predict whether the new visibility of Islam in a country would lead to a revolt against the central political authority has to take into account non-religious as well as religious variables. Following Lewy, I suggest that such a study has to look at such things as leadership, religious doctrine, ecclesiastical organization, and the "situational factors," i.e., cultural, economic, political, social, and psychological variables, to the extent that each such variable is significant at a given time and place.[10] Only such an approach would uncover distinct clusters and even unique cases within the usually undifferentiated "Muslim context."

the present study is an attempt in this direction. Its aim is to show some of the characteristics of the Ottoman-Turkish development that together make Turkey almost a unique case in herself. It also tries to explain some aspects of the visibility of Islam in that country.

2. The Ottoman Background

In the Ottoman polity one comes across a "Muslim state" where the influence of the religion was constrained by many factors. In that polity, the concept of *mülk*, i.e. temporal power, had been stretched to its limits. Drawing upon their *örf-i sultani*, or sovereign powers, the Ottoman sultans could issue laws and regulations which would do away with Islamic precedents.[11] From the seventh-century on, even the sultans lost their charisma; charisma was gradually attributed to the state. The sultans could now be deposed in the name of the state.[12] In other Muslim states the concept of the state as an instrument of worldly salvation is a rather recent development.[13] Thus, early in the game, the state in the Ottoman-Turkish polity was based largely upon "structural legitimacy," or independent belief in validity of the structures and norms.[14] In developing their state system, the Ottomans drew upon the Iranian example. Beginning in the sixteenth-century the Safavid state itself started to lose its relative autonomy *vis-à-vis* the influential Shi'ite hierarchy. In stark contrast, as early as the mid-sixteenth century the Ottomans began to freely flout the law of Islam.[15]

In the Ottoman case, there was little need for "institutional secularization as disengagement," or change from ecclesiatical control to public administration,[16] because the state as a distinct entity, i.e., with "sovereignty" and "autonomy," and the supporting resources, always existed. And even when the Islamic influences reached their apogee during the sixteenth century the Ottoman state was far from being a truly Islamic one, i.e., a complete theocracy. Thus, "institutional secularization as differentiation," i.e., giving religion a definite, though by no means a minor, place in the social scene, too, existed in the Ottoman polity.

In fact, the so-called Muslim institution in that polity was a prop for and subservient to the state. Unlike their Shi'ite brethren the Ottoman ulama did not equate temporal power with injustice. Instead, they thought that cooperation with, and an official status in, the political realm was the only way of exercising an effective restraining influence on the temporal power.[17]

Moreover, popular religious orders, which proved to be rather troublesome in some other contexts,[18] have not made life equally difficult for the Ottoman orthodox religious center. It is, in fact, possible, in the Ottoman case to talk about a process of "institutional secularization as routinization," i.e., the operative religion in a sociological sense to be replaced by a set of ideas, rituals, and symbols. In the West, this process emerged with the church being substituted for the sects, which in turn, led to greater conservatism. In the case of the Ottomans these orders were not replaced but coopted.[19]

During the nineteenth century the traditional Islamic concept of "justice" no longer meant "securing to each category of the ruled no less and no more than it deserved according to its function or state in the society." It now meant "promulgation of secular legislation outside the jurisdiction of the Islamic traditions and autonomous from them."[20] Secular legislation thus freed in certain areas from the shackles of the prescriptions of the Sharia, was promulgated by the civil and the military bureaucratic elite during the rest of the Ottoman period. The hold on politics of this group constitutes a vivid contrast to that of the Iranian political elite which both before and during the nineteenth century had to enlist the support of the ulama as well as the bazaar merchants.[21]

Thus, in the Ottoman empire it was as early as the nineteenth century that "normative secularization as desacralization," i.e., that life can be lived in accordance with human rationality, began to take shape. It is difficult to conjecture to what extent the Ottomans' Hanefi "school" of the Sunni branch, which deemphasized charisma and underlined analogy and reason, facilitated such a development. In any case, from the *Tanzimat* (Regulations) period (1839-1876) on policies of the Ottoman state did not in every instance need to be complementary to basic Islamic formulas; the most important criterion in promulgating such policies was going to be "reason." The Ottoman modernizers adopted the so-called "cast-iron theory of Islam," i.e., that Islam has fallen out of phase with life and cannot be adapted to modern circumstances.[22] A consistent policy of Westernization was followed throughout the nineteenth-century and the last two decades of the Ottoman Empire in the twentieth-century. Here, the contrast with the developments in Egypt is rather striking. Muhammed Ali Pasha's reform programs quickly disintegrated in the decade of the 1840s; his armed forces were dismantled and his schools were closed.[23]

In all of the Middle East, the Young Ottomans (of the 1860s) became the first and, for a long time, the only proponents of a highly elaborated political and intellectual movement. Their goals were articulated in terms of state and nationality. Ziya Pasha and Namık Kemal counterposed the concepts of fatherland and patriotism against the concept of umma, or religious community. Later in the century, Abdülhamid II's policy of Pan-Islamism was, unlike Pan-Arabism, an international rather than a supranational ideology. As such, it did not prove to be a serious obstacle to the emergence of a non-religious nationalism. At the turn of the century, Ziya Gökalp acted as an influential proponent of the separation of religion and state. The Young Turks, drawing upon Gökalp's ideas, agitated for the replacement of Islam by nationalism as the basis of the state. They developed a conception of nationalism that brought with it a secular image of government, and introduced the notion that the nation is the source of all authority.

3. Cultural Revolution in the Republic
3.1 Kemalist Reforms

If a significant Islamic revival ever occured in Turkey it was during the War of Independence (1919-1923). Islam was a means to mobilize the masses against "the infidel." It was used to legitimize the national struggle that was carried out against the wishes of the sultan in Istanbul.[24]

The Kemalist reformers refrained from using religion; their very target was the hold of religion on the polity and the society. In this sense, Atatürk and his associates were "coercive elites" who attempted to utilize many of the traditional orientations, but shorn of much of their concrete content and of their identification with any connection to the older order or to any part of it.[25] One basic goal was to bring institutional secularization as disengagement to its logical conclusion; to completely free the policy from religious considerations. Islam was not supposed to have even the function of a "civil religion" for the Turkish polity; Islam was not going to provide a transcendent goal for the political life.

The Kemalists took nationalism as a subtitute for Islam. This approach places Turkey in a unique position. The Kemalists attempted to adopt territorial and, later, linguistic rather than religious nationalism. This Anatolian nationalism did not oblige the Turks to annex new territory, which the ideology of pan-Arabism requires.[25] Besides, Atatürk did not place the moral responsibility of remaining backward solely upon the dominating tendencies of the advanced nations.[27] The situation in most other Muslim countries is somewhat different. As a consequence of their earlier colonization by the Europeans there seems to be a difficulty of responding positively to a West seen to be an attacker and the abode of infidels.[28] This leads to a continued emphasis on Islam.

At the level of the individual, too, what was attempted was unlike the situation in the Arab countries. In Turkey the aim was reformation rather than a renaissance of Islam. Again the baseline was the cast-iron theory of Islam. The aim was gradual crystallization of a Turkish concept of Islam as a religion in the Western, i.e., post-French Revolution sense of the term.[29] It was to resemble the Protestant tradition that placed emphasis on the absolute privacy of individual conscience.

With this goal in mind, religious orders and brotherhoods were closed. This was an attempt to suppress folk Islam. Measures were taken to improve the quality of religious personnel, all of whom were now members of the civil bureaucracy. Also, policies were developed that touched directly on religious observance and customs. The Koran and the Traditions of the Prophet were translated into Turkish. The use of Arabic in public acts such as the call to prayer from the minarets was forbidden. All public displays of religious observance were discouraged.

In retrospect, it may be surmised that three out of the four kinds of response to change formulated by Eisenstadt[30] did not exist in the Turkish case: neither the appearance of what may be called transformative capacity, nor different types of adaptability to change, and not even an active resistance to change through an organized "traditionalistic" response aiming at imposing at least some of the older values on a new setting.[31] What took place resembled a fourth type of response, which, as Eisenstadt reports, occurs in relatively rare cases - totally passive, negative attitude often resulting in weakening of the resisting groups. Both of what Eisenstadt predicts as likely causes for this state of affairs - a poor leadership and lack of organizational ability - were operative. I have already noted the process whereby the religious bureaucracy was subordinated to the civil bureaucracy. And when what is usually referred to as "religious revival" occurred in the 1950s most of the leaders hardly resembled the impeccable, let alone, the infallible Shi'ite imams.

Consequently, "institutional secularization" as "routinization," "differentiation," and "disengagement" gained increasing pace, and a favourable climate for a fourth type of institutional secularization was created, that of "decline," i.e., desertion of holy places and a drop in church, in this case mosque, attendance. It must be pointed out that the object was not to destroy religious beliefs. As Count Ostrorog, one-time French ambassador in Ankara noted, "...religion was merely caused to recede from the halls of human conflict. It was to ascend into the stronghold of conscience to dwell there in much greater dignity and security than when its ministers pretended to rule earthly interests as moral aspirations."[32]

The modernist-secularist policy of the Kemalists, particularly after Atatürk's, however, carried anti-religious features. Atatürkism itself became a transcendent goal. Atatürk's message was "bureaucratized." His value charisma was used for legitimizing the "sovereignty" and "autonomy" of the state. It was transformed into an official ideology.[33]

3.2 The Multi-Party Period: 1940s to Present

The transition to multi-party politics in the mid-1940s has not led to a *laissez-faire* policy concerning Islam. As Stirling perceptively observed, Republicans in Turkey can claim that the state has been freed from religion although religion has by no means been freed from the state.[34] The "concessions" granted during the multi-party period were no more than reintroduction of call to prayer in Arabic and somewhat expanded religious instruction in the grade schools. Out of these two concessions the resumption of instruction in religion may seem more critical. In fact such instruction constituted not even the remotest threat to the secular central authority. These courses were offered by lay teachers; the textbooks were duly approved by the Ministry of Education.

The Democrats did not consider repudiating the fundamental aspects of the Kemalist reforms concerning Islam. During the early 1950s, effective legal procedures were started against the leaders of a number of religious orders which tended to emerge after 1950. No comparison can be made between these orders and, for instance, the Muslim Brotherhood in Egypt that fully emerged in place of the declining Sufi orders by World War II. In Iran, a more elaborate, though, of course, different, type of religious organization existed.[35] When the principal leaders of the orders in Turkey received even light prison terms some of these orders quickly disappeared.

Other measures against revival of Islam included passing a law in 1951 that forbade belittling Atatürk's memory. The state continued to control religious education. The state has supervised even the selection of prayer leaders at the village and neighborhood level. As Dodd recently observed, "Turkey has always allowed Islam to use what means it can to spread itself provided that the Islamic institution is not recreated outside and apart from the state."[36]

Lewis once observed that if one had to describe modern Turkish Islam in one word, the word would be not "fanatical" but "simple."[37] This must be due to the fact that the "reforms" of the 1950s were not the product of profound soul searching or of a spiritual crisis but chiefly of utilitarian and political considerations - the quest for a secure foundation of common morality, the need for a united front against Communism, and, above all, the never-ending competition for electoral votes. It is for this reason that the state itself supported, and, still supports, the rise of popular Islam in Turkey by establishing new schools of preachers and prayer leaders and by contributing to the construction of new mosques.

In Turkey, apart from the initial years of the War of Independence, religion has not been used to mobilize the masses. In this sense there is again a basic difference between Turkey and Egypt. Toward the end of the 1950s Nasser discovered that the Egyptian masses could be reached and mobilized only by associating nationalism with Islam. Before long, nationalism came to mean Arab nationalism built upon a religious foundation. This was only to be expected as the only glory the Arabs value was achieved under the banner of Islam.[38] Turks, in contrast, based their nationalism upon their pre-Islamic history.

In the Turkish case, the role that religion has played in politics, too, should not be exaggerated. After the transition to multi-party politics those political parties which similarly emphasized religion in their programs could obtain little support as compared to the Democrat Party.[39] The Democrat Party itself placed greater emphasis on religion only when it faced serious economic problems after the mid-1950s.

The 1961 Constitution widened the scope of public liberties. Soon overtly religious political parties emerged. One such political party is the Turkish Unity Party (TUP). This party was supported by the Shi'ite population. The Shi'ites in Turkey had traditionally been supporters of the Republican People's Party in whose commitment to secularism they have seen the best guarantee against Sunni discrimination to the extent that it exists.[40] The TUP received 2.8, 1.1, and 0.4 percent of the votes in the 1969, 1973 and 1977 general elections respectively.

The major religiously-oriented political party during the 1970s was the NSP. It garnered 11.9 and 8.6 percent of the votes in the 1973 and 1977 general elections respectively. Recently, Rustow reported that the NSP is "emphatically Sunni in orientation and would feel profoundly repelled by any regime of Shi'ite ayatollahs. The elaborate hierarchy that made the Shi'ite clergy the best organized opposition to the Shah is absent among the Sunnis."[41] The party activities of the NSP during the 1970s which violated the secularist aspects of Kemalism[42] earned it indirect but stern rebuke in a letter that the military high command presented to the President on December 27, 1979. The recent military takeover in Turkey (12 September 1980) is, among other things, a reaction to the increased anti-secularism of the NSP.

There is little possibility for religion in Turkey to be a functional alternative to politics, which is not the same thing as a political movement taking on a religious colouring.[43] If, after Rustow,[44] one defines the prerequisites of political modernization as (1) authority - a strong authoritative linkage between governers and governed, (2) identity - a distinct sense of selfhood, and (3) equality - democracy, freedom, and socialism, Turkey seems to have a distinctly modern political system as compared to other Muslim polities. In Turkey, politics have become self-sustaining; politics as a field of human activity do make sense in their own right and can function without religious props. During the last thirty years, Turkey successfully replaced an authoritarian, bureaucratic, single-party system by a multi-party system dominated by peripheral forces, and furthermore started to produce a new party system based on functional rather than cultural cleavages.[45] It was pointed out that if effective yet democratic political development could succeed anywhere it would be in Turkey.[46] The pronounced motive behind the recent military takeover in Turkey is to restore the necessary conditions for a viable democracy.

The situation in Turkey may be better appreciated if one remembers that religious fervor accounted for more than a small fraction of the opposition movement to the Shah in Iran. In the eyes of the democratic middle class, the intelligentsia, the merchants, and the minorities the regime had no structural legitimacy.[47] While Turkey made a transition to multi-party politics early in the game, the Shah of Iran encouraged enormous economic, and some social, change while he prevented any basic political change. And in almost all of the Arab states, including the relatively secularized ones such as Egypt, Algeria, and Tunisia, the force of Islam as a legitimizing principle is still evident even at the highest levels.[48]

3.3 Impact of the "Cultural Revolution"

Among anthropologists there is a consensus that reforms concerning religion had a strong impact in Turkey.[49] As Spencer pointed out, there were two dimensions of change that followed.[50] First, there has been a continuing and consistent socialization to increase the awareness of one's identity as Turk and patriot. This socialization was carried out through mass media, school, People's Houses (1932-1954), flag saluting, national anthem singing, state parades, and non-religious holidays on national anniversaries. In the Turkish case there was no need for religion to be a carrier of identity. When asked, "How do you see yourselves...?" 50.3% of the workers in a textile factory considered themselves as "Turks" and only 37.5% as Muslims."[51] In a nationwide survey, too, nationalism as a characteristic of a Turk was found to be stronger than being a Muslim.[52] If earlier religion has been the primary component of one's identity, lately it seems to have lost its salience in this regard.

Secondly, there have been over the decades serious blows to religion. In many ways people had been touched deeply even before being affected by a market economy. These included a change in the structure of Islam, revolutionary measures which divided it from the state, adoption of Western dress and headgear, taking a surname, submitting to a system of education couched in the scientific terms of the West, learning to write in an alphabet of Latin rather than of Arabic origin, enlisting one's son in a modern military organization, having days of the week and calendrical year changed, and watching women vote.

In 1951 Jaschke arrived at the conclusion that Atatürk's revolution had taken hold permanently in Turkish society.[53] Jaschke's impressionistic observation is supported by empirical studies carried out in the following decades. In 1964, a nearby town and even a major city (Istanbul) were no longer viewed by the villagers as a conglomerate of humanity profaned by infidels.[54] In the early 1960s among the villagers the value of secular education was gradually being realized.[55] In 1968 and 1969, in two villages only 3 percent of the villagers thought that one is a powerful person because he is a pious man.[56] One of the findings in a study carried out in 1969 among migrant male workers at the Middle East Technical University in Ankara was that participating frequently in religious practices is weakly associated with believing that religion should not be separated from politics.[57] In the early 1970s, rural Turks were using the courts; the use of courts by citizens extended to areas formerly within the jurisdiction of religious law alone.[58] In a study conducted from August 1969 to July 1970 in a village, education was negatively correlated with superstitious beliefs and practices, and mass media exposure was likewise negatively correlated with religious strictness.[59]

These findings are in sharp contrast to what Israeli recently observed among the Egyptian public: insistence that modern civilization is bankrupt and that no substitute could match Islam.[60] Israeli also reports the findings of recent surveys in Egypt which show that religious faith is deeply ingrained in all sections of Egyptian society, including the middle and upper middle classes, the urban and rural populations, and university graduates.[61] In Turkey, at the level of the educated elite, the blow to religion has been even stronger. While for both the masses and the educated there has been a gradual "normative secularization as desacralization," it has been suggested that at the level of the educated there has also occurred "normative secularization as secularism," i.e., denial of the existence of sacred order. An entire generation was educated thinking religion to be some evil and irrational force of mere orthodoxy and blind tradition.[62]

This is probably true for the generation educated during the single-party years extending to the middle of the 1940s. Nobody in a group of upper echelon civil servants of the period 1945-1960 agreed with the following statement: "In order to alleviate some of the tensions and bottlenecks in Turkish political life it might perhaps be wise in political debates to compromise on some tenets of Atatürkism like secularism, nationalism, and etatism."[63]

In 1957, Reed reported that when pressed further to learn if renewed interest in religious duties involved a possible return to the Shariah, the majority of urban and educated Turks smilingly replied that there was no question of such a "retrogression" implied in their actions. They sought a revitalized, liberal, "protestant" type of Islam freed of its former "superstitious" or "outmoded" accretions. Reed added that the villagers he lived with were of like mind.[64]

It may be surmised that for a long time "normative secularization as desacralization" has been occurring *vis-à-vis* both the masses and the educated. The initial impetus for this process came from Atatürk's cultural revolution. Industrialization, urbanization, and exposure to mass media that gained increasing momentum from the 1950s on quickened the pace of this change. The absence of factors like a religious nationalism, a Turkish version of pan-Arabism, etc. that would have always kept Islam in the political agenda, further facilitated it.

The educated elite seem to be more ambivalent concerning religion than the masses. This must be due primarily to the fact that they rather than the masses had been under the spell of the cast-iron theory of Islam. If I may be allowed an impressionistic note, most of the educated elite in Turkey for long resembled "a majority in the West who believe in God, have a certain public respect for Him and His advocates, but the activities associated with his name are regarded as simply boring or incomprehensible. Some vague hopes are cherished concerning death. Meanwhile each sphere of life has been largely released from religious conceptualization and ecclesiastical influence: political ideology, education, economics and welfare."[65] It may be suggested that the educated elite in Turkey experienced not only "normative secularization as desacralization" but also "cognitive secularization as segmentation," i.e., some metaphysical aspects of life had been seen as problematic; they fitted uneasily into the wholly internalized non-religious world view; such areas continued to be experienced as different and mysterious.

3.4 The Recent Visibility of Islam in Turkey

If it is true that in Turkey the secularization process in its various dimensions started during the Ottoman era and gained further momentum under the Republic how can one explain the visibility of Islam in that country? There seem to be at least two mechanisms behind this phenomenon.

One such mechanism is related to the urban migrants, and perhaps more generally to the "transitionals." It is well-known that industrialization is accompanied by role-differentiation. Confronted with fragmentation and segmentation of his role, the individual may strive desperately for reintegration. Religion in America survived because it performed the task of stabilizing the immigrants' life while at the same time facilitating his assimilation into American life.[66] More relevant to my discussion is a study by Oscar Lewis which found that religiosity increases among the urban migrants once the migration is made, and continues for some time.[67]

I would like to suggest that one aspect of the new visibility of Islam in Turkey is likewise an emergence of a Durkheimian version of religiosity. In this version, religion refers to a class of statements and actions denoting social relationships. As a result of the superior powers of the collectivity, its cohesive force, and moral authority, group-ritual aspects become important.[68]

Kinship groupings in Islam had always been its basic social units. The Ottoman-Turkish social structure has been no exception. At the level of "little culture" it has traditionally been a society of close kin groups. For the individual, the family has been the most important mechanism of integration.[69] As Stirling argued, however, in recent decades, in one village, the family as an integrative mechanism experienced a sharp setback largely as a result of a decline in the father's authority. The young are less deferential, and less obedient because it is they who are able to exploit the new opportunities. Still another development is a decline in cultural consensus. Decline in consensus leads to decline in social control.[70]

If Turkey has been going through "cognitive secularization as segmentation," i.e., religion no longer playing a role as an agent of group solidarity, one aspect of the new visibility of Islam in Turkey is perhaps a reversal of this process. As Stirling reports, formal religion in Turkish villages is booming while "people know much more about alternative dogmas; ideas of causality, especially in relation to agriculture, medicine and mechanical technology are changing."[71]

Scott's finding that the least developed provinces in Turkey have the lowest rates of Qur'an courses and the most developed ones have the highest rates[72] also, supports our proposition. Thus, what is increasing is secular religion rather than an intensification of belief in the supernatural.

Levine's study already noted[73] shows that resort is made to secular religion by some of the urban migrants too. Levine found that three clusters of value systems are operative among the migrant male workers. One cluster he calls "rural identity:" the individual rejects city people; identifies with villagers and with the village; he may or may not be religious. A second cluster reflects "urban modern identity:" the individual has good economic prospects; is not being unrealistically aspiring; does not over accept the city; and is not religious. The third cluster - "urban identity" - is critical for our purposes. It represents a synthesis of conflicting values: the individual identifies strongly with the city people; aspires to ownership of consumer goods; and he is very religious. In another study it was found that, with the passage of time, religiosity among urban migrants increases; it begins to decrease with still more years spent in the urban environment.[74] The new visibility of Islam concerning these "transitionals" seems to be no more than a passing phenomenon for each such wave.

What has been happening in Turkish villages and among urban migrants only partially resembles recent developments in Egypt. Similar changes in Egypt have weakened the kinship structure and induced men to seek solidarity by returning to traditional religious brotherhoods[75] well known for their fundamentalist orientations. What we have been witnessing in Turkey is a revival of religious-based institutions rather than that of religion in its pristine form. In fact, the large numbers of religious-based local associations which have been organized in all Turkish communities have at least as many community functions as theological ones.[76]

A second aspect of the new visibility of Islam in Turkey is at the level of education. Here I have to draw largely upon impressionistic data. During the 1950's, Smith had made the following observation: If there is no transcendent justice in the universe to which a man's conscience can appeal, against the empirical actions and even the laws of a society, that man and that society are precarious in the extreme. He added that whether Turkey can generate an effective substitute, in this realm, for the divine laws of Islam is not yet clear.[77]

Kemalism, the official ideology comprising such principles as republicanism, nationalism, popularism, secularism, étatism, and reformism, could not be a substitute. Kemalism did not play any role at the level of personality development.[78] The end result was "the real impoverishment of Turkish culture": among the intelligentsia this state of affairs led to a type of human relations which have been vacuous, sentimental and yet devoid of compassion; "the continuing intensity of religious belief among large groups of Turks in the last twenty-five years" may be explained in terms of this culture pattern.[79] Earlier Rosenthal had detected among the student generation who grew up without religious teaching and, at least a number of them, without religion at home, a search for something to believe in.[80] Kağitcibasi's finding that among the high school students in Izmir there is a positive correlation between anomie and religiosity conceptualized in its metaphysical dimension, supports Rosenthal's observations.[81]

It is possible to conclude that Kemalism could not perform the metaphysical function of a religion, i.e., provide a system of beliefs and practices by means of which a group of people struggles with the ultimate problems of human life.[82] Thus, for at least some members of the educated elite, "normative secularization as generalization," i.e., religion becoming an over-reaching integrative factor in a differentiated society must have been replacing "cognitive secularization as segmentation." The non-religious dimension of their life must have been becoming increasingly dissatisfying; they must have felt the need to complement it with ethical principles that could not be derived from Kemalism.

There still remains, however, the question of why the visibility of Islam among the educated has become intensified particularly in recent years. One may speculate that some of the non-bureaucratic, educated elite, who, after 1950, adopted materialism shorn of humanism and professionalism - often referred to in Turkey as a one "apartment (flat) - one car philosophy" - might have become aware recently that something is missing.

Another group which might have felt likewise recently may come from the ranks of the traditional bureaucratic, educated elite. Until recently this stratum as a whole might not have felt sharply the impoverishment of culture that Mardin talks about. For a long time their cognitive map concerning Turkish society and polity consisted only of a center-periphery cleavage where they themselves made up the "center." In the absence of a more comprehensive world view or philosophy (that the rising "bourgeoisie" was unable to formulate)[83] they must have been quite content with Kemalism. That Kemalism did not provide the "cultural resources"[84] to tackle the ongoing processes of specialization and differentiation might have not bothered them because for a long time they did not feel threatened by those processes.[85] It is only recently that they realized their increasing subordination in the Turkish polity.[86] Thus the inevitable question: "Why do the just suffer and the unjust prosper?" And this has occurred when Kemalism as an ideology simply became less relevant despite the fact that a destruction of it by capitalism has not taken place. As Frey put it, "...the Kemalist paradigm is exhausted,...

this is obscurely recognized, and...no successor has been accepted."[87]

There may be two types of response to a situation of this sort:

In the case of economic, social, and organismic deprivation... religious resolutions are more likely to occur where the nature of deprivation is inaccurately perceived or those experiencing the deprivation are not in a position to work directly at eliminating the causes. The resolution is likely to be secular under the opposite conditions - where the nature of the deprivation is correctly assessed by those experiencing it and they have, or feel they have the power or feel they can gain the power, to deal with it directly.[88]

I would like to suggest that most members of the traditional bureaucratic, educated elite in Turkey, preferred the secular alternative; they found solace in hard ideologies of a mainly leftist and, to a lesser extent, rightist variety. The recent turmoil in Turkey that was often taken as a sign of Islamic resurgence[89] was in fact a spinoff from this polarization. Political democracy in Turkey, added to the self-confidence of the Turkish intelligentsia (including, of course, the students), made it possible for this elite to opt for secular politics rather than an Islamic mass movement. The more timid within this stratum must have provided additional stuff of which the present visibility of Islam is forged. Nevertheless, it is hard to imagine this group roaming the streets of Ankara like their Iranian counterparts; the Turkish bureaucratic, educated elite would not easily discard their essentially Kemalist orientation.

4. <u>Conclusion</u>

The "Cultural Revolution" in Turkey has been more successful than is usually presumed. Economic change that accelerated after the Second World War had a strong impact in the same direction. Successful institutionalization of political democracy provided alternatives to religious protest. In Turkey the secularization process in its various dimensions has been essentially a cumulative process. Thus, Dekmejian's general characterization of that process in the Middle East as "a cyclical pattern of ebb-and-flow between secularist trends and Islamic trends"[90] is not true concerning Turkey.

The most important dimensions of the recent visibility of Islam in Turkey are psychological and cultural. Inner need and the problems of meaning have been most significant. The "revival" in Turkey has not been an increase in the "force" of the religiosity, i.e., in the thoroughness with which such a pattern is internalized, but in its "scope," i.e. the range of social contexts within which religious considerations are regarded as having more or less direct relevance.[91] The religion that has spread has Durkheimian or metaphysical functions. There has been no intensification of belief in the supernatural.

Turkey represents a unique case within the Muslim context. There are significant differences between Turkey on one hand and Iran and Egypt on the other. There must be major differences with other Muslim countries.

SACRAMENTAL FOOD TRANSACTIONS AMONG
SOUTH ASIAN MUSLIMS AND HINDUS

John P. Thorp

1. Introduction

Food transactions comprise one of the "languages" in which the religious, social and political affairs of South Asian Muslims and Hindus are conducted. Various food stuffs are "lexemes" marked with specific significance which can be manipulated in syntactical patterns or codes of giving or receiving, sharing and exchanging. Like lexemes, various foods and food transactions are symbolic. Who gives - and/or - receives what kinds of food to - and/or - from whom on what occasions and in what manner are meaningful statements, "sentences," within both Hindu and Muslim societies. In this sense, food transactions are similar to Talcott Parson's "generalized media of social interaction" (1963a, 1963b). However, in South Asia food transactions are much more than generalized statements about, or arbitrary symbols of, religious and social and political reality. Instead, food transactions are constitutive of this reality. They embody the relationships they express; they are sacraments of social interaction. This paper expands upon Parson's concept of symbolic generalized media of social interaction in order to explore the cultural systems of food transactions in South Asia. In the context of South Asian ideas about the coded substantiality (Schneider, 1968) of all reality (Marriott and Inden, 1973; 1974), I will pay detailed attention to food transactions as they are conducted among South Asian Muslims. I will point out how the concept of effective sacrament more adequately than the concept of arbitrary symbol makes sense out of the data recorded in the literature about South

Asian Muslims and Hindus, and makes sense out of the data which I have gathered from rural, Bangladeshi Muslims.

2. **Generalized Media of Social Interaction**
According to Parsons (1963a: 41) a generalized medium is defined in terms of four institutional prerequisites: a category of value, a category of interest, a definition of the situation, and a normative framework. South Asian food transactions can be so defined. In any South Asian transaction, but especially in food transactions, a category of value is involved. There is a definite respect in which the values of both Muslim and Hindu transactors are at stake, because each transactor is concerned with the effect of the transaction on his own substantial composition, on his person. South Asian Hindus are especially concerned with protecting the very fluid boundaries of their persons (Marriott, 1976 Hindu Transactions: Diversity without Dualism in Transaction and Meaning, ed. Bruce Kapferer, Pp.109-142. Philadelphia: Institute for the Study of Human Issues. 1980). Hindus view themselves as very open to changes in personal substance. However, only certain kinds of changes are considered valuable. Secondly, a category of interests in objects is also present in food transactions. Food stuffs have properties in the action situation which are highly relevant in the light of the category of value. Different food stuffs communicate coded bodily substances differently. Hindus, in particular, believe that each person's coded bodily substance can be dispersed by means of food transfers, and a person may also accumulate others' differently coded bodily substances in these transactions. Third, Parsons calls for a definition of the situation in which generalized media are used by the acting units to obtain their interests. Generalized media function in a collective structure. In the case of food transactions the situation is defined in terms of birth. A person is born a Hindu or a Muslim, which is the source of that person's fundamental coded substance, and the orienting factor in the person's particular capacity to participate in different ritualized events of social existence.

Most of these events involve food transactions. Finally, a normative framework is necessary to discriminate between legitimate and illegitimate modes of action in pursuit of the actor's interests. Within the South Asian context the normative framework allows two basic modes of action: sharing with people of the same coded bodily substance, and exchanging with people of differently coded substances (Nicholas and Inden, 1977). These exchanges may be carried out according to one of four strategies: optimal asymmetric exchange, or pessimal asymmetric exchange; maximal symmetric exchange, or minimal non-exchange (Marriott, 1976).

South Asian food transactions meet Parsons' general requirements for generalized media of social interaction. A further criterion of these media, however, is that they be symbolic. For Parsons and others (see Morris, 1938; Langer; 1960, Geertz, 1973) a sign or a symbol "stands for" what it represents. Symbols have no intrinsic value of their own, (cf. Lévi-Strauss, 1967: 93-95) but are conventionally assigned to represent valued social objects or relationships. The lexeme is the primary analogue in the definition of any symbol. The assignment of a particular lexeme to represent a particular real object is considered arbitrary, and is meaningful only because the identification between lexeme and object is conventualized, or agreed upon by all the speakers of a particular language. If this definition of symbol is accepted, it is not possible to consider food a generalized symbolic medium of religious, social and political interaction in South Asia, and at the same time seriously account for everything South Asians themselves say about food. Food is considered an object with intrinsic value, a person becomes what he eats and what he can become is determined by what is available to eat. Not only that, but what people do with particular food stuffs in situations of interaction makes a real difference in the nature of their interrelationships. Food transactions do not stand for relationships that exist independently of the transaction. They are part of that very relationship. Communal sharing of a village feast is not "symbolic" of a disembodied, non-reified, Durkheimian community solidarity. Participation in the feast creates an embodied solidarity in which the participants vitalize those parts of their personal coded substance which they share in common. Food transactions in South Asia are sacraments, rather than symbols. They are a medium which is believed to actually effect what is represented.

3. South Asian Muslim Society

Although the Muslims of South Asia insist upon dissociating themselves from Hindus and things Hindu, nevertheless, they share with the Hindus a common sacramental approach to reality. The Muslim reformers of the nineteenth and twentieth centuries made attempts at purification (Khan, 1960; 1965), Arabization (Mutakar and Ansari, 1966), and Islamicization (Aggarwal, 1971) of South Asian Islam. The intention of these reform efforts was to rid the Muslim community of supposed Hindu accretions. However, not one of these attempts is reported to have objected to food transactions as un-Islamic. For example, the Fara'idi movement of Bengal objected to the common rite of offering *fatihah* in memory of the dead. This rite includes reading from the Quran, the performance of various prayers and the consumption of a meal by the participants. The reformers' objection was not to the inclusion of the meal with the reading of the Quran. Rather, they opposed this ritual because they could find no explicit reference to the particular combination of elements in the ritual in either the Quran or the Traditions, although each of the elements was perfectly acceptable Muslim behaviour (Khan, 1960). In Parsons' terms, Muslims and Hindus do not completely share the same definition of situation and category of value. However, they do share similar categories of interests in objects and normative frameworks. The Hindus and Muslims, as it were, speak dialects of the same "language."

Informative source material about South Asian Muslims is limited. But what is available exhibits a striking pattern of consistency across both space and time. Beginning with Jafar Sharif's work of 1832 and then jumping forward to Abbot's work of a century later (1932), and then moving into the social scientists' work of the 1960's and 1970's, material exists which treats the Muslim communities of the Indus and Ganges river systems and the Deccan plateau. Although these sources are seldom mutually corroborative on particular points of interest, and they in no way tell the whole story, nevertheless they do not contradict each other. My own research in Bangladesh (sponsored by Caritas-Bangladesh, 1975-76) also corroborates the consistency of South Asian Muslim beliefs and behaviour in regard to the importance of food. On the basis of this material it is possible to make coherent generalizations about the sacramental significance of food transactions in South Asian Muslim communities. To simplify Parsons' fourfold approach to generalized media, and to paraphrase Laswell (1958), it is possible to generalize about who gives and/or receives what, when and how.

3.1 <u>Who</u>
Transactions in food among South Asian Muslims have to be understood in terms of the particular worldview these Muslims adhere to. Rural Muslims, of Bangladesh in particular (Thorp, 1978), place great emphasis in all aspects of their lives upon their descent from Allah's first human creature, Adam. The reality of human creaturehood is the implicit but controlling value in food transactions. The very nature of being human is involved in these transactions. In particular, the "who" of being Muslim is the Parsonian "value" that is at stake for these "acting units," these transactors.

The categorization of value in food transactions revolves around Allah's creating Adam out of the first of the four primal elements: earth, air, fire, and water. Adam's creation from earth gave him primacy over all of creation, including the angels whom Allah had already created from fire. Earth is considered the most powerfilled of the elements, and the earthiness of his creaturehood imparted to Adam (and imparts to his descendants) physical strength and, more importantly, intellectual, moral capacity (in Bengali, *Khamatā*). In the Bengali view the Muslim, therefore, is particularly adept at being a farmer.

Allah gave his earthly creature, Adam, dominion or mastery (*adhikār*) over all of the earth, much to the chagrin of Iblis, the leader of the angels, a creature of fire. Rural Muslims see their own possession of cultivable land as directly related to the original bestowal of mastery upon Adam. Insofar as they possess even the tiniest plot of land, a (Bengali) Muslim considers himself a full heir of Adam and, therefore, a person of substance. It is obvious that some persons have more substance than others. Some are "rich," others are "poor." Still others who are completely landless are "beggars." Earth is the critical substance. Creation from it bestows on men strength and ability and moral responsibility to take possession of the earth in order to farm it, to bring forth food from it. Producing food allows a person to engage in food transactions which create the significant social relations of daily life.

Persons possess statuses and are organized into social groups in relation to this original creation of Adam, and in relation to food as a product of this creation. Significant collectivities for South Asian Muslims are numerous and they are not similarly named in different Muslim communities. However, the following collectivities are found throughout South Asia, whatever they are named. First of all, Allah also created Howa (Eve) from Adam's left side and together they bore many children who themselves bore children. Eve and these children were dependents (*paribār* in Bengali) of Adam, or Adam's "family" because he fed them from the produce of his land. Today, the master of land, the *mālik*, is also the master of a household whose members are dependent upon him for food. These persons are, thus, his "family" or *paribār*. A particular *mālik's* family is the result of a number of marriages over time, as well as being due to the birth of offspring. "Relatives" (*ātmīya-svajan*) are the total collectivity which results from births and marriages.

Various food transactions are used to unite the members of this collectivity and to distinguish sub-groups within it.

Unrelated families and groups of patrilineally related families (*kūl*, *gusthī*) form local residential communities that are variously named throughout South Asia. In Bengal local, residential communities are known as *samāj*, which may be translated as "residential brotherhood." The image of Adam surrounded by his sons and their sons and their dependents is the template for the organization of these residential brotherhoods. The masters of land and family consider themselves sons of Adam, substantively related to each other by the earthiness of their creation and by their common residence upon, and use of, land in a particular area. Their conceptualization is much more than that of "fictive kinship," as it is usually regarded by anthropologists (see Aziz, 1979: 76-82). Members of a residential brotherhood consider themselves brothers upon the land. Food transactions on various occasions sacramentalize this valued sharing of common substance.

Muslims of South Asia also organize themselves into a variety of religious brotherhoods which may be organized around mosques where prayers are regularly shared, or cemeteries where variously related persons are buried, or around particular holy men (*pīr*) from whom religious instruction is obtained, or around the shrines of deceased holy men where the saint's holiness is still active. Food is not the only medium of interaction in South Asia. In the case of holy men their "words" may also be considered another sacramental medium. However, food is also used to substantiate the reality of all these groups.

The ceremonies involved in the veneration of Muslim holy men or saints are particularly instructive in this regard. People approach such saints to obtain their help in solving problems in curing illness. On these occasions it is common to obtain a *tawiz* (amulet) from the saint which can either be worn or immersed in water and the water drunk. Should a person wish to become the disciple of a saint, a special initiation ceremony is performed during the course of which sweets brought by the prospective disciple are blessed by the saint and returned to the disciple and the assembled congregation for their consumption. Finally, at the annual celebration of a deceased saint the offering and reception of food as *tabarruk* (*sinni* in Bengal) is an important and enthusiastically participatory part of the celebration. Food purchased with money donated in memory of the saint is also widely distributed among the poor on these occasions and is generally considered a source of blessing (Census of India, 1962a). North Indian *pirs* (saints) are considered powerful people, possessed of *kudrat*, and by transacting with them in words and food their followers come in immediate contact with their power (*kudrat*) which produces blessings (*barkat*) (Abbot, 1932: 81, 95, 402). The words and food are the sacraments that not only represent but also produce these blessings.

Finally, South Asian Muslims recognize a variety of non-Muslims, usually Hindus, with whom they interact. Depending on the demographics of a particular situation, non-Muslims providing specialized services, e.g., washermen, carpenters, or potters, are more or less important to the Muslims. The more important that these non-Muslims are, the more likely it is that they will be involved in food transactions with Muslims. However, they are involved in a significantly different way, usually as the recipients of uncooked food grains.

Who a person is, is intimately bound up with the food transactions he engages in. Maintenance of this identity is highly valued among South Asian Muslims and Hindus. The category of value or the definition of the "who" is different for the Hindus, but both communities bring their whole identity to every food transaction which effects, creates, realizes this identity sacramentally. The common saying, "You are what you eat," could not be more true than it is in South Asia.

3.2 <u>What</u>
Particular products of the earth constitute the medium of these sacramental transactions. Food stuffs are the

Parsonian "objects of interest" for both Muslims and Hindus. Food stuffs have properties in the action situation which are highly relevant in light of the Muslims' and Hindus' evaluations of their separately conceived substantive personhoods. Although Hindus conceive of the person as a combination of air, water and fire, and Muslims conceive of themselves as created instead from earth, nevertheless both Hindus and Muslims are in agreement about the definition and the characteristics of food. For both communities rice is the premier food grain, and the basic element in food transactions around which other food items are assembled.

Both groups use raw food stuffs in their transactions with those whom they consider least like themselves. In most cases this means each other. Among the Hindus transactions with service castes are also conducted by means of uncooked food stuffs. Food in this potential form is least likely to have any serious transformative effect upon either donor or recipient. Rice specially cooked in milk and/or clarified butter, or foods prepared with various sweeteners or special spices, are the common foods used on special occasions by persons who consider that they share a common, particularly coded substantive nature. When food grains are simply boiled in water by the women of a family and consumed as daily fare, a statement is being made in both Muslim and Hindu communities about the similarity and the closeness of the persons consuming such food, that is, family members. To become such a member a person need only regularly consume his daily food within this group. For example, a new bride is incorporated into the family to which her husband belongs by turning her hand to the preparation of this ordinary food (Eglar, 1960). Although ordinary cooked food is not the only substance that creates families, it is considered capable of doing this. Clearly, food is sacramentally effective in this case.

As Muslims' and Hindus' conceptualizations about the composition of their substantive natures are different, so too their explanations of why food is able to effect particular results are different, though not unrelated.

The explanations of Bengali Muslims, at least, are part of their views about Allah's original creation of Adam. Of the four elemental substances earth is particularly power-filled (*sakti-sālī*). This "power" gave Adam his bodily strength, his mental capacity and his moral sense. As earth possesses this "power," so too creatures of earth possess it. As the produce of the earth, food also possesses this "power." Humans can possess themselves of more of this reality by consuming food. The more food and the better the quality of the food consumed, the more strength, wisdom, skill and responsibility a person may obtain. As my own colloquial Bengali improved with time in the research area, my informants inevitably and quite seriously attributed this improved linguistic performance to my consumption of locally produced food, and to the quality of food that I consumed. I daily consumed either fish, eggs, chicken or meat, all of which are considered to be especially power-filled by my informants. Muslims especially value meat from any animal sacrificed to Allah as particularly conducive to establishing and maintaining a person as a Muslim. Consumption of this kind of food, even more than circumcision ("making a Muslim"), which is limited to males, concretizes the distinctiveness of being a Muslim in the Hindu milieu which positively values vegetarianism. Animal sacrifice is essential to the Muslim commemoration of Abraham's sacrifice of his son, which is performed in conjunction with the sacrifices concluding the pilgrimage to Mecca.

The Muslim farmer of Bengal, at least, considers himself a creature of earth, constantly reconstituting himself by his labour upon the earth which produces his own and his dependents' food. A substantive relationship with the "natural" world exists for these farmers (Thorp, 1979) which is constantly being realized through the medium of food. Furthermore, it should be pointed out that food is only one of the media in which people transact. Words of blessing and instruction, clothes, jewelry, animals, money are all part of the total picture of transactions South Asians are involved in. Transactions of one kind are not always reciprocated (if that is necessary) in the same kind. Food, however, does represent the most generalized and potent of the possible media. It functions with definite meanings and specific effects across the spectrum of social, political, and religious situations that make up South Asian social existence.

3.3 When
The Muslim definition of situation is most obvious and accessible on occasion of ritualized activity (T. Turner, 1968: 129-30) when food transactions occur. Among the Muslims there are two sets of these ritualized situations that are distinguished. The first set is commonly considered to be composed of life-cycle rituals, dealing with birth and death, and the transformations that occur between these two events (see especially Aggarwal, 1971; Bhowmick, 1965; Eglar, 1960; Ellickson, 1972; Jafar Sharif, 1895; Thorp, 1978). Among the Muslims birth now establishes on the earth the actors who are transformed through circumcision in the case of males, by marriage, and who are finally and specially transformed by death. All these situations are alike in that their central focus is the status of a particular person at a particular moment as a Muslim. The result of the ritualized activity which occurs on these occasions is to identify the particular person with other persons sharing the same status, and to differentiate him from other statuses.

The second set of ritual situations comprises those usually referred to as calendric festivals (see especially Aggarwal, 1971; Census of India, 1962b; Jafar Sharif, 1895). Unfortunately, much less attention is given to these festivals in the sources than to the first set; and what attention is given is nowhere near as detailed. However, my own field experience (Thorp, 1978) has given me a wealth of detail about these festivals among Bengali Muslims. The main festivals begin in the first month of the Muslim lunar calender, Muharram, with the commemorations of the martyrdom of the Prophet's grandsons. Next comes the celebration of the birth and death anniversary of the Prophet, *Milad*. Following is the vigil of Shabi-barat during which night Allah records the fate of each person for the coming year. The Ramzan fast and the Eid (-ul-Fitr) celebrating its conclusion is the first of the two major Muslim festivals, and it occurs during and at the end of the ninth month of the Muslim calendar. The second major celebration, Buqr-Eid, commemorating Abraham's sacrifice of his son Ishmael, occurs in the twelfth month and coincides with the conclusion of the pilgrimage to Mecca. Although the calendar regulates the occurrence of these festivals throughout the year, their major focus is upon the common heritage as creatures of earth shared by the Muslims of any given area, at least. The food transactions on these festivals are more communitarian than those of the first set of life-cycle rituals which mark off particular persons in terms of various collectivities of persons. This clearly can be seen by examining how persons transact with each other in life-cycle feasting and during calendric festivals.

3.4 How

The fourth and final Parsonian institutional prerequisite of a generalized medium of social interaction is a normative framework which establishes the rules or norms discriminating between legitimate and illegitimate modes of action in pursuit of the transactors' interests. Among South Asian Muslims and Hindus there are two modes of transacting in food: sharing it and exchanging it. When the Muslims' attention is focused upon the communalities between persons, food is shared. This is the pattern of transaction characteristic of the calendric festivals, and the consumption of ordinary cooked food within the family. On the other hand, on those occasions when the masters of families, the *māliks*, specially mark the passage of one of their dependents to a new status, invitations to feasts in their homesteads are exchanged. Feasts are exchanged on a regular basis by relatives and members of residential brotherhoods over time in such a way that differences between persons and collectivities are made evident. How these familial, life-cycle rituals concretize differences between persons and collectivities will be examined first. Then the functioning of calendric festivals in overriding and blurring such differences through the equal sharing of food will be treated.

3.4.1. Familial Life-Cycle Rituals

Life-cycle rituals are clearly characterized by the presence of a specially marked person who is for the most part the passive focus of special attention. In the process of focusing this attention on a particular person various collectivities are also marked off. The foci of those rituals which concern birth are first the pregnant mother and then the new child. Both are specially fed. A boy to be circumcised is also specially fed "strengthening" foods, as are both the bride and groom at a marriage. A dying person is also given special sweet drinks, and after death special food transactions between his heirs and relatives occur. During a person's lifetime optional relationships of allegiance to a holy man or a patron are sometimes established. The disciple or client in these relationships also receives special food. Unlike the child, boy, groom or dying person the disciple or client is not totally passive. He is able to terminate his allegiance by failing or refusing to accept his patron's food.

The feasts that accompany these special feedings of particular persons concretize various statuses and collectivities of persons within rural society. The master of a family, a *mālik*, hosts these feasts. He provides meat, vegetables and rice specially prepared by male members of his residential brotherhood to his relatives and to all the members of his residential brotherhood. He might possibly also provide this food to fellow members of some religious brotherhood. Depending upon the concrete circumstances of the host *mālik*, non-Muslims may also be provided food, more often than not in uncooked form. The way these transactions are accomplished serves to concretize distinctions of status, of age, of sex, of "close" as opposed to "distant" relatives, of friendship, as well as distinctions between the living and the deceased. Relative distinctions of wealth or poverty are also evident in that "rich" *māliks* are able and expected to provide for their guests lavishly. "Poor" *māliks* are also expected to proffer invitations to such feasts within their families, but to fewer persons and for poorer fare. "Beggars," in both cases, are expected to attend such familial feasts uninvited. As is obvious, they never reciprocate.

These life-cycle rituals do far more than mark the passage of one person to a new status within a community. These rituals through their pattern of transacting in food concretize, give expression to, allow persons to experience the community of persons to which they belong as diversified but, nevertheless, one community. The collectivities of persons who make up this community are acknowledged and realized at a particular time and in a particular place. The diversity which marks rural social life is acknowledged and perpetuated through the transactions in food that occur at these feasts. On these occasions the host gives food to his guests. At subsequent feasts (as well as at prior feasts) he will himself be a guest and accept food from those whom he has fed. Over time as feasts are exchanged, South Asian Muslims are able to recreate for themselves the original community of Muslims, Adam and his sons and daughters and their sons and daughters.

3.4.2. Religious Calendric Festivals

Muslim calendric festivals, on the other hand, play down the differences between persons, and emphasize the common identity of the transactors as all heirs of Adam, as Muslims, as all equally creatures of earth. On these occasions the emphasis is upon sharing food, not on exchanging it. The distinction of host and guest, of donor versus recipient is absent. Instead, whole collectivities of persons, usually residential or religious brotherhoods, participate together as one unit in these food transactions. The 10th of Muharram is the first of these festivals in the calendric order. This is the commemoration of martyrdom of the Prophet's grandsons at Karbala. The major transactors during Muharram, and later at the celebrations of the Prophet's birth and death anniversary in the second month of the calendar, seem to be the religious brotherhoods responsible for the care of the martyr's symbols and the Prophet's relics. These two festivals seem to be more important and more vigorously celebrated by the Muslims of north and western South Asia than they are in the east. The religious brotherhoods display the relics or symbols during the festivals, and they share meals together. They also distribute this food to any wishing to partake of it. The religious brotherhoods and the local residential communities are all drawn together during Muharram at the public ceremonies commemorating the battle on the plains of Karbala. At these ceremonies various sweet liquids are generously dispensed and widely shared (Census of India, 1962b).

On the occasion of Shab-i-barat, Ramzan and Eid-ul-Fitr, and Buqr-Eid local residential brotherhoods are the focus of important food transactions. Besides praying together at the mosque and in their homesteads on Shab-i-barat, and at the local area's Eid Field on Eid-ul-Fitr and Buqr-Eid, local residential communities of Muslims in Bangladesh gather at the homestead of the residential brotherhood's leader for a ceremonial sharing of specially prepared rice. Each family in the brotherhood prepares as much of this special rice as they can afford. This is then carried to the leader's homestead by the children and the men. After all the contributions have been gathered together, first the children and then the men share in this food. Shares of this food are also sent with the children to the women of the brotherhood who remained at home. On Buqr-Eid special care is also taken in the division of the sacrificed animals so that each man, woman and child of the brotherhood receives one, equal share in the meat. The overall proportion of the meat devoted to this residential community sharing varies from one-third to one-half in different parts of South Asia. The remainder of the meat, whatever the proportions, is returned to the donor or donors of the animal for their own consumption within their families or for distribution to relatives who reciprocate in kind. The equal sharing of food on these occasions sacramentalizes the participants' common identity as Muslims despite the multitude of personal distinctions that mark their society. At least in these festivals mankind's common equality and brotherhood as Allah's creatures is recognized, positively acknowledged, and actually achieved for the participants.

Another aspect of Muharram, Shab-i-barat, and Buqr-Eid which links these festivals with the life-cycle feasts is the commemoration of ancestors (*fatihah*) which occurs on these occasions. The *Milad* of the Prophet is itself the commemoration of the most special ancestor, Muhammad (Sm). I am as yet uncertain how to interpret these commemorations of ancestors. It is unclear what they sacramentalize. Due to the efforts of reformers of Islam in the late nineteenth century in the area of my fieldwork *fatihah* was not performed there in the way it is reported in the literature. The literature does not specify in any detail who these ancestors are. I would speculate that not every ancestor, nor even a person's immediate ancestors are commemorated, but only those who are in some way significant to the commemorators. The commemoration could then be considered an attempt to sacramentally maintain that part of the commemorator's identity that can be traced to the one commemorated. There is no doubt that these commemorations are important since there are three named and ranked forms. The *fatihah* is the commemoration of ordinary ancestors performed by their families and relatives, and consists of reading at least the opening chapter of the Quran and offering various prayers "in the name of the deceased" over specially prepared food that is then consumed by the participants. An *urs* is a *fatihah* offered in the name of a deceased *pir*. Thirdly, the Prophet is commemorated in a celebration known as a *milad*. This yearly festival is considered the birthday of the Prophet, although it is celebrated on his traditional death anniversary. This conjunction of birth and death deserves far more treatment than the sources give it. It would appear to be very important in a system that is as birth conscious as South Asian Islam is. Beside the yearly festival, a *milad* in the Prophet's name may also be conducted on other auspicious occasions during the year by particular families (Ellickson, 1972). These occasions have the form of the *fatihah* and include a meal. These three ancestral commemorations, like the life-cycle rituals, are focused on particular and significant persons, but unlike the life-cycle rituals their performance emphasizes the sharing of specially coded common substance, rather than marking distinctions.

6. Sharing and Exchanging

The Muslims of South Asia share food, as well as exchange it. The most common food transaction is the sharing of ordinary food from the same cooking pot. This sharing is engaged in only by those with the greatest similarity of common coded substance, family members. As has been pointed out, Muslims gather together in brotherhoods of various sorts on the occasions of calendric festivals, and their interaction by means of food is basically that of an equal sharing of special foods. On the other hand, patterns of food exchange also occur when non-family members, usually relatives and fellow brotherhood members, are invited into the family and specially fed. Those who are hosts on one such occasion are, however, guests on other similar occasions. Food is also distributed to non-Muslims without any expectation or desire that it be reciprocated.

As was briefly referred to above, exchange transactions in South Asia can be patterned out to produce the fourfold schema of maximalizers, minimalizers, optimalizers, and pessimalizers (Marriott, 1976). This is so because giving is positively evaluated in South Asian culture, and receiving is negatively evaluated. An optimalizer is the person who only gives, e.g. the Brahman. A pessimalizer is someone who only receives, such as an Untouchable. A minimalizer is someone who neither gives nor receives. A maximalizer is someone who gives and receives from as many other persons as possible. Among

Hindus the middle-level castes tend to be either maximalizers or minimalizers. As a whole community South Asian Muslims appear to be best described as maximalizers. At least with other Muslims, they seem to pursue a pattern of balanced reciprocity with as many exchange partners as possible. However, some Muslims can be found in the other categories, with the possible exception of the minimalizers. Unfortunately, I have no information about the Khojas of Bombay or about the Shiite groups in South Asia, nor is there very detailed information about the different groups of "reformed" Muslims in the early years of this century, who quite possibly were minimalizers. The Bengali reformer, Titu Mir, is reported to have instructed his followers to inter-dine only among themselves, and especially to avoid the non-reformed Muslim. Khan (1965: lxiii), however, disputes that this could have been possible for a reformer. He points to the practice of even conservative theologians and holy men who would not receive food from anyone of questionable integrity, but who did not hesitate to feed these same individuals at their own tables. These persons could be described as optimalizers. This was the practice among the Fara'idis of the nineteenth century, and still occasionally happens among them today. Khan seems to deny the existence of any minimalizers. Be that as it may, South Asian Muslims more often than not are maximalizers. Although they recognize the other possibilities in a conceptual system that positively evaluates giving and negatively evaluates receiving, part of being a Muslim is to participate regularly in a pattern of reciprocal food exchanges. It is almost as if the acceptance of Islam necessitates a willingness to give and to accept invitations to feasts from any other person who identifies himself as a Muslim. Only those who are destitute cannot offer these invitations and are thus pessimalizers, but they will accept food nevertheless. As is true of food sharing on calendric festivals, so also even food exchanges during familial feasts promote the valued concept of equality, at least among fellow Muslims. This value is not at all characteristic of these Muslims' hierarchically organized Hindu neighbors.

4. Conclusions

Food transactions are a particularly important part of the cultural systems of both the Hindu and Muslim societies of South Asia. Food transactions are visible social behaviour and their observations can serve to map out many of the significant elements of South Asian social structure. Patterns of relationships can be established empirically. However, food is culturally defined; and transactions in this medium embody these cultural meanings and values. These transactions give definite shape to the empirical patterns of social relationships. Food transactions are conspicuous examples of meaningful (cultural) behaviour (social action), where the social and cultural systems interpenetrate. The study of food transactions allows not only the mapping of social relationships, but also allows these relationships to be positively evaluated and understood in their significance to South Asians, that is, if the observer knows the lexical code, and recognizes its sacramentality.

Both Hindus and Muslims transact in food, sharing as they do the same generalized interest in objects and normative framework, but differing in important ways in their categories of value and definitions of situation (for example, see Madan, 1972). I do not think it is an overstatement to say that at the epistemological level of culture South Asia is one. Hindus and Muslims share the same sacramental approach to identifying persons and collectivities, and to interrelating them sacramentally in substantive ways. Thus, Muslims and Hindus are able to order their societies, and, furthermore, make provisions for handling situations of potential conflict.

However, to share the same "language" does not mean always to say the same things. Muslims and Hindus are different, and the most obvious difference is that the Muslims are less hierarchical than the Hindus. Although categories of birth are important to the Muslims, and though they differentiate "classes" of persons, nevertheless they also emphasize their common membership in the community of believers (*ummat*) which results from the sharing of a common coded substance by each Muslim, as an heir of Adam. Communality of involvement in the same event is positively evaluated by minimalizing the differentiation in means of participation, especially in the sharing of food at those calendric festivals considered properly Muslim. The common element of their coded substance allows what hierarchy that does exist among the Muslims to be overridden and maximalizing tendencies to develop.

One concluding example of the relevance of this sacramental approach to social interaction can be taken from the political sphere of South Asian life. I would posit that as a consequence of this sacramentality significant cooperation or activity aimed at the achievement of public goals is limited in South Asia to situations where the actors can transact substantially and immediately with each other, that is, through some concrete medium. At the village level this medium has traditionally been food. A good example of this is the ward organization among the Pathans of Swat (Barth, 1960; 1965) that centres in the ward men's houses. The locally dominant Pathan supports this institution, principally by providing food to those who choose to be part of the institution. By receiving the dominant landlord's food the frequenters of the men's house are made the landlord's political dependents and supporters. This is not an irrevocable allegiance, but as long as a person receives the landlord's food, he will be called upon for support. This pattern is common throughout South Asia, and influences the pursuance of public activities in important ways. As the scope of political activity expands beyond the realm of immediate interaction, however, serious problems develop because of the South Asian emphasis on sacramental interaction. How do you treat individuals or institutions whom you can neither feed nor be fed by ? The most frequently decried solution to this problem of the need for immediate interaction through some medium is "graft." To make the bureaucratic system work at the local level a chain of relationships through a great variety of specific middlemen has to be established. As experience has shown, the attempt to construct chains of these kinds of immediate, substantialized relationships has rendered South Asian bureaucracies rather inefficient, if not ineffectual. South Asian sacramentality does not possess the degrees of freedom of Parsonian symbolic activity, and, therefore, will not produce the same kind of political and social product. One stance that might be taken is that the South Asian product is inferior in and of itself because of its limited existential efficiency; and its sacramentality, therefore, must be eradicated. Another, more practical approach, however, is the attempt to understand more clearly the nature of generalized sacramental media in South Asia. Although sacramental media do not possess the degrees of freedom of symbolic media, they do embody cultural values in concrete and immediate forms that seemingly have greater potential for the integration of society than do symbolic media. Further research into the distinction between the two approaches and their resultant products is essential.

OTATHA: PROBINGS INTO THE ISOKO CONCEPT OF PREDESTINY

S.G.A. Osovo Onibere

The Isoko[1] concept of predestiny (*otatha*) is so much entrenched in the traditio-religious milieu of the Isoko (in present day Nigeria) that it calls for a thorough analysis in order to understand its various ramifications. And prefatory to its understanding is a consideration of the constituents of man.

Man, the Isoko strongly hold, is a tripartite composition comprising body (*oma*), spirit (*ezi*) and soul (*emema* or *oma*).[2] Whereas the *oma* (body) is tangible and concrete, the *ezi* (spirit) is intangible and invisible. *Ezi* is responsible for animating the body, and by implication its withdrawal from its natural habitat betokens the termination of existence. *Ezi* is thus empirically discernible through its causal functions. On the other hand, the *emema* or *oma* (soul) is the essence of personality - ruling, guiding and controlling the life and activities of a person. More significantly, it is the *emema* which indissolubly connects man to Deity in a special way.

A close look at the concept of *emema* reveals a complication. "It is conceived as a semi-split entity in consequence of which it is at the same time the essence of the personality and the person's guardian or protector,"[3] known to the people as *osu*.[4] Perhaps a starting-point towards a resolution of the complexity is a discussion of the essays by William Ifode and James W. Welch. Ifode has written: "The child in coming to the world has a companion guide called *osu* (meaning leader or guide) and on arrival is known as *oma*."[5] Welch writes:

Oma is present when Oghene creates each individual, and assists [sic] but the chief function of *Oma* is to lead the person to earth and to watch over him there. *Oma* is often given another name at the birth of a child, "*osu*", meaning leader but once the leading part is over, *osu* is driven back to Oghene by giving him pieces of plantain outside the house, and by making a hole near the door and covering it with chalk to prevent his entrance; *Oma* is then officially received by the sacrifice of a hen. Throughout life one's prosperity depends upon the goodwill of one's *Oma*, who is thought as acting for Oghene.[6]

In the opinion of Ifode *osu* changes its name to *oma* on arrival in the world of mortals; whereas Welch reverses this order and makes *oma* the leader of the child to earth, at the conclusion of which it is given another name, *osu*.[7] It is clear that a measure of confusion reigns in the minds of both writers regarding the Isoko conception of a person's guardian (*osu*) and the soul (*oma*). It is this that has led them to merge the two different entities of *osu* and *oma* into one and to make it perform two functions which otherwise belong to the two seperately. Succinctly stated *osu* and *oma* are separate entities which exist side by side from the beginning to the end of the life of the individual. As a matter of fact, Welch confuses the situation the more when he says that the one thing given two names is simultaneously "driven back to God" and "officially received by the sacrifice of a hen". Evidently, both writers' interpretation of the oral traditions at their disposal at this point appears to be misleading.

A further look at Welch's work reveals more infelicities. He claims that

each individual has also two guardian spirits sent by Oghene, which are *Oma* and *Ezi*.... *Ezi* means life-bringer, and is a person's soul, and without him life is impossible. At death *Ezi* is said to have gone home to Oghene. While *Oma* arrives with the new child, *Ezi* delays his arrival until the child can speak and think, when *Ezi* is welcomed and a visible symbol made in the shape of a branch of the *ovo* tree with cowries and two strands of red cloth attached.[8]

The first point that strikes the present writer is the translation of the soul as *ezi*, which translation is certainly odious to the Isoko. Besides, Welch categorically asserts that *ezi* (his wrong translation is soul) and *Oma* (spirit) are "two guardian spirits sent by Oghene" (God) to every Isoko person. Apparently, it is not orthodox to regard the soul and the spirit as the guardians of an Isoko. The true picture, as already indicated, is that man consists of body, spirit and soul, the last of which can become a semi-split entity to include a person's guardian (*osu*). Again Welch is involved in a clear error when he says that the soul (his erroneous translation of *ezi*) "delays his arrival until the child can speak and think." Does he mean to say that a person has no soul from the day of his birth to when he "can speak and think"? Does this not contradict his earlier declaration that "without him [soul] life is impossible"? To be sure, some measure of inconsistency exists here. The fact of the matter is that Oghene creates each Isoko complete with body, spirit and soul, the latter including a person's guardian.[9] The question is: What is the preexistent state of man and how does he become a member of the community of mortals? To this we must now turn.

It is unambiguous in the oral traditions that the creation of man is the responsibility of the Supreme Being. Originally all were created equal and why some now function in a subordinate capacity finds solution in the following myth. According to this,[10] God created human beings equal and released them to go to the sensible world. As they were on their way he discovered that, for an orderly functioning of the world, statuses must be hierarchized. Consequently he had them recalled and caused the loads on the heads of some of them to be pushed off. It was those who were relieved of their loads that have become subordinates in the present world.

Nonetheless, there is imperceptibly introduced into the picture the idea of *emema* (soul) as an assistant to the Supreme Being in his creative activities.[11] And at this point we are faced with a dilemma. If the Supreme Being is the creator of the three constituent parts of man as we have made clear, does it mean that the *emema*, having been created in turn began to assist Oghene? If the *emema* was busy assisting God, does it mean that man as a finished product was lacking the *emema* constituent? Alternatively, if it is conceded that God created subsequent *emema* what relationship had these with the first created *emema*? What was the precise nature of the assistance? Does God, who is omnipotent, need an assistant? On this array of questions the oral traditions maintain a significant silence. A resolution of this dilemma seems to lie in the fact that *emema* in this context attracts a different meaning, making it coterminous with the Supreme Being. This view is given credibility because of etymological considerations. *Emema* is a variant of *Omemama*, the latter being a contraction of *o ma emama* (literally "he created things"). It is thus virtually certain that God is known as *Emema* in his capacity as the Creator; and any thesis that makes *Emema* a separate entity is likely to ruin a proper understanding of the phenomenon.

However this may be, once a person's creation has been completed he has to kneel or stand before God to choose or receive his destiny (*otatha*).[12] In this act, if a person chooses or receives a fortunate *otatha*, especially longevity, his relatives and associates in the spirit-world will release shouts of disapproval because they will be without him longer than necessary. Moreover, "some spirits coming to earth are said to be so scared by Oghene's awful presence... that they fear to declare boldly before him all that they wish to be and do. Such spirits, when reincarnated either "go back" that is, die shortly after, or live wretched lives."[13] When the conferring of *otatha* has been done, however, the spirit to be incarnated crosses the rubicon between the suprasensible and physical worlds by means of conception and birth. Anything forgotten cannot be retrieved; nor does the person remember the contents of his destiny, except that he has a destiny to fulfil. To all intents and purposes, therefore, the aim of human existence in Isoko thought seems to be the fulfilment of destiny.

The source of *otatha*, arising as it does from the immutable Deity himself, is enough for its unalterability. Hence when the people encounter an untoward happening they say in desperation: *emema me o ru ome* ("It is my Creator that has caused this") or *o no igwe me e ta ze* (literally, "that which has been said by my knee"). One would have thought that the concept of *otatha's* unalterability would be settled beyond any possible uncertainty; but surprisingly enough, the oral traditions also present a contrary view - that of alterability.

The following myth current among the people serves to underscore our present contention. In the distant past there lived a king in a certain town. One of his subjects was blessed with white and sparkling teeth, though he was unfortunately childless. Every year it was the wicked practice of this king to reduce the subject's teeth by one during the celebration of a festival. The citizen was so bitter and helpless on account of his childlessness that he decided to meet Oghene to alter his *otatha*.

Thither he went but Oghene was away attending a meeting. He was, however, lucky to meet the favourite wife of Deity to whom he unbosomed his problem. Oghene's wife was sympathetic to his cause but reminded him that it was because he did not choose a happy destiny that the problem of infertility had come upon him. As this conversation was taking place, Oghene arrived, whereupon she had the man hidden in one corner of the house. But their design was not unknown to Oghene, who demanded his immediate appearance. The mortal emerged from his hiding, prostrated, himself before Oghene and pleaded that he be granted a child who would rescue him from the hands of the king. Oghene acceded to his request, granting two children instead of one. With the discussion concluded, Oghene drew a circle round the mortal and touched the latter's head. And to his utter astonishment he was at once with his relatives in the physical world and so reduced a journey that took several months to a matter of a split second!

On arrival on earth he quickly performed his conjugal obligation towards his two wives, who became pregnant and eventually gave birth to two sons known as Oruerakpo and Ugbugbe. Whereas Oruerakpo, as the name indicates, was peace-loving and quiet, helping his parents in sweeping the compound, washing kitchen utensils and fetching water for his mother, Ugbugbe was rascally, pugnacious and seen by his parents only at mealtimes. (But his usefulness will be fully transparent as the myth unfolds.)

The celebration of the king's festival was again approaching and one of the teeth of Ugbugbe's father was, so the king thought, sure to change places. By now it had become very easy to count the number of teeth left in his mouth. Ugbugbe's military character naturally heightened his acrimonious resentment of the king's action and he was consequently armed to the teeth to prevent a reoccurrence. Before too long the king had sent his envoys to carry out their usual assignment on Ugbugbe's father. Indeed this time Ugbugbe's father was also destined to lose his tongue! The presence of the envoys filled Ugbugbe with anger untold. And while Oruerakpo was engaged in pleading with them to reduce the unwarranted punishment to be inflicted on his father, Ugbugbe, with the speed of lightning, fell upon the envoys, scattering their number. Ugbugbe was of course aided with traditional medicine (*ebo*). Oruerakpo himself was so frightened with the turn of events that he was forced to run for dear life. Ugbugbe's father who complained of the severity of the action, was threatened by Ugbugbe with extinction should he further obstruct him in his bid for vengeance. Secretly, it is sure, Ugbugbe's father was most pleased that at last a "saviour" had arisen to protect his interests.

All this was such a surprise to the envoys that they sat at close quarters at home discussing what to do with Ugbugbe. But before they could execute any plans they had, Ugbugbe had already appeared in town, plucking down any whom he encountered. And before long the whole town had succumbed to death, leaving only the king and his family. Ugbugbe repaired to the king's palace but could not enter because it was saturated with traditional medicine (*ebo*). Ugbugbe was not prepared to accept defeat. Thereupon he went back home and soaked himself with more *ebo*. He reappeared with more supernatural power, entered the king's palace and made for the king. But the king could not be found as he was ingeniously hidden. Fortunately for

Ugbugbe the king's favourite wife (*anase*) was caught and ordered to reveal the secret of her husband's power. She did. With this knowledge it was now possible to locate the king's hiding place and have him killed. The *anase*, who was still alive, prostrated herself before Ugbugbe and promised to marry him if only he would spare her life. By this time Ugbugbe had become impervious to all appeals. And so with characteristic brutality he had her liquidated amidst tears of pleas.

Not satisfied with one town, Ugbugbe spread his tentacles to contiguous towns. In one of these towns he encountered Uwhumedue, a man with a strange behavioural pattern. Ugbugbe met him sleeping on a rubbish-heap. At once Ugbugbe sent his machete into action but recorded no wounds. On the contrary, Uwhumedue laughed and told Ugbugbe to beware lest he meet his end. Ugbugbe thought that Uwhumedue was a man of no consequence. Little did he know that Uwhumedue was a more potent force to reckon with and that his presence meant that Ugbugbe's punitive expedition, now executed beyond the bound of propriety, was surely ill-omened. And so it was that after much fighting between both of them, Ugbugbe was overpowered and killed.

Apart from this myth, there are other belief strands which vindicate the concept of the alterability of predestiny. It is believed that diabolical forces[14] which perpetuate the evil principle are capable of damaging a good destiny. Protective measures are therefore taken against them and where their machinations have been set in motion attempts are made to render them powerless. So also is it true that indiscriminate acts of behaviour do promote the doctrine of the alterability of predestiny. As an individual goes through life he is expected to maintain a good character in order to guarantee a fulfilment of his good *otatha*. Again, one's personal spirits can undo one's fortunate destiny. That is why a person's *obo* (hand), *owo* (leg), *oma* (soul) and *ezi* (spirit) are objects of worship so as to keep them in a state of peaceful contentment.[15] It is here, it appears, that a complication unveils itself. If the *obo*, *owo*, *oma* and *ezi* are all constituents of a person why is it that they can constitute a threat to a person's prosperous *otatha*? Is this not a case of a house divided against itself? In the face of all this our sources offer neither explanation nor rationalisation. It is simply accepted as an integral part of human existence.

It is noteworthy that the theoretical assent to the concept of *otatha's* alterability is given a practical basis. In accordance with this, and given certain circumstances, practical steps are taken to rectify an unhappy lot. A miserable destiny includes premature death, barrenness, poverty, madness, and so on. In order to identify a particular bad destiny a diviner has to be consulted. Prior to this consultation the victim might have been known to exhibit some measure of eccentricity. There is a story,[16] quite historical, which graphically illustrates this. An Enhwe man by the name of Oji once lived and worked at Warri with his family. He indulged in a practice which made his family very uneasy. At night he usually cried without prior provocation. After a time it became so frequent that his family did not attach much importance to it any longer. One day, at midnight, he started crying again but this time it was his last because his days had been numbered in compliance with his *otatha*. He gasped for breath but no rescue came from anyone since all regarded it as his usual queer behaviour. One of his children however, noticed a difference on this particular occasion and reported it to his mother, who dismissed him with a wave of her hand. Things were taking their predestined course, eventually culminating in the death of Oji. Much trepidation and wailing followed; but of course it was too late. Had they consulted a diviner to know why he cried at night, his *otatha* would have been identified and the remedy effected.

Perhaps at this point it may be appropriate to describe in some detail how an unhappy *otatha* can be rectified. And here we have necessarily to take a trip to Olomoro where Peter Edhewarie specialises in the rectification of unhappy *otatha*. The ceremony, which usually takes place before the shrine in his compound, is initiated by fixing the price of the undertaking. The items for fixing the price - known as *eware unueki* - include a bottle of gin and one naira, twenty kobo.[17] This done, the suppliant places the following items on the ground: six naira, seventy kobo, ten kolanuts, a bottle of beer, two bottles of soft drinks, a cat, candles, rice (prepared), powder, scent, white cloth and biscuits.[18] These are used at the appropriate stage of the ceremony. With the settlement of the price and procurement of the preceding items, the ceremony can now start in earnest.

The suppliant is arrayed in white and made to wear an amulet (*ama*) around his hand and waist with a pot of concoction on his head and a mirror in his hand. He stands before the shrine in a house; whereupon the officiant prays:

>   Edho Olomoro wha te reho ore
>   ko edho ko edho kpobi wha te reho ore
>   Oghene to reho ore
>
>   Olomoro gods, come and take white chalk
>   All the gods, come and take white chalk
>   God, come and take white chalk

The victim is then told kindly to have a seat outside. He stretches out the hand around which the *ama* has been tied and the officiant sprays white chalk on it with these words:

>   Ivie oria no otatha na o ro kpobi
>   Nyani mu ei re o to lie ze
>
>   Please, wherever the bad destiny is
>   Possess the victim in order that he may lay his hands on it.

It is believed that the *otatha* spirit, through the agency of the *ama*, does possess the victim, thus giving him enough spiritual sensitivity to reveal where his bad *otatha* (usually viewed in terms of such things as snails, cowrie-shells, broken bottles, plates, etc.) has been hidden. While this is happening, however, there is much drumming, singing and dancing. Some of the songs are reproduced as follows:

(i) Ye de ma yare re, ye de-ee
    Ye de ma yare re, ye de-ee
    Ye de ma yare re, ye de-ee
    Ede ri nene ma yare re (solo)
    Ye de ma yare re, ye de - e e e

    It is a bright day we pray for
    It is a bright day we pray for
    It is a bright day we pray for
    It is this day we pray for (solo)
    It is a bright day we pray for.

(ii) Me je where, me je where
     Uwhere uwhere u wo agho ho me je where
     No me je where no me je where (solo)
     Uwhere uwhere u wo agho ho me je where
     No me je where no me je where (solo)
     Uwhere uwhere u wo agho ho me je where-ee

     I am just sweeping, I am just sweeping
     A broom sweeps without discrimination,
     I'm just sweeping
     I am just sweeping, I am just sweeping (solo)
     A broom sweeps without discrimination
     I'm just sweeping
     I am just sweeping, I am just sweeping (solo)
     A broom sweeps without discrimination,
     I'm just sweeping.[19]

The songs are meant to inspire the suppliant into action, while the scattering of the rice, powder, scent, biscuits, etc., is to appease his colleagues,[20] who remain securely invisible to the spectators, including the officiant.

Then comes the much awaited moment when the victim, under possession, becomes restless, running here and there and occasionally screaming or crying, searching for where his bad *otatha* has been hidden. He may even run two kilometres in an attempt to unearth the object of his bad *otatha*, the *ama* around his hand leading the way. Then he at last settles on the spot. And here all hands must be on deck to ensure that when the object is finally revealed, it does not find its way into his mouth, an occurrence which surely spells his death. After the discovery, the *otatha* object is snatched from him, washed and placed on a plate for all to see. The suppliant is made to give two naira, ten kobo and a bottle of gin to the officiant. He sits on a chair in a house and all his relatives and friends "spray" him with money. This is also the time to give him anything that was demanded in the course of the search for the *otatha* object. Clearly, this discovery naturally brings the ceremony to an end and the relatives of the suppliant can now pay the balance of the cost of the job completed.

However, a sacrifice takes place *ex eventu* in the officiant's compound, say, a month later. The suppliant buys the sacrificial items, which include a duck, goat, cock, a parrot's feather, seven sticks of white chalk, leather of an animal known as *evue* and three pence (*utoro*) and half penny (*epini*) pieces. The cock is slaughtered and its blood caused to drip on the bundle of herbs, seven sticks of white chalk, parrot's feather, *evue's* leather and the three pence and half penny pieces. Some of its blood is rubbed on the feet of the suppliant. Then the cock together with the goat and duck are used in preparing food for all the participants to eat, which merry-making is followed by dispersal. Thereafter the suppliant worships the spirit represented by the bundle or else he may once again be overtaken by misfortunes. If for any reason he cannot undertake this worship it can be trusted to the officiant to do it on his behalf. Nonetheless, he must pay an annual fee to the officiant for life.

Our discussion has already indicated that the belief in the alterability of *otatha* is very strong among the people and where it cannot be consciously altered it is resigned to the next reincarnation when the person can choose a better lot. Evidently, when this is weighed against that of unalterability a contradiction results, a situation which the people accept with utmost equanimity.

On the whole, however, the concept of *otatha's* alterability, especially as it pertains to character, attracts the concomitant of human responsibility. Indeed, that a person can choose his destiny in preexistence anticipates this latter concept. Surely, the element of human responsibility negates an automatic fulfilment of a good destiny; and hence a cast-iron predestiny cannot be predicated of the Isoko system.

RELIGIONS IN CONFLICT AND CHANGE IN THE WORKS OF MODERN AFRICAN NOVELISTS

Azim Nanji

1. Introduction

A considerable portion of East and West African fiction and poetry in English and French during recent decades has been devoted to presenting African societies, individuals and values in contact and conflict with extraneous influences and in transition towards a search of values that will reflect the African heritage of the post-colonial, independent era. Religious values and traditions have been at the heart of this clash and search.

The conflicts and dilemmas are evoked particularly well in the writings of Chinua Achebe, Ayi Armah, Hamidou Kane and Yambo Ouologuem from West Africa and Ngugi wa'Thiongo and Okot p'Bitek from the East. Rather than provide a mere summary of how their writings reflect the problem, I have chosen to develop certain major themes as illustrated through a clustering of titles of their works and have then traced in greater detail the pattern of encounter and response on the basis of Kane's *L'aventure ambiguë*.[1] This novel lends itself to such a role because it is not merely an expression of encounter, it portrays a philosophical response to the ambiguities and choices that result from such an encounter. Though the characters in the book are meant to represent "types," each position is articulated clearly, the search delineated without undue romanticizing of the past and the ambiguities recognized for what they are - dilemmas that are to be lived and experienced, rather than descriptions of ideological stances. An additional significance of Kane's work is that it incorporates the role of Islam as part of the traditional African landscape and shows it to be fully integrated into traditional society. In conjunction with the other works, Kane's novel thus enables us to explore the encounter in the context of the contact between African religions, including Islam, and Western Christianity and the secular traditions accompanying the advent of the European colonial period in African history.

Of the accompanying works, Laye's *L'enfant noir*[2] and the first part of Achebe's *Things Fall Apart*[3] represent the traditional setting before the period of encounter; Ngugi's two works - *The River Between*[4] and *Weep Not Child*[5] - and the second half of *Things Fall Apart* study the process of the encounter and the resulting dilemmas.

Three more works have been chosen to constitute a form of epilogue to this paper. They are Ngugi's *Petals of Blood*[6], Ouologuem's *Le devoir de violence*[7] and Ayi Armah's *Two Thousand Seasons*.[8] All attempt to assert a vision of what is to be or must not be, hinting perhaps of a time when the African personality is neither fully that of the past nor a mere product resulting from its encounters and contacts with Islam, Christianity or the secular *techno-science* of the modern world.

2. The Traditional World in Equilibrium

Whereas the notions of conflict and ambiguity best define the portrayal of African societies in transition, it is the idea of totality, a sense of oneness and equilibrium, that characterize in general the traditional world as it is evoked by our writers. Both Kane and Laye offer a view of such a world.

L'enfant noir is a novel that has often been criticized for its idealized portrayal of traditional African society. This it does, but self-consciously so, within the perspective of a boy emerging into adulthood entirely within a traditional setting, with the colonial and overseas experiences still to come. It is thus a portrayal of a world in touch with innocence. There are several religious symbols and activities that Laye uses to illustrate the boy's upbringing. The first is the snake, the eternal guiding spirit of the people, a symbol of interdependence between the material and spiritual worlds and of the transmission of knowledge from the world of spirits to the world of persons. The second important symbol is the Koran School where the sum total of all traditional knowledge is given and received. The Koran School is a significant symbol because it highlights a part of traditional learning and knowledge that was as essential to the Islamized African society as was the indigenous part, a part wherein intelligence expressed itself in the spoken or recited word; as Laye points out, "if intelligence seemed slower it was because reflection preceded speech and because speech itself was a most important matter."[9]

The Koran School thus embodies all three aspects of traditional knowledge and wisdom - speech, reflection and intelligence.

In *L'aventure ambiguë* a similar sense of wholeness is projected where the Koranic knowledge unifies what are referred to as the "visible" and the "invisible" worlds:

The word of God flowed pure and limpid from his fervent lips.... He contained within himself the totality of the world, the visible and the invisible, its past and its future. This word which he was bringing forth in pain, was the architecture of the world - it was the world itself.[10]

In parallel fashion, Achebe describes in the first part of *Things Fall Apart*, traditional Ibo society. The characterization is less idyllic but nonetheless one in which the fortunes of the main character, Okonkwo, unfold in a fully realized traditional framework. Life is dominated by the calendrical pattern of seed-gathering, planting and harvesting; personal life involves the extended family, the ancestors and the clan in all the villages; the realm of the unknown is personified in *Agbala*, the priestess, and the *iyi-uwa* stone which must be discovered if Okonkwo's daughter Ezinma, who is an *ogbanje* (a child who repeatedly dies and returns to its mother to be reborn), is to live. Even Okonkwo's exile and downfall are set within the limits of a tradition which he accepts and recognizes as the supreme arbiter of his destiny. Ambitious as he is, he cannot transcend the limits set by society or escape the consequence of going beyond these limits.

The above works then highlight an integrated, fairly homogeneous society. If I may paraphrase Ngugi, "night" and "day" are both part of life. Both are accepted in their entirety and related to through daily and ritual life to become the totality of what we might call an indigenous religious world view.

3. <u>The Traditional World in Contact and in Conflict</u>

In the second half of *Things Fall Apart* and in Ngugi's two works, *The River Between* and *Weep Not Child*, traditional society comes into contact with European and Christian values. The initial encounter at the level of government, Christian churches and mission schools creates a climate of tension and ambiguity. In *Things Fall Apart* there is a jarring of indigenous religious perspectives when the missions attract and absorb even the outcasts (the *osu*). Some of the converts become fanatical Christians. Even Okonkwo's son converts. Although aspects of Christianity appeal to them - the music, the mythology, the sense of history and community - in a striking passage the general Ibo attitude injects itself clearly: "If we leave our gods and follow your god who will protect us from the anger of our neglected gods and ancestors?"[11] Within the tribe the conflict continues until several sacred Ibo symbols have been violated, and yet it is felt that the Ibo divinities are quite capable of fighting their own battles. So the Ibo exercise restraint and tolerance and the Christian community continues to survive and even to grow.

Because Okonkwo cannot bear the violation of his world as he understands it, he finally lashes out, destroying others and himself in the process, dying an ignoble death - by suicide. Things have indeed fallen apart. Elsewhere a poet has used an image that I believe sums up the thrust of *Things Fall Apart*; the image is that of a shattered mirror, the pieces can never again be put together to reflect the world as it was.

But what is to be salvaged out of this encounter? What might be conceived as a sort of synthesis is hinted at in the early works of Ngugi.

In *The River Between*, Ngugi explores for a possible meeting point between Christianity and Gikuyu religion. Can one embrace the white man's faith and remain true to oneself? All protagonists in Ngugi's early works are idealists. Hence, in the *The River Between*, Muthoi, who has converted to Christianity, still wishes to be circumcized in the traditional way against the wishes of her Christianized family and friends; and she says to her sister:

Why? Are we fools? Father and mother are circumcized. Are they not Christians? Circumcision did not prevent them from being Christians. I too have embraced the white man's faith. However I know it is beautiful, oh so beautiful to be initiated into womanhood. You learn the ways of the tribe. Yet the white man's God does not quite satisfy me. I want, I need something more. My life$_{12}$ and your life are here in the hills, that you and I know.

For her, Christianity can only be meaningful if mediated through the idiom of indigenous tradition. Her goal is that of reconciliation.

In *Weep Not Child*, Njoroge encounters a similar dilemma and responds in a like manner. He idealizes about the new Gikuyu who has received education, who can go on to help his people and develop a society that will have the best of both worlds. His emotions are expressed through key biblical notions such as faith, hope and salvation. Even when the political reality of the harshness of the Mau Mau resistance to the British take-over of Gikuyu land intrude into his life, he finds solace in the message of hope and the future. There is a particularly touching scene in *Weep Not Child* in which Njoroge goes to church during the height of Mau Mau activity and listens to the preacher's words:

Our people, what shall we do to escape the greater plague that is to come? We must turn to God. Then all our wounds will heal at once. We shall be washed by the blood of the lamb. Let us pray. [There follows a reading from Matthew]: "...nation shall rise against nation and he that shall endure unto the end, the same shall be saved.... Verily I say unto you, this generation shall not pass till all these things shall be fulfilled.[13]

The expectation is still one of hope beyond suffering. If *The River Between* promised reconciliation and a middle way that would emerge from the confluence of Christianity and Gikuyu religion, then the finale of *Weep Not Child* presents a repudiation, in the context of political reality, of that hope. Njoroge contemplates suicide when all his hopes have been dashed and his family and the possibility of love have been destroyed; even then, I suspect the novel holds on to the glimmer of hope reflected in the title which is drawn from Walt Whitman's *On the Beach at Night*.[14] The current position that Ngugi's novels reflect is one we shall see later in the paper.

It is on returning to *L'aventure ambiguë* that we find ourselves in the midst of a far deeper psychic and global perspective of the encounter and the resulting ambiguity. Samba, as the hero of this fictional autobiography is called, grows to manhood in a world increasingly altered by the influence of the French presence. As the heir to the leadership and the traditions of his people, the Diallobé, Samba stands between the two apparently conflicting worlds. It is not he alone who must make a choice, charting his own personal destiny, but rather his choice must represent a decision on the part of his people, because his destiny is their own. Among leaders of the community who must decide as they too survey the choices, the key ones are his father, the "knight;" his cousin, the Chief of the community; the sister of the chief, the Most Royal Lady, and finally the carrier of traditional thought, the teacher; all of whom have a deep concern for him and for the continuity of the traditions and well-being of the people they lead and represent. Their positions on Samba's future and education thus represent the different issues at play in the society and the options that must be exercised to preserve the integrity and even the very survival of the group as a unified people.

Samba's teacher, the repository and transmitter of knowledge, fears the spiritual consequences of westernization. He has perceived from his limited contact with the French that the spiritual world in which the colonizer exists is a void. He senses that increasing westernization will plunge his people into a similar void. Therefore, he initially advocates a retreat from a technological and materialistically oriented educational system.

The emerging perception of Western education is worth pondering. The Western school in this view, "only teaches men to join wood to wood - to make wooden buildings."[15] There is a play upon the words "wood" and "school," for pronounced in the language of the region the words mean the same thing. It seems to me that herein lies the heart of the problem of acquiring knowledge. As he understands it, the teacher views traditional education as encompassing the person in relation to the total environment, where he, like the wood, is shaped to fit into the whole. For him Western education does the opposite by merely adding wood to wood in linear fashion, increasing knowledge but not relating knowledge, persons and cosmos to each other.

A second and opposite point of view is that of the sister of the Chief, the Most Royal Lady, a figure of authority and power in the land. Her attitude is one of acceptance of Western ways to ensure the continuity of her people and to assure well-being for the individual. She also sees the Western emphasis on rationality as a means of enabling the people to understand better their own colonized situation.

The Chief is the symbol of stability. He is perceived as the "landmark and the recourse" to whom his people look for a decision at what is for them a time of ambiguity and choice, a historical juncture. Yet as he ponders the dilemma, he is aware of the consequences of his decision, which is sure to cause division. This dilemma he conceives in polarized terms while reflecting on the desirability of Western, secular education - "can one learn *this* without forgetting *that*, and is what one learns worth what one forgets?"[16]

Samba's father, though part of the debate, articulates no given position, but seems by his very stature and bearing, to radiate the deep spirituality and tradition of faith, which is the hallmark of the totally integrated Diallobé man, the model of synthesis and equilibrium between outer and inner.

Ultimately there is only one choice: Samba must be offered to the altar of experimentation, he must be the guinea-pig for any future solution by going to the new school and embarking on an adventure into ambiguity.

Samba's acquisition of Western learning and his experience of the Western world is reduced by Kane to two essential conflicts. The first is the dichotomy that Samba discovers with the help of his father between two views of Man. His father defines the indigenous Diallobé view of God as the whole process encompassed in the Universe. Human beings are part of the wider cosmic system, and human destiny and effort are a reflection of their role within that system. That the Muslim roots of this view have combined with an indigenous African concept is evident - there has been a blend which has created what might at best be termed an Afro-Muslim synthesis. This vision is then contrasted with perhaps a somewhat simplified Western view where man through the mastery of technology continues to distance himself from God and from the Universe of which he is a part. The alienation causes a sense of loss, a deprivation of identity and an absence of belonging to a Universe of which one is a living part. Such a system creates an imbalance within man and within society which continues to feed upon itself, growing like a cancer and ultimately destroying itself.

The argument is that, prior to the encounter with Western values and colonialism, Africans did not know such alienation for it did not touch them. There was a sense of harmony, a sense of belonging, and a sense of interdependence nourished by ritual and sacrifice. A decision was reached by reference to the word, or that collective intelligence of the people symbolized by the word. Man was not so utterly dependent on himself as was the case in the

West; he did not face by himself the awful responsibility of having to make choices individually.

The book develops a second dichotomy in Samba's exploration, while in the West, into the thought of Descartes and Pascal: the dichotomy of an act of reason as opposed to an act of will or faith. Samba sides with Pascal whom he considers untypical of the West. Belief in God and morality are not ultimately epistemological issues to be speculated upon, but living issues that must be acted upon. This conforms to his understanding of the African religious impulse. Such are the essential dichotomies that Kane develops in his work. His main character, Samba, acts out these dichotomies, for as an African living in the Western world, he not only lives them but feels it. He experiences loneliness, the loneliness of the spirit with a sense of having been abandoned by God. The anguish is stated thus:

I am not a distinct country of the Diallobé, facing a distinct Occident, and appreciating with a cool head what I can take from it and what I must leave with it in return. I have become the two. There is not a lucid mind deciding between the two aspects of a choice. There is a strange nature, one, in distress over not being two.[17]

The consciousness is of having become a hybrid; the adventure finally leaves the seeker at the crossroads, still in the midst of ambiguity.

He returns to Africa in search of peace and harmony, but fails to find it. He is ultimately killed. Having survived the West physically, he succumbs to psychological and spiritual trauma. But death is, perhaps, only the final stage for him in this journey, for in the view of the Muslim Sufi tradition of which his African life was a part, he may have reached the final transcendental state of knowledge where death itself is the great transition. The ultimate solution is a mystical one, and Kane leaves us, as it were, grasping a strand that we cannot entirely hold or feel.

4. Beyond Ambiguity - Newer Assertions?

Kane's almost apocalyptic portrayal of the conflicts that engage Diallobé society and Samba in particular assert no one position or panacea. The mystical voice that speaks at the end is an attempt to rise above the contradictions without denying them. The tensions and the ambiguities are real but it is eternity that ultimately beckons the spirit.

Some fairly recent novels have in contrast tried to go beyond a mere analysis of conflict and have tried to assert new choices. Ngugi's *Petals of Blood*, Ouologuem's *Le devoir de violence* and Armah's *Two Thousand Seasons* belong to this category. As an epilogue to this paper, I have tried to sketch this recent trend to indicate the type of shifts that are taking place in African literature on the issue of religious conflict and change.

Petals of Blood explores the political and social ambiguities that follow independence. The inevitable passing away of the traditional society and the superficial westernization of African life create alienated individuals who, in their search for meaning, must retreat to the periphery of their respective societies. Out of their experience arises the motivation and eventually the need for action. This need expresses itself in a political revolution whose overtones are Marxist and populist. It was for this work and others that Ngugi was detained for a time in Kenya and had to relinquish his position at the University of Nairobi. In this work both indigenous values and those from outside are transcended through a revolution.

Ouologuem and Armah's two works offer no such millenium. Rather they are both brutal in their iconoclasm. The works devalue and debase both the Muslim and Western Christian component that has become part of the African cultural and religious landscape. There is an uncompromising rejection of the view represented by Kane's mystical quest or even that for a common point and a middle ground in the earlier writings of Ngugi.

Essentially, these two works leave one in a vacuum. The anger spent, the aggression ventilated, and the icons smashed, we are left with precious little. The iconoclasm is ultimately self-defeating. If the choices that result from contact are unacceptable, then the transition is towards a void, for the shattered mirror can never be put together again. In comparison one of the strengths of Kane's work is the degree of clarity with which the situation is presented. Samba's anguish is often objectified as an intellectual problem, the novel is meant to stimulate thought not merely to stun the senses.

The "Ambiguous Adventure" is ambiguous precisely because the issue is fraught with ambiguity: no one choice will suffice, though the adventure must continue to be pursued; the outside world cannot be shut out or ignored because the search must be conducted in a wider global context.

At the heart of Kane's novel is the ambiguity of the universal human condition. When the debate among the various characters takes place, the need for change and the giving up of tradition are seen as reflecting a desire for more "substance," for things relating to matter and the body - health, housing and food. The teacher uses the image of the gourd to describe human beings, containers whose very existence and nature demands that they contain substance. A gourd exists in order that it can achieve weight. And yet that very gourd wants in the teacher's words to "take flight.... Its happiness is a function of its vacuity, of the sonority of its response when breath stirs it. The gourd is right in both instances."[18] The teacher, however, lives for the world of flight which the material needs of human existence may threaten. He is aware of the exclusivity and perfection he demands in order to maintain the purity of the tradition. The Most Royal Lady in contrast argues for substance as the means to survival. Samba's adventure as the gourd that must attach itself to substance is the adventure that all religious traditions in contact and change must face - the quest to balance the desire to fly and be free and to be the gourd that is not overwhelmed by the substance it must contain. Kane's work seems to hint at possibilities that go beyond polarities by placing the notion of ambiguity at the heart of the argument. The implication of recognizing ambiguity as part of a search beyond encounter is that by passing through that particular stage African traditions might in fact become enriched and not necessarily suffer total erosion. In that sense the "Ambiguous Adventure," though full of anguish, is not totally without hope. David Rubadiri, the Malawian poet, captures this universal dilemma in a short poem, that sums up the main thrusts of the arguments analyzed in this paper:

>The tide that from the west
>washes the soul of Africa
>and tears the moorings of its spirit
>Till blood-red the tide becomes -
>And heartsick the womb -
>The tide that from the
>west with blood washes Africa
>Once washed a wooden cross.[19]

THREE TYPES OF RELIGIOUS ACCULTURATION
AMONG THE OGLALA LAKOTA

Paul B. Steinmetz, S.J.

The Native Americans of Pine Ridge Reservation in South Dakota are the Oglala, a sub-tribe of the Teton Indians who speak the Lakota language. The Teton are one of the Seven Fireplaces speaking the three dialects of Dakota, Nakota and Lakota. Since they did not have a common name, outsiders called them Sioux, a French corruption of an Algonkian word meaning "adder," which referred to their reputation for treachery. Since this is derogatory the term "Dakota" is frequently but incorrectly used for all three linguistic groups. I have used the accurate classification of Oglala Lakota in this paper. Shortly after 1700 the Oglala Lakota were nomadic buffalo hunters on the northern plains until their confinement to the Pine Ridge Reservation in 1878.

My material on the contemporary Oglala Lakota Religion is of ethnographic value because of the fast-paced historical changes taking place and of theoretical value because of the important insight it provides. There are three religious traditions among the Oglala Lakota today: the traditional Lakota Religion of the Sacred Pipe, the Peyote Religion and traditional Christianity. Even though the traditional religion of the Pipe as it is practiced today is probably only a few hundred years old, elements of it may be much older.

I think that William Powers is correct when he states in his book, *Oglala Religion*, that the majority of Lakota move back and forth on a continuum between Lakota Religion and Christianity as a white man's institution.[1] However, there has been a small group of medicine men and other

Lakota who have been religious thinkers in Paul Radin's sense.[2] They have been more reflective than the common people and they have developed new beliefs in their Lakota Religion in an effort to avoid the compartmentalization implied in the continuum just mentioned. In the past sufficient attention has not been paid to the beliefs of the Native Americans. During my studies at the University of Stockholm Dr. Åke Hultkrantz made the point that most of the ethnographic literature on Native American Religion, such as that of the Bureau of America Ethnology and the American Museum of Natural History, were largely external descriptions of ceremonies with a very little development of the beliefs connected with them. I will describe, at least in a preliminary way, some of the current religious beliefs among the Oglala Lakota.[3] The survival of these beliefs in coming years cannot be taken for granted. Continual research will be needed to determine this.

Frank Fools Crow, now in his eighties and a well known medicine man, told me that in the early days he never talked about the Pipe with a Catholic priest, since most of them condemned it, but that he brought the two religious traditions together on his own. Now this does not mean that he analyzed the relationship between Lakota Religion and Christianity to achieve a well-developed explanation. Rather, he made certain symbolic identifications and performed certain actions as a means of bringing out this relationship. In some way Fools Crow believes that the Lakota Pipe belongs in the Catholic Church. Cherry Seed, a man who passed his powers on to Fools Crow, told him as a teenage boy that the acceptance of the Pipe would be in a "holy house with all those strings attached to it," which referred to the obligations connected with the Pipe. Fools Crow told me that he later reflected that the "holy house is the Catholic Church." And so, at the Catholic funeral services for Ben Black Elk, he prayed along with me with the Sacred Pipe at the grave. Fools Crow also invited me to dance in the 1971 Sun Dance at Pine Ridge. He offered this invitation to me, a Catholic priest, since, in his mind, the priest is worthy to handle the Pipe and to participate in the Sun Dance.

But other medicine men have also been quietly making at least a beginning in formulating a modern Lakota religious belief, one influenced by Christianity. This has been taking place in their religious imagination. George Plenty Wolf, who was a practicing Catholic and a medicine man, prayed with the Sacred Pipe in the Catholic Church in the Slim Butte community. He shared a few of his Lakota Christian beliefs with me. In the Sun Dance ceremony the Lakota have always hung rawhide effigies of a buffalo and a man from the cottonwood tree.[4] To Plenty Wolf the rawhide effigy of the man stood for the return of Christ. He puts a new Christian interpretation on this religious symbol, one which goes beyond the Lakota symbol and yet forms a continuity with its tradition. This can be seen from an examination of the ethnographic literature. James Dorsey states that the effigy of the man was a phallic symbol of fertility.[5] This is most appropriate as a symbol of the return of Christ which is also a symbol of new life in a way that is unique and goes beyond the Lakota one but not in conflict with it. The new Christian identity simply raises the Lakota symbol to a new level. According to Frances Densmore the effigy of the man was a symbol of the enemy conquered through supernatural means.[6] The same pattern of continuity and discontinuity is present here. While the Lakota thought of overcoming a mortal in battle, Plenty Wolf, as a Lakota Christian, thought of Christ overcoming universal evil at the end of time.

I think that Plenty Wolf's discovering a Christian meaning in Lakota symbolism is a verification of what Mircea Eliade discussed in his "Methodological Remarks in the Study of Religious Symbol":[7]

> Symbols are capable of being understood on more and more "elevated" planes of reference.... But then one may ask if these "elevated" meanings were not in some manner implied in other meanings, and if, as a consequence, they were, if not plainly understood, at least vaguely felt by men living on archaic levels of culture.... The difficulty of the problem rests in the fact that symbols address themselves not only to the awakened consciousness, but to the totality

of the psychic life.... This admitted, two important consequences follow: (1) If at a certain moment in history a religious symbol has been able to express clearly a transcendent meaning, one is justified in supposing that this meaning might have been already grasped dimly at an earlier epoch. (2) In order to decipher a religous symbol not only is it necessary to take into consideration all of its contexts, but one must above all reflect on the meaning that this symbol had had in what we might call its "maturity."

Of course, Eliade's statement is beyond phenomenology. it presumes certain value judgements to determine what the maturity of a symbol is. But it is important to distinguish whether the value judgment is in the mind of the ethnographer or of the informant. Although not explicitly stated, the assumption in Plenty Wolf's mind is that the Lakota symbol finds its maturity in Christ. I feel that I am just discovering that assumption and not making it by raising Plenty Wolf's symbolic identification to a level of reflection. At least this is Plenty Wolf's assumption insofar as he is speaking from the viewpoint of his Christian faith. However, as with everyone else, the Lakota are sometimes ambivalent. Plenty Wolf at times may have moved back to the position conceptualized by Powers as the continuum between Lakota Religion and Christianity. In this position Plenty Wolf may even have regarded the Lakota Religion in practice as superior to his Christian one. He probably believed his practice of *yuwipi*, a Lakota ceremony of praying through the spirits, as superior to making a Christian novena to a saint. I suggest that Lakota symbols reach a maturity in Christ when I judge that the Lakota are speaking from a position of Christian faith. Unfortunately, this judgement is partially based on a personal experience with them over a number of years, an experience which I am unable to share with the reader in a short article. However, it should also be noted that Plenty Wolf's understanding of Christianity also acquires a new dimension. His concept of power in Lakota ceremonies influenced to a great extent his understanding of the power in the Christian sacraments. When Plenty Wolf's granddaughter had an epilepsy seizure, he told his relatives that he did not have power over this sickness, but rather she should receive the Sacrament of the Annointing for healing from a Catholic priest.

But let us gather more expressions of their religious belief. Plenty Wolf made another identification. The effigy of the Buffalo is the Old Testament; that of the man is the New Testament. Erikson describes so beautifully how the buffalo stood for the entire Lakota way of life.[8] What Plenty Wolf was saying was that the Lakota way of life, including their religion, was a preparation for Christ for the Lakota just as the Old Testament was for the Israelites. Plenty Wolf also told me that when a dancer is pierced, it is done in remembrance of the piercing of Christ. During the 1979 Sun Dance at Porcupine, S.D. I saw two women dancers wearing crosses around their necks. Several other dancers told me that they thought of Christ. Plenty Wolf said that according to the man who brought the Sun Dance from Montana to the Lakota "he was doing something like Noah did, bringing the people in a certain boat. We are going through the Sun Dance and we are reaching our destination just like Noah reached his."

Edgar Red Cloud, leader of the Sun Dance singers for twenty five years, offered still other examples. He sang a Sun Dance song, holding the Sacred Pipe, during the Communion part of a Mass celebrated on the Sun Dance grounds at Pine Ridge. He identified the woman who brought the Calf Pipe to the Lakota with the Blessed Virgin Mary who brought Christ (the same identification was made to Dr. Luis Kemnitzer, an anthropologist doing field work on the Pine Ridge Reservation). Red Cloud had an even more profound insight. He told me that when the Indians knew Mother Earth, they knew the Blessed Virgin Mary but they did not know her by name. Here we are getting into the area of the unknown presence of Christ and Mary which theologians and missiologists are developing and which is beyond the scope of anthropology. However, in my judgment, Edgar Red Cloud was speaking from a position of Christian faith so that in his mind the Lakota knowledge of Mother Earth found its maturity in the Blessed Virgin. However, Red Cloud's understanding of the Blessed Virgin is enriched and deepened by the Lakota concept. As a result both religious traditions are changed.

Pete Catches, a medicine man who had been a Catholic catechist, told me that he prays with the Pipe in memory of his vision just as the priest changes bread and wine into the Body and Blood of Christ in memory of the Last Supper. This comparison raises the whole practice of Lakota Religion to a sacramental level. To what extent Catches is consciously aware of this when he performs Lakota Pipe ceremonies is another question. But, I feel that this comparison in some way influences his Lakota Christian belief, perhaps even on an unconscious level.

The medicine man, John Iron Rope, told a Lakota in my presence: "I am glad that this Father is interested in the Pipe. He can use this Pipe at Mass.... Whatever he asks for will be granted.... He can take up this Pipe, put it on the altar as he says Mass." Now, this invitation by Iron Rope brought some Lakota a new understanding of the Pipe, one which is rejected by the militants or activists.

Some may judge this type of symbolic identification as a superficial manifestation of Christianity. For example, Weston LaBarre lists several pages of identification of peyote symbols with Christian ones and yet comes to the conclusion "that the layer of Christianity on peyotism is very thin and superficial indeed."[9] Also there is the pre-judgment against Christianity which Morris Opler makes in stating, "Indeed, far from becoming a weakened and Christianized version of native beliefs, the Mescalero Apache acceptance of peyote resulted instead in an intensification of the aboriginal values and concepts at many points."[10] However, in the minds of the Lakota we have been considering it was the very Christian version of their native beliefs which brought their aboriginal values to maturity. Again, according to Joseph Jorgensen and Richard Clemmer, Fools Crow inviting a Catholic priest to dance in the Sun Dance was a "denigration of the Sun Dance to a variable of Christianity."[11] But, is it a denigration in the mind of Fools Crow's or in the minds of Jorgensen and Clemmer? I do not think these assumptions should go unchallenged. It is my belief that the religious symbols of man express a deeper faith than rational dogmas. In the last few centuries the acceptance of dogma has been over-emphasized as a norm of religious commitment to the detriment of religious symbols. Our understanding of depth psychology today should help us to place a much greater importance on the religious symbols of man.

The most remarkable intergration of the Lakota and Christian traditions took place when Black Elk reflected in later years on his Messiah vision which he received when participating in the 1890 Ghost Dance on the Pine Ridge Reservation. The vision as presented in John Neihardt's *Black Elk Speaks* omits all reference to Christ. I have taken the material from the manuscript of the field notes from which the book was written. The omitted or changed parts will be indicated by parenthesis.

As I looked there I saw men coming towards me and they stood before me and said: "Our Father, the two legged chief, you shall see." Then I went to the center of the circle with these men and there again I saw the tree in full bloom. Against the tree I saw a man standing with outstretched arms. As we stood close to him these twelve men said. "Behold him." The man with outstretched arms looked at me (and I didn't know whether he was a white or an Indian. He did not resemble Christ. He looked like an Indian but I was not sure of it). He had long hair which was hanging loose. On the left side of his head was an eagle feather. His body was painted red. (At this time I had nothing to do with white man's religion and I had never seen any picture of Christ). This man said to me, "My life is such that all earthly beings that grow belong to me. My father said this. You must say this." I stood there gazing at him and tried to recognize him. All round him was a light. Then he disappeared all at once. (It seems as though there were wounds in the palms of his hands.... It seems to me on thinking it over that I had seen the son of the Great Spirit himself.)$_{12}$

The first observation is that Black Elk is reflecting on his vision as a Lakota Christian. He had been a Catholic catechist for close to twenty-eight years by the time he talked to Neihardt. Consequently, his reflection involved an explicit knowledge of Christ which he did not have at the time of the vision. At first the man in the vision was the Ghost Dance *Wanikiye* or Saviour and not the Christ of his Catholic faith since Black Elk told Neihardt that at the time he had nothing to do with the white man's religion and had never seen a picture of Christ. According to Leslie Spier the Ghost Dance was predominatly an aboriginal religous movement with little influence from Christianity.[13] Certainly, any Christian meaning was not an explicit one for Black Elk but at most an intimation, or, according to Eliade, Christ was perhaps vaguely grasped. At first, Black Elk experienced a Messiah manifestation on a phenomenological level, and it was only later after his conversion that the Ghost Dance *Wanikiye* would be recognized as the Son of the Great Spirit Himself in the sense of Christ. This is the most obvious interpretation since Black Elk is speaking after years of being a Catholic catechist. Secondly, there seemed to be wounds in the palms of his hands, making the man in the vision resemble the risen Christ with glorifed wounds. Third, at this late point in time Black Elk would not be identifying the Ghost Dance Messiah with Wovoka or Jack Wilson as the rumors had done at the time of the vision. However, Black Elk had to overcome a personal prejudice to do this. He stated that the man did not resemble Christ; that he looked like an Indian. But, he was able to rid himself of this false assumption to accept the Ghost Dance Messiah as the Christ of his Catholic faith.

Now, there are several remarks in Neihardt's published book which are contrary to this interpretation and must be examined. According to the published book Black Elk said: "...I heard the gossip that was everywhere now and people said it was really the son of the Great Spirit who was out there; that when he came to the *Wasichus* [that is, white man] a long time ago, they had killed him; but he was coming to the Indians this time."[14] What Black Elk actually told Neihardt was: "From the rumors and gossips I heard that the Messiah was the son of the Great Spirit that had come out there."[15] But this was simply the title given to the man Wovoka whom the white man called Jack Wilson.[16] There is no indication in the manuscript that Black Elk identified the Ghost Dance Messiah with Christ at this point in time. The first mention of Christ in the manuscript is when Black Elk reflects upon his Messiah vision as a Catholic catechist. Secondly, according to Neihardt's published account Black Elk said: "He was not a *Wasicuh* and he was not an Indian."[17] Black Elk actually told Neihardt: "I do not know whether he was a White or an Indian." And then he expresses an inclination: "He looked like an Indian but I was not sure of it."[18] In the total context I feel that this identification was strong enough that it did serve as an image of the Lakota Christ. In fact, this uncertainty expresses well the continuity and discontinuity or immanence and transcendence, that always occurs when Christianity confronts a non-Christian religion.

But contact and change have taken place not only between traditional Lakota Religion and Christianity. There has also been some interesting religious acculturation taking place between traditional Lakota Religion and the Native American Church. Traditional Lakota Religion has always had a profound effect on the use of peyote. The year 1904 can be given with great probability as the date for the introduction of peyote on the Pine Ridge Reservation from the Winnebago tribe in Nebraska. From the very beginning there was a Lakota named Red Bear who always prayed with the Pipe during his peyote meetings. This was at a time when there was a half-moon fireplace without smoking and a cross-fire fireplace with the Bible. In later years James Hawkins followed the practice and passed his Pipe on to George Gap, who on occassion prayed with it during peyote meetings. Solomen Red Bear, Jr., a great-grandson of the first Red Bear, prayed with the Pipe during a peyote curing ceremony for a little girl. I prayed with the Pipe during a peyote meeting for my safe journey overseas to study and during the thanksgiving meeting on my return so that I would complete the prayer in the same way it was begun. The actual use of the Pipe during peyote meetings may be a unique Lakota form of religious acculturation. The smoking of the ceremonial cigarette during meetings in the early 1910's seems to have been a direct influence from Oklahoma. However, even here the

Lakota put their stamp of traditional religion on it. For in talks and prayers the Lakota word, *cannunpa* or pipe, is used to refer to the cigarette instead of the word *canli*, the usual word for smoke. A prominent half moon-member told me that the cigarette is used instead of the Pipe in peyote meetings because some people attending may be unworthy to handle the Pipe, so that the traditional Pipe is present in half-moon peyote meetings symbolically if not actually. There are also religious symbols common to both traditions. These include the four water calls (at midnight, early morning, the ceremonial breakfast and the noon dinner), the offering of spiritual food, the roadman praying in the four directions outside the tipi at midnight and the half-moon altar.

Here we see religious symbols mediating between two Indian religious traditions. Half-moon members are not alienated from their Lakota Religion. They move back and forth between participating in sweat-lodge ceremonies, fasting on the hill with the Pipe, Sun Dancing and attending traditional Pipe ceremonies for healing and attending peyote meetings for some of the same purposes. They also discover a traditional Lakota meaning in their Native American Church symbols. Some Lakota seem to be more aware that these symbols are associated with their Lakota religion than with their peyote tradition. This association (feeling tones in Jungian psychology) gives some members a feeling of the Native American Church as Lakota although they know it is pan-Indian. For these the Native American Church acquires a Lakota identity on the level of depth psychology but not on one of ethnohistory. This relationship deserves a good psychological investigation. A remarkable example of the mutal influence of these two traditions was a traditional Lakota naming ceremony for a boy and a girl in the Potato Creek community on the Pine Ridge Reservation. During this ceremony a horse and other gifts were given away. Four tipis were set up. Asa Primeau, a roadman from the Yankton Reservation, conducted a half-moon meeting in one and Leslie Fools Bull, a minister from the Rosebud Reservation, conducted a cross-fire ceremony in another. Asa Primeau is also a traditional medicine man and he conducts, at times, peyote meetings when he puts a person on the hill to fast with the Pipe.

This leads us to the third type of religious acculturation among the Oglala Lakota, that between two divisions within the same religious tradition. The Native American Church has two fireplaces, the half moon with smoking and the cross-fire with the Bible. The half-moon has been described above. The cross fire is more explicitly Christian. The members not only use the name of Jesus in prayers and songs as the half-moon members do, but the Bible is behind the altar and the chief peyote sits on top of it. Someone reads from the Bible or gives a talk on Christ during the midnight water call. They reject ceremonial smoking during their meetings because of a moderate fundamentalism although Emerson Spider does instruct cross-fire members to take part voluntarily in smoking during half-moon meetings. Their leaders are ordained and called ministers. Ordination is a very simple ceremony of the laying on of hands and a spontaneous prayer outside the peyote meeting. Spider asked me to take part in the ordination of several minsters. To be considered a member of the church one must be baptized although one can attend meetings and eat peyote without baptism. In addition, because of Spider, who has the title of the State High Priest for the Native American Church in South Dakota, there is a strong evangelical spirit. Although this attitude may not characterize every single member of the cross-fire fireplace, Spider has a great influence on many of the members.

The mutual influence of those two fireplaces has an interesting history. In the early days members of the half-moon and cross-fire fireplaces did not attend each other's meetings but went considerable distances to attend their own meetings. Despite this, a mutual influence began to develop. The half moon influenced the cross fire through the introduction of spiritual food. This was accomplished over the opposition of Jim Blue Bird, one of the charter members of the Native American Church on the reservation. Spider introduced sixteen sets of songs instead of the twelve they had and the midnight water instead of only one water call at breakfast. But the cross-fire also influenced the half-moon. Tom Bullman, one of the early cross-fire members, claims that in the beginning the half-moon members did not use the name of Jesus in their meetings. So this may have been a cross-fire influence. In addition, baptism has been introduced into the half-moon through the Bernard Red Cloud family. Bernard is a prominent half-moon roadman. Bernard was baptized to express his total commitment to Christ. His wife, Christine, was baptized to guarantee her burial in the half-moon cemetery. She feels that so many of the Native American Church members are baptized in other Christian denominations and buried in their cemeteries. Half moon members have also been affected by Spider's intense evangelical spirit.

But there is still friction between the fireplaces. I attended a half-moon meeting in which Spider, before baptizing three children, made a long apology to anyone who might object. In a half-moon meeting in a cross-fire church, which is very infrequent, I was critized for using the traditional Lakota word for God, *tunkasila* or grandfather, in my prayer. Several years ago there was enough friction between the two fireplaces that Spider discussed it in the State Convention at Porcupine, S.D. He concluded that neither fireplace is of any value unless it leads to Christ. As a means of healing the divisions he encouraged roadmen and ministers to conduct meetings according to both fireplaces. Several, including Spider, stated that they intended to do so.

A number of both half-moon and cross-fire members told me that they consider the Native American Church Christian but not a white man's institution. I feel that Slotkin's remark that the Native American Church is an Indian version of Christianity[19] is verified on the Pine Ridge Reservation. The historical development of the half-moon fireplace to a more explicit Christian identity is too large a subject to be treated here. There has been a long standing debate between Weston LaBarre, insisting on the aboriginal character of peyote, and Omar Stewart on its Christian character.[20] But a half-moon roadman clearly expressed a Christian identity in a prayer at the midnight water call during a Mother's Day meeting. An excerpt of the prayer follows:

This evening we have the heart [the ash formation in the fireplace], the Sacred Heart of Jesus Christ. This Heart here means a lot of things to this religion, to the Native American Church. It has a lot of concern in there. Coming to Mother's Day. Even the Lord when He was crucified, He looked down upon His mother. His mother was standing below Him there. He didn't say anything to her. All He could do was to shed tears. He cried. That's all He could do. So His mother was standing below and looking up at Him. There was nothing she could do to help Him, to help her Son. There was nothing she could do. So the Lord gave Himself for the people that are here on this earth. Not only across the ocean but over here too, for the Indian people. He gave His life for you. The Great Spirit so loved the world that He died for you. From that time on that is the way this Sacred Heart of Jesus came about. If any person believes in God, the Great Spirit, He said thou shall love thy neighbor as thyself. That's what the teaching of the Native American Church is.

This prayer is taking place not in a Catholic Church where such devotion to Mary would be expected but during the morning water call at a half-moon peyote meeting. On a level of depth psychology the sacred fireplace becomes associated with the Sacred Heart of Jesus and the Blessed Virgin Mary with the peyote water woman. Whether one accepts this as a genuine Christian identity depends upon the importance one places on symbolic identification.

Two important conclusions can be drawn from these observations. First, acculturation among Native American traditions need not assume that "Indians acculturate to white culture," an accusation Jorgensen and Clemmer make against acculturational studies.[21] The contact and change between the traditional Lakota Religion and the Native American Church is between two Native American religious traditions. Secondly, acculturation can strengthen a Native American religious tradition and not necessarily weaken a "pure native religion," as Opler implies.

Certainly, for Frank Fools Crow, George Plenty Wolf, Edgar Red Cloud, Pete Catches, John Iron Rope and Black Elk their discovery of Christian meaning in their Lakota symbols added a new dimension to their Lakota tradition.

But recognizing the place of religious symbolism in these three types of religious acculturation is an even more important contribution. The common denominator seems to be the mediating symbol, or, in Jungian terms, the symbol of individuation. Between the traditional Lakota Religion and Christianity we find many such symbols. The effigy of the man hanging from the Sun Dance tree is the return of Christ; the Buffalo Calf Woman is identified as the Blessed Virgin Mary; the Lakota knows the Blessed Virgin in knowing Mother Earth but not by name; a medicine man prays with the Pipe in memory of his vision as the priest changes bread and wine into the Body and Blood of Christ in memory of the Last Supper. These are all mediating symbols. The Sacred Pipe is consciously looked upon by some Lakota as a mediating symbol between Lakota Religion and Christianity, an attitude associated with Dr. Luis Kemnitzer. But the most significant symbol of individuation was Black Elk's discovery of the Lakota Christ in his Ghost Dance Messiah vision. Power claims that some Lakota return to the traditional Lakota end of the continuum of religious practice, where they discover ideology and continuity, out of a symbolic illness for which no practitioner has a remedy at the white man's end of the continuum.[22] However, Black Elk avoided this symbolic illness since the image of the Lakota Christ mediated between his conscious Catholic life and the suppressed elements of his Lakota Religion, bringing his religious feelings into a harmony which was only imperfectly achieved in his conscious life.

In the second type of religious acculturation, between the traditional Lakota Religion and the half-moon fireplace of the Native American Church, there is the use of the Pipe in peyote meetings, the ceremonial cigarette standing for the Pipe, the four smokes, four water calls, the roadman going out to pray in the four directions, the sixteen sets of sons and the use of the word *tunkasila*, grandfather, for God. All these symbols mediate between the Lakota identity and pan-Indian identity, bringing them into an harmonious relationship.

In the third type of religious acculturation, between the half-moon and cross-fire fireplaces within the Native American Church, there is the use of spiritual food, the sixteen songs, the use of water, baptism, a strong evangelical spirit and the Name of Jesus, which serve as mediating symbols. It seems that whenever mediating symbols are strong, there is integration and harmony, and whenever they are weak, there is division and friction. I believe that it is the mediating symbol and not rational belief that is at the center of religious contact and change among the Oglala Lakota. This, perhaps, is the most important lesson to learn from this experience.

THE STRUGGLE AGAINST DEPENDENCY:
EQUALITY AS INDIVIDUALS OR AS PEOPLES

Patrick Kerans

In the early 1970's the energy crisis turned Canadians' attention towards the vast untapped potential of Canada's north. There were difficulties: technical problems occasioned by the severe arctic climate; concerns for the fragile ecology of the region; and ethical dilemmas as well. Several thousand Native Canadians, both Inuit and Indian (or Dene), live in a precarious yet relatively stable balance with that harsh land and sea. What would vast inroads of high technology do to their culture? Were the energy needs of industrialized southerners an ethically sufficient reason to risk destruction of the native northerners' environment or culture?

In 1974 a minority government in Ottawa was pressured into appointing Mr. Justice Thomas Berger to conduct a Commission of Enquiry into the question whether a pipeline should be built the length of the Mackenzie Valley.[1] Berger had already, as a practicing lawyer, fought successfully for Native aboriginal land claims. He now used the Commission in unprecedented ways. First, he took his enquiry to each native village in the north, and accepted the villagers' testimony as they were prepared to give it. In his report he gave them weight over against the expertise of the engineers and economists. Secondly, he held hearings in all major southern cities to provoke a political debate throughout the country.

During this process several "southern support groups" sprang up, the most effective of which was Project North, an interchurch committee which publicly involved the formal leadership of the five major Churches in Canada.[2]

But while the Natives were willing to accept political support, they rapidly emerged as the most creative political ethical thinkers in the debate. The position of the Dene (upon which I shall concentrate in this paper) arising as it does from their struggle for survival, it lends credence to a remark by Rubem Alves, "the seedbed of ethical ideas is the imagination of those who suffer." While they began with legal arguments, their position deepened, to find its roots in universal human values.

Because it is extremely difficult to have a conception of "universal human values" which is not in fact culture-bound, my intent here is to inquire more particularly into how the Dene have articulated this position. Since, within our political tradition, universality and equality are closely linked, I wish here to analyse the conception of equality which the Dene have articulated, and compare it with the notion of equality implicit in the Federal Government's position. The government's notion fits the long sanctioned liberal tradition, while the Dene's is sufficiently innovative, to evoke ethical reflection.

Whatever social theory can tell us of the interconnectedness of individuation and socialization, the Natives, out of their long and bitter experience, have been able to tell us clearly that if they lose their culture they will disappear. Bruno Apple told the Berger Commission: "When this pipeline gets through, it's going to be like the end of the world here."[3] For, as Paul Andrew told the same commission: "We do not want another way of life. We do not know enough of any other way of life."[4]

In sorting through the obstacles to their goal, they realized, as Roger Hutchinson has argued, that their subordinate status as a colonized group was the political root of their problem. Colonial status is a relationship whose terms are defined by the imperial power.[5] In reaction, they began to assert their identity and rights as a community, as a nation. In March 1975, the Dene Declaration insisted "...on the right to be regarded by ourselves and the world as a nation. What we seek is independence and self-determination within the country of Canada."[6]

In March 1980, they had worked their position through to where they had specific strategies and demands with respect to political structures. In a statement to the North West Territorial Council, they said:

One of our critiques of the present form of government...is that it promotes the interests of a privileged few in our society... The problem is not that the institutions of...government...are the political embodiments of a particular people, mainly the British. The problem is that those institutions are put to work to entrench a particular set of values rather than to *treat the values of each distinct community of people equally*. ...the government's task is *to make sure that all "value-communities" enjoy equal rights*.

I find this operational definition of equality innovative. While equality is and was considered central to the biblical tradition and to western Enlightment, I know of no major thinker who has probed the notion of equality of peoples. They have rather been unselfconsciously ethnocentric, assuming the superiority of western culture because of its faith or, later, its rationality. If pushed, many would latterly have fallen back on a utilitarian argument that the interests - and these merely cultural interests - of a minority simply could not have the weight of the economic interests of the vast majority. With these arguments, I would suggest that even as human responsibility for history was being widely accepted throughout the west, and indeed was becoming central to western modernity, notions such as "progress" and "*raison d'état*" were, so to speak, exempting wide areas of human historical activity from answerability to traditional ethical canons. The Dene's call for equality gives rise to ethical reflection on some of these historical exemptions.

I would like to examine the Federal Government's basic policy briefly, in order to compare its notion of equality with that of the Dene. In August, 1973, the government stated its basic policy with respect to Indian and Inuit claims. Therein they admitted the validity of aboriginal title as well as title based on treaty. They stated clearly that claims arising from these titles would best be settled through negotiations.[8]

Willingness to negotiate is an implicit affirmation of a certain sort of equality. It disclaims any superior wisdom to arbitrate disputes; it admits that superior strength is not necessarily a justification for imposing settlements. It becomes important, though, to ask just how an institution as powerful as a Federal Government negotiates with a few thousand impoverished Natives to determine the ethical limits of their notion of equality.

Two instances might help us get a clearer focus on these limits. First, the James Bay agreement signed in November 1975 between the Federal Government, the Quebec Government, the Cree and the Inuit of northern Quebec with respect to their traditional lands (some 379,400 square miles) was called by the then Minister of Indian Affairs and Northern Development a model.

On the other hand, the James Bay agreement is to other Native groups a model of what they don't want. First it was "a land extinguishment settlement."[9] This seems to mean that, despite the government's insistence that the preservation of Native culture and way of life must be a goal in negotiations, the government thinks that this goal can be met if the Natives have enough money. This in turn seems to imply that the government does not really accord equal weight to the values of the Native cultures, and tends instead to feel that a fair deal within the terms of our market culture is the best the Natives should hope for.

Why then did the Natives accept the agreement? As one of them said, they had "guns to their heads."[10] Construction of the hydroelectric project had already begun - without consultation with Natives. When the Natives obtained an injunction to halt construction, this injunction was overturned by the Court of Appeal within a week. The Natives could then either try to stop the project through the courts (on the basis of aboriginal title to the land) or take what they could from negotiations. Since they could not afford the all-or-nothing gamble of the first alternative, they took the second.

Some might wish to argue that putting the Natives under this kind of pressure is, in effect, negotiating in bad faith. However, I would argue that this sort of pressure is well within the bounds of a liberal sense of fairness and equality. As I have argued elsewhere, not only does the liberal tradition not guarantee equality of outcomes, it is positively against them. It holds instead for a notion of justice and equality with respect to process: each person is entitled to a chance at maximizing his/her individual utility through the interactions characterized by the market - in our case, negotiating. If one side is sufficiently strong (because, after all, it represents the interests of a vast majority) to be able to bring pressure on the other, this is simply bringing legitimate reality factors into the bargaining.[11]

This again seems to suggest that the government was not according equal weight to the values of the Natives, among whom decisions are made by consensus and who consider such pressure illegitimate. Insisting on the norms of legitimacy of our technological culture is tantamount to using naked force on Natives.

The second incident to examine is the Federal Government's decision to suspend funding for MacKenzie Valley native claims negotiations in September 1978. This decision was taken just two weeks before a scheduled meeting of the Dene to draw up their negotiating position. The government's stated reason for this decision was: "...the lack of substantive progress by the Dene and Metis leadership during the past year to agree on a mechanism for conducting joint negotiations with the federal government on their overlapping claims."[12]

Some have insisted that the government cut off funding because it foresaw how radical the Dene's demands would be. However, I find it illuminating that the government was willing to associate itself publicly with the stated reason. For thereby they go on record as stating that not only is negotiation the best way to achieve accord over disputed claims, but that it is the only legitimate way. No person or group can legitimately claim that their position is right, the other position bad (or at least worse than theirs), such that a compromise would be unreasonable or even immoral. All positions are negotiable; every interest is compromisable.

I have argued elsewhere that the liberal understanding of equality is fundamentally amoral: each person's interests were to be considered equal because, so far as the public authority was concerned, moral differences between them were to be treated as insignificant.[13] Only if the pursuit of one person's interests were to result in direct harm to those of another would the public authority be entitled to intervene. Within this context, if two sets of interests were irreconcilable (such as, in the case of the North, two incompatible land uses) then there needed to be compromise; and, on the original assumption, all interests are compromisable.

This notion of equality which implies the negotiability of all interests is, of course, "amoral" only if one is arguing from the perspective of an ethics of principle. There are ethical criteria at work within the liberal vision; but they are utilitarian criteria.

Compromise becomes a more acceptable ethical course than insistence upon rights, if actions are judged only by their consequences, and if the basic consequential criterion is the greatest good for the greatest number. Historically, this criterion has come to be understood as the maximum feasible aggregate economic good.

By contrast, the Dene had come to realize that any compromise was defeat. Alexis Arrowmaker, a chief of the Dogribs, explained that what white society means by ownership of land is very different from what the Dene meant. He went on:

Cabinet ministers do not understand this Indian concept or the way we see ourselves in relation to this land. They are stuck inside their own society and concepts, and they try to impose their view on us. We cannot compromise because it means giving up our concept and accepting theirs. We are not talking only about land, but also about Dene people and how we see ourselves as a group.[14]

I would like to contrast their position with a more usual one. When an urban citizens' group contests the intense use of some land (say for an airport), they are calling into question neither our culture's fundamental relationship to land nor the notion of ownership. They base their legitimacy on their ownership of adjacent land. They also affirm that land should be a commodity on the market, for their legitimate interest is that their land should not be devalued through incompatible uses nearby. Protesters who accept our culture, then, do not call into question the basic logic of land use; they simply want that logic arrested mid-way. While they affirm a rising land market they don't want land values rising so high that uses incompatible with their enjoyment of their land become economically unavoidable. Thus most protest groups have an ambiguous relationship to development and are seen to be intransigent if they do not compromise. The Natives, however, stand in an unambiguous relationship to our notions of land use and ownership; and cannot compromise if they wish to survive.

In summary, the federal policy of negotiation, as clarified by its subsequent actions, fits very neatly within the framework of a liberal vision of equality. They have declared themselves ready to negotiate, but have also clarified this to mean that all claims should be negotiable, since, according to the liberal vision, various claims and interests are *a priori* equal since moral differences between them are insignificant. While negotiating, they have brought insuperable pressure to bear on the Natives by allowing construction projects to proceed. This is considered legitimate because outstanding claims are in effect weighed against the basic utilitarian criterion, the maximum feasible aggregate economic good.

Over against this liberal vision, the Natives have made their statement concerning equality. They insist that the values at the heart of their culture and their consequent interests be judged not according to the technocratic criteria of our culture, but according to criteria which would encompass both our culture and theirs - in short, universal human values.

To try to spell out the ethical implications of this demand, I would like to locate it within a theoretical framework. I would, by way of preliminary remark, like to insist that this theory does not serve to legitimate their demand. Indeed, the reverse is true: their own experience and struggle is the basis of their legitimacy, and lends weight to the theory. Theory serves only to bring into relief the differences between their position and the liberal tradition, and thus to bring out various ethical implications.

The first implication I would like to stress is that these questions are ethical. They cannot be collapsed into technical, managerial considerations. The churches seem to be learning this from the Dene. In June 1976, before the Berger Commission, Project North pledged "...to stand openly and officially and wholeheartedly with the Dene and Inuit..." and this they did "...for there to be equality in this struggle...."[15] At that point they seem to have adopted the liberal framework in their understanding of negotiations, and saw their intervention as lending moral weight to a group under pressure. However, when in September 1978 the government cut off funds for an important Dene assembly, the churches provided the money. That decision involved a serious and difficult judgment: the Dene did not wish to compromise their position; the Metis were willing to compromise; the government was pressing the Dene to fall into line. The churched decided, in effect, that the Dene were right and the Metis wrong. The assembly went ahead; Dene claims were clarified; eventually the Metis came to agree.

The second implication to notice is that the Dene call for equality as a people makes visible the ethical limits of our culture. To elucidate this, I turn to the thought of Juergen Habermas. Over several years of negotiating, the native leaders kept complaining that the people in the south did not understand them. It was this breakdown in communication which has pushed them to their innovative articulations of their position. Habermas has noted that for comprehensibility and consensus, there must be both linguistic competence and communicative competence.[16] His analysis of the latter has led him to note that not only must language be grammatically comprehensible and propositionally true, but when a person wishes to enter an interpersonal relationship based upon communicative interaction, that person must also give - at least implicitly - grounds that his communicative act is both sincere and appropriate.[17] Each of these four validity claims must be open to question and, if necessary, settled through rational discussion.

Spokespersons for industry and government are perfectly willing to challenge and be challenged on the first three points - their grammaticality, their factual accuracy and their sincerity - but they tend to take the appropriateness of their position, and behind that, the validity of their cultural norms, for granted. Thus, when the Roman Catholic Church sided with the Dene and referred to their colonized status, industry spokesmen characterized that as "inaccurate, emotional language."[18] "Inaccurate" refers to the propositional truth of the Church's statement; "emotional" takes for granted the normative context of liberal negotiation and accuses the Church of an utterance inappropriate for that context.

However, if one party in a conversation is able to take its normative background for granted even when the other challenges its validity, that is exactly what is meant by domination. For equality, within this framework, means that each party has symmetrical chances to raise any question about any of the four aspects of the conversation.[19] In insisting upon their right to equality as a people, as a community with its own value-centres, the Dene have put their finger on the root of the government's insistence - despite their protestations - to continue to keep the Dene in a colonized position.

What has this to say about the limits of our culture? While admitting that a basic function of society is continuity - survival in the face of increased complexity -

Habermas rejects the metaphors of society as organism and society as cybernetic through discourse[20], that is, that the ability of a society to adapt and survive is fundamentally a question of ethics.[21]

Thus, as Project North has been saying in more concrete terms for some years, if Canadians through their government and industry spokesmen, insist on leaving technological criteria unquestioned, if they continue to collapse fundamental political questions into technical, managerial considerations, if they thereby continue systematically to distort communication both among themselves and with the Natives, then their technological culture's ability to adapt to the real complexities articulated by the Dene is curtailed. Domination in a society which insists on democratic forms and processes can only be achieved through a distortion of communication which cuts its members off from insitutional learning possibilities.

In their effort to be heard, the Native people of Canada's north have begun to develop language which bursts the ethical limits of our liberal, technocratic culture. They are appealing to values which are not confined within our cultural perspective, but which enable us to grasp the limits of our present cultural criteria.

HUMANISTIC AND THEOLOGICAL HISTORY OF RELIGIONS WITH SPECIAL REFERENCE TO THE NORTH AMERICAN SCENE

Joseph M. Kitagawa

1. Introduction

Any attempt to assess the development of the History of Religions during the past 100 years, especially in North America, cannot ignore the impact of two of the major international assemblies on the discipline, namely the World's Parliament of Religions, held in Chicago in 1893, and the first Congress of the History of Religions, held in Paris in 1900.

The World's Parliament of Religions reflected the growing interest of Americans in exotic non-Western religions. Significantly, many professors from leading universities were involved in the Parliament as representatives of their respective denominations. To be sure, many of them were scholars of Comparative Religion or History of Religions, but they were inclined - theologically and religiously - to share the motto of the Parliament: "To unite all religion against all irreligion; to make the Golden Rule the basis of this union; to present to the world...the substantial unity of many religions in the good deeds of the Religious Life...and [to demonstrate] the marvelous Religious progress of the Nineteenth century...."[1] Ironically, in the minds of many Americans the cause of the Parliament became inseparably related to the aim of Comparative Religion or History of Religions.

Elsewhere I have touched upon the checkered career of the comparative and historical study of religion in North America, its popularity throughout the 1910's and 1920's, its uneasy alliance with theological liberalism and certain types of philosophy of religion, and its sudden decline in the 1930's. Through it all, a serious "humanistic" study of religions, especially the History of Religions, did not take root in North America until after World War II.

Today there seems to be a kind of confusion in many quarters. The fundamental distinction between the two genuine enterprises of "humanistic" and "theological" approaches to the History of Religions is not adequately appreciated. This confusion impoverishes both approaches, as I will discuss presently.

The 1900 Paris Congress set the tone in four ways for subsequent congresses, and, indirectly, the later development of the discipline of the History of Religions: (1) Unlike the 1893 World's Parliament of Religions, the Paris Congress was a scholarly, rather than a religious conference. (2) There was a variety of scholarly approaches and competencies represented at the Congress. Indeed, there were many scholars who were not "Historians of Religions" in terms of academic and disciplinary affiliations. However, they were engaged in critical and humanistic, social-scientific research into the rich phenomena of religions for the purpose of "understanding" the nature of religions. This "unified concern" characterized the Paris Congress. (3) In spite of the "unified concern" with a strong historical bent, the format of the Paris Congress was more "horizontal" in nature, dividing its program into separate sessions, each dealing with religions of non-civilized peoples of the pre-Columbian Americas, religions of the Far East, Indo-Iranian religions, Christianity, etc. The format of the Paris Congress was followed without much deviation by the subsequent Congresses for the History of Religions. (4) The Paris Congress did little, if anything, to move from the "unified concern" of the History of Religions to a "unified discipline," as envisaged by Burnouf and other pioneers of the discipline.

2. <u>Discussion on the Nature of the History of Religions</u>
Since 1950, when the IAHR was officially formed in Amsterdam, the leaders of the IAHR have urged historians of

religions to be self-conscious about the nature, objective, and methods of the discipline. For example, in Amsterdam Professor van der Leeuw stressed both the independence of the History of Religions from theology, as well as the necessity of the History of Religions to maintain rapport with philosophy, archaeology, anthropology, psychology and sociology in order to attain a "synthetic view." In the 1960 Congress at Marburg a number of participants signed a statement that stressed the following points: (1) Although the *religionswissenschaftliche* method undoubtedly is a Western creation, it would be misleading to juxtapose "occidental" and "oriental" methods in the History of Religions, as some scholars were inclined to do. (2) *Religionswissenschaft* "understands itself as a branch of the Humanities." It studies the religious phenomena as a creation of human culture. (3) As such, the notion that "the value of religious phenomena can be understood only if we keep in mind that religion is ultimately a realization of a transcendent truth" is not a legitimate foundation of *Religionswissenschaft*. (4) "The study of religions need not seek for justification outside itself," for every quest of historical truth is "its own *raison d'être*."[2] In the 1970 Congress in Stockholm, Professor Geo Widengren expressed his concern over the excessive "compartmentalization of scholarship" and its implication to the common enterprise of the History of Religions. He was unhappy about the myopia of specialists who think they can study specific religions without any reference to the general history of religions. In fact, the general history of religions requires the cooperation of all specialists, this then provides the proper perspective to the study of specific religions.

Even such a spotty account of the discussions at previous congresses reminds us that wherever we may be situated, and whatever our competencies may be, all of us must make every effort to clarify the nature of our discipline for the sake of our common task. With this in mind, let me present my own assessment of the state of the

History of Religions in North America and my own understanding of the nature of our discipline.

3. The History of Religions in North America

Earlier I mentioned that Comparative Religion and the History of Religions became popular subjects in North America following the Parliament of Religions and during the first three decades of our century. Both disciplines suddenly declined due to the impact of theological neo-orthodoxy, the depression, the impending war, and other factors.

The impetus for the renewed interest in the History of Religions - or at least certain aspects of it - after the end of World War II came from several factors: (i) a sudden interest in things Eastern, including historic Asian religions and modern Eastern cults; (ii) the proliferation of Religion Departments in colleges and universities that pursue the non-theological nature of the History of Religions as well as general studies of non-Western religions; (iii) the growing fascination among some social scientists in non-Western myths, symbols, cults, social structures and cultural patterns, and (iv) a new interest among influential theologians in a dialogue not only with Judaism but also with Eastern religions.

It is particularly interesting to note that while mainline church groups in North America have lost much of their incentive for overseas missionary enterprises, they show increasing interest in "dialogues" with other religions. Numerous seminars, workshops, and conferences (to which a number of historians of religions have been invited) have been held for this purpose, to exhibit a wide range of qualities and perspectives. These range from simplistic exhanges of the main tenets of various faiths - reminiscent of the 1893 Parliament - to more sophisticated searches for a common language or common frame of reference as a basis for a meaningful dialogue with other religions. In addition, some theologians have attempted to develop the viable enterprises of the "Theology of Religions," "Comparative Theologies," and "Theological History of

Religions." One of the most serious attempts to set forth the principles of a "Theological History of Religions" was made by Paul Tillich.

Tillich was engaged in a theological enterprise, even though he wanted to use data provided by the History of Religions. In his own words:

> A theological history of religion should interpret theologically the material produced by the investigation and analysis of the pre-religious and religious life of mankind. It should elaborate the motives and types of religious expression, showing how they follow from the nature of the religious concern and therefore necessarily appear in all religions, including Christianity in so far as it is a religion.[3]

Tillich was convinced of the importance of the phenomenological approach. But, realizing that the phenomenological method is only partially competent in dealing with spiritual realities like religion, he advocated a "critical phenomenology" - the method which supplies a normative description of spiritual meaning - in the theological enterprise.[4] Tillich's methodological procedure in his proposed "theological history of religion(s)" rested on what he called a "dynamic typology," which he claimed to be more adequate than Hegel's teleological dialectics. Using the means of a dynamic typology, Tillich wanted to characterize the typical structures within the unique form of various historic religions and to compare them with the typical structures appearing in Christianity as a historic religion. For example, he proposed to use two *telos*-formulae in the dialogue between Christianity and Buddhism, namely, the Kingdom of God and Nirvāna. "These, of course," he stated, "are abbreviations for an almost infinite number of presuppositions and consequences; but just for this reason they are useful for the beginning as well as for the end of a dialogue."[5]

My reference to Tillich does not imply that he was the only advocate of a Theological History of Religion(s). There are many other serious attempts being made today along this line of inquiry. Although he dealt with concrete data only in his small book, *Christianity and the*

Encounter of the World Religions, I refer to Tillich because to me personally his assumptions and methodological principles are clearer than others. Since dialogues among Catholic, Protestant, and Jewish groups have been going on in North America, and since various religious groups are beginning to engage in dialogues with non-Western religious groups, a variety of theological approaches to the history of religions will continue to be devised. Some North American historians of religions have already been involved in such dialogues in various capacities.

As I see it, the present danger is that the line of demarcation between "theological" and "humanistic" approaches to the history of religions is not safeguarded - much to the disservice of both enterprises.

4. The State of the "Humanistic" History of Religions

Inasmuch as my assessment of the North American scene is made from my limited perspective, I should state briefly what I understand the History of Religions to be, acknowledging of course that my own understanding is not the only, or perhaps the best, one. I have a sneaking suspicion that today in North America - and probably in other places, too - the designation "History of Religions" refers to many different enterprises that share no "unified concern." Therefore, this term is losing its own integrity. I do not want to restrict the term "History of Religions" to mean only the historical aspect of our study, leaving out the phenomenological and other legitimate dimensions of our discipline. I realize that there are different emphases and approaches within our discipline. This is why I have been encouraged by discussions on the nature of the discipline that have been carried on at previous Congresses, and I certainly hope we compare notes and learn from each other on this subject at this Congress. My concern arises from my observation that today any study that touches on historical dimensions of any religion, usually non-Western religion, from any perspective and utilizing any methodological principle, is accepted as the History of Religions. I have already cited the "theological" History of Religions as a legitimate theological enterprise, but not to be confused with the "humanistic" History of Religions. I also have indicated that the popular equation of the History of Religions with the study of "World Religions" goes back to the Chicago Parliament of 1893. Regarding the use of the category of "World Religions" as such, which is used widely in academic circles in North America, I refer you to the insightful critique of my colleague, Jonathan Z. Smith, as expressed in his recent book entitled *Map Is Not Territory*.[6] Another broad category, "Asian Religions," which has been made an acceptable term by programs of Asian Studies, has now crept into the vocabulary of religion departments and of the American Academy of Religion. The popularity of this subject, however loosely interpreted, is illustrated by the recent survey that lists 1,653 professors who teach Asian religious traditions in colleges and universities in Canada and the United States. However, this list does not indicate the disciplinary training and/or affiliation of these professors; we are not told who among all of these scholars are theologians, comparative ethicists, social scientists, philosophers of religion, or historians of religions.

    I do not wish to suggest that the History of Religions is the most important discipline in the study of religions. However, I am persuaded that the History of Religions is a legitimate scholarly enterprise in spite of many problems involved, and that it is not merely a collective title for a number of related studies, such as the historical studies of Islam, Christianity, Buddhism, Hinduism, and primitive religions, for example, or the comparative studies of doctrines, practices, and ecclesiastical institutions of various religions. Following my mentor Joachim Wach, I interpret the History of Religions as an approximate – and not altogether satisfactory English term for *Allgemeine Religionswissenschaft*, which is an autonomous discipline situated between normative studies, such as philosophy of religion and theology, and descriptive studies such as sociology, anthropology, and psychology. *Religionswissen-*

schaft is composed of two complementary aspects - the "historical" and the "systematic" procedures of study. The historical task requires a mutual interaction between the historical studies of specific religions and the study of the general history of religions, while the systematic task aims at disciplined generalizations and structuring of data, and depends on a collaboration of phenomenological, comparative, sociological, psychological, and other studies of religions.

Like other historians of religions, I affirm that the point of departure of *Religionswissenschaft* is the study of the historical forms of religions as humanity's response to the sacred dimension of life and the world, recognizing that each religion is an individual totality, incomparable in its uniqueness. The goal of an historical study in *Religionswissenschaft* is to gain understanding into the various facets of each religion, facets that together have come to form the totality of the various religions, but which do not remain the same from one historic stage to the next without losing their *Lebensgefühl*. In this endeavor we must study a specific religion in its environment. Following Raffaele Pettazzoni's advice, we also study "its relation to other cultural values belonging to the same environment, such as poetry, art, speculative thought, social structure and so on."[7] It also must be mentioned that in this historical study of specific religions, a "humanistic" historian of religions - unlike a "theological" historian of religions or philosopher of religion - does not have a speculative purpose, nor does he resort to an a priori deductive method. At the same time, while the historical task of *Religionswissenschaft* has to abide by descriptive principles, its inquiry must be directed to the "meaning" - which links, in a sense, the descriptive and normative concerns - of the religious data which constitute its subject-matter. In this respect, my learned colleague Professor Mircea Eliade reminds us that the meaning of a religious phenomenon can be understood only if it is understood to be something religious. "To try to grasp the essence of such a phenomenon by means of physiology, psychology, sociology, economics, linguistics, art or any other study is false; it misses the one unique and irreducible element in it - the element of the sacred."[8] It might also be mentioned that the comparative method is a necessary tool for the understanding of the nature and meaning of specific religions.

Of course, the historical study of specific religions within the framework of *Religionswissenschaft* has much in common with, say, histories of Hinduism, Buddhism, and other religious traditions. But the historical study within *Religionswissenschaft* must view specific religions not only as entities in themselves but also parts of the total history of the religions of humanity. This is why at Stockholm in 1970 Professor Widengren suggested that we need more scholars who are oriented from the viewpoint of the History of Religions in general to study Islam and other religions. We realize, of course, that our audacious aim to gain an "integral understanding" of the general history of religions depends on our limited horizon to view the total religious history of humanity. Such a task - here the historical task borders the systematic task - requires a selectivity of data and a telescoping of the long and complex historical tapestry of various religions. In this respect, the task of the historian of religions is something analogous to that of the historian of cultures and civilizations; to use the phrase of Robert Redfield, it involves "thinking about a civilization." According to Redfield, "thinking about" is "something different from getting information and acquaintance, though this third activity requires and is guided by the first two. It is to develop formed and nameable thoughts about the civilization. It is to conceive it, and make it a mental artifact, a shaped work of the intellect."[9] If such "thinking about" civilization involves risks, then thinking about the religious history of the human race involves far greater risks and difficulties. And yet this is precisely what the historian of religions is expected to contribute to the humanistic study of religion.

I must humbly confess at this point that the longer I

study the History of Religions the more difficulties I encounter in relating the historical and the systematic dimensions of *Religionswissenschaft*. I have almost come to the simple conclusion that some people are born to be more historically oriented, while others are systematically oriented. I also recognize the rarity of the kind of encyclopedic mind that can develop adequate systematic works. And yet I also am inclined to believe that in the long run *Religionswissenschaft* will stand or fall with the systematic structuring of the data on its own ground. Certainly, the task of *Religionswissenschaft* is not the gathering of data for the benefit of other academic enterprises. To be sure, philosophers and theologians are at liberty to utilize our research, but their interpretations must remain within the philosophical or theological discipline. Conversely, the exclusive utilization of philosophical or theological data by *Religionswissenschaft* turns ours into a philosophical or theological discipline. The common danger I find in our discipline is to fall into the temptation of systematizing our data on the basis of a framework borrowed from philosophical, sociological, anthropological or psychological models.

Our discipline is haunted by the difficulties in deriving systematic categories to focus and study. The forebearers of our discipline seemed to have borrowed not only data but also categories from various other disciplines, especially from philosophy. Even C. P. Tiele, who rejected a metaphysically or religiously colored philosophy, resorted to philosophical categories because, in his view, *Religionswissenschaft* was essentially a philosophical inquiry into the universal human phenomenon called religion.[10] According to Wach, it was Max Scheler who first envisaged an independent, religio-scientific mode of inquiry called the "concrete phenomenology of religious objects and acts," whose object was to study religious phenomena by means of religio-scientific categories.[11] Nevertheless, the systematic or phenomenological inquiry of *Religionswissenschaft*, in spite of its use of religio-scientific categories, often has been mistaken by others as a philosophical or pseudo-theological endeavor. More recently, due to strong influence of the social sciences on *Religionswissenschaft*, our discipline's systematic study appears to look, at least to some people, more like anthropology or psychology. These and other kinds of misunderstandings notwithstanding, the primary task of the systematic dimension of *Religionswissenschaft* is not so much to unfold novel generalizations as much as to articulate its research procedures and methods.

Rightly or wrongly, I feel that it is crucially important for historians of religions to begin their work with "classical" religions. Our scholarly categories, inadequate though they may be, are derived primarily from the classical forms of religions in which religious manifestations are more clearly discernible than in the ambiguities of modern or less-known pre-civilized situations. Thus, unlike social-scientific disciplines which have refined research procedures to deal with modern as well as primitive religious phenomena, the "humanistic" History of Religions must first develop sufficient understanding of classical forms and types of religious phenomena. These forms may then provide a means with which to deal with other religious modalities. In this connection, I would also add a word of caution against the uncritical use of the "traditional versus modern" formula, which often appears to our anti-historical contemporaries to offer simple resolutions for the complex problems presented by the discipline of the History of Religions. Such a stereotyped dichotomy, however, fails to do justice to the rich historical heritage or the tradition (*traditio*) which has remained alive and resourceful to the present. I am keenly aware of a series of difficult problems that confronts the History of Religions, methodological or otherwise. But, I believe, our problems will find their solutions - to the extent that any scholarly problems are ever solved - by our asking important religio-scientific questions and by our refining our research procedures and categories.

THE SIGNIFICANCE OF THE JAPANESE INTELLECTUAL TRADITION FOR THE HISTORY OF RELIGIONS

Michael Pye

It is widely held that the application of Western concepts in the study of Asian religions is a distorting imposition of alien modes of thought. It is sometimes even argued that the very names given to well-known religious traditions are misleading abstractions which should be abandoned. It is also widely held that the historically oriented, critical study of religion is essentially a product of the European Enlightenment and hence is alien to the Asian intellectual tradition. The history of the Japanese intellectual tradition, however, provides reasons for a drastic qualification of these views. The central reason is that there was an independent historical critique of the religion in early eighteen-century Japan, exemplified most dramatically in the work of Nakamoto Tominaga (1715-1746). Analogies between his ideas and those of Lessing (17291781) have already been pointed out.[1] It is particularly striking that Tominaga discussed the three "teachings" of Buddhism, Confucianism and Shinto as developing historical entities subject to analysis and criticism by reflective observers. This work of Tominaga has been followed through, after some fits and starts, and with significant Western stimulus in the nineteenth century, to the point where there is now a major non-western discipline of religious studies in Japan. Although in recent decades there has been much borrowing of Western concepts in the analysis of religion, there is every reason to hope that Japanese scholars will contribute increasingly to the refinement of the abstract concepts needed for any study of religion.

At the time of the earlier paper mentioned above there had not been any sustained consideration of the international or intercultural significance of Tominaga's work. Indeed there still has not been. R. Tsunoda's excellent *Sources of Japanese Tradition* contains some extracts from one of Tominaga's works, but the explanatory passages simply place Tominaga in the context of the history of Japanese ideas without attempting any wider discussion.[2] The same is true in principle for the introductory piece by S. Kato in *Monumenta Nipponica* where he published the first integral translation of one of Tominaga's works into a non-Japanese language.[3] Indeed it is most interesting that the intercultural, methodological significance of Tominaga's achievement does not seem to have occurred to Japanese scholars who have written about him in Japanese. They have dwelled on his methodology, but not on its intercultural or comparative significance. More will be said on this point later.

For these reasons it seemed important to chart some of the similarities between Tominaga's historically relativist critique of Asian religions and the work of a suitable counterpart representing the European Enlightenment. In the intervening years more detailed studies have been carried out on Tominaga's work in the original Japanese and Sino-Japanese texts. These studies have included a new translation of the work previously translated by Kato (the *Okina no Fumi*), which is complete as to the text itself, and a first translation into English of Tominaga's other extended work (the *Shutsujō Kogo*), which is three-quarters completed. These more detailed studies indicate that there is an entirely satisfactory and solid foundation for meaningful comparison with Western historical critiques and analyses of religion. This does not mean of course that Tominaga's preferred concepts for explaining the development of religion are just the same as those produced in the Western world. There are important reasons in the background of ideas, especially religious ideas, why this could not be so. Moreover his preferred concepts are extremely difficult to translate. The concept of *kajō*, for example, is used to explain the accumulation of religious teachings through time. While literally it means both adding to and going beyond, there seems to be no English term which quite fits. To avoid the danger of wresting Tominaga's idea from its moorings and equating it over-simply with some Western idea, it will probably prove necessary to familiarise people with the original term. However, while key terms are not necessarily exactly parallel (and therein lies much of the attraction), what is clear is that in Tominaga's work important presuppositions are discernible which provide an entirely adequate base for the development of modern, critical and systematic reflection on religion. Such a base was by no means prepared in Europe alone, and therein lies the rest of the attraction.

The trend in European and North American research to doubt the applicability of western-derived concepts to the religions of other cultures has been extremely healthy. Researchers in a variety of relevant disciplines have laboured to shed undue reliance on the concepts of God, of faith, of the nature of religious experience, and indeed of rationality, which were derived from European theology and philosophy. Anthropologists tried to grasp the nature of presumedly different primitive mentality, or of archaic religious consciousness, rightly perceiving that to study the beliefs of less complex civilizations as if they were so-called superstitions or fundamentally erroneous was to ignore their symbolic value and their consistency and meaning within the society in question. Orientalists and comparative religionists came to see, with some fits and starts, that the traditions of India, China, Japan and so on, could not be adequately considered in theistic terms, or at least not in theistic terms alone. The trend has been strongly reinforced by the popularity of the Wittgensteinian concept of language games, which has encouraged people to be satisfied with staring at self-contained sets of discourse without seeking external criteria for their elucidation or criticism. The trend has also been reinforced by those voices from Asia itself, especially from India and Japan, which stressed the ineffability of

Oriental religious experience over against that of a Western mind supposedly trapped at a secondary level of rationalist discriminative thought. Others pointed to the lack of historical consciousness in Buddhism, for example, with the suggestion that therefore questions about the nature and development of Buddhist tradition are not appropriate. The latest version of the Western scruples is that in which the names of the major religions are rejected as alien impositions, or in a popular term, as "reifications." Cantwell Smith's influence has been great in this regard, and so too has that of Robert Baird's recent work *Category Formation in the History of Religions*.[4] This work would leave us with few verbal tools to discuss the nature or structure of religious traditions, and it is notable that the important abstract term "syncretism" is rejected as useless.

It must be admitted that this whole trend, which has such diverse and powerful stimuli from West and East alike, is in line in an important sense with the concerns of those who would study religion phenomenologically. That is, it encourages the study of religion, at least in the first instance, in terms of the believers' own consciousness, and not in terms of preconceived ideas about truth and falsity, about the nature of reality, and so on. In this sense the trend is an extremely healthy one which calls for self-examination and restraint on the part of observers and interpreters wherever they were born and brought up.

However, the study of religion is sufficiently painful to demand work against this trend also, namely towards those critically refined abstractions which alone enable us to reflect comparatively, that is, upon more than one case at a time. This is also essential if anthropologists are to do more than simply disappear forever in the village of their choice, if historians of religion are to do more than relapse into antiquarianism, and if those who study religion (or something like it) in cultures other than those in which they grew up are to do more than become mere converts and enthusiasts. In other words, it is essential to make use of critically refined abstractions to bring particular sets of observed data into a wider area of intelligible discourse and reflection. We need to use such words as shamanism, mysticism, tradition, doctrine, myth, or else to come up with alternatives which are better suited to their task. We need them, that is, if the study of religion is in any sense to be understood as a public science.

The general characteristics of Tominaga's thought have already been indicated here and there, but the argument now requires some reminder in order to proceed. In a sense the more difficult of Tominaga's two extended works has the simplest methodological assumptions, for it deals with one religion only, namely Buddhism. This work, entitled *Shutsujō Kōgo*, makes extensive use of quotations from Buddhist sutras and treatises to show that there was great diversity in the teaching on all major topics at an early time. In particular, the Mahayana sutras were not the direct utterances from the golden mouth of the Buddha which popular piety supposed, a stunning thesis for Tominaga's time. The saying "Thus I have heard" at the beginning of Buddhist sutras was always meant to be an indication of their authenticity, but in his chapter bearing this saying as its title Tominaga deftly transforms it into a symbol of the later creation of these sutras by the Buddha's followers. He also claimed that the various forms of Buddhist teaching represented constant efforts by different groups to supersede each other, thus giving rise to ever more complex scriptural deposits. This is regularly summarized by the term *kajō*, referred to earlier. Tominaga also stressed the relativity of language in this work (Section 11), saying that the meaning of a term is affected by three conditions: the intention of the individual user, the conventions of the milieu, and the type to which the term belongs (any one of five). Those interested in cosmology and psychology may be more interested in Section 4, where many variations of teaching about Mount Sumeru and the heavens are reviewed. This has a typical and particularly interesting ending:

"The theory that there are five worlds of which the Sumeru world is one was first propounded by the brahmins and is the basis for the others. When they speak of the small thousand-fold world, the medium thousand-fold world, and the three-thousand fold great thousand-fold world, or again of ten worlds apart from the three thousand-fold world, these are all later supersedings. The *Bonmō* teaching of the lotus world is another superseding layer which extends as far as the world sea of *Kegon* teaching. Teachings about the cosmos are really quite vague and go no further than describing the workings of the mind. There is no way of knowing whether they are right or wrong. Hence I say that the worlds arise in conformity with people's minds."5

This paragraph clearly shows the use of Tominaga's theory of *kajō*. It also suggests a most interesting demythologization of cosmology. Note carefully that the different versions of cosmology are not relativized in terms of variations in the Buddha's teaching to suit different recipients, which would be a classic Mahayana explanation. The psychologised view arises because there are no criteria for assessing the truth or falsity of cosmologies. The world is different and the terms are different, but the presupposition is clearly akin to that of modern Western thinking about religion. In fact, the terms are not as distant as one might imagine, because the phrase "workings of the mind" translates two characters used in modern Japanese to mean "psychology" (*shinri*).

The principle of *kajō* is taken up again in Tominaga's second extant work, the *Okina no Fumi*. This title may be translated as *Writings of an Old Man*, a literary form which Tominaga adopted to provide a certain indirectness for what he had to say. In fact the text offers three standpoints, that of the basic statements ostensibly made by an old man whom Tominaga knew, comments ascribed to the Old Man, and comments made directly by Tominaga himself. The text begins with an uncompromising statement of religious relativism. The Old Man declares that Buddhism was proper to India, Confucianism to China and Shinto to the Japan of an earlier time. Each was subject to its time and place, and the forms there assumed could not simply be transferred to another time and place. Tominaga poured scorn on those who slavishly imitated Indian, Chinese or ancient Japanese practices on the assumption that the meaning of the "ways" would thereby appear (Sections 2-5). In Section 6 the Old

Man is then made to expound what is termed "the way of ways" or "the way of truth" (*makoto no michi*), which turns out to be a very simple moralism, more strongly reflecting the neo-Confucianism of his own time than Tominaga probably realised (Sections 6-8). We then come to a very short, pivotal section in which Tominaga's view of the genesis of religious traditions is made quite clear. This may be quoted in full:

But here this old man would like to make his point. Since ancient times it has generally been the case that those who preach a moral way and establish a law of life have had somebody whom they have held up as an authoritative precursor, while at the same time they have tried to emerge above those who went before. Later generations, however, being unaware of this regular practice, are quite confused by it.[6]

This general principle behind the genesis of "ways" is then illustrated for Buddhism (a tiny summary of the *Shutsujō Kogo*), Confucianism and Shinto respectively in Sections 10, 11 and 12, the last of which will be taken up in more detail shortly. After that the work concludes with a further critique of each of the three religions or ways in terms of a particular habit ascribed to each. For Buddhism the habit is magic, for Confucianism it is rhetoric and for Shinto it is secrecy. Tominaga argued that none of these was appropriate to the Japan of his time. For us today it is interesting to observe that all three of these habits are enemies of reason.

Tominaga did not use a word which can be translated as tradition. However, he did constantly refer, with specific names, to coherent patterns of teaching and practice which he analysed and explained. The specific relevance of his work to the methodological concerns of the history of religions today may be most clearly shown by attending to this aspect of his work. This leaves on one side his moralism, which is, however, not closely related to his analytical efforts. It also leaves on one side the immensity of his critique of the growth of Buddhism which entirely anticipated the shock of nineteenth-century critical study. What follows is restricted to some reflections on the names which Tominaga used to refer to the religions of his day, and the way in which he himself viewed this naming process as part of his nascent theory of religious tradition.

At the beginning of the *Okina no Fumi* we find the expression *Shin-Ju-Butsu*. *Shin* is short for *Shindō* (or *Shintō*), a term which Tominaga himself used freely. *Ju* and *Butsu* are what we today would refer to as Confucianism and Buddhism. The modern Japanese ending *-shugi*, which was coined to parallel the Western "-ism" (in its various forms), was not in use in Tominaga's time. However, to say merely *Butsu*, as Tominaga often did, is to fail to say *Butsudō* (Buddha-way) or *Buppō* (Buddha-Dharma) and thus to give a somewhat off-hand nuance. *Butsu* does not refer to any particular Buddhist saint, nor indeed to the historical founder of Buddhism whom Tominaga calls Shaka (Śākyamuni), nor to a specially venerated scheme of teaching. The term *Butsu* is quite simply a name for the system of Buddhism in general, and the word "Buddhism" is the nearest translation for it in modern English. The same may be said for *Ju*. This is the name Tominaga gives to the whole range of Confucian teaching with its representative teachers and institutions, in short, for what in English is referred to as Confucianism. Hence, while it would be gratuitous to add an "ism" to Shinto as Kato did in his translation, it would be equally wrong to go to special lengths to avoid saying Confucianism and Buddhism. On the same basis it is appropriate to refer to Confucianism for *Jushi* and *Jukyōto* when these appear in various places in the *Shutsujō Kōgo*.

In case the tender-hearted harbour scruples on this point the line of thought needs to be considered as well. The opening sentences of the *Okina no Fumi* are: "In the world today one learns that the three ways Buddhism, Confucianism and Shinto are the three teachings of India, China and Japan respectively. Some people say that these three coincide, while others dispute about the rights and wrongs of each."[7] This more extended phrasing illustrates that *Shin*, *Ju and Butsu* can be called both "ways" and "teachings." It also shows that Tominaga assumed people in general, not just himself, to have a sufficiently clear conception of these ways or teachings as distinct entities or patterns for discussions about them to take place. Such discussions were on the same basis as many which take place today, namely on the relations between religions (or is it essential to say ways, or teachings?) and about their respective claims. However the point is not that such disputes have progressed so little since that time, but that in the early eighteenth century, a very long way from Europe, people used summary terms to refer to patterns of practice and teaching whose similarities and differences mattered to them. Tominaga of course went way beyond the mere assumptions of his time. He was attempting to put forward a coherent explanation as to how these patterns had come to be as they were, and why people were confused by things which seemed not to fit with the underlying purpose of these patterns. His line of thought may be further illustrated by an extended quotation from Section 11 of the *Okina no Fumi*, which has the particular advantage of showing that Tominaga himself thought there was a time when our names for these patterns were not appropriate. (It was an extremely long time ago.)

As for Shinto, in semi-antiquity they all claimed that it went back as far as the age of the gods and gave it the name of the Way of Japan, thus trying to come out above Confucianism and Buddhism. To offer analogies, at the time of the deva Abhasvara in India, or at the time of the P'an Ku clan in China, there was no fully-fledged defined way which could be called Buddhism or Confucianism. If Buddhism and Confucianism were made up on purpose by people in later times, Shinto too could scarcely have existed in some ancient age of the gods. What was given out first was called *Ryōbu Shūgō* (Twofold Combination). This was made by combining elements of Confucianism and Buddhism and adding or subtracting as desired. The next to appear was the *Honjaku Engi* (The Story of Origin and Manifestation). This was compiled by Buddhists of the time who were jealous of the rise of Shinto and who taught Shinto on the surface while inwardly redirecting it towards Buddhism. Then the next teaching was called *Yuiichi Sogen* (Single Great Source). This was a departure from the ways of Confucianism and Buddhism and only taught pure Shinto. While these three kinds of Shinto all come from semi-antiquity, there has recently appeared something called *Ōdō Shinto* (Kingly Way Shinto). According to this there is no such thing as a separate way called Shinto. It teaches that the Kingly Way *is* Shinto. Yet again, there has appeared a Shinto which teaches Shinto on the surface and inwardly is identical with Confucianism. None of these existed in the age of the gods, but, as explained, each was expounded to come out above the others. When foolish people today fail to realise this and think that one or other of these teachings is the true way, they wrong themselves and argue disputatiously with each other. This seems to an old man to be vexing, pitiful and ridiculous.8

The last thought in this paragraph reflects Tominaga's moralism, that is, his view of the "true way" as consisting of practical, moral behaviour. The quotation is taken this far to avoid giving a misleading impression of Tominaga's interests, for in this work he is indeed a moralist as well as an analytical critic. However the main argument in this section makes it quite clear that Tominaga saw the story of Shinto as a succession of consciously devised systems, having varied relations with Confucianism and Buddhism. It is interesting that he saw the first emergence of Shinto as a coherent system to have depended on the presence of the older systems from China and India. He also saw that the linking of diverse systems is not always as simple as might at first seem. In other words he had a complex view of what has later been called syncretism. Above all he is concerned with the genesis and the consecutive phases of coherent patterns of practice and belief, in short, with religious systems which have names. Since these nameable, if not easily definable systems had an interesting diachronic existence for Tominaga, we are justified in seeing his work as an early contribution to the theory of religious tradition. There can be absolutely no question of thinking that such ideas are in principle the creation and property of the Western mind alone.

If we take together the ideas of Tominaga's two extant writings it is fair to say that he not only offered a historical critique of many a pious assumption, but that he went on to mount a theory of tradition. This theory may be said to be partly psychological and partly historical. Tominaga held that religious leaders experienced an urge both to adduce some past authorities and at the same time to put a new gloss on their teaching, thereby "coming out above" those who had gone before. In his view the Buddha and Confucius were no exception to this. They too had their precursors whom they had sought to supersede. Thus there is no one point in the continuing chain of tradition which has an absolute authority *de novo*. The idea of "coming out above" is prominent in the *Okina no Fumi*, but it runs closely parallel to that of "adding and going beyond" (*kajō*) which seems to occur more frequently in the *Shutsujō Kōgo*. Tominaga's historically conceived idea of tradition is of course completely different from some doctrinal stance giving a particular perspective on past movements. His idea depends on a freedom from doctrinal authorities, on the ability to perceive the character of specific phases and forms of tradition, to compare them, and to reflect on the activity and intentions of those who promote them. It depends on the use of abstractions which can be applied to more than one case.

Tominaga was in interesting respects an innovative thinker. This does not mean, however, that he was an aberration. Biographically he can be located, though with no surfeit of details, in the merchant society of eighteenth-century Osaka, a society which by then was sufficiently well-to-do to promote learning in independent schools. Such a culture does not lack parallels with the city bourgeois society of Europe which provided the social base for the European Enlightenment. This may be a new starting point for a discussion of the significance of Tominaga and other Tokugawa Period thinkers in terms of the sociology of knowledge, although it cannot be pursued further in the present argument. Leaving aside the social conditions for the moment, let us be content with noting that there was a general movement of critical investigation and reflection which gathered momentum during the Tokugawa Period in Japan. This movement had empiricist, rationalist, moralist, historicist and romantic threads, and it provided the intellectual base for Japan's ability to respond almost instantaneously to the dramatic stimuli of Western culture in the nineteenth century. The plain fact is that in many important respects Japanese thinkers had thought in modern modes long before they were called upon to modernise.

It is a most important principle in understanding the significance of Tominaga's work to recognize that it was an autonomous achievement within the context of the Japanese intellectual tradition. There is no question whatever of Western influence on his ideas, in principle or in detail. Paradoxically, it is because he was culturally insulated that he now takes on a universal significance. The universal significance lies in the fact that the kind of presuppositions which he brought to bear on the analysis of religion are not Japanese or European alone, but belong to a wider rationality. Thus we are left today with a transcultural base for developing the historical and comparative study of religion.

When we come to the modern study of religion it is time that the supposed dependence of nineteenth-century Japanese beginnings upon the West was reappraised. This cannot be attempted in detail here though a few suggestions may be made. In general it may be argued that the influence which Max Müller and others exercised in the nineteenth-century was effective in Japan only because of the prior development of modern critical ideas. It might be well to ask for closer definitions of what in principle was learned from Western studies of religion which had not already been tried out in Japan. One needs to bear in mind not only Tominaga's thorough critique of Buddhist history and canonical authority but also Sorai Ōgyū's critique of Confucian texts and traditions and Norinaga Motoori's extremely modern interest in the archaic sources of Shinto. The latter almost like a European Romantic, consciously preferred the *Kojiki* to the more Sinified *Nihongi*, and his linguistic commentary thereon may be seen as the major starting point for all later Japanese folklore studies.

As to Tominaga's personal influence, it should not be overlooked that his works, though later falling into near oblivion, were read for some time by people associated with all three of the main traditions with which he dealt. An early critique of Confucianism was so subversive, and evidently considered by others to be dangerous, that it was banned and is now lost. The points made in it were clearly not lost on his enemies. Motoori and his follower Hirata both referred to Tominaga's work in influential writings. Among the Buddhists some written responses were composed to counter his critique, but these seem to have remained at the level of pious horror. The direct impact of Tominaga on those who knew him cannot easily be assessed. However he was without doubt part of a wider intellectual community based in Osaka and there would certainly have been those who understood his messages.

Although the connections between persons, places and writings no doubt provide material for much ramified research, it may not be too far-fetched to suggest that Tominaga and Motoori, different as they are from each other, will eventually come to be seen as the main forefathers of modern Japanese studies of religion, just as the European discipline finds its main origins in the Enlightenment and in Romanticism. At least there is no doubt that Japanese scholarship in the history of religions has significant independent roots. Today it is also closely sensitive to Western work. Given this double strength it is to be expected that significant contributions will be made in the refinement of those abstract concepts which are necessary for the study of religion.

This returns us to the starting point. There may be cases when particular concepts drawn from one tradition are not applicable to another. Indeed contributions from various viewpoints are extremely desirable in order to produce the qualifications and refinements needed for using abstract and comparative concepts in the study of religion. However it can no longer be held that such abstractions are in principle cultural impositions emanating from the Western world. On the contrary, they are a natural feature of modern reflection about religion which can be documented in at least two distant and thoroughly distinct cultures as early as the first half of the eighteenth century.

WOMEN'S STUDIES IN RELIGION:
THE STATE OF THE ART, 1980

Rita M. Gross

During the past ten years a significant new focus, usually called the "women and religion movement," has emerged within the academic study of religion. The first section of this paper will briefly review the development of that movement. Then I will discuss the basic rationale of the women and religion movement as a whole in terms that apply to both the historical/comparative and the theological sides of religious studies. In this section, I will also discuss the significance of the movement for the whole field of religious studies. My paper will end with a more detailed look at the history of religions and some of the needs of our discipline.

Ten years ago, in 1970, the "women and religion" movement existed mainly in the frustrations of some graduate students and a few younger professors of religious studies. No institutional format existed at that time and neither the American Academy of Religion nor the International Association for the History of Religions paid much attention to the topic of women and religion. If someone brought up the idea of specifically focusing on women and religion, the response was a combination of indifference, hilarity and hostility. Now, in North America at least, the topic is somewhat well-known; the American Academy of Religion has had a section on "Women and Religion" since 1972 and it has become one of the liveliest and best-attended sections of the AAR. For the first time, the International Association for the History of Religions has programmed the topic "Femininity and Religion," a somewhat strange heading that I suspect betokens the goodwill, general interest, and naivete of the organization as a whole. While the percentage of journal articles on women and religion remains small, some important journals have published significant articles on women and religion. In addition, quite a number of books have appeared, especially in the more theological side of religious studies. Why? What is it about?

The phenomenon could be viewed simply as spillover from a general social-political movement, in which case it would probably be assessed as an intrusion into academia whose popularity is dependent on the fate of the "women's movement." However, I do not think that the need to study women and religion can be so easily dismissed nor do I think that the relevance of women's studies for religious studies is dependent in any way on the success or failure of the women's movement.

One could also regard the study of women and religion as merely the religious studies component of the field of women's studies. Then it would be considered another distinct subject area within religious studies with various facts and figures to be researched and theorized about. Women's studies as a distinct focus within religious studies exists, and must exist, because in the past, the field of religious studies has really been the study of men and religion. Well over 90 per cent of the contents of most books on religion actually concern only *men's* religious lives and thought. There may or may not be a paragraph or chapter about women. Most often that chapter primarily discusses men's attitudes toward and relationships with women, so it is questionable whether even that chapter really is about women. Therefore, the women and religion movement as a separate focus that fills innumerable missing links and unreported gaps in data vital to students of religion is essential.

However, I feel that the women and religion movement is fundamentally more challenging. It is not merely an academic fashion nor merely more information. I have always felt that if the women and religion movement fulfills its potential, it will effect a paradigm shift in religious studies that would also be paralleled in all the humanistic and social scientific disciplines. Making that paradigm shift possible is the true *raison d'être* of women's studies. Furthermore, the mark of this success would be not "women and religion" as a separate subject area patronized only by those who choose to do so. Rather true success would involve a shift in the scholarly mind-set so thoroughgoing that we would not need a separate "women and religion" section because religious studies would no longer be the study of men and religion.

The fundamental challenge and potential of women's studies in religion, as in other fields, is its delineation and critique of androcentrism. The tasks of laying bare the fundamental unconscious preconceptions of androcentrism, demonstrating their inadequacy, and providing a more adequate alternative are the most important and central contributions of the women's studies perspective to the fields of religious studies and comparative religions. It is important to remember throughout the following discussion that, though I am speaking in broadly applicable terms, I am also speaking self-consciously and directly about methodology in the history of religions. The broad applicability of my critique and reconstruction should in no way become an excuse to overlook its specific applicability to the history of religions.

Both the essential promise of women's studies to induce a paradigm shift in scholarship, and the necessity of a phase during which the women's studies perspective manifests as a separate focus researching lost or suppressed data on religion, are results of the prevailing conventional mind-set of most scholars. That mind-set utilizes an androcentric, one-sex model of humanity. The women and religion movement criticizes that model of humanity as inadequate and offers instead a two-sex, androgynous model of humanity. All these terms need to be defined.

Definitions of androcentrism could easily be multiplied. However, three central characteristics of the androcentric worldview will suffice to demonstrate both the nature and the inadequacy of androcentrism.

First of all, in androcentric thought, the male norm and the human norm are collapsed and become identical. In fact, recognition that maleness is but one facet of human experience is minimal or non-existent. As de Beauvoir states,

> In the midst of an abstract discussion it is vexing to hear a man say: "You think thus and so because you are a woman," but I know that my only defense is to reply: "I think thus and so because it is true," thereby removing my subjective self from the argument. It would be out of the question to reply: "And you think the contrary because you are a man," for it is understood that the fact of being a man is no peculiarity. A man is in the right in being a man; it is the woman who is in the wrong. It amounts to this: just as for the ancients there was an absolute vertical with reference to which the oblique was defined, so there is an absolute human type, the masculine. Woman has ovaries, a uterus; these peculiarities imprison her in her subjectivity, circumscribe her within the limits of her own nature. It is often said that she thinks with her glands. Man superbly ignores the fact that his anatomy also includes glands, such as the testicles, and that they secrete hormones. He thinks of his body as a direct and normal connection with the world, which he believes he apprehends objectively, whereas he regards the body of woman as a hindrance, a prison, weighted down by everything peculiar to it.[1]

Thus in androcentric thinking maleness is normal; in addition, it is the norm. Any awareness of a distinction between maleness and humanity is clouded over and femaleness is viewed as an exception to the norm.

The second major characteristic of androcentrism follows directly from the first. If the male norm and the human norm are identical, it follows that the generic masculine habit of thought, language and research will be assumed to be adequate. So we might say that scholarship dependent on the androcentric model of humanity utilizes generic masculine language. As a result, research about the religions of other times and places as well as about our own religious situation deals mainly with the lives and thinking of males. It seems unproblematic to include only a few stray comments about women's religious lives as a footnote or a short chapter towards the end of the book.

The generic masculine habit of language, thought, and research is so pre-reflective and so strong that many scholars are genuinely unaware that one has studied only part of a religious situation if one has studied only the religious lives and thoughts of men. The need to present a full account of women and religion thoroughly integrated into the account of men and religion simply is not perceived. The generic masculine covers the feminine, as I was told by my mentors when I first questioned the completeness of current understandings of *homo religiosus*.

The problem, of course, is that it really doesn't, which brings up the third, and perhaps most problematic aspect of androcentrism. The third constituent of the androcentric outlook is its attempt to deal with the fact that, since men and women are taught to be different in all cultures, the generic masculine simply does not cover the feminine. The generic masculine would work only in a religious-cultural situation where there were no sex roles either explicit or implicit. That situation, of course, does not exist, not even in modern Christianity or Judaism, to say nothing of the religio-cultural situations of other times and places more normally investigated by the historian of religions. Therefore, women *per se* must sometimes be mentioned in accounts of religion. At this point, adherents of the androcentric model of humanity have reached a logical impasse. Their solution to this impasse is the most devastating component of the androcentric outlook. Because they differ from the male (presumably human) norm, women must be mentioned, at least in a cursory fashion. But *because* they deviate from these norms, when women, *per se*, are mentioned, androcentric thinking deals with them only as an object exterior to mankind, needing to be explained and fitted in somewhere, having the same epistemological and ontological status as trees, unicorns, deities, and other objects that must be discussed to make experience intelligible. Therefore, in most accounts of religion, males are presented as religious subjects, as namers of reality, while females are presented only in relation to the males being studied, only as objects being named by the males being studied, only as they appear to the males being studied.[2]

As a corrective to this situation, a basic re-orientation of the scholar's consciousness is called for. We need a basic paradigm shift from models of humanity and modes of research and thought that perceive males at the center and females on the edges to modes that perceive both females and males at the center and reflect the essential "femaleness-maleness" of androgynous humanity. That would be a "two-sex" model of humanity, as opposed to a "one-sex" model of humanity.

The most important aspect of what I have called "androgynous methodology" or "the androgynous model of humanity" is this characteristic of being a "two-sexed" or "bisexual" model of humanity. This concept requires clarification, for what I have in mind when I speak of androgynous models or methods differs considerably from both conventional notions of androcentric "mankind" and from the unisexual or sex-neutral meaning of androgyny that is popular at the present time.

What I mean by androgyny as a two-sex model of humanity and why such a model of humanity is mandatory should be clear from what has already been stated. Very simply, we are in need of a model of humanity that accurately reflects two basic facts. First, biologically, for the most part humans are of one sex or the other, with little overlap at the most obvious level. Second, and even more important, the two-sexed biology of the human species is augmented and enhanced rather than minimized by culture, society, and religion, so that today in all cultures, there is more stress on behaviours proper to and limited to one or the other sex than would be required by basic biology. As a result, men's and women's lives are more separate and different from each other than is biologically dictated. No scholarship prior to the current women's studies movement has come close to dealing adequately with the sheer massive unyielding presence of such sex-role differentiation in all religio-cultural situations, which is the major reason why all previous scholarship and theology failed so abysmally to understand women and religion. So, clearly, a model of humanity is needed that compels recognition that humans come in two sexes and that both sexes are human at the same time as it forbids placing one sex in the center and the other on the periphery. Androgyny as a two-sex model of humanity, as the notion that humanity is both female and male, meets those requirements, while traditional androcentrism and a sex-neutral model of humanity both fail completely. (By way of brief definition, a sex-neutral model of humanity is one that minimizes sexual differentiation, that regards distinct maleness and femaleness as irrelevant, and that urges pursuit of a "common humanity." While one could debate the utility of such a model of humanity as a prescription for the future, it is obviously quite useless as a guide to descriptions of the past or present.)

These critiques and agendas have been worked out in some detail by specialists in the area of women and religion both in the historical and theological wings of the discipline.[3] However, it is appropriate to ask to what extent the field of religious studies now reflects the critique or follows the agenda of the women and religion movement. Two generalizations can be made.

First, the ultimate goal of so transforming the mind-set of scholars in religious studies that "women and religion" is no longer needed as a special topic or a necessary subject area is still very far away. If we did not have our little topic of "femininity and religion" I suspect that very few of the discussions of religion occurring at this conference would include any discussion of women or femininty. In other words, the two-sex androgynous model of humanity is by no means pervasive yet.

Second, the theological side of religious studies is quite a bit ahead of disciplines like the history of religions in working through the implications of moving from a one-sex to a two-sex model of humanity. I find this situation a bit puzzling and while I really have no explanation for it, would like to explore the problem further. I find the situation puzzling because the whole critique is actually much less controversial for history of religions than for theology. One hardly needs to be a feminist in one's personal beliefs or life style to recognize that most religions have both female and male participants. That adequate scholarship about such religions would have to include and be based on data about both women and men does not seem to be a particularly startling or radical contention. On the other hand, in theology, the theologian's basic symbol systems really are at stake. Also it is not as absurd for a theologian to claim that s/he is dealing with abstractions that are beyond sexual identity and gender as it is for a historian of religions to ignore half the data - the religious experiences and reflections of women - and still claim to be describing and analyzing human religiosity. Perhaps this curious situation is simply due to the fact that history of religions is still a rather small field and has fewer women proportionally than other areas in religious studies. Or perhaps the shifts in the scholar's worldview that are required to do androgynous scholarship are even more momentous for the historian of religions than for the theologian, but so much more subtle, and, therefore, much easier to ignore.

In any case, at the beginning of a more specific discussion of women's studies in the history of religions, my major comment has to be that thus far the whole critique and subject matter has not been taken very seriously; there really is not that much literature allowing a discussion of "the state of the art." The two major journals in history of religions, *Numen* and *History of Religions*, have yet to publish articles directly cognizant of the women and religion movement and its critique of conventional methodologies, though in fairness it must also be stated that at least the latter journal has published a significant number of articles whose context is useful in the study of women and religion and that the percentage of such articles has increased in recent years. *Numen's* record is far less encouraging.[4] On the other hand, by way of hopeful contrast, the mainline North American journal in the field of religious studies as a whole, the *Journal of the American*

Academy of Religion, has published several significant articles that directly deal with the women and religion movement in the past few years, and the majority of these articles are actually in the area of history of religions.[5] Other journals, less relevant to history of religions, such as the *Journal of Religion* and *Religious Studies*, also publish an occasional article dealing directly or indirectly with women and religion, but such articles are few and far between.

Books seem to be appearing more readily than articles, especially in theology and in Western religions, but books on women in non-Western religions are not that plentiful. Only two general books on women in world religions have appeared; a third is in preparation.[6] Monographs will fill in detailed material that surveys cannot hope to provide, but again the progress is slow.[7] All this is quite a contrast, by the way, to our sister discipline of anthropology, which is quite aware of androcentrism and is producing books and articles quite rapidly.[8]

Given the relatively 'lightweight' character of our discipline, in the remainder of this paper I would like to suggest some specific areas of research and appropriate guidelines in each case and then to comment on a few significant books in each area of research.

First, the relevant subject areas. Any truly androgynous, complete consideration of a religio-cultural situation would include three subjects under the general heading "femininity and religion." First, one must investigate the actual religious lives and experiences of women. Second, one should study the general cultural norms and attitudes vis-à-vis women, which may or may not coincide with women's own experiences. Third, mythical personifications of femininity as goddesses, which may or may not have much resemblance to either women's experiences or to stereotypes about women, are also significant. Failure to consider all three of them, confusing them with one another, or, even more serious, considering only one of them and concluding that one's studies are complete, would be serious failings.

Of these three topics, the most important, the most often neglected, and the most often confused with the other two, is women's actual religious lives and experiences. That is typical of an androcentric perspective which confuses men's experiences of women with women's own lives, reflections, and experiences. The lack of attention to women's own lives and experiences is the greatest single failing of history of religions literature in general and of history of religions when it purports to discuss "femininity and religion." The book, *Unspoken Worlds*, which Nancy Falk and I have recently published, is a model both for what the subject matter is and how important and interesting it is. I think that our book contrasts significantly with most other recent books in history of religions in that it is truly about women's religions, not just about attitudes, most often men's attitudes, about women's religious inclinations. I would like to see many more similar books.

Another fruitful approach to the same topic has been taken by Penelope Washbourn in her recent book, *Seasons of a Woman* (San Francisco, Harper and Row, 1979) a collection of original expressions by women, commenting on various phases of their life cycles. There is no analysis of these expressions, no scholarly comments and no cultural context. This is obviously not conventional history of religions but this book does bring together much material not otherwise readily available and presents these materials in a provocative fashion. Still another approach to the same topic is Bruce Lincoln's *Emerging from the Chrysalis: Studies in Rituals of Women's Initiation* (Cambridge: Harvard University Press, 1981), which studies one theme in women's religious lives in several cultural contexts. The three approaches in these works are only the beginning of what could be done with the topic of women's own religious lives and expressions.

The single greatest barrier to scholarship on the topic of women's lives and experiences, apart from androcentric consciousness, is that it is much more difficult to find the data in historical than in contemporary situations because fieldwork is more likely than texts to contain the potential information. However, as the historical articles in our book demonstrate, it is possible at least to reconstruct something if one's consciousness about androcentrism and androgyny has been transformed. In any case, even if the materials simply are not available to us because of the androcentrism of the culture and time period being studied, at least one's scholarship can reflect these lacunae, which would be an important concession and one I would like to see much more frequently.

As for cultural stereotypes about women or norms for women, they are, of course, interesting and important. However, it is crucial to recognize them as such, noting that they may not have too much to do with women's realities, as Wendy O'Flaherty has cleverly indicated in the title of her most recent book, *Women, Androgynes and Other Mythical Beasts* (Chicago, University of Chicago Press, 1980). The title expresses a point quite well, I think. In many, if not most, traditional cultures, women are somewhat mythical to men, due to rigid sex roles and sexual segregation. If in addition, as is usually the case, only men write the texts or only men are interviewed by field workers, we end up with women as symbols and mythic creatures in the imagination of men. Obviously that is part of the data of a religio-cultural situation and it should be studied - but for what it is, only for what it is, and nothing more. The contribution of the women's studies perspective here is to encourage careful delineation of the degree to which these stereotypes conform or do not conform to women's religious experiences and thinking. Additionally androgynous scholarship may sometimes have to point out ways in which androcentric scholarship has completely misinterpreted the information we do have on men's ideas about women.[9] I might also add that data in this area are no problem: law codes, epics, myths, folk sayings, and folk tales, all contain numerous stereotypes about women. But most need to be looked at more closely, not just accepted at face value as information about women.

Much the same could be said about goddesses and other mythical and symbolic representations of femininity. Even more than stereotypes or conventions about women, history of religions has always studied goddesses to some extent. But I would want to add that, even more than in the case of stereotypes of the feminine, typical scholarship shows quite androcentric tendencies. First and foremost, among these tendencies is the basic tendency to place goddesses after gods in book outlines and similar endeavors and to provide many fewer pages for goddesses than for gods.[10] This tendency is perhaps the most basic evidence that history of religions, even though it studies goddesses, tends to regard them as far more peculiar than gods - a tendency that could exist only if male is normal and female is other. This flavor of dealing with something foreign is not only quantitative; it haunts the presentations and interpretations of goddesses as well. How many times can all the goddesses be lumped together as the Goddess and eyed curiously as Attractive-Destructive Mother before the whole thing becomes slightly hollow?[11]

Second, historians of religion have paid curiously little attention to the effects of goddesses on their devotees, especially their effects on women. The old generalization that goddesses are a one-for-one reflection of women's status and the culture's attitudes towards women simply does not hold up. Goddess worship and misogyny go together too often for such to be the case. But obviously, the relationship between goddesses and women is not random either. Much more study of the actual impact of goddesses on religious experience and expression is needed.

As with stereotypes about women, there is no particular problem finding data about goddesses: the folk or "little tradition" stratum of every religion and less orthodox texts abound with material. In addition, the visual arts present a wealth of information that one can barely begin to assimilate and interpret. All that is needed is more imagination and willingness to work with the materials in less androcentric ways.

Finally, I would like to sound a concluding note about the more theological side of religious studies. As I have already said, for theology the basic issue of androcentrism versus androgyny is the same as it is for history of religion. Additionally, as I have also already said, theology is considerably ahead of history of religions in dealing with the women's studies critique and reconstruction, and it would be impossible in a short paper even to summarize that development.[12] However, I would like to suggest that historians of religion study the development of feminist theology as it is occurring because it offers a fascinating example of the process by which myths and symbols are revalorized as well as a fascinating study in the relationship between myth/symbol and socio-political awareness and power. This is especially the case with the revival of goddess imagery and worship that is occurring now, right under our scholarly noses.

So, in summary and conclusion, I would like to state that a good beginning has been made in the study of women and religion. Awareness that the topic exists has grown quite a bit in the last ten years and I believe that sufficient methodological critiques and reconstructions have been offered, at least to serve as a foundation. But much work remains to be done, especially on the topic of women as religious persons. And another look at stereotypes of the feminine and at goddesses, in the light of the basic women's studies critique of androcentric consciousness, would provide fascinating material. To me it seems that no area of history of religions or of religious studies in general is as interesting or as rich and productive as the study of women and religion and I would certainly like to invite more of my colleagues to join in this venture.[13]

WESTERN PERCEPTIONS OF ASIA:
THE ROMANTIC VISION OF MAX MÜLLER

Ronald W. Neufeldt

1. Introduction

Max Müller (1823-1900) is still a familiar name in the field of Indology, principally for his contributions in the area of Vedic studies and for his editorship of the *Sacred Books of the East*. Largely unnoticed, however, is his work in developing and popularizing the comparative study of religion in spite of the fact that he has been referred to as a pioneer if not a founder of this field of study.[1] Central to Max Müller's concern for the development of the "science" of the comparative study of religion was his preoccupation with India and her literary tradition as represented in her ancient texts. This preoccupation arose out of the belief that India had much to teach the West. Indeed this was made the exclusive subject of one of his many volumes. His concern with and love for the ancient texts, particularly the *Rig Veda*, arose out of his belief that here lay the key to understanding the religious, mythological, linguistic, and mental developments of mankind. Max Müller, however, brought to the study of India and her texts certain presuppositions which resulted in a highly questionable vision of India's intellectual and religious heritage. Chief among these were his commitment to an evolutionary scheme culminating in Christianity, his commitment to textual/philological studies as the key to understanding India in particular, and human civilization in general, and his commitment to certain religious and philosophical texts (i.e., the *Rig Veda*, the Upanishads and Vedanta) as the true or essential representatives of India.

The concern of this paper is to show that Max Müller's vision of India and her texts was both narrow and romantic and that this vision was based on particular presuppositions which he brought to his study of India. It is important to recognize that elements of these presuppositions are still very much alive in the field of Indology resulting in rather narrow if not faulty approaches to, and views of India, just as they did in the case of Max Müller. To place these presuppositions in context, it is necessary first to recall some aspects of Max Müller's interest in India.

2. India and Indians

It is common knowledge that Max Müller never set foot in India. When he had the chance he refused to go citing the burdens of his age and his duties, and the uselessness of a short visit.[2] His acquaintance with India was based on texts, correspondence with Indians, and visits by those Indians who came to Europe to study or to travel.[3] However, he had much to say about India and Indians. His views can perhaps be summed up in an excerpt of a lecture delivered in 1882 at Cambridge for candidates of the Indian Civil Service:

If I were to look over the whole world to find out the country most richly endowed with all the wealth, power and beauty that nature can bestow - in some parts a very paradise on earth - I should point to India. If I were asked under what sky the human mind has most fully developed some of its choicest gifts, has most deeply pondered on the greatest problems of life, and has found solutions of some of them which well deserve the attention even of those who have studied Plato and Kant - I should point to India. And if I were to ask myself from what literature we, here in Europe, we who have been nurtured almost exclusively on the thoughts of Greeks and Romans, and of one Semitic race, the Jewish, may draw that corrective which is most wanted in order to make our inner life more perfect, more comprehensive, more universal, in fact more truly human, a life, not for this life alone, but a transfigured and eternal life - again I should point to India.[4]

It is clear from this quotation that Max Müller entertained an optimistic view of India's past, her people and her potential as a teacher for the West. For him,

India's past was full of lessons concerning man and his development, particularly his religious development. In India Max Müller believed that one could study the origin, natural growth, inevitable decay and regeneration of religion.[5] Here he felt one could see historical developments from the first predicative and demonstrative roots of language to the development of rational thought in its highest stages.[6] Thus he could say:

Whatever sphere of human mind you may select for your special study, whether it be language, or religion, or mythology, or philosophy, whether it be laws or customs, primitive art or primitive science, everywhere, you have to go to India,....[7]

Given this optimistic view of India, it is not surprising that the people of India themselves should receive from Max Müller similar laudatory compliments. Just as India was the land of beauty and promise both physically and intellectually so the people were to be seen as beautiful people both physically and intellectually. His interest was of course, more the intellectual than the physical. On this basis he claimed the "Aryas of India" as

...our nearest intellectual relatives, the framers of the most wonderful language, the Sanskrit, the fellow-workers in the construction of our fundamental concepts, the makers of the most transparent of mythologies, the inventors of the most suitable philosophy, and the givers of the most elaborate laws.[8]

The people of India, Max Müller claimed, had arrived at a purer, higher, and more consistent idea of Godhead than had the Greeks, Romans, and Hebrews. Having passed through the various stages of development, henotheism, polytheism, and monotheism, they had arrived at a pantheism which asserted that "everything has its being in God".[9]

The needed correctives which Max Müller derived from India were of a religious and social nature. The religious is related to the pantheism of India. The only true answer to the identity of Self, a common Self beyond the limited I and free from accidents and limitations, is to be found in the Upanishads and Vedanta.[10] Closely associated with this assertion is Max Müller's belief that India can teach the

West to develop the passive, meditative and philosophical side of man in order to balance the active side which has been developed in the West. This side of man he claimed has seen its fullest growth in India after a period of activity in which India was conquered by invading Aryans.[11] Indeed, he spoke of an Indian character as basically philosophical and religious and of the Hindus as a nation of philosophers whose concerns were primarily metaphysical and religious ideas.[12]

The lesson concerning the development of the contemplative and philosophical side of man had some clear social implications for Max Müller which he used to defend his life as a scholar against the accusations that might arise out of the activism of a man like Ruskin. In this context Max Müller saw a positive use for caste. He states:

What India teaches us is that in a state advancing toward civilization, there must always be two castes or two classes of men, a caste of Brahmans or of thinkers, and a caste of Kshatriyas, who are to fight£ possibly other castes also of those who are to work and of those who are to serve.[13]

If one can trust Max Müller's recollection of his early introduction to India and Indians in the form of a picture in a textbook, it would appear that his attitude to India and Indians remained basically the same throughout his life. He began with being enamoured by the beauty and stateliness of people in a picture and ended with a glowing report of the lessons which the country and its people have for the West. If anything his vision or attitude was amplified or expanded, moving beyond a fascination with the surface appearances of a picture.

The comments concerning lessons or correctives which India has to offer the West ought to have a ring of familiarity at least to those involved in the field of study known as Indology. The emphasis on the Upanishads and Vedanta as the repository of truth concerning the identity of Self serves to underline the all too prevalent practice of depicting the Upanishads and Advaita Vedanta not only as the height of Indian philosophical developments, but also as the essence of Indian religiosity. The implication of course is that as a teacher and student of Indian religious traditions, and particularly Hinduism, this is where one ought to spend one's time and effort. One might, of course, want to "dabble" from time to time in more "peripheral" and "exotic" interests such as Puranic texts, devotional literature in the vernaculars, modern attempts to re-define and reform the tradition, the daily devotional practices of ordinary people, and even modern-day *gurus*, but one should never mistake these for the true or essential India. One might want to argue that the view that India is predominantly passive, meditative and philosophical is merely a popular one, but surely there is a relationship between the perpetuation of this view in the popular imagination and the approaches to the study of India in the world of Indology.

3. Sanskrit and the Veda

In spite of his acquaintance with Indians both personally and by way of correspondence, Max Müller's vision of India was largely controlled by his interests in the literature of India, particularly Sanskrit and the *Rig Veda*. This is indicated in the first instance by his concern that a knowledge of Sanskrit be a necessity for Indian Civil Servants. In the second instance it is shown by his preoccupation with Sanskrit literature and the *Rig Veda*, a preoccupation which continued unabated from 1845 to the end of his life. Aside from the actual edition of the *Rig Veda*, his views on its nature and content formed major parts of his works on language, mythology, religion, and thought. In addition to the *Rig Veda*, he is said to have been strongly drawn to the Upanishads and Vedanta as compatible with Alexandrian Christianity, the culmination point of all religion for Max Müller.[14] By his own admission his real interest lay not in the actual people of India but in the Sanskrit language and the ancient religious texts, particularly the *Rig Veda*. In this respect it is interesting to note his stated reason for refusing to go to India when he had the chance. His India, he claimed, was the India which lay many centuries beneath the surface, and therefore he could see no value in going to India on a globe-trotter's visit to get a taste of the surface of India.[15] This statement coupled with a quotation from Max Müller's lecture on the "Human Interest of Sanskrit Literature" gives one an accurate picture of his India. He states:

Do not let us be deceived. The true history of the world must always be the history of the few; and as we measure the Himalaya by the height of Mount Everest, we must take the true measure of India from the poets of the Veda, the sages of the Upanishads, the founders of the Vedanta and Samkhya philosophies, and the authors of the oldest lawbooks, and not from the millions who are born and die in their villages, and who have never for one moment been roused out of their drowsy dream of life.[16]

One suspects that statements like these were as important as his political statements in earning for Max Müller the title "Friend of India".

These statements serve to underline the fact that Max Müller's India was primarily the India of Sanskrit literature, particularly the India of the ancient religious texts rather than the India with its people which existed in his day. Furthermore, his interest in the texts was confined to the historical development of the "inward and intellectual world" from the origin of language to the development of rational thought in its highest stages.[17] Early in his life he had shared in the high expectations that were placed on the study of Sanskrit and the Veda, that through such study one should be able to discover the origins and development of language, thought, mythology, and religion.[18] Throughout his life Max Müller continued to entertain such high expectations using the ancient texts, particularly the *Rig Veda*, as a laboratory to find the necessary empirical evidence to support his theories on the origin and development of language, mythology, thought and religion.[19] The interest in Sanskrit literature defined in terms of a few ancient texts is still prevalent particularly in the narrow textual/linguistic approach which characterizes much of the study of India's religious heritage. While Max Müller's concern for origins may no longer be a dominant issue, certainly the emphasis on the "inward and intellectual world" and thus on the thoughts of the few to the exclusion of the thoughts and activities of the masses remains.

When Max Müller spoke of the human interest of Sanskrit literature he meant the answers he claimed to be able to derive from this literature concerning his theories on the development of the human mind. Thus he claimed to find in ancient Sanskrit literature, particularly the *Rig Veda*, an unparalleled chapter in the education of mankind and asserted that whoever cared to study origins and growth in language, thought, religion, mythology, astronomy, metronomy, grammar, and etymology, etc., would have to pay close attention to the literature of the Vedic period.[20]

This is precisely the value that the *Rig Veda* had for Max Müller - it served to bring the scholar closer to the study of beginnings than anything else available. In the *Rig Veda* he heard "articulate voices reaching us from a distance from which we never heard before the faintest whisper".[21] He saw here a period in the intellectual life of man for which there is no parallel anywhere else, for here one could see man developing out of a child-like state of animal nature, seeking to unravel the mysteries of his world and his existence.[22] He insisted that in the *Rig Veda* we have "one of the earliest and rudest phases in the history of mankind".[23] This is the thrust of his repeated assertions that in the *Rig Veda* we have the oldest book, the literary relic which takes us back farther than any other literary relic.[24] His optimistic views are well summarized in a speech delivered in 1874 in which he states:

> ...it is because it stands alone by itself and reveals to us the earliest germs of religious thought, such as they really were; it is because it places before us a language, more primitive than any we knew before; it is because its poetry is what we may call savage, uncouth, rude, horrible, it is for that very reason that it is worth while to dig and dig till the old buried cable was recovered, showing us what man was, what we were, before we had reached the level of David, the level of Homer, the level of Zoroastor, showing us the very cradle of our thoughts, our words, and our deeds.[25]

4. Presuppositions

In his assessment of Max Müller J. Voigt states:

The weakness of Max Müller's conclusions...was the lack of actual acquaintance with India. Max Müller was a brilliant interpreter of Indian literature but not of Indian reality. He was a philologist and philosopher drawing his conclusions from literature only.[26]

It is clear from any thorough study of Max Müller's life and work that his India was defined by the conclusions he drew from ancient Sanskrit literature, principally Vedic literature. Voigt's conclusion concerning the narrowness of Max Müller's vision is essentially correct. His vision is not simply narrow in that it concentrates on the literature only, it is also narrow in that it concentrates on only a part of India's literary tradition, i.e., Vedic literature and within the Vedic corpus, the *Rig Veda*. In his assessment of Sanskrit literature Max Müller let it be known that the other Vedas, besides the *Rig Veda*, were merely sacrificial books containing curious remnants of poetry, incantations, medical formulae, etc., whose loss would not be great as long as we still possessed the *Rig Veda*, and that the Puranas which for some Indians supersede the Vedas are morally and intellectually bankrupt.[27]

Max Müller's interest lay in learning who man is by learning what man had been. This he regarded as the principle aim of philology.[28] As far as he was concerned one did this by studying only those texts worthy of consideration, the literary monuments of India. In his own words, his studies were concerned to clear away "the rubbish which passing ages have left on the monuments of the human mind," never mistaking the rubbish for the monuments themselves.[29] Such a restriction resulted not only in a narrow vision, but also in a highly idealized or romantic vision of India, its past, and its meaning, a vision which Max Müller acknowledged as idealistic but defended as realistic:

...I have known for many years the beauties of its literature, the bold flights of its native philosophy, the fervid devotion of its ancient religion, and these together seem to me to give a much truer picture of what India really was, and is still meant to be in the history of the world, than the Bazaars of Bombay, or the Durbars of Rajahs and Maharajahs at Delhi. Of course, I shall be told that my picture of India is purely ideal, but an ideal portrait may sometimes be truer than even a photograph.[30]

He admitted that his concern was the "high mountain path of literature," remote from the millions of people living and dying daily on India's plains and travelled by only a few who are to be regarded as "the true representatives of India from age to age".[31]

Throughout his career as a scholar, Max Müller was concerned to draw certain lessons from the study of ancient Sanskrit literature. There are personal lessons drawn from Vedanta, the caste system, and the meditative and passive character of the Hindus which served to sustain him as a scholar and religious individual. These, however, pale in significance beside the lesson concerning the development of the human mind, particularly in the areas of language, mythology, thought and religion. Very early in his career, Max Müller enunciated his concern to discover such developments when he defined the sole aim of philology as learning "what man is by learning what he has been" and the aim of Sanskrit philology as supplying "one of the earliest and most important links in the history of mankind".[32] This link was, of course, the Vedic literature, particularly the *Rig Veda*. The real beauty of India for Max Müller was not the physical beauty of the country or its people but the answers he could derive from the literature concerning the development of the human mind. More than anything else, it was this which caused him to exult and to break out in poetic characterizations concerning India's past and her place in history.

Such answers, however, are derived not so much from the ancient literature as from an evolutionary framework which Max Müller brought to bear on all his work, and particularly on his views of India. His characterization of India's ancient literature as showing origins and developments as no other evidence can, make this evolutionary framework abundantly clear. Familiar with the work of Darwin, he welcomed it as supporting views which philologists had long held and claimed that students of language, thought, and religion were more fortunate than students of nature since they could study developments without missing links.[33] Presumably the missing links had been uncovered in the discovery of the *Rig Veda*.

Max Müller claimed always to have been an evolutionist, explaining that his object had always been to discover continuous intelligible growth, and vowed to remain an evolutionist in his studies.[34] He proposed the evolutionary principle as basic for proper historical and scientific research.[35] As an evolutionist his concern was to show developments in a variety of ways. He believed in growth from lower to higher stages. For him this meant movement from the simple to the complex, the material to the spiritual, the concrete to the abstract, the visible to the invisible, and the unsystematic to the systematic. Such growth was found in the Vedic literature, indeed in the *Rig Veda* itself. Max Müller claimed to see here a movement from simple invocations of natural phenomena through appellatives as proper names for deities, to the unsystematic stage of henotheism which itself shows trends to the more systematic and sophisticated stages of polytheism, monotheism, and monism.[36] Such developments were to be seen as inevitable in the sense that each stage is an intelligible and natural development of what is contained in a preceding stage and in the sense that there is a movement to a goal. In the case of the *Rig Veda*, the culmination of its developments is reached in the thought of the Upanishads and Vedanta which in turn finds its completion in Max Müller's understanding of Christianity. Thus he could speak of the Indian nation as having an important mission to fulfill in producing a new form of "subjective" religion out of empty idolatry and the "objective worship of nature". And this in turn was to be regarded as part of the gradual education of the human race, the exhausting of all the "fallacies of human reason" before mankind "could be admitted to the truths of Christianity."[37]

The basic tools for the discovery of these evolutionary stages were philological. This is perhaps not surprising since Max Müller's training was that of a philologist. He believed that the most significant ingredient in the development of human civilization was language. Thus to study man in his essence was to study language.[38] But, more than just a tool, his linguistic studies and the theory of the origin and development of language served as a paradigm for his views as to origins and developments in mythology, thought and religion. He looked for the same order and wisdom, the same growth, decay, and regeneration of primary elements as he found in language.[39] Thus the *Rig Veda* provided the missing link and philology became tool and paradigm to interpret the missing link correctly.

5. Conclusion

Max Müller's evolutionary commitments and his use of philology as tool and paradigm explain his attention to only a segment of India's religious heritage, his interpretation of the "Indian reality" through that segment, and his dismissal of all else as either unimportant or rubbish. In the final analysis, the result is not simply a narrow idealistic view of India, but a myth of major proportions which speaks of the Hindus as a nation of philosophers, of the Indian character as passive and meditative and of the Indian mind as caring little for history, as being concerned primarily with the religious and the metaphysical, and as preparing the East for its fulfillment in Christianity. In part this myth may be a function of Max Müller's attempts to correct views of India and Indians which he considered to be erroneous and derogatory. And most certainly it is a result of his commitment to find and reconstruct an evolutionary system and to do this primarily through the glasses of philology.

Given his picture of India and his concerns to trace origins and developments using philological tools and paradigms, one is forced to ask if the reasons Max Müller cites for not going to India tell the whole story. Of primary significance here is the apparent ease with which he dismissed as unimportant those aspects which radically challenged his picture of the "real" India. Clearly, this suggests that as far as Max Müller was concerned, to understand India did not necessarily mean to take into account everything Indian, nor did it necessitate the first-hand experience of life in India. In other words, a visit to India simply was not necessary.

There were perhaps three reasons for this. First, Max Müller was interested only in the "true" India, or in the "true representatives" of India; that is, in that aspect of India which could teach us what man should be by revealing his inward evolution. In this respect the millions who live and die in the villages could be dismissed and need not be experienced first-hand for their lives were largely unconscious. They were not the poets, sages and philosophers who could give us the "true measure" of India. Nor did one need to visit the latter, for much of their thought could be had through written texts. Secondly, Max Müller's evolutionary commitment and system was complete without such a visit. The data needed to support and fill in the details of the system was to be culled not from the present reality of India, but from the ancient texts and his knowledge of philology. Thirdly, Max Müller's own training as a philologist in the classical tradition meant that the materials on which he would exercise his philological tools would be ancient texts. He simply transferred his philological training from Greek and Latin to Sanskrit and Sanskrit texts. If these suggestions are correct it is questionable whether a visit to India would have made an appreciable difference in his views. One is reminded here of Carl Jung who merely looked to India for supporting evidence for theories developed through his work in Switzerland, who refused to see more than a few Indian villages because the villagers lived largely unconscious lives, who refused to see more than a few sages since one was the same as another and who preferred reading Western alchemy texts aboard ship in Bombay harbour to going ashore because visits ashore would not teach him anything he did not already know.[40]

It is important to recognize that aspects of the approach to and the myth concerning India entertained by Max Müller persist in the world of Indology whether East or West in both the study of and teaching about Indian and particularly Hindu religious traditions. The approach is seen in the continuing commitment to a narrow textual and linguistic approach as the only proper approach to the interpretation of the Indian reality. The myth remains in a commitment to create out of India's manifold and varied religious expressions a grand synthesis called "Hinduism," a synthesis which takes on a decidedly theological/philosophical and textual character. It is to be found in the view that "Hinduism" is essentially a matter of metaphysics, or a metaphysical system to be found in common scriptures, beliefs and ideals. Strangely enough, the metaphysical system put forward as the sum and substance of "Hinduism" usually turns out to be Advaita Vedanta, and this because Advaita is seen as the apex of Indian and idealistic thought, and thus the only system worthy of lengthy religious and scholarly attention. All too prevalent is the view that Advaita Vedanta is the fulfillment of the thought and aspirations of all Hindus, indeed of all religions, in the sense that all developments tend towards Advaita, and in the sense that all Hindus if scratched deeply enough below the surface turn out to be advaitins either consciously or unconsciously. Admittedly this is a twist on Max Müller's view that Vedanta finds its fulfillment in Christianity, but the spirit is the same. Aside from the philosophical, the myth is found in the view that India is the land par excellence of meditative and spiritual practices. Both the approach and myth are brought together in the all too prevalent assumption that the "real" India is to be found only in the study of Sanskrit and through Sanskrit, the Upanishads and the philosophical schools.

If one views Max Müller's approach to and depiction of India and Hindus as narrow and idealistic, resulting in mythical views of India, surely the same criticism must be made of the continuing controlling influence of the theological/philosophical and textual/linguistic approach to the understanding of India's religious heritage. The difficulty lies not so much with the fact that such an approach should exist but with the continuing presupposition that there is little else of importance in the study of India's religious traditions. One suspects that the basic problem lies with an underlying commitment to the notion of the "real" or "true India" which can be seen only in certain texts and through certain approaches. In its simplest form this view is expressed by Carl Jung when he states that to grasp the spiritual life of India or to see "purest India" one need only read an Upanishad, any discourse of the Buddha or the thought of Shri Ramana.[41]

LES REINS ET LES COEURS: PEUT-ON ECRIRE UNE HISTOIRE RELIGIEUSE SUR TRACES?

Michel Vovelle

Le débat que l'on souhaite ouvrir ici, malgré les apparences, n'a rien d'académique. Il voudrait conduire à un état actuel d'une question aujourd'hui singulièrement fluide, celle des méthodes d'approche des attitudes et des pratiques religieuses.

Domaine en total renouvellement dans les derinères décennies: d'évidence on n'écrit plus aujourd'hui l'histoire religieuse comme hier. Mais si, sur le terrain les chantiers se multiplient, les méthodes s'expérimentent, et le mouvement se prouve en marchant, on reste trés loin d'un consensus méthodologique; ce qui, dira-t-on, n'est peut-être pas indispensable. Mais dans ce foisonnement d'ouvertures tous azimuthe, on est fondé à s'interroger: l'histoire religieuse, comme le christianisme de Jean Delumeau, va-t-elle mourir? Entendons, va-t-elle se fondre dans l'histoire des mentalités, ou même dans une ethnographie historique, dont l'annexionisme est évident?

Telle question ne peut être esquivée, en toile de fond d'une interrogation qui, plus prudemment, souhaite s'en tenir aux méthodes et aux techniques d'approches: mais tout est lié.

Sans remonter au déluge, il est évident que lorsque l'abbé Brémond, voici plus de cinquante ans, prospectait en hardi découvreur les domaines d'une "histoire littéraire du sentiment religieux," le problème se posait en termes tout autres. Ce sont des témoignages élaborés et mis en forme, et non point des traces souvent infimes qu'il analysait, même si la nouveauté méthodologique était grande de se référer à la foule anonyme des écrits peu ou mal connus de la littérature religieuse du quotidien. Un ample corpus (dirions-nous aujourd'hui) virtuel se dessine, même si le traitement, refusant la systématisation, reste impressionniste.

Brémond avait ouvert une voie: tel itinéraire n'est pas totalement désuet, qui conduit aux productions les plus récentes de l'histoire de la spiritualité, attentive aux aventures spirituelles du petit nombre des élus.

Mais pour introduire notre thème, c'est d'une autre révolution méthodologique qu'il convient de partir: quitte à l'apprécier elle-même historiquement: celle de la sociologie religieuse dont Le Bras et Boulard ont frayé les voies, et façonné les techniques. En cet été 1980, François Isambert, assisté de Jean-Paul Terrenoire, viennent de publier l' "Atlas de la pratique religieuse des catholiques en France" à partir des papiers et documents du chanoine Boulard. Un monument certes, et qui n'a pas fini de servir et d'interroger par sa série de cartes de pascalisants, de messalisants, de cénalisants, hommes et femmes ventilés entre villes et campagnes, entre statuts sociaux hierarchisés.... Mais en même temps qu'on reste ébloui des richesses de cette moisson scientifique, étroitement associée à une étape de la pastorale - entre 1955 et 79 - en taillant large, offrant un flash instantané de la pratique religieuse française à un moment essentiel de son histoire, on ne peut manquer de se dire: voilà une histoire telle qu'on n'en fera plus jamais. Ne serait-ce, pourrai-ton dire un peu méchamment, que parce qu'on ne fera plus de comptages à la sortie des églises, et que la pastorale de missions de l'intérieur n'est plus celle d'aujourd'hui. Mais si le monument dressé par F. Isambert, de même que la publication en cours des matériaux Boulard, apparaissent comme plus commémoratifs qu'ouverts sur l'avenir, et si, sans trop oser le dire, on est en train aujourd'hui de brûler la perruque de Gabriel Le Bras, il nous reste toutefois l'apport demeuré révolutionnaire de cette socsiologie religieuse, qui eut tant de peine voici 30 à 40 ans à se tailler droit de cité.

En premier rang, cette hypothése de travail, ou cette féconde imprudence de méthode, d'affirmer qu'entre les gestes de la pratique et la fidélité religieuse il y a une corrélation, grossiére certes mais positive et indiscutable. Premiére réponse, au moins implicite, au probléme central de cette communication. A partir de ces bases, il devient légitime de compter messalisants, pascalisants, cénalisants, délai au baptême, mariages et obséques religieuses, taux d'ordinations et vocations monastiques. Autant de "traces" qui ont en commun avec celles qui vont nous préoccuper d'être, somme toute, pauvres, massives, mais en même temps directes, mesure sans détour de l'appartenance religieuse.

Un tournant a pris place, me semble-t-il, quelque part dans les années 60 - en chronologie française s'entend - au temps même où les méthodes de comptage de la sociologie religieuse connaissaient une sorte d'apogée dans le cadre de la pastorale qui les questionnait. Ce tournant, c'est d'abord l'inscription dans une perspective historique plus large de ce qui était surtout resté une technique d'enquête de l'époque contemporaine. Non que Gabriel Le Bras en premier n'ait pas engagé les historiens dans les voies d'une enquête régressive, à l'époque moderne voire médiévale, insistant sur les richeses potentielles des visites pastorales de l'ancien régime.

Mais cette découverte s'est faite par étapes: pour plus d'un chercheur français, la Révolution Française représentait bien une sorte de point origine, en amont duquel se situait un état de chrétienté, caractérisé par l'unanimité ou la quasi-unanimité des gestes caractéristiques: grands sacrements "saisonniers," communion pascale .... Les premiers modernistes qui se soient risqués dans ce type d'enquête tel L. Perouas, dans sa thèse sur le diocése de la Rochelle aux XVIIé et XVIIIé siécles, ont buté sur ces 97 à 98% de pascalisants, ou de pratiquants saisonniers qui semblaient lui enlever presque toute signification.

L'extension régressive dans la durée historique confrontait ainsi l'historien à la nécessité d'une remise en cause de la batterie d'indicateurs opératoires et significatifs à l'époque contemporaine, et de la découverte d'autres indices appropriés: obstacle stimulant, qui faisait apparaitre le caractére relatif de ces "traces" auxquelles on s'était confié.

Les deux autres traits, qui m'apparaissent caractériser le tournant des années 60, s'associent assez directement au premier. C'est d'abord la *banalisation* d'une technique de comptage et de mesure qui commence à cesser de choquer ou de paraitre incongrue. L'histoire religieuse s'apprivoise alors à la sociologie historique et commence à sortir du cadre choisi des élites et de la spiritualité pour se pencher sur les attitudes et comportements des masses. Non sans tâtonnement parfois, ainsi Toussaert découvrant chez les paysans de la Flandre française au XVe siécle une force de résistance insoupçonnée à la christianisation. En cette phrase, les réticences à venir à l'égard du décompte des gestes n'ont pas encore cours, et c'est une découverte confiante qui l'emporte. Qui dit banalisation de ces méthodes, dit également changement d'esprit de la recherche, et si l'on veut me passer l'expression, au sens le plus neutre du terme, sa *déclericalisation*. La préoccupation pastorale sous-jacente, consciente ou non, de la plupart des enquêtes sur le présent ou le passé immédiat, qui en faisaient une méditation inquiéte sur las déchristianisation et ses origines, s'estompe à mesure que l'on remonte dans le temps. Puis, parallélement, en ces années, l'histoire des mentalités plus aggressive, plus gourmande, tend à s'annexer des territoires qui empiétent de plus en plus sur l'histoire religieuse classique-ceux des attitudes collectives devant la vie, la famille, l'amour ou la mort: autant de sollicitations pour de nouvelles pistes.

L'histoire des attitudes et des pratiques religieuses s'est faite quantitative, ou plus précisément sérielle, organisant dans la longue durée l'évolution des "indicateurs" qu'elle sélectionne, ou qui s'offrent à elle. On ne prétendra pas être exhaustif-tâche vaine-en évoquant quelques-uns des chantiers qui se sont ouverts depuis une vingtaine d'années. L'héritage, entendons celui de la sociologie religieuse de l'école Le Bras, n'a pas été rejeté. On a simplement affiné, et sophistiqué les méthodes pour la mesure des gestes de la pratique: ne serait-ce que pour aller au-delà de l'impression de monolithisme que peuvent laisser les registres paroissiaux avant le partage laïc né de l'événement révolutionnaire. On se penchera donc sur des tests plus indirects: l'empressment au baptéme, le respect des temps interdits (caréme et avent) au mariage, et par suite les demandes de dispenses de bans...

Puis le flux des vocations religieuses et sacerdotales, même si - significativement - on a pu s'interroger sur sa pertinence comme indicateur du zéle et de la ferveur religieuse (Perouas), semble avoir affronté avec succés l'examen de passage: on dispose actuellement d'une brassée de courbes d'ordinations et de titres cléricaux pour plus de moitié des diocéses français. Les avatars du peuple des clercs sous la Révolution-schisme, serment constitutionnel, dechristianisation et abdications de prêtrise-livrent pour leur part d'autres indices cartographiables qui permettent souvent d'anticiper de près de deux siécles sur l'instantané que les cartes de la pratique religieuse dressées par le chanoine Boulard ont livré dans les années 1960.

Ce ne serait encore qu'une extrapolation régressive des méthodes, et des problémes de la sociologie de la pratique: mais il est notable de relever la diversification des supports nouveaux pris en compte, tant dans le domaine des sources écrites que de l'archéologie et l'iconographie.

Sources écrites? J'ai donné, voici une dizaine d'années, le mauvais exemple en proposant une approche du réseau des dévotions "baroques" en Provence et de leur déstructuration au XVIIIe siécle, à partir de la source massive de plusieurs dizaines de milliers de testaments: contamination évidente et volontaire de l'analyse en histoire religieuse par les méthodes d'une histoire sociale quantitativiste qui, suivant la formule de Simiand "compte, mesure et pèse." Cette pesée n'a pas été admise immédiatement sans réticences: on s'est interrogé sur la signification de la brassée d'indices que les testaments me

permettaient de prendre en compte: des élections de
sépultures aux pompes funêbres, aux "messes de mortuis,"
aux legs pies et charitables, et à l'appartenance aux
confréries. Et it s'est trouvé un historien anglais sans
humour pour s'indigner de la courbe du poids moyen des
cierges en Provence que j'avais, en malicieuse provocation,
glissée dans mon oeuvre.

Nous voici au coeur de ces enquêtes d'un nouveau
style, qui valorisent tel "indicateur" pertinent pour
analyser dans la longue durée pluriséculaire une évolution
de la sensibilité ou du sentiment religieux: dans cette
voie, les possibilités sont multiples, et j'ai moi-même
récidivé dans le cadre de mes recherches sur les attitudes
devant la mort, exploitant ici tel corpus d'un millier
d'épitaphes américaines de 1660 à 1820, compilées au XIXe
siécle par un clergyman érudit, Thomas Alden, traitant
ailleurs un corpus de centaines de faire-parts de décés
d'aristocrates et de notables française du début du XIXe
siécle au XXe siécle.

Autant d'exemples qui ne prétendent qu'à une illustration ponctuelle d'une procédure actuellement généralisée: là où les testaments m'ont permis de suivre le
discours collectif sur la mort, l'analyse sérielle des
demandes de dispenses de bans de mariage pour consanguinité
ou compaternité conduit tel autre chercheur (J.M. Gouesse)
à reconstituer le discours sur le couple, le mariage et la
famille. Particuliérement significatif est de voir en
quels termes, et suivant quelles méthodes on peut reprendre
aujourd'hui le corpus utilisé voici soixante ans par l'abbé
Brémond de la petite littérature de dévotion: Daniel Roche,
dans tel article remarqué sur "La mémoire de la mort"
substitue à l'analyse thématique impressionniste de l'historien littéraire, une recension exhaustive et
systématique, suivie de l'analyse d'un certain nombre de
traits pertinents de ce corpus de la littérature chrétienne
autour de la mort à l'âge classique.

Dans cette prospection, l'importance des sources
écrites se trouve relativisée par celle d'autre "traces"
que propose l'iconographie ou l'archéologie par exemple.

Ne prétendons pas, en ce domaine non plus, avoir découvert l'Amérique: on n'a pas attendu les 20 dernières années pour étudier ces témoignages d'une sensibilité religieuse. Mais c'est l'approche qui a changé. Tel chercheur (B. Cousin) qui a rassemblé l'impressionnant corpus de 5.000 ex-voto peints en Provence du XVIe au XIXe siécle, en fait jaillir de façon éclairante, par une étude sérielle à partir d'un grille de traitement élaborée, les moments et les étapes d'un rapport au sacré par le biais du miracle demandé et obtenu.

A partir d'un série comparable, quoique beaucoup plus restreinte, nous avions, Gaby Vovelle et moi-même, tenté d'analyser les représentations de la mort et de l'au-delà à partir des autels et rétables des âme du purgatoire suivis dans le Midi français dans leur continuité du XVe au XXe siécle.

Actuellement, pour prendre un exemple à la fois proche et différent, je dirige dans le même cadre géographique une enquête sur l'archéologie des cimetiéres urbains, du XIXe siécle à nos jours, pour y analyser les traits de ce qu'on a défini parfois-abusivement peut-être, mais significative- ment, comme "le nouveau culte des morts" dont le cimetiére est le lieu.

Voici assez d'exemples peut-être, si partiel que soit un inventaire qui avoue son caractére subjectif, pour nous permettre d'analyser les traits originaux qu'offrent en commun ces nouvelles procédures: et dont la quantification n'est qu'un des éléments.

Plus profondément, ce qui apparaitra essentiel dans le parti pris de ces études nouvelles, reste bien, à mon avis le projet de connaissance des masses anonymes-celles qui n'ont pu se payer le luxe d'une expression individuelle, si peu que ce soit, littéraire. C'est donc à ce stade, ou à ce niveau de la religion moyenne, dans ses pratiques comme dans les représentations collectives qui les soustendent que se situe l'enquête.

A ce titre, elle refléte sans doute cette évolution dont l'oeuvre de Philippe Aries est par ailleurs une illustration, et qui privilégie dans l'histoire actuelle des mentalités plutôt que le niveau de la pensée claire, et des expressions mises en forme, celui qu'Aries dénomme d'une expression qui demanderait à être explicitée l'"inconscient collectif." Car c'est bien là que l'interrogatoire indirect ou la confession extorquée qu'autorisent nos sources se révéle le plus rentable.

Car il faut bien prendre conscience des limites, et en même temps du cahier des charges astreignant que comporte tel type d'enquête. La premiére limite étant sans doute la relative *pauvreté* de ces sources massives. Expliquons-nous en illustrant; l'ex-voto peint, par exemple, peut à premiére vue décourager par sa répétitivité apparente, le caractére stéréotypé des attitudes, le nombre de scénarios finalement réduit-scénes d'intérieur "gisant au lit malade," scénes d'extérieur des aggressions de la mort violente-qu' il illustre et commente. On en pourrait dire autant de l'iconographie des cimetiéres ou a fortiori des faire-part. Sources de la répétition, témoignages qui n'ont pas été éloborés pour les fins auxquelles on les fait servir: tout un décryptage s'impose à partir d'indices fragiles. Scrutant les ex-voto, le chercheur mesurera patiemment la surface respective de l'espace céleste de l'apparition et de la scéne terrestre; comme il analysera le gestuel et le jeu des regards par lequel s'établit le lien entre les deux univers. Analysant les représentations du purgatoire dans leur évolution, on relévera les mutations caractéristiques d'un panthéon d'intercesseurs qui se dépeuple du XVIIe au XVIIIe siécle...

Puis le "cahier des charges" impose également au chercheur une réelle ingéniosité et un flair sans défaut dans le choix comme dans l'interprétation de ces "indicateurs" que l'héritage de l'histoire a placés à sa disposition. Tel support, comme les testaments dont l'importance et la signification s'enflent du XIVe siécle à l'âge classique, en même temps que la pratiques se diffuse, perdent brutalement à la fois leur base statistique et leur intérêt intrinséque dans une France (voire une Europe) post-révolutionnaire où le Code Civil a sanctionné le partage laîc en même temps qu'il portait une atteinte

Vovelle: Les Reins et les Coeurs 615

irréversible aux pratiques anciennes de dévolution des biens.

Il faut savoir passer d'un support à l'autre: suivre les expressions de la survie individuelle de l'art funéraire des églises, à celui des cimetiéres, voire de la place publique quand les morts quittent le lieu saint, entre 1770 et 1850, pour se regrouper en d'autres lieux.

Ces lourdeurs, ces contraintes, qui ne tolérent pas l'erreur ni la lecture pauvre, ou réductrice, expliquent en partie les réticences, voire le contestation radicale, dont cette enquête sur traces a parfois fait l'objet, à mesure même que ses chantiers se multiplient. Telles critiques peuvent être fortes, et ne sauraient être traitées par le mépris. Ces traces que l'on reléve pour les organiser en séries sont par définition le reflet de pratiques sociales. Elles passent par des filtres et par des médiations propres à en altérer la signification. Qui fait le testament: le testateur ou le notaire? Et ces ex-voto, souvent préparés plus qu'à demi, et que l'artisan peintre de série n'a plus qu'à compléter à la demande.... Médiations, distorsions, contraintes: ces documents massifs et pauvres ne seraient-ils à tout prendre que le reflet de la pression sociale, ou de la convention d'un moment? Par là même, la faiblesse de ces enquêtes sérielles sur traces ne serait elle pas de nous laisser à la surface des choses, confinés à connaissance à la fois superficiele et grossiére, limités aux apparences? Et peut-on espérer à partir de là approcher un phénoméne aussi secret que la foi?

Le dialogue amical qui m'a affronté à Philippe Aries sur l'interprétation du tournant spectaculaire de sensibilité collective qui s'inscrit quelque part au cours du XVIIIe siécle, entre 1740 et 1770, quand les clauses de dévotion et le discours religieux désertent les testaments français, est tout à fait significatif de l'enjeu du débat. Déchristianisation commencée: telle était, et demeure, mon hypothése. Changement de convention, reflet d'une sensibilité modifiée répond Aries, pour qui, à l'ére rousseauiste de l'affectivité triomphante, le pére de famille n'a plus besoin de stipuler égoîstement les précautions à prendre pour sa dépouille comme pour son âme,...assuré qu'il est que ses héritiers s'en chargeront. Intériorisation plutôt que changement: il y a toujours un for intérieur, et qui peut se flatter d'eu avoir percé le secret? Je dois avouer que sur plus de 20.000 testaments, je n'en ai rencontré aucun qui s'ouvre sur "joie, joie, pleurs de joie..." Dans toutes ces recherches, l'une des difficultés majeures reste bien la lecture et l'interprétation des silences, cependant si chargés de sens. Quand la source devient muette, que faut-il en conclure? Dans mes testaments provençaux du XVIIIe siècle, se rencontraient ainsi un silence janséniste, aussi bien qu'un silence du libertin, s'élargissant en silence d'indifférence généralisée dans la seconde partie du siècle...

A ces critiques, qui sont fortes, l'historien quantitativiste n'est point sans réponse. Il sait la fragilité d'un indice pris isolément, et l'impérieuse nécessité de corréler. Il m'est facile de répondre à Philippe Aries que le changement d'affectivité familiale n'explique pas pourquoi les confréries se vident, ni pourquoi la nébuleuse des clercs et religieux, parents et amis, importante dans les testaments de la fin du XVIIe siècle et du début du XVIIIe, s'étrique en peau de chagrin à la fin du siècle...

Il serait aisé également d'interpréter en termes de conjoncture historique ce retour au qualitatif qui caractérise en partie l'histoire toute récente des mentalités, et singulièrement l'histoire religieuse. La tentation quantativiste a correspondu dans l'historiographie catholique française et européenne à une étape de pastorale volontariste, acceptant comme hypothèse de travail l'adéquation de la vitalité de la foi et de la régularité des gestes de la pratique. D'où l'importance de l'étape qu'a représenté la sociologie religieuse de G. Le Bras et de ses successeurs. Mais aujourd'hui, en présentant comme un point final son "Atlas de la pratique religieuse des catholiques en France," François Isambert annonce la mist sur pied de la nouvelle formation qu'il dirige sur le thème "Ethique et pratiques symboliques."

D'évidence, toute une orientation a changé, et point seulement parce que la débacle des gestes formalisés de la pratique dans la Chrétienté post-conciliaire imposait cette révision fondamentale.

Chercheurs d'indices, compteurs des traces anonymes, serions-nous, nous autres historiens, les attardés d'une autre guerre, d'une époque révolue?

Je n'en crois rien; mais bien plutôt à la possibilité d'une utilisation féconde, dans les voies même d'une historiographie religieuse nouvelle, de ces enquêtes sur traces anonymes de l'histoire sérielle.

Tout d'abord, parce qu'elles sont porteuses, convenablement décryptéss, d'éléments qui n'ont rien de pauvre, et vont même bien au-delà des questions initiales que l'on avait pu formuler, au départ de l'enquête.

Qu'on me pardonne de revenir une derniére fois à ces testaments, qui ont été mon chantier premier d'expérimentation. Parti d'une problématique initiale qui peut rétrospectivement apparaitre pauvre - une interrogation sur les origines de la déchristianisation au siécle des Lumiéres - j'ai trouvé dans cette source plus, et autre chose, que ce que je n'y attendais: les traits d'une sensibilité à la mort, le réseau des gestes qui l'entourent, les formes symboliques qui l'accompagnent.

Ne pourrait-on en dire autant de ces sources si diverses puisqu'elles vont des dispenses de bans au comptages de l'illégitimité, ou aux faire-part de décès et à l'art funéraire des cimetiéres, et qui toutes convergent autour du pôle de la famille et des attitudes devant la vie?

On dira que c'est là une maniére ambigue, et somme toute discutable de retrouver l'histoire religieuse, qui se trouve ici comme phagocytée par l'envahissante histoire des mentalités.

J'en conviens: mais au niveau des attitudes proprement et plus profondément religieuses, si tant est qu'on puisse les dissocier des précédentes, il me semble qu'il est toute une série de résultats qu'on ne saurait atteindre que par ce détour ou cette ruse méthodologique.

Tout d'abord, dans la perspective de l'histoire des comportements, attitudes et représentations collectives des masses, ce que j'appelerai la diffusion des idées-forces. La dialectique qui associe dans un rapport complexe le surgissement dans les élites spirituelles de thèmes et de notions nouvelles, et leur diffusion dans le peuple chrétien ne peut être perçue dans ses progrès comme ses inerties que par le recours aux tests de la pratique. C'est entre 1620 et 1640 que l'abbé Brémond situe la grande période de ce qu'il appelle "l'invasion mystique": c'est vers 1660-1680 que j'en retrouve la petite monnaie dans les clauses de dévotion des testaments provençaux. Ces formes de décalage ou d'inertie peuvent être analysées avec précision au regard des sources convergentes dont nous disposons: si le flux ascendant de la littérature des fins dernières, pièce importante de la pastorale post-tridentine, se "casse" dès le début du XVIIIe siècle dans les statistiques de la production livresque dressées par Daniel Roche, faisant du Siècle des Lumières celui des rééditions, ce n'est pas avant 1750, ou 1730 au plus tôt, que tel repli s'inscrit sur les courbes des dévotions testamentaires.

Une démonstration comparable à celle dont on rappelle ici trop briévement les thèmes, a été faite dans la très longue durée, s'agissant du dogme et des dévotions autour du purgatoire, très anciennement implantée chez les clercs et surtout les religieux au Moyen Age, mais ne commençant dans les masses sa diffusion qu'à partir du XIVe et surtout du XVe siècle, pour culminer dans la période de la reconquête post-tridentine. Pour percevoir ces faits de diffusion, de gauchissement et d'adaptation aussi, il semble bien que le recours aux sources écrites ou iconographiques dont on vient de parler représente un détour indispensable: c'est ce que nous avons tenté de faire, Gaby Vovelle et moi même à partir des autels des âmes du purgatoire.

J'irai plus loin encore: il me semble bien qu'il est toute une série de traits de représentations collectives qui ne peuvent se saisir dans leurs structures comme dans leur évolution inconsciente qu'à partir de ce type de sources. La psychologie du miracle, suivie au jeu des regards dans l'ex-voto, l'évolution qui s'enregistre au fil des tableaux des âmes du purgatoire, confidence inattendue sur les représentations du troisiéme lieu: autant découvertes qu'aucun texte écrit ne nous livrera. Et ce n'est pas chercher le paradoxe, aprés avoir parlé du poids de l'inertie dans la diffusion des nouveautés, que d'opposer au contraire, à la stabilité d'un discours religieux qui se fige, à partir de la Contre-réforme, le patient travail d'adaptation, voire de gauchissement qui s'opére dans les masses.

Pour percevoir ces évolution obscures, méconnues le plus souvent des contemporains, parce qu'elles se situent en deça d'une prise de conscience formalisée, les nouveaux moyens d'enquête que nous venons d'évoquer sont plus que jamais nécessaires. Et l'on en trouvra d'autres.

Qu'on ne me fasse pas dire que les vérités globales et d'approximation auxquelles ils conduisent, livrent le grand secret, et permettent-par ruse-de sonder les reins et les coeurs. Car ceci est une autre affaire.

STRUCTURE IN JUNG AND LÉVI-STRAUSS

Adrian Cunningham

In comparing Jung and Lévi-Strauss one may appear to be explaining the obscure by the yet more obscure, and especially so since neither line of thought is entirely self-consistent. I hope to exploit these inconsistencies to bring the two closer together. My interest in seeing if the gap between them can be narrowed arises from two practical concerns. The first is a dissatisfaction with using sometimes anthropological and sometimes psychological approaches to religious data, just as they happen to be applicable. The second concern, one with tradition and change in the study of religion, is that Jung seems to offer the most thoroughgoing account of those similarities of motif and content in religions which have been a staple part of their study since the Enlightenment, whilst Lévi-Strauss would seem to have drawn a sharp line between all such studies and any claim to a science of religion.[1]

Of the various points of similarity and difference between these two men which I shall discuss, three issues seem crucial:

1. The difference between the *orderly* nature of the phenomena studied and their *meaningfulness*;

2. The question whether this orderliness is to be thought of as *purposive*;

3. Certain misunderstandings, in both writers, of the notion of *category*, as it relates to talk of archetypes and structures.

Both of the theorists I am concerned with discover in the material they study (1) basic patterns which they relate to (2) structuring factors underlying material from different periods and cultures, although (3) these are not seen by the symbol-users themselves. These patterns relate to basic structures of mind or psyche and probably derive from properties of organic matter itself.

They agree that the fundamental difference between the primitive and the modern resides, in Jung's words, not in "a difference in mental functioning but rather in the premises upon which the functioning is based."[2] They agree that a symbol may have its effect without this being consciously recognised or understood. They agree in thinking that if a search for fundamental structures of experience is involved then it may not matter greatly if the foreigners' material finds its form in the operation of the investigator's thought or if it finds its form in the operation of theirs.

They further agree that *some* sort of comparison can be made between phenomena of myth, of dream, and of "primitive thought" - though as we shall see they differ profoundly on the nature of the relationship. They both see myth as a means of escape from time and agree that the modern world sees an attenuation of the social dimension of mythic time, so that it now has only a personal sense.[3] They find "pensée sauvage" in folk traditions and, in sophisticated form, in alchemy.[4] They study the ways in which human beings give cultural significance to natural objects: the cultural exploration of the raw and the cooked, the psychological meaning of kitchens and ovens. For Lévi-Strauss the myth mediates contradictions, for Jung the transcendent function of the symbol is that it can offer a *tertium datur* in the clash of opposites. For both men, their key concepts, structure and archetype, respectively, are not directly observable but only to be inferred: they use an identical image, of tracing rays of light back to an invisible, "virtual centre."[5]

Lévi-Strauss insists that "ethnology is first of all psychology"[6] and he is interested in psychoanalysis: "the comparison with psychoanalysis has allowed us to shed light on some aspects of shamanistic curing. Conversely, it is not improbable that the study of shamanism may one day serve to elucidate obscure points of Freudian theory."[7] In

Tristes Tropiques and elsewhere the indebtedness to Freud is clear and explicit. If I have chosen Jung rather than Freud, whom Lévi-Strauss favours for comparison, it is not just for the perversity of making a case the hard way. Many of Jung's concerns with the universality and continuity of fundamental patterns of meaning in human experience have a direct connexion with the history of religions that Freud's critique has never had.[8]

In Jung's scheme the relations between conscious and unconscious areas of experience are basically compensatory. Life is a conflict of opposites in the personality which can never be satisfactorily won by one side or the other. Whilst there are as many archetypes as there are recurrent experiences, the function of the symbol can be not only the sign of a solution of a paradox but the means of its achievement. *Symbols have transforming power*.

Jung does not observe a clear-cut distinction between mind and body, and thus on many occasions takes the imagination as equivalent to a natural organ. This is not just a manner of speaking; it has important consequences for his overall psychology. It means, for instance, that symbols are mostly, like the functioning of any other organ, natural. They are not, as would be the case with Freud, primarily investigated for their evasive, substitutive or deceptive functions. Further, taking it that organic functioning is *purposeful*, Jung sees in the symbols we come upon in fantasy a discoverable purpose. He often compares the archetypal processes of imagining to the functioning of instincts; as instincts may prompt us to certain lines of action, so certain images may prompt us to definite forms of apprehension.

In comparison with Jung, Lévi-Strauss typically differs about what it is that structures structure. Where Jung speaks of psyche, Lévi-Strauss speaks of "mind." For Lévi-Strauss the affective or emotional side of man cannot be part of an explanation because it is itself opaque to explanation, being arational. For Jung it is precisely emotional states that are the key to interpreting human experience, and it is Jung's endeavour to provide as precise a vocabulary and syntax as he can for the analysis of such states. For him emotional states give particularity, earthiness, to the intellect's endless spinning of rational patterns. On the other hand, the move from the emotional particularity of an individual in therapy to the collective phenomenon of, say, myth is notoriously difficult. In the case of Lévi-Strauss, his work is rigorously intellectual and is so, in part, because he too is aware of the pitfalls of the endless compilations of symbols. It is this suspicion which leads him away from content to what it is that *relates* item to item. To do this he appeals to models derived from linguistics, where Jung appeals to ideas borrowed from theories of instinct. On one side, then: psyche, archetype, emotion, image, instinct; on the other, mind, logic, rationality, communication, linguistics.

My intention is to show that if one questions carefully Lévi-Strauss's rejection of the emotional life as resistant to scientific investigation and his sense of the pertinence of linguistic models, then the difference between himself and Jung is more finely described. Whilst Lévi-Strauss's forté may be the analysis of logical relations, the applications that are persuasive do in *practice involve serious and often detailed considerations of content and context*. Contrariwise, in his laborious pursuit of comparable symbols Jung is always careful to stress the *formal* elements in the underpinning theory.

Attempts at positive comparison, however, might seem to founder on Lévi-Strauss's clear rejection on several occasions of the notions of collective unconscious and of archetypes.

Jung's work is thought to depend upon comparison of dreams and myths at the level of identical or comparable *contents*, where one of the distinctive features of structuralism is attention to the *relations* between contents, indeed to a logic of relations in which the contents, as bearers of the pattern of relationship, may be arbitrary. Thus, for Lévi-Strauss, "myths are not contents endowed with permanence and continuity: they are only forms."⁹ And, "It is only forms and not contents which can be common."¹⁰ By contrast, Jung urges that "An image can be considered archetypal when it can be shown to exist in the records of human history in *identical form* and with the *same meaning*," such that an American black "dreams of motifs from Greek mythology and a Swiss clerk re-experiences in his psychosis the vision of an Egyptian gnostic."¹¹ Lévi-Strauss urges that the notion of a collective unconscious might be acceptable if it concerned only the "ensemble of *logical* constraints" in human experience. The error of Jung, he says, is to pretend to find universal *contents* in such a collective unconscious. Ethnological experience shows that such contents are not constant. What the structuralist is seeking is *invariant forms within different contents* and not - as he sees the Jungians doing - seeking *recurrent contents under variable forms*.¹²

For Lévi-Strauss, if contents of different mythic systems do turn out to be comparable then this is either a matter of cultural diffusion and borrowing or lies in recognition of the objective properties of specific empirical data.¹³ In either case the similarity is "*hors de l'esprit*," it does not reside in the human psyche. But one can ask, if there are universally recognizable properties of common objects, may there not be universally recognizable properties of common human experiences and relationships, as the psychoanalysts assume? And would these not be "inside" as well as outside the human psyche? It is to deny such possibilities that Lévi-Strauss turns to linguistic theory:

Jung's idea that a given mythological pattern - the so-called archetype - possesses a certain meaning...is comparable to the long-supported error that a sound may possess a certain affinity with a meaning: for instance the "liquid" semi-vowels with water, the open vowels with things that are big, large, loud or heavy, etc.¹⁴

As against this, "the...principle of the *arbitrary character of linguistic signs* was a prerequisite for the accession of linguistics to the scientific level."¹⁵

On this constant appeal to linguistics, which cannot be pursued here, I follow those critics of Lévi-Strauss who are suspicious of his tendency to assimilate the ordering of meaning to the ordering of the sounds that convey this meaning. The slogan of the arbitrariness of the linguistic sign can lead to the position being illegitimately extended. As both de Saussure and Lévi-Strauss allow, within a particular language or mythic system symbolic relationships do obtain; the anthropological structuralist's scepticism really and strongly applies to comparison of symbols in different systems. The difference between Lévi-Strauss and Jung is about the meaning of meaning. For both of them, meaning is *at least* the non-arbitrary nature of phenomena - their orderliness regardless of a human perceiver. Where they differ is that Jung relates this order to *purpose*. The patterns in the material are not just patterns, they show a purposiveness, an intentionality which connects matter and psyche: they show something which is not only orderly but *meaningful*. The patterns culminate in opportunities for their existentially relevant symbolic fulfilment in human living.

The basic objection of Lévi-Strauss is to any idea that structure is of a Platonic kind, imagining that there are imperishable, contentful, archetypes which dominate the life of all possible societies. The reason why, for example, as Merleau-Ponty says,

Contemporary American society may have rediscovered a path in its mythology which has already been taken in another time or place, is not that a transcendent archetype has been embodied three times in Roman Saturnalia, Mexican katchinas, and the American Christmas. It is that this mythical structure offers a way of resolving some local, present tension, and is recreated in the dynamics of the present.[16]

The example is instructive. We may, with benefit, accept that it is often a mistake to look for comparison in the overt content of myths - classifying together all attitudes towards the moon or towards cabbages - and should attend, rather, to an underlying *logic* which uses different *materials* indifferently. But some of the most compelling exemplifications of structuralism have been to show how these logical arrangements *do* work with similar contents. For example, there are *meaningful* relations between Saturnalia and Christmas - I am thinking of Leach's demonstration, on structural grounds, that rites of marking the switch between times (old year, new year) are represented by switches in role and gender; New Year rites of role-reversal and sex-reversal in parties and pantomimes.[17] In sum, we may be able to say that invariant logical patternings of human perception come to bear upon commonly recurring patterns of human experience: the deep grammar of human syntax articulates recurrent features of human semantics. Ordering is not only logical but *satisfying*, and this satisfying nature of order is present in common human situations which are *both* conceptual and emotional: how do humans differ from nature; how does male differ from female; how does human sexuality differ from animal; how do children differ from parents; how do humans and nature differ from gods?

The matter of structure and content can be illustrated by considering two examples Lévi-Strauss offers. Replying to a critic for whom, he says, social structure is like a kind of jigsaw puzzle and everything is achieved when one has discovered how the pieces fit together, Lévi-Strauss comments:

But if the pieces have been arbitrarily cut, there is no structure at all. On the other hand, - if the pieces were automatically cut in different shapes by a mechanical saw, the movements of which are regularly modified by a camshaft, the structure of the puzzle exists, though not at the empirical level (since there are many ways of recognizing the pieces which fit together). Its key lies in the mathematical formula expressing the shape of the cams and their speed of rotation. This information does not correspond in any perceptible manner to the puzzle as it appears to the player, but it alone can explain the puzzle and provide a logical method to solve it.[18]

The analogy is a fascinating one, but it seems to me that Lévi-Strauss may be using it in a one-sided way. Note that the relation between the shape of the pieces and the picture they comprise is arbitrary: *any* picture could be "structured" in the same way, on the same machine. Indeed, it looks as if the *arbitrariness of the relationship is the necessary condition of the invariance of the structure*. But this feature *may be* of limited use in solving the puzzle. The pieces could be fitted together in a different order, but there would be no picture, only a jumble of colour. On the other hand, if the pieces were arbitrarily cut there would be no structure, though there would still be a picture and the puzzle would still therefore be solvable. It is, then, *not* the structure which "alone can explain the puzzle and provide a logical method of solving it." It seems to me that here we may have an interesting parallel to Jung's notorious difficulties with the inaccessibility of the fundamental sources of archetypal patterning and the archetypal images or pictures which alone are accessible. In both theorists we may need to maintain a dual perspective between the deep logic of the structural patterning and the meaningfulness of the material structured.

I hope to illustrate the advantages and limitations of Lévi-Strauss's denial of the recurrence of archetypes by taking two more examples from his work. In chapter 7 of *The Elementary Structures of Kinship*, "The Archaic Illusion," as "proof" of the anthropologist's need to seek beneath the surface strangeness of foreign institutions for the underlying principles which are "in fact very simple and universal," Lévi-Strauss offers a story that seems very like Jung's Swiss clerk re-experiencing in his psychosis the vision of an Eygptian gnostic. At the end of one of his lecture courses a woman who was hearing of dual organization in primitive societies for the first time, outlined the fantasy world of her four-year-old son and the two different locations in it of his father and mother. Lévi-Strauss's comment on this is striking. This Egyptian child has reconstructed a dual system, with unequal moieties, stylistic creation of place-names, "so evocative of a Melanesian onomatic system," even with a suggestion of exogamy. If the child had been an Australian aborigine this fantasy would have found valuable confirmation later in his social experience. Growing up as an Egyptian, however, the model can have little instrumental value and in a year or two will be abandoned and repressed. For Lévi-Strauss the adult world of thought, mediated by a specific language and culture, is a selection and elaboration from *one* of the vast number of possibilities present in the world of the infant, in the same way that the speech of the adult is a specification within the range of sound which the infant is capable of - a specification which makes it very hard for the adult to pronounce "foreign" sounds it spontaneously uttered in infancy. Thus the rational core of the tendency to combine primitive and childhood thinking and set them off against our adult one is that it is with reference to the undifferentiated world of *any* child that contrasts in adult thought-worlds can be thought. It is because both our own and primitive adult thought-worlds derive from that of a common childhood that we refer back to childhood to identify the thought of the stranger. Primitives may compare *us* with *their* children: "The analogies between primitive and child thought are not based on any so-called archaism of primitive thought, but merely on a difference of extension which makes child thought a sort of meeting place, or point of dispersion, for all possible cultural syntheses."[19] It is on this same basis that the frequent parallels made between the world of the child and the mentally ill are to be properly understood. These worlds are too close to the multiple possibilities of the generic human being, and it is this that renders them unstable and only intermittently intelligible:

...the mental schemata of the adult diverge in accordance with the culture and period to which he belongs. However, they are all derived from a universal resource which is infinitely more rich than that of each particular culture. Every newborn child provides in embryonic form the sum total of possibilities but each culture and period of history will retain and develop only a chosen few of them. Every newborn child comes equipped, in the form of adumbrated mental structures, with all the means ever available to mankind to define its relations to the world in general and its relations to others. But these structures are exclusive. Each of them can integrate only certain elements out of those that are offered... child thought is a sort of universal substratum the crystallizations of which have not yet occurred, and in which communication is still possible between incompletely solidified forms.[20]

The difference from Jung is crucial.[21] The apparent "recurrence" of exotic or archaic material in this child is *not* meaningful and purposive, it is dysfunctional.

My last example from Lévi-Strauss is his paper on the therapeutic effectiveness of a shamanic ritual, in a case of difficult childbirth. As he says, it has a strong parallel with psychoanalytic treatment, and I think it brings out further aspects of the relation between structure and content.

In the shaman's case the cure comes about in the shaman's enacting a myth of search and struggle for the "soul," or vital power responsible for the uterus, with the goddess Muu and her daughter and various monsters. This quest is *clearly* thought of as taking place inside the patient's body: "a transition is made...from the most prosaic reality to myth, from the physical universe to the physiological universe, from the external world to the internal body."[22]

There are many obvious passages of Jung on the way in which our psyche is set up in accord with the structure of the universe which could be set alongside Lévi-Strauss's affirmation that:

The effectiveness of symbols in the cure of organic disorder would consist in precisely this "inductive property," by which formally homologous structures, built out of different materials at different levels of life - organic processes, unconscious mind, rational thought - are related to one another.[23]

He agrees with Rimbaud that metaphor can change the world. That is, as with Jung, *symbols have transforming power*.

However, whilst we may need to posit some fundamental pattern in reality which makes a link between organic processes and rational thought possible, it is by *identifying* with the shaman as the protagonist of the battle that the incoherent and arbitrary pains are organized in a meaningful way: the myth provides a means of articulating repressions and emotional disturbances at the root of the organic problem. Thus when Lévi-Strauss says that "the shaman provides the sick woman with a *language*, by means of which unexpressed, and otherwise inexpressible, psychic states can be immediately expressed," it is the content and meaning that are important.[24] The pattern of this meaning is somehow related to a pattern of behaviour inside the body. One may want to say that the myth and the body have an homologous structure but this is a structure of meanings. Would a change of the items structured work the cure? No! Thus, if, as Lévi-Strauss argues, the unconscious is structured like a language, we need to ask further whether there are not *several* types of structure present: some of these may be expressible as logical relations but not all of them need be exhaustively expressed in those terms.

In raising the question about different types of structure or fundamental patterning, we can turn to analogous issues in Jung. On the question of structure, of archetypal patterns and archetypal images, Jung invariably stresses the distinction between (1) specific images which emerge in personal experience combining with forgotten or repressed elements of personal history, and (2) their underlying formative principles which are common to all psychical experience: that is, objective, collective. To take some typical formulae: archetypes are "pre-existent forms of apprehension, congenital forms of intuition, the a priori determining of all human experience. Just as instincts *compel* a man to a life that is specifically human, so the archetypes or categories a priori *compel* institutions and apprehension to forms specifically human."[25] They are "systems of preparedness...inherited with the structure of the brain of which they represent the psychic aspect."[26]

Apart from the purposive implication of compulsion perhaps, when Lévi-Strauss would favour "constraints," these formulations are compatible with Lévi-Strauss's talk of structures.

Many of Jung's archetypes, however, are "contentful" – the tree of life, for instance. Shorn of outdated notions of the inheritance of acquired characteristics, millenia of experience somehow imprinting themselves on the human psyche, it is very hard indeed to see how archetypes of this kind can be inherited with the structure of the brain. It seems to me that in talking of archetypes, Jung often fails to distinguish between *universality* and *uniformity*. By claiming that something is universal we may be claiming no more than, important as such a claim is, that something occurs in the experience of many or most people and cultures, the particular form and intensity of its occurrence being variable. By claiming that something is uniform ("invariant" in Lévi-Strauss's sense) we are claiming that something occurs in each and every instance and that variation of form or intensity is excluded.

The kinds of things which Jung describes as archetypal are of *different* kinds. Some may be uniform, some may be universal, but nowhere that I know of does he systematically distinguish them. These different classes of material occur in the traditions themselves. In Christianity, for instance, the Spirit may be represented anthropomorphically, theriomorphically, materially or formally: as old man, dove, fire, triangle. Such differences also occur and are not always clearly distinguished in the lists of polarities that feature in both Lévi-Strauss and Eliade. Clarifying this confusion confirms, I think, the possibility of overlap between Lévi-Strauss and Jung, offering some clues for rapprochement and future work on symbolic systems.

1. A first class of archetypal material has a purely formal or geometrical character - the circle or square, for instance. It might be reasonable to take these as basically innate patterns, a preference for regular over irregular shapes, and akin to those found in contemporary research on "phosphenes."[27]

2. Other material shows a consistent binary structure which may also have an innate character and be related to the necessity for orientation in space; for example, contrasts of inner-outer, high-low, centre-periphery,

right-left, before-behind.[28] These may in turn generate further "neutral" contrasts, like hot-cold, dry-moist.

3. A further class of archetypal material consists of images whose Gestalt derives in part from common experience of the outer world - the tree, or fire, for instance, and perhaps those of male and female.

4. Another class and that which occurs most frequently in Jungian writings, is composed of personal figures - the great mother, the hero, the wise old man, and so on.

In all these instances, the particular motivation that is given to the symbols may vary, but it is the latter two classes that pose the problem. We are dealing increasingly with meaning and not just with order.[29] The formal, category-like, nature of archetypes seems compatible with the ordering processes of the square or centre, but it is hard to see how something that is present as a person can be a category. I think, however, that there may be a solution.

Jung once remarked that what he was trying to establish with the term archetype was something metaphysically overvalued by Plato and undervalued by Kant. It was the Platonism which he detects in Jung which is the object of Lévi-Strauss's criticism. I think the Kantianism in some of Jung's formulations is *equally* misleading.

Here, again, I think one needs to distinguish between universality and uniformity. Kant's categories are *a priori*; that is, they occur universally *and* uniformly. They apply with absolute sameness; there are no instances where they can be absent or where it would make sense for them to be either more, or less, present. By clear contrast, whilst Jung speaks of archetypes as categories, his work shows that they do *not* occur uniformly either in individuals or in cultures. Their strength and specific features will vary greatly.

A similar point can be made with regard to Lévi-Strauss. He once accepted the description of his own system as "Kantianism without a transcendental subject."[30] But it is not Kantianism. Whilst many of his examples claim uniformity, as the example of the Egyptian boy shows, what he is sometimes talking about is a *repertoire* of possible combinations from which we select. The pattern common to society X's hygiene laws and society Y's caste system may *not* be useful in looking at society Z. With regard to Kant's categories this is inconceivable.

Jung may have tended to put together the notions of the inaccessibility of what ultimately undergirds experience and the notion of categories. The conclusion that I draw here is that there may be categories of apprehension and ordering principles that are formal and inaccessible; some of these may be both universal and uniform, others may not, but neither of these exclude the possibility of there also being predispositions in us to form images in response to common experiences, particularly of childhood, which are "personal" and, as predispositions, inaccessible.

Distinguishing these *different* types of archetypal material and the uses of the term category brings my comparison of Lévi-Strauss and Jung to a close.[31] I hope to have shown that Lévi-Strauss provides a severe criticism of cultural comparisons in terms of content, including archetypal content, but that this may issue in a modification and supplementation of such comparisons and not their abandonment.

Outside of their existence within particular traditions I think we shall have to be sceptical of Jung's talk of an absolute sameness of meaning of highly specific motifs occurring at different times and places. This apart, it does seem to me that a revised Jungian view of structure need not be fundamentally at odds with, at least, one stream in contemporary structural anthropology.

AN ANALYTICAL PHILOSOPHER LOOKS AT ORIENTAL MYSTICISM

James R. Horne

Arthur Danto's *Mysticism and Morality* has drawn heavy fire from reviewers whose condemnations range from Frits Staal's "an astonishing collection of errors and misinterpretations"[1] to Gitlin's milder remark that Danto's book fails to do justice to the issues because "his approach itself is self-limiting."[2] These negative reactions are understandable, because Danto's overall idea is that Western analytical philosophers can learn nothing from Eastern mysticism. That is, one specific tradition, in meeting another, has no prospect of responding with sympathy. Furthermore, his book as a whole suggests that this would be true in general of contacts between traditions. Therefore his thesis has serious implications, and should be examined carefully.

Danto compares Western thought (which he thinks of as secular and non-mystical) with Eastern thought (which he thinks of as religious and mystical). In this comparison, his main interest is in the relationship which each form of thought has to morality. As an essential preliminary to his comparison he briefly states a theory of the relationship of factual beliefs and moral beliefs, his main idea being that moral beliefs presuppose factual beliefs. As an example of what he means he points out that we can neither obey nor disobey a command that is based on a false factual presupposition. We cannot obey a command to stop running if we are not running, or to close the window if there is no window. At a more complex level, we cannot obey a command not to covet our neighbour's belongings if none of us ever does that anyway.[3] With this Danto states something that is true, but uncontroversial. He adds that other kinds of factual beliefs may provide what he calls "application conditions" for moral judgments. Thus, if we have certain factual beliefs about what hurts people and what pleases them this will establish guidance for us as we try to decide how to implement a moral command that tells us to act so as to make people happy.[4] Given these connections, loose though they may be, between factual beliefs and moral judgments, Danto adds that groups of factual beliefs and moral judgments in combination serve as part of the definition of what he calls "a form of life."[5] So, he continues, "a *form of life*, as I understand it, is partially defined by a set of moral rules that participants in that form hold as binding upon each other and by a set of factual beliefs, some of which constitute application conditions for the former."[6] (Communal and individual customs for intensifying both beliefs and rules are also involved.) A total form of life, with such components, is a way of imposing "a degree of rationality upon existence." It "holds chaos at bay."[7] Now, a form of life, defined in this way, is obviously a complex thing in which there is interdependence between the parts. As Danto observes, our moral beliefs may be undermined if we discover that our factual beliefs about their application conditions have been inaccurate. Also, certain beliefs about reality (I shall specify the sort shortly) can break down if they arouse moral repugnance. Putting it another way, relative to his thesis, Danto says that if we consider adopting the moral rules of another community without adopting the factual beliefs those moral beliefs presuppose, we will find that the "delicate connection" between the two will require us either to give up the venture or else go further and adopt the factual beliefs too, in a "transformation in the form of life itself."[8] If you change your moral beliefs alone, you may find that they are not well grounded in factual beliefs. If you change your factual beliefs alone, you take the risk of establishing factual grounding for radically different moral beliefs. This tenuous but nevertheless strong two-way bridge over the is-ought gap is, for Danto, what constitutes the problem for a Westerner who hopes to learn something about the conduct of life from Eastern mysticism. If he is looking for insights into reality he may find that they are tied to a morality which he cannot accept. If he is looking for moral guidance, he may find that it is not given, because moral guidance is not the ultimate point of that form of life. These are statements of the two aspects of Danto's one thesis, which is: "The factual beliefs they take for granted are, I believe, too alien to our representation of the world to be grafted onto it, and in consequence their moral systems are unavailable to us."[9]

Danto illustrates his thesis with his own explications of four Eastern mystical "forms of life." He points out that Hindu mysticism, for example, involves belief in *moksha*, in *karma*, in the cyclical nature of time, and in reincarnation. This whole set of beliefs about the nature of reality, which is keyed to the idea of *karma*, is presupposed, Danto says, with the same finality as the Western belief in the uniformity of nature.[10] However, the Hindu factual beliefs about the world ground (in the manner previously explained) actions (or rather measures to achieve the cessation of action) that, in Danto's opinion, seek to take the person right out of moral situations. As he sums it up: "*Moksha*...is not a moral concept. It *contrasts* with moral concepts, and in pursuing *moksha* we occupy a station beyond good and evil, and so beyond morality."[11]

Danto has similar things to say about the other forms of life he considers. On Hinayana Buddhism, with its concern for achieving Nirvana, and its advice that although we have no power to change our lives or the world, we can find Nirvana in "accepting this world as sanctified," he says, "This is a teaching it is difficult not to respect. But I do not believe it will do as a moral philosophy."[12] He says this because, in his judgment, the Buddhist "way" that he is discussing is concerned only with a change in the quality of our experience, and would therefore have us treat all occasions and incidents, even tragedies and atrocities, as things to be accepted rather than changed.[13]

But, he says, "Ethics has to do with how we should treat one another, not merely with how we are treat ourselves alone."[14] Thus, "...the demands of salvation and the demands of morality are not automatically and simultaneously fulfilled, and they may even be antithetical."[15] This is a true, well known, and intensely interesting insight, although we may doubt Danto's further assertion, to the effect that morality *cannot* be a technique of salvation.[16] He never really states clearly why it cannot.

The contrast between ways of salvation and ways of morality appears again in Danto's discussion of the *Bhagavad-Gita*. As he sees it, that work concentrates on the transformed consciousness of the "saved" man, with the result that there is no attention paid to his specific moral decisions. Krishna advises Arjuna to do nothing different from what one in his station in society would do in fulfilling his role. Since Arjuna is a member of the warrior caste he is to kill people in battle. There is therefore no discussion of the morality of killing, and Danto finds this conception of human character and behaviour "a picture of a self that has been located itself beyond good and evil."[17]

The *Tao Te Ching*, his fourth example, goes beyond (or aside from) morality in another way. The Taoist discussion of the ideal way of life is concerned with moments of high creativity or perfect functioning. It reminds us of the need to assume, on occasion, an attitude of passivity toward the world's processes, and to co-operate with them.[18] It prescribes loss of the self in the universe, and regards morality as an artificial structure, one of those productions of man's will which impedes him in his efforts to be at one with reality's ongoing processes.[19]

In summary, Danto's philosophic discussion of factual beliefs and moral beliefs tells us five things. First, moral rules presuppose factual beliefs. Second, factual beliefs provide the application-conditions for moral rules. Third, there are forms of life, involving factual pre-suppositions, moral rules and intensification procedures, which people use to impose order on their experience. Fourth, neither factual beliefs nor moral rules can endure if they are obviously counter to facts. Fifth, a way of life cannot be adopted if it involves morally repugnant action guides.

Applying these five rules to his four examples of Oriental mysticism, he concludes that Westerners cannot accept such mysticism as a form of life because it is not moral and its factual presuppositions are unrelated to their experience of life. My comments on his arguments will be, first, that he ought to distinguish more clearly between religious factual presuppositions and practical factual presuppositions, and, second, that while he has identified an amoral tendency that can appear in religious life, he is mistaken in thinking that it is found in all forms of Oriental mysticism or that it is found exclusively in such mysticism. His mistake is based partly on his misunderstanding of certain Oriental religious themes, and partly on his incomplete formulation of a potential for amorality that exists in religious forms of life in general.

First, with regard to presupposed beliefs, Danto has not recognized that his four Oriental examples embody as "incorporated interpretation" (Moore)[20] factual beliefs which are the same as those held in Western secular and religious forms of life. All of them recognize such obvious facts as the existence of persons and of objects in space, so the beliefs characteristic of Oriental mysticism must be of a different order. *Karma* is his favorite example of such a presupposition, and his discussion indicates that he realizes that the belief that a person eventually suffers commensurately with his evil acts, even if that suffering must occur in further reincarnations, is not a belief that can readily be proven true or false. Danto says, however, that this belief is accepted without question, "like the ebb and flow of tides or the wheeling of the planets," and it plays "so profound a presuppositional role" that belief in it can be compared to belief in the regularity of nature in Western science.[21]

In a way this is true, in that the two beliefs he compares are presuppositional in nature, and both are known as examples of strongly-held beliefs whose truth cannot be determined. Yet, in another way, Danto has not recognized that these two presupposed beliefs are not comparable. *Karma*, as a religious presupposition, is very different from the regularity of nature, which is a practical presupposition. Any workman who relies on his tools, any farmer who uses his knowledge of the characteristics of plants and animals, anyone who uses his knowledge of human nature in his business, presupposes the regularity of nature. The need for such practical presuppositions is demonstrated in G.E. Moore's presentation of his "truisms," wherein he argues that belief in such things as objects in space and the relationship of events in time is unavoidable. Such practical presuppositions, including that of the regularity of nature, have to be adopted by anyone, anywhere, who is going to survive in the world. Therefore, when Danto says that we cannot adopt the factual beliefs which the Oriental mystics take for granted because they conflict with those that "the logic of belief requires us to hold as true,"[22] and then later in the book compares *karma* and the regularity of nature, he is misleading. The latter is a presupposition that cannot be avoided by any sane and practical person. *Karma*, on the other hand, can be, and the variety of such presuppositions in the world shows us that they do have an optional and avoidable character, even though they are strongly believed by the faithful. Danto would have done better to compare *karma* with the last judgment in Western thought. He could have pointed out that each of these beliefs implies an evaluation of history. Each deals with moral consequences. Each can exist as an attitude persisting in a secular form of thought within its culture, so that one could argue that the secular Westerner sees history as a record of progress while the secular Oriental sees it as cyclical, even if each has consciously dismissed the religious beliefs that inspired his attitude. Each belief about history could, however, be ignored, and a person could survive and do practical things without holding it at all. Thus, while such general religious presuppositions as *karma* are very hard to dismiss, once one has them, dismissing them is not impossible. They do have the optional character that alternative religious beliefs have, and this suggests that none of them is totally closed to the Westerner. If by "our reality" Danto means our *religious* factual presuppositions, then he need not say that "...our reality must be regarded by us as reality *tout court*."[23] Our religious presuppositions are not adopted with such finality. If, on the other hand, "our reality" refers to beliefs in the regularity of nature or the existence of objects in space, he has not been fair to the oriental mystics he discusses. It is reasonable to conclude, from their actions as artisans, etc., that they too hold these practical presuppositions, along with their religious beliefs, and that we do share a picture of reality as a basis for communication between traditions.

This qualification, that Danto's principal comparison does not serve well to illustrate his thesis, does not, however, vitiate his main line of argument, which is that the four religious schools whose teachings he explicates in his own way, sometimes calling them Oriental and sometimes mystical, have factual beliefs that "ground" characteristically non-moral action-guides. If his thesis is stated in precisely this limited way, that he proves that four specific schools, understood in the way he sees them, can provide religious but not moral guidance, then he seems to be on to a problem that can beset religious traditions, either internally or in contact with others. He attempts to explain just what that problem is, and numerous passages in the book expand his essentially limited thesis significantly. The expansions occur in two directions, for he sometimes says that mysticism provides no grounding for morality, but finally that religion provides no moral guidance. Are these expansions of his thesis correct? Let us consider each in turn. First, with regard to mysticism, we must notice that every example of mysticism Danto discusses has as its ideal the attainment of a state of serene consciousness beyond personal relationships. They are all, in other words, examples of the same general type of mysticism, that type which Otto and Zaehner called "soul mysticism," Stace "monistic mysticism," and Tillich "pure mysticism." Such mysticism, in its purest form, is concerned with meditative techniques for stilling sensation and thought, for "hypoarousal," as Roland Fischer calls it.[24] Its concern is with the individual consciousness, and with techniques for transforming it, and for it morality is aside from the point. As Danto depicts the *Bhagavad-Gita*, for example, Krishna advises Arjuna to fight not because that is morally good but because it is a technique for salvation. It is the way to play his role, work through his *karma*, and finally achieve *moksha*. Danto says that to view your actions in this way is to locate yourself "beyond good and evil."[25] Similarly, he argues that when some Buddhist philosophies culminate in the thought that *samsara* is Nirvana that amounts to telling you that you should accept your fate, and that you should have a positive attitude to whatever you find yourself doing in life, whether that activity be "good" or "evil."[26]

Of course the four mystical schools that Danto cites illustrate his thesis so well because he interprets them as monistic mysticism, which Buber, for example, describes as only a necessary stage in the spiritual life, saying, "First, the soul may become one."[27] This form of mysticism does readily omit moral concerns in just the way that Danto describes, because its overriding aim is unity of consciousness. However, it may not be the only form of mysticism there is. Another major form is variously named "theistic," (Zaehner), "God-mysticism," (Otto), or "dualistic" (Stace). There seems to be little doubt that such mysticism exists, at least in the form of reports of the experience. It is that mysticism which the mystic reports as an encounter with an ultimate Other in a personal relationship which establishes some of the important conditions for morality.

The typology of mysticism is a complex and vexed question. In particular, it involves doubts about the mystic's reports. Are they simple reports, or subsequent interpretations? In this short paper, I can only note that recent discussions of this subject by, for example, John Hick, Terence Penelhum and Steven Katz, take the mystics' (supposedly) interpretative or doctrinal statements seriously, because the way mysticism is approached and attained, and whether it is "seen as" a certain sort of situation (Hick) or "sought and found in the context of the right sort of doctrines" (Penelhum), makes a very important difference to the kind of experience it actually is.[28] The mystic's actions and attitudes will be formed and conditioned by his presuppositions about the kind of problem he is solving and the kind of deliverance he seeks. Also, his religious beliefs will determine whether he seeks salvation through self-directed techniques of hypoarousal or through the more outward looking and active practices which may be very much concerned with social and moral considerations such as purification from sin or the development of moral virtues. Whether, therefore, mysticism is experienced as mysticism of the void, or soul-mysticism, or God-mysticism is a function of the mystic's beliefs, which help to form the experience.

However, Danto clearly thinks of mysticism as all of one type. In a later article explaining *Mysticism and Morality* he writes that "...mysticism calls all factual beliefs, save the factual beliefs of mysticism itself, into question, and, in so doing, immediately renders the imperatives of any such systems inapplicable."[29] Danto refers to just one set of "beliefs of mysticism," and, as he says a little further on, "it seems to involve a transvaluation of values, or a devaluation of all values, save those revealed to him at the high moment of insight, and he returns to a phenomenal world so transfigured as virtually to be discontinuous with the one he lived in before."[30] Danto does not believe that the beliefs and values revealed to any mystic could be or could intensify those involved in morality. Yet in theistic mysticism this is exactly what does happen. The theistic mystic is very frequently called to morality and social concern. In neglecting that form of mysticism Danto is implying either that theistic mystics are not what he means by "mystics," or that they are mistaken or insincere in what they report.

But this is not the end of the complications. Wayne Proudfoot argues that religious forms of life based on numinous experiences (which would seem to presuppose interpersonal encounter and consequently morality) can be as nonmoral as mysticism if the assumed relationship with the Wholly Other abolishes the "distance" that is necessary for morality. Thus even a theistic form of belief, whether coming from mystics or prophets, might involve authoritarian beliefs so extreme as to constitute an elimination of all true relationship and all need for interpretation or judgment by the individual believer.[31] This too could wipe out the factual grounding for moral rules. Therefore my criticism of Danto for omitting theistic mysticism from his account must include the qualification that while theism can easily accomodate morality, it need not always do so. Any religious belief that tells me either that I am essentially the same as God or that I operate as one who is constrained by undoubted knowledge of God's will eliminates the factual beliefs that ground morality. By eliminating the "distance" between the self and God, some types of mystical religion become antinomian, but so do some forms of nonmystical religion. In fact, by a similar elimination of "distance," some secular forms of life could do the same thing.

Danto's other expansion of his thesis states that since the particular forms of mysticism he discusses enjoin "the collapse of the conditions that made morality possible," Oriental religions in general "dissolve any relations we may have to one another and replace them with the relationship we have to the universe at large."[32] Critics (cf. notes 1 and 2) have rightly pounced on this and similar generalizations in Danto's text. In fact, his explanation of Oriental religious thought is so obviously incomplete and erroneous that one is inclined to forgive and overlook it, while considering what he has to tell us about the relationship of religion, morality and mysticism in the abstract. However, justice to the Oriental traditions requires that one note his failure to recognize strong concerns for personal relationships, for morality, and for social and political ideals, as they exist in the religious movements he discusses. For example, here is an error mentioned by Gupta:

> Danto rightly says that *moksha* is the highest goal in life (p.50) but wrongly says that *moksha* is opposed to the other three goals - *artha*, *dharma* and *kama*. The spiritual side of man's nature can be fulfilled only when man's economic, ethical, and emotional needs are satisfied. Hence there is nothing "inhuman in the concept of *moksha*" (p.63) as Danto suggests.[33]

I cite this particular error, which is one among many, because it illustrates Danto's major problem in understanding Oriental mysticism. As Gitlin and de Nicholas explain, his logic leads him to believe that a person can be either moral or religious, but not both, in performing a given action. Thus he cannot understand the religious ideal which presents us with the exemplary religious person as one who has mastered practical skills, prudence and morality as prerequisites for spiritual discipline. Danto's strict and narrow rationality apparently cannot comprehend a personal integration of morality and religion in one and the same act, and this leads him to his final generalization, which is that if the schools he has dealt with are paradigms of religious thinking, religion may give us no moral guidance at all.[34]

That final expansion of his thesis occurs as his last statement in *Mysticism and Morality*, and it does, in a way, appear to be a defiant parting shot. Yet, in spite of the fact that he has considered neither all schools of Oriental religious thought nor all forms of mysticism, and so must be faulted for a hasty generalization, it is only fair to Danto to recognize that he has pointed out a moral problem that exists potentially in all religious forms of life. After all, his point throughout the work is not that religious factual beliefs *give* moral guidance, but that they provide grounding and application conditions for it, in the form of presuppositions. Thus, religious action-guides can be distinct from moral action-guides, even if they sometimes appear to us in the form of moral action-guides. They tell us more than how to behave morally. They are concerned with our relationship to *whatever* is conceived to be our ultimate concern, and, as Danto says, they are part of a "form of life" that imposes order on the potential chaos of our total experience. Considering this, and that there may be practical, psychological, aesthetic, and perhaps other criteria added to moral considerations in deciding upon the suitability of religious beliefs and decisions, it is not surprising that, even as Danto's examples (or, as he calls them, paradigms) illustrate, the broader action-guides of religion may come into conflict with the more specialized action-guides of morality. If this is what Danto's second extension of his thesis refers to, he is right, for he reminds us of genuine conflicts between religious guidance and moral guidance such as that in the story of Abraham setting out to obey God's seemingly immoral and savage command that he sacrifice his son Isaac. We are reminded of such puzzles as that in the *Euthyphro*, or of those apparently insoluble moral problems in the Gospels, about whether to keep God's ceremonial law or obey a moral law by relieving someone's suffering. In all such cases, even in those traditions that clothe religious action-guides in moral terms, as when God gives moral commands, religious guidance with its ultimate concern can conflict with morality *per se*. Thus, there is an important point to Danto's second generalization. Religious commands are different from moral commands and they do not give moral guidance pure and simple. In fact, they could sometimes not give moral guidance at all. As Paul Tillich summarizes the relationship of religion, mysticism and morality:

A religion which relates itself to the "ultimate" in terms of "being" only results in a world-denying, static mysticism, without ethical dynamics and without a world-transforming will and power. A religion which relates itself to the "ultimate" in terms of "ought to be" only results in a world-controlling technical activism, without a spiritual substance and a world-transcending will and power.[35]

What Danto has accomplished in his pioneering work (and his accomplishment is not a small one) is an extended explanation of Tillich's first statement, plus some suggestions for further identifying the nonmoral form of mysticism. However, his conclusions do not apply to all mysticism (nor to all Oriental mysticism), do apply to more religious forms of life than mysticism, and do not negate the possibility of traditions learning from each other.

TRUTH AND DIALOGUE IN RELIGION:
SOME COGNITIVE-DEVELOPMENTAL SPECULATIONS

Thomas Dean

The problem giving rise to this paper is a basic ambiguity in the way certain philosophers and theologians have formulated an otherwise positive response to the contemporary phenomenon of religious pluralism and inter-religious dialogue. On the one hand, John Hick states that "It is necessary, in the 'one world' of today, to face the problem of the apparently conflicting truth-claims of the various religions of the world. This issue constitutes one of the main growing points of the philosophy of religion today."[1] On this model the logic of dialogue appears to be the logic of conflict among opposing claims to truth. On the other hand, Wilfred Cantwell Smith tells us that dialogue among world religions does not involve conflicting truth-claims, or even apparently conflicting truth-claims.[2] On his model dialogue means shared conversation, mutual openness, a two-way process of learning from as well as contributing to the spiritual world of one another in a way that enriches both. The logic of dialogue is not a logic of conflicting or opposing truth-claims, it is a logic of mutually supportive truth-claims. Therefore, the conflict, if there is one, is not at the ground-level of the truth-claims of various religions, it is at the meta-level of these two different models or ways of thinking about truth in the situation of inter-religious dialogue.

To clarify these two models, I have turned for help to recent psychological theories about the phenomenon of cognitive development. In particular, I have compared the way cognitive-developmental psychology deals with pluralism and relativism in the transition from conventional to post-conventional thinking in religion, on the one hand, with the way John Hick deals with the problem of conflicting truth-claims in his transition from an exclusivist to a pluralist perspective in his theology of other religions. The thesis I wish to advance is that cognitive-developmental psychology not only helps to clarify the various models of truth and dialogue found in contemporary philosophy and theology, it also offers theoretical support for the claim that a pluralist perspective is cognitively more adequate than, and therefore philosophically and theologically superior to, an exclusivist way of thinking about the truth of one's own beliefs or the beliefs of others. I shall argue that the distinction between exclusivist or conflict models of truth and dialogue and pluralist or dialogical models of truth and dialogue is not simply a distinction between different but equally plausible models on the same logical and epistemological level; rather it represents a distinction between different levels or stages of thinking, one of which is "higher," that is, more rational, universal and objectively true than the other.

In what follows I shall first (I) describe some of the major features of a cognitive-developmental approach to knowledge. Next I shall (II) give a cognitive-developmental reading of John Hick's shift from an exclusivist to a pluralist way of thinking about truth and dialogue in religion. Finally I shall (III) draw out the implications of these cognitive-developmental speculations for the question about universal criteria of truth or rationality in philosophy and theology of religion.

I

To begin with, what are the general features of a cognitive-developmental approach to the nature of knowing and thinking?[3] According to Piaget, our thinking processes develop in a sequence of stages. It has often been noted that different minds construct different interpretations of the same data. But what Piaget noticed was that these differences of interpretation are not always random. Often they are functions of different patterns or structures of thinking which can be accounted for in terms of a developmental sequence of levels or stages of thought. The overall direction of change in these patterns or structures is from a stage of relatively simple, diffuse, undifferentiated structures to ones which are successively more complex, differentiated and comprehensive. They progress from an initially self-referential perspective through a successively increased capacity to see and interpret things from a variety of possible perspectives. It is important to note that, according to Piaget, it is not just the contents of our beliefs that change; it is the fundamental patterns or structures of our thinking that change as well. By patterns or structures Piaget means the rules, laws, or procedures we follow in our thinking and reasoning about the subject-matter or contents of our beliefs.

What triggers the process of cognitive development and structural change, or stage transition, is an awareness of new knowledge or a new context of thinking which pose a cognitive challenge to one's current way of thinking. There arises an awareness of the ways in which one's present cognitive framework proves structurally inadequate to assimilating, or making sense of, the new situation. This cognitive-structural dissonance is usually twofold: there is the external conflict between the new facts and the old framework, but there is also an internal contradiction between two elements within one's current framework that have previously not been differentiated from one another. Thus is generated a need to restructure one's old cognitive framework in order to accomodate the facts of the new cognitive situation, to provide a cognitively more adequate resolution of what would otherwise remain a disturbing or unassimilable phenomenon.

The dissolution of one way of thinking and its replacement by a new way of thinking is made possible by what cognitive-develomental theorists call "cognitive differentiation." This is the introduction of a new cognitive distinction, or differentiation, within a previously undifferentiated pattern of thinking. Once this distinction is seen, one can never go back to the old way of thinking. What is now required is a more complex, differentiated and comprehensive way of thinking about that particular matter.

These features characterize the dynamics of stage transition in general. But there is one particular stage in the sequence of development that is characterized by an additional feature, by the need for a new way of thinking of a very special sort - and that is the transition from the stage of conventional thinking, where one is guided primarily by the norms and rules of one's own particular tradition, to the qualitatively different stage of post-conventional thinking, where one's thinking must establish its compatibility with a plurality of other ways of thinking. What is required is a way of thinking that is in principle universal, open to all possibilities of thinking and valuing - a post-traditional way of thinking that is as "global" as the new, global setting of, say, morality or religion to which it must now respond.

Building on Piaget, James Fowler has developed a sequence of stages of development in what he calls our "faith-thinking," that is, the complex process of thinking and valuing whereby we relate ourselves to the ultimate conditions of existence. In Fowler's theory the transition between conventional and post-conventional faith-thinking occurs between stages four and five in a sequence of development that has six stages in all. To give a cognitive-developmental interpretation of Hick's structurally analogous transition from an exclusivist to a pluralist perspective on other religions, it is useful to have in mind the major features that distinguish stages four and five in Fowler's scheme of faith-development. As the following summary of these features shows, stages four and five involve markedly different patterns or ways of thinking and reasoning about one's own faith and the faith of others. They represent, says Fowler, qualitatively distinct structures, stages or levels in the development of faith-thinking.[4]

1. Whereas stage four appeals to the ideological consensus of its own doctrinal community for the norms of authoritative insight or criteria of truth to the exclusion of the claims or insights of other ideological communities, stage five is ready to consider multiple points of view or alternative sources of truth in a more complex world-view not reducible to any one doctrinal framework, including its own. Although the norms of one's own tradition are still important, they are no longer solely determinative. The pattern of thinking here is not the dichotomous one of "either/or," but the dialectical one of "both/and."

2. In appealing to the authority of one's own doctrinal group, stage four does so in explicit awareness that it is holding a point of view in conscious opposition to and potentially vulnerable to those of others, and that this point of view is consciously and freely chosen, not simply inherited. Stage five's willingness to consider the viewpoint of others, by contrast, rests on an awareness of growing tension within oneself between one's loyalty to one's own tradition and one's loyalty to a more inclusive community embracing other groups and potentially extending to humanity itself. The need is therefore somehow to embrace these tensions, accepting the truth of one's own tradition as somehow compatible with the truth of others' traditions, thus suggesting that tension or paradox is an essential feature of all truth in religion.

3. Stage four's world-view, logically regarded, represents an effort to provide an explicit systematization to the otherwise loosely organic web of symbols and narratives that make up one's tradition, and is marked by concern for such features as the inner consistency, coherence and comprehensiveness of one's system of beliefs. This system has an "ideological" quality in that it tends to an excess of assimilation over accomodation, that is, it tends to distort the views of others in order to fit them into one's own framework. It rests on the explicit assumption that the differences between world-views are to be seen in dichotomous terms, as opposed to or conflicting with the truth-claims of one's own tradition. Stage five,

on the other hand, is explicitly aware of the partial, limited character of its own world-view, in fact doubly so, for it sees not only the theological but the historical-cultural relativity of its own symbols and concepts. Yet stage five is not simply a relativist one, for it holds to its own view with a kind of "provisional ultimacy" - open to the possibility of new truth from other sources, but also committed to the "absoluteness" of the truth it already expresses, however inadequately.

4. Stage four is primarily concerned for the identity and integrity of its own group or tradition as is reflected in its concern for group or doctrinal boundaries, exclusive or inclusive. Stage five, by contrast, involves an expanded capacity to enter sympathetically into the world-views of others, and is correspondingly aware of the extent to which the "choice" of one's own tradition is limited by the accidents of one's "fate." The essential principles of morality and faith must somehow be seen as extending to all persons and groups, not confined within the boundaries of one's own.

5. The task of stage four is to become self-consciously aware and sure of the boundaries of one's previously "conventionally" held beliefs, a need often arising through confrontation with different coherent systems of belief. The task of stage five, by contrast, is to integrate into one's thinking that which previously was rejected or repressed as discordant or threatening - integration, not exclusion; permeation of boundaries, not clarity of boundaries; in short, *dialogue*, not *conflict*, with the truth-claims of others.

II

We are now ready to give a cognitive-developmental account of John Hick's movement from an exclusivist to a pluralist way of thinking about truth and dialogue in the encounter of the world's religions. First we shall (1) look at Hick's description of the exclusivist attitude toward other religions, what Hick calls the "Ptolemaic" perspective, in which the universe of religions is seen as centered around the religion of one's own tradition. Then we shall (2) look at the cognitive differentiation which enables Hick to make the transition from a Ptolemaic to what he calls his new "Copernican" way of thinking, in which the religions of the universe, including one's own, are seen as centered around that Ultimate Reality which transcends them all. Finally we shall (3) look at the cognitive solutions offered by Hick's new Copernican or pluralist perspective on the truth of other religions as well as one's own.

(1) The traditional Christian (Ptolemaic) attitude toward other religions displays many of the features of the stage four structure of faith-thinking described by Fowler. This will become clearer as we look at Hick's charactierization of the cognitive schema underlying the traditional Christian attitude, *extra ecclesiam nulla salus*. Following Wilfred Cantwell Smith, Hick notes that the traditional Christian attitude assumes that to be religious is to belong to one or another of a group of mutually exclusive cultural-historical systems or "entities," each of which is based on its own set of systematic beliefs.[5] Along with this perception of the nature of (a) religion, one's own and others, goes an understanding of one's theology as a body of directly revealed truths restricted to or identified with a particular cultural-historical tradition. The assumption that there is a fixed set of correct beliefs, carried to excess, can lead to dogmatic claims to possess "the truth" and to an equally rigid intolerance of all other claims to possess any truth.[6] In its milder form this Ptolemaic attitude toward one's own and other religious traditions consists simply in distinguishing and separating Christianity from other religions as the religion at which all individuals, or other religions, will eventually arrive. What is logically interesting about this Ptolemaic sort of claim, from a cognitive-structural point of view, is that it appears to possess the "triumphant invulnerability" of what R. M. Hare referred to as a *blik*, a cognitive structure which no amount of contrary evidence seems able

to dislodge, because it is able to interpret, to "assimilate," all such evidence to its own Ptolemaic standpoint.[7]

And so it had seemed to Hick before his own move to the multi-cultural, multi-ethnic, multi-religious city of Birmingham in 1968. The problem for a Ptolemaic or one's-own-religion-centered perspective on the universe of faiths commences when what appears to be a closed system in fact develops openings to incongruent facts or experiences. First there is the evidence, acquired through personal friendship, of the reality of salvation in the lives of members of other faiths. This gives rise to the cognitively discrepant notion that something like true piety or religious truth is possible outside the borders of Christianity and within the borders of other religions. Second, triggered in part by this first discrepancy, there is the sudden realization that, despite the weight of traditional authority to the contrary, the Ptolemaic perspective in Christianity may ultimately be ruled out by a deeper reflection on the logical implications of its own universalistic perspective on God as a God of love whose love extends impartially to all persons whatever their outward religious identities. Not only does the Ptolemaic scheme fail to make sense of the truth of other religions, it appears to have the seeds of internal dissolution and transformation already within it. Indeed, as Hick confesses, the state of mind he was in when he moved to Birmingham was already "thoroughly illogical"; he had simply failed or refrained from examining the consequences of this Ptolemaic attitude for his other equally if not more strongly held beliefs. It needed only the spark of actual personal encounters with the spiritual reality of other living faiths in the persons of their adherents to trigger the total collapse of his old Ptolemaic schema and launch him upon the construction of a new, post-Ptolemaic or Copernican way of thinking about the universe of faiths.

If Hick seems himself to have passed directly from a Ptolemaic (stage four) to a Copernican (stage five) response to other faiths, he notes that most Christian theologians have opted for another response short of radically dismantling the traditional Christian schema. The preferred choice of traditional Christian theology when faced with the need to "rethink" the dogma *extra ecclesiam nulla salus*, is not to reject the Ptolemaic standpoint altogether but to submit it to a series of smaller adjustments designed to accomodate the evidence of salvation "outside" Christianity by assimilating it, that is, somehow bringing it "inside" the circle of Christian faith. Hick calls these adjustments "epicycles," because "they are so powerfully reminiscent of the epicycles that were added to the old Ptolemaic picture of the universe, with the earth at the centre, to accomodate increasingly accurate knowledge of the planets."[8] Some instances of Christian "epicycles" designed to acknowledge the reality of salvation for members of other religions include such notions as that persons "invincibly ignorant" of the truth of the Christian faith may still be saved even though they die outside the church; or that some people may have "implicit faith" in the form of "a sincere desire to do God's will," so that though not "outwardly" baptized, they are "in" the church by a "baptism of desire," even though they do not yet "know what the truth" is.[9] Hick does not mean to imply that there is no saving merit in these various epicycles. Such epicycles in Christian theology initially and, for some, still do perform the useful service of acknowledging, albeit in terms of the original dogma, that there is salvation "outside" the church, or Christianity, or Christ. To this extent the solution via epicycles represents in cognitive-developmental terms "a real movement in response to a real problem." Nevertheless, Hick maintains, all such "solutions" are only *epicycles* of theory, "complicating a basically dubious dogmatic system and not going to the heart of the problem."[10]

Theoretically, says Hick, it is possible to go on adding epicycles to "reconcile the dogma with the facts," but the whole effort becomes "increasingly artificial and burdensome." There comes a time when one feels that the original dogma "has been stretched beyond recognition and is due to be replaced."[11] And once one's firm stand within the Ptolemaic framework, suitably modified by one or more epicycles, begins to falter, one is confronted by a fresh problematic, unresolvable within the framework of one's former assumptions, stimulated by contact with people of other faiths, and that is the disturbing fact or at least possibility of any number of other "Ptolemaic centres" in the universe of faiths. In addition to the problematic fact that one's own faith is apparently determined more by the geographical accidents of one's birth than by any necessities of theological doctrine, there is the added realization that *in principle* the Ptolemaic way of thinking could be adopted "not only from within Christianity but equally from within any other faith - just as men on Mars or Jupiter, if there were any, could formulate their own Ptolemaic astronomy with their own planet as the centre of the system."[12] It begins to appear, therefore, that one's own theological tradition is "not so much monotheistic as henotheistic, and is ripe for important further development and enlargement."[13] The Ptolemaic attitude of Christian theology toward other religions, as modified by various Catholic or Protestant epicycles, begins to seem like a *cognitively inadequate* theology, a failed attempt to square an old way of thinking with the emerging facts of a new and more complex universe of faiths - an attempt to hold on to "the husk of the old doctrine after its substance has crumbled."[14] The initial perceptual grid or cognitive structure of the dogma of Christianity as the true religion outside of which there is no salvation has ended up generating cognitive perplexities in which Christian theology of religions, including its most recent variations, has become "hopelessly entangled." If a Christian theology of religions is to get to the "heart" of the problem, it must undergo a revolutionary change or restructuring at the very "centre" of its cognitive framework. It will have to abandon its exclusivist pattern of centering on the perspective of its own tradition, and adopt instead a pluralist or multi-centered perspective on the universe of faiths. In other words, what is needed is a cognitive structure of a qualitatively new and different sort, and this means a stage-transition to a higher level of thinking.

(2) It will be recalled that according to cognitive-developmental theory the transition to a qualitatively "higher" or more adequate level of cognition requires the ability to make a conceptual differentiation not made at the prior stage of cognitive development. For Hick this occurs once one stands back from the arena of competing faith-systems and tries to gain a perspective on the scene of human religiousness as a whole. For then one sees something that is hidden from the Ptolemaic believer, and that is that the particular standpoint of the Ptolemaic believer seems to depend more on the accidents of birth - on external, contingent, non-religious factors - than it does on any considerations intrinsic to the nature of divine reality or faith itself. This suggests that the Ptolemaic understanding of religion (or religions) rests on a failure to distinguish that which is intrinsic to religion from factors which, however closely associated with religion, should not be confused or identified with it. External or non-religious facts of human birth or geography are not yet fully differentiated from the inner form or principles of religion as a distinctive form of human life. Universal principles about the reality of, or our relationship to, Ultimate Reality are not yet fully diferentiated from the particular cultural-historical traditions or modes of expression through which they are experienced or conveyed. Thus Hick, drawing on conceptual distinctions employed by Wilfred Cantwell Smith, proposes to move beyond the Ptolemaic standpoint by making a cognitive differentiation within the total phenomenon of religion between *faith*, the inner-personal and universal core of religion, and historical-cultural *tradition*, the outer, empirical manifestation, in ritual, belief, doctrine and institution, of the personal and universal core of human religiousness.

When we apply this new cognitive differentiation to the problem which the Ptolemaic standpoint failed to resolve - namely, the intelligibility of salvation outside the circle of one's own religion (i.e., one's own cultural-historical tradition) - we see at once the outlines of a possible post-Ptolemaic or Copernican solution. For we are now able, as the Ptolemaic standpoint logically or cognitively could not, to distinguish between a Ptolemaic concept of salvation as "incorporation into the Church of Christ" (i.e., an undifferentiated identification of the inner or universal reality of religion, salvation, with a particular cultural-historical tradition) and a post-Ptolemaic or Copernican, differentiated concept of salvation as "a right relationship to the divine reality as variously known in the different religious traditions."[15] Here the inner reality of religion, faith or "a right relationship to the divine," is clearly differentiated from the outer aspect of religion, "the different religious traditions."

(3) From this new Copernican perspective Hick no longer views the religious life of humanity as a multiplicity of competing, mutually exclusive ideological systems but rather as "a dynamic continuum within which certain major disturbances have from time to time set up new fields of force, of greater or lesser extent, displaying complex relationships of attraction and repulsion, absorption, resistance and reinforcement."[16] Against the background of a newly emerging "global human consciousness," the future of the relationship between these major religious traditions or "fields of force" within the continuum will be one of an ever closer growing together. Hick is quick to add that this global vision of the future of religions does not entail the emergence of a single world religion, but rather a new way of meeting between the various traditions, in which they will increasingly see each other as "parts of the one world of our common humanity." What is emerging as single or one is not a religion but our shared humanity, a "global human consciousness" within which our religious traditions are so many "variations" or "parts." In this new cognitive environment of the "one world" of the future, the religions

will increasingly relate to each other and influence one another by way of the positive attraction of elements which each finds good in others, and thus by "a cumulative sharing of religious insights and ideals." This interpenetration of positive values has now, for all practical purposes, replaced the attempt at the mass conversion of the adherents of one world religion to another."[17] In other words, in cognitive-developmental terms, we are leaving behind our stage four perspective and entering into a stage five way of thinking about, and relating to, the spiritual reality of the world's religions.

In this changed global setting of the relationship between the world's religions, there arises a corresponding Copernican vision of the new task of theology. Hick argues that "the varied but continuous field of the religious life of mankind demands unified theories of commensurate scope."[18] Our concept of this new kind of theory, or theology, must first of all be differentiated from the older, Ptolemaic concept of theology: "The older view of theology was that it was a body of divinely revealed truths. It is now construed as a continuing process of human reflection and theorising aiming to clarify the meaning of man's religious experience. And given this new understanding of the nature of theology the restriction to the religious data of a single culture becomes artificial."[19] Given that the world in which the theology of religions is to be done is rapidly becoming a "communicational unity," we are entering into "a new situation in which it is proper for theological thinking to transcend these cultural-historical boundaries."[20] A stage five theology of religions can no longer safely assume, as does a stage four theology of "other" religions, that culturally or historically *different* apprehensions of God are necessarily *mutually exclusive* apprehensions of God. A Copernican or global theology of religions, on the contrary, will be *compatible* with "the continued existence of a plurality of religions as concrete forms of religious life." In fact, Hick predicts, such global theologies, viewed from a Copernican rather than a Ptolemaic perspective, "will not be christian theologies, or islamic theologies, or buddhist theologies, but human theologies, which are not sectional but global in their use of the religious data."[21]

It might be thought, however, that, because Hick formulates his "global" or Copernican theology in terms of a centre variously referred to as "God" or "an Ultimate Reality," in fact it would not be applicable to those religions which are non-theistic such as the Hindu school of Advaita Vedanta or most forms of Buddhism. Hick tries to deal with this issue in two ways. First, while acknowledging that "in Hinduism as interpreted by the Advaita Vedanta school, and in Theravada Buddhism, ultimate reality is apprehended as impersonal," he argues that "differences in modes of experiencing the divine reality...as personal and as nonpersonal...can be understood as complementary rather than as incompatible." Further, this formal or abstract reference to "ultimate reality" (i.e., without reference to any particular religion's preferred mode of expression) gets added support from the fact that most religions themselves similarly distinguish between reality and the various modes of apprehending or expressing it. Second, while acknowledging that his view is itself a theological proposal, he argues that it is "speculatively projected" into a still-developing history of human thought. If further doctrinal developments (e.g., in Buddhist-Christian dialogue in the Kyoto school of Japanese philosophy, or in "global theology" as exemplified in his own book, *Death and Eternal Life*) lead to a rethinking of the doctrinal conflicts between, say, theistic and non-theistic modes of thought, then his hypothesis would be confirmed.[22]

From Hick's new cognitive perspective, therefore, the assertion of an exclusivist claim to truth by any religious tradition, not just Christianity, is firmly and unequivocally rejected as "a sheer dogma, as impossible to support as to refute," not least because from a Copernican perspective one now sees clearly what was hidden from the Ptolemaic believer, namely, that such a claim is "a dogma of a kind which can equally well be directed against one's own religion as for it."[23] When that happens the ultimate *arbitrariness* of the Ptolemaic cognitive schema stands clearly exposed.

III

With this matter of the cognitive arbitrariness of the Ptolemaic view of religion and theology, we come to our final question concerning the way in which the cognitive structure of stage five or Copernican thinking forms a higher level or more adequate stage of thinking than the stage four model of truth and dialogue in religion. How does a Copernican perspective avoid ending in a sceptical or relativist position when faced with the apparently conflicting or in any case multiple truth-claims of the various religions? To what criteria of cognitive or theological adequacy can it appeal if it is to solve the logical and epistemological impasse represented by a plurality of traditions each adopting a Ptolemaic standpoint toward the others? From the point of view of cognitive-developmental theory there are at least three sorts, or sources, of criteria which can be employed in evaluating the cognitive success of a Copernican perspective on the truth-claims of the various religions: first there are those provided by the general requirements of cognitive-developmental theory; next there are those provided by the particular structure of stage five thinking; and finally there are those which are specific to faith as a distinctive form of life or mode of consciousness.

1. *General Criteria of Cognitive Development.* Hick comments at the end of his chapter on "The Copernican Revolution in Theology" that "It remains possible to retain the Ptolemaic point of view; but when we are conscious of its historical relativity we may well feel the need for a more *sophisticated, comprehensive* and *globally valid* theory."[24] Contained in this comment are the elements of the first and most general set of criteria which determine

the comparative adequacy or superiority of one developmental stage relative to its immediate predecessor. According to Piaget and, following him, Fowler these are three: degree of differentiation or internal complexity; degree of integration or unification; and degree of comprehensiveness or universality. As Fowler points out, the criteria for the adequacy of any particular theological schema are, first of all, those of cognitive-developmental theory in general: "more complex and more highly differentiated forms of thought are more adequate than the less complex and less differentiated," since "each higher stage of faith incorporates in itself the qualities and abilities of each of the preceding stages, combining them in transformed ways." The corollary is that "the higher stages are more adequate because they call for a more comprehensive, inclusive, and accurate way of knowing of a complex world."[25] It is these general criteria of cognitive development to which Hick's comment indirectly refers: a Copernican theology of religions shows its greater cognitive adequacy to the challenge posed by cultural-historical relativism than does a Ptolemaic schema, because it displays a greater degree of conceptual sophistication (i.e., internal complexity or differentiation) and is more comprehensive, inclusive and accurate in its understanding of other religions (i.e., integrated, universal and globally valid).

2. *Criteria of Stage Five Thinking*. As William Perry discovered in his study of the transition of college students from an initially dualistic to a more contextual-relativist perspective in thinking and valuing, what prevented them from adopting one of the variants of cognitive "retreat" or "escape" into ideological dogmatism, on the one hand, or scepticism or relativism, on the other, was the accompanying insight that within an overall pluralistic framework there were "not only a multiplicity of points of view *about* such matters as literature, history or politics, but a patterning *within* each point of view, an interdependency of parts within the whole, which gave each 'point of view' its special character, its coherence, its integrity."[26] The students discovered that from within

their new cognitive schema they could not only talk about "assumptions and frames of reference," but could also argue about "the degree of coherence of interpretations or their congruence with data." In other words, appeal to such criteria of cognitive adequacy as coherence and congruence with data provided students with a way to continue to distinguish, within a post-Ptolemaic universe of multiple frameworks of interpretation, between "*an* opinion" and "a *supported* opinion," and thus enabled them to avoid the ever-present threat, in a "contextualist" universe, of scepticism or relativism.[27]

Thus, cognitive-developmental theory, both in its general criteria of structural adequacy - differentiation, integration, comprehensiveness - and in its specification of criteria which continue to hold (which in fact come into their own) in post-conventional stages of development - criteria such as internal coherence, empirical fit, existential relevance - supplies "a framework outside their tradition" by which each religion can evaluate its claims "in the light of a standard that is applicable also to other religious groups."[28] The fact that at stage five there are many different frameworks of interpretation (other religions than one's own) and that one can no longer simply appeal to the traditional criteria associated with some one of them in particular (one's own tradition) does not mean that there are no longer *any* criteria to which one can appeal in evaluating the cognitive adequacy or truth of one's own or another person's (or tradition's) beliefs.

Hick's own views seem to fit those of Perry and Fowler here. As he observes, the traditional Ptolemaic criteria of meaning and truth in religion involve an appeal to authority or to the alleged "orthodoxy" of a particular "unchanging" set of beliefs. But this represents simply an appeal to myths, *criteriological* myths, which inhibit rather than encourage the kind of rethinking and restructuring that is required of theology today. Hick wishes his own program of theological reconstruction to be judged rather by the criterion of its own merits rather than by "conformity to some previous stage of Christian development."²⁹ For where the Ptolemaic form of Christian theology claims, for example, to have a primarily biblical basis, Hick lays greater stress on the role of reason. "Not only must Christian beliefs be a reasonable, coherent body of belief, but they must be seen to be such."³⁰

3. *Criteria Provided by the Differentiation of Faith.* Finally, there are additional criteria of meaning and truth in religion disclosed by the differentiation of faith from cultural-historical tradition. The formal definition of faith employed by Fowler is, like Hick's, dependent on that of Cantwell Smith: "Faith is the knowing or construing by which persons apprehend themselves as related to the transcendent" or to "the limiting boundaries or depths of experience" or to "one's ultimate environment."³¹ This formal definition of faith, Fowler points out, also constitutes, or at least implicitly contains, a normative criterion of faith as well.³² It embodies a critical principle of theological adequacy, a standard of evaluation, which can be applied to the fundamental beliefs of the various religious traditions. It serves, among other things, to further the differentiation between the culturally and historically relative expressions of faith and the spiritual centre of each tradition - that spiritual reality and core of religious values which is the human experience or realization of salvation, of a "right relationship to the divine." These "core religious values" are "possible determinants of the human spirit whereby it relates itself to the ultimate goal of existence." These "principles of the Spirit" which lie at the centre of any religious tradition represent the possibility within that tradition of "transcending relativity." As principles of transcendence, of faith as a distinctive category or universal form of the human spirit, they are "the only non-relativistic criteria of the subsequent development of the tradition."³³

When we inquire more closely as to what these "principles of the Spirit" are which provide "non-relativist criteria" for the evaluation of the religious beliefs of various traditions, we find that, like their analogues in moral thought, they are formal and universal rather than culturally or historically specific in content, and that they rest on the prior differentiation between the culturally relative or historically particular content of religious beliefs and the underlying universal principles of faith of which the beliefs or religious traditions are the particular expression or manifestation. They are typically expressed in such formal and abstract terms as those of the fundamental Quaker conviction that "there is that of God in everyone," or the biblical insight that "he who would find his life must first lose it." They find expression in such universally applicable rules as that of "the Protestant principle" applied by the Christian theologian, Paul Tillich, to the Christ-event. According to Tillich, what is of ultimate spiritual validity in Jesus is that "he crucified the particular in himself for the sake of the universal."[34] Similarly, Tillich speaks of the history of all religions as the ongoing expression, in its various types and stages of development, of "a fight of God within religion against religion."[35] And in his own systematic theology he can speak of "the God beyond God." These are specifically Christian, or theistic, expressions of universal spiritual truths that find their counterpart expressions in the various religious traditions.

From a Copernican point of view, therefore, the critique of the criteria of truth that characterize a Ptolemaic or one's-own-religion-centered standpoint does not mean the end of all criteria of truth in religion, or the dissolution of the truth-claims of the various religions in the acid bath of scepticism or cultural-historical relativism. Such criticism is only made possible by, and in fact signals the birth-pangs of, a cognitively "higher" or theologically more adequate, post-Ptolemaic and Copernican perspective - the emergence and differentiation of a universal or globally valid set of criteria of truth in religion through a process of cognitive development that is analogous to the emergence of universal principles of truth in other domains of the human spirit such as morality. They are criteria that herald the arrival of a "global" perspective in theology that can contribute to and in turn be enriched by the collective efforts and insights of thinkers and believers in each of the converging streams that make up the dynamic continuum of the religious life of humankind.

From a cognitive-developmental perspective, therefore, the choice in current philosophy of religion and theology between the logic of "apparently conflicting truth-claims" and the logic of "mutually supportive truth-claims" is not a choice between two equally plausible same-level models but a choice between two qualitatively different levels or stages of thinking about truth and dialogue in religion, one of which, it has been argued, is "higher" or cognitively more adequate and hence philosophically and theologically *truer* than the other.

Postscript: Stage Six. Hick's Copernican theology of religions is, as we have argued, to be understood in stage five terms as a pluralistic perspective open to the multiple truths of the various religions. But beyond stage five there is, in Fowler's developmental schema, a further and final sixth stage of faith-thinking whose implications for an even more comprehensive or universal perspective in theology and philosophy of religion are not explored in this paper. It could be argued that the historical situation among the world's religions has not yet reached the stage where this more unitive style of thinking is realizable on a large scale (unlike the situation for Hick's more pluralistic theology of dialogue). Nevertheless, we can perhaps discern in the general features of stage six thinking what such a fully "global" style of theology might look like.[36] In contrast to stage five, stage six faith-thinking:

1. overcomes the tension of being committed to one's own truth while being open to the truth of multiple other points of view by appealing to an enlarged vision of a universal community that reveals the narrowness of our more particular identities;

2. thinks in a style that is not dichotomous or dialectical, but synthetic and unitive, grounded in an experience of oneness or unity with ultimate reality that involves the union of opposites rather than paradoxical tension, a sense of oneness beyond but inclusive of the manyness of being;

3. sees symbols as transparent to the reality they mediate, displaying a directness and immediacy in its own relation to and participation in the mystery of being;

4. adopts the perspective of an ideal, inclusive commonwealth of being, concerned to realize the full potentials of all its members;

5. is capable of relating to persons and issues of earlier stages with compassion, and ready for fellowship with persons of any faith-tradition.

From these general features of stage six faith-thinking, we could project that a stage-six style of theological thinking would no longer be primarily concerned, as is stage five theology, with formulating an acceptable theory of the truth of "other" religions, or of "inter-religious" dialogue, but would be primarily concerned to express in a clear and simple way its own direct and immediate sense of the mystery of being *wherever* it is found or *however* it is expressed - seeing *all* of its manifestations as *equally* vessels of that universal mystery. (One of Fowler's subjects judged to be at stage six responded to the question, "Are some systems of religious belief truer than others?" in the following way: "I don't - I think we are dealing here radically with mystery, and mystery is incapable of systematization." He went on to speak of people reaching "greater union and harmony, but without systematization," that is, without formulating "one philosophy and one way of life, and then trying to impose it on others as if it were an absolute, as if that were taking the place of mystery...nothing can take the place of mystery."[37]) In other words, here the stage five emphasis on openness to the truths of, and dialogue with, others would be superceded by a sense of universal sharing in a transcendent mystery common to all.

END NOTES AND BIBLIOGRAPHIES

NOTES TO J.C. HEESTERMAN, "THE FLOOD STORY IN VEDIC RITUAL"

1. Cf. M. Winternitz, "Die Flutsagen des Altertums und der Naturvölker," *Mittungen der Anthrop. Gesellschaft in Wien* 31 (1901), 305-44, who observes (p.315): "In zahlreichen Sagen wird gar keine Ursache angegeben, sondern einfach constatiert, dass eine Überschwemmung hereinbrach." Man's sinfulness seems to be a prominent motif in a minority of 73 floodstories listed by Winternitz.

2. Śatapatha Brahmana 1.8.1.1-11. See J. Eggeling, *Sacred Books of the East*, 12: 216-19; A. Weber, *Indische Studies*, 1: 161ff; H. Usener, *Die Sintflutsagen*, (Bonn: 1899), 25-28; A. Hohenberger, *Die Indische Flutsage und das Matsyapurāṇa*, (Leipzig: 1930), 4-6; S. Lévi, *La Doctrine du sacrifice dans les brāhmaṇaas* (reprinted, Paris: 1966), 115-17.

3. Cf. M. Winternitz, "Flutsagen", 327. For Manu being instructed to take seeds on board his ark see Mahābh. 3, 187, 32; Matsyapurāṇa 2.11; Agnipurāṇa 2.11; Bhāgavatapurāṇa 8.24.34; Daśāvatāracarita 1.32.

4. As Eggeling observes, (*Sacred Books of the East*, 12: 219, n.1), *iḍayā carati* has the double meaning of proceeding with the Iḍā ceremony and of living with the Iḍā.

5. Kāthakasamhitā 11.2: 146, 6-8; cf. W. Caland, *Altindische Zauberei: Darstellung der altindische Wunschopfer*, (Amsterdam: 1908), 117 (no.170), for the sacrifice for which the story should account.

6. See e.g. Rgveda 4.42.4; 7.86.1; cf. also 1.103.2; 2.11.7; 2.15.2. In 10.31.6, the statement that "This benefactor's favour having spread out with [to the extent of] the earth became the primordial cow" may contain a hidden reference to the Iḍā or, as suggested by Geldner, the *dakṣiṇā* cow (the two are intimately connected). Such conflation of different themes is proper to the rhetoric of the Rgveda, but in order to be rhetorically effective the themes have to be different. For the cosmogonic scenario involving the *instabilis terra*, its riveting and spreading, cf. F.B.J. Kuiper, "Cosmogony and Conception: A Query," *History of Religions* 10 (1970), 91-138, exp. 107-10.

7. Kāthakasamhitā 29.3:171.14.

8. Cf. A. Hillebrandt, *Vedische Mythologie*, 2nd ed. (Breslau: 1927), 1:145-53, on Agni's flight and hiding place in the waters.

9. W. Caland, "Vierte Mitteilung über das Vādhūlasūtra," *Acta Orientalia* 6 (1927), 110-20. The ritual context is the offering cake for Agni, made of rice or barley.

10. For a similar succession of immolation of the *medha* cf. Śatapathabr. 1.2.3. 5-7.

11. W. Caland, *Altindische Zauberei*, 119.

12. See M. Defourny, "Note sur le symbolisme de la corne dans le Mahābhārata et la mythologie brahmanique classique," *Indo-Ir. Journal* 18 (1976), 17-23. In so far as the fish in both cases can be put on a par, Vādhula seems to lend credibility to Defourny's suggestions, but the possible associations of the horn seem too diverse to allow a confident identification. If Defourny were right, it would make Manu and his ark the victim attached to the *yūpa*. This is in itself not impossible, the sacrificer (represented by

the sacrificial victim) being, ideologically, himself the victim. But the Śatapatha's telling of the floodstory in no way supports this consequence. At any rate the fish in the flood story does indeed seem to represent, if not sacrifice itself, at least the life-creating force that is also inherent in sacrifice.

13. Cf. W. Caland and V. Henry, *L'Agniṣṭoma*, (Paris: 1906), 397 (no. 254d).

14. Cf. ibid., 406-409.

15. Cf. Śatapathabr. 1.1.1.12; 3.1.4.15; Taittirīyabr. 3.2.4.1; Maitrāyaṇī S. 4.1.4:6.1; Aitareyabr. 2.20.11; Kausītakibr. 12.1.

16. For the invocation (*idopahvāna*) see Śaṅkhāyanaśrautas. 1.11-12. For the complex rites involved in the Idā ceremony, see A. Hillebrandt, *Das altindische Neu- und Vollmondsopfer*, (Jena: 1880), 122-30; Āpastambaśrautas. 3.1.-3.1.

17. Cf. "Reflections on the significance of the *"dakṣiṇā"*, *Indo-Ir. Journal*, 3 (1959), 241-58.

18. Taittirīyā par. 2.6.7.1. The verb *karoti* in this passage is rendered by Keith with "to produce," by Caland (ad ĀpŚS. 3.1.7) with "verwenden." The expression is rather cryptic and possibly goes back to a sacrificial riddle. In this connection it may be mentioned that the verb *karoti* can, in the context of the ritual, occur in the sense of "to kill." In that case the passage may originally have referred to the miraculous capacities of the cow as a sacrificial victim. As will be argued, this may be relevant for the Idā.

19. Cf. Maitrāyaṇī S. 4.2.13:36.3-7 where Mitra and Varuna fashion the (Idā) cow out of an *indigesta moles* produced by the gods.

20. Cf. Ṛgveda 1.128.1; 2.10.1; 3.23.4; 3.29.4; 6.1.2; 10.1.6; 10.70.1; 10.191.1; Taittirīyā S. 3.5.11.1(d). For the ghee-footed goddess Idā, cf. Ṛgveda 10.70.3. For "the head of the earth," on which the ghee libation is made, as the archetypal place of sacrifice, cf. Taittirīyā S. 6.1.8.2.

21. Cf. Ṛgveda 3.29.3 and 6.52.16. Also A. Bergaigne, *La Religion védique* (reprinted, Paris: 1963), 2,11.

22. Cf. W. Caland and V. Henry, *L'Agniṣṭoma*, 37-40 (no. 31).

23. Cf. Śatapathabr. 3.3.1.12.

24. See *Indo-Ir. Journal* 3 (1959), 254.

25. Maitrāyaṇī S. 4.2.1:21.11-12.

26. Maitrāyaṇī S. 4.2.13.

27. Cf. W. Caland and V. Henry, *L'Agniṣṭoma*, 36f. (no.30). For the mantras see Taittirīyā S. 1.2.4f-o.

28. Cf. S. Lévi, *La Doctrine du sacrifice*, 118-20. In most versions the wife is let off, but according to Śatapathabr. 1.1.4.14.17 she is immolated without scruple.

29. Śatapathabr. 11.4.3.1-2.

30. Cf. Āpastambaśrautas. 8.11.12. This sacrifice is part of the autumnal Sākamedha.

31. Cf. Āpastambaśrautas. 5.19.4. For many cows being slaughtered cf. Baudhāyanaśrautas, 2.15:57.12-15. Significantly, the cow staked in the gambling may be replaced by a (vegetal) rice mess (*odana*).

32. Taittirīyā S. 1.2.5d-e.

33. Maitrāyaṇī S. 4.2.3:24.16-25.5.

34. For the rivalry of gods and asuras for the Iḍā (and cattle), cf.Taittiriyā S. 1.7.1.3. In connection with violent conflict one might also adduce Rudra's shooting at and fatally wounding Prajāpati to punish him for his incestuous behaviour toward his daughter. This theme is associated with the "fore-portion" (*prāśitra*) of the sacrificial cake given to the *brahman* priest. Though relevant to our argument, it is mythologically kept apart from the Iḍā theme and ritually dealt with separately. It would, therefore, need a separate treatment, for which space is lacking here.

35. See Taittiriyā S. 1.7.1.4: 2.6.8.2: Śatāpathabr. 1.7.4.19.

36. Cf. Taittiriyā S. 1.7.1.1.

NOTES TO N. HEIN, " HINDU FORMULAS FOR CHANGE"

1. "Vedānta" does not mean "Veda's End" in the sense of "the Veda's *purpose*." Vedic revelation was conceived as too-impersonally given to have had a purpose.

2. Ganganath Jha, *Purva-Mimamsa in its Sources* (Varanasi: Benares Hindu University, 2nd ed. 1964), p.192.

3. P.V. Kane, *History of Dharmaśāstra* vol. III (Poona: Bori, 1946), p.830.

4. op. cit., vol. V, p.1258.

5. *The Gathapatha Brahmana*, ed. A. Weber (1849; Varanasi, Chowkhamba Sanskrit Series Office, 1964), 4:5.7. 2. & 5:1.2.13; tr. J. Eggeling SBE XXVI (1885) p.411 & XLI (1894) p.9. Cf. Taittiriya Brahmana 2:7.13 ed. R. Mitra (Calcutta: Bib. Ind. 1862).

6. Eggeling, op. cit., SBE XXVI p.424, SB 4:6.4.

7. Arthur Berriedale Keith, *The Religion and Philosophy of the Veda and Upanishads* (Cambridge: Harvard U. Press, 1925) 11 p.443.

8. See S.N. Dasgupta, *History of Indian Philosophy*, Vol.I p.217. Also A.B. Keith, *The Samkhya System* (Calcutta: Y.M.C.A. Publishing House, 1918, 1949), pp.39, 68; Edward Washburn Hopkins, *The Great Epic of India* (New York: Charles Scribner's Sons, 1901), pp. 125-138. Some theistic groups introduced Iśvara into the system as the Twentyfifth, rather, by reconceiving Purusha, the last principle, as having its true identity in the Lord.

9. M. Winternitz, *History of Indian Literature*, I (University of Calcutta, 1927), p.110.

10. Maurice Bloomfield, *Hymns of the Atharvaveda*, 1897; (Delhi: Motilal Banarssidass, 1964) pp. xxix n.2.

11. Kane, op. cit., II p.830; C. Sankararama Sastri, *Fictions in the Development of Hindu Law Texts* (Adyar: Vasanta Press, 1926), pp.71ff.

12. *Mahābhārata*, crit. ed., Poona, 12:327.18, "vedān adhyāpayām asa mahabharata pañcaman." For other readings of the kind see Hopkins, op. cit., p.53 and *passim*.

13. H. Von Glasenapp, *Madhva's Philosophie des VishnuGlaubens* (Bonn and Leipzig: 1923), p.25

14. Sir John Woodroffe, *Śakti and Śakta* (Madras: Ganesh & Co., 1918 6th ed. 1965). p.84. M.P. Pandit, *Studies in the Tantras and the Vedas* (Madras: Ganesh & Co., 1964), p.95.

15. Letter translated by André Rocaries, *Robert De Nobili S.J.* (Toulouse: Editions Priere et Vie, 1967), Textes choises No.4, pp.145-147. J. Bertrand, *La Mission Madurē* (Paris: 1848), pp.15-21. Bibl., Peter Bachmann, *Roberto Nobili* (Rome: Institutum Historicum S.I., 1972), pp.76-80.

NOTES TO K. SIVARAMAN, "THE ŚAIVĀGAMA AND THE ŚAIVASIDDHĀNTA"

1. The enumeration as six, nine and sixteen needs no comment. Śaivasiddhānta literature enumerates twenty-four *pūrva-paksa* traditions under the rubric of *"bāhyātbāhyam," "bāhyam," "bāhyāntaram"* and *"antaram"* spanning all religious traditions, non-Vedic, Vedic and Tantric in relation to which it sought to understand itself as "Siddhānta." *Svacchanda Tantra* inflates the list to three hundred and sixty three and more : *"itvevam vādinām tesām bhedānām tu śata trayam trisastiradhikaścanya vādinām bhrānta cetasām,"* etc. Verse 680 vol. 5 (Kashmire Series of Texts and Studies, 1933) p.287.

2. A term which, in the words of the *American Anthropologist*, has become the intellectual trademark of Professor M.N. Srinivas, used by him, technically to refer to the process by which a low Hindu caste or group changes its customs, ritual or even ideology and way of life in the direction of a high, twice-born caste. (See for the debate regarding sanskritization, J.F. Staal, *Journal of Asian Studies* vol. XII, no.3 p.265) Professor Srinivas, however, is not precluding by the use of his term the reciprocal assimilation between regional and local elements and Sanskritic Hinduism. See his *Social Change in Modern India*, (University of California Press, Berkeley: 1966,) pp.482,484,496.

3. The age of the texts is co-terminous with the temple culture of South India stretching back to 2nd century A.D. and continued perhaps till the 13th or 14th century A.D. For an up-to-date account see chapter XI; "The Sivaite Agama Literature" in J. Gonda, *Medieval Religious Lieterature in Sanskrit*; A History of Indian Literature vol. II, (Otto Harrassowitz, Wiesbaden: 1977).

4. The devotional and doctrinal texts in Tamil are spread over a period of a thousand years from 4th Century onwards, and the tradition itself becomes self-conscious *vis-à-vis* the religio-philosophical schisms within Vedanta in the 13th century after the advent of Meykanta lineage. For in-depth study and analysis of Meykanta literature see Dhavamoni, *Love of God according to Saiva siddhanta*, (Oxford: 1971) and for a fuller exposition and analysis of two of basic texts see V.A. Devasenapati, *Saiva Siddhanta*, (University of Madras 1974) and Sivaraman, K. *Saivism in Philosophical Perspective* (Motilal Banarsidass Delhi: 1972). Schemerus's *Der Caiva Siddhanta*, Eine Mystik Indiens (Leipzig) although out-dated is still the most complete account todate in a European language, scanning the entire corpus of the Tamil Meykanta literature.

5. A text of the *Makuta Agama* anticipates the spirit of the Tamil tradition : *"Vedasāram idamtantram tasmāt vaidikam ācaret. Vedāntārtham idam jñānam siddhāntam paramam śubham ūrdhva scrototbhavan srestram asta vimśati tantrakam vedasārārthedam jñeyam anyatatvanyartha sādhanam."* Cited in the Introduction of Ambalavana Navalar, *Pauskara Āgama* with Umapati's *bhāsya*, Grantha ed., (Madras: 1925) p.53.

6. *Anuṣṭubh* is a form of Sanskrit metre consisting of four word-units or pādas of eight syllables each, the whole stanza consisting of thirty-two syllables.

7. "And thus shall one understand the settled Śaiva truth in *Śivajñānabodham*." (or alternatively interpreted) "in the realization of the Gnosis of Sivam." For a literal rendering of the twelve sutras of the text into English see G. Mathews, *ŚivajñanaBodham*, A Manual of Saiva Religious Doctrine, (Oxford: 1948) pp.81,82; *Dhavamoni*, op. cit. pp.327-329.

8. G. Mathews op. cit. is to-date the best translation from the Tamil into English, with synopsis, exposition etc.

9. The literature is vast and only names of prominent participants in the debate over the issue, in the chronological order may be mentioned : P. Sundaram Pillai (1894) who was the first to raise the issue, Swami Vedacalam (1924) better known under the "translated" name of Maraimalai Adikal (who, incidentally, inaugurated so to speak, the vogue of Tamilising Sanskrit proper names thus reversing the age-long and the once-hallowed convention of "Sanskritizing" Tamil names of persons, places, hills, rivers, shrines, deities, kings, commerce, agriculture, assembly halls, art-work, musical instruments, every conceivable item, in short, of nature and culture) K. Subramania Pillai (1931) who also vigorously propounded the thesis of "original" four Vedas in Tamil, and M. Balasubramania Mudaliar (1949). The last one lists one hundered and twenty reasons in support of the view that *Civananapotham* is a Tamil original and not a translation from Sanskrit. *Siddhantam* Vol.22 No.5, Madras. For a defence, feeble but spirited, of the traditional point of view J.M. Nallaswami Pillai's *Studies in Saiva-Siddhanta* (1911) is still worthy of notice. pp.109-145; 244-315. Part of this book is reprinted by Dharmapura Adeenam (1962). The debate is, in terms of shifted interest, out-dated and looks in retrospect sterile being mere reactions, against or in favour but seldom responses supported by responsible indepth scholarship and study of the literatures involved.

10. Cf. Jean Filliezat's introductory remarks : "Les relations de la literature agamique avec l'école civaite aujourd'hui dominante dans le pays tamoul du Saiva siddhanta, sont certaines mais elles restent à préciser. Un des traités classiques fondamentaux de cette école, le *Civañānapotam* de Meykanta Tevar se presente comme un developement de douze stances sanskrites données come tirées du *Rauravagama*." vol. 1 p.xiv. The French preface to Raurava Agama vol. II (1972) after citing *"evam vidyāc chivajñāna bodhe śaivārtha nirṇayam,"* observes with scholarly reserve : "Il semble d'après cela qu'il s'agisse d'une oeuvre indépendante. Il n'est cépendant pas possible d'avoir sur ce point une opinion définitive taut que nous n'aurons pas un manuscript complète en notre possession" p.iii.

11. In addition to writing in Sanskrit and alternately in Tamil both of them also wrote in a style involving a mixture of the two languages - which is called the *manpravala*, literally, stringing together of ruby and coral. Incidentally, Sivagra yogin is the only writer in Tamil Saivism to employ the *manipravala* in his commentary on *Siva Nana Siddhi*, Supakkam. See M. Arunachalam, *An Introduction to the History of Tamil Literature*, Gandhi Vidyalayam, Tirucchitrambalam. (1974) p.206. There is no systematic expression in Saivism of acknowledging a twofold scriptural tradition and of

two religious languages - Sanskrit and Tamil as in Srivaisnavism. For an account of the development of *ubhayavedanta* and its relation to *manipravala* in Srivaisnavim see *Srivaisnava Manpravala*, K.K.A. Venkatachari, (Bomby 1978). pp.1-46.

12. *Philosophical thermeneutics* tr. and ed. by David E. Linge, (University of California Press, Berkley: 1977) p.16.

13. For an account of the literature of devotion comprising Tamil, Śaiva and Vaisnava religious texts see Zvelebil, Kamil Veith, *Tamil Literature*, vol. X,1 A History of Indian Literature ed by J. Gonda, (Otto Harrassewitz, Wiesbaden: 1974) pp.88-127.

14. For an analysis of India's written traditions and their impact on Indian life from the angle of Cultural Anthropology see Sharati, Swami Agehananda *Great Traditions and Little Traditions*, (Chowkhamba Sanskrit Series, Varanasi: 1978.)

15. For statements by some of them see Singer, Milton ed. *Traditional India* : Structure and change, American Folklore Society No.X (Philadelphia: 1959.) Raghavan, V. *The Indian Heritage*, 2nd revised edition, introduction, (Bangalore: 1958).

16. The twelve devotional books of the Saivite canon, different from doctrinal works, are called *Tirumurai*. For a chart of names of the authors and their works constituting them see Zvelebil Kamil *The Smile of Murugan* on Tamil Literature of South India, (E.J. Brill, Leiden: 1973) pp.188,189.

17. The issue of assimilation of Sri-Vaishnavism into the body of Vedanta did not immediately involve the question of *ubhava vedanta*. The early exponents of the Viṡiṣṭādvaita school, who laid the philosophical foundation of the tradition, were rather seized with the more urgent one of establishing the Vedic character of *Pancarātra*. It is only in the post-Ramanuja period of development of SriVaishnavism as systematised in the *manipravala* writings - commentaries on *Divva prabandham* and on Sanskrit works of Yamuna as well as *rahasva* and *sampradava granthas* that the issue of intergrating the Tamil component of the religion with vedanta surfaces as a theological problem. See *Srivaisnava Manipravalam* op. cit. chapter 1.

18. An awareness of this dual meaning of Vedanta is decisive for the self-interpretation of Śaivasiddhānta. Two of the three prasthanas of Vedanta viz. *Brahma Sutras* and *Bhagavad Gita* are accorded a qualified recognition, while the *Upanisads* are accepted unquestionably as an integral part of vedic authority; viewed necessarily as continuous with the *Mantras* and the *Brahmanas* on the one side and including, preeminently, the Śaiva Upanisads besides the classical ten.

19. Cf. the *parā-vidyā* spoken of in the *Mundaka-Upanisad* i, 1.5 : "*atha parā vidyā tad aksaram adhigamyate.*" According to Sankara the generality of *Veda* and *Vedanga* is to be considered "*aparā*" and the *Upanisads* alone, strictly are "*parā*." Ramanuja equates *aparā* and *parā* respectively with *paroksa jñāna* (indirect knowledge *via* texts) and *aparoksa jñāna* (intuition) answering to *bhakti*, (*adhigamyate* meaning *prāpyate i.e.* directly attained.) It is striking that this crucial distinction is preserved in the Śaivāgama : "*Śivasya Samavetayaśaktir Jñānatmikamala, Śivajñānam itiprektam śabd am tadanumpakam.*" *Pauskara Āgamam*, 1.7 : "The consciousness-power coeval with the Benign, of the very soul of taintless gnosis *is*, verily, 'knowledge', knowledge through

language being only manifester hereof." Umapati commenting on this says "śaiva jñānam - param jñānam" and "tad anumāpakam = anumāna pramānam, aparamjñānam."

20. The Saivagamas themselves use "Siddhānta" as a proper name for their corpus of twenty-eight: "Kāmikādi prabhedena śisyebhyah samprakāśitah. Astavimśatisamkhyosau siddhānta iti samnitāh." This is part of a citation alleged to be from Pauskara Samhitā given in the Introduction of Mrgendrāgama (Devkottai edn.p.2.) though I have not been able to trace it in the existing grantha editions. The Kāmika at the close of its Tantrāvatāra patala mentions "Śaivasiddhānta" as the label for referring to twenty eight Agamas beginning with itself. The Dharmapuram Publication no.109 (1946) has the following as the citation from the Kāmika (P.59) : "Śaivabhedam pravksyāmi aikya pāsāna vādinau, bhedavādi samavādi samkrānti cavikāravān, parināmi'ca śaivaśca siddhānti para īritah" which sounds suspiciously apocryphal in view of the use of the term "siddhānta" to refer to the theological interpretation contra-distinguished from interpretations which are, purvapaksas, - a later development.

21. Abhinava Gupta refers to "Siddhānta" when he says "siddhānta Karmabahulam malamāyādi rūpitam" (Tantrāloka XII, 400) but it is doubtful if he is referring by that name to the Śaivāgama or to the "Śaivasiddhānta" ortho-praxis school. The latter seems likely because he continues, in the same verse, to express his reservations about it : "Svalpa punyam bahullesam svapratiti vivarjitam, meksa vidyā vihīnahca vinayam tyaj dūratah." If he had intended the teachings of the twenty-eight Agamas as a whole, as Pandey believes (Pandey, K.C. Abhinavagupta, Chowkamba, Varanasi: 1963 p.168) it does not make sense that he (Abhinava Gupta) cites some of these Agamas, some of them more than once (Kāmika is cited seven times) in support of his conclusions in Tantrāloka as Pandey himself lists them in his Appendix B (pp.911-924) of his book. Tantrāloka I, 35 of course clearly refers to the "ten plus eighteen of the Agamas" and his Commentator Jayaratha lists many of them and describes them as "Siddhānta" and those accepting their guidance as "Saiddhāntika".

22. Tirumantiram 2397 : The Veda and the Agama, thus obtain the two-fold truth, that is , the word of God (iraivan nul, literally God-book), respectively, as general (pothu) and as special (chirappu). The Lord's Speech (natanurai), if one were to exegete (nadil), (leads to) two ends, different (from each other) they say : to the great they are indeed non-different.

23. Cf. Brahma Sutra II, 3, 1 Sankara's commentary.

24. Ibid II, 2,37. Appyaya Disksita's Dipika elucidates the parity between the Veda and the Śaivāgama further illustrating Srikanth's observations.

25. Umpati in his comentary on Pauskara Āgama cites the classical statement of Srikantha but adds : "Kiñca vedāstvapakvādhikāri visayah Śaivāgamastu pakvādhikāri visayah." The text variation cited in the grantha edition (p.10) under "padāntaram" reads "apeksādhikāri" and "paksādhikāri." Likewise the author of Siva-nana Siddhi does not endorse or even imply caste as the basis of distinction.

26. One of the frequent refrains recurrent in the Saiva Hymns describing the unapproachable nature of Śivam is that He is, eminently, one whom even the

Veda and the Vedanta do not comprehend. Cf. *Tiruvācakam* 5,89 : "Thou art he of the Veda (maraiyon) but whom (even) the Veda's end knows not." *Saiviom in Philophioal Perspective* op. cit. pp524-526.

27. *Śiva-dharmottara* cited in Nanavarana Vilakka Mapadiam (in Tamil) p.31.

28. *Tirumandiram* 73 : "Hara's feet daily contemplating did I commence to discourse the Āgama."

29. The *Pauṣkara Āgama* and the *Mataṅga-Parameśvara Āgama* in the entirety of their respective "knowledge-sections" are expositions of the thirty six tattvas. Umapati and Bhatta Ramakantha have respectively exegeted the texts with unusual fulness, a model of a critical edition complete with introduction and notes. The second text is also recently published in Devanagari script with concordances, introduction, analytic table of contents, glossary and other editorial features by the Publications de l'institut français d'Indologie, (Pondicherry: 1978).

30. The text of *Sarva-jñānottara* was printed in grantha script accompanied by Tamil translation in verse and notes by P. Muthia Pillai in 1923. I came across manuscripts of the text with Aghera Siva's *vṛtti* with gaps in copying in the Madras Oriental Manuscript Library. A critical edition of the Āgama is over-due, and when successfully accomplished will provide the missing link between the general corpus of *Śaivāgama* and *Sivajñānabodham*.

NOTES TO E.J. SHARPE "THE WEST AND THE BHAGAVAD GĪTĪ"

1. Welbon, *The Buddhist Nirvāna and its Western Interpreters* (1968), viii.
2. Ibid., loc. cit.
3. *Dictionary of National Biography*, 61 (1900): 259f.
4. P.J. Marshall (ed.), *The British Discovery of Hinduism in the Eighteenth Century* (1970), 12.
5. Reprinted, together with Wilkins' preface, in ibid., 184 ff.
6. Hastings, in Wilkins, in ibid., 5; Marshall, ibid., 184.
7. Wilkins, 7; Marshall, 185f.
8. Wilkins, 10; Marshall, 187.
9. See A.M. Davies, *Strange Destiny: A Biography of Warren Hastings* (1935), pp.343 ff.
10. Wilkins, 23; Marshall, 192 ff.
11. Although it will be argued at a later stage (though not in this paper) that the Gita did not become "popular" much before the 1880's, it should be noted that, in his pamphlet Ram Mohun Roy states that "The Geeta is not a rare work..." and that "the Geeta and its Commentaries are available to all." There is no contradiction here. Previously it was indeed well known and widely read, but only among the learned (Roy: "Let the learned decide the point.") Here Roy is writing as a pundit to pundits, not as a mass communicator to the general public. It was only during and after the 1880's that the Gita came to be produced and widely and freely circulated.
12. The quotation is from Karl Barth, *From Rousseau to Ritschl* (ET 1959), 226.
13. Cf. G.D. Bearce, *British Attitude to India, 1784-1858* (1961), 112 ff.

14. Ibid., 103.
15. Ralph L. Rusk (ed.), *The Letters of Ralph Waldo Emerson* (1939), 3:290.
16. Quoted by George Hendrick, in his introduction to the 1959 (New York) reprint edition of Wilkins, xi.
17. *The Selected Writings of Ralph Waldo Emerson* (Modern Library ed. 1964), edited by Atkinson, 276.
18. Thoreau, *A Week on the Concord...* (1906 ed.) 117.
19. Ibid., 120
20. Ibid., 126
21. Ibid., 127f.
22. Ibid., 129
23. Thoreau, *Walden* (New York: New American Library edition 1964) 198f.
24. Emerson, *Journals* 7:511, quoted by Arthur C Christy, *The Orient in American Transcendentalism* 1932), 23.
25. Quoted in Christy, *Orient*, 240.
26. Rudolf Haym, *Wilhelm von Humboldt* (1856, reprinted 1965), 581.
27. Ibid., 582
28. Ibid., 583: "Wie Musik wiegten ihn die Verse der Bhagavad-Gita ein."
29. Cowan, *Humanist without Portfolio* 23.
30. Ibid., 24.
31. Quoted in ibid., 169
32. As we shall see, R.A. Vaughan, *Hours with the Mystics* (1856; 6th ed., 1893) appears to take a diametrically opposite view.
33. Haym, *Wilhelm von Humboldt*, 580.
34. Ibid., 581
35. Vaughan, *Hours* (6th ed., 1893), 52.
36. Loc. cit.
37. Franz Lorinser, trans. and commentary, *Die Bhagavad gita* (1869), v. Cf. Richard von Garbe, *Indien und das Christentum* (1914), 244.
38. Monier Monier-Williams, *Hinduism* (1878), 212n. Cf. idem, *Indian Wisdom* (1875), 143f.
39. Idem, *Hinduism*, 207.
40. Ibid., 207f.
41. F. Max Müller, *India: What Can it Teach Us?* (2nd ed., 1892), 90.
42. Ibid., 94.
43. Ibid., 252.
44. Müller, *Natural Religion* (1889), 97.
45. Ibid., 99.
46. K.T. Teland, *The Bhagavadgītā* (Sacred Books of the East, 2: 1882), 1f.
47. M.K. Gandhi, *The Story of my Experiments with Truth* (1969) 50.
48. Quoted in Brooks Wright, *Sir Edwin Arnold? Interpreter of Buddhism to the West* (1957), 18.
49. Ibid., 71.
50. Ibid., 127
51. E. Arnold, *Poems Narrative and Lyrical* (Oxford University Press: 1853), 34.
52. Op. cit. Brooks Wright.

NOTES TO K. YOUNG "WOMEN OF THE NEHRU FAMILY"

1. See *Indira Gandhi: Speeches and Writings* (New York: Haper & Row, 1975), 158-59.
2. I thank my colleague Alaka Hejib for the following analysis of the compound *satyāgraha*.
3. See Alaka Hejib and Katherine Young, "Power of the Meek (*abalā*): A Feature of Indian Feminism" (to be published).
4. Erik H. Erikson, *Gandhi's Truth: On the Origins of Militant Non-Violence* (Toronto: George J. McLeod, 1969) 335.
5. Uma Vasudev, *Indira Gandhi: Revolution in Restraint* (Delhi: Vikas Publishing House, 1974), p.21. Herafter cited as *Indira Gandhi*.
6. Vijaya Lakshmi Pandit, *The Scope of Happiness: A Personal Memoir* (New Delhi: Vikas Publishing House, 1979), 313; hereafter cited as *Scope of Happiness*.
7. Kakasaheb Kalelkar (ed), *Bapu's Letters to Ashram Sisters* (Ahmedabad: Navajivan Publishing House, 1960), xii; hereafter cited as *Bapu's Letters*.
8. *Bapu's Letters*, xv, xviii, 6,6,98,103.
9. Ibid., xix
10. *Indira Gandhi*, 6.
11. *Scope of Happiness*, 69.
12. Ibid., 144.
13. Ibid., 66.
14. Idbid., 110.
15. *Toward Freedom: The Autobiography of Jawaharlal Nehru* (Boston: Beacon Press, 1958), 332-33; hereafter cited as *Toward Freedom*.
16. *Indira Gandhi*, 22.
17. Ibid., 22.
18. Ibid., 66.
19. Ibid., 113.
20. Ibid., 89
21. Ibid., 170.
22. Ibid., 22-23.
23. Ibid., 59.
24. *Bapu's Letters*, 116.
25. *Indira Gandhi*, 170.
26. Ibid., 55.
27. Indira Gandhi, *My Truth* (New Delhi: Vision Books, 1981).
28. Ibid., 187.
29. Ibid., 189.
30. Ibid., 190.
31. Ibid., 186.
32. I thank my colleague Alka Hejib for this observation of popular parlance.

NOTES TO J.R. HINNELLS "TWENTIETH CENTURY BOMBAY PARSIS"

*It is with pleasure that I record my great indebtedness to my friend and collaborator, Dastur Dr. K.M. Jamaspasa, High Priest of the Anjuman Atash Bahram and Secretary of the K.R. Cama Oriental Institute, Bombay, for all his guidance and especially for his translations of the Parsi Prakash. I also wish to record my thanks to my postgraduate students, notably C. Lucy Mitchell, Nora Firby, and Hilary Langstaff, whose work and questions have provided much stimulation. The research for this paper and my attendance at the congress were made possible by grants from Manchester University and the British Academy, to whom I offer sincere thanks.

1. E. Kulke, *The Parsees in India* (Munich: 1974), 123-26.

2. Ibid., 122, and R.S. Rungta, *Rise of Business Corporations in India 1851-1900* (Cambridge: 1970), 23,26, 28,57.

3. Rungta, *Rise*, 58.

4. K.N. Seervai and B.B. Patel, "Guajarat Parsis," *Bombay Gazetter 9/2* (1899), 247-51.

5. May 5, 1899, N.J. Wadia Andheri Charitable Dispensary opened; January 6, 1900, foundation stone layed of Naoroji Eye hospital Ahmedabad; February 23, 1900, a charitable dispensary opened near Surat; January 15, 1902, Dr. Masina Hospital, Bombay, opened; September 19, 1904, money given to Nadir E. Dinshaw Dispensary in Karachi; March 5, 1906, Parsi Fever Hospital, Bombay, opened; June 4, 1906, Sir Jehangir Cowasji J. Jehangir donated Rs 30,000 to start an opthalmic hospital (renovated with a further donation January 10, 1910); June 5, 1906, Charitable Dispensary at Santa Cruz opened; April 1, 1908, Dr J.N. Bahdurjee started the "Poor Man's Eye Clinic" in Bombay; December 23, 1911, foundation stone layed of Parsi Maternity Hospital; March 27, 1912, opening of B.D. Petit Parsi General Hospital, Bombay; June 26, 1912, opening of N.W. Wadia hospital; May 1, 1912, the Masina hospital moved to larger premises; June 9, 1912, the Parsi General Hospital opened in Navsari. The above information was obtained from the entries under the relevant dates in the *Parsi Prakash*, B.B. Patel (ed), Bombay.

6. See the entries in the *Parsi Prakash* for September 2, 1900 (vol.3, 705f.), and May 5, 1901 (vol.4, 22ff.).

7. *Parsi Prakash* for March 6, 1905 (vol.4, p.6).

8. R.P. Masani, *N.M. Wadia and his Foundation* (Bombay: 1961) ch.14.

9. J.R. Hinnells, "Parsis and British Education," *Journal of the K.R. Cama Oriental Institute 46* (1978), 42-64.

10. For a biography of Naoroji see R.P. Masani, *Dadabhai Naoroji: The Grand Old Man of India* (London: 1939).

11. For a biography of Mehta see H. Mody, *Sir Pherozeshah Mehta: A political Biography* (reprinted, Bombay: 1963).

12. The only biographical account of Bhownagree is contained in Natesan (publishers, no author/editor named), *Famous Parsis* (Madras: 1930), 475-88.

13. Again the only biography is Natesan (publisher), *Famous Parsis* 283-329.

14. See F. Harris, *Jamsetji Nusserwanji Tata: a Chronicle of His Life* (2nd ed., Bombay: 1958).

15. See G. Smith *The Life of Johnson, D.D., F.R.S.* (London: 1879); for an autobiography of one of his converts see Dhanjibhai Nauroji, *From Zoroaster to Christ* (Edinburgh: 1909). Two other missionaries who wrote about Parsis are H.G. Briggs, *The Parsis; or modern Zerdusthians* (Bombay: 1852) and Dr. Murray Mitchell, "A Lecture on the Parsis and the Zend Avesta," *Proceedings of the Bethune Society* (Calcutta: April 21, 1870), which he elaborated in his *The Great Religions of India* (Edinburgh: 1905). Mitchell was not without respect for what he considered to be Zoroastrian monotheism (1905:142). He commented that "Undoubtedly the purest of the Gentile creeds is Zoroastrianism; it stands nearer to Revealed truth than any other. It seems only natural, then, that it should be the first of existing Gentile systems to merge in Christianity" (1905:168). The theme that Zoroastrianism prepared Parsis for Christianity was developed by the scholar J.H. Moulton who during his stay in Bombay in 1916 spoke of himself as a Christian missionary to the Parsis, see his *The Teaching of Zarathushtra* (eight lectures and addresses delivered to Parsis in Bombay; Bombay: 1916), esp. p.3, and *The Treasure of the Magi* (London: 1917), esp. ch.8 in part II. Unlike Mitchell, Moulton did have a definite influence on the Parsi community, but as this was felt at the end of and later than the period covered by this paper his arguments are not examined here, even though his visit and lectures took place during the period covered.

17. Ibid., 377-79.

18. See Masani, *Dadabhai Naoroji*, 48-50. Naoroji's own assessment of the reform movement was given in a paper read before the Liverpool Philomathic Society, March 13, 1861 and published that year entitled "The Manners and Customs of the Parsees."

19. Two biographies have been written of Cama: S.M. Edwardes, *Kharshedji Rustamji Cama, 1831-1909* (Oxford: 1923), and J.J. Modi, *K.R. Cama* (Bombay: 1932).

20. One of the earliest such translations was by (the layman) K.R. Cama, who translated *The Religiion and Customs of the Persians and other Iranians as described by the Grecian and Roman authors*, from the German of Adolf Rapp in 1876. In 1879 Cama also translated works of Spiegel and Rhode and in 1883 the work of A. Kohut. Another leading translator was the high priest Darab Peshotan Sanjana. In 1885-86 he translated Geiger's two volume *Civilization of the Eastern Iranians* and in 1884 and 1897 he translated further works by Geiger. Also in 1897 he translated the work of F. Windischmann, *References in Ancient Writings to Zoroaster and his Doctrines*. In the 1890s M.P. Madan translated the work of de Harlez.

21. A survey of manuscripts and work in Gujarati is in J.C. Katrak, "Gujarati Literature on Iranology," *Acta Iranica*, 1 (1974) 360-78.

22. An excellent example of this knowledge is the book of J.J. Motivala and B.N. Sahiar, *Enlightened Non Zoroastrians on Mazdayasnism, The Excellent Religion* (Bombay: 1897-99), which collects favourable comments by Westerners (e.g., Haug and Lang) as well as by ancient authors.

23. M. Menant, *Les Parsis: histoire des communautés zoroastriennes de l'Inde*, (Paris: 1898). Three chapters of this were translated into English by Miss Ratanbai A. Vakil in 1902.

24. There is a short biography of Modi in Natesan (publ.), *Famous Parsis*, 454-74. His two English publications of this nature which were written during our period are, *The Religious System of the Parsis* (2nd ed., 1903), expanded from his paper to the World Parliament of Religion in Chicago; *A Catechism of the Zoroastrian Religion* (Bombay: 1911). Between 1902 and 1919 he published six volumes of lectures and sermons on Zoroastrianism in Gujarati. Modi was probably more orthodox than most scholarly Parsis of the period, which was probably why he was appointed secretary of the Panchayet and is shown in his opposition to the admission of converts in the court case discussed below.

25. A collection of his papers delivered during the period covered by this paper was published as *Studies in Parsi History* (Bombay: 1920).

26. *Speeches and Writings of Dadabhai Naoroji* (publ. by G.A. Natesan & Co., no editor or date given), 59, from his Presidential address to the 1893 Lahore meeting of the Indian National Congress. In a similar vein Mehta, in his presidential speech at the 1890 Congress, declared, "To my mind, a Parsi is a better and truer Parsi, as a Mahomdan or a Hindu is a better and truer Mahomedan or Hindu, the more he is attached to the land which gave him birth" (in J.R.B. Jeejeebhoy, *Some Unpublished and Later Speeches and Writings of the Hon. Sir Pherozeshah Mehta* [Bombay: 1918], 315n).

27. B.R. Chowdhury, *Madame Cama: A Short Life Sketch* (Delhi: 1977).

28. The literature on this is quite large. The Parsi involvement in the very English game of cricket was considerable. In 1886 Parsis organised the first Indian team to tour England. They were so good at the game one English observer, C.A. Kincaid, concluded it must be because Alexander the Great's invasion of Iran had infused Greek blood into the veins of the Parsis' ancestors, just as he believed there was Greek blood in English veins! ("The Parsis and Hellenic Influence," *The Parsi*, [March, 1905] 90-94.) There have been two histories of Parsi cricket, M.K. Patel, *History of Parsi Cricket* (Bombay: 1892), and M.E. Pavri, *Parsi Cricket* (Bombay: 1901). A later publication, H.D. Darukhanawala, *Parsis and Sports* (Bombay: 1935), gives an account of Parsis involved in a number of Western sports during the period relevant to this paper (e.g., pp. 16f.,64,67,135,145,147,201,218f.,221,225,286, 367,397, 408f.,413) covering body building, running, tennis, horse riding, badminton, motorcycling, and shooting. Parsis were leading figures in the development of drama and the Western theatre in Bombay. The columns and cartoons of the magazine *Hindi Punch* (started in 1854 by a Parsi as *Parsi Punch*) caricature an evident westernised trend among Parsis in the early twentieth century.

29. *The Parsi* (August, 1905), 324.

30. This is not to deny Hindu influence on the Parsis. Influence is evident in the marriage ceremony and ideas of caste clearly affected Parsis. But unlike the period of the inter-war years and later, Parsis do not appear to have been influenced by such Hindu teachings as rebirth (except through the mediation of Theosophy) or the avatar in the period 1900-1918.

31. *Dastur Dhalla: An Autobiography* (E.T. Gool and Behram S.H.J. Rustomji, Karachi: 1975), 156-58.

32. Most of Dhalla's writing during our period were in Gujarati, but an important English work was his *Zoroastrian Theology* (New York: 1914).

33. *Study of the Gathas* (Bombay: 1916) 5); see also his *Revelation Considered as a Source of Religious Knowledge with Special Reference to*

Zoroastrianism (1909). A Similar theme is developed by S.D. Bharucha, *A Brief Sketch of the Zoroastrian Religion and Customs* (2nd ed., 1903), 13. An earlier rationalising and abrasive reformer was B.J. Billimoria, *A Warning Word to Parsees* (Bombay: 1900; in 2 parts).

34. This was the theme of the K.R. Cama Prize essay, (1900; published 1906) by S.E. Dubash, "The Zoroastrian Sanitary Code," which attempts to interpret the Vendidad (the text attacked by Wilson) in the light of contemporary medical knowledge. It is a theme emphasised by S.A. Kapadia, *The Teaching of Zoroaster and the Philosophy of the Parsi Religion*, (London: 1905) 33f., in a book written to give a good impression of his religion to the West. M. Pithawalla, *Steps to Prophet Zoroaster* (Poona: 1915) 174f., develops the same argument. He also argues that Darwin's theory of evolution supports Zoroastrian teaching on the progress of the world towards the renovation. Other examples are J.J. Modi, *Religious System of the Parsis* (2nd ed., Bombay: 1903), 41 (a theme he elaborated in his later works); and A.S.N. Wadia, *The Message of Zoroaster* (London: 1912), 93f., who is clearly dependent on Laing (see p.88).

35. Perhaps the foremost interpreter of Zoroastrianism for the West was P.A. Wadia; "The Philosophy of the Gathas," *East and West* (January, 1903), 121-32, and (July, 1904) 1ff. See also his *An Inquiry into the Principles of Modern Theosophy* (Bombay: 1904). A similar tendency to view Zoroastrianism in terms of Western philosophies is in J.C. Coyajee, *The Spirit of the Gathas* (Bombay: 1903). Authors from this period who emphasise Zoroastrianism as a universal religion include R.H. Mistri, *Zoroaster and Zoroastrianism* (Bombay: 1906), 57,64ff.; and Pithawalla, *Steps to Prophet Zoroaster*, 68,103f. In a book published just after the end of our period Pithawalla argued that the best hope for a reconstructed postwar Germany was Zoroastrian ideals. As far as I can trace, little attention was paid to the new American Mazdaznan cult which claimed Zoroastrian heritage. It was started by Dr. Otoman ZarAdusht Ha'nish; see his *Mazdaznan Health and Breath Culture* (U.S.A edition, 1902; published in Britian in 1913). When "Mother Gloria" visited the Parsis in the 1930s the community was outraged - this they did not see as Zoroastrianism for the West! Parsis have often argued for Zoroaster's date as early as 4,000 or 6,000 B.C. thereby making him the archetypal prophet (see from this period V. Dinshaw, *The Date and Country of Zoroaster* [Hyderabad: 1912]), but this is not necessarily, nor even normally nowadays, used to argue for the universality of his religion.

36. K.J.B. Wadia, *Fifty Years of Theosophy in Bombay* (Madras: 1931). The figures are drived from the lists of office bearers in ch.14.

37. *The Journal of the Iranian Association* was started in April, 1912, edited by P.A. Wadia, with the declared aim "To expose and counteract the effects of such teachings of Theosophists and others as tend: (a) to corrupt the religion of Zarathushtra by adding elements foreign to it, and (b) to bring about the degeneration of a progressive and virile community like the Parsis, and make them a body of superstitious and unpractical visionaries." The *Journal* was an active supporter of Dhalla, who also attacked the Theosophists; see his *Theology*, ch.45.

38. Vimadalal's articles are on pp.69-78,154-60, 261-68. An active writer who sought to demonstrate the compatability of Theosophy,

Zoroastrianism, and modern science was N.F. Bilimoria, *Zoroastrian Ceremonies* (Bombay: 1896). See also his *Zoroastrianism in the Light of Theosophy* (Bombay: 1898).

39. For the account of Shroff's life see N.F. Mama, *A Mazdaznan Mystic* (Bombay: 1944). The first Khshnoomic book in English was a "review" of Dhalla's *Zoroastrian Theology*: P.S. Masani, *Zoroastrianism, Ancient and Modern* (Bombay: 1917).

40. The source of the idea of an Iranian cave of treasures is unknown. I suspect Shroff took it from Co. Olcott. In his 1881 lecture, and subsequently, he urged Parsis to form a research society, comparable to the Christian "Palestine Exploration Fund," to search for treasures in Iran. In his diary entry for February 19, 1991 (*Old Diary Leaves*, 5:438f.) Olcott wrote that the Master "Illarion is here en route for Tibet" who "...happily unknown by the public and even the majority of our members, who had but recently gone over the ground in Armenia, where the ancient Parsis lived." He told H.P.B. [Madame Blawatsky] that "...in a certain large mountain cave, effectually closed against all intruders and vandals, and, like the many other of the same kind scattered throughout the world, constantly watched over and guarded by the Masters of Wisdom, the whole body of valuable Zoroastrian literature is stored up against the proper time for its restoration to mankind." Ilm-i Khshnpm occupies a place among twentieth-century Parsis somewhat akin to the circle interested in the *Dabistān* and *Desatir* some hundred years earlier (see Dhalla, *Theology* ch.36). Indeed there may be a direct lineage. Nineteenth-century travellers refer to secret caves in Armenia which were linked with Mithraism, then understood as a form of Zoroastrianism. See, e.g., Sir Robert Ker Porter, *Travels in Georgia, Persia, Armenia, Ancient Babylonia &c &c during...1817,1818,1819 & 1820*, 2 vols. (London: 1821) 1:495-97. (I am indebted to one of my research students, Miss Nora Firby, for this reference). Could it be that these travellers heard of the oral tradition which lies behind the Armenian Mher legend (see J.A. Boyle, "Mher in the Carved Rock," *Journal of Mithraic Studies* 1/2 (1976) 107-118). Was this oral tradition passed on through travellers to the circle associated with the Destair and Dabistān, thence to Theosophists and Kshnoomists?

41. See M. Boyce, *Zoroastrians: Their Religious Beliefs and Practices* (London: 1979), ch.13. Conditions began to ease in the late nineteenth century because of the work of the Parsi, Maneckji, Limji Hataria; see Boyce in the *K.R. Cama Oriental Institute Golden Jubliee Volume* (Bombay: 1969) 19-31.

42. Reprinted in *The Parsi* (February 1905), 208-10. The Parsi then became something of a forum for such appeals and discussions. On the impact of Japan's victory on India as a whole, see J.N. Farquhar, *Modern Religious Movements in India* (reprinted, Delhi: 1967), 360.

43. *Zarathushtra and Zarathustrianism in the Avesta* (Leipzig: 1906). The reason for the German publication was Sanjana's international travels, which included not only Britain and the United States (where he met the President), but also Germany.

44. The main newspaper associated with orthodox opinion was, and is, *Jam i Jamshid*. The leading orthodox individuals were M.H. Cama, "Mansukh" (Muncherji Cawasji Langdana), B.F. Billimoria, B.K.M. Dordi, J.J. Vimadalal,

Dastur K.E. Pavri, and later Mr. Justice Davar. An illustration of the form of orthodox reactions in the letter of the Parsi Punchayat signed by two dasturs and 309 priests from Bombay and throughout Gujarat protesting at the title of Dhalla's conference as the "Zoroastrian" conference. They argued that it was organised by reformists and was not, therefore, typical of the religion (*Parsi Prakash* 5:17). Their point was that published proceedings should not be taken as representing majority opinion.

45. The debate and lawsuit were reported in all Parsi newspapers and journals and even in *The Times* of London. The following account is conflated from diverse newspapers and from *Parsi Prakash*.

46. *Parsi Prakash* 4:14.

47. For example, he had the Punchayat's decision to purchase copies of Dhalla's *Thoelogy* reversed because it did not represent "typical" parsi beliefs.

48. See *Journal of the Iranian Association* 3/5 (1914), 167-74.

49. The *Journal of the Iranian Association* played an active part, pleading the cause of Bella. G.K. Nariman, the distinguished Parsi historian, was a leading campaigner against Bella. The case is reported in *Parsi Prakash* 5:10 (1914).

50. *The Hindi Punch* is the most obvious, and humorous, example.

NOTES TO P. GERLITZ "DIE KHASI - RENAISSANCE"

1. Die missionarische Arbeit der christlichen Denominationen wird z.B. von Nalini Natarajan, *The Missionary among the Khasis*, (Sterling Publishers, New Delhi: 1977), 90ff., 184ff., durchaus positiv bewertet: "...the intentions of missionaries as a class were humanitarian and their efforts have yielded positive results for the nation as a whole" 122; cf. S. Barkataki, *The Khasis*, A.P. Choudhury, (Pathsalas: 1977), 12. Frau Natarajan muß sich allerdings eine heftige Kritik ihres Buches in der Wochenzeitung "Meghdoot", Shillong, 16.9.(1978), p.3-5, gefallen lassen, in der ihr christliche Überheblichkeit vorgeworfen wird. Die Vf. verschweigt natürlich die antichristlichen Tendenzen des Seng Khasi nicht, 114f.

2. Etwa dort, wo die Jurisdiktion des Syiem eingeschränkt wurde (P.R.G. Mathur, *The Khasi of Meghalaya, Study in Tribalism and Religion*, (Cosmo Publications, New Delhi: 1979), 30.72ff., und natürlich während der Freiheitskämpfe der Khasi und Jaintia, im Verlaufe derer U Tirot Singh im Gefängnis von Dacca starb (1834) und U Kiang Nong Bah, der Freiheitsheld der Jaintia, (1862) von den Briten hingerichtet wurde (ibid., 30).

3. J.B. Bhttacharjee, *The Messenger of Khasi Heritage*, (Shillong: 1979), 3.

4. H. Bareh, *A Short History of Khasi Literature*, (Don Bosco Press, Shillong: 1969), 36.

5. die er in der von ihm gegründeten Ri Khasi Press in Shillong herausgab.

6. *The Khasis*, repr. Cosmo Publications, Delhi 1975.

7. Später Welsh Presbyterian Foreign Mission genannt.

8. Cf. Bareh, l.cit., 38f. Bei Singh handelt es sich um einen christlichen Konvertiten, der zeitlebens eine besondere Vorliebe für die Religion seiner Vorfahren behalten hat (J.B. Bhttacharjee, l.cit.,14).

9. Besonders in der von Diengdoh begründeten Zeitschrift U Khasi Mynta, aber auch in Monatsblättern wie U Nongpyrta (Der Rufer), begr. 1921, und Ka Sngi (Die Sonne), begr. 1924.

10. Bareh, loc. cit., 50f.; Bhttacharjee, loc. cit.,13.

11. 2. erweiterte Aufl., (Shillong: 1979).

12. Printed Constitution, (Shillong: 1913); cf. Bhttacharjee, *The Messenger*, 8ff.

13. Der Grundsatz erscheint auch umgekehrt als Ka Niam Tipblei - Ka Niam Tipbriew. In jedem Falle wird die Anerkennung der Khasi-Gesellschaftsordnung für die Erkenntnis Gottes und gleichwertig mit dieser vorausgesetzt; cf. Kynpham Singh, "Khasi and Jaintia Religion" in: *Khasi Heritage, A Collection of Essays on Khasi Religion and Culture*, ed. U. Hipshon Roy, rev. and enlarged ed., (Ri Khasi Press, Shillong: 1979), 96.

14. P.R.G. Mathur, *Khasi of Meghalaya*, 90; cf. N. Natarajan, loc. cit., 113 (dort steht das Gebot an zweiter Stelle).

15. Bhttacharjee, l.cit., 7.

16. Mathur, loc. cit., 90.

17. U Hipshon Roy, (Khasi Heritage, 1979), 11f.; Mathur, loc. cit., 90, hat "adherence to the tenets of kinship as specified by the khasi ancestors (1), righteousness through service, love and truth (2), respect for one's own fellowmen with humility and faith (3), belief in God, the Sovereign Lord, the Creator and giver of all (4)."

18. So mein gleichnamiger Aufsatz in : *Studi Storico Religiosi*, ed. G. Piccaluga, II,2 (Romé 1978), 243ff.

19. Eine solche Aufspaltung erfolgt häufig dann, wenn der Begräbnisplatz des Clan (mawba) belegt ist und ein neues Gelände dafür ausgesucht werden muß.

20. Chie Nakane, *Garo and Khasi, A Comparative Study in Matrilineal Systems*, (Mounton, Paris/The Hague: 1967), 103ff.,117ff.

21. Wenngleich Rymbai ihn auch dort als U Kpa (Kpa als Ehrentitel) uba lah ba iai, a father able and steadfast, bezeichnet (*Khasi Heritage*, 113).

22. Cf. U.R. von Ehrenfels, Khasi Kinship Terms in Four Dialects, in : *Anthropos* 48, 1953, 396ff.; Gerlitz, l.cit., 250f.

23. Nakane, loc. cit., 121.

24. Ibid., 112.

25. F. Stegmiller, "Aus dem religiösen Leben der Khasi," in, *Anthropos* 16/16, 1921/22, p.418f.,420f.

26. Ibid., 421

27. Gurdon, loc. cit., 112.

28. Ibid., 113.

29. Stegmiller, loc. cit., 407ff.; cf. Gerlitz, loc. cit., 254ff.

30. Gerlitz, loc. cit., 257f. Hier ist vor allem das bei Stegmiller, loc. cit., 425, zitierte Dankgebet zu erwähnen: "Höre denn, of Gott! O Jawbei (to sngew ko blei ka jawbei)! Nachdem ich deine Gründe und Wege erkannt habe, woher dein Verderben und Verschulden gekommen ist (das du in mir gefunden hast), so, mein Herr (te kynrad), danke ich dir tausendmal,/und erhöre mich

gnädig,/da ich unwissend./da ich wider dich gehandelt habe,/ich, dein Kind und Enkel (nga u khun u ksiew)!"

31. So sein gleichnamiger Artikel in Paideuma 6, 1957, 285ff.; cf. ebenfalls von Ehrenfels, "The Double Sex Character of the Khasi Great Deity," in: *Journal of the University of Madras* 23/1, (July 1950), 26ff.

32. Von Ehrenfels, *Doppelgeschlecht und Götterpaar*, 292.

33. Cf. R.F. Rymbai, in: *Khasi Heritage*, 116.

34. Ibid., 410-412; cf. Gurdon, loc. cit., 106ff.,114ff.

35. Cf. R. Singh Lyngdoh, in *Seiner ungedruckten Philosophischen Dissertation*. "Government and Politics in Meghalaya," (Gauhati 1976), 162ff. In Frage kommt wohl der Abschnitt p.109-113 in Gurdons Buch.

36. U Hipshon Roy in *einer persönlichen Mitteilung* vom 29.3.1979; cf. auch R.T. Rymbai, "Some Aspects of the Religion of the Khasi-Pnárs," in: *Khasi Heritage*, 114.

37. Lyngdoh, loc. cit., 162ff.; R.T. Rymbai *im persönlichen Gespräch* vom 27.3.1979 in Shillong.

38. Lyngdoh, loc. cit.

39. Barsh, *A Short History ect.*, 39.

40. *Khasi Heritage*, 83f.; cf. die Definitionen von Rymbai, Ibid., 115f.; Lyngdoh, loc. cit., 162ff.

41. Ibid., 83.

42. Ebenfalls in *Khasi Heritage*, 97; Kynpham Singh im Gespräch vom 26.3.1979 in Shillong.

43. *Khasi Heritage*, 95.100f.

44. Ibid., 95.

45. Cf. P. Gerlitz, *Außerchristliche Einflüsse auf die Entwicklung des christlichen Trinitätsdogmas*, (Brill, Leiden: 1963), 243ff.

46. Singh, l.cit., 100; Rymbai in *einer persönlichen Mitteilung* vom 27.3.1979.

47. In diesem Falle erhält Gott den Namen U Blei Shihajar Nguh Shillong 1919.

48. Mit den Pnár ist der Stamm der Jaintia, auch Synteng genannt, gemeint.

49. Rymbai, Some Aspects, in: Khasi Heritage, 114.

50. Loc. cit., 117.

51. Gurdon, loc. cit., 106.117; Mathur, *Khasi of Meghalaya*, 62.

52. Der "Sündenfall" in der Khasi-Mythologie geschieht durch das frevelhafte Abhacken des Dinghiei-Baimes, der Himmel und Erde miteinander verband; cf. diese Sage Bei S. Barkataki, *The Khasis*, (Purbodoya Press, Calcutta: 1976), 90ff. Gurdon, loc. cit., 117; und Stegmiller, loc. cit., 408, berichten sogar von einem Sündenbekenntnis, das "nga briew nga la pop", "Ich, Mensch, habe gesündigt", heßt.

53. Beide Stellen bei Gurdon, loc. cit., 117; Stegmiller, loc. cit., 408. Gurdon ist selbst unsicher bei der Frage, wie es zu einer solchen Bedeutung des Hahnes gekommen sei und gesteht schließlich ein: "On how the cock came to occupy such an important position, tradition is vague and self-conflicting" (ibid.).

54. Kaum ein Einfluß des hinduistischen "Sündenverständnisses", wie S. Barkataki, loc. cit., 44, annehmen möchte.

55. Loc. cit., 420ff.; cf. Gerlitz, loc. cit., 257f. Ich gebe das Gebet hier auszugsweise wieder:/"Und nun, du Opferhahn,/du Sohn der Göttin (ko khun ka blei),/du Hüpfer und Springer, du Kräher..../So höre nun, ich frage, ich erwäge,/ich werfe Orakel, ich befrage Orakel:/Was ist der Grund,/was ist das, was den NN schlägt/und so sehr auf seinen Körper herniederprasselt?/Sage, o Göttin (ka blei):/Ich bin es, die ihn schlägt,/ich bin es, die auf ihn herniederprasselt,/und ich, die ihn geißelt und schlägt./Und ich gehe hin und her und auf und ab/und frage: Woher kommt denn das Verbrechen, das Verschulden, /woher denn der Verdruß und Ärger, o, du Göttin?/So sage doch, o Göttin (ka blei),/du Tochter der Lüge (ko khun ka lamler),/damals, nicht wahr,/an jenem Tage, hast du verlangt/das Bild des Menschen,/den Bestand der Familie vor meinem Angesichte,/vor mir, der Göttin,/vor mir, der Jawbei,/so sage ich!/Stehe auf und erinnere dich!.../Hast du keine Erzählung davon,/vor mir, der Göttin?/Vor meinem Angesichte?/Du vergräbst, du verbirgst es vielmehr und daher das Verderben,/sage ich, die Göttin, die Jawbei (ka blei ka jawbei)! /Du aber, o Gott und Herr (te ko blei trai kynrad),/da ich nun einmal auf deinen Grund,/den Weg des Verderbens, der Schuld, gekommen bin,/so erhebe ich mich./Die Erinnerung, die Betroffenheit/von wegen jenes Weges,/wo immer ich auch wohne,/soll sein der Dank, die Ehrerbietung,/das Brot und der Kuchen, der Kürbis und die Kürbisflasche;/friedlich und wohlgemut bist du,/o Göttin (ka blei) Jawbei,/an jenem Wege.../Rasch erhebe dich, Mensch!/Voll befriedigt sei du, o Gott (u blei)!/Nimm hinweg die Makel, die Fleken,/das Band und die Schlinge!.../Das Blut des Hahnes (snam syiar).../Hei! Siehe da,/ich zerreiße ihm den Nabel, das Gedärm,/damit gut sei die Beratung...."

56. *A Short History etc.*, 96f.
57. *Khasi Heritage*, 11.
58. Gurdon, loc. cit., 76ff.; Nakane, loc. cit., 117ff.
59. *Notes on Khasi Law*, (1934), (reprinted Ri Khasi Press, Shillong: 1974).
60. Cf. so lapidare Sätze wie "The origin is the mother, and the mother is the person who stands between the father and the son" (David Roy, in: K. Cantlie's *Notes on Khasi Law*, 88).
61. Cf. Gerlitz, loc. cit., 244; auch von Ehrenfels sieht eine Verbindung zwischen moderner Frauenemanzipation und matrilinearer struktur bei den khasi "Matrilineal Joint Family Patterns in India," in: *The Family in India, a Regional Review*, ed. G. Kurian, (Mouton, The Hague/Paris: 1974), 98.102ff.
62. Schon K. Cantlie, loc. cit., 75.
63. Some Aspects etc, in: *Khasi Heritage*, 111.
64. *Khasi Heritage*, 106f.
65. Shad Suk Mynsiem, in: *Khasi Heritage*, 129; cf. Mathur, loc. cit., 91. Wörtlich übersetzt heißt es "tanz für den Frienden der Seele."
66. Ganz im Gegensatz zum Shad Nongkrem, das als opferfest und Schwertertanz von der Familie des Syiem, des Königs des Khyrim-Staates, vor dessen Palast in Smit - also an höchst offiziöser Stelle - ausgerichtet wird. Diesem Fest Kommt eine eminent religionspolitische Bedeutung zu, weil im Verlauf der Feierlichkeiten der Staatsgott Shillong (U Blei Shillong) mehrfach vom König um Beistand für alle Khasi-Stämme angerufen wird. Dazu cf. die noch immer unübertroffene Darstellung von C. Becker, Die Nongkrem-Puja in den Khasi-Bergen, in: *Anthropos* 4, 1909, 892ff. Daß sich der Seng Khasi auch

dieses Festes besonders angenommen hat, zeigt die Stellungnahme von Maham Singh in: *Khasi Heritage*, 146ff.

67. Eine gute Beschreibung bei Mathur, loc. cit., 91ff.
68. Shad Suk Mynsiem, in: *Khasi Heritage*, 131; Mathur, loc. cit., 91.
69. Shillong 1979, 91. Der Artikel "The Messenger of Khasi Heritage" ist jetzt in den Sammelband "Khasi Heritage," 1979, aufgenommen worden und findet sich dort auf p.1ff. Auch N. Natarajan, loc. cit., 114, bestätigt die Bedeutung der Revitalisierung dieses Festes für den Seng Khasi.
70. Bhattacharjee nach Kynpham Singh, *Khasi Heritage*, 16. Auch U Hipshon Roy reagiert heftig auf die britische Herrschaft: "The British conquest was an organised attempt to destroy Khasi tradition and faith, aided by the Missionary who was given complete charge of education in these hills; the religion of these hills could be killed." (in einem persönlichen Schreiben vom 29.3. 1979); cf. Barkataki, loc. cit., 62f.
71. Natanajan. loc. cit., 114f.
72. Mathur, loc. cit., 93f.; Natarajan, loc. cit., 181.
73. Es entspricht zweifellos nicht den Tatsachen, daß z.B. der universale Gottesbegriff, den der Seng Khasi entwickelt hat, auf hinduistische Vorbilder zurückgeht, wie P.R.G. Mathur, loc. cit., 139, meint, wenn auch Riten und Zeremonien einige wenige Ähnlichkeiten mit dem Hinduismus aufweisen. Daraus, daß auch die Khasi ihre Toten verbrennen, läßt sich keine Ableitung aus dem Hinduismus postulieren. Durch die jahrhundertelange Isolierung der Khasi Hills ist es praktisch nur zu hinduistischen Einflüssen unter den Wár-Khasi am Südabhang des Plateaus gekommen.
74. Hier mag man an Soso Tham's Traum von einem Goldenen Zeitalter in den khasi Hills denken den sich der Seng Khasi ideologisch angeeignet hat (cf. Bareh, *A Short History*, 70).
75. Besonders deutlich wird das bei Hipshon Roy, der dem Vf. auf die Frage, ob die Khasi-Religion die Chance haben werde, die säkularisierung zu bestehen, antwortete: "In Khasi religion things worldly do not nullify things that are divine and vice versa. The Khasi religion creates a thinking man and does not expect him to accept the impossible; it allows him even to argue with the divine, this is rational and accepts things that would stand the test of reason." (29.3. 1979). Eine solche Aussage wäre ohne voranggangene westliche Aufklärung undenkbar.
76. Mathur, loc. cit., 138.
77. Natarajan, loc. cit., 181.

NOTES TO G.E. YOCUM "BUDDHISM THROUGH HINDU EYES"

*The original draft of this paper was written in 1977 under the auspices of a summer seminar at the University of Chicago sponsored by the National Endowment for the Humanities and directed by Professor Frank Reynolds.

1. The edition of the hagiography I have used is that of Pu. Ci. Puṉṉaivaṉanāta Mutaliyār (ed. and commentator), *Tiruvātavūratikaḷ Purāṇam* (Madras: South India Saiva Siddhanta Works Publishing Society, 1967). There is a complete German translation of this work by H.W. Schomerus (trans.), *Śivaitische Heiligenlegenden (Periyapurāṇa und Tiruvātavūrar-purāṇa)* (Jena:

Eugen Diederichs, 1925), 193-286; and Pope summarizes the text in the introduction to his translation of the *Tiruvācakam:* G.U. Pope (Trans. and commentator), *The Tiruvāçagam or 'sacred Utterances' of the Tamil Poet, Saint, and Sage Māṇikka-Vāçagar* (Oxford: Clarendon Press, 1900) xvii-xxxii, lxvii-lxxii.

2. On the date of the *Tiruvātavūrar Purāṇam* and other texts which relate some of the same events, see K.V. Zvelebil, *Tamil Literature* (Leiden: E.J. Brill, 1975), 220-21. In assigning dates to Tamil texts, I have relied upon this work.

3. Please address requests for copies of the translation to Glenn Yocum, Department of Religion, Whittier College, Whittier, CA. 90608, U.S.A.

4. See Radha Kumud Mookerji, *Ancient Indian Education (Brahmanical and Buddhist)* (London: MacMillan, 1947), 317-22. A recent work which discusses the Vedic disputation-contests of the sacrificial symposium as the precursors of institutionalized debate in India is Willard Johnson, *Poetry and Speculation of the Ṛg Veda* (Berkeley: University of California Press, 1980); see especially pp.61-63.

5. See Hsuan Tsang, *Buddhist Records of the Western World*, 2 vols., trans. by Samuel Beal (London: Kegan Paul, Trench, Trübner & Co., 1906), 1:217-21; Hwui Li, *The Life of Jiuen-Tsiang*, Trans. by Samuel Beal (London: Kegan Paul, Trench, Trübner & Co., 1914), 158-65, 176-81; and René Grousset, *In the Footsteps of the Buddha*, Trans. by J.A. Underwood (New York: Grossman, 1971), 196-203.

6. Sukumar Dutt, *Buddhist Monks and Monasteries of India* (London: Allen and Unwin, 1962), 267.

7. Kitsiri Malalgoda, *Buddhism in Sinhalese Society 1750-1900: A Study of Religious Revival and Change* (Berkeley: University of California Press, 1976), 60.

8. *Buddhist Records of the Western World*, 2:231-32, Where Hsuan Tsang describes the ruins of Buddhist monasteries and monuments, and the flourishing *deva* temples in the Cōḻa country (Malakūṭa). See also Grousset, *In the Footsteps of the Buddha*, 175.

9. See George W. Spencer, "The Politics of Plunder: The Cholas in Eleventh-Century Ceylon," *Journal of Asian Studies* 35/3 (May 1976), 405-419, esp. 407-408.

10. Recorded in the *Cūlavamsa*, ch.51. See Wilhelm Geiger (trans.), *Cūlavamsa* (Colombo: Ceylon Government Information Department, 1953), Part I, pp.150-151. For a sceptical view of the accuracy of the *Cūlavamsa's* account of this invasion, see K.A. Nilakanta Sastri, *The Pāndyan Kingdom: From the Earliest Times to the Sixteenth Century* (1929: reprinted, Madras: Swathi Publications, 1972) 62-64.

11. My translation based on the text as found in Cuvāmi Citpavaṉantar (ed. and commentator), *Tiruvācakam* (Tirupparāyturai: Śrīrāmakiruṣṇa Tapōvaṉam, 1970) 558. "Tillai's hall" refers to the sanctum of the Naṭarāja Temple in Chidambaram.

12. The major source for Campantar's biography is the twelfth-century *Periyapurāṇam* ("The Great Purāna"), sometimes called the *Tirurttontar Purāṇam*, by Cēkkiḻār. This is the principal hagiographical text of Tamil Śaivism and recounts the life stories of 63 leading devotees called Nāyaṉārs - "masters").

The following account of Campantar's encounter with Buddhists is based on this text. A modern edition of Cēkkiḻār's work used here is Pa. Irāmanāta Pillai (ed. and commentator), *Tiruttoṇṭar Mākkatai* (Madras: South India Saiva Siddhanta Works Publishing Society, 1970) 353-561 for Campantar's biography. There are also English and German summaries of the text: J.M. Nallaswami Pillai, *St. Sekkiḻar's Periyapuraṇam* (Madras: Rajan, 1955); Suddhananda Bharati, *The Grand Epic of Śaivism* (Madras: South India Saiva Siddhanta Works Publishing Society, 1970); and Schomerus, *Śivaitische Heilegenlegenden*.

13. K.A. Nilakanta Sastri, "An Episode in the History of Buddhism in South India," *B.C. Law Volume, Part 1*, ed. by D.R. Bhandarkar et al. (Calcutta: Indian Research Institute, 1955), 43. This essay includes a good translation of thirty-one verses of the *Periyapurāṇm* describing Campantar and the Buddhists, and I have, for the most part, relied on it here.

14. The only reference to this particular incident in Campantar's debate with the Buddhists which is prior to Cēkkiḻār is found in the *Ālutaiya Piḷḷaiyār Tiruttokai*, a brief poem (65 lines) in praise of Campantar by Nampi Āntār Nampi, a well-known Tamil Śaiva poet who probably lived about the end of the tenth century. Lines 39-40 state that Campantar "recited an accomplished song [*vittakap pāṭal*] which caused the Buddhist's head to tumble onto the ground." Here it is Campantar himself who sings the portentous song. For the text, see *Patiṉōrān Tirumuṟai* (Śrīvaikuntam: Śrī Kumarakuruparaṉ Caṅkam, 1973), p.487. Also Nilakanta Sastri's discussion in ibid, 41.

15. Nilakanta Sastri also noted that the analogical reasoning employed is similar to that found in the Milindapañha; ibid., 47-49.

16. My translation of verse 11 of *Campantar Tēvāram patikam* 173 as found in Catāciva Cettiyār (ed), *Tēvārap Patikaṅkaḷ*, 2nd ed., 2 vols. (Madras: South India Saiva Siddhanta Works Publishign Society, 1973), 1:286.

17. My translation of *patikam* 366 in ibid., 614-15.

18. The following verse from the Tamil Śaiva Siddhānta philosophical tradition is a good example of the way in which the Vedas are cited by Tamil Śaivism. The verse is found in John H. Piet, *A Logical Presentation of the Śaiva Siddhānta Philosophy* (Madras: Christian Literature Society for India, 1952), 14: "The *Veda* is the cow; its milk the true *Āgama*; the Tamil sung by the Four [i.e., Appar, Campantar, Cuntarar, and Māṇikkavācakar] is the ghee extracted from it; and the virtue of the Tamil work, full of wisdom (bodha) of Meykantār of the celebrated (city of) Vennai is the fine taste of the ghee [i.e., the *Civañāṉapōtam* by the thirteenth-century Siddhānta philosopher Meykantār]."

19. *Tiruttoṇṭar Mākkatai* 659-62.

20. K.A. Nilakanta Sastri, *A History of South India from Prehistoric Times to the Fall of Vijayanagar*, 3rd ed. (Madras: Oxford University Press, 1966), 144-45.

21. Ibid.

22. K.A. Nilakanta Sastri, "Buddhism in the Tamil Country," *The March of India* 8/124 (November 1956), 52. See also K.A. Nilakanta Sastri, the *Cōḷas*, 2nd ed. (Madras: University of Madras, 1955), 101-102.

23. Nilakanta Sastri, *History of South India*, 144.

24. Kamil Zvelebil, *The Smile of Murugan: On Tamil Literature of South India* (Leiden: E.J. Brill, 1973), 197.

25. See *Akanāṉūṟu* 98:19; 114:2; 182:17; 242:11; *Puṟanāṉūṟu* 362:22; *Kuṟuntokai* 53:8; 318:3; and *Tirumurukāṟṟuppaṭai* 223, as cited in K. Kailasapathy, *Tamil Heroic Poetry* (Oxford: Clarendon Press, 1968), 64. For additional references, see N. Subrahmaniam, *Pre-Pallavan Tamil Index* (Madras: University of Madras, 1966), 785-86.

26. See George L. Hart III, *The Poems of Ancient Tamil: Their Milieu and Their Sanskrit Counterparts* (Berkeley: University of California Press, 1975), 29, for references to *Puṟanāṉūṟu* 22; 129; and *Kuṟuntokai* 105; 366.

27. For example, the possession and frenzied dance of a Maṟavar woman in canto 12 and the possession of Tēvantikai by the god Pācaṉtaṉ in the 30th canto.

28. For example, see Louis Dumont, *Une sous-cast de l'Inde du sud: Organization sociale et religion des Pramalai Kallar* (Paris: Mouton, 1957), 350-52; Clarence Maloney, "Religious Beliefs and Social Hierarchy in Tamil Nāḍu, India," *American Ethnologist* 2/1 (February 1975), 188; and moving outside the Tamil speaking areas of South India, see Edward B. Harper, "Shamanism in South India," *Southwestern Journal of Anthropology* 13 (1957), 265-89; and E. Kathleen Gough, "Cults of the Dead among the Nāyars," *Traditional India: Structure and Change*, ed. by Milton Singer (Philadelphia: American Folklore Society, 1959), 243.

29. Hart *Poems of Ancient Tamil*, 29.

30. Louis Dumont "World Renunciation in Indian Religions," *Religion/Politic and History in India: Collected Papers in Indian Sociology* (Pairs: Mouton, 1970), 57.

31. On the significance in the Hindu tradition of sacred presence manifested at specific places, see the insightful essay by Kees W. Bolle, "Speaking of a Place," in *Myths and Symbols: Studies in Honor of Mircea Eliade*, ed. by Joseph M. Kitagawa and Charles H. Long (Chicago: University of Chicago Press, 1969), 127-39. On the localization of the sacred in Tamil Śaivism, see George Spencer, "Sacred Geography of the Tamil Shaivite Hymns," *Numen* 17 (December 1970), 232-244; and David Dean Shulman, *Tamil Temple Myths: Sacrifice and Divine Marriage in the South Indian Śaiva Tradition* (Princeton: Princeton University Press, 1980), 40-89.

32. Zvelebil, *Smile of Murugan*, 198-99.

33. Hart, *Poems of Ancient Tamil*, 25.

34. Ibid., 65-80, 191-96.

35. Ibid., 81-137, esp. 86-119. See also Hart's article "Women and the Sacred in Ancient Tamilnad," *Journal of Asian Studies* 32 (1973), 233-50.

36. With regard to this point, see my article, "The Goddess in a Tamil Śaiva Devotional Text, Māṇikkavācakar's *"Tiruvācakam,"* *Journal of the American Academy of Religion*, 45/1 supplment (March 1977), 369-90.

37. See Shulman, *Tamil Temple Myths*, passim.

NOTES TO A. RAWLINSON "THE ORIGIN OF MAHAYANA"

1. A. Bareau, *Les Sectes Bouddhiques du Petit Véhicule* (Saigon: École Française d'Extrême-Orient, 1955), esp. appendix III.

2. E. Lamotte, *Histoire du Bouddhisme Indien* (Louvain: Biblithèque du Muséon 43, 1958), 689-95.

3. E. Conze, *Buddhist Thought in India* (London: Allen & Unwin, 1962), 195-98.

4. Additional support for this view comes from A. and H. Wayman, *The Lion's Roar of Queen Śrīmālā* (New York & London: Columbia University Press, 1974), 1-3, who argue that this text arose from within the Mahāsamghikas.

5. Bareau, *Les Sectes Bouddhiques*, 58-59, thesis 6,7,8.

6. Ibid., 57, thesis 1. The *lokottara* theme is common to many of the sub-schools of the Mahāsamghikas (ibid., 76) - in fact, all the main tenets of the Lokottaravādins (ibid., 76-77) are also found among the parent Mahāsamghikas (ibid., 58-61). The exact significance of this is impossible to assess since none of Bareau's sources (Vasumitra, Bhavya, Vinītadeva, Paramārtha, Hsuan-tsang, Tāranātha) agree as to which school (out of the Mahāsamghikas, Ekavyāvahārikas, Lokottaravādins and Gokulikas) teaches what their relationship to each other is, or even whether they all exist (ibid., 75-77).

7. Ibid., 81-86.

8. *The Prajñāpāramitā Literature* ('S-Gravenhage, Holland: Mouton, 1960), 12.

9. If only because we need *some* explanation of why ch. 21 of the Saddharmapundarīka is entitled *dhāranī-parivarta*.

10. See M. de Mallmann, *Introduction à l'étude d'Avalokiteśvara* (Paris: Press Universitaires de France, 1948) 86-95. Cf. E. Conze's review, reprinted in his *Further Buddhist Studies* (Oxford: Cassirer, 1975), 150-54.

11. See the list (Les Incomposés) given in Bareau, *Les Sectes Bouddhistes*, 285-86

12. At A i 16 and A vii 177 (all references are to Mitra's ed.), see *prajñapti* in E. Conze, *Materials for a Dictionary of the Prajñāpāramitā Literature* (Tokyo: Suzuki Research Foundation, 1973).

13. Bareau, *Les Sectes Bouddhistes*, 72 thesis 78.

14. Ibid., 79.

15. The two terms are common in the *Laṅkāvatāra* (see D.T. Suzuki, *An Index to the Laṅkāvatāra Sutra* (Kyoto: The Sanskrit Buddhist Texts Publishing Society, 1934); [reprinted by the Suzuki Research Foundation, n.d. for reference], and are seminal to the *Tathāgatagarbha* texts (e.g., Śrīmālādevīsimhanāda and Ratnagotravibhāga).

16. See P.S. Jaini, "The Sautrāntika Theory of *Bīja*," *Bulletin of the School of Oriental and African Studies*, 22 (1959), 236-49.

17. Thesis 18 (Bareau, 61): "*Les Sectes Bouddhistes*, "Quand les Bodhisativa entrent dans une matrice (*garbha*), ils ne reçoivent pas les formes embryonnaires...comme leur *svabhava*." Thesis 29 (Ibid., 64): "Les Srotāpanna peuvent comprendre la *svabhāva* de leur pensée (*citta*) et de leur choses mentales (*caitta dharma*)." Thesis 43 (Ibid., 67) [among the nine *asamskrta-dharma*]: *pratītyasamutpādāṅgasvabhāva* and *mārgāṅgasvabhāva*. Thesis 71 (ibid., 71): "La causalité (*paccayatā*) est determinée (*vavatthitā*)." In fact, the term *śūnya* occurs only once, as a synonym of *anātmya* (thesis 23, ibid., 62) - a purely non-Mahayana sense. There is no evidence whatever that the Mahāsamghikas held any version of the *śūnyatāvāda*. (Conze's references in *Buddhist Thought in India*, 198, are completely misleading - they are all to

later sub-schools of the Mahāsaṃghikas.) On the contrary, they seem to have held a sort of *lokottaradharmasvabhāvavāda*.

18. Bareau, *Les Sectes Bouddhistes*, 79.

19. This is even true of the famous *daśabhūmika* section of the Mahāvastu (pp.53-157 of vol.1 of Senart's ed.). The connection between these ten *bhūmis* and the ten *bhūmis* of the later Mahāyāna is so tenuous as to be worthless as evidence of Mahāsaṃghika influence (see Lamotte, *Histoire du Bouddhisme Indien*, 695).

20. The ascription of a *Bodhisattva-piṭaka* to the Bahuśrutīyas - and also to the Dharmaguptakas - is a sticky point, but personally I do not find the evidence (Bareau, *Les Sectes Bouddhistes*, 296-97) convincing:

(1) Paramārtha (6th century), Hsuan-tsang (7th century) and Harivarman (3rd century) do not agree with one another as to the composition of the Mahāsaṃghika canon.

(2) The existence of the *Bodhisattva-piṭaka* of the Bahuśrutīyas is based *soley* on the following chain of reasoning:

(a) the Śatyasiddhiśāstra makes this claim;
(b) it was written by Harivarman;
(c) it is a work of the Bahuśrutīyas (according to Paramartha).

This is very tenuous evidence, to put it mildly.

(3) Both Paramārtha and Hsuan-tsang are much too late for their assertions to be any more than pious traditionalism.

In other words, the argument that the Bodhisattva ideal emerged from the Mahāsaṃghikas is based on evidence that will support only a much weaker conclusion: namely that the Mahāsaṃghikas contained elements in their teaching that are sympathetic to the influence of the Mahāyāna (in the same way as a minor chord is sympathetic to a major chord).

No one, as far as I am aware, has ever suggested that the Bodhisattva ideal is *derived* from the Sarvāstivādins, even though the Abhidharmakośa (5th century) contains a very detailed account of the *Bodhisattva-caryā*. And the reason is clear: there is no obvious sympathy between Sarvāstivādin soteriology and that of the Mahāyāna. Hence the *Bodhisattva-caryā* portions of the Abhidharmakośa are either part of the common tradition of the Bodhisattva that we find in the Jātaka/Avadāna literature (of all schools), or they are themselves the result of the influence of the Mahāyāna on the Sarvāstivādins, and not the other way round. I suggest that the evidence for the influence of the Mahāsaṃghikas on the Mahāyāna is no stronger than that for the influence of the Sarvāstivādins, and should be interpreted in the same way; i.e. it is an element in the Mahāyāna but not the source of it.

To emphasize this point it is worth remembering that we have no way of explaining how it is that the earliest Mahāyāna sutras are evidently quite at home with such Bodhisattvas as Mañjuśrī and Avalokiteśvara, whose very existence and names cannot be found in any traditional Buddhist school, Mahāsaṃghika or otherwise.

Such considerations lead me to the conclusion that the whole Bodhisattva ideal (in the specific Mahāyāna sense of [a] all beings are potentially Buddhas, and [b] there are innumerable Bodhisattvas working for the benefit of all beings) is of independent origin, i.e., it was based on a quite distinct experience of the Dharma (and the Buddha) that was then dovetailed into traditional Buddhism - and thereby transformed it - by Buddhists who had to find *something* to hand their experience on. Their starting point was Śākyamuni as a Bodhisattva but they very quickly moved beyond this into a new dimension, where the Bodhisattva stands for a means of transformation that is so devastating as to be revolutionary. I see nothing in the Mahāsaṃghikas that can account for this departure (apart from their obvious openness to innovation, but this is not a sufficient explanation in itself).

21. E.g., A i 5-8.

22. E.g., ch.2, v.33.

23. *Les Sectes Bouddhistes*, 299. Even Buddhaghosa (5th century) and the Vibhāṣā (3rd century) are silent. As Bareau admits, this is odd, since on the whole the Hinayanists were very concerned to refute false views. It is sometimes claimed (e.g., by Lamotte, no less, *Histoire du Bouddhisme Indien*, 590), that the Mahayana *is* referred to by Buddhaghosa in his commentary on Kathāvatthu 17.6 and 18.1 under the name of the Vetulyas, also known as the Mahāsuññavādins (though one edition has the v.r. Mahāpuññavādins); the terms *Vetulyavāda* and *Vedalja-piṭaka* are also found in three late Theravādin texts (see *The Dictionary of Pali Proper Names* under *Vetullavāda* for reference) in which nothing is made clear except that the authors disapprove of them. I fail to see how any conclusion whatever can be drawn from these fragmentary assertions. Moreover, the supposed connection between the terms *vetulla/vetulya/vaitulya* on the one hand, and *vepulla/vepulya/vaipulya* on the other, which would then connect the Vetullavādins and the *vaipulya-sūtras* of the Mahayana, is extremely suspect. I have discussed this problem in Appendix II of my thesis, "Studies in the Lotus Sutra," 2 vols. (University of Lancaster, 1972). Bareau's own answer to this silence on behalf of the Hinayana school is simply that neither the Sarvāstivādins nor the Theravādins knew of the Mahayana because it arose around the second century A.C. far away from Kashmir and Sri Lanka. Indeed, there is little else he could say. By contrast, our view is that the Mahayana was a pan-Buddhist inspirational movement that swept through the continent like wild-fire. It did not consider itself to be a school and was, in turn, not regarded as one by the Hinayanists - they therefore ignored it (insofar as they bothered to find out about it in the first place).

24. A. Rawlinson, "The Position of the Aṣṭasāhasrikāprajñāpāramitā in the Development of Early Mahayana," in L. Lancaster (ed.) *Prajñāpāramitā and Related Systems (Studies in Honor of Edward Conze)* (Berkely: Berkeley Buddhist Studies Series, 1977) 3-34.

25. Evidence: (1) Chs. 1-9 of the Saddharmapuṇḍarīka never refer to writing the sutra, though they frequently mention the merit that follows from reciting it, chanting it, and holding it in mind. From Ch. 10 onwards, however, writing *is* mentioned (along with reciting, chanting, and holding in mind); (2) Chs. 30 and 31 of the Aṣṭasāhasrikāprajñāpāramitā (the *avadāna* of Sadāprarudita) is very similar to ch. 22 of the Saddharmapuṇḍarīka and ch. 33 of the Samādhirāja (see Rawlinson, "Position," 6, for details). This is best explained as three separate adaptations of a single *avadāna* - and such adaptations are to be expected in oral transmission; (3) the Kashgar and Nepalese mss. of the Saddharmapuṇḍarīka sometimes contain differences that

cannot be easily explained by scribal errors or emendations. Two verses from ch. 8 will illustrate this:

Nepalese (Kern-Nanjio ed.)

v. 37 Saṃtarpayitvāna ca bhojanena
anekamūlyaṃ ratanaṃ sa dadyāt
baddhvo 'ttarīye vasanānti granthiṃ
dattvā ca tasyeha bhaveta tuṣṭaḥ
v. 38 so cāpi prakrāntu bhaveta bālo
utthāya so 'nyaṃ nagaraṃ vrajeta
so kṛcchraprāptaḥ kṛpano gaveṣī
āhāra paryeṣati khidyamānaḥ

Kashgar (Toda transliteration)
(folio 202a -202b)

saṃtarpayitvāna ca bhojanena
anarghamūlyaṃ ratano 'sya dadyāt
bandhitva ca antarime nivāsane
granthīni kṛtvā ca bhaveta tuṣnīm
sa cāpi prakrrānta bhaveta bāla
utthāya so nagara vrrajeya anyam
sa Kṛcchrapprapto kṛpano vrrajeta
āhāravastrāṇi paryeṣmānaḥ

The most striking differences are: (1) the last two lines of v. 37, which are simply different ways of saying the same thing (as one would expect in oral transmission); (2) the last two lines of v. 38, which diverge very considerably judged by the normal standards of variations in mss., and must, in my view, represent slightly different recensions of the same story.

26. Evidence: (1) References to "my secret (rahas) that the Bodhisattvas should hold in mind (dhārayantu)" (Saddharmapundarīka, ch. 2, v. 139, of Kern-Nanjio ed. = v. 40 in Wogihara-Tsuchida ed.); and to "hidden/mysterious/ esoteric speech" (saṃdhābhāṣya [28.10 of Kern-Nanjio ed.] or saṃdhāvacana [ch. 2, vv. 143 and 144 of Kern-Nanjio ed. = vv. 144 and 145 of Wogihara-Tsuchida ed.]). The meaning of this phrase, and how it relates to the concept of upāya, is discussed at length in my thesis (cited in n.23 above), esp. n. 221; (2) Vv. 137ff of ch. 3 of the Saddharmapundarīka say that the highest truth (paramārtha; perhaps "real meaning") should only be taught to those who have seen many Buddhas, planted innumerable good roots (kuśala[-mūla]), have a firm resolve (dṛḍhādhyāśaya), are full of vigour (vīryavanta), with a mind that is constantly suffused with friendliness (sadā maitrīcitta), who have given away (utsṛṣṭa; possibly: "abandoned attachment to") their body (kāya) and life (jīvita), whose morality (śīla) is flawless like a gem, who are endowed with pity (kṛpā) for all living beings, who are searching for all-knowledge ...etc., etc. This is the classic "minimal" description of the Bodhisattva, and though that term is not used in these verses (though "sons of the Buddha" is), it seems obvious to me that we are dealing with a special group (not unlike "those who are called to the Spirit," as the Pentecostalists say).

27. This really follows necessarily from the fact that transmission of the new Dharma was both oral and secret. But additional evidence is the existence of self-contained parables, avadānas and dharmaparyāyas, in the early Mahayana sutras; (see Rawlinson, "Positions," 3-7). Independent works like this could only exist in such profusion if there were a relatively large number of groups amongst whom they circulated.

28. I have made a somewhat sketchy attempt to show this in my thesis (cited in n.23 above), paras. 1095ff. Also relevant here are pp.19-21 of my Conze Festschrift article (cited in n.24 above), in which I try to explain the occurrence of various concepts in the early sutras as the result of cross-

fertilization, so to speak, from the different strands that made up the Mahayana.

29. L. Lancaster, "An Analysis of the Aṣṭasāhasrikāprajñāpāramitā from the Chinese Translation," Ph.D thesis (Wisconsin: 1968), 36-57. The main tenets of the thesis are summarized in L. Lancaster, "The Oldest Mahayana Sutra: Its Significance for the Study of Buddhist Development," *The Eastern Buddhist*, 8/1 (May 1975) 30-41.

30. See my thesis, paras. 425-53; summarized in my Conze Festschrift article p.8. The crucial passage is ch. 2, vv. 1-17, of which vv. 1-7 (in śloka) expressly contradict vv. 8-17 (in Triṣṭubh).

31. Bareau, *Les Sectes Bouddhistes*, 49-50; Rawlinson, "Position," 18.

32. This very useful term, which I have not found in any Sanskrit text, was suggested to me by A. Hirakawa, "The Rise of Mahayana and its Relation to the Worship of Stupas." *Memoirs of the Research Department of the Toyo Bunko* 22:57-106. The term occurs on p.85, and Hirakawa gives references to the second-century Chinese translation of the Ugradattaparipṛcchāsūtra (Taisho 12, no.322, p.20a; no.323, p.28a; Taisho 11 no.310, p.477c).

33. I have discussed these three dimensions in a slightly different context in "The Ambiguity of the Buddha-nature Concept in India and China," in L. Lancaster and W. Lai (eds.), *Early Ch'an in China and Tibet* (Berkeley: 1979).

34. E.g., "Homage to you, the infinite" (p.62 of Wayman's translation of the Śrīmālādevīsimhanādasūtra, cited above n.4).

35. E.g., "Le Śūraṃgamasamādhi est tellement immense (apramāṇa) qu'il révèle la toute puissance miraculeuse du Buddha et que d'innombrables êtres en retirent avantage" (E. Lamotte, *La Concentration de la Marche Heroique* [Śūraṃgamasamādhisūtra] [Brussels: Institut Belge des Hautes Études Chinois, 1965], 140).

36. E.g., "This perfection of wisdom, Subhuti, is a great perfection, unlimited (apramāṇa), measureless (aparimāṇa), infinite (ananta)" (E. Conze, *The Perfection of Wisdom in Eight Thousand Lines and Its Verse Summary* [Bolinas, CA: Four Seasons Foundation, 1973], 100, =p.45 of Mitra's ed.).

37. E.g., 132.11 of the Kern-Nanjio ed., where the Buddha says that there is only the *ekayāna*, the *buddhayāna*. But the reading *buddhayāna* is supported by only three Nepalese mss; another three have *mahāyāna*, which is also supported by the Gilgit ms. (Ga folio 50b = 61.29 of S. Watanabe, *Saddharmapuṇḍarīka Manuscripts Found in Gilgit* [Tokyo: The Reiyukai, 1975], pt.2). But *buddhayāna* is supported by the Kashgar ms. (folio 132a). (There is a gap in the Gilgit ms. Gb. here; and this second half of ch. 5 is omitted in Kumarajiva, so we have no reading from him either.) Similarly, Kern-Nanjio 82.10 has *mahāyāna* (supported by both Gilgit fragments: Ga 33b [=34.11 of Watanabe] and Gb 27b [=210.25 of Watanabe]), where the Kashgar ms. has *buddhayāna* (90a), which is supported by Kumarajiva (13c17 of the Taisho ed.).

38. Mitra's ed., p.319

39. Mitra's ed., p.23

40. See the clichés collected at the end of Lamotte's translations of the Śūraṃgamasamādhisūtra (cited in n.35 above) and the Vimalakīrtinirdeśa (Louvain: Bibliothèque du Muséon 51, 1962); the passages noted by Lamotte, *Histoire du Bouddhisme Indien* (cited in n.2 above), 650-52; the concepts and

passages noted by Conze, *Buddhist Thought in India* (cited in n.3 above), 196-221.

NOTES TO J. STRONG "FILIAL PIETY AND BUDDHISM"

1. Jean Przyluski, "Les rites d'Avalambana," *Mélanges Chinois et Bouddhiques* 1 (1931-32), 221.

2. See e.g., D.R. Shastri, *Origin and Development of the Ritual of Ancestor Worship in India* (Calcutta: 1963), i.

3. E.W. Hopkins, *Religions of India* (reprinted, New Delhi: 1977), 57; G. Bühler, (trans.), *The Law of Manu*, in *Sacred Books of the East*, 25 (reprinted, New Delhi: 1975): 57.

4. A.L. Basham, *The Wonder That Was India* (New York: 1954), 156; J. Gonda, *Les religions de l'Inde* (Paris: 1962), 1:164-68.

5. On all of these, see Kenneth Ch'en *The Chinese Transformation of Buddhism* (Princeton: 1973), ch. 2. See also P. Pelliot, "Meou-tseu ou les doutes levés," *T'oung-pao* 19 (1920), 255-433; Arthur Wright, "Fu I and the Rejection of Buddhism," *Journal of the History of Ideas* 12 (1951), 31-47; Galen Sargent, "Tchou-hi contre le Bouddhisme," *Mélanges publiés par l'Institut des Hautes Etudes Chinoises* (Paris: 1957) 1:1-158.

6. T.W. and C.A.F. Rhys Davids, *Dialogues of the Buddha*, Part 3, *Sacred Books of the Buddhists*, 4 (London: 1921): 180.

7. The introduction to the sermon itself makes this clear: the Buddha comes across Sigāla early in the morning as he is engaging in Brahmanical devotions enjoined on him by his father and tells him he is not carrying them out properly. There then follows the sermon preaching the Buddhist way of doing devotions which includes the injunction to worship one's parents in the manner described.

8. Ch'en, *Transformation*, 19.

9. This Vinaya rule was often pointed at to show that the monastic life was not against the parents' wills. See Erik Zürcher, *The Buddhist Conquest of China* (Leiden: 1972), 283.

10. E.B. Cowell and W.H.D. Rouse (Trans.), *The Jātaka Stories* (reprinted, London: 1957), 6:39. The *Sāma* (Skt. *Śyāma*) *jātaka* may be found in its Sanskrit version in J.J. Jones, (trans.), The *Mahāvastu* (London: 1952), 2:199ff. For one of the several Chinese versions, see Edouard Chavannes, *Cinq cents contes et apologues extraits du Tripitaka Chinois* (Paris: 1910), 1:156ff.

11. Cowell, 39.
12. Ibid.
13. Ibid.
14. Ibid.
15. Ibid., 40-50.
16. Ibid., 51.
17. Ibid., 2:34; 4:257; 5:164ff; 4:58-61. The last of these is the *Mātuposaka-jātaka*, not to be confused with the Mātuposaka-*sutta*, nor with the popular story of the bodhisattva swimming with his mother on his back which is often depicted in Sinhalese temples and called the *Mātuposaka Jātaka*. See

Richard Gombrich, "Feminine Elements in Sinhalese Buddhism," *Wiener Zeitschrift für die Kunde Südasiens* 16 (1972), 82, n.8.

18. Begging to maintain one's father and mother was an acceptable practice for Brahmanical ascetics and questers. See Bühler, *Manu*, 430.

19. The Mātuposaka sutta of the *Samyutta Nikāya*. See C.A.F. Rhys Davids (trans.), *The Book of Kindred Sayings*, 1. (Pali Text Translation Series, 7; reprinted, London: 1971). 230ff. For a discussion of the sutta, see Léon Feer, "Maitrakanyaka-Mittavindaka - La Piété filiale," *Journal Asiatique* 11 (1878), 388.

20. Rhys Davids, *Kindred Sayings*, 230.

21 Ibid.

22. John Marshall, *A Guide to Sānchī* (reprinted, New Delhi: 1955), 81.

23. James Legge (trans.), *A Record of Buddhistic Kingdoms* (New York: 1965), 106.

24. Visited by Hsüan-tsang. See Thomas Watters, *On Yuan Chwang's Travels in India* (reprinted, Delhi: 1961), 1:217.

25. Sylvain Lévi (ed.), *Mahākarmavibhanga (La grande classification des actes)* (Paris: 1932), 127-28.

26. Ch'en, *Transformation*, 20.

27. Chavannes, 4:113.

28. Ch'en, *Transformation*, 23.

29. Ibid.

30. Ibid., 18.

31. Ibid., 45.

32. Ibid., 29.

33. See e.g., S. Beal (trans.), *The Fo-Sho-Hing-Tsan-King*, Sacred Books of the Buddhists, 19 (reprinted, Delhi: 1975), 218ff.

34. Ch'en, *Transformation*, 44. For a similar sutra, the *Fo-shuo fu-mu en-chung ching* (Sutra on the importance of parental love), see ibid., 36ff., and Harold J. Isaacson, *The Throat of the Peacock* (New York: 1974), 11-24.

35. Ch'en *Transformation*, 44.

36. Ibid., 43.

37. The text specifies jewels, pearls, cat's eye, conch, crystal, coral, silver, gold, emeralds, sapphires, ruby, and right-turning shells.

38. P.L. Vaidya (ed.), *Divyāvadānam* (Buddhist Sanskrit Texts, 20; Darbhanga: 1959), 31-32.

39. Quite to the contrary, as the story progresses, it is *she* who offers a meal to both her son and the Buddha, and once she is converted, Mahā Maudgalyāyana, having fulfilled his filial duty, quickly returns to Jambudvīpa.

40. Ch'en, *Transformation*, 45.

41. Har Dayal, *The Bodhisattva Doctrine in Buddhist Sanskrit Literature* (reprinted, New Delhi: 1975), 54.

42. In this case, it should be noted, relief for the mother comes not in the form of food but in rebirth elsewhere in a better mode of life. However, in other practices in Chinese Buddhism, it was clearly thought possible to make direct offerings of food to the ghosts to alleviate their suffering.

43. See, for references, J.J.L. Duyvendak, "The Buddhistic Festival of the All-Souls in China and Japan," *Acta Orientalia 5* (1935), 82-107; Arthur Waley, *Ballads and Stories from Tunhuang* (London: 1960), 216-35.
44. The same word, it should be noted, is used for the rice offerings given to Buddhist monks.
45. Shastri, *Origin and Development*, 94ff. See also Lawrence A. Babb, *The Divine Hierarchy* (New York: 1975), 92.
46. Shastri, *Origin and Development*, 307; Gonda, *Les Religions*, 164.
47. On the parallelism between Buddhist peta and Hindu pitṛ, see Richard Gombrich, "Merit Transference in Sinhalese Buddhism," *History of Religions* II (1971), 208.
48. See, e.g., the Tirokudda Sutta of the *Khuddakapātha*, translated in G.P. Malalasekera, "Transference of Merit in Ceylonese Buddhism," *Philosophy East and West* 17 (1967), 87. See also E.W. Burlingame, (trans.), *Buddhist Legends (Dhammapada Commentary)*, 1, (Harvard Oriental Series, 28; reprinted, London: 1969), 103-104.
49. Malalasekera, "Transference...," 87; Gombrich, "Merit Transference," 211.
50. F.L. Woodward (trans.) *The Book of the Gradual Sayings*, 5. (Pali Text Society Translation Series, 27; reprinted, London, 1961) 180-81.
51. Ibid., 182.
52. In some versions of the story, she is reborn in the Avīci Hell, but this is often but one of her rebirths, which usually include the preta realm as well. See Ch'en *Transformation*, 28.
53. A more thoroughgoing resolution to this dilemma was to come with the notion of the transfer of merit; the offerings were to be made to the monks for the sake of the departed ancestors *wherever they might be*. It is in this light, perhaps, that we should consider the fully developed stories of Mu-lien in which his mother is portrayed as a hungry ghost, a denizen of hell, or even as a dog.
54. There does seem to be a different emphasis in the two countries, however, concerning the specific methods of support. In India, the stories focus on supporting one's parents by begging, i.e., essentially burning their lives towards the monastic mode. In China, the feature of begging is less stressed.
55. The same conclusion was reached by Glen Dudbridge in his interpretation of the figure of Miao-shan, who continues many of the filial themes we have seen in this paper. See Glen Dudbridge, *The Legend of Miao-shan* (London: 1978), 97.
56. Edwin O. Reischauer, *Ennin's Diary* (New York: 1955), 344.

NOTES TO C. HYERS "ONCE-BORN, TWICE-BORN ZEN"

1. William James, *The Varieties of Religious Experience* (New York: Longmans, Green, 1902), 79.
2. Shunryu Suzuki, *Zen Mind, Beginner's Mind* (New York: Weatherhill, 1970); Hakayu Taizan Maezumi and Bernard Tetsugen Glassman, *The Hazy Moon of Enlightenment* and *The Way of Everyday Life* (Los Angeles: Center Publications, 1978).

3. E.g., Francis Dojun Cook, *How to Raise an Ox: Zen Practice as Taught in Zen Master Dōgen's Shōbōgenzō* (Los Angeles: Center Publications, 1978); Reiho Masunaga, *A Primor of Sōtō Zen: A Translation of Dōgen's Shōbōgenzō Zuimonki* (Honolulu: East-West Center Press, 1971). Abe Masao has also been translating portions of the Shōbōgenzō in issues of *The Eastern Buddhist* over the past decade.

4. Suzuki, *Zen Mind*, 9.

5. Philip Yampolsky, *The Zen Master Hakuin: Selected Writings* (New York: Columbia University Press, 1971), 116.

6. Ibid., 118.

7. Ibid.

8. Winston and Jocelyn King (trans.), "The Fourth Letter from Hakuin's *Orategama*," *The Eastern Buddhist*, n.s., 5/1 (May 1972), 95.

9. Yampolsky, *Zen Master*, 143.

10. James, *Varieties*, 142.

11. Yampolsky, *Zen Master*, 122.

12. Ibid., 65 (my emphasis).

13. Ibid., 31-32.

14. James, *Varieties*, 165.

15. Ibid., 89.

16. Ibid., 99.

17. Ibid., 78.

18. Hee-jin Kim, *Dōgen Kigen, Mystical Realist* (Tucson: University of Arizona Press, 1975), 87. Biographical material on Dōgen has been taken largely from Kim, whose work also contains an excellent philosophical analysis.

19. Abe Masao, "Dōgen on Buddha Nature," *The Eastern Buddhist*, n.s., 4/1 (May 1971), 39.

20. Abe Masao and Norman Waddell (trans.), "Dōgen's *Bendōwa*," *The Eastern Buddhist*, n.s., 4/1 (May 1971), 128.

21. King, "Fourth Letter", 86.

22. Christmas Humphrey, *Buddhism* (London: Penguin Books, 1951), 184.

23. Alan W. Watts, *The Way of Zen* (New York: Pantheon Books, 1957), 155.

24. Charles Luk, *Ch'an and Zen Teaching*, 2 (London: Rider, 1961): 114.

NOTES TO L.S. KAUFMAN "RELIGIOUS CONTENT IN JAPANESE ART"

1. For complete illustrations of the paintings, see *Nihon emakimono zenshū*, Tanaka Ichimatsu, general editor, vol. 10, *Ippen Hijiri-e*, Miya Tsugio, editor (Tokyo: Kadokawa shoten, 1960).

2. Controversy surrounds the question of the identity of Hōgen En'i. Scholarly opinion is divided as to whether Hōgen En'i was the same person as the En'i who, as a high priest of Onjōji, was active in court ceremonies in the early fourteenth century. For a review of the issue, see Miya Tsugio, "Ippen Hijiri-e to En'i," *Bijutsu Kenkyū*, 244 (Jan. 1959), 163-78; and in English, Laura S. Kaufman, "*Ippen Hijiri-e*: Artistic and Literary Source in Buddhist Handscroll Painting of Thirteenth-century Japan," Ph.D. dissertation (New York University, 1980), 283-325.

3. For a survey of the Pure Land founders' biographies, see Terukazu Akiyama, "New Buddhist Sects and *Emakimono* (Handscroll Painting) in the Kamakura Period," *Acta Asiatica* 20 (1971), 58-76.

4. This translation from the *Ippen Hijiri-e* and those that follow are based upon the transcription of the text in *Nihon emakimono zenshū*, 10:64-82. For the Shakadō episode, see p.72.

5. On the *Ippen Shōnin Ekotoba Den*, see *Nihon emakimono zenshū*, vol. 23, *Yūgyō Shōnin Engi-e*, Miya Tsugio, editor (Tokyo: Kadokawa shoten, 1968).

6. *Nihon emakimono zenshū*, 10:66.

7. Ibid., 69.

8. The most important works in the poetic manner, the screen paintings that decorated the houses of the courtiers, have all been lost. For the remaining evidence of this tradition, see Saburō Ienaga, *Painting in the Yamato Style*, trans. by John M. Shields, Heibonsha Survey of Japanese art, 10 (New York and Tokyo: Heibonsha, 1973), 37-93; 104-107.

9. *Nihon emakimono zenshū*, vol. 11, *Saigyō Monogatari Emaki, Taima Mandara Engi*, Shirahata Yoshi, editor (Tokyo: Kadokawa shoten, 1958), 44.

10. *Nihon emakimono zenshū*, 10:69.

11. Asayama Enshō, *Ippen Hijiri-e: Rokujō Engi* (Tokyo: Sankibō busshorin, 1940), 176, n.98. For the version of Saigyō's poem cited here, see Watanabe Tamotsu, *Saigyō Sankashū zenchūkai* (Tokyo: Fūkan shobō, 1971), 633-34.

12. The practice of composing Buddhist verse in the vernacular may be traced to India. For example, the Mahāsiddhas, the yogis of early vajrayā Buddhism, such as the great Saraha, wrote *dohās* or songs. The tradition was transplanted to Tibet, producing most notably the *Mila Grubum*, the Hundred Thousand Songs of Milarepa (1052-1135). In China, the Fifth Patriarch of the Ch'an sect, Hung-jen (601-675), challenged his disciples to express their understanding with a poem, and on this basis selected as his successor Hui-neng, who had hitherto worked in the monastery kitchen.

13. *Togano-o Myōe Shōnin Ikun*, as translated in Hajime Nakamura, *Ways of Thinking of Eastern Peoples: India, China, Tibet, Japan*, Philip P. Weiner, editor (rev. ed., Honolulu: East-West Center Press, 1964), 553-54.

14. Ippen stated his teachings on renunciation with particular clarity in his letter to Bishop Kyōgan, recorded in the *Ippen Shōnin Goroku*. See Shizutoshi Sugihira, "The Teaching of Ippen Shōnin," *Eastern Buddhist* 6 (1934), 287-88.

15. *Nihon emakimono zenshū*, 10:64.

16. Ibid., 77.

17. See the survey of all the sites represented in the scrolls in Kaufman, "*Ippen Hijiri-e*," 23-124.

NOTES TO F. STRENG "THREE RELIGIOUS ONTOLOGICAL CLAIMS"

1. *Systematic Theology*, 1 (Chicago: University of Chicago Press, 1952), 191, 189.

2. Ibid., 188.

3. Ibid., 179.

4. Ibid., 191.

5. Ibid., 189.

6. Ibid., 190.
7. Ibid., 191.
8. Ibid., 202.
9. *What is Religion?* edited by J.L. Adams (New York: Haper & Row, 1961), 56-57.
10. Ibid., 57.
11. Ibid., 59.
12. Ibid., 64.
13. Chün-i T'ang, "Cosmologies in Ancient Chinese Philosophy," *Chinese Studies in Philosophy* 5/1 (Fall 1973), 17.
14. Ibid.
15. Ibid., 12.
16. Ibid., 16.
17. Ibid., 17.
18. Ibid., 24.
19. Ibid., 22.
20. Ibid., 22-23.
21. Chün-i T'ang, "Religious Beliefs and Modern Chinese Culture, Part II: The Religious Spirit of Confucianism," *Chinese Studies in Philosophy* 5/1 (Fall 1973), 56.
22. Ibid., 51.
23. Ibid., 56.
24. "The Standpoint of Śūyatā," trans. by Jan van Bragt, *Eastern Buddhist*, n.s., 6/2 (October 1973), 66.
25. Ibid., 64.
26. See K. Nishitani, "Nihilism and Śūnyatā," trans. by Yamamoto Seisaku, *Eastern Buddhist*, n.s., 4/2 (October 1971), 30-49; 5/1 (May 1972), 55-69; 5/2 (October 1972), 95-106. For another useful examination of negativity in certain Buddhist and Western formulations see Masao Abe, "Non-being and *Mu*: The Metaphysical Nature of Negativity in the East and West," *Religious Studies* 11/2 (June 1975), 181-92.
27. "The Standpoint of Śūnyatā," 66.
28. Ibid., 67.
29. Ibid.
30. Ibid., 68.
31. Keiji Nishitani, "What Is Religion?" in *Philosophical Studies of Japan*, 2 (Tokyo: Japan Society for the Promotion of Science, 1960), 35.
32. Ibid., 24.
33. Ibid., 25.

NOTES TO M. LATTKE "DIE BEDEUTUNG DER APOKYPHEN SALOMO-ODEN"

1. Hennecke/Schneemelcher II 575f. - Der volle Titel des Sammelwerkes: E. Hennecke, *Neutestamentliche Apokryphen in deutscher Übersetzung*. 3., völlig neubearbeitete Auflage herausgegeben von W. Schneemelcher. I. Band: Evangelien, II. Band: Apostolisches, Apokalypsen und Verwandtes. Tübingen 1959 (I), 1964 (II). 4. Auflage 1968 (I), 1971 (II).
2. Hennecke/Schneemelcher II 576-625.

3. Bilderbibeln und andere künstlerische Darstellungen zeigen, dass nicht nur die kirchlich anerkannten Schriften (vor)gelesen wurden, sodern dass auch die romanhafte und oft viel buntere "apokryphe" Literatur sich bleibender Beliebtheit erfreuen konnte.

4. Hennecke/Schneemelcher I 18-26.
5. Hennecke/Schneemelcher I 26-31.
6. Hennecke/Schneemelcher I 4.
7. Vgl. ein SNTS-paper von K.M. Fischer.
8. M. Lattke, Die Oden Salomos in *ihrer Bedeutung für Neues Testament und Gnosis*. Fribourg Suisse/Göttingen 1979ff. Band I: Ausführliche Handschriftenbeschreibung, Edition mit deutscher Parallel-Übersetzung, Hermeneutischer Anhang zur gnostischen Interpretation der Oden Salomos in der Pistis Sophia, 1979 (= Orbis Biblicus et orientalis 25/1), Band Ia: Der Syrische Text der Edition in Estrangela, Faksimile des griechischen Papyrus Bodmer XI, 1980 (=OBO 25/1a), Band II: Vollständige Wortkonkordanz zur handschriftlichen, griechischen, koptischen, lateinischen und syrischen Überlieferung der Oden Salomos, Mit einem Faksimile des Kodex N, 1979 (=OBO 25/2).
9. OBO 25/1 207-225.
10. W. Bauer in Hennecke/Schneemelcher II 577, dort weitere Literatur.
11. Ein jüdisch-christliches Psalmbuch aus dem ersten Jahr-hundert. (The Odes...of Solomon, now first published from the Syriac version by J.R. Harris, 1909). Aus dem Syrischen übersetzt von J. Flemming. Bearbeitet und herausgegeben von A. Harnack, (Leipzig: [=Texte und Untersuchungen 35,4] 1910), S.111.
12. C.H. Kraeling, The Odes of Solomon and their Significance for the New Testament, in *LCR* 46 (1927) 226-41, hier 227.
13. J.H. Charlesworth/R.A, Culpepper, The Odes of Solomon and the Gospel of John, in *CBQ* 35 (1973) 298-322, hier 298. Dort weitere Literatur, auch von J.H. Charlesworth selbst, der seine Edition hinzuzufügen ist: The Odes of Solomon edited with translation and notes, (Oxford: 1973).
14. H. Jordan, Geschichte der altchristlichen Literatur, 1911, S.455.
15. Hennecke/Schneemelcher I 20.
16. R.P. Martin, Carmen Christi, Phillippians II.5-11 in *Recent Interpretation* and in *the Setting of Early Christian Worship*, (Cambridge: 1967), S.7.
17. J. Kroll, *Die christliche Hymnodik bis zu Klemens von Alexandreia*, 2., überprüfte Auflage, (Darmstadt: 1968), S.36.
18. G. Schille, *Frühchristliche Hymnen*, (Berlin: 1965), S.9
19. Charlesworth/Culpepper (s.o. Anm. 13), 320.
20. W.G. Kümmel, *Einleitung in das Neue Testament*, (Heidelberg: 1973) u.ö., S.183.
21. A.a.O., S.189.
22. J.R. Harris, The Odes and Psalms of Solomon, now first published from the Syriac version, (Cambridge: 1909, vgl. die 2nd. ed. 1911), S.13.
23. Auswahlsweise nenne ich hier: J.H. Bernard, The Descent into Hades and Christian Baptism (A study of 1 Peter III. 19ff.) in: The Expositor 42 (1916, 8th Ser. No.64) 241-74. - W. Bieder, *Die Vorstellung von der Höllenfahrt Jesu Christi*, (Zürich: 1949) (=AThANT 19), bes. S.172-82. - W.K.L. Clarke, The First Epistle of St. Peter and the Odes of Solomon, in: *JThS* 15

(1913/14), 47-52. - K. Gschwind, *Die Niederfahrt Christi in die Unterwelt. Ein Beitrag zur Exegese des Neuen Testaments und zur Geschichte des Taufsymbols*, (Münster i.W: 1911) (=Ntl. Abh. II Band, 3/5. Heft). - J. Menard, Le "descensus ad inferos", in: *Festschrift G. Widengren* (1972) 269-306. - Bo Réicke, *The Disobedient Spirits and Christian Baptism. A Study of 1 Pet. III. 19 and Its Context*, (København: 1946).

Wie man sieht, ist die Untersuchung dieses Themas eng verbunden mit der Frage nach der Bedeutung der Taufe. Auf den Zusammenhang zwischen der Taufliturgie und den Oden Salomos kann hier nicht näher eingegangen werden, nur soviel: die Oden primör oder gar ausschliesslich mit der Taufe als ihrem soziologischen Sitz im Leben der Frühkirche zu verknüpfen, scheint mir viel zu eng.

24. R. Abramowski, Der Christus der Salomooden, in: *ZNW* 35 (1936) 44-69. - R. Bultmann, Die Bedeutung der neuerschlossenen madäischen und manichäischen Quellen für das Verständnis des Johannesevangeliums, in: *ZNW* 24 (1925) 100-46, wieder abgedruckt in: Exegetica (1967) 55-104. - Charlesworth/Culpepper (s.o. Anm. 12). - P. Kleinert, Zur religionsgeschichtlichen Stellung der Oden Salomos, in: *ThStK* 84 (1911) 569ß611. - E. Massaux, *Influence de l'évangile de saint Matthieu sur la littérature chrétienne avant saint Irénée*, (Louvain: 1950), bes. S.205ß227. - F. Spitta, Die Oden Salomos und das Neue Testament, in: *MPTh* 7 (1910), 91-100. - R.H. Strachan, The Newly Discovered Odes of Solomon, and their Bearing on the Problem of the Fourth Gospel, in: *The Exp. Times* 22 (1910) 7-14.

25. Die Frage der Originalsprache der Oden Salomos ist bis heute ungeklärt und kontrovers. Wenn man aber - wie für das Johannesevangelium, vgl. M. Lattke, *Einheit im Wort*, (München: 1975), S.4 - als Entstehungsort das zweisprachige Gebiet der Provinz Syria annehmen kann, dann relativiert sich das Problem der Ursprache.

26. M. Lattke (s.o. Anm. 25), 227.

27. Vgl. dazu U. Wilckens, *Weisheit und Torheit. Eine exegetisch-religionsgeschichtliche Untersuchung zu I, Kor. 1 und 2*, (Tübingen: 1959) (=BHTh 26), bes. S.135-39.

28. W. Bauer in: Hennecke/Schmeemelcher II 601, Anm.7.

29. Zum Problem des Kanons vgl. E. Käsemann (Hg.), *Das Neue Testament als Kanon. Dokumentation und Kritische Analyse zur gegenwärtigen Diskussion*, (Göttingen: 1970).

30. Zu dieser Teildisziplin der Alten Kirchengeschichte vgl. vor allem B. Altaner/A. Stuiber, Patrologie. Leben, Schriften und Lehre der Kirchenväter, 8., durchgesehene und erweiterte Auflage, Freiburg u.a. 1978.

31. Zu Begriff und Sache vgl. H. Köster/J.M. Robinson, Entwicklungslinien durch die Welt des frühen Christentums, Tübingen 1971 (übersetzt aus dem Amerikanischen).

32. Zur Geschichte des Urchristentums vgl. das 1980 erschienene de Gruyter Lehrbuch von H. Köster, das hier allerdings nicht mehr berücksichtigt werden konnte.

33. Zum Problem dieser Tatsache vgl. N. Brox (Hg.), Pseudepigraphie in der heidnischen und jüdisch-christlichen Antike, Darmstadt 1977 (=Were der Forschung, Band 484).

34. Ph. Vielhauer, *Geschichte der urchristlichen Literatur. Einleitung in das Neue Testament, die Apokryphen und die Apostolischen Väter,* (Berlin/New York: 1975) (=de Gruyter Lehrbuch). Hier findet sich öfter der wichtige Hinweis darauf, dass im 2. Jahrhundert (was für das 3. Jh. auch noch gilt) Kanonische und nicht-kanonische christliche Literatur unbedenklich nebeneinander zitiert wurde.

NOTES TO W. TYLOCH "L'IMPORTANCE DU 'ROULEAU DE TEMPLE'"

1. Voir R. de Vaux, *L'archéologie et les manuscrits de la Mer Morte*, (Londres: 1961), et aussi *Archaeology and the Dead Sea Scrolls*, (Londres: 1973), surtout pp.121-26.

2. Voir entre autres F.M. Cross Jr., "The Development of the Early Jewish Scripts", dans: G.R. Wright (éd.), *The Bible and the Ancient Near East. Essays in Honour of William Foxwell Albright*, (Londres: 1961), pp.133-202.

3. Voir entre autres, dans C. Rabin et Y. Yadin, *Aspects of the Dead Sea Scrolls* (col. "Scripta Hierosolymitan," 4 - Jérusalem² 1965), les articles de C. Rabin, "The Historical Background of the Qumrân Hebrew," pp.144-61, et de Z. Ben-Hayyim, "Traditons in the Hebrew Language, with special Reference to the Dead Sea Scrolls", pp.200-14. Voir aussi E.Y. Kutscher, *The Language and Linguistic Background of the Isaiah Scroll*, (Jérusalem: 1959), pp.1-70 (en hébreu).

4. Flavius Josèphe, *La Guerre Juive* II, VIII, 2. Texte grec dans l'éedition des oeuvres de Flavius Josèphe publiée par B. Niese, vol. VI (Berlin: 1895).

5. Flavius Josèphe, *Antiquités judaïques* XVIII, I, 6 (B. Niese, vol. III, Berlin: 1892).

6. Voir *Talmud yerushalmi, Sanhedrin* 29a; *Mishna, Rosh Hashshanah* II, 1; *Talmud babli, Shabbat* 116a; *Tosephta, Sanhedrin* 13,5. Voir aussi Hégésippe, cité par Eusèbe, *Historia ecclesiastica* 4,22,7; Epiphane, *Adversus Haeresses* I, 1,10 (Migne, *Patrologia Graeca* XLI, 232-233).

7. *Mĕgillôth gĕnûzôth*, (Jérusalem: 1948).

8. *Aperçus préliminaires sur les manuscrits de la Mer Morte*, (Paris: 1950)

9. *Quod omnis probus liber sit*, paragraphes 75-91 (texte grec des oeuvres de Philon publiées par C. Cohn et S. Reiter, *Philonis Alexandrini opera quae supersunt*, vol. VI, (Berlin: 1915). pp.21-26; *Apologia pro Judaeis* (vol. VI, pp.46-71); *Apologia pro Judaeis*, dans Eusèbe, *Preparatio evangelica* VIII, XI, 1-22 édité par K. Mayoff, *Eusebius Werke*, vol. VIII, p.2 (Berlin: 1954).

10. *Antiquités judaïques* XIII, V, 9; XVIII, I, 2-6; *La Guerre Juive*, II, VIII, 2-13; *La Vie*, paragraphes 7-12, (édité par B. Niese).

11. *Historia naturalis* V, 17,13 (édité par K. Mayoff, Teubner).

12. *Philosophoumena* (=*Refutatio omnium haeresium*) IX, 18-29 (édité par P. Wendland, *Hippolyt*, vol. III, Leipzig: 1916, pp.255-64 - GCS, vol XXVI).

13. Par example R. North, "The Qumrân Saducesse": *The Catholic Biblical Quarterly* 17 (1955) 164-88; A.M. Haberman, *Mĕgillôth Midbar Yehuda*, (Jérusalem: 1959), pp.25-30 (en hébreu).

14. Par example S. Lieberman, "The Discipline in the So-called Dead Sea Manuel of Discipline": *The Journal of Biblical Literature* 71 (1952) 199-206; C. Rabin, *Qumrân Studies*, (Oxford: 1952), pp.199-206.

15. Par example C. Roth, *The Historical Background of the Dead Sea Scrolls*, (Tel Aviv: 1958); G.M. Livshitz, *Kumranskije rukopisy i ikh istoritsheskiye znatsheniye*, (Minsk: 1969); G.K. Driver, *The Judean Scrolls*, (Oxford: 1965).

16. Voir surtout E. Dabrowski, *Odkrycia nad Morzem Martwye a Nowy Testament*, (Varsovie: 1960); J.D. Amousine, *Rukoposy Miertvogo Moria*, (Moscou: 1960).

17. C'était l'hypothèse de S. Zeitlin, et aussi de P.R. Weis, "The Date of the Habakkuk Scroll": *The Jewish Quarterly Review* 41 (1950), 125-54.

18. Voir H. del Medico, *Le mythe des Esséniens*, (Paris: 1958).

19. W. Tyloch, *Apekty spoleczne gminy z Qumrân*, (Varsovie: 1968).

20. Voir 1QS VI, 3,6: Flavius Josèphe, *La Guerre Juive* II, VIII, 9,13; Hippolyte, *Philosophoumena* (cité note 12) IX, 25; CDCXIII, 2-3.

21. 1QS V, 8; VI, 14-23; CDC XV, 5-10; Flavius Josèphe, *La Guerre Juive* II, VIII, 7,10.

22. Hippolyte, *Philosophoumena* (cité note 12) IX, 23. Voir A. Dupont-Sommer, *Nouveaux aperçus sur les manuscrits de la Mer Morte*, (Paris: 1963), pp.123-26, et *Les écrits esséniens découvert près de la Mer Morte*, (Paris: ³1964), p.43.

23. Philon, *Quod omnis probu liber sit* (cité note 9), paragraphe 81; Flavius Josèphe, *La Guerre Juive* II, VIII, 5; Hippolyte, *Philosophoumena* (cité note 12) IX, 25; 1QS VI, 8-13; VII, 10-15.

24. Voir Flavius Josèphe, *La Guerre Juive* II, VIII, 9; Hippolyte, *Philosophoumena* (cité note 12) IX, 25; R. de Vaux, "Une hachette essénienne": *Vetus Testamentu* 7 (1957), 399-407.

25. Flavius Josèphe, *La Guerre Juive* II, VIII, 6; Philon, *Quodomnis probus liber sit* (cité note 9), paragraphes 81-82; Hippolyte, *Philosophoumena* (cité note 12) IX, 22; 1QS VI, 6-8.

26. 1QS VI, 24 à VII, 26; Flavius Josèphe, *La Guerre Juive* II, VIII, 8-9; Hippolyte, *Philosophoumena* (cité note 12) IX, 24-26.

27. "The Temple Scroll": *The Biblical Archaeologist* 30 (1967) 135-139, et *Comptes rendus de l'Académie des Inscriptions et Belles-Lettres* 8/12 (1967) 607-617, ainsi que "The Temple Scroll", dans: D.N. Freedman et J.C. Greenfield, *New Directions in Biblical Archaeology*, (Garden City (N.Y.): 1971) pp.156-166.

28. *The Temple Scroll. Hebrew Edition*, edited by Yigael Yadin (Jérusalem: 1977). vol. I: *Introduction*, 308; vol. II: *Text and Commentary*, 323; vol. III: *Plates and Text*, p.8, pl.82 et p.7, *Supplementary Plates*, pl.40.

29. Voir Y. Yadin (cité note 28), vol. I, pp.10-15.

30. Voir N. Avigad, "The Paleography of the Dead Sea Scroll", dans: C. Rabin et Y. Yadin, *Aspects of the Dead Sea Scrolls* (col. "Scripta Hierosolymitana", 4), (Jérusalem: 1958), pp.56-87; F.M. Cross Jr., "The Development..." (cité note 2), pp.131 ss.

31. Voir Y. Yadin (cité note 28), vol. I, p.295.

32. Voir Y. Yadin (cité note 28), vol. I, pp.61 ss.

33. Voir les articles d'A. Jaubert, "Le calendrier des Jubilés et la Secte de Qumrân: *Vetus Testamentum* 3 (1953) 250-264, "Le calendrier des Jubilés et les jours liturgiques de la semaine": *Vetus Testamentum* 7 (1957) 35-61, et "Aperçus sur le calendrier de Qumrân", dans: J. van der Ploeg, *La secte de Qumrân et les origines du christianisme*, (Paris/Bruges: 1959), pp.113-120. Voir aussi S. Talmon, "The Calendar Reckoning of the Sect from the Judean Desert", dans: C. Rabin et Y. Yadin (cité note 3), pp.162-199.

34. Y. Yadin (cité note 28), vol. I, pp.69-72 et 231-232. Les chiffres entre parenthèses indiquent les versets dans les solonnes du rouleau, d'après la reconstitution de Yadin.

35. Sous l'expression "à partir du lendemain du sabbat" (Lv 23,15) qui formait la base du calcul de toutes les fêtes, on comprenait à Qumrân le premier jour de la semaine, c'est-à-dire le dimanche, et non le jour après le premier jour de la fête de Pâques, comme on le fait dans le judaïsme orthodoxe. A Qumrân on commençait le calcul des fêtes au 26ème jour du premier mois (voir D. Barthélémy, "Notes en marge de publications récentes sur les manuscrits de Qumrân": *Revue Biblique* 59 [1952] 187-218, surtout pp.200 ss.), puisqu'on comptait le cinquantième jour à partir du premier dimanche après la fête des Azymes, et non à partir du premier dimanche qui tombait au milieu de la fête (voir S. Talmon [cité note 33], p.174).

36. Selon le calendrier de Qumrân, la communauté essénienne célébrait la Fête de la Nouvelle Huile le dimanche, 22ème jour du sixième mois.

37. Le terme hébreu $hîn$ désigne la mesure pour des matières liquides: environ 6.5 à 7.5 litres. Donc, toutes les tribus devaient offrir au total six setiers (hînîm) d'huile, c'est-à-dire entre 39 et 45 litres.

38 Voir Exode 29,40.

39. En hébreu: $h\bar{a}$-$^c\hat{o}l\bar{a}(h)$ $bikkûrîm$. $lipnê$ $Yahvé$.

40. En hébreu: $^c iśśarôn$, mot désignant un dixième de $epa(h)$ (environ 4 litres), mesure de capacité pour les matières sèches.

41. En hébreu: $b^e l\hat{u}l\bar{a}(h)$. Voir Nombres 15,9.

42. Voir Lévitique 1,17.

43. Voir Exode 27,20.

44. Voir Deutéronome 15,20.

45. D'après le fragment concernant la Fête du Nouveau Vin (co. XXi, 4), on peut supposer que pendant cette fête, les membres de la communauté mangeaient des olives. Voir Y. Yadin (cité note 28), vol. II, p.73.

46. Flavius Josèphe, *La Guerre Juive* II, VIII, 3 (paragraphe 123).

47. Voir Y. Yadin (cité note 28) Vol.II p.73, et aussi vol. I, p.305.

48. Voir Y. Yadin (cité note 28), vol. I, p.92.

NOTE TO M. SMITH "TERMINOLOGICAL BOOBYTRAPS"

1. Johannes Hempel in *Die althebräische Literatur und ihr hellenistisch-jüdisches Nachleben*, (Wildpark-Potsdam: 1930), at least saw the problem and in his title promised to deal with it. However, the fifteen pages (180-194) he gave to the period from Nehemiah's retirement to the completion of the Gospels do little more than list some of the works he should have studied.

NOTES TO J.H. CORBETT "THE FOSTER CHILD"

1. Josephus, *Jewish War* 2. 120/1 (adoption among the Essenes); Augustine, *The Good of Marriage* 10, *The Good of Widowhood* 9-11, 23-28 (procreation to be left to the pagans).

2. Tacitus, *History* 5:5; "it was a crime among them [the Jews] to kill any newly-born infant" - clear evidence, for Tacitus, of the anti-social desire of the Jews to be different.

3. For evidence and discussion see F.W. Albright, *Yahweh and the Gods of Canaan* (London: 1968), 204ff.; R.de Vaux, *Studies in Old Testament Sacrifice* (Cardiff: 1964), ch. 3, cf. D. Harden, *The Phoenicians* (Pelican ed., 1971), 94-95; and for social implications of sexuality in the ancient world see J. Pitt-Rivers, *The Fate of Shechem* (Cambridge: 1977), ch. 7.

4. For evidence and discussion see W.W. Tarn and G.T. Griffith, *Hellenistic Civilization* 3rd ed. (Meridian ed., 1961), 100-102; P.A. Brunt, *Italian Manpower 225 B.C. - A.D. 14* (Oxford: 1971) esp. 148-54; S.B. Pomeroy, *Goddesses, Whores, Wives and Slaves: Women in Classical Antiquity* (London: 1976), esp. 164, 228. The older studies are useful, for the most part, only as a guide to the evidence: G. Glotz and G. Humber, s.v. "Expositio," in *Dictionnaire*, ed. by Daremberg and Saglio, 2/1 (Paris: 1892): 930-39; E. Weiss, s.v. "Kinderaussetzung," in *Real-Encyclopädie der Classischen Altertumswissenschaft* 11/1 (1921), 463-72.

5. E.A. Wrigley, *Population and History* (New York: 1969), ch. 4, esp. 125-26; cf. M. Harris, *Cannibals and Kings: The Origins of Culture* (New York: 1977), Index, s.v. "Infanticide."

6. For a concise yet thorough review of the evidence concerning *alumni* see H. Leclercq, s.v. "Alumni," in *Dictionnaire d'Archéologie Chrétienne*, ed. by F. Cabrol, 1/1 (Paris: 1907): 1288-1306. P. Allard, *Les esclaves chrétiens*, 5th ed. (Paris: 1914), 34ff., covers much of the same ground; his account is marred by some inaccuracy and, more seriously, by his strong bias against "pagan" practice.

7. For the text of the *Code of Gortyna* see *Inscriptiones Creticae*, vol. 4, *Tituli Gortyni*, ed. by M. Guarducci (Rome: 1950): 126-42; for the interpretation of this fascinating document see R.F. Willetts, *Aristocratic Society in Ancient Grete* (London: 1955).

8. Slavery must have been the fate of many foundlings; see *Oxyrhynchus Papyri*, vol. 1 (London: 1898), ed. by B.P. Grenfell and A.S. Hunt, nos. 37,38 for evidence of a male foundling picked up from the gutter and probably destined to be reared as a slave. But many foundlings were probably trained to trades, whether slave or free; see *Code of Justinian* 8,51,1. (A.D. 224) for sums spent *ad discendum artificium*.

9. For the jurists' definition of *alumnus* see Paulus, *Sent.* 5,6,16, and Ulpian in the *Digest* 20,1,8; cf. 29,5,1, 10 where the *alumnus* is contrasted with *concubina* and *filii naturales*; cf. *Digest* 45,1,132pr.; 40,2,13,14; Gaius 1.19; *Institutes* 1,6,5, where the *alumnus* is contrasted with *filius* and *cognatus*.

10. For the interpretation of these letters and references to the major modern studies see A.N. Sherwin-White, *The Letter of Pliny: A Historical and Social Commentary* (Oxford: 1966), 650ff. Essential for the legal background

is E. Volterra, "L'efficacia delle costituzioni imperiali emanate per le provincie a l'istituto dell'espostio," in *Studi....Besta* (Milan: 1939), 449-77. The Roman requirement that the cost of maintenance be repaid as a pre-condition of the return of a foster-child to natural father or master is most clearly stated in Pseudo-Quintilian, *Orations* 278 (p.132 in Ritter ed., Leipzig: 1884); *accipere illum* [i.e., *expositum*] *nisi solutis alimentis non potuisti.*

11. For the texts of the documents concerning Petronia Iusta see G.P. Caratelli, "Tabulae Herculanenses II," *Parola del Passato* 3 (1948), 165-84. Most important for the interpretation of these unique documents are V. Arrangio-Ruiz in *Parola del Passato* 3 (1948)), 129ff., and 6 (1951) 116ff.; A. Piganiolin, *Studi in onore di V.E. Paoli* (Florence: [1956]), 563ff.

12. For the epigraphic evidence relating to foster-children in the Greek East see T.G. Nani, *"Threptos,"* *Epigraphica* 5 (1943), 45-84; for the Latin west see E. De Ruggiero, *Dizionario Epigrafico di Antichità Romane*, 1 (Rome: 1895): 437-40, s.v. "alumnus"; cf. G.N. Olcott, *Thesaurus Linguae Epigraphicae*, 1 (rome: 1904), 261-64 s.v. "Alumna," and 264-68 s.v. "Alumnus."

13. For the experience of secularization in the modern world as viewed by a sociologist see P.L. Berger *The Sacred Canopy* (New York: 1969), esp. ch.5. Mary Douglas has argued convincingly that secularization is not simply a "modern trend attributable to the growth of cities or the prestige of science, or just to the breakdown of social forms." It is rather "an age old cosmological type, a product of a definable social experience, which need have nothing to do with urban life or modern science"; see M. Douglas *Natural Symbols* (Penguin ed., 1978), esp. 36ff.

14. For fears of pollution and their relationship to anxieties about group self-definition see M. Douglas, *Purity and Danger: An Analysis of Concepts of Pollution and Taboo* (London: 1966); for social images of the body and their relationship to social structure see Douglas, *Natural Symbols*.

15. See Ibid., esp. ch. 4, "Grid and Group."

16. For the concept of liminality see V. Turner *The Ritual Process: Structure and Anti-Structure* (Chicago: 1968), esp. ch. 3, "Liminality and Communitas"; Turner notes (107) that symbols of liminality "often relate to the physiological processes of death and birth," the implication being that these processes are widely conceived of as "liminal" in the extreme; cf. Turner Ibid., 125, for the structural inferior as moral and ritual superior (cf. Ibid., ch. 5, "Humility and Hierarchy: The Liminality of Status Elevation and Reversal"). For the association of Turner's work with the theories of Mary Douglas see Ibid., 109. Turner has developed his theory of liminality in great detail in a number of studies; it is conveniently summarized by him in the essay "Variations on a Theme of Liminality," in *Secular Ritual*, ed. by S.F. Moore and B.G. Myerhoff (Amsterdam: 1977).

17. The concept of rites de passage was adopted by Turner from the work of A. Van Gennep, *The Rites of Passage*, trans. by M.B. Vizedom and G.L. Caffee (London: 1960).

18. For the liminalty of shamans and initiates into ancient mystery cults see V. Turner, *Ritual Process*.

19. Athenagoras, *A Plea for the Christians* 35; Clement of Alexandria, *Instructor* 3.3; Tertullian, *To the Gentiles* 1.16 (cf. *Apology* 9); Lactantius,

Divine Instututes 5.9, 6.20; Origen, *Against Celsus* 8.55; *Epistle to Diognetus* 5.

20. For a convenient, if limited, review of the epigraphic evidence relating to fostering among Christians see H. Leclercq, s.v. "Alumnus," in *Dictionnaire d'Archéologie Chrétienne* 1.1 (Paris: 1907), 1288-1306.

21. See Ibid., 1296-98.

22. Cf. *Cod. Theod.* 5.10,1 of A.D. 329 and *Cod. Theod.* 5.9,1 of A.D. 331.

23. In 389 Ambrose deplored the fact that poor women were continuing to expose their children and the rich were continuing to practice abortion in Milan; see Ambrose, *Hexaemeron* 5,18 (cf. *De Nubuthe Jesraelita* 5,21-4); and Basil, *Hamil.* 6.4, directs his efforts against the sale of children at the same time.

24. It might appear that his malicious gossip consisted of speculation to the effect that exposed children really were the children of the "virgins" who took them up. This seems rather unlikely in view of the fact that the Canons are directed to regulating attempts to *reclaim* exposed infants, something which does not appear altogether consistent with gossip directed against holy "virgins"; but certainly is impossible in such a situation.

25. For the Canons of the councils of Vaison and Arles see J.D. Mansi, *Sacrorum Conciliorum Nova et Amplissima Collectio*, 6 (Florence: 1761): 451ff. for Vaison, and 7 (Florence: 1762): 875ff. for Arles.

26. In several pages of perceptive comments devoted to outlining the social basis of the strength of the "orthodox" church in Rome (by contrast to the "non-orthodox" churches with which he is so much concerned) Walter Bauer has stressed the importance of the church's commitment to the buying back of slaves and prisoners from bondage and prison, laying the foundations of the new social order by acts of "redemption" in the fullest sense; see W. Bauer, *Orthodoxy and Heresy in Earliest Christianity*, English trans. ed. by R.A. Kraft and G. Krodel (Philadelphia: 1971), esp. 122-23. Although Bauer does not mention *alumni*, I believe that foster children fit into the picture which he outlines; for they too had been "redeemed" - from death by exposure, as had prisoners and slaves from bondage.

27. See *Thesaurus Linguae Latinae*, 1 (Leipzig: 1900): 1793-99, s.v. "*alumnus (alumna)*".

28. See Leclercq (cited in no.20 above), 1299ff.

29. J.H. Corbett, "The Saint as Patron in the Work of Gregroy of Tours," *Journal of Medieval History* 7 (1981), 1-13.

30. For infanticide as a possible course of action see Gregory of Tours, *Miracles of St. Martin* 2.24.

31. For some indication of the evidence regarding Christian foster-children to be found in the later Roman law codes see Leclercq (cited in no.20 above), 1304ff. This evidence deserves further close study.

32. For a tentative analysis of those themes in the Gospel of Mark see now F. Kermode *The Genesis of Secrecy: On the Interpretation of Narrative* (Harvard University Press: 1979), esp. 129-36.

33. The Greek word *agapētos* used in the Gospels (e.g., Mark 1:11) and usually translated "Beloved (Son)" itself translates in the Septuagint the Hebrew word *yachid* which is used most frequently to describe children chosen for sacrifice (including Isaac). This deserves more careful investigation.

34. See P. Brown, *Relics and Social Status in the Age of Gregory of Tours: The Stenton Lecture 1976* (University of Reading: 1977).

NOTES TO J.J. BUCKLEY "MANI'S OPPOSITION TO THE ELCHASAITES"

1. Albert Henrichs and Ludvig Koenen, "Ein griechischer Mani-Codex," *Zeitschrift für Papzrologie und Epigraphik* (cited hereafter as *ZPE*) 5, (1970), 97-216.
2. Henrichs and Koenen, "Der Kölner Mani-Codex (P. Colon. inv. nr. 4780) *Peri tēs gennēs toy sōmatos ayoty*, Edition der Seiten 1-72," *ZPE* 19 (1975), 1-85; "Der Kölner Mani-Codex (P. Colon inv. nr. 4780) *Pari tēs gennēs toy sōmatos ayoty*, Edition der Seiten 72,8-99.9," *ZPE* 32 (1978), 87-199. The last, very fragmented part of the book remains to be edited and translated. An English edition and translation is also available: Ron Cameron and Arthur J. Dewey, *The Cologne Mani Codex: "Concerning the Origin of His Body"* (Text and Translation, 15, Early Christian Literature Series, 3: Missoula: Scholars Press, 1979). In the following, references to the text of the codex will be given to the English edition and translation, unless otherwise indicated. The codex will be referred to as *CMC*.
3. *ZPE* 5, (1970), 104f.; *ZPE* 32, (1978), 147, n.208.
4. Bayard Dodge, *The Fihrist of al-Nadim*, 2 (New York/London: Columbia University Press, 1970): 811. See also ref. in *ZPE* 5 (1970), 133-34.
5. A. Henrichs, "Mani and the Babylonian Baptists: A Historical Confrontation," *Harvard Studies in Classical Philology* 77 (1973), 23-59, deals only marginally with the issues raised in my paper. L. Koenen, "From Baptism to the Gnosis of Manichaeism," *Proceedings of the International Conference on Gnosticism at Yale 1978*, ed. by Bentley Layton (Leiden: Brill), is still in press at the moment of writing.
6. See Wilhelm Brandt, *Elchasai: Ein Religionsstifter und sein Werk* (Amsterdam: Philo Press, 1971; repr. of 1912 ed.) 7-8.
7. Ibid., 25,41. See also *New Testament Apocrypha 2*, ed. by Edgar Hennecke and Wilhelm Schneemelcher (Philadelphia: Westminster Press, 1964): 747, Johann C. Irmscher's introduction to his translation of the so-called *Book of Elchasai*; *ZPE* 32 (1978), 182-83, n.272.
8. *ZPE* 32 (1978), 170, n.243.
9. *CMC*, 72-73 (90, 11-15).
10. Ibid., 18-19 (17-18); see also *ZPE* 5 (1970), 119f.; *ZPE* 19 (1975), 77-78, n.40; excerpt from al-Nadim's *Fihrist*, in Alfred Adam, *Texte zum Manichäismus*, Kleine Texte für Vorlesungen und Übungen, 175 (2nd ed. Berlin: de Gruyter, 1969), 25; see also Henrichs, "Mani and the Babylonian Baptists," 32, n.34.
11. *CMC*, 64-65 (80,23-81,13). (Brackets and parentheses occuring in *CMC* quotations do not constitute my additions, but are given in Cameron and Dewey's translation of the text).
12. Ibid., 66-67 (82, 23-84,9).
13. Ibid., 74-75 (94,2-95,15).
14. Professor Helmut Koester (in a personal communication) has drawn attention to the interesting parallel between Jesus and Mani here. Both have predecessors who are water-baptizers.

15. *CMC*, 76-77 (96,6-17).

16. Ibid., 66-67 (84,9-85,12). The last expression of the quotation shows the awkwardly rendered Greek translation of Aramaic idioms, *bna* and *qm*: see *ZPE* 32 (1978), 149-50, n.215.

17. *ZPE* 32 (1978), 146-47, n.208, with ref. to *ZPE* 5 (1970), 137, n.102.

18. *CMC* 68-69 (86,17f.); *ZPE* 5 (1970), 142f.; *ZPE* 32 (1978), 160-61, n.225.

19. *ZPE* 5 (1970), 139-40; 140, n.113.

20. Ibid., 120-32; *ZPE* 32 (1978), 120-22, n.139; see also n.10 above.

21. See n.11 above.

22. See n.16 above.

23. Ibid.

24. Only the moon is made out of good water; see François Decret, *Aspects du Manicheisme dans L'Afrique Romain*, Etudes Augustiniennes (Paris: 1970), 227, n.3 (ref. to Augustine, *De Haer*. 46, PL 42:35).

25. J.P. Asmussen, *Manichaean Literature*, Persian Heritage Series, 22 (Delmar, New York: Scholars' Facsimiles and Reprints, 1975), 26.

26. Ibid.

27. The problem of the historical development of the Manichaean ecclestiastical organization will not concern me here, since that issue lies beyond the task at hand. Suffice it to say that the class-structure is mentioned early, both within and outside of the Manichaean corpus.

28. *CMC*, 28-29 (35,4-7).

29. Ibid. (32,8f.). L. Koenen, "Augustine and Manichaeism in Light of the Cologne Mani Codex." *Illinois Classical Studies* 3 (1978), 154-65, sees the Manichaean organization as *Corpus Manichaei* or *Corpus Christi* (pp.164-65). See also Cameron and Dewey's introduction to *CMC*, 2.

30. Pointed out by Arthur Vööbus, *History of Asceticism in the Syrian Orient, I: Origin of Asceticism. Early Monasticism in Persia* (Louvain: CSCO 1958), 135-36.

31. For Mani's indebtedness to Indian, particularly Buddhist, religious organizations, see, e.g., ibid., 166-69, and Geo Widengren, *Mani and Manichaeism* (New York: Holt Rinehart & Winston, 1965), 95-96.

32. As Henri-Charles Puech has it, "Der Begriff der Erlösung im Manichäismus," *Eranos Jahrbuch* 4 (Zürich/Rhein: 1936), 196.

33. Alexander Böhlig and Hans J. Polotsky (ed.), *Kephalaia 1,1* Manichäische Handchriften der Staatlichen Museen Berlin (Stuttgart: 1940), 191,16f.

34. Asmussen, *Manichaean Literature* 59, gives no specific reference, but see n.44 below.

35. This formula comes from Hegemonius, *Acta Archelai*, quoted and translated in Widengren, *Mani and Manichaeism*, 97.

36. Vööbus, *History*, 137, reference to Walter B. Henning, "Ein manichäisches Betund Beichtbuch," *APAW* (Berlin: 1936), 141.

37. See Asmussen, *Manichaean Literature*, 50, ref. to Augustine, *De Mor. Man.* 39; ibid., 15, ref. to Augustine, *Epist*. 236,2: Jaap Mansfeld and P.W. van der Horst, *Alexander of Lycopolis' Treatise "Critique of the Doctrine of Manichaeus*," (Leiden: Brill, 1974), 79.

38. Adam, *Texte*, 7. See also Prosper Alfaric, "Un manuscript manichéen," *Revue d'histoire et de littérature religieuses* 6 (n.s.), (1920), 62-98, p.67; *Kephalaia*, 220,27f.; L.J.R. Ort, "Mani's Conception of Gnosis," in *Le Origini dello Gnosticismo*, ed. by Ugo Bianchi, Colloquio di Messina 13-18 Aprile, 1966 (Leiden/Brill: 1967), 604-13, (p.611., ref. to Text M 8251, I, in W.B. Henning, "Ein manichäischos..." 308-11.)

39. *Kephalaia* 228,22-27.

40. Ibid., 229,16-230,20. See also Asmussen, *Manichaean Literature*, 34.

41. *Kephalaia*, 232,4 and 233,26-27.

42. P. Alfaric, *L'Évolution intellectuelle de Saint Augustine* (Paris: E. Nourry, 1918), 154. See also al-Nadim's comment in Dodge, *Fihrist*, 788.

43. Observed by Henrichs and Koenen, *ZPE* 5 (1970), 150-54; also, see pp.4-5 and n.13 and 14 above.

44. *CMC*, 78-79 (96,18-97,10).

45. Ibid., 70-71 (87,18-23; 89,14-18); 72-73 (90,1f.).

46. Ibid., 72-75 (91,22-93,2); see n.34 above.

47. Ibid., 74-75 (93,17-20).

48. see ibid., 78-79 (97,11-17).

49. Ibid., 72-73 (91,12-12).

50. Ibid., 74-75 (93,8-9).

51. Ibid., 78-79 (97,18-98,8).

52. Alfaric, *L'Évolution*, 152.

53. *CMC*, 12-13 (9,4-13); see also 72-73 (91,14-18).

54. For religious organization in Elchasaism, see e.g., *CMC* 70-71 (89,5-8).

NOTES TO J. HELGELAND "THE TRANSFORMATION OF CHRISTAINITY"

1. For a recent example of the application of sociological methods to the study of early Christianity see John Gager, *Kingdom and Community* (Englewood Cliffs, N.J.: 1975).

2. The category of time became predominant because of the mobility of the nomadic life of the ancient Israelites. See Yi-Fu Tuan, *Topophilia: A Study of Environmental Perception, Attitudes and Values* (Englewood Cliffs, N.J.: 1974), 146-49. Tuan makes an explicit connection between mobility and religious styles which approximate the categories of conversion and adherent religion. "Long-distance travel and migrations may in themselves have had an effect in breaking up cyclical time and the vertical cosmos, substituting for them linear time and horizontal space." "Sedentary peoples of the middle latitudes tend to accept the course of the seasons as an inexorable fact of nature: like the movement of the stars it is an apt image of eternity." (149).

3. A.D. Nock, *Conversion* (Oxford: 1933). Nock defines these terms in ch. 1, pp.1-6.

4. For example, Acts 6:14, 7:44, 7:48-50. These verses demonstrate that Stephen regarded the spatiality of the temple as idolatrous. In Gal. 4:8-10 Paul criticizes the spatiality and the cyclical pattern of time which revolves around sacred centers, navels of the universe, as Eliade would put it.

5. Ephesians 20.2.

6. Mary Douglas, *Purity and Danger: An Analysis of the Concepts of Pollution and Taboo* (London: 1966), definitely emphasizes spatial models in her analysis. For example, the concept of dirt arises from a spatial structure. When loam is in the field it is soil, but when it is on the living room rug it is dirt. The mind "creates" dirt and pollution by determining the proper places for things; there is no such thing as "absolute" dirt, for "where there is dirt there is system" (48). So whenever one refers to pollution and defilement, spatial categories are implicit. See also Douglas' article, "Pollution," *International Encyclopedia of the Social Sciences* 12 (London: 1968): 336-41.

7. This process can be observed in creating a spatial mental construct. See S. Stein, "The Dietary Laws in Rabbinic and Patristic Literature," *Studia Patristica* 2 (1957), 141-54. For a demonstration of how foods and animals fit into a conceptual spatial system see Edmund Leach, "Anthropological Aspects of Language: Animal Categories and Verbal Abuse," in *New Directions in the Study of Language*, ed. by Eric Lenneberg (Cambridge, Ma.: 1964), 23-63.

8. *Archaic Roman Religion*, trans. by Philip Krapp (Chicago: 1970), 1:18-32.

9. See the author's chapter "Roman Army Religion," in *Aufstieg und Niedergang der Römischen Welt*, II/16/2, ed. by W. Haase (Berlin/New York: 1978): 1473-78.

10. *Ecclesiastical History* 5.1.3-2.8.

11. Ibid., 5.1.62.

12. W.H.C. Frend, *Martyrdom and Persecution in the Early Church* (Garden City, N.Y.: 1967), 321. The fact that cemeteries had become an important issue is shown by Gallienus' specifically returning cemeteries to the Christian community; Eusabius, *Eccl. History* 7,13.3.

13. Herbert Musurillo, *The Acts of the Christian Martyrs* (Oxford: 1972), 175.

14. Ibid., 249.

15. Ibid., 183.

16. Ibid., 229.

17. Ibid., 29,35.

18. See n.9 above.

19. John M. McColloh, "The Cult of Relics in the Letters and 'Dialogs' of Pope Gregory the Great: A Lexicographical Study," *Traditio* 32 (1976), 145-84; see p.149.

20. *Dialogs* 2.38.

21. Helgeland "Roman Army Religion," 1488-95, 1500-1504.

22. Numa Denis Fustel de Coulanges, *The Ancient City*, trans. by Willard Small (Garden City, N.Y.: n.d.), 34-39.

23. Bede, *Ecclesiastical History of the English People* 2.4.

24. Ibid., 3.25.

25. Ibid. R.W. Southern, *Western Society and the Church in the Middle Ages* (Grand Rapids, MI: 1970), 30: "Even the pope, whatever theoretical claims were made for him, in practice owed most of his authority to the fact that he was the guardian of the body of St. Peter. This brought men to Rome and made them listen to the voice of St. Peter mediated through his representative on earth."

26. Bede, *Eccl. Hist.* 5.21.

27. Angelus Haussling, *Mönchskonvent und Eucharistiefeier: Liturgiewissenschaftliche Quellen und Forschungen.* Veröffentlichungen des Abt-Herwegen-Instituts Maria Laach, 58 (Münster: 1973) 69, 84-85, 223.

28. *Adversus Haereses* 3.3.2.

29. Cf. *The Scillitan Martyrs* and *The Acts of Perpetua and Felicitas*; see Musurillo, *Acts of the Christian Martyrs*, 86-89, 106-131.

30. Patrick J. Geary, *Furta Sacra: Thefts of Relics in the Central Middle Ages*, (Princeton, N.J.: 1978), 33.

31. For an example of how geography affects religious institutions see Peter Brown, "The Rise and Function of the Holy Man in Late Antiquity," *Journal of Roman Studies* 61 (1971), 80-101. He argues (83) that the difference in Syrian and Egyptian monasticism is related to the nature of the respective deserts: in Syria it is possible to live by oneself because the desert is not as severe a climate as in Egypt where monks were forced to live in communities.

BIBLIOGRAPHY FOR P. BOGLIONI "LE SOPRAVVIVENZE PAGANE NEL MEDIOEVO"

P. Audin, "Unexemple de survivance païenne à l'époque contemporaine: le culte des fontaines dans la France de l'ouest et du centre-ouest," in *Annales de Bretagne et des Pays de l'Ouest*, 86 (1979), p.83-107 (resoconto di tesi di terzo ciclo; prima parte).

L.J.-B Bérenger-Féraud, *Superstitions et survivances étudiées au point de vue de leur origine et de leurs tansformations*, (Parigi: 1895), 5 vol. in-8^0.

Wilhelm Boudriot, *Die altgermanische Religion in der amtlichen kirchlichen Literatur des Abendlandes* vom 5. bis 11. Jahrhundert (Bonn: 1928, ristampa Darmstadt: 1964), VIII p.79

Mourant Brock, *Rome: Pagan and Papal*, (Londra: 1883), XII-270 p.

Franco Cardini, *Magia, stregoneria, superstizioni nell'Occidente medievale*, (Firenze, 1979), 241 (bibl., p.103-141).

—— "La christianisation des pays entre Loire et Rhin, IVe-VIIe's.", in *Revue d'hist. de l'Eglise de France*, 62 (1976), p.5-526 (contributi vari).

Giuseppe Cocciara, *Storia del folklore in Europe*, (Torino: 1971, 1^a ed., 1952), 622.

—— "Paganitas. Sopravvivenze folkloriche del paganesimo siciliano", in *Atti del I Congr. internaz. di studi sulla Sicilia antica*. Kokalos, Studi pubblicati dall'Ist. di storia antica dell'Univ. di Palermo, X-XI (1964-1965), p.401-416 (ora in *Preistoria e folklore*, Palermo: 1978).

Stanley A. Cook, *The Study of Religions*, (Londra: 1914) pp.149-234; *Survivals and their significance*.

—— *La conversione al cristianesimo nell'Europa dell'Alto Medioevo*, (Spoleto: 1967), 865; (Settimane di studio, XIV) (contributi vari).

M. Crampon, *Le culte de l'arbre et de la forêt en Picardie. Essai sur le folklore picard*, (Amiens-Parigi: 1936) 584.

Carlo Ginzburg, *I Benandanti. Stregoneria e culti agrari tra Cinquecento e Seicento*, (Torino: 1966) 250.

Laurence George Gomme, *Folklore as an Historical Science*, (Londra: 1908), XVI-371.

Dieter Harmening, *Superstitio. Überlieferungs- und theoriegeschichtliche Untersuchungen zur kirchlich-theologischen Aberglaubensliteratur des Mittelalters*, (Berlin: 1979), 379; (bibl., p.340-364).

Woodburn Walter Hyde, *Greek Religion and its Survivals*, (New York: s.d.) (ristampa, 1963), IX-230.

Richard Kieckhefer, *European Witch Trials. Their Foundations in Popular and Learned Culture, 1300-1500*, (Londra: 1976), 176.

Gordon J. Laing, *Survivals of Roman Religion*, (New York: s.d., ristampa, 1963), XIV-257.

John Cuthbert Lawson, *Modern Greek Folklore and Ancient Greek Religion. A Study in Survivals*, (Cambridge: 1910, ristampa, New York: 1964), XXII-620.

Jacques Le Goff, "Culture cléricale et traditions folkloriques dans la civilisation mérovingienne", in *Annales. ESC*, 22 (1967), p.780-91 (tr. it. in *Tempo della Chiesa e tempo del mercante*, (Torino: 1977) 193-207).

Godfrey Charles Leland, *Etruscan Roman Remains in Popular Tradition*, (Londra: 1892), VIII-385.

Stephen McKenna, *Paganism and Pagan Survivals in Spain up to the Fall of the Visigothic Kingdom*, (Washington: 1938), X-165.

Raoul Manselli, *La religion populaire au moyen âge. Problèmes de méthode et d'histoire*, (Montréal/Parigi: 1975), 234.

R.R. Marett, *Psychology and Folklore*, (Londra: 1920), (p.120-142: The interpretation of survivals.)

Margaret A. Murray, *The Witch-Cult in Western Europe*, (Oxford: 1962; 1ª ed., 1921), 303.

Rudolf Neuwinger, *Die Herkunft des Christentums. Christliche Lehren, Sitten und Gebräuche in religionsgeschichtlicher Beleuchtung*, (Berlino: 1941), 247.

Pierre Saintyves, *En marge de la légende dorée. Songes, miracles et survivances. Essai sur la formation de quelques thèmes hagiographiques*, (Parigi: 1931), VIII-596.

Édouard Salin, *La civilisation mérovingienne d'après les sépultures, les textes et le laboratoire*. IV: *Les croyances* (Parigi: 1959), 580.

Jean-Claude Schmitt, *Le saint lévrier Guinefort, guérisseur d'enfants depuis le XIIIe's.*, (Parigi: 1979), 278.

Paul Sébillot, *Le Paganisme contemporain chez les peuples celto-latins*, (Parigi: 1908), XXVI-378.

Jean Seznec, *The Survival of Pagan Gods. The Mythological Tradition and its Place in Renaissance Humanism and Art*, (Princeton: 1972), XIV-376.

Ronald Sheridan - Anne Ross, *Grotesques and Gargoyles. Paganism in the Medieval Church*, (Newton Abbot: 1975), 127p. + ill.

G. Storms, *Anglo-Saxon Magic*, (L'Aja: 1948), IX-336.

Th. Trede, *Das Heidentum in der römischen Kirche. Bilder aus dem religiösen und sittlichen Leben Süditaliens*, 2 vols., (Gotha: 1889-1891).

Edward B. Taylor, *Primitive Culture. Researches into the Development of Mythology, Philosophy, Religion, Language, Art and Custom*, 2 vol., (Londra: 1920; 1ª ed., 1871).

Arthur Weigall, *The Paganism in our Christianity*, (Londra: s.d.), 253.

NOTES TO J. WORTLEY "ISRAEL AND BYZANTIUM"

1. Edward Gibbon, *The History of the Decline and Fall of the Roman Empire*, ch. 32.

2. See Alexander Schmemann, "The 'Orthodox World,' Past and Present," and other essays in his *Church, World, Mission: Reflections on Orthodoxy in the West*, (Crestwood, N.Y.: 1979).

3. Gibbon, loc. cit.

4. It is in the apocalyptical literature of the Eastern Empire that one encounters the full extent of the Byzantine sense of destiny, a destiny at once glorious and tragic, since this last great world empire must inevitably pass away. See John Wortley, "The Literature of Catastrophe," *Byzantine Studies/Etudes Byzantines* 4 (1977), 1-17.

Peter Richardson, *Israel in the Apostolic Church*, (Cambridge: 1969). esp. p.ix, noting Justin Martyr, *Dialogue with Trypho*.

6. Constantine Manasses' *Synopsis Istorikē* (*CSHB*, 29; *PG*, 127), written in the 1080s, and a very influential work in the popular or "vulgar" chronicle-tradition, certainly succeeds in creating this impression.

7. See especially Paul J. Alexander, "The Strength of Empire and Capital as Seen through Byzantine eyes," *Speculum* 37 (1962), 346ff.

8. *Le Typicon de la Grande Eglise*, ed. by Juan Mateos, 2 vols. (Rome: 1962, 1963), 1:5.

9. The growing popularity of Old Testament heroes can be traced in the *synaxaria* of the tenth through thirteenth centuries. See *Synaxarium Ecclesiae Constantinopolitanae*, ed. by Hippolyte Delehaye (Brussels: 1902), *passim*.

10. See Raymond Janin, *La Geographie ecclesiastique de l'Empire byzantin*, Part 1. *Le Siège de Constantinople et le Patriarcat oecuménique*, vol. 3, *Les Eglises et monastères*, 2nd ed., (Paris: 1969) 110-11, 132-38, 272-73, 313-14, 449-50 etc. The number of the shrines dedicated to Old Testament heroes is disproportionately small in comparison with the host of names commemorated in the calendar, and even less than the number of those whose relics were venerated at the Capital. According to E. Lucius, *Les Origines du culte des saints dans l'église Chrétienne*, trans. by Jeanmaire (Paris: 1908), 192, nn. 3 and 7; of all the Old Testament heroes whose cults flourished in the east, only that of the Maccabees, originally an Antiochene cult which spread to Constantinople in the fourth century and there enjoyed considerable popularity, really ever gained much credence in the west. Little is heard of it after the thirteenth century in the west.

11. Mansi, 13:347. This was a re-affirmation and fortification of a declaration of the Council held at Hieria in 754 (Mansi 13:347-48D) expressly rejecting the views of the Emperor Leo III, but stating a long-standing belief based on Heb. 13; thus John Damascenus, *De Fide Orthodoxa* 4:15 (PG, 94:1153C).

12. The earliest extant "world chronicle" is that of John Malalas (sixth century.) The works of George the Monk, Theophanes Confessor, and George Cedrenus are typical of the genre.

13. Constantine Manasses (*Synopsis Istorikē*, lines 968-70) leaves little doubt that he regards the history of the Hebrews to be of greater importance than that of the Hellenes, and elsewhere (lines 4358-63) he expressly refers to the orthodox (i.e., iconodoule) Byzantines as Israel.

14. See John Wortley, "The Legendary History of Byzantium," *Canadian Historical Papers* (1977), 215-29, illustrating the way in which the chronographers adjusted their story (with legends) to fit their beliefs.

15. The inhabitants of the Sinaitic peninsula were first known as Saracens (Ptolemy, Geography 5.16), but from the first century A.D. this term came to be used more generally of people in or from the east, especially by Ammianus Marcellinus. Eusebius (PG, 19:354) and Epiphanius (Adversus Haereses 1.1.8, PG, 41:196B) seem first to have identified the Saracens as Ishmaelites and/or as Hagarenes, in the fourth and at the beginning of the fifth centuries respectively. Nicephorus the Patriarch (A.D. 806-15) in his *Breviarium* still consistently uses the term Saracens, but this is frequently rendered *Hagarenes* by Theophanes Confessor, his contemporary. In the twelfth century, Zonaras speaks frequently of the Muslims as Ishmaelites or as Hagarenes rarely as Saracens.

16. The words of Psalm 79 LXX were often quoted in this context. Constantine Manasses speaks of the defeated Byzantium as "Sion, the daughter of God, mourning in sackcloth and ashes the widowed bride" (*Synopsis Istorikē*, lines 4671-74.) The oblique reference to the Daughter of Sion (cf. Isaiah 62:11, and frequently in Isaiah, Lamentations etc.,) is of course unmistakeable, and intentional.

17. The principle of dynastic succession, though never firmly established in Israel, was always observed in Judah (though this did not convey the *right* to rule). Only in the tenth century was this principle established at Byzantium, and never unshakeably so nor did it convey the right to rule there either. Women were excluded from the succession in Old Testament times, hence the condemnation of Athaliah's reign (2 kings 11,) and hence perhaps the condemnation of the reign of the Empress Irene (*sola* A.D. 797-802.) The point at which Byzantine practice differed markedly from the Old Testament pattern was the frequent adoption into the imperial family, usually by marriage, of a suitable outsider, a process which provided such outstanding rulers as Marcion, Zeno, Anastasius and Maurice. Here Byzantium was certainly more Roman than Hebraic.

18. For example, in *Vita Constantini*.

19. Leo I Makelles appears to have been the first emperor to have accepted Christian coronation, but the prevailing principle seems always to have been that, whenever possible, one emperor crowned another. Only when this was not possible did the Patriarch, as second person of the the Empire rather than as priest, impose the diadem.

20. *Narratio de structura templi S. Sophiae*, ch. 27, ed. by Th. Preger, *Scriptores Originum Constantinopolitanarum*, 2 vols., continuous pagination (Leipzig: 1901. 1907), p.105.3-5. This has to be read in the light of Justinian's restoration of Solomon's treasure to Jerusalem, albeit to the Christians there, at the protest of a Jew, when they were brought from Africa by Belisaurius (Procopius, *Wars* 4.9.5-10 cf. 3.5.3 and 5.12.42). Telling of Justinian's boast, Michael Glycas continued: "...and at the imperial cistern he set up a statue of Solomon looking at the Great Church of God, holding his jaw, thus showing that Solomon was superceded in the building of the New Jerusalem." It is rare to find the Great Church thus described. *CSHB*, 27:498.15-20.

21. Proverbs 14:34.

22. Thus D.S. Bailey, *Homosexuality and the Western Tradition*, (London: 1955). This is the outstanding example of Justinian's attempts to enforce morality by law his determined attempts to extinguish homosexuality are noted, e.g., by Malalas (p.436.3-16) and Theophanes Confessor (*ad* A.M. 6021).

23. Genesis 19:4-11.

24. Theophanes Confessor, ed., by De Boor, 1:328.2-10. The mystical overtones of this event have been much emphasised by Theophanes, who points out that, after six years of fighting, Heraclius was now entering a seventh of rest. But cf. Nicephorus, *Breviarium*, De Boor ed., p.22, from whose account the mystical and messianic implications are absent.

25. *Vita Constantini* 4.60.

26. *BHG* 1061, ed. by Leo Sternbach, *Analecta Avarica* (Cracow: 1900), 298-320. Another document which maintains a similar analogy between Israel and Byzantium to an extent which goes beyond being a mere figure of speech is *BHG* 1058, which for that reason has been frequently (though unconvincingly) claimed to be from the same pen as *BHG* 1061. It is concerned with the attack on Constantinople in 860 by the Rôs, who are compared to the wild boar who breaks in and destroys (the Lord's) cultivated garden. See John Wortley, "The Oration of Theodore Syncellus (*BHG* 1058) and the Siege of 860," *Byzantine Studies/Etudes Byzantines* 4 (1977), 111-26.

27. Suzanne Spain Alexander, "Heraclius, Byzantine Imperial Ideology and the David Plates," *Speculum* 52 (1977), 217-37. This article draws attention to a number of aspects of Byzantine pseudo-Sionism.

28. Reigned A.D. 717-40 and 740-75 respectively.

29. "Since therefore having delivered to us the Sovranty of the Empire, as it was His good pleasure, He added this thereto, to make manifest our love with fear toward Him, in that He bade us, as He bade Peter the supreme Head of the Apostles, to feed His most faithful flock: We can conceive nothing more acceptable by way of thanksgiving to Him than the righteous and just government of those entrusted to us by Him, so that henceforward the bonds of wickedness may be broken, the unjust breaches of covenants may be stopped, and the attempts of transgressors may be crushed, and thus by victories over our enemies, through his almighty hand, we may be crowned with the encircling diadem and the throne may be confirmed, more precious and honourable, and in peace to ourselves, and the republic established on a firm foundation."

One may also note what Leo III meant by improving the Roman Law "in the direction of humanity": "The Appendix to the *Ecloga* contains much more than mere quotations of scriptural texts. In it are reproduced textually the Ten Commandments and a number of austere precepts of the Jewish Law taken from the Pentatench. These are grouped together under the title 'Synopsis of the law given by God through Moses to the Israelites'" *A Manual of Roman Law, the Ecloga, published by the Emperors Leo III and Constantine V of Isauria at Constantinople, A.D. 726, Rendered into English by Edwin Hanson Freshfield*, (Cambridge: 1926), 66-67, and *Introduction*.

30. Stephen Gero, *Byzantine Iconoclasm during the reign of Leo III with particular attention to Oriental Sources*, SSCO, 346, Subsidia 41 (Louvain: 1973), esp. 57-58.

31. *Theophanes Continuatus* (*CSHB*, 33:84.12-86.8), Scylitzes (*CFHB*, 5:50.14-15) cf. Zonaras, *Epitomē* 12.25. 1-9.

32. For example, *Life of Saint Andrew the Fool*, ch. 208 (*PG*, 111:853A) the so-called *Oracle of Leo the Wise*, *PG*, 107:1119 Photius, Homily 3 *passim*, in *Sancti Patris nostri Photii Patriarchae Cpoleos Orationes et Homiliae LXXXIII*, ed. by S. Aristarches 2 vols. (Constantinople: 1900), trans. by Cyril Mango, *The Homilies of Photius, Patriarch of Constantinople*, (Cambridge, MA: 1958) Nicolaos Hydruntinus, quoted in Edouard Didier Riant, *Exuviae Sacrae Constantinopolitanae* 2 vols. (Geneva: 1877, 1878), 2:233. On the designation of Constantinople as the New Jerusalem, see E. Fenster, *Laudes Constantinopolitanae: Miscellanea byzantina Monacesia*, 19 (Munich: 1968), 121.

33. "On the very spot which witnessed the Saviour's sufferings, a new Jerusalem was constructed over against the one so celebrated of old....and it may be that this was that second and new Jerusalem spoken of in the predictions of the prophets, concerning which such abundant testimony is given in the divinely inspired records." *Vita Constantini* 3.33, referring to Revelation 21:2. It is to Gilbert Dagron, *Naissance d'une Capitale: Constantinople et ses institutions de 330 a 451* (Paris: 1974), that we owe our better understanding of this matter. Popular tradition notwithstanding, not a single specifically Christian building (which the heroön obviously was not) at Constantinople can be confidently attributed to Constantine I.

34. *Vita S. Danielis Stylitae*, ch. 10, ed., by Hippolyte Delehaye, *Les Saints Stylites*, *Subsidia Hagiographica*, 14 (Brussels: 1923), 12. Note also this, from the end of the fourth century: "ubi cum venissem [cpolim] per singulas ecclesias vel apostolos necnon et per singula martyria quae ibi plurima sunt, non cessabam Deo nostro Iesu gratias agere..."; *Peregrinatio Aetheriae*, ed., by Otto Prinz, 5th ed., (Heidelber: 1960), 33.9 (p.30.22-24).

35. For example, Constantine Manasses, *Synopsis Istorikē*, line 3272-83: "If I might liken this City, this blessèd City, this/City of Constantine, to the sphere of heaven,/And all it churches to the twinkling of the stars -/I do not think this would be stretching a point too far,/For each is resplendent in points of perpetual light/And they all seem like shining stars to the creatures of earth./ But when the sun arises above the horizon in all its beauty,/The lights of all the stars are extinguished/And it alone shines brightly. So, like little stars/Are all the churches in comparison to this great sun/Which is the temple of divine foundation, the beauty of the whole earth."

36. Procopius, *De Aedificiis* 1.1.61-62. Cf. Constantine Manasses, lines 3267-81: "[Justinian] built the great and glorious temple,/The precinct of my God, the heaven on earth/Which I think even the seraphim must wonder at as they sing./ If God were to deign to dwell in temples made with hands/He would certainly dwell in this one; where else, indeed?" At one point in the *Life of Saint Andrew the Fool* (chs. 141,142 *PG*, 111:788D-89B) it is bluntly asserted that the Great Church is every bit as much the dwelling-place of God as ever the body of the *Theotokos* had been.

37. *Life of Saint Andrew the Fool*, ch. 224; *PG*, 111:868B.

38. The table of the Last Supper, the tools used to make the cross, a portion of the true cross, the door, key, lock and seal of the Holy Sepulchre together with the lintel and two paving-stones thereof are some of the items

mentioned by visitors to Constantinople in the twelfth century as located in the Great Church. Riant, *Exuviae*, 2:293ff.

39. "*Le Livre du Pelerin d'Antoine de Novgordo*," trans. by Marcelle Ehrhard, *Romania* 58 (1932), 44-65, pp.53,54. Anthony seems to have realised that the tables were replicas in silver.

NOTES TO E. JOHNS "THE CHANGE IN STATUS OF WOMEN IN ICELAND"

1. Else Mundal, "Kvinner i norrøn litteratur," *Norskrift* (preliminary paper) 27 (Oslo: 1980), 1-16, postulates that there is a difference in the role of women in the family sagas and in the heroic sagas ("fornaldar soger") and poems. In the heroic texts, she says, a powerful even cruel woman is given much more influence than in the former. In the first place, her argument that women are not given an influential role in the family sagas is not convincing. Secondly, although correctly pointing out that the heroic sagas appear late in the Middle Ages and that their description of women therefore is not so realistic, she does not at all convincingly answer the very interesting question why this is so.

2. Around 1100, bishop Jón tries to get rid of "witchcraft and sorcery and magic formulas." *Flateyarbok II* tells about phallus cults in Christian times.

3. The best example is the *jól* traditiion, where the old midwinter rites were combined with Christmas.

4. "Make *runes* and pray for the help of the *dises*" (*Edda*, Sigurdskveda, v.7) was changed to praying to *Mary* for help, but up till 1300 runes were still in use to give birth magical help. *Vaette-nyren* (vaette-Kidney) was the most used amulet; it is a fruit stone of the West Indian plant *pusaetha scandens*, brought to Iceland by the Gulf Stream. It was said to help the delivery. The women would also open and loosen everything - doors, windows, knots - and after the delivery lock and tighten everything; the spirit of the house, embodied in the house itself, gave birth. These customs were still in use after the Reformation.

5. In all of Europe a female underground culture (often represented by midwives and "wise" women) was connected with sorcery, and many practitioners of pagan knowledge and magic ended up on the witch-stake. It is remarkable, however, that in Iceland only two female witches were killed, one burned and one on the stake. Twenty-seven men were killed, twenty-four of them burned. Iceland had, in all 120 witch-trials, but only nine against women. There is no reason to believe that men practiced sorcery more often than women did in Iceland; the explanation of the statistics may be that magical powers, in spite of Christian influence, was regarded as belonging to the female sphere, and if a man practiced sorcery, he did something *ergi*. The fear of mixing the sex-spheres could have been stronger than the fear of "the feminine mystique" that swayed the rest of Europe. This interesting problem has not been seen and discussed thoroughly, and an authority like Prof. Else Mundal in Oslo asks the following questions on a totally wrong basis: "Does this [namely, that women were more easily accused of sorcery in the sagas] show that the negative attitude towards women that later finds expression in the witch-trials already

is growing when the Icelandic sagas were written?" (my translation; Mundal, "Kvinner...," 8).

6. Freed slaves could be given economic assistance, but there is reason to believe that the abolition of slavery had small *practical* results; often it was only a change in status from slave to servant. Another church reform which possibly meant an improvement, especially for women, was the prohibition of exposure of frail children or, in poor families, even of healthy girls.

BIBLIOGRAPHY FOR E. JOHNS "THE CHANGE IN STATUS OF WOMEN IN ICELAND"

J.H. Adalsteinsson, *Under the Cloak: The Acceptance of Christianity in Iceland with Particular Reference to the Religious Attitudes Prevailing at the Time*. (Uppsala: 1978).

T.M. Anderson, *The Icelandic Family Saga: An Analytic Reading*, (Cambridge, Ma.: 1967).

Thomas Bredsdorff, *Kaos og Kaerlighed: En Studie i Islaendingesagaenes Livsbillede*, (Copenhagen: 1971).

Olafur Davidsson, *Galdur og galdramal a Islandi* I-III, (Reykjavik: 1940-43).

Joan Ferrante, *Woman as Image in Medieval Literature*. (New York/London: 1975).

Bjarne Fidjestøl, "Ut no glytter dei fagre droser," *Syn og Segn* 8 (Oslo: 1976).

Peter Hallberg, *Den isländska sagan*, (Stockholm: 1956).

Rolf Heller, *Die literarische Darstellung der Frau in den Isländersagas*. (Halle: 1958).

Jón Jóhannesson, *Islands historie i mellomalderen*, (Bergen: 1969).

Finnur Jónsson, *Den Old Norske og Old Islandske Litteratur-Historie* 2d printing, (Copenhagen: 1923).

Hans E. Kinck, "Et par Ting om AEttesagaen: Skikkelser den ikkje forstod," in *Sagadebatt*, Else Mundal (ed.,) (Oslo: 1977).

W. Krause, *Die Frau in der Sprache der altisländischen Familiengedichten*. (Göttingen: 1926).

Kulturhistorisk leksikon for nordisk middelaider, (Copenhagen: 1956-75).

Preben Meulengracht Sørensen, *Saga og Samfund*. (Copenhagen: 1977).

Else Mundal, editor, *Sagadebatt*, (Oslo: 1977).

Else Mundal, "Kvinner i norrøn litteratur", *Norskrift*, (Preliminary paper) 27, 1-6. (Oslo: 1980).

Marina Mundt, "Kvinnens forhold til ekteskapet i Njåls saga," *Edda* I/II (Tromsø: 1976).

M.C. van den Toorn, *Ethics and Moral in Icelandic Saga Literature*. (Assen: 1955).

BIBLIOGRAHPHY FOR L. ROUSSEAU "LA SACRALISATION DE L'ESPACE"

*Il n'a pas été possible d'intégrer à cet article l'étude exaustive du corpus des croix de chemin que vient de publier Paul Carpentier, *Les Croix de chemin: au-delà du signe*, Ottawa, Muées nationaux du Canada, 1981 XXIV-476p., et dont les conclusions s'accordent avec notre interprétation.

F. Choay, *L'urbanisme, utopies et réalités*, (Paris: Seuil, 1965).

P. Deffontaines, "Le rang, type de peuplement rural du Canada Français," dans *La société canadienne-française* (Montréal: HMH, 1971), 19-32.

M. Eliade, "Architecture sacrée et symbolisme," dans *Mircea Eliade*, (Les cahiers de l'Herne, Paris: de l'Herne, 1978), 141-156.

A.J. Greimas, "Pour une sémiotique topologique," dans *Sémiotique de l'espace: Architecture, urbanisme, sortir de l'impasse* (Médiations 185 Paris: Denoël/Gonthier, 1979), 11-44.

R.C. Harris, *The Seigneurial System in Early Canada: A Geographical Study* (Madison: University of Wisconsin Press, 1968).

R.C. Harris, J. Warkentin, *Canada Before Confederation: A Study in Historical Geography* (New York: Oxford University Press, 1974).

P. Jacob, "Croix de chemins et dévotions populaires dans la Beauce," *SCHEC*, Rapport (1976), 15-33.

Y. Lacroix, *Les origines de Lapraire*, (Montréal: Bellarmin,1981).

A. -Ph. Lagopoulos, "L'image mentale de l'aglomération," dans *Communications*, 27, (1977), 55-78.

Ed. Z. Massicotte, "Nos croix de chemins," dans *Bulletin des recherches historiques* (1923-24).

J. Porter, L. Dezy, *Calvaires et croix de chemin du Québec* (Cahiers du Québec - 15 Montréal: Hurtubise-HMH, 1973).

B. Ray, "Sacred Space and Royal Shrines in Buganda," dans *History of Religions*, 16/4 (1977), 364-73.

J. Simard, "Cultes liturgiques et dévotions populaires dans les comptés de Portneuf et du Lac-St-Jean," dans *Société canadienne d'histoire de l'Eglise catholique*, Rapport (1976), 5-14.

—— "Croix de chemins et frontières culturelles des francophones au Québec et au Canada," dans *Mélanges en l'honneur de Luc Lacourcère*, (Montréal: Leméac, 1978), 353-412.

—— *Un patrimoine méprisé: La religion populaire des Québécois* (Cahiers du Québec, 46 Montréal: Hurtubise-HMH, 1979), 7-26.

—— *Corpus des croix de chemin du Québec*, Rapport général d'inventaire, département d'Histoire, Université Laval, Québec, (1980) polycopié.

NOTES TO N. PAGÉ "ARCHITECTURE RELIGIEUSE CONTEMPORAINE"

1. Christian Norberg-Schulz, *La Signification dans l'architecture occidentale* (Bruxelles: Mardaga, 1977), 412.

2. Le Corbusier, *Textes et dessins pour Ronchamp* (Genève: Coopi, 1965), 24.

3. Bolle-Reddat, *Ronchamp*, Munich: Verlag Schnell, 1976), 14.

4. Paolo Soleri, *Matter Becoming Spirit*, (New York: Anchor Press, 1973), 253.

5. Norberg-Schulz, *La Signification*, 412.

6. K.J. Conant, *Carolingian and Romanesque Architecture*, (Harmondsworth and Baltimore: Penguin Books, 1959), 4.

7. Baboulene-Brion-Delalande, *Faut-il encore construire des églises?*, (Paris: Fleurus, 1970).

8. F. Debuyst, *Art d'Eglise*, no 139, p.33.

9. Joseph Comblin, *Théologie de la ville*, (Paris: Ed. Universitaires, 1968).
10. J. Joedicke *K. und H. Siren*, (Stuttgart: Kramer Verlag, 1977), 68.
11. Norberg-Schulz, *La Signification*, 120.
12. Ibid., 119.
13. Le Corbusier, *Textes et dessins*, 37.
14. Ibid., 21.
15. Ibid., 21.

NOTES TO A. HAMDANI "SHADES OF SHĪ`ISM"

*This article is a revised version of a paper read, under the same title, at the Fourteenth International Congress of the International Association for the History of Religions, Winnipeg, August 17-22, 1980. I would like to acknowledge with gratitude a travel-grant from the University of Wisconsin-Milwaukee which enabled me to attend this conference and the careful typing of this article by Ms. Margaret Kleiber.

1. *Encyclopaedia of Islam* (new edition) article "Ikhwān al-Safāʾ."
2. The quotations from the *Rasāʾil Ikhwān al-Safāʾ* are from the Beirut edition 4 vols. (Dār Sādir: 1957), those from *Al-Risālat al-Jāmiʿa* are also from the Beirut edition, ed. by Mustafā Ghālib, (Dār Sādir: 1974). The volume and page numbers are given in the text of the article. Earlier editions of the *Rasāʾil* are (a) ed. by Wilāyat Husayn (Bombay: 1888) and (b) ed. by Khayr al-dīn al-Zarkalī, 4 vols. (Cairo: 1928) with two separate introductions by Tāha Husayn and Ahmad Zakī Pasha and of the *Risālat al-Jāmiʿa*, ed. by Jamīl Slība, 2 vols. (Damascus: 1969; the editor considers the attribution of this work to al-Majrīṭī's authorship as valid). The Beirut editions are chosen because they are the latest and are used by most scholars. They are, however, reprints of earlier Cairo and Bombay editions. None of them is collated from the oldest manuscripts available and none has indexes for convenient reference. There was a great temptation to quote in the Arabic original, but it has been avoided because of the printing difficulties and also because the Arabic text is available in print for reference. Crucial Arabic expressions have, however, been transliterated.
3. The Dāʿī al-Husayn b. ʿAlī b. Muhammad b. al-Walīd (d. 667/1268) in his *Al-Risālat al-Wahīda fī tathbīt arkān al- aqīda* (ms. of the Hamdani collection), pp.19-24, interprets al-Siddīq as referring to ʿAlī b. Abī Tālib, al-Fārūq to al-Hasan b. ʿAlī, and Dhūʾn-Nurayn to al-Husayn b. ʿAlī. See H.F. al-Hamdani, "*Rasāʾil Ikhwān al-Safāʾ* in the literature of the Ismāʿīlī Taiyibī Daʿwat," *Der Islam*, 20 (1932), 289.
4. Ms. no. 4707 of Majlisi-Shūrā-i-Millī, Tehrān (no pagination), copied in very good hand by Khalīl b. Yūsuf b. Sallār b. ʿAlī in 686/1287; microfilm of the same, no. 172, at the Arab League Institute of manuscripts, Cairo (Irān hand-list, p.19).
5. "The Arrangement of the *Rasāʾil Ikhwān al-Safāʾ* and the Problem of Interpolation," a paper read at the Annual Meeting of the American Research Center in Egypt, San Francisco, April 14, 1980.
6. S.H. Nasr, *An Introduction to Islamic cosmological Doctrines* (Cambridge: Harvard University Press, 1964), 27-28, 31.

7. A.L. Tībawī, "The Idea of Guidance in Islām" *Islamic Quarterly* 3 (1956), 148.

8. S. Diwald, *Arabische Philosophie und Wissenschaft in der Enzyklopädie: Kitāb Ihwān as-Safā'* (III) *Die Lehre von Seele und Intellekt*, (Wiesbaden: 1975), 22, 27. See my review of this book in the *Journal of the American Oriental Society* 98/2 (1978), 158-59.

9. L. Massignon, *Receuil de Textes inedits concernant l'histoire de la mystique en pays d'Islam*, (Paris: 1929), 130. See also A.L. Tībawī, "Ikhwān as-Safā' and their Rasā'il: A Critical Review of a Century and Half of Research," *Islamic Quarterly* 2 (1955), 44.

10. A.L. Tibawī, "Ikhwān ...," 34.

11. In Ismāʿīlī thought, "haqā'iq" is the term used for philosophy based on *ta'wīl* (esoteric interpretation). The expressions *ta'wīl* and *baqā'iq* usually go together, as do *zāhir* and *bātin*.

12. There are Zaydī polemical works against the Ismāʿīlī whom the Zaydī writers particularly call Bātinīs, as e.g., Yahya b. Hamza al-ʿAlawī (d. 745/1344) *Al-Ifhām Af'idati'l-Bātiniyyat al-Tughām*, ed. by Faysal ʿAwn (Alexandria: Al-Maʿārif publication, no date).

13. The English translation given here is of Bernard Lewis, *Origins of Ismāʿīlism* (Cambridge: 1940), 94-95.

14. A section of this chapter (II, 203-377) was translated into Urdu by Ikrāmʿ Alī in 1810 then edited by Shaykh Ahmad b. Muhammad al-Yamānī under the title *Tuhfat Ikhwān al-Safā'* with an English preface by T.T. Thomason (Calcutta: 1912). A later revision entitled *Fragment on the Controversy between Man and Animals* was published by Duncan Forbes and C. Rien (London: 1861). An English translation of the same was published by J. Platt *Dispute between Man and Animals* (London: 1869). In fact these initiated the earliest studies of the *Rasā'il Ikhwān al-Safā'* by A. Sprenger (1848), F. Dietirici (1858-1872), G. Flügel (1858), and S. Lane-Poole (1888). They also occasioned the first full edition of the *Rasā'il* entitled *Kitāb Ikhwān al-Safā'*, ed. by Wilāyat Husayn and published by Nūral-dīn jīwā Khān (Bombay: 1888). The authorship of the *Rasā'il*, on the title page, is attributed to the pre-Fātimid Ismāʿīlī Imām Ahmad b. ʿAbd Allah b. Muhammad b. Ismāʿīl b. Jaʿfar al-Sādiq.

15. Zāhidʿ Alī, *Ta'rīkh-i-Fātimiyyīn-i-Misr* (Hyderabad: 1948), 522-26.

16. W. Madelung, "Karmatī," *Encyclopedia of Islam* (new edition).

17. Abū Hayyān al-Tawhīdī *Kitāb al-Imtāʿ wal-Mu'ānasa*, ed. by Ahmad Amīn and Ahmad al-Zayn, 3 vols. in 1, (Beirut: 1939-44 2d ed., 1953), 2:3-6.

18. "Abū Hayyān al-Tawhīdī and the Brethren of Purity," *International Journal of Middle East Studies*, 9 (1978), 345-53.

19. "Al-Fārābī and the Brethren of Purity," a revised version of a paper given under this title at the Ninth Annual Meeting of the Middle East Studies Association at Louisville, November 1975, now being prepared for publication.

20 see n. 5 above. We do not know of any ms. of the *Rasā'il* earlier than Istanbul, Atif no. 1681, copied between 549/1154 and 578/1182 some seventy years after the death of al-Ghazzālī by a Sunnī copyist. By that time many glosses of orthodox respectability must have already been added on to an anonymous Shīʿite work; and in the long history of editing and copying the *Rasā'il* many references from a later time would have been interpolated. For example, in the body of the text itself, we find the expression *kamā*

qāla ͐l-muḥaqqiq shi ͨran ("as the editor has cited the verses;" 4:76). If such an editorial note could be introduced in the text, it seems certain that many others have also found their way into it and have after passed as the text itself.

21. "An early Fāṭimid Source on the Time and Authorship of the *Rasā ͐il Ikhwān al-Ṣafā ͐*" *Arabica* 26/1 (1979), 62-75.

22. Persian verses are cited in 1:139 (7vss.), 209 (2vss.),235 (6vss.), and Persian words are used, such as *kāghadh* (paper) in 1:281 and *āsmānjū ͐ī* (sky-coloured) in 4:226.

23. The authors usually refer to themselves in the plural but sometimes the singulaur is used, as in 1:372.

24. There is no use made of it in the works of the *dā ͨīs* of the early Fāṭimid period. In case of the Dā ͨī Ḥamīd al-dīn al-Kirmānī (d. ca. 411/1020) this is particularly noticeable.

25. Such was the case with the *Kitāb al-Maḥṣūl* of the early Dā ͨī al-Nasafī (d. 331/942) and the *Sīra* of the Dā ͨī Ja ͨfar b. Manṣūr al-Yaman (d. ca. 360/970), probably due to a ban imposed on them. Both of these works surfaced in part in later quotations. In fact the *Rasā ͐il* fared better. It was preserved in fact both by the Nizārī and Ṭayyibī Da ͨwas branching off from the Fāṭimid Caliphate.

26. The first known reference is by the Syrian Nizārī Dā ͨī Abū Ma ͨālī Ḥātim b. ͨImrān (or Maḥmūd) b. Zuhrah (d. 498/1104). The book is edited by Aref Tamir in *Khams Rasā ͐il Ismā ͨīliyya* (Beirut: 1956).

27. The first known reference in the Ṭayyibī tradition is by the Yamanī Dā ͨī Ibrāhīm b. al-Ḥusayn al-Ḥāmidī (d. 557/1162): *Kitāb Kanz al-Walad*. The book is edited by Mustafa Ghālib (Beirut: 1971).

28. Ibnal-Athīr, *Al-Kāmil*, under the year 545 H., and Al-Maqrīzī *Itti ͨāz*, ed. by Muhammad Hilmy (Cairo: 1973), 3:316-17. See also Syed Ameer Ali, *Spirit of Islam*, 450, and J.N. Hollister, *The Shī ͨa of India* (London: 1953), 209.

29. Yūsuf Najmuddin, *Masā ͐il Sayfī Fī ͐l-Fiqh* (as given in Ismail Poonawala, *Bibliography of Ismā ͨīlī Literature* [Malibu, CA: 1977], 210) or *al-Masā ͐il al-Sayfiyya* (as given by W. Ivanow, *Guide to Ismā ͨīlī Literature*, 74). See H.F. al-Hamdani, article cited above in n.3, 291.

NOTES TO M. HEPER "ISLAM AND SOCIETY IN TURKEY"

*An earlier version of this article was submitted at the annual meeting of the British Society for Middle Eastern Studies, London, U.K., July 7-10, 1980 and at the Fourteenth Congress of the International Association for the History of Religion, Winnipeg, Canada, August 16-22, 1980. The Author is grateful to the Harry S. Truman Research Institute of the Hebrew University of Jerusalem for support that made this study possible. Yilmaz Esmer, Carter Findley, Nikki Keddie, Serif Mardin, Howard Reed, Ilkay Sunar, and Paul Stirling have given an earlier draft of this essay the benefit of careful criticism. Needless to say, the final responsibility rests with the author.

1. James A. Curry, "Church-State Development Around the World," *Annals*, AAPSS, 446 (1979), 19-31.

2. Bernard Lewis, "The Return of Islam" *Commentary* 1 (January 1974), 39-49; reprinted in *Middle East Review* 12 (1979), 17-30.

3. Although there is some ambivalence concerning Turkey such a prediction is nevertheless made for that country, too: Curry, "Church-State Developments Around the World," 23; Cherl Benard and Zalmay Khalizad "Secularization, Industrialization, and Khomeini's Islamic Republic," *Political Science Quarterly* 94 (1979), 229; Joseph Pincus, "Syria: A Captive Economy," *Middle East Review* 12 (1979), 56; and Raphael Israeli, "The New Wave of Islam," *International Journal* 34 (1979), 369. One comes across the same line of thought in popular literature, too: John Laffin, *The Danger of Islam* (London: Sphere Books, 1979); G.H. Jansen, *Militant Islam* (London and Sydney: Pan Books, 1979).

4. Benard and Khalilzad, "Secularization, Industrialization, and Khomeini's Islamic Republic," 229.

5. I take these categories from Israeli, "The New Wave of Islam," 370ff.

6. See, inter alia, Lewis, "The Return of Islam," 40 C.A.O. van Nieuwenhuijze, "Islam as a Determinant of Middle East Civilization," *Islam and Modern Age* 1 (1970), 18.

7. Robert K. Merton, *Social Theory and Social Structure* (New York: Free Press, 1957), 398; Max Weber, *Economy and Society: An Outline of Interpretive Sociology*, 1 (paperback ed.; Berkeley/Los Angeles/London: University of California Press, 1978), 399.

8. Roger Owen, "Islam and Capitalism: A Critique of Rodinson," *Review of Middle East Studies* 2 (1976), 92. See also David Laitin, "Religion, Political Culture, and the Weberian Tradition." *World Politics* 30 (July 1978), 570-71.

9. H.H. Gerth and C. Wright Mills (ed.), *From Max Weber: Essays in Sociology* (New York: Oxford University Press, 1958), 291.

10. Guenther Lewy, *Religion and Revolution* (New York: Oxford University Press, 1974), 237ff. For two such excellent studies see Ernest Gellner, "Post-Traditional Forms in Islam: The Turf and Trade, and Votes and Peasants," *Daedalus* 102 (1973), 191-206 and Clifford Geertz, *Islam Observed: Religious Development in Morocco and Indonesia* (Chicago: University of Chicago Press, 1968).

11. Halil İnalcık, "Islam in the Ottoman Empire," *Cult Turcica* 5-7 (1968-1970), 21. Elsewhere Inalcik points out that even during the period of decline after the sixteenth century the idea of a state of power independent of the religion never lost its importance in the Ottoman polity: "On the Secularism in Turkey," *Orientalistische Literaturzeitung* 64 (1969), 438. Thus, the Ottoman sultan resembled the Mughal King who was supposed to "act as time demands": Ibn Hasan, *The Central Structure of the Mughal Empire* (London: Oxford University Press, 1936), 61.

12. For an elaboration of this point, see my "Center and Periphery in the Ottoman Empire with Special Reference to the Nineteenth Century," *International Political Science Review* 1 (1980), 85.

13. M.S. Agwani, "Religion and Politics in Islamic Theory and Practice," *Islam and Modern Age* 2 (1971), 49.

14. For ideas that make up this non-Islamic legitimation system, or an Islamic system only in a looser sense, see Carter Findley, *Bureaucratic Reform in the Ottoman Empire. The Sublime Porte 1789-1922* (Princeton: Princeton

University press, 1980), 8-12. Even today "structural legitimacy" is an alien concept in the Middle East. Most states stand on the "ideological legitimacy" and the remaining few on the "personal legitimacy" of their rulers. See Michael C. Hudson, *Arab Politics: The Search for Legitimacy* (New Haven/London: Yale University Press: 1977).

15. For example, see Majid Khadduri, *War and Peace in the Law of Islam* (Baltimore: Johns Hopkins University Press, 1955), 274.

16. Unless otherwise indicated, the conceptions of institutional, normative, and cognitive secularization and their sub-dimensions used in this essay draw upon Peter E. Glasner, *The Sociology of Secularization: A Critique of a Concept* (London: Routledge and Kegan, Paul, 1977).

17. Muhsin Mahdi, "Modernity and Islam," in Joseph M. Kitagawa (ed.), *Modern Trends in World Religions* (La Salle, IL: Open Court, 1959), 14-15. Also see Avigdor Levy, "The Ottoman Ulema and the Military Reforms of Sultan Mahmud II," *Asian and African Studies* 7 (1971), 13-39.

18. See, *inter alia*, Jamil M-Abun-Nasr, *The Tijanniyya: A Sufi Order in the Modern World* (London/New York/Toronto: Oxford University Press, 1965); Michael Gilnesan, *Saints and Sufism in Modern Egypt: An Essay in the Sociology of Religion* (Oxford: Clarendon Press, 1973).

19. Uriel Heyd, "The Ottoman Ulema and Westernization in the Time of Selim III and Mahmud II," *Scripta Hierosolymitama* 9 (1961), 64ff.

20. Niyazi Berkes, *The Development of Secularism in Turkey* (Montreal: McGill University Press, 1964), 94-95.

21. Roger M. Savory, "The Problem of Sovereignty in an Ithna Ashari (Twelver) Shi's State," *Middle East Review* 11 (1979), 5-11.

22. Nur Yalman, "Islamic Reform and the Mystic Tradition in Eastern Turkey," *Archiv. Europ. Sociol.* 10 (1969), 41-42.

23. On the contrast with other Muslim countries, see M.E. Yapp, "Contemporary Islamic Revivalism," *Asian Affairs* 11 (June 1980), 181.

24. Dankwart A. Rustow, "Politics and Islam in Turkey 1920-1955," in Richard Frye (ed.), *Islam and the West* (The Hague: Mouton, 1957), 74.

25. I take this concept from S.N. Eisenstadt, "Some Observations on the Dynamics of Traditions," *Comparative Studies in Society and History* 11 (1969), 454. Their substitution of the integrative version of populism for *umma* is a case in point. See Serif Mardin, *Din ve ideoloji* (Ankara: Sevinc Matbaasi, 1969)

26. Nikki Keddie, "Intellectuals in the Modern Middle East: A Brief Historical Consideration," *Daedalus* 101 (1972), 52; Bernard Lewis, "Turkey: Westernization," in Gustave E. von Grunebaum (ed.) *Unity and Variety in Muslim Civilization* (Chicago: University of Chicago Press, 1955), 312; Wilfred Cantwell Smith, *Islam in Modern History* (Princeton University Press: 1957 reprinted, New York: New American Library, 1959), 174, 176.

27. Niyazi Berkes, "The Two Facets of the Kemalist Revolution," *The Muslim World* 64 (1974), 305.

28. Nikki Keddie, "Intellectuals in the Modern Middle East," 44. See also Carl Leiden, "Arab Nationalism Today," *Middle East Review* 11 (1978-79), 45.

29. Erwin J.J. Rosenthal, *Islam in the Modern National State* (Cambridge: Cambridge University Press, 1965), xviii.

30. Eisenstadt, "Some Observations on the Dynamics of Traditions," 459.

31. As Mardin points out, only much later (1970s) did the National Salvation Party (NSP) attempt "a synthesis of Islam and economic growth of the type exemplified by rational capitalism." Its "success," however, "is not as much due to the infiltration of the secular - and to the extent that it has developed - the capitalistic sector of the Turkish Republic by Islamic structures as it is due to the infiltration of Islamic structures by the organizational concomitants (i.e. civil society) of the Turkish Republic." Serif Mardin, "Religion in Modern Turkey," *International Social Science Journal* 24 (1977), 295.

32. Quoted in Henry E. Allen, "The Outlook for Islam in Turkey," *The Muslim World* 24 (1934), 116. See also Smith, *Islam in Modern History*, 193-4.

33. See my "Atatürkcülük: Karizmanin Emredici 'Siyasal Cerceve'ye Dönüsümü," Prof. Dr. Bülent N. Esen'e Armagan (Ankara: Ankara Üniversitesi Hukuk Fakültesi Zayini, 1977).

34. Paul Stirling, "Religious Changes in Republican Turkey," *The Middle East Journal* 12 (1958), 339.

35. On the elaborate organizations and critical functions of the religious orders in Egypt and Iran, see Gilsenan, *Saint and Sufi in Modern Egypt*, 202-203, and James A. Bill, "Iran and the Crisis of '78," *Foreign Affairs* 57 (1978/79), 332.

36. C.H. Dodd, *Democracy and Development in Turkey* (Hull: The Eothen Press, 1979), 76.

37. Geoffrey Lewis, "Islam in Politics - A Muslim World Symposium: Turkey," *The Muslim World* 56 (1966), 237.

38. Lewy, *Religion and Revolution*, 445.

39. Binnaz Sayari, "Türkiye'de Dinin Denetim Islevi," *Ankara Üniversitesi Siyasal Bilgiler Fakültesi Dergisi* 33 (1978), 181-82 (published in 1979). Yapp has suggested that the involvement of the masses in politics in the Middle East has made political life more Islamic ("Contemporary Islamic Revivalism," 183). This has not occurred in Turkey.

40. Dankwart Rustow, "Turkey's Travails" *Foreign Affairs* 58 (1979), 98-99.

41. Ibid., 99. Perhaps a more basic reason why the hierarchy is absent among the Turkish Sunnis is that the state first made the top ulema into a kind of bureaucracy (*ulemâ-yi resmiye*), and then abolished it under the Republic.

42. See my "Recent Instability in Turkish Politics: End of a Monocentrist Polity?" *International Journal of Turkish Studies* 1 (1979-80), 102-13. See also Jacob Landau, "The National Salvation Party in Turkey," *Asian and African Studies* 11 (1976), 1-57.

43. I take this distinction from David Martin, *A General Theory of Secularization* (New York: Harper and Row, 1978), 31.

44. Dankwart A. Rustow, *A World of Nations: Problems of Political Modernization* (Washington, DC: Brookings Institution, 1967).

45. Ergun Özbudun, *Social Change and Political Participation in Turkey* (Princeton: Princeton University Press, 1976).

46. Frederick W. Frey, "Patterns of Elite Politics in Turkey," in George Lenczowski (ed.) *Political Elites in the Middle East* (Washington, DC: American

Research Enterprise for Public Policy Research, 1975). See also Joseph Szyliowicz, "Elites and Modernization in Turkey," in Frank Tachau (ed.), *Political Elites and Political Development in Turkey* (New York: Wiley, 1975), and Ersin Kalaycioglu, "Why Legislatures Persist in Developing Countries: The Case of Turkey," *Legislative Studies Quarterly* 5 (1980), 123-40. Here, my point is that political democracy has been established in Turkey more firmly than is the case in other Middle Eastern countries. This does not mean that Turkey has no problem vis-à-vis political democracy. I take up some of these problems in my "Recent Instability in Turkish Politics: End of a Monocentrist Polity?"

47. L.P. Elwell-Sutton, "The Iranian Revolution," *International Journal* 34 (1979), 405-406.

48. Hudson, *Arab Politics: The Search for Legitmacy*, 50. See also R. Stephen Humphreys, "Islam and Political Values in Saudi Arabia, Egypt, and Syria," *The Middle East Journal* 33 (1979), 1-19.

49. See, *inter alia*, Robert N. Bellah, "Religious Aspects of Modernization in Turkey and Japan," *American Journal of Sociology* 64 (1958), 1-15.

50. Robert F. Spencer "Aspects of Turkish Kinship and Social Structure," *Anthropological Quarterly* 33 (1960), 1-11.

51. Mardin, *Din ve ideoloji*, 132.

52. Frederick Frey, "Socialization to National Identification Among Turkish Peasants," *Journal of Politics* 30 (1967), 934-65. See also Spencer, "Aspects of Turkish Kinship and Social Structure," 42.

53. Gotthard Jaschke, *Yeni Türkive'de Islâmlik* (Ankara: Bilgi Yayinevi, 1972), 111. (Trans. of *Der Islam in der neuen Türkei: Eine rechtsgeschichtliche Untersuchung* [1951]).

54. Peter Suzuki, "Encounters with Istanbul: Urban Peasants and Village Peasants," *International Journal of Comparative Sociology* 5 (1964), 213.

55. "The New Wave of Islam," 385.

56. Richard B. Scott, "The Turkish Religious Attitudes Toward Religious Education," *The Muslim World* 55 (1965), 227.

57. Ayse Kudat, "Derivative Analysis of Reputational Power Structure," (typescript, Center for International Studies, MIT, 1972).

58. Ned Levine, "Value Orientations among Migrants in Ankara, Turkey: Case Study," *Journal of Asian and African Studies* 8 (1973), 58. More recently George S. Harris, too, concluded that in Turkey practice of Islam does not necessarily challenge the system: "Islam and the State in Modern Turkey," *Middle East Review* 12 (1979), 26.

59. June Starr and Jonathan Pool, "The Impact of a Legal Revolution in Rural Turkey," *Law and Society Review* 8 (1974), 552.

60. Deniz Kandiyoti, "Some Social Psychological Dimensions of Social Change in a Turkish Village," *British Journal of Sociology* 25 (1974), 56.

61. "The New Wave of Islam," 385,388.

62. Yalman, "Islamic Reform and the Mystic Tradition in Eastern Turkey," 47.

63. See my "Political Modernization as Reflected in Bureaucratic Change: The Turkish Bureaucracy and a 'Historical Bureaucratic Empire' Tradition," *International Journal of Middle East Studies* 7 (1976), 517.

64. Howard A. Reed, "The Religious Life of Modern Turkish Muslims," Frye (ed.), *Islam and the West*, 116.

65. David Martin, *Dilemnas of Contemporary Religion* (Oxford: Blackwell, 1978), 13.

66. Alasdair MacIntyre, *Secularization and Moral Change* (New York: Oxford University Press, 1967).

67. Lewis, "Some Perspectives on Urbanization with Special Reference to Mexico City," in Aidan Southall (ed.), *Urban Anthropology: Cross-Cultural Studies of Urbanization* (New York: Oxford University Press, 1973), 131.

68. On different conceptions of religion used here see Ernest Krautz, "Religion and Secularization: A Matter of Definitions," *Social Compass* 17 (1971-72), 203-12.

69. Mardin, *Din ve ideoloji*, 103 Spencer, "Aspects of Turkish Kinship and Social Structure," passim.

70. Paul Stirling, "Cause, Knowledge and Change: A Turkish Village Revisited," in William Hale (ed.), *Aspects of Modern Turkey*, (London: Bowker, 1976), 85-86.

71. Ibid., 88.

72. Richard B. Scott, "Qu'ran Courses in Turkey," *The Muslim World* 61 (1971), 239-55. Abadan-Unat and Yücekök, too, found that Qu'ran courses and religious organizations are concentrated in the more developed regions of Turkey. Their conclusions differ. They argue that in the more developed parts of Turkey, "the Islamic religion is the 'status qou ante' ideology of a part of the petit bourgeoisie, directed against the capitalist development and expansion." They add that "Islamic religion in the underdeveloped parts of Turkey is a 'Conservative' ideology in the hands of the classes that benefit from underdevelopment." See Nermin Abadan-Unat and Ahmet N. Yücekök, "Religious Pluralism in Turkey," *Turkish Yearbook of International Relations* 10 (1969-70), 24-49. The data that they use are reported in greater detail in Ahmet N. Yücekök, *Türkiye'de Dini Sosyo-Ekonomik Taban (1946-1968)* (Ankara: Ankara Üniversitesi Siyasal Bilgiler Fakültesi, 1971), 175ff.

73. See n. 56 above.

74. Kemal Kartal, *Kentlesme ve insan, Kentlesme Sürecinde insan Tutum ve Davranislarinda Meydana Gelen Degismeler: Cankiri Köylerinden Ankara'ya Göc Edenler Uzerinde Bir Arastirma* (Ankara: Türkiye ve Orta Doğu Amme Idaresi Enstitüsü, 1978), 111.

75. Morroe Berger, *Islam in Egypt Today: Social and Political Aspects of Popular Religion* (Cambridge: University Press, 1970), 75-79. On the fundamentalist approach of the Muslim Brotherhood in Egypt, see Israel Altman, "Islamic Movements in Egypt," *The Jerusalem Quarterly* 10 (1979), 87-105.

76. Walter F. Weiker, *The Modernization of Turkey: The First Half Century of the Republic* (New York: Holmes and Meier, 1980), 105ff.

77. *Islam in Modern History*, 200.

78. Mardin, *Din ve ideoloji*, 120.

79. Mardin, "Religion in Modern Turkey," 279.

80. *Islam in the Modern National State*, 314.

81. Cigdem Kagitcibasi, *Sosyal Degismenin Psikolojik Boyutlari: izmir Lise ogrencileri Uzerinde Bir inceleme* (Ankara: Türk Sosyal Bilimler Dernegi Yayini, 1972), 92-93.

82. I take this definition from J.M. Singer, "Pluralism, Religion, and Secularism," *Journal for the Scientific Study of Religion* 6 (1967), 18.

83. Mardin, *Din ve ideoloji*, 120.

84. I take "cultural resources" here as in Clifford Geertz, "Ideology as a Cultural System," in David Apter (ed.), *Ideology and Discontent* (New York: Free Press, 1964), 64.

85. See my "The Recalcitrance of the Public Bureaucracy to 'Bourgeois Politics' in Turkey: A Multi- Factor Political Stratification Analysis," *The Middle East Journal* 30 (1976), 485-500.

86. See my "Negative Bureaucratic Politics in a Modernizing Context: The Turkish Case," *Journal of South Asian and Middle Eastern Studies* 1 (1977), 65-84.

87. "The Patterns of Elite Politics in Turkey," 70.

88. C.Y. Glock and P. Stark, *Religion and Society in Tension* (Chicago: Rand McNally, 1965), 249.

89. See, *inter alia*, R. Hrair Dekmejian, "The Anatomy of Islamic Revival: Legitimacy Crisis, Ethnic Conflict and the Search for Islamic Alternatives," *The Middle East Journal* 34 (1980), 4.

90. Ibid., 2-3.

91. I take this distinction from Geertz, *Islam Observed*, 111-12.

BIBLIOGRAPHY FOR J.P. THORPE "SACRAMENTAL FOOD TRANSACTIONS"

John Abbot, *Keys of Power: A Study of Indian Ritual and Belief* (New York: E.P. Dutton, 1932).

Partap C. Aggarwal, *Caste, Religion and Power: An Indian Case Study* (New Delhi: Sri Ram Center for Industrial Relations, 1971).

K.M. Ashraful Aziz, *Kinship in Bangladesh* (Dacca: International Centre for Diarrhoeal Disease Research, Bangladesh, 1979).

Lawrence Babb, "The Food of the Gods in Chhatisgarh: Some Structural Features of Hindu Ritual." *South West Journal of Anthropology* 26 (1970), 287-304.

Fredrick Barth, "The System of Social Stratification in Swat, N. Pakistan." in *Aspects of Caste in South India, Ceylon and N.W. Pakistan*, ed. by E.R. Leach (Cambridge: University Press, 1960).

―――― *Political Leadership Among Swat Pathans* (New York: Humanities Press, 1965).

Ranjit K. Bhattacharya, "The Concept and Ideology of Caste Among the Muslims of Rural W. Bengal." in *Caste and Social Stratification among the Muslims*, ed. by I. Ahmad (Delhi: Monahar Book Service, 1973), 107-32.

P.K. Bhowmick, "Kasba Narayangarh, A Muslim Village." *Man in India* 45 (1965), 201-22.

Census of India, 1961, *Beliefs and Practices Associated with Muslim Pirs in Two Cities of India*. Vol. 1 (monograph series VII-B, mongraph 1, 1962a) ed. by B.K. Roy Burman.

―――― *Moharram in Two Cities*. Vol. 1 (monograph series VII-B, monograph 3, 1962b) ed. by B.K. Roy Burman.

Victor S. D'Souza, "Social Organization and Marriage Customs of the Moplahs on the South West Coast of India." *Anthropoa* 54 (1959), 487-516.

Zekiye Eglar, *A Punjabi Village in Pakistan* (New York: Columbia University Press, 1960).

Jean Ellickson, "Symbols in Muslim Bengali Family Rituals." in *Prelude to Crisis: Bengal and Bengal Studies in 1970* ed. by P. Bertocci (E. Lansing: Michigan State University Asian Studies Center, 1972), 65-78.

Clifford Geertz, *The Interpretation of Cultures* (New York: Basic Books, 1973).

G.E. Von Grunebaum, *Muhammadan Festivals* (New York: Schuman, 1951).

Sharif Jafar, *Qanoon-Islam, or the Customs of the Mussalmans of India, Comprising a Full and Exact Account of Their Various Rites and Ceremonies from the Moment of Birth till the Hour of Death*, trans. by G.A. Herklots (Madras: Higgenbotham, 1895).

Abdul Karim, "Research into the Social Heritage of the Muslims in Bengal (a Historical Study up to A.D. 1538)." in *Social Research in E. Pakistan*, ed. by P. Bessaignet (Dacca: Asiatic Society of Pakistan [Publication no.5], 1965), 66-90.

Muin-ud-din Ahmad Khan, "Research in the Islamic Revivalism of the 19th Century and its Effect on the Muslim Society of Bengal." in *Social Research in E. Pakistan*, ed. by P. Bessaignet (Dacca: Asiatic Society of Pakistan [Publication no.5], 1960), 38-65.

―――― *The History of the Fara'idi Movement in Bengal (1818-1906)* (Karachi: Pakistan Historical Society, 1965).

Susanne K. Langer, *Philosophy in a New Key* (Cambridge: Harvard University Press, 1960).

H. Laswell, *Politics: Who Gets What, When, How* (New York: Meridian Books, 1958).

C. Lévi-Strauss, *Structural Anthropology* (New York: Anchor Books, 1967).

Shirley Lindenbaum, "Women and the Left Hand: Social Status and Symbolism in E. Pakistan." *Mankind* 6 (1968), 537-44.

T.N. Madan, "Religious Ideology in a Plural Society: The Hindus and Muslims of Kashmir." *Contributions to Indiana Sociology* 6 (1972), 106-41.

Mckim Marriott, "Caste Ranking and Food Transactions: A Matrix Analysis." in *Structure and Change in Indian Society*, ed. by M. Singer and B. Cohen (Chicago: Aldine Press, 1968), 133-72.

―――― "Hindu Transactions: Diversity without Dualism." in *Transaction and Meaning: Directions in the Anthropology of Exchange and Symbolic Behaviour*, ed. by Bruce Kapferer (Philadelphia: Institute for the Study of Human Issues, 1976), 109-42.

―――― "The Open Hindu Person and Interpersonal Fluidity." (Paper read at the meetings of the Association for Asian Studies, March 1980, Washington, D.C.).

M. Marriott and R. Inden, "An Ethnosociology of South Asian Caste Systems." (1973) typescript.

―――― "Caste Systems." in *Encyclopedia Britannica* 3 (1974), 982-91.

Charles W. Morris, "Foundations of the Theory of Signs." in *International Encyclopedia of a Unified Science* vol. 1/2 (Chicago: University of Chicago Press, 1938).

R.K. Mutakar and A. Ansari, "Muslim Caste in an Indian Town: A Case Study." *Bulletin of the Deccan College Research Institute* 25 (1966), 163-90.

R. Nicholas and R. Inden, *Kinship in Bengali Culture* (Chicago: University of Chicago Press, 1977).

Talcott Parsons, "On the Concept of Influence." *Public Opinion Quarterly* 27 (1963a), 37-62.

—— "On the Concept of Power." *Proceedings of the American Philosophical Society* 107 (1963b), 232-62.

David Schneider, *American Kinship: A Cultural Account* (Englewood Cliffs, N.J.: Prentice-Hall, 1968).

M.K.A. Siddiqui, "Caste Among the Muslims of Calcutta." in *Caste and Social Stratification Among the Muslims*, ed. by I. Ahmad (New Delhi: Monahar Book Service, 1973), 133-56.

John P. Thorp, "Masters of Earth: Conceptions of 'Power' Among Muslims of Rural Bangladesh." Ph.D. dissertation (University of Chicago: 1978).

—— "Bengali Muslims and the Symbolism of Earth: An Analysis." in *Understanding Religion and Culture: Anthropological and Theological Perspectives*, ed. by John H. Morgan (Washington, D.C.: University Press of America, 1979), 15-34.

Terrence Turner, "Parsons' Concept of 'Generalized Media of Social Interaction' and its Relevance for Social Anthropology." *Social Inquiry* 38 (1968), 121-34.

NOTES TO S.G.A. OSOVO ONIBERE "ISOKO CONCEPT OF PREDESTINY"

1. The Isoko are located in the Niger Delta, Bendel State of Nigeria. They are one of the Edo-speaking peoples of Southern Nigeria.

2. $\bar{O}ma$ (body) and $\bar{o}ma$ (soul), as can be seen, are only distinguishable through the tones.

3. E.B. Idowu, *Olodumare: God in Yoruba Belief* (London: Longman, 1962), 172.

4. R.E. Bradbury, *The Benin Kingdom and the Edo-speaking Peoples of South-Western Nigeria* (London: International African Institute, 1970 ed.), 160.

5. W.O.A. Ifode, "Priesthood in the Traditional Religion of the Isoko People of Mid-West State of Nigeria," a B.A. Long Essay (Department of Religious Studies, University of Ibadan, 1972), 16.

6. James W. Welch, "The Isoko Tribe," *Africa* 7/2 (1934), 163ff.

7. Bradbury, *Benin Kingdom*, 160.

8. James W. Welch, *"Isoko Tribe,"* 163ff.

9. *Ezi* and $\bar{o}ma$ as objects of worship will be fully indicated further on in the paper.

10. Interview with Pa Adube, c.120, at Aviara town, December 3, 1978.

11. Bradbury, *Benin Kingdom*, 160.

12. "$\bar{O}tatha$" is a contraction of *o no o ta ze* = "that which he said when coming." The $\bar{o}tatha$ conferment is known as *a re dhu* or *a re di igwe* ("they do kneel down').

13. S.U. Erivwo, "Christianity in Urhoboland," Ph.D., thesis (University of Ibadan, 1972), 30.

14. See P.A. Dopamu, "The Forces of Evil and their Social Function," a paper presented to the fifth Annual Conference of the Nigerian Association for the Study of Religion (NASR), University of Ilorin, September 10-14, 1979.

15. Cf. M.Y. Nabofa, "Erhi: The Concept of the Human Double and the Paradox of Self-predestination in the Religion of the Urhobo," Ph.D., thesis (University of Ibadan, 1978), 161-82.

16. Interview with elders at Enhwe, December 3, 1978.

17. In former times cowries were used in the recantation ritual then came pounds, shillings and pence in which case the amount was twelve shillings (12/-). Now it is naira and kobo hence we have one naira and twenty kobo in our context.

18. It is noteworthy that beer, soft drinks, candles, powder, scent, and biscuits were not used in the ritual. This is the consequence of social change. All that was needed was three pounds and seven shillings (£3 7/-), ten kolanuts and a cat.

19. This song is intended to appease the forces around to make it possible for the suppliant to see his bad ɔtatha in time.

20. An ɔtatha victim usually has colleagues who basically remain invisible. They are present in such a ceremony, helping to delay the discovery of the ɔtatha.

NOTES TO A. NANJI "MODERN AFRICAN NOVELISTS"

1. Hamidou Kane, *Ambiguous Adventure*, trans. by K. Woods (London: Heinemann, 1972).

2. Camara Laye, *The Dark Child*, trans. by James Kirkup et. al. (New York: Noonday Press, 1954).

3. Chinua Achebe, *Things Fall Apart* (Greenwich, Conn: Fawcett, 1959).

4. Ngugi wa'Thiongo, *The River Between*, African Writers Series, 17 (London: Heinemann, 1965).

5. Ngugi wa'Thiongo, *Weep Not Child*, African Writers Series, 7 (London: Heinemann, 1964).

6. Ngugi wa'Thiongo, *Petals of Blood* (New York: Dutton, 1978).

7. Yambo Oulouguem, *Bound to Violence*, trans. by Ralph Manheim, African Writers Series, 99 (London: Heinemann, 1971).

8. Ayi Kwei Armah, *Two Thousand Seasons*, African Writers Series, 218 (London: Heinemann, 1979).

9. Laye, *The Dark Child*, 49.

10. Kane, *Ambiguous Adventure*, 5.

11. Achebe, *Things Fall Apart*, 136.

12. Ngugi, *The River Between*, 30.

13. Ngugi, *Weep Not Child*, 89-90.

14. The full quotation at the beginning of *Weep Not Child* is: Weep not, child/Weep not, my darling/With these kisses let me remove your tears,/The ravening clouds shall not long be victorious,/They shall not long possess the sky...."

15. Kane, *Ambiguous Adventure*, 9.

16. Ibid., 34.

17. Ibid., 150-151.

18. Ibid., 33-34.

19. David Rubadiri, "The Tide that from the West Washes Africa to the Bone" in *African Voices*, ed. by Howard Sergeant (New York: Lawrence Hill, 1973), 114.

NOTES TO P.B. STEINMETZ "THE OGLALA LAKOTA"

1. William K. Powers, *Oglala Religion* (Lincoln NB/ London: University of Nebraska Press, 1975), 205.

2. Paul Radin, *The World of Primitive Man* (New York: Henry Schuman, 1953), 37-67.

3. The original field material is taken from Paul B. Steinmetz, *Pipe, Bible and Peyote among the Oglala Lakota*, Stockholm Studies in Comparative Religion 19 (Stockholm: Almqvist & Miksell International, 1980).

4. James Owen Dorsey, "A Study of Siouan Cults," *Eleventh Annual Report of the Bureau of Ethnology* (Washington D.C.: Smithsonian Institution, 1895), 456.

5. Ibid., 456-57.

6. Frances Densmore, "Teton Sioux Music," *Bulletin of the Bureau of American Ethnology* 61 (Washington, D.C.: Smithsonian Institution, 1918), 118.

7. Mircea Eliade, "Methological Remarks on the Study of Religious Symbolism," in Mircea Eliade and Joseph Kitagawa (eds.) *The History of Religions: Essays in Methodology* (Chicago: University of Chicago Press, 1959), 106-107.

8. Erik Erikson, "Childhood and Tradition in Two American Indian Tribes," *The Psychoanalytic Study of the Child* 1 (1945), 320.

9. Weston LaBarre, *The Peyote Cult*, 4th ed. (New York: Schocken Books), 165.

10. Morris E. Opler, "The Influence of Aboriginal Pattern and White Contact on a Recently Introduced Ceremony, the Mescalero Peyote Rite." *Journal of American Folklore* 49 (1936), 144.

11. Joseph Jorgensen and Richard Clemmer, "America in the Indian's Past," *The Indian Historian* 11 (1978), 43.

12. John G. Neihardt, "Fieldnotes for *Black Elk Speaks*," unpublished manuscript, n.d. (Columbia, MO: University of Missouri Library), 135-39.

13. Leslie Spier, *The Prophet Dance of the Northwest and Its Derivatives: The Source of the Ghost Dance* (New York: AMS Press, 1979).

14. John G. Neihardt, *Black Elk Speaks: Being the Life Story of a Holy Man of the Oglala Sioux* (Lincoln NB: University of Nebraska Press, 1961), 239.

15. Neihardt, "Fieldnotes for *Black Elk Speaks*," 130.

16. Ibid., 129.

17. Neihardt, *Black Elk Speaks*, 249.

18 Quoted above.

19. J.S. Slotkin, *The Peyote Religion: A Study in Indian-White Relations* (Glencoe, IL: Free Press, 1956). 46.

20. Omer C. Stewart, Book review of Weston La Barre, *The Peyote Cult*, *American Anthropologist* 19 (1977), 930-31.

21. Joseph Jorgensen and Richard Clemmer, "America in the Indian's Past," 39.

Notes to pages 540-551

22. Powers, *Oglala Religion*, 205-206.

NOTES TO P. KERANS "THE STRUGGLE AGAINST DEPENDENCY"

1. Berger's report was tabled in the House of Commons on May 9, 1977. He called for a five year moratorium. Cf. Mr. Justice Thomas Berger, *Northern Frontier, Northern Homeland: The Report of the Mackenzie Valley Pipeline Inquiry: Volume One*. (Ottawa: Ministry of Supply and Services, 1977).
2. This paper is part of a larger study, conducted by Professor Roger Hutchinson, into the position and role of Project North. I am appreciative of the clarity and wealth of information derived from the consultation sessions of Professor Hutchinson and his team.
3. Berger, *Northern Frontier*, 148.
4. Ibid., 111.
5. Hugh McCullum, "The Dene: A Struggle for Decolonization" (typescript, March 1977), 8.
6. *The Dene: Land and Unity for the Native People of the Mackenzie Valley* (Yellowknife: The Dene of the Northwest Territories, 1975).
7. Bob Overvold, "Address to the Ninth Legislative Assembly of the Northwest Territories" (transcript, March 1980), 8. My italics.
8. "Statement Made by the Honourable Jean Chretien, Minister of Indian Affairs and Northern Development on Claims of Indian and Inuit People," August 8, 1973 communique of DIAND #1-7339.
9. Project North, "A Call for a Moritorium: Some Moral and Ethical Considerations Relating to the Mackenzie Valley Pipeline" (typescript, June 1976), 14 cf. also Hugh and Karmel McCullum, *This Land is Not for Sale* (Toronto: Anglican Book Center, 1975), 66.
10. Cf. ibid., 68.
11. Patrick Kerans, "Philosophic Barriers to Equality," in Allan Moscovitch and Glenn Drover (eds.), *Inequality: Essays in the Political Economy of Social Welfare* (Toronto: University of Toronto Press, 1981).
12. "Funding Suspended for Mackenzie Valley Native Claims Negotiation," communique of DIAND #1-7839, 1.
13. Cf. Kerans, *"Philosophic Barriers"* also George P. Grant, *English-Speaking Justice* (Sackville, N.B.: Mount Allison University Press, 1974), 39.
14. Cited by Hugh McCullum, *This Land is Not For Sale*, 6.
15. Project North, "A Call for a Moratorium," 12-13,21. I am grateful to Russell Halton, one of Project North's founders, for pointing out this development in the churches' position.
16. Thomas McCarthy, "Translator's Introduction" in Jürgen Habermas, *Communication and the Evolution of Society* (Boston: Beacon Press, 1979), xviii. cf. also McCarthy's "Translator's Introduction" to Jürgen Habermas, *Legitimation Crisis* (Boston: Beacon Press, 1975), xiii-xviii.
17. J. Habermas, *Communication*, 50-65.
18. Patrick D. O'Connell, President, Canadian Institute of Mining and Metallurgy, "Comments on the Canadian Catholic Bishops' Labour Day Message," September 1, 1975 (typescript, January 6, 1976).

19. Jeremy J. Shapiro, "The Slime of History," in John O'Neill (ed.) *On Critical Theory* (New York: Seabury Press, 1976), 156.
20. Habermas, *Legitimation Crisis*, 8 cf. also F.W. Sixel, "The Problem of Sense," in O'Neill, *On Critical Theory*, 196.
21. Jürgen Habermas, *Towards a Rational Society* (Boston: Beacon Press, 1980), 112-13.

NOTES TO J. KITAGAWA "THE HISTORY OF RELIGIONS"

1. The World's Religious Congress, *General Programme* (preliminary ed., 1893), 19.
2. Statement drafted by Professor R.J. Zwi Werblowsky, and signed by Professor Abel (Brussells), Brandon (Manchester), Brelich and Brezzi (Rome), DuschesneGuillemin (Liege), Eliade, Kitagawa and Long (Chicago), Goodenough (Yale), Hidding (Leiden), Hoffman (Munich), Kishimoto (Tokyo), Lanternari and Pincherie (Rome), Simon (Strasbourg), and Zaehner (Oxford). This statement was presented in response to the statement by Professor C.J. Bleeker.
3. Paul Tillich, *Systematic Theology* (Chicago: University of Chicago Press, 1951), 1:39.
4. Ibid., 108.
5. Tillich, *Christianity and the Encounter of the World Religions* (New York: Columbia University Press, 1963). 56.
6. Jonathan Z. Smith, *Map is Not Territory: Studies in the History of Religions* (Leiden: E.J. Brill, 1978), 295-97.
7. Raffaele Pettazzoni, *Essays on the History of Religions* (Leiden: E.J. Brill, 1954), 216.
8. Mircea Eliade, *Patterns in Comparative Religion* (New York: Sheed & Ward, 1958), xi.
9. Robert Redfield, "Thinking about a Civilization," in Milton Singer (ed.), *Introducing India in Liberal Education* (Chicago: University of Chicago Press, 1957), 3.

Joachim Wach, *Religionswissenschaft: Prolegomena zu ihrer wissenschaft-theoretischen Grundlegung* (Leipzig: J.C. Hinrichs, 1924), 117-19.

NOTES TO M. PYE "THE JAPANESE INTELLECTUAL TRADITION"

1. Michael Pye, "Aufklärung and religion in Europe and Japan," *Religious Studies* 9 (1973), 201-207.
2. Ryūsaku Tsunoda et al., *Sources of Japanese Tradition* (New York: Columbia University Press, 1958), 479-88.
3. Shūichi Katō, "The Life and Thought of Tominaga Nakamoto, 1715-46, a Tokugawa Iconoclast," *Monumenta Nipponica* 12/1-2 (January 1967), 1-35.
4. Robert Baird, *Category Formation in the History of Religions* (The Hague: Mouton, 1971).
5. Translated from text as given in N. Mizuta and T. Arisaka (eds.), *Nihon Shisō Taikei* 43 (Tokyo: Iwanami Shoten, 1973), 112.
6. Translated from text as given in Y. Nakamura (ed.), *Nihon no Shisō* 18 (Tokyo: Chikuma Shobō, 1971), 160.
7. Ibid., 145.

8. Ibid., 169-70.

NOTES FROM R.M. GROSS "WOMEN'S STUDIES IN RELIGION"

1. Simone de Beauvoir, *The Second Sex* (New York: Bantam Books, 1961), xv.

2. To demonstrate what I mean by androcentrism in the history of religions, I will discuss only one classic, Mircea Eliade's *Patterns in Comparative Religion* (Cleveland: Maridian Books, 1963). If the androcentrism of this one example is understood the point is easily transferred to the literature of the whole discipline. Simply in looking over the chapter titles, one notices something strange. The book is basically a catalogue of the major hierophanies and symbols through which *homo religiosus* apprehends the sacred and constructs a religious symbol system. After chapters on the sky and sky deities, the sun and sun-worship, the moon and its mystique, waters and water symbolism, and sacred stones, we find a chapter on "the earth, woman, and fertility." The next chapters are on vegetation, agriculture and fertility cults, sacred space, sacred time, etc. There is no chapter on maleness or men as a symbol. There is no indication that women experience hierophanies and create symbol systems only that they are experienced as hierophanies by men and then intergrated into other aspects of the world "out there." It is all so one-sided. Why are women symbols to men but not vice versa? Why is womanhood but not manhood a symbol? Such patterns permeate the history of religions literature.

3. For history of religions, see Rita M. Gross, "Methodological Remarks on the Study of Women and Religion: Review, Criticism, Redefinition," in Judith Plaskow and Joan A. Romero (eds.), *Women and Religion* (Missoula, MT: Scholars Press, 1973): "The Issues and Non-Issues in the Study of Women in World Religions," *Anima* 2/1 (Fall 1975) "Androcentrism and Androgyny in the Methodology of History of Religions," in Rita M. Gross (ed.) *Beyond Androcentrism: New Essays on Women and Religion* (Missoula, MT: Scholars Press, 1977) and Nancy Auer Falk and Rita M. Gross, "Introduction: Patterns in Women's Religious Lives," in Falk and Gross, *Unspoken Worlds: Women's Religious Lives in Non-Western Cultures* (New York: Harper & Row, 1980). For theology, see Carol Christ and Judith Plaskow (eds.), *Womanspirit Rising: A Feminist Reader in Religion* (New York: Harper & Row, 1979), which contains valuable introductions and reprints the most valuable essays in feminist theology to date. See also Carol Christ, "The New Feminist Theology: A Review of the Literature," *Religious Studies Review* 3/4 (October 1977).

4. For *History of Religions*, the index of the ten years 1961-1971 reveals nine articles with content relevant to the study of women and religion. In the next nine years, through May 1980, there are fourteen such articles, with four of them appearing in the last four issues. *Numen* has not published an article with relevant data for twelve years since 1968. In the earlier years of the journal, from 1958 to 1968, there were three articles with content at least tangentially discussing women's invovlement in religion.

5. Three articles directly take up issues central to the women and religion movement: Carol Christ, "Feminist Studies in Religion and Literature: A Methodological Review," *JAAR* 44/2 (June 1976): Rita Gross, "Menstruation and Childbirth as Ritual and Religious Experience in the Religion of the

Australian Aborigines," *JAAR* 45/4 (December 1977): Rita Gross, "Hindu Female Deities as a Resource in the Contemporary Re-discovery of the Goddess," *JAAR* 46/3 (September 1978). Several other recent articles, while they are not as explicitly positioned within the women and religion movement, obviously were inspired by it. They are Jane Smith, "Women in Islam: Equity, Equality, & the Search for the Natural Order," *JAAR*, 47/4 (December 1979), and Mary Bodnarowski, "Outside the Mainstream: Women's Religion and Women Religious Leaders in Nineteenth Century America," *JAAR* 48/2 (June, 1980).

6. Falk and Gross, *Unspoken Worlds* and Denise Larner Carmody, *Women and World Religions* (Nashville: Abingdon, 1979). A volume to be published by the University of Queensland Press, edited by Arvind Sharma, is in preparation.

7. One of the best examples of such work is Diana Paul, *Women in Buddhism: Images of the Feminine in Mahayana Tradition* (Berkeley: Asian Humanities Press, 1979).

8. For a review essay, see Rayna Rapp, "Anthropology," *Signs: Journal of Women in Culture and Society* 4/3 (Spring 1979).

9. For one example, see Gross, "Menstruation and Childbirth."

10. My favorite examples are found in any overview of Hindu theism. Long discussions of Visnu and Siva dominate the discussion: all the goddesses are lumped together in a short third chapter. This seems to be a basically inaccurate model of Hindu theism, in which the goddesses are certainly co-equal with the gods and may even dominate them.

11. David Kinsley's interpretation of Kali in *The Sword and the Flute* (Berkeley: University of California Press, 1977) should be cited as an example that does not fall into such simple-minded generalities and thus should be emulated.

12. See n.2 above.

13. In addition to articles already cited above see Starhawk, *The Spiral Dance* (New York: Harper & Row, 1980), and recent issues of *Anima: An Experiental Journal*. *Lady-Unique-Inclination-of-the-Night*, *Heresies*, and *Womanspirit* are feminist periodicals that have devoted special focus to goddess worship. Merlin Stone's book *When God Was a Woman* (New York: Harcourt, Brace, Jovanovich, 1976), has been especially influential.

NOTES TO R.W. NEUFELDT "THE VISION OF MAX MÜLLER"

1. See J. Waardenburg, *Classical Approaches to the Study of Religion* (The Hague: Mouton, 1973), I:14 S. Hardy, "Zur Geschichte der vergleichenden Religionsforschung," *Archiv für Religionswissenschaft* 4 (1901), 195-96 J. Wach, *The Comparative Study of Religions* (New York: Columbia University Press, 1956), 3.

2. F. Max Müller, *Auld Lang Syne*, 2nd Series (New York: Scribner's, 1899), 5.

3. Ibid., see especially his reminiscences about Indians whom he met and with whom he corresponded.

4. F. Max Müller, *India: What Can It Teach Us?* (London: Longmans, Green, 1919), 6.

5. Ibid., 13.

6. Ibid., 14.

7. Ibid., 15.
8. Ibid.
9. F. Max Müller, *Auld Lang Syne* 2nd Series, 180-81
10. F. Max Müller, *My Autobiography: A Fragment* (New York: Scribner's, 1901), 42.
11. Max Müller, *India: What Can It Teach Us?*, 95.
12. F. Max Müller, *A History of Sanskrit Literature* (Varanasi: Chowkhamba Sanskrit Series Office, 1968), 28.
13. Max Müller, *My Autobiography*, 316-317.
14. J. Voigt, *Max Müller: The Man and His Ideas* (Calcutta: Firma K.L. Mukhophadhyay, 1967), 32-33. See also F. Max Müller, *Psychological Religion* (London: Longmans, Green, 1903), lectures 9,12 and 15, where he discusses Vedanta, Alexandrian Christianity, and Christian Theosophy.
15. Max Müller, *Auld Lang Syne*, 2nd Series, 5.
16. Max Müller, *India: What Can It Teach Us?*, 84.
17. Ibid., 14.
18. Max Müller, *My Autobiography*, 148.
19. For a comment on the *Rig Veda* as a laboratory see N.C. Chaudhuri, *Scholar Extraordinary: The Life of Professor the Rt. Hon. Friedrich Max Müller, P.C.* (London: Chatto and Windus, 1974), 176. See F. Max Müller, *Natural Religion* (London: Longmans, Green 1887), 18,20 for his argument that the *Rig Veda* puts his theories on a firm foundation.
20. Max Müller, *India: What Can It Teach Us?*, 89.
21. Ibid., 123.
22. F. Max Müller, *Chips From a German Workshop* 1 (New York: Scribner's, 1891): 67-68.
23. Ibid., 72.
24. See F. Max Müller, *I Point to India*, 60, and *Chips From A Germany Workshop* 4 (New York: Scribner's 1895), 3-4.
25. Ibid., 353.
26. Voigt, *Max Müller*, 30.
27. Max Müller, *Auld Lang Syne*, 2nd Series, 30-31, 74.
28. Max Müller, *A History of Sanskrit Literature*, 7.
29. Ibid.
30. Max Müller, *Auld Lang Syne*, 2nd Series, vi-viii.
31. Max Müller, *India: What Can It Teach Us?*, 84.
32. Max Müller, *A History of Sanskrit Literature*, 7-8.
33. Max Müller, *Physical Religion* (London: Longmans, Green, 1891), 191-92.
34. Max Müller, *Natural Religion*, 143.
35. Max Müller, *My Autobiography*, 198.
36. F. Max Müller, *Contributions to the Science of Mythology* (New York: Longmans, Green, 1897), 824-25.
37. Max Müller, *A History of Sanskrit Literature*, 29
38. Max Müller, *My Autobiography*, 31.
39. Max Müller, *Chips From A German Workshop*, 1: Preface, ix-x,xxi.
40. See C.G. Jung, "The Holy Men of India," in *The Collected Works of C.G. Jung*, V-1.II (Princeton: Princeton University Press, 1969) and H.G.

Coward, "Jung's Encounter with Yoga," *Journal of Analytical Psychology* 23/4, 340,343.

41. C.G. Jung, *Collected Works*, 2:576-79.

NOTES TO A CUNNINGHAM "STRUCTURES IN JUNG AND LEVISTRAUSS"

1. Much of the discussion that follows has an obvious and close bearing on Mircea Eliade's style of history of religions. Comparison of the chapters on sun and moon symbolism in his *Patterns in Comparative Religion*, trans. by Rosemary Sheed (London: Sheed and Ward, 1958 original, 1948), Lévi-Strauss's 1969 essay "The Sex of the Sun and the Moon", *Structural Anthropology*, vol. 2, trans. by Monique Layton (New York: Basic Books, 1976), and Eliade's "Prolegomena to Religious Dualism: Dyads and Polarities," in his *The Quest: History and Meaning in Religion* (Chicago: University of Chicago Press, 1969), shows a refinement of Eliade's stance in the light of structuralism. The substantial differences that remain can be pinpointed by saying that Lévi-Strauss is concerned with the appplication of methods derived from linguistics and information theory to the study of myths as the *transmission of messages*. Eliade is concerned with *traditions* - the appropriation of a body of traditional materials in a group and their handing on to another generation. The differences of resonance and of method implied by this contrast of transmission and tradition, of the neutral logic of transmission and the motivated patterns of tradition, will be noted throughout this paper.

As Eliade puts it, for Lévi-Strauss "there is no solution of *continuity* between the polarities and oppositions grasped at the level of matter, life, deep psyche, language or social organization and those grasped at the level of mythological and religious creations" (*The Quest*, 132 my emphasis). For Eliade, the dichotomies and polarities - of cosmic, religious, and sexual kinds, for instance - "*imply each other mutually*" (ibid.,174). For Lévi-Strauss they do not; they imply only an underlying and neutral logic. What Eliade wants is a "reading [of] nature and human nature through the cypher of polarity..." (ibid., 141), "the cypher through which man unveils both the structures of the universe and the significance of his own existence" (ibid., 174). For Lévi-Strauss, whilst there may be an aesthetic satisfaction in the orderliness of our logical operations, they are devoid of existential significance.

2. C.G. Jung, forward to Charles Roberts Aldrich, *The Primitive Mind and Modern Civilization* (1931), in Jung's *Collected Works*, 18 (London: Routledge and Kegan Paul, 1957-79), 562.

3. Lévi-Strauss *Structural Anthropology*, 1, trans. by Claire Jacobson and Brooke Grundfest Schoepf (New York: Basic Books, 1963), 204.

4. Lévi-Strauss, "Sur le caractère des faits ethnologiques," *Revue des Travaux de l'Academie des Sciences morales et politiques* 115 (1962), 215.

5. Lévi-Strauss, *The Raw and the Cooked*, trans. by John and Doreen Weightman (New York: Harper & Row, 1969) Jung, *Collected Works*, 8:323.

6. Lévi-Strauss, *The Savage Mind* (Chicago: University of Chicago Press, 1966), 131.

7. Lévi-Strauss, *Structural Anthropology*, 1, 202.

8. In suggesting areas of fruitful comparison between Lévi-Strauss and Jung, I am leaving to one side those questions of correlating theories of social data and theories of individual data which beset any work drawing on both anthropological and psychoanalytic material.

9. Lévi-Strauss, "Sur le Caractère," 214.

10. Lévi-Strauss, *Savage Mind*, 65.

11. Jung, *Collected Works*, 17:273. In his later writings Jung distinguishes between the inaccessible archetype itself and the images it produces - a distinction Lévi-Strauss ignores in his criticism of Jung.

12. Lévi-Strauss, *Structural Anthropology*, 2:255.

13. "S'il existe des contenus communs, la raison doit en être cherchée, soit du côté des propriétés objectives de certains être [sic] empiriques, soit du côté de la diffusion et de l'emprunt, c'est-à-dire, dans les deux cas, hors de l'esprit" (*"sur le caractére,"* 218).

14. Lévi-Strauss, *Structural Anthropology*, 1:208.

15. Ibid.

16. Maurice Merleau-Ponty, "From Mauss to Claude Lévi-Strauss," in his *Signs*, trans. by Richard C. McCleary (Evanston, IL: Northwestern University Press, 1964), 117.

17. E.R. Leach, "Two Essays on the Symbolic Representation of Time," in his *Re-thinking Anthropology* (London: Athlone Press, 1961).

18. Lévi-Strauss, *Structural Anthropology*, 2, 79-80.

19. Lévi-Strauss, *The Elementary Structures of Kinship*, trans. by Jame Harle Bell, ed. by John Richard von Sturmer and Rodney Needham (Boston: Beacon Press, 1969), 95.

20. Ibid., 93

21. Lévi-Strauss's discussion of parallels between childhood and primitive thought in "The Archaic Illusion" (ch. 7 of *The Elementary Structure of Kinship*) are a response to Jean Piaget's work on this topic. Interestingly enough, the chapters of Piaget's *La formation du symbole chez l'enfant* (1945) cited by Lévi-Strauss contain a rebuttal of Jung's theory of archetypes. I suspect that Lévi-Strauss's latter objections to Jung are based upon Piaget's critique. See also Judith K. Brown, "'The Archaic Illusion': A Re-examination of Lévi-Strauss's View of the Developing Child," in Thomas R. Williams (ed.) *Psychological Anthropology* (The Hague: Mouton, 1975), 103-108.

22. Lévi-Strauss, *Structural Anthropology* , 1:193.

23. Ibid., 201.

24. Ibid., 198.

25. C.G. Jung, *Collected Works*, 8:133, (my emphasis).

26. C.G. Jung, *Collected Works*, 10:31. To explain the relation between archetype itself and specific archetypal images, Jung often uses the analogy of the axial system of a crystal which structures the crystal although it has no material existence of its own. (See, for instance, Jung's *Collected Works*, 9:172-73.) Interestingly enough, it is to just such an analogy that Lévi-Strauss appeals in the essay where he rejects Jung's position (*Structural Anthropology*, 1:229).

27. Phosphenes are endogenously arising lumonous patterns seen with the eyes closed; with the eyes open they can arise in visually clueless situations, driving in fog or snow for instance. They can be artificially

produced by gentle pressure on the eyeballs or by chemical or electrical stimulus. The phenomenon has been known since at least the late seventeenth century. The regularity of the patterns perceived - arcs, radials, waves, circles, spirals, meanders etc. - and their endogenous origin may suggest that they represent, as it were, the brain looking at itself. For a synopsis see M. Knoll and J. Kugler, "Subjective Light Pattern Spectroscopy," *Nature* (December 5, 1959), 1823-24. Phosphene patterns have been correlated with Kellogg's well-known studies, with Jungian affiliations, of children's drawings; See Rhoda Kellogg, M. Knoll and J. Kugler, "Form-Similarity between Phosphenes of Adults and pre-School Children's Scribblings," *Nature* (December 11, 1965), 1129-30. See also Lorna McDougall, "Symbols and Somatic Structure," in John Blacking (ed.), *The Anthropology of the Body* (London: Academic Press, 1977).

28. Eliade, *Quest*, 128.

29. In an appendix to *Memories, Dreams, Reflexions* (not in the English edition), Jung seems to touch on the difference between order and meaning. "Since a creation without the reflecting consciousness of man has no *recognizable* meaning, the hypothesis of a latent meaning invests man with a cosmogonic significance, a veritable "raison d'être" (*Erinnerungen, Traüme, Gedanken* [Zurich: Rascher, 1963], 377). But he does not pursue the matter.

30. *Esprit* 31/ 322 (Nov. 1963), 633.

31. Other discussions of structuralism and psychoanalysis which I have consulted are R.J.Z. Werblowsky, "Structure and Archetype," *Journal of the Ancient Near Eastern Society of Columbia University* 5 (1973), 435-42; Roy C. Calogeras, "Lévi-Strauss and Freud: Their 'Structural' Approaches to Myths," *American Imago* 30 (1973), 57-79; Ino Rossi, "The Unconscious in the Anthropology of Claude Lévi-Strauss," *American Anthropologist* 75 (1973), 20-48; John Raphael Stande, "From Depth Psychology to Depth Sociology: Freud, Jung and Lévi- Strauss," *Theory and Society* 3 (1976), 303-38; Martin Thom, "The Unconscious Structured Like a Language," *Economy and Society* 5 (1976), 435-69; Paul Filmer, "Durkheim, Jung and Symbolism: The Necessity of a Sociology of the Unconscious," *Harvest* 23 (1977), 62-88; Thomas Shalvey, *Claude Lévi-Strauss: Social Psychotherapy and the Collective Unconscious* (Amherst, MA: University of Massachusetts Press, 1979).

NOTES TO J.R. HORNE "ORIENTAL MYSTICISM"

1. Frits Staal, review of *Mysticism and Morality*, in *The Journal of Philosophy* 71 (1974), 175.

2. Todd Gitlin, "Again the Yogi and the Commissar," *The Nation* 217 (1973), 245. Orientalists reviewing *Mysticism and Morality* uniformly condemn Danto for his oversimplified account of oriental religions. Staal, in the review just cited, and Bina Gupta, in a review in *The Review of Metaphysics* 29 (June, 1976), 730-1, cite various specific errors of interpretation. Antonio T. de Nicholas, in "Cultural Lobotomy: The Failure of Philosophy," in *Philosophy East and West* 27 (Jan. 1977), 97-113. Minette Marin, "Beyond the Grasp of the West," *Far Eastern Economic Review* 93 (July 16, 1976), 41, and Gitlin see Danto as hampered by excessive reliance on a strict and narrow idea

of rationality. Both lines of criticism seem to be correct, and so supplement each other.

3. Arthur C. Danto, *Mysticism and Morality* (New York: Harper Torchbooks, 1973), 10.
4. Ibid., 12-13.
5. Ibid., 13.
6. Ibid.
7. Ibid., 14.
8. Ibid., 13.
9. Ibid., x-xi.
10. Ibid., 41.
11. Ibid., 63.
12. Ibid., 81.
13. Ibid., 81-82.
14. Ibid., 82.
15. Ibid.
16. Ibid.
17. Ibid., 95.
18. Ibid., 110-11.
19. Ibid., 119.
20. Peter Moore, "Mystical Experience, Mystical Doctrine, Mystical Technique," in Steven T. Katz (ed.), *Mysticism and Philosophical Analysis* (New York: Oxford University Press, 1978), 108.
21. Danto, *Mysticism and Morality*, 41.
22. Ibid., xi.
23. Ibid.
24. Roland Fischer, "On Creative, Psychotic and Ecstatic States," in John White (ed.), *The Highest State of Consciousness* (Garden City, NY: Doubleday, 1972), 190.
25. Danto, *Mysticism and Morality*, 95.
26. Ibid., 81.
27. Martin Buber, *I and Thou*, trans. by Walter Kaufman (New York: Scribner's, 1970), 134.
28. Cf. John Hick, "Mystical Experience as Cognition," 45, and Terence Penelhum, "Unity and Diversity in the Interpretation of Mysticism," 73, both in Harold Coward and Terence Penelhum (eds.), *Mystics and Scholars* (Waterloo, Ontario: Wilfred University Press, 1977). Cf. also Steven T. Katz, "Language, Epistemology, and Mysticism," in Katz (ed.), *Mysticism and Philosophical Analysis*; 25.
29. Arthur C. Danto, "Ethical Theory and Mystical Experience: A Response to Professor Proudfoot and Wainwright," *The Journal of Religious Ethics* 4 (1976), 41.
30. Ibid., 45.
31. Wayne Proudfoot, "Mysticism, the Numinous, and the Moral," *The Journal of Religious Ethics* 4 (1976), 15.
32. Danto, *Mysticism and Morality*, 118.
33. Gupta, review of *Mysticism and Morality*, 731.
34. Danto, *Mysticism and Morality*, 120.

35. Paul Tillich, "Vertical and Horizontal Thinking," *American Scholar* 15 (1946), 103.

NOTES TO T. DEAN "TRUTH AND DIALOGUE IN RELIGION"

1. John Hick, *Philosophy of Religion*, 2d ed. (Ithaca: Cornell University Press, 1973), 3.
2. Wilfred Cantwell Smith, "Conflicting Truth-Claims," in John Hick (ed.) *Truth and Dialogue in World Religions: Conflicting Truth-Claims* (Philadelphia: Westminster, 1974), 156-57.
3. For the following account see James Fowler, "Life/Faith Patterns: Structures of Trust and Loyalty," in *Life Maps: Conversations on the Journey of Faith*, by James Fowler and Sam Keen (Waco, TX: Word Books, 1978), 25-29, 34-39.
4. For the following see Fowler, *Life Maps* 69-87, 96-99 and James Fowler, "Stages in Faith: The Structural Developmental Perspective," in Thomas Hennessey (ed.) *Studies in Moral Development* (Paramus, NJ: Paulist Press, 1976). Fowler's own full-length account of his work has just appeared as *Stages of Faith: The Psychology of Human Development and the Quest for Meaning* (San Francisco: Harper & Row, 1981).
5. John Hick, "Foreword," *The Meaning and End of Religion*, by Wilfred Cantwell Smith (New York: Harper & Row, 1978), x.
6. John Hick (ed.) *The Myth of God Incarnate* (Philadelphia: Westminster, 1977), 39.
7. John Hick, *Death and Eternal Life* (New York: Harper & Row, 1976), 30.
8. John Hick, *God and the Universe of Faiths* (New York: St. Martin's, 1973), 124.
9. Ibid., 123-30.
10. Hick, *Philosophy of Religion*, 129.
11. Hick, *God and the Universe of Faiths*, 124, 130.
12. Ibid., 130.
13. Ibid., 100.
14. Hick, *Myth of God*, 180.
15. Hick, *God and the Universe of Faiths*, 124.
16. Ibid., 101-102.
17. Hick, *Myth of God*, 181-82.
18. Hick, *God and the Universe of Faiths*, 103.
19. Ibid., 104.
20. Ibid., 103.
21. Ibid., 106, 103.
22. For Hick's two arguments, see *Philosophy of Religion*, 127-28. For an account of the contributions of the kyoto school to rethinking the alleged doctrinal incompatibilities of theistic and non-theistic modes of thought, see Hans Waldenfels, *Absolute Nothingness: Foundations for a Buddhist-Christian Dialogue* (New York: Paulist Press, 1980).
23. Hick, *God and the Universe of Faiths*, 177.
24. Ibid., 132 (italics mine).
25. James Fowler, "Faith, Liberation and Human Development," *The Foundation* (Atlanta: Gammon Theological Seminary), 79 (1974), 21-22.

26. William Perry, *Forms of Intellectual and Ethical Development in the College Years* (New York: Holt Rinehart and Winston, 1970), 111.
27. Ibid., 100.
28. James Fowler, "Interview with James Fowler," *Havard Divinity Bulletin* 6/a, (June, 1976), 6.
29. Hick, *Myth of God*, x.
30. Julius Lipner, "Does Copernicus Help? Reflections for a Christian Theology of Religions," *Religious Studies* 5/13 (1977), 349.
31. Fowler, *Life Maps*, 17-25.
32. Ibid.
33. Don Cupitt, in Hick, *Myth of God*, 205.
34. Paul Tillich, *Christianity and the Encounter of the World Religions* (New York: Columbia University Press, 1963), 81.
35. Paul Tillich, *The Future of Religions* (New York: Harper & Row, 1966), 88.
36. The following summary is from Fowler, *Life Maps*, 87-90, 96-99.
37. Ibid., 93-94.

AUTHORS

1. P. Boglioni — Université de Montréal
2. J.J. Buckley — Harvard Divinity School
3. J.H. Corbett — University of Toronto
4. A. Cunningham — University of Lancaster
5. T. Dean — Temple University
6. P. Gerlitz — West Germany
7. R.M. Gross — University of Wisconsin - Eau Claire
8. A. Hamdani — University of Wisconsin - Milwaukee
9. J.C. Heesterman — Rÿksuniversiteit te Leiden
10. N. Hein — Yale University
11. J. Helgeland — North Dakota State University
12. M. Heper — Bogazici University
13. J.R. Hinnells — University of Manchester
14. J.R. Horne — University of Waterloo
15. C. Hyers — Gustavus Adolphus College
16. E. Johns — University of Utrecht
17. L.S. Kaufman — Manhattanville College
18. P. Kerans — Dalhousie University
19. J.M. Kitagawa — University of Chicago
20. J. Langlais — Champlain Regional College
21. M. Lattke — University of Queensland
22. A. Nanji — Oklahoma State University
23. R.W. Neufeldt — University of Calgary
24. S.G.A. Onibere — University of Ife
25. N. Page — Université d'Ottawa
26. M. Pye — University of Leeds
27. A. Rawlinson — University of Lancaster
28. L. Rousseau — Université du Québec à Montréal
29. H. Sakurai — Kogakkan University
30. A. Schimmel — Harvard University/University of Bonn
31. E.J. Sharpe — University of Sydney
32. K. Sivaraman — McMaster University
33. M. Smith — Columbia University
34. W.C. Smith — Harvard University
35. P.B. Steinmetz — St. Peter's Rectory
36. F.J. Streng — Southern Methodist University
37. J. Strong — Bates College
38. J.P. Thorp — St. Mary's College
39. W. Tyloch — University of Warsaw
40. M. Vovelle — Université de Provence
41. J. Wortley — University of Manitoba
42. G.E. Yocum — Whittier College
43. K. Young — McGill University

ACKNOWLEDGEMENTS

INTERNATIONAL ASSOCIATION FOR THE HISTORY OF RELIGION (IAHR)

EXECUTIVE COMMITTEE
M. Simon, President
University of Strasbourg, France

R.J. Zwi Werblowsky, Secretary-General
Hebrew University of Jerusalem

H.J. van Lier, Honorary Treasurer
Utrecht, Netherlands

M. Abe, Vice-President
University of Kyoto, Japan

J.M. Kitagawa, Vice-President
University of Chicago, USA

Michael Pye, Assistant
Secretary-General
University of Leeds

CANADIAN SOCIETY FOR THE STUDY OF RELIGION (CSSR)
NATIONAL POLICY & PLANNING COMMITTEE
Peter Slater, Chairperson
University of Toronto

Manabu Waida, Treasurer
University of Alberta

William Klassen, Vice-Chairperson
McMaster University

Earle Waugh, Treasurer
University of Manitoba

Yun-hua Jan, Vice-Chairperson
University of Calgary

Donald Wiebe, Executive Director
University of Trinity College

Louis Rousseau
Université du Québec à Montréal

Darlene Clare, Administrative
Assistant

Harold Coward, Chairperson
Academic Programme Committee
University of Calgary

IAHR ACADEMIC PROGRAM SECTION COMMITTEES
African Religions - Section One
Benjamin C. Ray, Coordinator
University of Virginia

Near Eastern/Mediterranean Antiquity - Section Two
William Klassen, Coordinator
University of Manitoba

Daniel Fraikin
Queen's University

Peter C. Craigie
University of Calgary

Buddhism - Section Three
L.S. Kawamura, Coordinator
University of Calgary

A.K. Narain
University of Wisconsin-Madison

Christianity - Section Four

Michel Despland, Coordinator
Concordia University

G. Vallée
McMaster University

W. Principe
Pontifical Institute of Medieval Studies

P. Boglioni
University of Montreal

East Asian Religions - Section Five

Y.-h. Jan, Coordinator
McMaster University

M. Waida
University of Alberta

D. Overmeyer
University of British Columbia

Indian Religions - Section Six

R.W. Stevenson, Coordinator
McGill University

Alaka Hejib
McGill University

Katherine Young
McGill University

Paul Younger
McMaster University

Clifford Hospital
Queen's University

Islam - Section Seven

Earle H. Waugh, Coordinator
University of Alberta

C. Adams
McGill University

L. Librande
Carleton University

Judaism - Section Eight

Alan F. Segal, Coordinator
University of Toronto

J. Lightstone
Concordia University

R. Goldenberg
Jewish Theological Seminary

Native Traditions in the Americas - Section Nine

Peter Hordern, Coordinator
Brandon University

Methodology and Hermeneutics - Section Ten

Willard G. Oxtoby, Coordinator
University of Toronto

Donald Wiebe
University of Trinity College

Comparative and Phenomenological Studies - Section Eleven

Yvon Desrosiers, Coordinator
University of Quebec at Montreal

Peter Slater
University of Toronto

Anthropology of Religion - Section Twelve
Joan Townsend, Coordinator
University of Manitoba

Linguistics and Textual Interpretation - Section Thirteen
Eugene Combs, Coordinator
McMaster University

R. Polzin
Carleton University

K. Post
McMaster University

Psychology of Religion - Section Fourteen
Harold G. Coward, Coordinator
University of Calgary

Sociology of Religion - Section Fifteen
R. Lemieux, Coordinator
Laval University

Philosophy of Religion - Section Sixteen
Terence Penelhum, Coordinator
University of Calgary

Cathleen Going
Thomas More Institute

Bruce Alton
University of Trinity College

Femininity and Religion - Section Seventeen
Penelope Washbourn, Coordinator
University of Manitoba

S. McDonough
Concordia University

D. Kinsley
McMaster University

Literature and Religion - Section Eighteen
William C. James, Coordinator
Queen's University

Charles Davis
Concordia University

Carl Ridd
University of Winnipeg

Art and Religion - Section Nineteen
Phyllis Granoff, Coordinator
McMaster University

N. Pagé
University of Ottawa

Religion, Ethics and Society - Section Twenty
Roger Hutchinson, Coordinator
University of Toronto

E. Best
University of Toronto

CONTRIBUTORS

We are pleased to acknowledge the generous support given to the National Planning Committee by the organizations, foundations and various businesses listed below. Without their support, the organization of this Congress would not have been possible.

Government Agencies

Government of Canada through the Social Sciences and Humanities Research Council of Canada (SSHRCC)

Government of Manitoba through the Department of Cultural Affairs and Historical Resources, Cultural Development Branch

City of Winnipeg

Academic Institutions

Canadian Corporation for Studies in Religion (CCSR)
Canadian Society for Study of Religion (CSSR)
Council on the Study of Religion (CSR)
International Council for Philosophy and Humanistic Studies

Acadia University
Bishop's University
Brandon University
Carleton University
Conrad Grebel College
Dalhousie University
Huntingdon College
McGill University
McMaster University
Mount St. Vincent University
Queen's Theological College
St. Jerome's College
St. Michael's University

Trinity College, Toronto
Thorneloe College
University of Alberta
University of Calgary
University of Manitoba
Université de Montréal
Université d'Ottawa
Université du Québec à Montréal
University of Saskatchewan
Univesity of Sudbury
University of Toronto
Wilfrid Laurier University Press

Foundations

David D. Friesen Family Foundation
James Richardson and Sons Limited
Sellers Foundation
St. Stephen's Broadway Foundation
University of Manitoba Alumni Association
Winnipeg Jewish Foundation

Businesses and Corporations

Assiniboine Travel Services Limited
Blackstone Group

Canada Cement Lafarge Limited
Canada Steamship Lines Limited
Central Optical Company
DeFehr, C.A. & Sons
Eaton's
Friesen, D.W. & Sons, Limited
Great West Life Assurance Company
Henry Armstrong's Instant Printing
Huntingdon Holdings Limited
Investors Syndicate Limited
Mackie Travel Service Limited
Robinson Little & Company Limited
Southam Company Limited
Versatile Manufacturing Company

SUPPLEMENTS

1. **FOOTNOTES TO A THEOLOGY**
   The Karl Barth Colloquium of 1972
   Edited and Introduced by Martin Rumscheidt
   1974 / viii + 151 pp. / OUT OF PRINT

2. **MARTIN HEIDEGGER'S PHILOSOPHY OF RELIGION**
   John R. Williams
   1977 / x + 190 pp. / $8.00 (paper). In U.S.A. $9.25 (paper)

3. **MYSTICS AND SCHOLARS**
   The Calgary Conference on Mysticism 1976
   Edited by Harold Coward and Terence Penelhum
   1977 / viii + 121 pp. / AVAILABLE IN LIMITED QUANTITY

4. **GOD'S INTENTION FOR MAN**
   Essays in Christian Anthropology
   William O. Fennell
   1977 / xii + 56 pp. / $2.50 (paper). In U.S.A. $3.00 (paper)

5. **"LANGUAGE" IN INDIAN PHILOSOPHY AND RELIGION**
   Edited and Introduced by Harold G. Coward
   1978 / x + 98 pp. / $5.50 (paper). In U.S.A. $6.50 (paper)

6. **BEYOND MYSTICISM**
   James R. Horne
   1978 / vi + 158 pp. / $6.50 (paper). In U.S.A. $7.50 (paper)

7. **THE RELIGIOUS DIMENSION OF SOCRATES' THOUGHT**
   James Beckman
   1979 / xii + 276 pp. / OUT OF PRINT

8. **NATIVE RELIGIOUS TRADITIONS**
   Edited by Earle H. Waugh and K. Dad Prithipaul
   1979 / xii + 244 pp. / OUT OF PRINT

9. **DEVELOPMENTS IN BUDDHIST THOUGHT**
   Canadian Contributions to Buddhist Studies
   Edited by Roy C. Amore
   1979 / iv + 196 pp. / $6.95 (paper). In U.S.A. $8.25 (paper)

10. **THE BODHISATTVA DOCTRINE IN BUDDHISM**
    Edited and Introduced by Leslie S. Kawamura
    1981 / xxii + 274 pp. / $6.95 (paper). In U.S.A. $8.25 (paper)

11. **POLITICAL THEOLOGY IN THE CANADIAN CONTEXT**
    Edited by Benjamin G. Smillie
    1982 / xii + 260 pp. / OUT OF PRINT

12. **TRUTH AND COMPASSION**
    Essays on Judaism and Religion in Memory of Rabbi Dr. Solomon Frank
    Edited by Howard Joseph, Jack N. Lightstone, and Michael D. Oppenheim
    1983 / vi + 217 pp. / $8.95 (paper). In U.S.A. $10.50 (paper)

EDITIONS

1. **LA LANGUE DE YA'UDI**
   Description et classement de l'ancien parler de Zencircli dans le cadre des langues sémitiques du nord-ouest
   Paul-Eugène Dion, O.P.
   1974 / viii + 511 p. / $9.00 (paper). In U.S.A. $10.50 (paper)

2. **THE CONCEPTION OF PUNISHMENT IN EARLY INDIAN LITERATURE**
   Terence P. Day
   1982 / iv + 328 pp. / $7.00 (paper). In U.S.A. $8.00 (paper)

3. **TRADITIONS IN CONTACT AND CHANGE**
   Selected Proceedings of the XIVth Congress of the International Association for the History of Religions
   Edited by Peter Slater and Donald Wiebe with Maurice Boutin and Harold Coward
   1983 / x + 758 pp. / $14.50 (paper). In U.S.A. $16.75 (paper)

STUDIES IN CHRISTIANITY AND JUDAISM / ETUDES SUR LE CHRISTIANISME ET LE JUDAISME

1. A STUDY IN ANTI-GNOSTIC POLEMICS
Irenaeus, Hippolytus, and Epiphanius
Gérard Vallée
1981 / xii + 114 pp. / $5.00 (paper). In U.S.A. $5.75 (paper)

THE STUDY OF RELIGION IN CANADA / SCIENCES RELIGIEUSES AU CANADA

1. RELIGIOUS STUDIES IN ALBERTA
A State-of-the-Art Review
Ronald W. Neufeldt
1983 / xiv + 145 pp. / $8.50 (paper). In U.S.A. $10.00 (paper)

Also published / Avons aussi publié

RELIGION AND CULTURE IN CANADA / RELIGION ET CULTURE AU CANADA
Edited by / sous la direction de
Peter Slater
1977 / viii + 568 pp. / $8.50 (paper). In U.S.A. $9.75 (paper)

Available from / en vente chez:
WILFRID LAURIER UNIVERSITY PRESS
Wilfrid Laurier University
Waterloo, Ontario, Canada   N2L 3C5

**Published for the
Canadian Corporation for Studies in Religion/
Corporation Canadienne des Sciences Religieuses
by Wilfrid Laurier University Press**